THE HARVARD BOOK

THE

Harvard
Book

Selections from Three Centuries

Revised Edition

EDITED BY

William Bentinck-Smith

.

Harvard University Press

Cambridge, Massachusetts
London, England

Library of Congress Cataloging in Publication Data

Main entry under title:

The Harvard book.

    1. Harvard University—History—Sources.   I. Bentinck-
Smith, William, 1914–
LD2151.H29   1982   378.744′4   81-20078
ISBN 0–674–37301–4   AACR2

CONTENTS

I
WHAT IS THIS PLACE?

II
PEDAGOGUES AND PUPILS

III
TROUBLE UNDER THE ELMS

IV

YOU CAN TELL A HARVARDIAN . . .

V

SPORTS AND SPORTING TYPES

VI
HER SOLITARY CHILDREN

VII
THE OTHER SIDE

VIII
THESE FESTIVAL RITES

IX
THE ALUMNI

X
SOME VISITORS FROM AFAR

PREFACE

THIS anthology appeared almost thirty years ago in what now seems a very different, distant Harvard era. The depression, the Harvard Tercentenary, the Second World War, and the brief, magnificent, crowded days of the G.I. Bill were all in the immediate past. Despite the Korean conflict and the antics of Senator Joseph McCarthy, the colleges of America had settled into a fairly predictable course, and so had the students. Though Radcliffe women shared Harvard classrooms, they had yet to share Harvard dormitories, and Harvard College was still primarily male in habit and outlook. It was also primarily white. The Supreme Court had not yet ruled in *Brown v. Board of Education,* and the coming of impressive numbers of American ethnic minorities to Harvard was still in the future. The College, however, had become geographically national, while on the graduate and professional level there were new, large contingents of students from other countries.

Three decades are but a tenth of Harvard history, and it is a wonder that an anthology conceived in the spirit of quite another time has managed to hold its own through such a tumultuous period of change in the intellectual, social, and economic complexion of this country and of Harvard. A very practical reason for the book's modest popularity has been the steady support of the Harvard alumni clubs which continue to use the volume as one of the Prize Books awarded annually nationwide to leading high-school juniors—regardless of college destination. Additionally, its continued readership may lie in the fact that it provides a rather pleasant way to dip into Harvard history, sampling by the case method, if you will, what Harvardians and a few other observers have been saying about Harvard during the past three centuries and a half.

It is still as true today as it was thirty years ago—and, let us hope, ever will be—that there comes a time in the life of almost every Harvardian when he or she suddenly awakens to the fascination of Harvard. Very likely it may be the moment when the long line of the alumni marches past at Commencement or some other academic ceremony, as Emerson saw them at the bicentennial and noted in his journal:

> Cambridge at any time is full of ghosts; but on that day the anointed eye saw the crowd of spirits that mingled with the procession in the vacant

spaces, year by year, as the classes proceeded; and then the far longer train of ghosts that followed the company, of the men that wore before us the college honors and the laurels of the State—the long winding train reaching back into eternity . . .

Emerson's observation—something which the visitor Rupert Brooke also noticed—is an eerie moment, when the Harvardian becomes briefly a part of the passage of time in a way which is curiously elusive and hard to describe. It is a rare experience and yet it occurs over and over in different individuals.

In a similar mood many Harvard people had thought that somewhere and sometime a Harvard anthology should be put together. There had been Harvard anthologies before—the collections of stories and poems from the *Harvard Advocate* are examples, and more recently collections of the best from the *Lampoon* and the *Crimson*—but none which sample material from all three centuries of Harvard history. The origin of the task can be blamed upon three Harvard friends who made the original suggestion in the early 1950s and did the urging—Thomas J. Wilson, Director of the Harvard University Press, David McCord, Executive Secretary of the Harvard Fund Council, and William M. Pinkerton, Director of the Harvard University News Office.

From the beginning it was agreed that the project should not be just an anthology of writing, related or unrelated to Harvard, by Harvard people; nor should it be simply writing about Harvard by anyone; but that the field should be limited in general to Harvard teachers, students, or alumni (I use the term collectively), writing about Harvard subjects—an essence of "Harvard literature."

So much has been written about the first American college that it was almost a physical necessity from the beginning to put some limitations on the book. Yet Harvard has not suffered thereby. This method has served as a more intimate and subtle way of illustrating the historical and intellectual growth of Harvard as well as showing something of what Harvard has meant to its great and near-great offspring. Every educational institution is, after all, merely a refinement of the ancient combination of teacher, student, and log. The reader, therefore, should not expect to find in this volume much educational detail in the form of descriptive passages about courses and professional teaching methods. The book is intended to amuse, to stimulate the interest, to reflect something of the spirit of Harvard.

After testing a chronological arrangement, the present form was decided upon where a simple collection of prose and a single poetical sample are arranged in approximate chronological order under headings suggesting some of the aspects of Harvard life. To facilitate the pleasure of reading, antique spelling and punctuation have, in most cases, been modernized.

One of the features of the original volume was an introductory essay discussing ironically whether Harvard people know how to write. Taking as a text an editorial tirade by Bernard DeVoto on the subject of "Writing Like a Harvard Man," the anthologist pasted up a collection of comments by Harvard writers on Harvard writing and discussed in passing the general topic of Harvard fiction and poetry, Harvard history, memoirs, and letters. Much of the essay is amusing and perhaps still pertinent. Yet in the nobler and more gracious state of mind and heart that has come with his senescence, the essayist now feels he can leave the earlier work for those who may wish to consult it for possible antiquarian interest. *The Harvard Book* seems to speak for itself in suggesting the scope and interest of what may be called Harvard literature. For the purposes of this new edition it suffices simply to report the findings of Bliss Perry, Williams graduate and professor of English, after twenty-three years at Harvard, that

> there was a comfortable creed that the graduates of Harvard wrote better than the graduates of other colleges. I kept to myself the dreadful secret that in ten years of reading manuscript for the *Atlantic* I had never observed that Harvard men wrote any better than Yale men or Bowdoin men or men like Howells and Aldrich and John Burroughs who had never gone to college at all! It seemed to me that writing was a highly personal craft, to be perfected only after long practice, and that it made little difference where or how the practitioner learned the rudiments of his trade. Many years afterward, I admired Professor Grandgent's courage in declaring his fear that Harvard students "write rather poorly and speak worse."

Summing it all up, the anthologist concluded that taking pen in hand as a representative of Harvard is a dangerous thing: the rule of thumb is that when you are good, you are very, very good, and when you are bad, you are no better than any other bad college writer anywhere.

A second point of the original essay was the danger of generalizing about Harvard. The English A instructor in George Weller's *Not to Eat, Not for Love*, warned: "Generalizing about Harvard is a great Harvard vice. You began doing it before you came here, and the habit had you. You came to Harvard to find out why you had been so possessed. You will wallow in it four more years and still you won't know the answer."

There is much generalizing about Harvard in *The Harvard Book*. By Harvard presidents, historians, professional writers, politicians, sages, scoundrels, snobs, sensitive souls, the wise and the witty, the warm and the cold, the innocent and the sophisticated—all joined in the avocation of self-criticism—that inalienable right, which every Harvardian has earned, to wear a hair shirt in public. Borrowing another observation of Bliss Perry

> Indifference was surely not a characteristic of the alumni. If they disliked some fact or tendency pertaining to Harvard, they never hesitated in public or private to express their views. Astonished as I was at first by this broad latitude of criticism, I came gradually to see that it was one of the priceless traditions of a freedom-loving university.

Freedom-loving university! Along with *veritas,* words like freedom and liberty constantly recall, in Harvard literature, the often stated ideal with which those who value the privileges of higher education ally themselves. In the Harvard historical record there is much bold talk of freedom, that ancient principle asserted to be essential to the proper functioning of a university. It is always at challenge, for *veritas* implies the willingness to defend principle, to dare to be true. In a beautiful little tribute to Harvard, contained in this volume, one of Harvard's alumni elders declared, in the spirit of John Milton, that the right to utter is the first condition of personal rectitude and national progress, an aspiration to which Harvard has adhered. "The shining moments" of Harvard history, John Lord O'Brian declared, have been the moments of sacrifice when Harvard people stood against the tide of public opinion even though such an action might have been "peculiarly disagreeable, not to say difficult or impossible" in the face of the emphasis on conformity. O'Brian's statement was made in 1957, under no pressure from the heated and unhappy mood of public opinion ten or twenty years later, when shouts, slogans, and overamplification often drowned out the voices of those struggling to keep classroom doors open, to encourage rational discussion of issues, and to promote calm consideration of problems.

While crises of principle have spoiled the repose of many presidents and deans, the night thoughts of others, as *The Harvard Book* amply illustrates, have from time to time dwelt on more carefree pursuits. From the seventeenth century onward there has been a strain of idleness and frivolity in Harvard affairs as well as one of solemnity and nobility, incidents of sporting life as well as of ceremonial, youthful effusions as well as the settled charm of age.

From the simple honesty of Henry Dunster's wintry appeal for consideration from an unbending General Court, to the light-hearted naïveté of the boyish Oliver Wendell Holmes longing for a "petticoat," something of Harvard's ever varied character comes clear in successive examples culled from the amazing wealth of material to be found in the University Archives and in publications about Harvard.

The original search for material for *The Harvard Book* took several years of part-time exploration in many corners. The recent review has been a matter of months, for it seemed clear that much of the book ought to stand unchanged, because there would have to be some reasonable limitation on length and subsequent production cost. The search has led through the major publications and anthologies—*Crimson, Lampoon, Advocate, Independent, Harvard Magazine (Harvard Alumni Bulletin), Harvard Today, Harvard University Gazette,* and recent memoirs, reminiscent articles, collections of letters, and insiders' accounts of how matters really stand at Harvard, like Scott Thurow's *One L* about the first year at the Law School and Charles LeBaron's *Gentle Vengeance,* dealing with the first year at the

Medical School. The harvest has been impressive—from Frankfurter to Finley, so to speak. One regrets the need to omit much—and the alas-too-late glimpse of treasures like the undergraduate reminiscences of Robert Fitzgerald and Robert Coles, written for the new anthology, *Our Harvard,* edited by Jeffrey Lant.

As to poetry, most in the early years was of the humorous or satiric variety, with a few splendid exceptions, such as James Russell Lowell's "Commemoration Ode" (1865). The undergraduate work of later great men, such as Robinson or Eliot, Stevens or Cummings, has been frequently excerpted from the *Advocate* or *Monthly.* In the twentieth century, however, Harvard or Cambridge crept modestly into the verse of matured poets such as Robert Lowell, John Updike, Adrienne Rich, Donald Hall, or Robert Fitzgerald, to mention but a few. In general, however, our poets have not spent much time with the symbols of Harvard life, and this anthology does not attempt to include poetry.

On the other hand fiction writers have frequently turned to college and university themes. The several samples in this book provide evidence of a gradual maturing of attitudes by writers and readers toward the college experience. Whether we can point to a perfect college novel seems doubtful, even if we have passed beyond Mr. Verdant Green to Zuleika Dobson. In American letters a list of personal favorites would surely include Alison Lurie's *The War Between the Tates,* Howard Nemerov's *Homecoming Game,* May Sarton's *Faithful Are the Wounds,* and Theodore Morrison's *Stones of the House.* Some of the stories of Charles Macomb Flandrau still stand up well, and George Weller's much praised *Not to Eat, Not for Love* (imitative though it is of John Dos Passos' distinctive style in *U.S.A.*) recalls the very different Harvard just before the changes wrought by the under-graduate Houses.

Nearly fifty years after its publication one of Weller's contemporaries dealt somewhat harshly with the novel. Nathan Pusey in a reunion address to his class of 1928 brushed it off as "not ... a very good book then, nor when I looked at it again some years later." But where is a better total literary treatment of Harvard for this period in Harvard letters? At least Weller tried to deal with the whole Harvard (including, as Pusey remarked, "some rather fancy goings-on, at Revere Beach and other places"). Have later books improved on this topic?

Weller's book was never a best-seller. On the other hand, Erich Segal's *Love Story* (1970), brief, swift, episodic, was a smashing commercial success, appealing in a strange way to the reader's yearning for something a little naive, pathetic, and tender in a cynical age. Some of the same elements gave *The Paper Chase* wide popularity in its transformation from novel to motion picture to television series. This depiction of law school life by John Osborn, A.B. 1967, J.D. 1970, is about a place that might be Harvard, and, like *Love Story,* it has credible characters and reasonable plot. Other recent popular successes with a trace of Harvard or Radcliffe background are Rona

Jaffe's *Class Reunion, The Last Convertible,* by Anton Myrer, and *The Women's Room,* by Marilyn French.

The one new element which has extended the popular readership of college fiction, including that of Harvard, is the franker treatment of young love. Those curious enough to dip into this shallow amatory pool may wish to investigate *Fume of Poppies,* by Jonathan Kozol, A.B. 1958, *Girl with a Zebra,* by Perdita Buchan, A.B. 1962, *Love with a Harvard Accent,* by Leonie St. John (pseudonym for Nancy Harmon and William S. Bayer II, A.B. 1960), or the chapter "Jennifer's Story" in the late Nicholas Gagarin's *Wind Song* (1970), which approaches, but does not match, the insight, freshness of observation, and mature vision of Sallie Bingham's touching undergraduate love story of 1957, "Winter Term."

Harvardians with a craving for the saucepan can taste *Cooking with a Harvard Accent,* by Melanie Marcus, a former staff member of *Harvard Magazine,* while, for those with a satanic bent, the way might lead to the cauldron of William S. Burroughs, A.B. 1936, author of *Junkie,* although his underworldly domicile may be hard to find, since the latest Harvard Alumni Directory records his name with "address unknown."

That there was a Harvard underworld was clear in the days before the Second World War when Timothy Fuller of the Class of 1936 wrote a detective novel about murder at the Fogg Museum, and Damon Runyon produced a long short story, "Undertaker Song," depicting a gangland slaying at the Harvard-Yale football game. In more recent years painstaking Jane Langton has given us *The Memorial Hall Murder,* and Amanda Cross (Carolyn G. Heilbrun) the deft *Death in a Tenured Position.* In the latter volume the feminist detective (like her creator, a Columbia professor) is associated with the Bunting Institute, as was Mrs. Heilbrun not so long ago. And what shall we say of *Darconville's Cat,* wandering around Cambridge, in Alexander Theroux's intoxicating, intensely verbal novel, which is only peripherally about Harvard?

Although the idea of revising *The Harvard Book* had long been on the indolent editor's attenuated list of unattained ambitions, it took the helpful prodding of Chairman Peter Toulmin and the Harvard Prize Book Committee to bring action. Much appreciated financial backing for research and editorial expense came from the offices of Fred L. Glimp, Vice President for Alumni Affairs and Development, and David Aloian, Executive Director of the Associated Harvard Alumni, each of whom has been generous with time, suggestions, and background knowledge of the University. They and other long-time friends, such as John T. Bethell, Christopher Reed, Franklin L. Ford, Robert Shenton, John P. Reardon, and Peter J. Gomes, were wonderfully helpful. Harley P. Holden and the ever accommodating staff of the Harvard University Archives have been warm and welcoming. With such ready assistance, students of Harvard's past find an unusually happy research setting in the beautiful Archives reading room, associated with the names of Mr. and Mrs. Alexander M. White.

The memory of many favors from those who helped with the original compilation thirty years ago remains still vivid. The obliging Archives staff was then headed by Dr. Clifford K. Shipton, with Kimball C. Elkins as Senior Associate. Their assistance was matched by the counsel and practical aid of my former colleagues of the *Alumni Bulletin,* Henry M. Mahon, Norman A. Hall, Jane E. Howard, Barbara Gibbins Duffy, Nancy Shaw Esty, and Natica Bates. At strategic moments in the volume's progress David W. Bailey, Secretary to the Harvard Corporation, and G. W. Cottrell, former editor of the *Harvard Library Bulletin,* offered invaluable criticism.

I must also thank George Weller of the *Chicago Daily News* for several enjoyable discussions, over the years, of his novel *Not to Eat, Not for Love,* and am grateful as well to Frederick L. Gwynn, former head tutor of Adams House and a great admirer of Weller's book, for his analysis of the college novel as a type of literature. In the field of Harvardiana, Hamilton Vaughan Bail, author of *Views of Harvard,* and my college classmate, I Bernard Cohen, now Victor S. Thomas Professor of the History of Science, made a number of appreciated suggestions.

Above all, my constant and friendly mentor has been the Tercentennial Historian, Samuel Eliot Morison, through the medium of his several volumes on Harvard. No one investigating a Harvard subject can fail to be impressed by his sure and skillful pioneering, and anyone writing about Harvard owes him a tremendous debt.

Two good friends of some thirty years' standing were partners in this project. For the original edition Marjory Perry Johnson materially shortened a long job of research with her cheerful, patient, and competent assistance. For the revision, it was Elizabeth Stouffer, exemplary editorial and research colleague, whose long familiarity with Harvard people and events made her sharp eyes and refreshing common sense especially valuable. She also edited the index.

In conclusion, grateful mention should be made of the late Burton J. Jones of the Harvard University Press, who designed the original book and was honored by having it selected by the American Institute of Graphic Arts as one of the fifty best books of 1953; of Marion L. Hawkes, who prepared the original manuscript for the printer; and of Rose Udics, who gave the necessary editorial polish to the revised edition.

In 1875 two members of the Class of 1874 published a mammoth two-volume work designed for the library table, containing contributions of general and historical interest on the subject of Harvard. It is to that lavish example of printing and illustration and to its editors, F. O. Vaille and H. A. Clarke, that the present volume owes part of its title.

William Bentinck-Smith

January 1982

I

WHAT IS THIS PLACE?

"Is that you,
John Harvard?"
I said to his statue.
"Aye—that's me," said John,
"and after you're gone."

DAVID MC CORD (1940)

Harvard was founded by dissenters. Before two generations had passed there was a
general dissent from the first dissent. Heresy has long been in the air. We are proud
of the freedom which has made this possible even when we most dislike some particular form of heresy we may encounter.

JAMES BRYANT CONANT (1936)

All my memories of the four years were happy ones: there was everything to remember, nothing to forget. And I think, as I left the Yard behind me, there were two
feelings uppermost in my mind. The one was how humbling an experience four years
at college was—to begin to have realization of the vast stores of learning and
thought that had been made available to us; the wonderful minds and men at whose
feet, so to speak, we had sat . . . The second emotion that kept coming back to me
was the sense of freedom that the atmosphere of Harvard and the years we had spent
in it had brought home to us.

THOMAS W. LAMONT (1946)

IN RESPECT OF THE COLLEGE
(1643)

The most important early statement of the aims of the founding fathers in establishing a college in New England was contained in the "promotion pamphlet," New England's First Fruits, and the section "In Respect of the College" is thought almost certainly to have been compiled with the help of Master Henry Dunster himself. That he was not the actual author is probable because of the complimentary references to Dunster in the text, which contained also an outline of the curriculum and a summary of the college laws.

AFTER GOD had carried us safe to New England, and we had builded our houses, provided necessaries for our livelihood, reared convenient places for God's worship, and settled the civil government, one of the next things we longed for and looked after was to advance learning and perpetuate it to posterity; dreading to leave an illiterate ministry to the churches, when our present ministers shall lie in the dust. And as we were thinking and consulting how to effect this great work, it pleased God to stir up the heart of one Mr. Harvard (a godly gentleman, and a lover of learning, there living amongst us) to give the one half of his estate (it being in all about £1700) towards the erecting of a college, and all his library; after him another gave £300; others after them cast in more, and the public hand of the State added the rest: the college was, by common consent, appointed to be at Cambridge (a place very pleasant and accommodate) and is called (according to the name of the first founder) Harvard College.

The edifice is very fair and comely within and without, having in it a spacious hall (where they daily meet at commons, lectures, exercises) and a large library with some books to it, the gifts of divers of our friends, their chambers and studies also fitted for, and possessed by the students, and all other rooms of office necessary and convenient, with all needful offices thereto belonging; and by the side of the college a fair grammar school, for the training up of young scholars, and fitting of them for academical learning, that still as they are judged ripe, they may be received into the college of this school: Master Corlet is the master, who hath very well approved himself for his abilities, dexterity and painfulness in teaching and education of the youth under him.

Over the college is Master Dunster placed, as president, a learned, conscionable and industrious man, who hath so trained up his pupils in the tongues and arts, and so seasoned them with the principles of divinity and Christianity, that we have to our great comfort (and in truth beyond our hopes) beheld their progress in learning and godliness also; the former of these hath appeared in their public declamations in Latin and Greek and disputations logical and philosophical, which they have been wonted (besides their ordinary exercises in the college hall) in the audience of the magistrates, ministers, and other scholars, for the probation of their growth in learning, upon set days, constantly once every month to make and uphold. The latter hath been manifested in sundry of them, by the savoury breathings of their spirits in their godly conversation. Insomuch that we are confident, if these early blossoms may be cherished and warmed with the influence of the friends of learning, and lovers of this pious work, they will by the help of God, come to happy maturity in a short time.

New England's First Fruits (1643).

Samuel Eliot Morison

JOHN HARVARD AND THE NOTE OF FREEDOM

(1636-1936)

Just as no anthology of American letters would be complete without a selection from the writings of Francis Parkman, so would no collection of Harvardiana be complete without a portion from the Tercentenary historian, Samuel Eliot Morison, whose sensitive interpretation of Harvard history is the best yet written. On the opening day of the Tercentenary Celebration— November 8, the Founder's birthday—Professor Morison read an essay which has never been equaled as an eloquent statement of the part Harvard has played "in the great stream of learning and enlightenment which sprang from antiquity and has pursued its course uninterruptedly during all the intervening centuries." Running through this historical treatment is one aspect of Harvard's tradition which most Harvardians, no matter how much they abhor the term "tradition," will defend to the last—the principle of liberty of the mind. The Harvard Alumni Bulletin *commented on Professor Morison's essay: "During the greater part of its history Harvard was compelled to resist the interference of religion, as today it must resist the interference of political and economic creeds. There is always some orthodoxy whose adherents are afraid of thought, and against which a great university must guard its independence. Freedom does not mean heresy any more than it means orthodoxy, but it means that the honest love of truth, the discipline of science, and the accumulation of learning must be allowed to bring forth their own fruits in their own time. It means that only by such a general grant of freedom, scrupulously observed, can society profit by its universities. Professor Morison has sounded the keynote of the Tercentenary Celebration: the reinvigoration of the soul of Harvard by the recollection of its past and a rededication to its essential and abiding purposes."*

AUTUMN has crushed her vintage from the wine-press of the year. November has come, the days of family reunions and New England anniversaries. In November the *Mayflower* sighted Cape Cod, and the Compact was signed; it is the month of Thanksgiving, the important football games, and John Harvard's birthday. The *Old Farmer's Almanac* advises us to observe November by taking in cabbage, casting up accounts, and filling the cellar with good cider, "that wholesome and cheering liquor." So let us pause, and take stock of the past, and for a moment forget about Mussolini, Ethiopia, and our own politics. Let us take down from our shelves Bradford's *History of Plimmoth Plantation* and turn to that noble and prophetic passage where the Governor of the Pilgrim Fathers in his old age summed up the history of his Colony:

"Thus out of small beginnings greater things have been produced by His hand that made all things of nothing, and gives being to all things that are; and as one small candle may light a thousand, so the light here kindled hath shone to many; yea, in some sorte, to our whole Nation."

Another such light was kindled at New Town in the Bay Colony in 1636. But the spark that touched it off came from a lamp of learning first lighted by the ancient Greeks, tended by the Church through the dark ages, blown white and high in the medieval universities, and handed down to us in direct line through Paris, Oxford, and Cambridge.

In the elder Cambridge across the seas another small beginning had been made near the end of Queen Elizabeth's reign. Sir Walter Mildmay, Chancellor of the Exchequer, founded and endowed a new college, to which he gave the Puritan name Emmanuel—God with us. Puritanism was not in favor with Her Majesty, who, at her next meeting with this aged public servant, burst out with:

"So, Sir Walter, I hear you have erected a Puritan foundation?"

"No, Madam," said he, "Far be it from me to countenance anything contrary to your established laws; but I have set an acorn, which when it becomes an oak, God alone knows what will be the fruit thereof.'

One of the first fruits was Harvard College; and from that acorn, planted in the new Cambridge, has grown a goodly oak, nigh three centuries old, whose own fruits in the arts and sciences, in law, medicine, and letters, are spread through the length and breadth of this land.

John Harvard was one of the thirty-five graduates of Emmanuel College who came to New England in the great Puritan migration. He settled at Charlestown and filled the pulpit on alternate Sabbaths. In the summer of his arrival a committee composed largely of Cambridge alumni, appointed by the General Court of Massachusetts, were busying themselves about a College, for which the Court had appropriated £400 in the autumn of 1636. In the "New Towne" they found a site that recalled their *Alma Mater* on the Cam. A spacious plain, "smooth as a bowling green," sloped to a quiet river winding among salt marshes to the sea. The small village, New Town, was clustered near a good landing-place; and Thomas Shepard, the minister, an Emmanuel man, was perhaps judged to be more effective than others as an inspirer of youth, because in college days he had been a rather wild youth himself. On the north edge of the village stood Master Shepard's dwelling, and next it another; behind them was a row of cow-yards where the people kept their cattle at night behind palings, to protect them from prowling wolves and Indians. The house next Shepard's and the cow-yard behind it were purchased by the committee; a master was engaged; and there the first freshman class of the College, a dozen strong, was gathered in the early summer of 1638; and the New Town was promptly renamed Cambridge.

Shortly after, perhaps on the opening day, John Harvard rode over from Charlestown to look at the College. A well-to-do young man from London's middle class, married but childless, he was touched by this brave effort to reproduce in New England a Christian college like his own Emmanuel; he decided to help it. But John had not long to live. A "consumption," as the early chroniclers called it, had marked him down as victim; and that autumn he died, in his thirty-first year. On his deathbed John Harvard dictated a will that gave him an endless series of sons; for to the College he left his library, and half his estate. And the General Court at the next session "Ordered, that the colledge agreed upon formerly to bee built at Cambridg shalbee called Harvard Colledge."

Thus Harvard College was established *hic in silvestribus et incultis locis*, on the edge of the wilderness, in a colony eight years old, numbering less than ten thousand people, who had barely secured the necessities of existence; and with no help from any church, government, or individual in the Old World. No similar achievement can be found in colonial history; and in the eight centuries of university annals, there have been few nobler examples of courage in maintaining intellectual standards amid hard material circumstances, than the founding and early history of the Puritans' college by the Charles.

No university can pretend to be an end in itself. Universities are founded and maintained in order to serve mankind; but the ideas prevalent in some communities regarding the services proper to universities are, to say the least, peculiar; and if a university, to be popular, tries to be all things to all men, it is likely to become of slight value to anyone. Harvard has been singularly happy in having been permitted, even encouraged, to function in an atmosphere of freedom; to decide for herself what she shall contribute to learning; and how. She has never abused that freedom to her own advantage, or the community's prejudice. On the contrary, she has used the corporate autonomy with which the Commonwealth endowed her in 1650, and the wealth poured into her treasury, to pour forth ever greater services, on a constantly widening watershed.

It is not an easy matter to explain these services, or to defend learning to the unlearned. Most of what a university does cannot be measured by statistics, represented by graphs, weighed, or counted—or where it can be counted, as in Harlow Shapley's work on stellar galaxies, we cannot follow him much beyond the first hundred million light-years! The public can understand a university supporting teaching, or research in the natural and social sciences—provided historians forbear close inspection of idols' feet. But what of this ripe scholar, spending a lifetime editing and translating the works of a Greek dramatist a long time dead; of that modest man of science, working in his laboratory of cryptogamic botany on algae and fungi that even some of the botanists consider mildly obscene? How can we explain and defend the expenditure of money on these things? The answer is, we cannot; until the scholar is dead, or unless he becomes world-famous. Many of the state universities of this country, where professors are dependent for their daily bread on annual appropriations, have to do good by stealth, while maintaining shows in the way of extension lectures and football games, to get the votes and the money. Many things that members of a university write, do, and say, must be unpopular; for it is a university's business to be wiser, more liberal, and more hospitable to new ideas, *and more critical of them,* than the community. Badgering, bridling, and blindfolding the universities is cheap and popular, although the community hurts itself in the end more than it does the college. A professor with blinders on can see no farther than his feed-bag.

At the time of her foundation, Harvard was unique among the universities of the western world, in having no statutory oaths imposed on her teachers or students. The reason is clear: Harvard was founded by Puritans whose consciences had been troubled by the oaths to support the state religion that they had had to take at Oxford or Cambridge. In order to obtain a degree in an English university they had been forced to subscribe to principles that they abhorred; yet, as the lesser evil, they had taken the oaths and gone their way, as conscience dictated. Personal experience taught them the vanity of trying to control opinion by tests and oaths; and they made no such attempt here.

While the universities should lead, it is also true that no leader can afford to run too far ahead of his followers, or he becomes isolated and lost. Harvard has had plenty of experience of that during her three centuries of life. Henry Dunster, our first president, was pulled up short when he opposed infant baptism. The Governing Boards wished him to continue, regardless; but the General Court forced him to resign. A few years later there was another small but significant controversy. Someone more liberal than the majority wished to print on the College press a translation of that beautiful manual of Christian devotion, *The Imitation of Christ.* President Chauncy and his board of censors gave their consent, and the copy went to press. But when the General Court of Massachusetts got wind of it, they resolved that, whereas "there is now in the press reprinting a book entitled Imitations of Christ by Thomas a Kempis a Popish minister, wherein is conteyned some things that are unsafe for the people of this place ... there shall be no further progress in that work." And the *Imitatio Christi* was not reprinted in Massachusetts—for some time. This taught the College authorities that their efforts to liberalize the community must be done quietly, almost imperceptibly, through a gradual process of education, and not by shocking departures from the Puritan canon. How well they succeeded may be seen in the Unitarian movement of the early nineteenth century.

President Mather once boasted of the "liberal manner of Philosophizing" at Harvard; but of liberal theology he would have none; and his attempt to incorporate an oath of orthodoxy in a new College charter was only foiled by the veto of a hearty Irish peer, Lord Bellomont, then Governor of Massachusetts. Oxford and Cambridge, less fortunate, had a stringent set of tests and oaths imposed on them by Charles II. The consequence was that the dissenters and Roman Catholics were excluded from the benefits of university education, and college tutors found that the safe way to hold their fellowships was to give up writing, or research; and both universities for a long period became contemptible as places of learning.

Another oath bill for Harvard was threatened in the 1740's, as a punishment for Harvard indifference toward the evangelical revival; but it failed to pass. As long as Massachusetts was a Royal Province, the Harvard Presidents were charged by the Royal Governor at their inauguration, to perform their duties "with loyalty to our Sovereign Lord, King George, and obedience to His Majesty's Laws." The last colonial President, Langdon, was installed in 1774. On a fine June morning the next year he might have been heard preaching rebellion against George III to the American army, just before it marched from Cambridge to Bunker Hill.

John Adams saw to it that Harvard University had a chapter to herself in the Massachusetts Constitution of 1780; but no oath of allegiance was required of the President or Professors. The Commonwealth was represented on the Board of Overseers until 1866; but never once, to my knowledge, did these official representatives of government use their positions to restrain or repress. Finally, in 1866, forty years after she had ceased to contribute to the support of the College, Massachusetts handed over the Board of Overseers to the Harvard alumni. On them now rests the responsibility of representing the community in the University constitution.

President Eliot's administration, coming in the greatest era of progress and liberalism, democracy, and optimism that America has ever known, was little troubled by problems of academic freedom. Commonwealth and University alike took it for granted that scholars and professors had complete liberty, within the limits of decency, to write, speak, and publish their minds. Free speech was regarded as an axiom of democracy, and the guardian of liberty.

But the Great War brought back that spirit of intolerance that Thomas Jefferson had hoped to bury forever. It took the form of demands for the dismissal of certain professors, either because they had the misfortune to be Germans, or because they spoke or wrote in a manner to alarm patriots or property-holders. And these demands came most sharply from some of our own alumni; from men who had benefited from the very freedom that they sought to restrain. It is the greatest glory of Mr. Lowell's administration that he maintained, in theory and in fact, this ancient principle of academic freedom, as an essential condition for the proper functioning of a university. In conferring upon him an honorary degree in 1934, his successor characterized Mr. Lowell as "our resolute captain who enlarged and deepened the life of this University, and preserved untainted the vitalizing spirit of liberty." And if Harvard and her sister universities are to serve the Great Republic in the future as they have in the past, they must be confirmed in their freedom to function as republics of learning.

Three centuries is a mere moment in human history; but a long era in the history of universities, over one-third of the time that has elapsed since groups of masters and scholars first organized as *universitates* in Bologna and Paris. As an institution for promoting the intellectual labors of mankind, the universities have had no rivals or competitors. Almost the whole of what we call civilization, certainly the nobler and more ideal aspects of it, have been wrought through the unselfish and devoted studies of their sons. In this noble pageant of learning, from the era of Gratian and St. Thomas to our own day, Harvard has worked up from a humble position in the rear ranks, to a place among the captains and the kings; and that place, God willing, she means to hold.

"Thus out of small beginnings greater things have been produced by His hand that made all things of nothing, and gives being to all things that are; and as one small candle may light a thousand, so the light here kindled hath shone to many; yea, in some sorte, to our whole Nation."

Harvard Alumni Bulletin, November 22, 1935.

William James

THE TRUE HARVARD

(1903)

During the course of his distinguished teaching career, William James, M.D. 1869, LL.D. 1903, made many statements about his Alma Mater, including the offhand remark to his sister, shortly after his appointment as Professor of Philosophy, that "although I serve Harvard College to the best of my ability, I have no affection at all for the institution, and would gladly desert it for anything that offered better pay." Fortunately, he did not desert Harvard and he came to love and understand it better, as his address at the Harvard Commencement dinner in 1903 seems to indicate.

WE ARE glorifying ourselves today, and whenever the name of Harvard is emphatically uttered on such days, frantic cheers go up. There are days for affection, when pure sentiment and loyalty come rightly to the fore. But behind our mere animal feeling for old schoolmates and the Yard and the bell, and Memorial and the clubs and the river and the Soldier's Field, there must be something deeper and more rational. There ought at any rate to be some possible ground in reason for one's boiling over with joy that one is a son of Harvard, and was not, by some unspeakably horrible accident of birth, predestined to graduate at Yale or at Cornell.

Any college can foster club loyalty of that sort. The only rational ground for preeminent admiration of any single college would be its preeminent spiritual tone. But to be a college man in the mere clubhouse sense—I care not of what college—affords no guarantee of real superiority in spiritual tone.

The old notion that book learning can be a panacea for the vices of society lies pretty well shattered today. I say this in spite of certain utterances of the President of this University to the teachers last year. That sanguine-hearted man seemed then to think that if the schools would only do their duty better, social vice might cease. But vice will never cease. Every level of culture breeds its own peculiar brand of it as surely as one soil breeds sugar-cane, and another soil breeds cranberries. If we were asked that disagreeable question, "What are the bosom-vices of the level of culture which our land and day have reached?" we should be forced, I think, to give the still more disagreeable answer that they are swindling and adroitness, and the indulgence of swindling and adroitness, and cant, and sympathy with cant—natural fruits of that extraordinary idealization of "success" in the mere outward sense of "getting there," and getting there on as big a scale as we can, which characterizes our present generation. What was Reason given to man for, some satirist has said, except to enable him to invent reasons for what he wants to do. We might say the same of education. We see college graduates on every side of every public question. Some of Tammany's stanchest supporters are Harvard men. Harvard men defend our treatment of our Filipino allies as a masterpiece of policy and morals. Harvard men, as journalists, pride themselves on producing copy for any side that may enlist them. There is not a public abuse for which some Harvard advocate may not be found.

In the successful sense, then, in the worldly sense, in the club sense, to be a college man, even a Harvard man, affords no sure guarantee for anything but a more educated cleverness in the service of popular idols and vulgar ends. Is there no inner Harvard within the outer Harvard which means definitively more than this—for which the outside men who come here in such numbers, come? They come from the remotest outskirts of our country, without introductions, without school affiliations; special students, scientific students, graduate students, poor students of the College, who make their living as they go. They seldom or never darken the doors of the Pudding or the Porcellian; they hover in the background on days when the crimson color is most in evidence, but they nevertheless are intoxicated and exultant with the nourishment they find here; and their loyalty is deeper and subtler and more a matter of the inmost soul than the gregarious loyalty of the clubhouse pattern often is.

Indeed, there is such an inner spiritual Harvard; and the men I speak of, and for whom I speak today, are its true missionaries and carry its gospel into infidel parts. When they come to Harvard, it is not primarily because she is a club. It is because they have heard of her persistently atomistic constitution, of her tolerance of exceptionality and eccentricity, of her devotion to the principles of individual vocation and choice. It is because you cannot make single one-ideaed regiments of her classes. It is because she cherishes so many vital ideals, yet makes a scale of value among them; so that even her apparently incurable second-rateness (or only occasional first-rateness) in intercollegiate athletics comes from her seeing so well that sport is but sport, that victory over Yale is not the whole of the law and the prophets, and that a popgun is not the crack of doom.

The true Church was always the invisible Church. The true Harvard is the invisible Harvard in the souls of her more truth-seeking and independent and often very solitary sons. *Thoughts* are the precious seeds of which our universities should be the botanical gardens. Beware when God lets loose a thinker on the world—either Carlyle or Emerson said that—for all things then have to rearrange themselves. But the thinkers in their youth are almost always very lonely creatures. "Alone the great sun rises and alone spring the great streams." The university most worthy of rational admiration is that one in which your lonely thinker can feel himself least lonely, most positively furthered, and most richly fed. On an occasion like this it would be poor taste to draw comparisons between the colleges, and in their mere clubhouse quality they cannot differ widely:—all must be worthy of the loyalties and affections they arouse. But as a nursery for independent and lonely thinkers I do believe that Harvard still is in the van. Here they find the climate so propitious that they can be happy in their very solitude. The day when Harvard shall stamp a single hard and fast type of character upon her children, will be that of her downfall. Our undisciplinables are our proudest product. Let us agree together in hoping that the output of them will never cease.

Harvard Graduates' Magazine, September, 1903.

Walter Prichard Eaton

HERE'S TO THE HARVARD ACCENT!

(1936)

After twenty-five years of writing, newspaper work, and college teaching, Walter Prichard Eaton went to Yale in 1933 as a reluctant substitute for the late George Pierce Baker. Instead of a three-year stint at the most, he stayed to teach playwriting until the age of sixty-eight, became a full professor, and "had a very happy time." He was the author of nearly forty books, among them a series of juveniles.

GEORGE ADE once declared that his Alma Mater, Purdue, "gives you everything that Harvard does, except the pronunciation of *a* as in *father*." George did not intend this remark to be complimentary to the university on the Charles, but as a matter of fact it is, for it points out one of the chief reasons for Harvard's greatness. Words, as Professor Kittredge has so often told us, are vastly important things. But the pronunciation of words is vastly important, too. A way of pronouncing not only betrays the speaker's regional origin, but carries with it most of the associative ideas which belong to the region, and wakes them in the hearer. Regional pronunciations are symbols of provincialism. They may be none the worse for that; indeed they may often have a special charm on that account, nor would we see them lost in the general uniformity of "correct" speech. But they are provincialisms nonetheless.

Probably to Ade's ear (as to many others across the Continent) the pronunciation of *a* as in *father* is also a provincialism, the provincialism of Massachusetts Bay. Certainly he would not admit that because Boston and Harvard employ it, it is therefore standard. But the fact remains that for the best speakers of the language as a whole, on both sides of the Atlantic, it is standard; it is the pronunciation which has brought the music of Shakespeare most magically to our ears, whether spoken by Edwin Booth or Ellen Terry or John Gielgud or Walter Hampden. It is the pronunciation which has trumpeted the noblest prose in our language from the loftiest pulpits, and without which even Isaiah loses some of his rolling majesty. It is a kind of hall mark of oral dignity and of English style; it is a syllabic sound around which cluster the associative ideas of richest dignity and least provincial scope, least because they embrace the whole confines of the language on both sides of the water. Those associative ideas are so subtly and constantly playing upon any sensitive man who spends four years at Harvard that whether he knows it or not they color his life, and whether he can express it or not in words they are much of what Harvard comes to mean to him.

So let him cling proudly to his broad *a*, and to his not always secret belief that any other pronunciation is provincial. Let the Mid-West laff. It is a prerogative of the young.

Boston Herald, Harvard Tercentenary Supplement, September 13, 1936.

David McCord

THE LIGHTS COME ON

(*1941*)

Emerson once wrote in his journal, "the sky is the daily bread of the eyes," and David McCord has felt that those nine words have meant a great deal to him over the years. They have stuck with him longer than simply the moment when they suggested to him his early essay, "Cambridge Sky." Few Harvardians have written of their University with so much affectionate perception and literary skill as the former executive director of the Harvard Fund Council and former editor of the Harvard Alumni Bulletin. *"By pure chance," he said at the time of his twenty-fifth anniversary of graduation from Harvard, "vocation and avocation combined to anchor me to Harvard. Though my list of natural regrets has enjoyed the happy accretive growth of 25 years, I have never for a minute regretted this. Harvard has given me everything: a living, a reasonably useful pen—perfecto size—a catholic attitude toward art, and the winds of more doctrine than I can halfway handle." McCord has written more than thirty books, including* Oddly Enough, Stirabout, Notes on the Harvard Tercentenary, The Crows, Bay Window Ballads, About Boston, A Star by Day, *and* In Sight of Sever. *He has edited several anthologies, among them* What Cheer. *In his years of retirement he has been in great demand as a lecturer and reader of poetry, particularly before student groups.*

YOU NEVER KNOW just when, for there are not in all the buildings together filaments enough to make the Yard a brilliant place, even by any city backstreet standard. Murky Cambridge dusk—how damp, how murky!—and then of a sudden you turn a corner and there is the familiar outdoor bracket beacon, like the carriage lamp of another age, brightening a segment of brick and showing a pool of amber on the rotting snow beneath. Now half a dozen other lights are winking from the windows of Weld, Grays, and the rest. Back of tall pillars the curtain of Widener slowly rises and inward illumination comes up as on a vast but silent stage. A voice calls far across from the steps of Hollis. Figures about the Yard grow shadowy and soft and moist. A match flares to a cigarette. Evening becomes official, and the gloom is gradually filtered everywhere with the innocent pin-points of sixty-cycle sunlight.

Down in the Basin, half the Harvard Bridge—the Boston half, perhaps—has already responded to the throwing of a giant switch. From shore to center the dwindling silhouette is brilliant with little bulbs: an accusing finger in the direction of Cambridge, warning her to forget the budget and mounting taxes and turn on the juice of the other half. This (in good time) the servants of the City Fathers will surely do.

Up the river sweep the beams and half-beams of homeward suburban cars against the slower-moving glitter of inbound Boston traffic. The Weeks Bridge, a pretty Georgian fragment thrown across the Charles, and her less beautiful elder sister to the west, flank the batteries of increasing window light from the Houses and the Business School. It is Monday evening—high table, that means, at Lowell House—and the graceful Lowell tower emerges in the gloom, touched off by your modern reflectors, cunningly concealed. Cambridge is a city of spires now, even by night, and at other times there are three of them ablaze at once. In the river, where the ice is going out in jigsaw-puzzle fragments, float the images of phosphorous. A pretty sight, with spring so faintly stirring in the night air: a moment of security, almost, in a world so pitifully insecure.

The lights of Harvard's Cambridge come on with a greater front and a steadier shine than they did for our more somnolent ancestors. Even the now old-fashioned arc of hotly sputtering carbon, still casting weird tree-shadows on a wall in Plympton Street, has probably more candle-power within one cracked globe than half the Yard could muster in the rosy days of *The Rebelliad.* And what would the ancients say to the milk-white Taj Mahal, the Good Gulf gas station on the site of dead Beck Hall, the dreary?

Light has always been one of the first symbols of colleges and learning. Centuries and electrons have not changed us there. The point is that at Harvard the lights *can* still come on—in fair weather or in rain, in a time of free thinking, or of the soul's own darkness, when man shall save his birth-right only by a masterful resolve.

Harvard Alumni Bulletin, March 22, 1941.

Donald Moffat

ONE VIEW OF HARVARD
(1948)

With true affection and the felicity of a master craftsman, Donald Moffat, A.B. 1916, turned his hand to the introduction of Samuel Chamberlain's Fair Harvard *and brought forth a beautifully ordered essay on the character of Harvard, one of the best items in all Harvard Literature. A writer by trade, Moffat, who died in 1958, was the author of* A Villa in Brittany, The Mott Family in France, *and* The Prejudices of Mr. Pennyfeather.

HERE AND THERE in the pages of Samuel Eliot Morison's *Three Centuries of Harvard* occurs a phrase which might well have been taken for the College motto, to stand beside the celebrated *Veritas:* "Harvard men were divided in opinion."

In a present alumni army of some ninety thousand you will find, where Harvard is concerned, no two elements agreeing on anything. Among undergraduates the same law runs, and among the faculty too. Harvard means conflict and conflict means passion and the only sensible rule for identifying a Harvard man is to call him a minority of one. United by a mystic loyalty which not only cements the family but forms a useful shield to hold up against the world, Harvard is rent by polite but fearful discord on every point worth mentioning from the function of education to the function of the catch in rowing. There is no escaping this truth, which is called John's

Law, after the founder. Historians are sharply divided on the question of John Harvard's right to the title of founder.

For if education may be defined in a word, that word is controversy. Where concord reigns, learning withers; where conflict rules, it flourishes. And the cumulative effect of three hundred years of conflict results—in the best, or Harvard, opinion—in a university three times as great as one which has been at it only one hundred years, and so on.

Harvard can point to no moment in her history and truthfully say, "Here we were in equilibrium." No college generation has known an armistice in the age-old war between the orthodox and the radical, the conservative and the progressive points of view towards current controversy among her student or faculty scholar-servants, whether it be academic, religious, political, social, or trivial. Every day is crisis day at Harvard, and on few of them, be it said to her credit, has she failed to take the line leading up and on.

She has been called godless from the beginning, a serious charge during her first two hundred years, when religious orthodoxy was the only passport to fair repute; and radical almost as long as godless. In fact, the dangerous radical at godless Harvard emerges as a stock figure in her history. Yet the important point is this: in all the long roster of Harvard heretics and rebels I find no instance of a student or teacher being disciplined purely because of his opinions. In this respect Harvard's tradition stands firm as a rock, the record is clear. Tomorrow's dissenters like yesterday's may be reviled by the press, the public, and the pulpit; they may be, as they have been, called atheist, imperialist, communist, or merely unAmerican: the College fathers will uphold their right to be heard. Of this we may be sure . . .

Four years are none too long: so many skins must be shed, so many new layers grown or grafted. If it be true that the first milestone on the road leading out of childhood is the discovery that your mother and father don't like spinach either, the next is perhaps the ability to tell an honest man from a scoundrel, and a third the precious lesson that because a thing is new, or because it is old, it is not therefore necessarily good: that the word "modern," fetish of youth and the advertising profession, is no more synonymous with "excellent" than the word "ancient." The knowledge that the integrity of the man who pushes the button is more important than the reliability of the machine the button starts is another item that hopeful but incredulous youth finds hard to accept, but must accept, if his education is to do him any good. The lesson of humility—hallmark of the truly great—can hardly be learned in four years; but a beginning can be made, a glimpse caught. The downy freshman looks at a classmate a little timidly, a little truculently, thinking "I'm just as good as you are!" Four years later he may have learned to change the emphasis, saying "You're just as good as I am." Simple humility is not easily won. But it is a step on the road to becoming a free man and an educated man, and may at last enable one to apply to himself the aphorism "that man is free who is conscious of himself as the law which he obeys."

Who is wise enough to swear that the air he breathes, the sound of echoing footsteps of generations of great men who have gone before, the impalpable influences which shape and form the spirit as well as the mind, do not play their part in these beginnings? ...

Since the vanished elms were planted in 1815 and the original paths laid out from building to building, door to door, a crisscross of new walks have appeared in the Yard, beaten out by the students' footsteps. Here and there are fences, some high, some low. But the short cuts are not fenced: the muddy or dusty tracks appear, then one fine morning the impatient undergraduate finds that official notice has courteously been taken of his trespasses, in the form of fresh gravel. A new dormitory, chapel, or library is built, a new star discovered, a great teacher is born, science pushes the mysterious curtain back another millimeter: presto! the new pathways appear. Harvard is too experienced to call them royal roads, wise enough to know that time is the precious factor which alone may prove their worth.

Fair Harvard (Cambridge, 1948).

John F. Kennedy

SOWER OF THE SEED

(1957)

During his years as United States senator and later as president, John Fitzgerald Kennedy became the symbol of youthful aspiration to millions of American young people and to thousands at Harvard. He crossed political lines. He was "one of ours"—hero to the humblest freshman, man of destiny to most of the faculty, Harvard's sixth president of the United States. Even in middle age he was a rather boyish figure, charismatically appealing. Harvard conferred on him the honorary LL.D. degree in 1956, and the alumni elected him an Overseer in 1957. In the following tribute to his undergraduate mentor, Professor Arthur Holcombe, the future president reiterated a favorite theme that he often used in speakinig of his alma mater.

PROFESSOR George Lyman Kittredge is supposed to have stopped in the Harvard Yard one day, pointed to the Widener Library, and remarked that every other building could burn to the ground, but if the Library continued to stand, "we should still have a University."

I share Professor Kittredge's admiration for the Library. But I am inclined to think that even the Library could be devoured in a general conflagration and the essence of Harvard would endure if teachers like Kittredge and his fellows survived. For the real meaning of Harvard is not in the buildings or the Library, however important their supporting functions may be; it is in the teachers and the students and the interrelationship between them. The teachers, not the Library, serve as the organ of memory, distilling the knowledge of the past, and, in the words of Woodrow Wilson, transmitting to the future the best traditions of the State.

I have known many great teachers at Harvard, many who excelled in showing the enchantment of thought to young men who, in this springtime of youth, were more enchanted with life itself. But the one teacher known to generations of Harvard students who stands out in my memory and personal affections is Arthur Holcombe. Under his direction in a course in American Government, I discovered for the first time the distractions of the Congressional Record, as I studied for one term the rise and eventual political extinguishment of an obscure Republican Congressman from upstate New York.

But Professor Holcombe's greatest impact was not in his erudition but in his personality and character. Dispassionate, reserved, self-restrained, without illusions yet persistently idealistic, he was extraordinarily well equipped with qualities and principles to meet his responsibilities as a teacher and as a citizen. He taught and inspired my father. Forty years later he taught and inspired, with equal brilliance, my younger brother. To them, to me, to all his students, he set a standard to which in later life we could repair.

Shortly after the 1946 election he remarked to me with unconcealed pride: "I had the pleasure on election day of voting for three of my former students—one for Senator, one for Governor and one for Congressman— and they were all elected." It did not matter to him that the party labels were different; they had been his students, they were graduates of Harvard, he respected their capabilities and motives—and that was enough.

I trust that fire is not about to envelop the Harvard Yard, and that Widener Library will be standing long after all the present faculty and students are gone. But I am even more confident that the spirit of the Holcombes and the Kittredges and all the rest will endure even longer. And Harvard will endure with it.

Brooks Atkinson, ed., *College in a Yard* (Cambridge, 1957).

Archibald MacLeish

WHEN WE THINK NOW OF THE GREATNESS OF THE UNIVERSITY, WE THINK FIRST OF THE DEAD

(1976)

Remembered for his long, distinguished, and busy life as writer and public servant, Archibald MacLeish will always be revered in Harvard circles as the ninth incumbent of one of the College's oldest and most important chairs, the Boylston Professorship of Rhetoric and Oratory. As such he taught at Harvard—both poetry and advanced writing—from 1949 to 1962, completing at age seventy an association with Harvard that began in 1938 with a one-year stint (preceding his service as Librarian of Congress) as the first curator of the Nieman fellowship program for journalists. This beautiful tribute to Harvard and a deceased colleague says in another way what Mac-Leish remarked of Harvard at his retirement, "Perhaps the reason why grown men, mature men, give themselves to this place with such wholeness of heart is precisely that here the life of the mind, which is a metaphor in ordinary speaking, is a presence, a reality. And that here the free society of which we talk is truly free."

IT IS only at your life's end, when your generation in this place begins to ravel out and vanish, that you come really to understand the greatness of the University. When you were a student here, or a young instructor, or even a middle-aged writer appointed to an historic chair, you were lost in a daydream of the present in which you saw the University as the possession of the living: a daydream in which the piled-up clouds of greatness back behind the living were just that—piled-up clouds. You may have caught a glimpse of Whitehead once, or talked to men who once had talked with William James, or heard of Santayana from his students, but all this talk was only talk—irrelevant remembrance.

Not until a man's own generation comes to its last few survivors, not until the generations of the dead include his own contemporaries, does he see what Harvard is and who has made it what it is—that long succession of the famous dead who bear the living on their shoulders and conceive the always-changing future. Ten generations of the dead there are now in this College—in this University. It is they who thrust the living forward like the breaking of a wave that never breaks but lifts and runs and reaches.

This, to me and to my old colleagues, is the significance of Kenneth Murdock's death. He was not the first of us to die. Matthiessen we lost a long time back and Theodore Spencer and Perry Miller, but we were younger then and what we thought of was the loss to us, not the change in the great company behind us. Now we see more clearly. When we think now of the greatness of the University we think first of the dead. And when we think of the dead we think not only of those distant and immortal names, those famous strangers, but of the men we knew and still know there among them. We think of this new latest name, this elegant, tall figure we have seen so often, always sauntering, never hurried. We recall the lazy-seeming wit that darted like a lizard's tongue, the intellectual power that never preened itself as power, or called attention to itself as intellect, but simplified and clarified and cleared away.

We have friends now in that company and the past becomes *our* past— our generation's past as well as all the others'.

For Kenneth Murdock *is* both ours and theirs. Some who live their lives out in this University, die elsewhere—are remembered elsewhere—but not Murdock. His life was given to the University, and so now is his death. He still belongs to it. And not as scholar only but as himself. He knew the Puritan past as few others have ever known it, but what he bears into the University's long past is not that scholarly knowledge but his living life. He was a learned man, whose learning even Cotton Mather would have recognized, but he was also Kenneth Murdock, man of his own time. He was modern in his generation's sense of that ambiguous word, meaning that he was worldly—what his generation meant by worldly: a sophisticated and adroit intelligence and an informed aesthetic feeling to which Mozart was the measure of all music and Keats's famous aphorism was not only true as poetry, but, being poetry, was true.

Harvard's Puritan past needs Mozart and the poets to be true to what this ancient Harvard has become, and Murdock's presence in that past has changed it for his friends, for his survivors. We in our diminishing generation who remember him, who know the triumph and the tragedy of his life, who lost him years before his death and who, for years, turned back to better years to find him, think of him now, restored to his bright self, secure among his peers and his companions of the many generations: part forever of the greatness he so loved.

Harvard Magazine, February, 1976.

Five Presidents

TOWARD A DEFINITION OF HARVARD

(1869–1980)

Many have sought to put into words something of the meaning of Harvard; but none should be more qualified to speak on the subject than the presidents from Eliot to Bok. In the more than a century of expansion and consolidation represented by their administrations, Harvard grew from a small New England college into the great educational institution of today. Yet, despite Harvard's changing needs and vastly altered educational pattern, there is little essential difference to be found in the way these five presidents interpret Harvard's mission. The following passages, culled from notable presidential statements, define in noble terms the spirit of a great university.

CHARLES W. ELIOT

THIS UNIVERSITY recognizes no real antagonism between literature and science, and consents to no such narrow alternatives as mathematics or classics, science or metaphysics. We would have them all, and at their best. To observe keenly, to reason soundly, and to imagine vividly are operations as essential as that of clear and forcible expression; and to develop one of these faculties, it is not necessary to repress and dwarf the others. A university is not closely concerned with the applications of knowledge, until its general education branches into professional. Poetry and philosophy and science do indeed conspire to promote the material welfare of mankind; but science no more than poetry finds its best warrant in its utility. Truth and right are above utility in all realms of thought and action . . .

The notion that education consists in the authoritative inculcation of what the teacher deems true may be logical and appropriate in a convent, or a seminary for priests, but it is intolerable in universities and public schools, from primary to professional. The worthy fruit of academic culture is an open mind, trained to careful thinking, instructed in the methods of philosophic investigation, acquainted in a general way with the accumulated thought of past generations, and penetrated with humility. It is thus that the university in our day serves Christ and the church . . .

Harvard College is sometimes reproached with being aristocratic. If by aristocracy be meant a stupid and pretentious caste, founded on wealth, and birth, and an affectation of European manners, no charge could be more preposterous: the College is intensely American in affection, and intensely democratic in temper. But there is an aristocracy to which the sons of Harvard have belonged, and, let us hope, will ever aspire to belong—the aristocracy which excels in manly sports, carries off the honors and prizes of the learned professions, and bears itself with distinction in all fields of intellectual labor and combat; the aristocracy which in peace stands firmest for the public honor and renown, and in war rides first into the murderous thickets.   (1869)

The brief history of modern civilization shows that in backward ages universities keep alive philosophy, and in progressive ages they lead the forward movement, guiding adventurous spirits to the best point of onward departure. They bring a portion of each successive generation to the confines of knowledge, to the very edge of the territory already conquered, and say to the eager youth: "Thus far came our fathers. Now press you on!" The hope of mankind depends on this incessant work of the philosophical pioneer, who may be years, or generations, or centuries in advance of the common march.

And universities are among the most permanent of human institutions. They outlast particular forms of government, and even the legal and industrial institutions in which they seem to be embedded. Harvard University already illustrates this transcendent vitality . . .   (1886)

Universities have three principal, direct functions. In the first place, they teach; secondly, they accumulate great stores of acquired and systematized knowledge in the form of books and collections; thirdly, they investigate, or, in other words, they seek to push out a little beyond the present limits of knowledge, and learn, year after year, day after day, some new truth. They are teachers, storehouses, and searchers for truth.   (1891)

ABBOTT LAWRENCE LOWELL

THE INDIVIDUAL STUDENT ought clearly to be developed so far as possible, both in his strong and in his weak points, for the college ought to produce, not defective specialists, but men intellectually well rounded, of wide sympathies and unfettered judgment. At the same time they ought to be trained to hard and accurate thought, and this will not come merely by surveying the elementary principles of many subjects. It requires a mastery of something, acquired by continuous application. Every student ought to know in some subject what the ultimate sources of opinion are, and how they are handled by those who profess it. Only in this way is he likely to gain the solidity of thought that begets sound thinking. In short, he ought, so far as in him lies, to be both broad and profound . . .

Surely the essence of a liberal education consists in an attitude of mind, a familiarity with methods of thought, an ability to use information rather than in a memory stocked with facts, however valuable such a storehouse may be . . . The best type of liberal education in our complex modern world aims at producing men who know a little of everything and something well . . .

The university touches the community at many points, and as time goes on it ought to serve the public through ever increasing channels. But all its activities are more or less connected with, and most of them are based upon, the college. It is there that character ought to be shaped, that aspirations ought to be formed, that citizens ought to be trained, and scholarly tastes implanted. (1909)

The usefulness of a great university is by no means exhausted by its teaching. It has two functions, both so essential that neither can be said to be more important than the other. One is that of preserving and imparting the knowledge slowly acquired in the past, the other is that of adding to it. The question a university should ask is not whether an idea is old or new, but only whether it is true, and the universities have shown that there is no difficulty in combining the retention of what is good in the old with the strenuous search for new truth. (1916)

The teaching by the professor in his classroom on the subjects within the scope of his chair ought to be absolutely free. He must teach the truth as he has found it and sees it. This is the primary condition of academic freedom, and any violation of its endangers intellectual progress . . . The gravest questions, and the strongest feelings, arise from action by a professor beyond his chosen field and outside of his classroom. Here he speaks only as a citizen . . . In spite, however, of the risk of injury to the institution, the objections to restraint upon what professors may say as citizens seem to me far greater than the harm done by leaving them free . . . It is not a question of academic freedom, but of personal liberty from constraint, yet it touches the dignity of the academic career . . . If a university or college censors what its professors may say, if it restrains them from uttering something that it does not approve, it thereby assumes responsibility for that which it permits them to say. This is logical and inevitable but it is a responsibility which an institution of learning would be very unwise in assuming . . .

Surely abuse of speech, abuse of authority and arbitrary restraint and friction would be reduced if men kept in mind the distinction between the privilege of academic freedom and the common right of personal liberty as a citizen, between what may properly be said in the classroom and what in public. But it must not be forgotten that all liberty and every privilege imply responsibilities. Professors should speak in public soberly and seriously, not for notoriety or self advertisement, under a deep sense of responsibility for the good name of the institution and the dignity of their profession. They should take care that they are understood to speak personally, not officially. When they so speak, and governing boards respect their freedom to express their sincere opinions as other citizens may do, there will be little danger that liberty of speech will be either misused or curtailed.

(1918)

We have believed that the problem of Harvard College is really a moral problem. We want men to think, and think seriously. We do not want them to think alike. That is an entirely different matter. We have stood, and we always shall stand, for absolute freedom of thought under any circumstances, both with our professors and with our students. We do not want them made in a pattern. We want them to think. In other words, if I may parody the motto of the University, what we desire here is not truth, but the search for truth.   (1933)

As wave after wave rolls landward from the ocean, breaks and fades away sighing down the shingle of the beach, so the generations of men follow one another, sometimes quietly, sometimes, after a storm, with noisy turbulence. But, whether we think upon the monotony or the violence in human history, two things are always new—youth and the quest for knowledge, and with these a unversity is concerned. So long as its interest in them is keen it can never grow old, though it count its age by centuries. The means it uses may vary with the times, but forever the end remains the same; and while some principles, based on man's nature, must endure, others, essential perhaps for the present, are doomed to pass away . . .

(1936)

JAMES BRYANT CONANT

ACCORDING to the account written nearly three hundred years ago, Harvard was founded "to advance learning and perpetuate it to posterity." We can all agree that these few admirable words still describe our aims, although the methods of advancing learning and the modes of perpetuating it have changed greatly in the course of three centuries. Our Puritan ancestors thought of education and theology as inseparably connected. It is hard for us to recapture their point of view; today, learning has become secular. Indeed, the universities are now the residuary legatees of many of the spiritual values which were guarded by the church three centuries ago. Our responsibilities are correspondingly increased and our ideals must be clearly defined. If future generations are to have that high regard for the achievements of the human mind which is essential to civilization, there must be a true reverence for learning in the community. It is not sufficient to train investigators and scholars, no matter how brilliant they may be; a large body of influential citizens must have a passionate interest in the growth of human knowledge. It is our ambition to inspire the undergraduates in Harvard College with an enthusiasm for creative scholarship and a respect for the accumulated intellectual treasures of the past. This is one way in which we today perpetuate learning to posterity.

Learning must be advanced as well as perpetuated. Indeed, in the last analysis it is only by advancing learning that it is possible to perpetuate it. When knowledge ceases to expand and develop, it becomes devitalized, degraded, and a matter of little importance to the present or future. The community loses interest, and the youth of the country responds to other challenges. Able young men enlist in an enterprise only if they are persuaded that they, too, may contribute by creative work. A zest for intellectual adventure should be the characteristic of every university. In the future as in the past, our teachers must be scholars who are extending the frontiers of knowledge in every direction. I hope there will never be a separation of our faculty into those who teach and those who carry on creative work. No line should be drawn between teaching and research. Our strength in the past has lain in the fact that the spirit of scholarship has pervaded our teaching and our scholars have seen the importance of perpetuating the ideals of scholarship as well as advancing knowledge in their own specialty.

A university is a group of men—a community of scholars and students—and here lies the real problem in regard to the future of all institutions of higher learning. Harvard's success will depend almost entirely on our ability to procure men of the highest caliber for our student body and for our faculty . . . Together with other institutions of higher learning, we are the trustees in whose hands lies the fate of the future of human knowledge . . .   (1934)

The primary concern of the University today should be what it always has been, to foster the search for truth; only secondarily should a university concern itself with the immediate applications of knowledge.   (1936)

If we attempt to sum up in one phrase the aim of higher education, we can do no better than to speak of "the search for truth . . ."

When the Puritans wrote *Veritas* upon the open books, they had in mind two paths by which truth could be obtained: one, Revelation as interpreted with the aid of human reason; the other, the advancement of knowledge and learning.   (1936)

The bedrock on which the scholarly activities of a university are founded is a charter of free inquiry; without this you may have an institution of advanced education, a technical school or a military college, for example, but you do not have a university. I am sure we are all agreed on that. There should be no barriers to an objective analysis of every phase of our national life. No compromise with this principle is possible even in days of an armed truce. The nation has a right to demand of its educational institutions that the teachers dealing with controversial subjects shall be fearless seekers of the truth and careful scholars rather than propagandists. But granted honesty, sincerity and ability there must be tolerance of a wide diversity of opinion.   (1948)

The old cliché that "education is what is left after all that has been learnt is forgotten" is worth repeating in any discussion of education. Through our departmental offerings we assist the student in learning many difficult skills ranging from the ability to handle mathematics or ancient and modern languages, to manipulation of both the concepts and the apparatus of the social and the natural sciences. By the same means we provide opportunities for absorbing a vast amount of knowledge. Along with the acquisition of knowledge and skills within an area comes the unerstanding and appreciation of an embryonic specialist, one who sees what the mastery of a field would mean. Even if twenty years later the student has forgotten nearly all that he learned through his field of concentration, he will know something of what it means to master a subject. On this point President Lowell used to insist repeatedly in expounding his philosophy of education.   (1950)

NATHAN M. PUSEY

HARVARD is great primarily because of what it has stood for through the years—a bulwark in the maintenance of freedom of the mind, that freedom upon which all the other freedoms depend. It is great because it has repeatedly stood for this at times when it would have been quite easy to forget its responsibility to defend and maintain the university idea.   (1954)

Education begins to do its full work only when the materials of learning, ably and imaginatively presented, penetrate into the very marrow of the learner and set up there a process of desiring that will not be stilled. When the impact of the thing learned, bursting into the self and filling it with excited awareness of the far-reaching implications in the thing studied, engenders a thrilling realization that the self really matters, and urges on irresistibly to new effort, education of the deepest kind is taking place. It is the awesome power of the great teacher, who must himself have had such experience, to work this kind of magic.   (1955)

What makes a college good is its magic power, perennially renewed, to widen experience and in so doing to work those transformations in young minds and hearts that draw us into fuller and deeper life and engender processes of learning which enable us later in less favorable circumstances still to care when the bloom of fresh excitement shall have passed.   (1960)

What Harvard wants more than anything now to give to our country and the world is educated men and women of character. It is her hope that there will develop here generation after generation, now as in the past, thoughtful people who through their beliefs and actions will go on to renew and strengthen true quality in the world's life; men and women of knowledge and faith who, ready to learn from others, will make an effort at honest appraisal of their culture, will recognize both its strength and its weakness, will try to see these aspects separately and fairly, and who then, not complaining, or criticizing unreasonably, or turning way in supercilious indifference, will steadfastly set about working where they can—first of all perhaps with themselves—to improve that culture and to make not its shabbiness but its goodness available to others.   (1962)

Morehouse, Harvard, and all of ours belong with Delhi and other colleges and universities, new and old, everywhere, in one common tradition. We are all members of an ancient fellowship of educated men and women whose numbers though relatively small and whose voices though relatively feeble are, I am convinced, the best hope of mankind. It is a thin and fragile chain that binds Morehouse and Harvard with Delhi and a thousand other institutions where learning flourishes and is honored, and where the noblest qualities of man stand revealed in that simple and unpretentious Indian "commandment": truth and righteousness, and with them courage, modesty, sympathy, belief, understanding, and joy.

At any commencement there is little more we can say than what they [at Delhi] said:

> This is the precept;
> This is the advice;
> This is the commandment;
> Follow it; follow it.

In the widespread observance of such commandment, under God, lies our hope for a better world.   (1962)

DEREK C. BOK

ONE HOPES that the vital areas of research and education will always have first claim on the president's attention. Nevertheless, it has been clear for a long time that the president is neither equipped nor empowered to produce the blueprints for educational policy that some forceful presidents were able to draft in the changeful decades surrounding the turn of the century. The president's influence will remain more indirect, centering upon his power to appoint deans of the different Schools and to participate in the appointments process to insure that selections have been made with the necessary thoroughness and care. In addition, the president's role will take subtler forms; discerning new opportunities for others to consider—especially opportunities that do not fall within the exclusive province of a single Faculty; creating an atmosphere and a set of incentives that stimulate innovation and maintain a sound balance between teaching and research; encouraging needed collaboration between Schools and searching for better organizational frameworks for marshaling interested people and adequate resources to work on problems cutting across traditional intellectual boundaries. In the end, the president must recognize that the progress of the University will always depend fundamentally upon the imagination and ability of faculty, students, and staff. But there will be much for him to do in suggesting new directions and helping to maintain an environment in which the great talents of the University are encouraged to express themselves as freely and creatively as possible.   (1971)

Despite the need for devoting more thought to the aims of undergraduate education, a sense of purpose will only carry us so far. The variety of interests within the student body and the subtlety of the educational process require a diversity that can never be wholly captured in any set of institutional goals. It is also infinitely more important for the College to assemble a talented, motivated student body and a faculty of the highest intellectual distinction. With these ingredients, the experience of college will usually prove interesting and valuable to the student. Without them, the experience will probably be shallow and uninspiring however carefully the institution's goals are defined. For these reasons, I can argue for paying closer attention to our purposes while still emerging from my first year in office with a feeling of awe and respect for the richness of talent and activity that gives such value to a college education at Harvard.   (1972)

For Harvard, the challenge is not to avoid a financial crisis or even to stave off chronic deficits. The challenge is to maintain the great quality and distinction of its scholarship and education at a time when distinguished scholarship and education are more important than ever. As always, the challenge will depend on the combined efforts of many people. From the faculty must come the inspiration to meet our intellectual challenges creatively. From administration must come the skill to husband resources wisely and create the framework in which talented students and professors can do their best work. And from our friends and alumni must come the moral and financial support that will be needed for Harvard to maintain the essential quality it must have in order to capitalize fully on the opportunities before it.   (1976)

In serving Harvard, we serve an institution with a remarkable capacity for human good—an institution that can help us surmount the innumerable problems that afflict us, a community that offers a memorable experience to thousands of able young people, a forum of ideas which can produce the occasional works of intellect and imagination that illumine man's condition long after we are gone. Other institutions may succeed in one or another of these endeavors. But few can aspire to do them all, and among those few, I do believe that Harvard stands unsurpassed. To me, it will always be the highest privilege to do what little I can to further an institution so dedicated to the welfare of mankind.   (1979)

Does anyone imagine that we can remove all of our racial barriers and misunderstandings without the help of able, determined, and well-prepared minority leaders? Can anyone suppose that we will achieve genuine equality without the understanding and active support of dedicated whites? Would anyone recommend that Harvard refrain from doing its best to participate fully in the education of these leaders—or suggest that we would not rejoice in any success they might ultimately achieve? It is already a source of satisfaction to have had a part in the education of many students of all races who have later made significant contributions to breaking down the barriers of discrimination in this country . . . This is not a tradition that should engender anxiety or hesitation for the future, but one that enables us to hope that our present efforts will bear even greater fruit in the future. To participate in so constructive a quest brings to us all a chance to enlarge our own understanding and to help in creating a better society for the future. Such opportunities are worthy of our best efforts, and I hope that we will accept them in this spirit.   (1981)

II

PEDAGOGUES AND PUPILS

The uses of adversity are beyond measure strange. As a professor, he regarded himself as a failure. Without false modesty he thought he knew what he meant. He had tried a great many experiments, and wholly succeeded in none. He had succumbed to the weight of the system . . . The only part of education that the professor thought a success was the students. He found them excellent company. Cast more or less in the same mould, without violent emotions or sentiment, and, except for the veneer of American habits, ignorant of all that man had ever thought or hoped, their minds burst open like flowers at the sunlight of a suggestion. They were quick to respond; plastic to a mould; and incapable of fatigue. Their faith in education was so full of pathos that one dared not ask them what they thought they could do with education when they got it.

HENRY ADAMS (1907)

I perceive that I got almost nothing of intellectual value from Harvard University. It was my fault, no doubt; if I had been a real student, I should have found genuine instruction. But, for all my assumption of superiority, the crudeness of my mind at the age of twenty wakens amazement in me.

LOGAN PEARSALL SMITH (1938)

Henry Dunster

CONSIDERATIONS

(1654)

Henry Dunster, the first and youngest of the long line of Harvard presidents, at thirty-three took over the reins of the College after the infant institution had been forced to close down for a year following the miserable regime of the Eatons. "Dunster's genius for organization was such," wrote Samuel Eliot Morison, "that the curriculum, the forms, and the institutions established under his presidency long outlasted his time, and even his century . . . and the Charter of 1650 that he obtained . . . still serves as constitution of the modern University." Dunster's outspoken conviction that only adult believers should be baptized resulted finally in his resignation on October 24, 1654. Three weeks later he wrote with "simple, touching pathos" to the General Court, begging leave to remain in the president's house throughout the winter; his request was granted in this case, although in other respects he was not treated with much consideration, particularly as to his meager salary.

FIRST. The time of the year is unseasonable, being now very near the shortest day, and the depth of winter.

Second. The place unto which I go, is unknown to me and my family, and the ways and means of subsistence, to one of my talents and parts, or for the containing or conserving my goods, or disposing of my cattle, accustomed to my place of residence.

Third. The place from which I go, hath fire, fuel, and all provisions for man and beast, laid in for the winter. To remove some things will be to destroy them; to remove others, as books and household goods, to hazard them greatly. The house I have builded, upon very damageful conditions to myself, out of love for the College, taking country pay in lieu of bills of exchange on England, or the house would not have been built; and a considerable part of it was given me, at my request, out of respect to myself, albeit for the College.

Fourth. The persons, all besides myself, are women and children, on whom little help, now their minds lie under the actual stroke of affliction and grief. My wife is sick, and my youngest child extremely so, and hath been for months, so that we dare not carry him out of doors, yet much worse now than before. However, if a place be found, that may be comfortable for them, and reasonably answer the obstacles above mentioned, myself will willingly bow my neck to any yoke of personal denial, for I know for what and for whom, by grace, I suffer.

The whole transaction of this business is such, which in process of time, when all things come to mature consideration, may very probably create grief on all sides; yours subsequent, as mine antecedent. I am not the man you take me to be. Neither if you knew what, should, and why, can I persuade myself that you would act, as I am at least tempted to think you do. But our times are in God's hands, with whom all sides hope, by grace in Christ, to find favor, which shall be my prayer for you, as for myself,

Who am, honored Gentlemen, yours to serve,

HENRY DUNSTER

Josiah Quincy, *The History of Harvard University* (Cambridge, 1840).

Cotton Mather

HARVARD FROM HOAR TO MATHER

(1702)

One of the most extraordinary personages in early Harvard history was Cotton Mather (1663–1728) whose prodigious learning and amazing energy were applied both to his ministry and to his voluminous writings. Disappointed twice in the expectation of becoming president of Harvard, he nevertheless left as his monument an early history of his alma mater in his greatest work, the Magnalia Christi Americana. *Until the histories of Peirce, Quincy, and Eliot, this was the standard general account of the early Harvard and despite its annoying pedantry and a humor strange to modern ears, it preserved much valuable information about the early years of the College. The following selection, with certain long-winded passages removed, gives the flavor of the famous book.*

AFTER the death of Mr. Chauncy ... the Alma Mater Academia must look among her own sons to find a President for the rest of her children; and accordingly the Fellows of the College with the approbation of the Overseers,

July 13, 1672, elected Mr. Leonard Hoar, unto that office; whereto, on the tenth of September following he was inaugurated.

This gentleman, after his education in Harvard College, travelled over into England, where he was not only a preacher of the Gospel in divers places, but also received from the University in Cambridge the degree of a Doctor of Physick. The doctor, upon some invitations relating to a settlement in the pastoral charge with the South Church at Boston, returned into New England; having first married a virtuous daughter of the Lord Lisle, a great example of piety and patience, who now crossed the Atlantic with him; and quickly after his arrival here, his invitation to preside over the college at Cambridge superseded those from the church in Boston. Were he considered either as a scholar or as a Christian, he was truly a worthy man; and he was generally reputed such, until happening, I can scarce tell how, to fall under the displeasure of some that made a figure in the neighborhood, the young men in the College took advantage therefrom to ruin his reputation as far as they were able. He then found the rectorship of a college to be as troublesome a thing as ever Antigonus did his robe . . . The young plants turned cud-weeds, and with great violations of the Fifth Commandment set themselves to travesty whatever he did and said, and aggravate everything in his behavior disagreeable to them, with a design to make him odious; and in a day of temptation, which was now upon them, several very good men did unhappily countenance the ungoverned youths in their ungovernableness. Things were at length driven to such a pass that the students deserted the College, and the doctor on March 15, 1675 resigned his presidentship. But the hard and ill usage which he met withal made so deep an impression upon his mind that his grief threw him into a consumption, whereof he died November 28 the winter following, in Boston, and he lies now interred at Braintree . . .

After the death of Dr. Hoar, the place of president *pro tempore* was put upon Mr. Urian Oakes, the excellent pastor of the church at Cambridge, who did so, and would no otherwise accept of the place; though the offer of a full settlement in the place was afterwards importunately made unto him. He did the services of a president even as he did all other services, faithfully, learnedly, indefatigably; and by a new choice of him thereunto, on February 2, 1679, was at last prevailed withal to take the full charge upon him. We all know that Britain knew nothing more famous than their ancient sect of Druids, the philosophers whose order, they say, was instituted by one Samothes, which is in English as much as to say, An Heavenly Man . . . Reader, let us now upon another account, behold the students of Harvard College as a rendezvous of happy Druids, under the influences of so rare a President; but alas! our joy must be short lived, for, on July 25, 1681, the stroke of a sudden death felled the tree.

—Qui tantum inter Caput extulit Omnes,
Quantum Lenta solent, inter Viburna Cypressi.

Mr. Oakes, thus being transplanted into the better world, the presidentship was immediately tendered unto Mr. Increase Mather; but his church upon the application of the Overseers unto them, to dismiss him unto the place where to he was now chosen, refusing to do it, he declined the motion. Wherefore, on April 10, 1682, Mr. John Rogers was elected unto that place, and on August 12, 1683, he was installed into it. This worthy person was the son of the renowned Mr. Nathanael Rogers, the pastor to the church of Ipswich, and he was himself a preacher at Ipswich until his disposition for medicinal studies caused him to abate of his labors in the pulpit. He was one of so sweet a temper that the title of *deliciae humani generis* might have on that score been given him; and his real piety set off with the accomplishments of a gentleman, as a gem set in gold. In his presidentship, there fell out one thing particularly for which the College has cause to remember him. It was his custom to be somewhat long in his daily prayers (which our presidents used to make) with the scholars in the college hall. But one day, without being able to give reason for it, he was not so long it may be by half as he used to be. Heaven knew the reason! The scholars returning to their chambers found one of them on fire, and the fire had proceeded so far that, if the devotions had held three minutes longer, the College had been irrecoverably laid in ashes, which now was happily preserved. But him also a premature death, on July 2, 1684, the day after the Commencement, snatched away, from a society that hoped for a much longer enjoyment of him, and counted themselves under as black an eclipse as the sun did happen to be at the hour of his expiration . . .

The College was now again by universal choice cast into the hands of Mr. Increase Mather, who had already in other capacities been serving of it; and he accordingly, without leaving either his house or his church at Boston, made his continual visits to the College at Cambridge, managing as well the weekly disputations as the annual Commencements, and inspecting the whole affairs of the society; and by preaching often at Cambridge he made his visits yet more profitable unto them.

Reader, the interest and figure which the world knows this my parent hath had in the ecclesiastical concerns of this country ever since his first return from England in the twenty-second until his next return from England in the fifty-third year of his age makes it a difficult thing for me to write the church history of the country. Should I insert everywhere the relation which he hath had unto the public matters, it will be thought by the envious that I had undertaken this work with an eye to such a motto as the son of the memorable Prince of Orange took his device, *Patriaeque Patrique.* Should I on the other side bury in utter silence all the effects of that care and zeal wherewith he hath employed in his peculiar opportunities with which the free grace of Heaven hath talented him to do good unto the public, I must cut off some essentials of my story. I will however bowl nearer to

the latter mark than the former, and if nobody blame Sir Henry Wotton for still mentioning his father with so much veneration as that best of men, my father, I hope I shall not be blamed for saying thus much: My father hath been desirous to do some good. Wherefore I will not only add in this place that when the Honorable Joseph Dudley, Esq., was by the King's Commission made President of the Territory of New England, this gentleman, among other expressions of his hearty desire to secure the prosperity of his mother whose breasts himself had sucked, continued the government of the College in the hands of Mr. Mather, and altered his title into that of a Rector. But, when wise persons apprehend that the constitution of men and things, which followed after the arrival of another governor, threatened all the churches with quick ruins, wherein the College could not but be comprehended, Mr. Mather did by their advice repair to Whitehall, where being remarkably favored by three crowned heads in successive and personal applications unto them, on the behalf of his distressed country, and having obtained several kindnesses for the college in particular, he returned into New England in the beginning of the year 1692, with a royal charter full of most ample privileges. By that royal charter under the seal of King William and Queen Mary, the country had its English and its Christian liberties as well as its titles to its lands (formerly contested) secured to it; and the Province being particularly enabled hereby to incorporate the College (which was the reason that he did not stay to solicit a particular charter for it); immediately upon his arrival, the General Assembly gratified his desire, in granting a charter to this University. Mr. Mather now reassuming the quality of president over the College, which in his absence had flourished for divers years under the prudent government of two tutors, Mr. John Leverett, and Mr. William Brattle, he does to this day continue his endeavors to keep alive that river, the streams whereof have made glad this City of God
. . .

And now, I hope that the European churches of the faithful will cast an eye of some respect upon a little university in America, recommended by the character that has been thus given of it. Certainly they must be none but enemies to the Reformation, the sons of Edom (which the Jewish rabbins very truly tell us is the name of Rome in the Sacred Oracles) that shall say of such an university, Raze it! Raze it!

Magnalia Christi Americana (1702).

Clifford K. Shipton

THE NEPHEW OF UNCLE EXPERIENCE

(c. 1730)

*The perils of a twentieth-century Pauline were as nothing to the torments
suffered by the tutors who kept a painful watch over the behavior of Harvard undergraduates in the seventeenth and eighteenth centuries. A familiar
target for undergraduate pranks was tutor Joseph Mayhew of the Class of
1730 who spent two postgraduate years in Cambridge and sixteen other
years serving the College as disciplinarian, Tutor, and member of the Corporation. Because no detailed contemporary accounts exist, a reconstruction
can be made only by compiling and editing the few scraps of isolated information which have been preserved through the forethought of antiquarians.
Such scholarly detective work, combined with good writing, distinguishes
Clifford K. Shipton's fourteen volumes of* Sibley's Harvard Graduates, *now
our principal secondary source of information about the men who went to
Harvard in the early days. Shipton resumed in 1930 the task which had come
to a hull with the death of John Langdon Sibley (1804–1885), the indefatigable Harvard librarian and archivist, part of whose substantial estate was assigned to the Massachusetts Historical Society for the completion of the biographical studies begun in 1859. Mr. Sibley brought the records down to
1690; Mr. Shipton continued them to 1771, and also found time to serve as
Custodian of the Harvard University Archives and as Librarian of the
American Antiquarian Society. No collection of Harvardiana would be
complete without an example of one of "Shipton's Lives."*

TUTOR JOSEPH MAYHEW was born on February 26, 1709/10, the eldest son of
Deacon Simon and Ruth Mayhew of Chilmark. No member of this distinguished family had as yet been graduated at Harvard, and Simon, who was a
farmer, might not have sent Joseph to college if Harvard had not in 1723
forced an honorary M.A. on Uncle Experience Mayhew in recognition of his
work as a missionary to the Indians. At Cambridge, Joseph's career was
marked by the unusual combination of the highest scholastic honors and a
gnawing appetite which the regular issue of college commons could by no
means satisfy. When he was a freshman, Thomas Hollis, who had no doubt
heard of him from Uncle Experience, wrote to the college suggesting that
he be awarded one of his rich scholarships, but the Corporation saw fit to
ignore the donor's suggestion. It did, however, appoint him a monitor and
award him the Hopkins prize for excellence in his studies. The prize consisted of copies of Cotton Mather's *Ratio Disciplinae* and *Manuductio.*

After he had taken his first degree, Mayhew was awarded a Hopkins fellowship, but he did not qualify by residing in Cambridge and performing academic exercises. At least a part of the year he spent keeping the Roxbury school. On February 22, 1730/1, he was offered a Boyle fellowship of £20 "provided his Father first give Bond for refunding the Said Sum to the College in Case his Son should live, & decline the Indian Service, or should not be imployed statedly in the said Service within the Space of five years." He did not, however, resume residence at the college until after he had taken his M.A. in 1733, on which occasion he presented a negative answer to the *Quaestio,* "An Damnati puniantur, ob Peccata in Inferno commissa?" About this time he was nominated to the Society for Promoting the Gospel in New England and Parts Adjacent to be a missionary to the Nantucket Indians, but in February 1733/4, he again took up residence at the college.

After another year at Cambridge, Mayhew was appointed by one of the Boston endowments to preach to the little congregation of Indians and Whites on Block Island ... After a year on Block Island he returned to Cambridge where he was again awarded a Hopkins fellowship. In August 1737, he left the college, but in May 1738 he returned, and the following spring he was awarded Flynt and Gibbs fellowships to enable him to meet the bills which he had accumulated.

It was then the practice to choose the tutors from among recent graduates, but in August 1739 the Corporation departed from it to elect Mayhew. The Overseers stood upon their right to investigate his religious principles:

> Mr Joseph Mayhew having been Chosen by the Corporation a Tutor for three years he was now presented to the Overseers for their acceptance— and such of the Gentlemen of the Corporation as are present having Signified that the Corporation had Examined him as to his religious principles The Question was put Whether the Gentlemen of the Corporation here present be desired to give Some account of the said Examination and it passed in the affirmative and an account thereof was given accordingly and then the Overseers voted their Acceptance of Mr Joseph Mayhew as a tutor.

The worst that could be said of Mayhew's religious views was that he did not favor revivals, an attitude which he later demonstrated by subscribing for the *Seasonable Thoughts* of Charles Chauncy (A.B. 1721). He also subscribed for the *Chronological History* of Thomas Prince (A.B. 1707), which was at that day the mark of an intellectual. There is no reason to question the statement of a contemporary that he was "a man of superior abilities and learning."

Why any man of his age would want to be a tutor is a puzzle. In the years which followed his appointment he grew accustomed to being greeted in the yard with "Contemptuous Noise & Hallowing" and to being subjected to "Heinous Insults." He was defied by drunken students and his orders were resisted with physical violence. Logs were rolled down the stairs by his study door, his door knob was broken off, and his cellar was broken open and his beer and brandy stolen. He fought back, and when his window was broken by a stone he detected and apprehended the culprit by calculating the arc of the missile. He also had to contend with Overseers like Lieutenant Governor Andrew Oliver (A.B. 1724) who had no hesitation about using their influence in behalf of any boy of good family who was detected in such crimes.

Once when Mayhew ordered a Freshman to go to aid a sick upperclassman, Tutor Nathan Prince (A.B. 1718) interfered. To expose Prince, Mayhew insisted on a Faculty hearing:

> Mr. Mayhew bro't a complaint that he had been ill treated by Winslow a Senior Sophister, viz by his detaining a Freshman from him. On which Mr. Prince (said Winslows Tutor) told Mr. Mayhew, He thought it improper to bring so trifling an Affair before the President & Tutors but that if Mr Mayhew would consent he doubted not, They might make up that Affair amicably between themselves, which the President consented to, but when Mr Mayhew insisted upon its being consider'd then, Mr. Prince Said he had urgent Business & couldnt tarry; Mr Mayhew repeating his desires of a present Consideration, The President told Mr Prince that if Mr Mayhew insisted upon the Affair, He would proceed then to consider it, Mr Prince again repeating the Necessity of his going away, mov'd off abruptly, while Mr Mayhew was still declaring his desires to have the Affair then consider'd.

After other encounters of the sort, Prince came to the considered conclusion, publicly announced, that Mayhew was "a Rascall & a Rascally Fellow."

When Prince finally drank himself out of the college in 1742, it was Mayhew who succeeded him as a Fellow of the Corporation. He served this body on committees to audit the accounts, to visit and report on the college farms, to inspect the library, and to make a college inventory. The Corporation supported him in matters of discipline, and with some degree of regret accepted his resignation on July 24, 1755. the reason for his action was apparently the recent death of his father.

Mayhew settled on the family farm on Martha's Vineyard where he remained in quiet obscurity until the tremors of the approaching Revolution shook even that remote corner of the Province . . . Mayhew was still active in civil affairs when death overtook him on March 31, 1782. He was unmarried.

Sibley's Harvard Graduates, VIII, 1726–1730 (Boston, 1951).

David Sewall

FATHER FLYNT'S JOURNEY TO PORTSMOUTH

(1754)

It is regrettable that time has partly obliterated from the record the full per-
sonality of Tutor Henry Flynt (1676–1760), whose academic ministrations
to Harvard men spanned nearly six decades, beginning shortly after his
graduation, and continuing until his death at the age of eighty-four. Occa-
sional flashes in the records have revealed him to us, the stalwart son of
Harvard who served fifty-five years as Tutor, sixty years as Fellow, forty-six
years as Secretary to the Board of Overseers, and one year, after the death of
Wadsworth, as Acting President. In the spring of his final year as Tutor the
venerable Flynt decided to make a trip to Portsmouth, New Hampshire, and
engaged as his driver a member of the junior class, David Sewall. The nine-
teen-year-old undergraduate recorded the events of the journey like a true
Boswell, and for years his manuscript account was preserved among the
papers of his classmate, John Adams. Aside from this first-hand portrait,
there are few such human characterizations of this remarkable personage.
The Latin of Father Flynt's tombstone proclaims him "a man of sound
learning, of acute and discriminating intellect; firm but moderate, steadfast
in opinion, but without obstinacy; zealous and faithful in the discharge of
his various duties."

IN THE MONTH of June, 1754, after the Senior Sophisters, agreeable to the
usage of Harvard College in those times, had left off attending and reciting
to their tutor, and were making the necessary arrangements for graduating
in July then next, the time of commencement, Henry Flynt, the senior tutor
of the institution, who had then the care and instruction of the senior class
of undergraduates, sent for me to his chamber, in the old Harvard Hall, on
Saturday afternoon, and told me he intended to take a journey to Portsmouth, N.H.; and, being informed that I was an excellent driver of a chair,
he wished to know if I would wait upon him in that situation, and return
home for a few days. I replied, the proposition was to me new and unexpected, and I wished for a little time to consider of it. He replied "Aye,
prithee, there is no time for consideration: I am going next Monday morning." I paused about a minute, and then replied that I would wait upon him
in the journey.

I afterwards learned that he had applied to T. Atkinson, a student from
Portsmouth, who had declined, and who had recommended me as a skilful
and careful driver of a chair. In those days a single horse and chair, without

a top was the usual mode of conveyance. A covered chair, then called a calash, was very seldom used.

After my consenting to attend Mr. Flynt, he says, "Go to the President (Holyoke), and give my sarvice to him, and desire him to give leave for you to return home," that I might attend him in his proposed journey. I accordingly went, and obtained leave of absence, and was then directed to go to Mr. Stedman's, and procure a horse and chair for him to go the journey.

On Monday, after breakfast, I went with the horse (which was a pacing mare) and chair to the college yard, from whence we proceeded on the journey across the common, and up the Menotomy Road, until we came to the cross road, passing near the Powder House to Medford, and from thence through Malden to Lynn. The first stop we made was at the noted public-house kept in that day by landlord Newall, where we oated the horse; and, as it was a warm forenoon, Mr. Flynt had a nip of milk punch; after which Mr. Flynt took from a leather purse (of considerable bulk, filled with small silver change) a small piece of money, and gave me to discharge the reckoning, with this injunction: "Be careful, and take the right change." Which being done, we proceeded through Salem plain to Danvers, by the country seat of King Hooper (so called) of Marblehead, through Ipswich, and a little before sunset we reached the dwelling of the Rev. Mr. Jewett of Rowley; where we called, and Mr. Flynt acquainted him he meant to tarry there that night. We were cordially entertained, and at bed-time we were introduced to a chamber where was only one bed; upon getting into which, says Mr. Flynt to me, "You will be keeping well to your own side" (an injunction I had no disposition to disobey). The next day, Tuesday, we passed through Newbury, over Merrimack River, at the ferry called Salisbury Ferry. He conversed freely and sociably on many topics (a thing then unusual for a tutor with an undergraduate), and, among other things, that he had lately sold a farm to cousin Quincy, for £500 or thereabouts; but, as he had no present need of the money, he had taken his security for the purchase sum, payable at a future period on interest.

Mr. Flynt intended to call and dine with Parson Cotton of Old Hampton; and, as we came to the road that led from the post-road to Cotton's house, we met the parson and his wife walking on foot. Upon which Mr. Flynt informed Mr. Cotton that he intended to have called and taken dinner with him; but, as he found he was going from home, he would pass on and dine at a public-house. Upon which, says Mr. Cotton, "We are going to dine, upon an invitation, with Doctor Weeks, one of my parishioners; and Mr. Gookin and his wife, of North Hill, are likewise invited to dine there; and I have no doubt you will be as welcome as any of us; and, besides, the Doctor has a son who he intends shall enter college next commencement; and I will with pleasure introduce you to Doctor Weeks." After pausing a small space, Mr. Flynt agreed to go, provided Parson Cotton would pass on before us, [and] make the necessary explanation to show that we were not interlopers. Upon which Mr. Cotton and wife passed on before us, and I halted the chair, and moved on slowly behind them (about 100 rods) to Dr. Weeks's; and Mr. Cotton introduced us to him, where we were cordially received and hospitably entertained. After dinner, while Mr. Flynt was enjoying his pipe, the wife of Dr. Weeks introduced her young child, about a month old, and the twins of Parson Gookin's wife, infants of about the same age, under some expectation of his blessing by bestowing something on the mother of the twins (as was supposed), although no mention of that expectation was made in my hearing; but it produced no effect of the kind.

After dinner, we passed through North Hampton to Greenland; and after coming to a small rise of the road, hills on the north of Piscataqua River appearing in view, a conversation passed between us respecting one of them, which he said was Frost Hill. I said it was Agamenticus, a large hill in York. We differed in opinion, and each of us adhered to his own ideas of the subject. During this conversation, while we were decending gradually at a moderate pace, and at a small distance, and in full view of Clark's Tavern, the ground being a little sandy, but free from stones or obstructions of any kind, the horse somehow stumbled, in so sudden a manner, the boot of the chair being loose on Mr. Flynt's side, threw Mr. Flynt headlong from the carriage into the road; and the stoppage being so sudden, had not the boot been fastened on my side, I might probably have been thrown out likewise. The horse sprang up quick, and with some difficulty I so guided the chair as to prevent the wheel passing over him; when I halted and jumped out, being apprehensive from the manner in which the old gentleman was thrown out that it must have broken his neck. Several persons at the tavern noticed the occurrence, and immediately came to assist Mr. Flynt; and, after rising, found him able to walk to the house; and, after washing his face and head with some water, found the skin rubbed off his forehead in two or three places,—to which a young lady, a sister of William Parker, Jr., who had come out from Portsmouth with him and some others that afternoon, applied some pieces of court plaster. After which we had among us two or three single bowls of lemon punch, made pretty sweet, with which we refreshed ourselves, and became very cheerful. The gentlemen were John Wendell, Willliam Parker, Jr., and Nathaniel Treadwell, a young gentleman who was paying suit to Miss Parker. Mr. Flynt observed he felt very well, notwithstanding his fall from the chair; and, if he had not disfigured himself, he did not value it. He would not say the fault was in the driver; but he rather thought he was looking too much on those hills. John Wendell was just upon the point of marrying to a Miss Wentworth; and he [Flynt] was asked if he had come at this time to attend the wedding. He replied he had not made the journey with that intent; but, if it happened while he was at Portsmouth, he should have no objection of attending it.

I was directed to pay for one bowl of the punch, and the oats our horse had received, after which we proceeded on toward Portsmouth; Mr. Tread-well and Miss Parker preceded us in an open chair. William Parker was going on to Kensington, where he was employed in keeping school; and J. Wendell returned on horseback to Portsmouth. The punch we had partaken of was pretty well charged with good old spirit, and Father Flynt was very pleasant and sociable. About a mile distant from the town, there is a road that turns off at right angles (called the Creek Road) into town, into which Mr. Treadwell and Miss Parker (who afterward married Captain Adams) entered with their chair. Upon which Mr. Flynt turned his face to me, and said, "Aye, prithee, I do not understand their motions; but the Scripture says, 'The way of a man with a maid is very mysterious.' "

The time and manner of this observation was such that, in order to suppress my risible faculties, the water fell in several drops from my eyes. We passed on the usual road to Portsmouth, to the dwelling-house of Thomas Wibird,—a respectable merchant, a bachelor, who kept house with several domestics. There I tarried on Tuesday night, and slept again in the same bed with Mr. Flynt. The next day, being Wednesday, after receiving directions at what day of the succeeding week he should commence the journey back to Cambridge, I passed the ferry, and walked on foot to York, and tarried there until the time assigned for my return, when I came again to Portsmouth.

We left the town, and, passing through Greenland, North Hampton, Hampton Old Town to Hampton Falls, stopped at Mr. Whipple's, the minister of the place, where Mr. Flynt intended to dine. But it so happened that dinner was over, and Mr. Whipple had gone out to visit a parishioner; but Madame Whipple was at home, and very social and pleasant, and immediately had the table laid, and a loin of roasted veal, that was in a manner whole, placed on it, upon which we made an agreeable meal. After dinner, Mr. Flynt was accommodated with a pipe; and, while enjoying it, Mrs. Whipple accosted him thus: "Mr. Gookin, the worthy clergyman of North Hill, has but a small parish and a small salary, but a considerable family; and his wife has lately had twins."—"Aye, that is no fault of mine," says Mr. Flynt.—"Very true, sir; but so it is." And, as he was a bachelor, and a gentleman of handsome property, she desired he would give her something for Mr. Gookin; and she would be the bearer of it, and faithfully deliver it to him. To which he replied, "I don't know that we bachelors are under an obligation to maintain other folks' children." To this she assented; but it was an act of charity she now requested for a worthy person, and from him who was a gentleman of opulence, and who, she hoped, would now not neglect bestowing it. "Madam, I am from home, on a journey, and it is an unseasonable time." She was very sensible of this; but a gentleman of his property did not usually travel without more money than was necessary to pay the immediate expenses of the journey, and she hoped he could spare something on this occasion. After some pause, he took from his pocket a silver dollar, and gave her, saying it was the only WHOLE DOLLAR he had about him. Upon which Mrs. Whipple thanked him, and engaged she would faithfully soon deliver it to Mr. Gookin; adding, it was but a short time to commencement, when it was probable Mr. Gookin would attend, and she hoped this was but an earnest of a larger donation he would then bestow upon Mr. Gookin. Father Flynt upon this replied, "Insatiable woman, I am almost sorry I have given you any thing."

Soon after which we pursued our journey, and, riding over the sandy road to the ferry, the easy motion of the chair lulled the old gentleman into a sleep for some time; upon which I carefully attended the boot of the chair, to prevent his being thrown from the carriage a second time, in case of the stumbling of the horse. We passed on through Newbury and Rowley, without calling upon the minister of either of the places, and reached Ipswich toward evening; when we stopped at the dwelling of Mr. Rogers, the clergyman of the old parish, who seemed much pleased with the visit, and introduced his wife (who, I understood, was a daughter of President Leverett); when Mr. Flynt accosted the lady, "Madam, I must buss you," and gave her a hearty kiss.

We enjoyed a social evening; and, upon his being asked some questions about the scholars, related the following anecdote: "One morning my class were reciting, and stood quite round me, and one or two rather at my back, where was a table on which lay a keg of wine I had the day before bought at Boston; and one of the blades took up the keg, and drank out of the bung. A looking-glass was right before me, so that I could plainly see what was doing behind me. I thought I would not disturb him while drinking; but, as soon as he had done, I turned round, and told him he ought to have had the manners to have drank to somebody." And this was all the reprimand made on the occasion.

We again slept in the same bed, together. In the morning I arose before him, and he slept on until breakfast-time, when I went upstairs to acquaint him of it. We had toast and tea. He was interrogated by Mrs. Rogers whether he would have the tea strong or weak, that she might accommodate it to his liking. He replied, he liked it strong of the tea, strong of the sugar, and strong of the cream; and it was regulated accordingly.

Breakfast being over, we departed, and passed through the hamlet now called Hamilton, to Beverly, and a ferry (where a toll-bridge is now erected), into Salem, and stopped at the home of Mr. Browne, an opulent merchant of the place, where we dined. This Mr. Browne was related to my classmate, William Browne; and, from the conversation which passed during dinner, I found he was a great genealogist. After dinner was over, we proceeded on our way, without any other remarkable occurrence, until we reached Cambridge, and finished the journey.

Proceedings of the Massachusetts Historical Society, First Series (Vol. XVI, 1878–1879).

Andrew Preston Peabody

OLD POP

(c. 1830)

Few Harvard teachers of the first half of the nineteenth century were better known to the students at our little New England college than "Old Pop" (John Snelling Popkin, A.B. 1792). Professor Popkin was teacher of Greek and college disciplinarian in a time when Harvard was little other than a boarding school. This pleasant sketch of a remarkable man was written by Andrew Preston Peabody (1811–1893), himself one of the most admirable of Harvard servants, who was connected with the College as student and teacher, off and on, for some three score years, beginning with his entrance as a junior at the age of thirteen. He was Plummer Professor of Christian Morals and Preacher to the University (1860–1881); on two occasions he was Acting President; he edited the North American Review (1852–1863); he wrote a half-dozen books, largely on religious and ethical subjects, and published two volumes about Harvard—Graduates Whom I Have Known and Harvard Reminiscences. It is from the latter that this excerpt comes.

DR. POPKIN was a bachelor, and for many years led a very lonely life. It was said that he had in his early days been strongly attached to a lady whose affections were bestowed elsewhere; and it is certain that when she died, in his old age, he sent for a carriage, and attended her funeral, though he had not been a wonted visitor at her house, nor, indeed, in any house. Till near the close of his professorship he lived in a college-room, for most of the time in the second story of Holworthy. He at first boarded in the college commons: but, finding the dining-hall too noisy and tumultuous, he after a little while took his meals in his own room; the venerable Goody Morse cooking his food, bringing it to him at the regular college hours, and in various ways taking the most assiduous care for his comfort. Shortly before he resigned his office, a widowed sister and two orphan nieces of his came to Cambridge; and he established himself as the head of their family, in the old Wigglesworth house, which stood next to the president's house in Harvard Street. He afterward built a house on North Avenue, adjacent to a house then recently built by his classmate and lifelong friend, Dr. Hedge. The two ex-professors used to hold the most pleasant intercourse on their several sides of the dividing fence, but neither ever entered the other's house; as Dr. Popkin, while the kindest of men, and social in his way, neither made nor invited visits.

Dr. Popkin was undoubtedly the best Greek scholar of his time; and there is a mine of recondite learning stowed away in his edition of the Gloucester Greek Grammar, and in the notes in the American edition of Dalzel's "Collectanea Graeca Majora" signed "P," and generally, with his characteristic modesty, pointed with an interrogation-mark, though no one was better entitled than he to employ the affirmative form of statement. I can hardly say that he gave instruction in the recitation-room, though he muttered in what seemed a breathlessly rapid soliloquy a great deal that would probably have been instructive, could it have been heard and understood. The criterion of a good recitation with him was not grammatical knowledge, but the accuracy and elegance with which the Greek was rendered into English. He had at the same time a singularly delicate ear for the detection of a rendering which was not the student's own; and, though he seemed to see very little, if a printed translation was brought in, he was not unlikely to discover and confiscate it. In like manner he accumulated a little library of interlined "Majoras," which had been made with assiduous care, transmitted from class to class, and held at a high price in the college market. But the students who cared little for the Greek language or literature could appear reasonably well at very small cost. He commonly called up the members of a division in alphabetical order, and one could always determine within a few lines the passage which he would have to construe. Once in a great while, however, Dr. Popkin would spread consternation by striking midway in the seats; but those who on such occasions utterly failed, felt entire security for many subsequent days. Those of us who really studied our whole lessons had a wearisome task. There was no Greek-English lexicon obtainable. Our chief dependence was on the often inadequate Latin definitions of Schrevelius, and we were not sufficiently good Latin scholars not to need the mediation of a Latin dictionary between the Greek and the English. There were in my class two or three copies of the more copious lexicon of Hedericus; and round one of these half a dozen of us would sit, each with his Schrevelius, depending, when he failed us, upon the fuller supply of Latin meanings in the larger vocabulary. Under such difficulties, the actual amount of Greek scholarship fell far short of the estimate which it had in the professor's generous credulity.

Dr. Popkin would have had a majestic presence, had he so chosen. He was tall, with a massive frame, with a broad and lofty brow, and with features indicative of superior mental power. But shyness and solitude gave him an aspect and manners more eccentric than can easily be imagined in these days, when, under the assimilating influence of modern habits, idiosyncrasies have faded out, and every man means and aims to look like every other. His dress, indeed, was, in an historical sense, that of a gentleman; but his tailor must have been the last survivor of an else long extinct race. He never walked. His gait was always what is termed a dog-trot, slightly accelerated as he approached its terminus. He jerked out his words as if they were forced from him by a nervous spasm, and closed every utterance with a sound that seemed like a muscular movement of suction. In his recitation-room he sat by a table rather than behind it, and grasped his right leg, generally with both hands, lifting it as if he were making attempts to shoulder it, and more nearly accomplishing that feat daily than an ordinary gymnast would after a year's special training. As chairman of the parietal government, he regarded it as his official duty to preserve order in the college yard: but he was the frequent cause of disorder; for nothing so amused the students as to see him in full chase after an offender, or dancing round a bonfire: while it was well understood that as a detective he was almost always at fault.

Oddities were then not rare, and excited less surprise and animadversion than they would now. The students held him in reverence, and at the same time liked him. His were the only windows of parietal officers that were never broken. Personal insult or outrage to him would have been resented by those who took the greatest delight in indirect methods of annoying him. Once, indeed, when he was groping on the floor in quest of smothered fire, in a room that had been shattered by an explosion of gunpowder, a bucket of water was thrown on him by a youth, whose summary expulsion was the only case of the kind that I then knew in which the judgment of the students was in entire harmony with that of the Faculty. As may be supposed, he was not without a nickname, which he accepted as a matter of course from the students; but hearing it on one occasion from a young man of dapper, jaunty, unacademic aspect, he said to a friend who was standing with him, "What right has that man to call me 'Old Pop'? He was never a member of Harvard College."

Dr. Popkin's only luxury was the very moderate use of tobacco. Every noon and every evening, Sundays excepted, he trotted to an apothecary's shop, laid down two cents, then the price for what would now cost five times as much, and carried to his room a single Spanish cigar. Of course, though the shop was open, he would not go to it on Sunday; and he would not duplicate his Saturday's purchase, lest he might be tempted to duplicate his Saturday evening's indulgence. A friend who often visited him on Sunday evening always took with him two cigars, one of which the doctor gratefully accepted.

Dr. Popkin took his turn in officiating at the daily college prayers, and his peculiarities of manner were almost always merged in the sacred dignity and the profound solemnity with which he conducted the service. While in his own soul it was evidently the utterance of sincere devotion, and not mere routine, there were certain phrases, scriptural for the most part, that recurred so often as to attach themselves indelibly to my memory of him. Thus, among his ascriptions of gratitude, he seldom failed to offer thanks for "wine that maketh glad the heart of man, and oil [*ile,* as he pronounced it] to make his face to shine, and bread which strengtheneth man's heart,"— wine having not yet fallen under the ban of even the Society for the Suppression of Intemperance, of which he must have been a member, as were the president and most of the Faculty. In the chapel service Dr. Popkin was apt to falter and hesitate, and even to sink into an unconscious bathos, when there was any thing unusual in the occasion, especially at the close or the beginning of a term, when he in vain attempted to embody the homegoing or the re-assembling of the students in the stately phraseology which he was wont to employ. He seldom preached in the chapel; but on the rare occasions on which he supplied the president's place, he plainly showed that the pulpit was the fitting fulcrum for his life-power. He was a heedful listener to sermons, and a wise and discriminating critic. Some of us younger college officers sat with him on Sundays in the chapel gallery, and descended the stairs at his side, to hear what he had to say about the sermon; though we never knew whether he was talking to himself or to us, as he made his comments *sotto voce.* Once, when a minister from a neighboring town had been preaching on the choice between Baal and Jehovah, offered to the people of Israel by Elijah, Dr. Popkin indicated the strange, but actual omission of the preacher, by saying, "If we are going to choose Baal, I see no need of being in such a hurry about it."

Dr. Popkin resigned his office in 1833. With his inexpensive habits, he had acquired a competent provision for his remaining years. He lived till 1852, retired from the outside world, still reading the Greek poets; but most of all loving the Bible, studying the New Testament in the original, and, while a good Hebraist, preferring the Old Testament in the Septuagint version. While never entirely in gearing with the machinery of this world's life, no man ever lived in more genuine fellow-citizenship with those whose blessed company he joined in dying.

Harvard Reminiscences (Boston, 1888).

FOUR LETTERS FROM FOUR PRESIDENTS

(1829-1862)

Harvard presidents have unhappily not always been noted for their tactful and blameless handling of great decisions. Forthright Quincy stirred up a disagreeable mixture of undergraduate pottage with his too strict treatment of the undergraduates. A century later aristocratic Lowell was widely criticized for his racial policy in rooming assignments. Fortunately Harvard presidents have sometimes shown remarkable diplomacy and determination, as the following group of four communications demonstrates. None of these letters (culled from the presidential letter books) has ever before been published; and the one from President Sparks is, of course, the answer to the action taken on April 23, 1849, to which Longfellow referred cryptically in his diary: "We have had at Faculty meeting an application from a young lady to enter College as a regular student."

PAINFUL FACTS COMPEL ME TO WRITE PLAINLY

Cambridge, July 30, 1829.

My dear Sir

You are apprised that circumstances have placed me at the head of Harvard University. I did not know until very recently that a son of yours was a member of it,—and the facts which have brought it to my knowledge are of that painful character which I would willingly conceal from you, did not duty compel me to write plainly, and without keeping back any of the truth.—During the last six or eight months such a series of depredations have been committed on property of the college, in its different public rooms, & buildings, that the Government were satisfied that access was had by means of false keys.—

In the same manner there was reason to believe that the public Arsenal, had been opened, and hand grenades, or shells, & powder pilfered.—

Although the last articles were not traced into the College, there was little doubt that the same person or persons who had been engaged in depredations in the college rooms were concerned in taking the public property;—and notice to that effect was given to the Adjutant General, that he might take measures for their detection and its preservation.—

Some time in May last, a set of carpenters who were working on the President's House, & who had their tools secured in a chest in the stable of that house, had their chest forced, and tools of various descriptions to the value of near fifty dollars taken away together with the key of the chest.—

The circumstances were of so gross & atrocious a kind, that they had no suspicion that it could have been done by any scholar, they accordingly ordered advertisements to be made offering a reward for the detection of the thief,— and actually took search warrants against houses suspected in the vicinity.

The loss was to the persons suffering under it very heavy, they being journeymen, and almost all they were worth vested in tools.—About a month afterwards however, a considerable number of the tools much abused, were found concealed in the garret of Massachusetts, which satisfied every one that the injury must have been done by some scholar, probably an inmate of that College.—No suspicion however attached to any one until yesterday, when I was called upon by the College carpenters, requesting that I would accompany them to the room occupied by your son, (I think Number 18, or 19) Massachusetts.—They informed me that being engaged in making the usual repairs of the rooms of scholars, always done in vacations, and having occasion to move a small table in your son's room they were satisfied by the rattling, that something not usual in college drawers, was contained in it.—

They had accordingly found a key that would open the lock, and in the drawers discovered a great number of false keys, suited to various locks, which however they would not touch until I had been called.—I went to the room, and found as they had stated in a table drawer, containing one or more letters to your son, & his receipted quarter bill, forty five keys, of which I took possession, and which on trial & inspection have been found to open almost all the public rooms in the College. Among the keys was that of the Carpenter's Chest,—broken open at the stable of the President's House,—before mentioned, and on farther search some of the tools taken from the Chest were found concealed in your son's room, and also various articles the property of the College.—A hole also was cut through the floor of his study,—into the cellar, and a sort of trapdoor adjusted to it.—The Carpenters' key to tools have been identified beyond all manner of question.—

It is not for me to dwell in writing to you, on the nature of this evidence.—It is of that character, & the depredations have affected so many persons, that if your son returned here, he will probably be subjected to a judicial process.—The usual college refuge of round denial, in such cases cannot I apprehend be resorted to with any success, and whatever should be the result of a judicial investigation, the disgrace which will attach to him must be such, that it is impossible his connexion with the College could longer be permitted.—

On this point however, I write after no consultation with any one, *not as the Head of the University,* but as a friend to a friend, on a subject of a very delicate and critical nature.—

If you ask me what I advise you to do, I am compelled to say, that were I placed under the same circumstances, I should by settling with the parties injured, preclude all possibility of farther publicity.—I should take my son immediately from the University, and under a most rigorous *surveillance.*—

It gives me great pain to be necessitated to communicate facts so distressing to a parent.—But there is no alternative.—I ought to add perhaps that on an inspection of the scale of merit of his class, I find he stands the lowest of any students now members of the University, & his continuance cannot probably be of any advantage to him, even should it be permitted.—

Respectfully yrs.,
Josiah Quincy.

Note [by Eliza Susan Quincy, the President's daughter]:

"Some months after the date of this letter, workmen repairing Harvard Hall, found under the floor of the Library, between it & the ceiling of the room beneath;—hand grenades, charged with powder, & a train of powder laid to them.—"

A SOLITARY FEMALE AT HARVARD?

Harvard University,
Cambridge, April 25th, 1849.

Miss Sarah Pellet,

Your letter, making inquiry whether you could be admitted into this University upon presenting the proper credentials of character and scholarship, was duly received. I am not aware that any law exists touching this point, and, as it is a novel case, it would be decided by a vote of the Corporation.

As the institution was founded, however, for the education of young men, all its departments arranged for that purpose only, and its rules, regulations, internal organization, discipline, and system of teaching designed for that end, I should doubt whether a solitary female, mingling as she must do promiscuously with so large a number of the other sex, would find her situation either agreeable or advantageous. Indeed, I should be unwilling to advise any one to make such an experiment, and upon reflection I believe you will be convinced of its inexpediency.

It may be a misfortune, that an enlightened public opinion has not led to the establishment of Colleges of the higher order for the education of females, and the time may come when their claims will be more justly valued, and when a wider intelligence and a more liberal spirit will provide for this deficiency.

Very respectfully yours,
Jared Sparks.

Mrs. Stoughton
New York

Cambridge, Oct. 16, 1861

Dear Madame.

It is with great regret that I have to inform you that your son, John Fiske, of the Junior Class, has incurred a public admonition by misconduct at the Episcopal Church. The particular acts complained of by the officers of the church were neglecting to conform to the customary modes of worship, and on two occasions, reading a secular book, which he had taken with him, during the service. These repeated marks of his contempt for the Episcopal service, and for the religious feelings of those among whom he had chosen to worship, exhausted the patience of the officers of the Church, and he was reported to the Faculty. Our laws require the attendance of every student at Church; but all are allowed to attend the church in which they are brought up, or which they prefer from "conscientious motives." Your son last year attended the College Chapel. He changed to the Episcopal Church, permission having been granted on your written request. Under these circumstances, the misconduct reported against him caused me great surprise: for he is a studious young man, and, so far as I know, of good moral character. I sent for him to ask an explanation. He very frankly admitted the facts charged against him, and added that he was not a Christian, i.e. a believer in Christianity. He further added in answer to a question of mine, that he had changed from the Chapel to the Church, from no conscientious motive, but in order to have a "pleasanter time."

We never attempt to control the religious opinions of young men. But I consider it a great and lamentable misfortune to a young man, when, in the conceit of superior wisdom, he openly avows himself an infidel. He has neither studied, nor reflected, nor experienced enough to make such an avowal anything more than a foolish, shallow, and whimsical affectation of superiority. I respect the doubts of a studious and enquiring mind, and would always treat such doubt with tenderness. But I have no such respect for open and positive denial by a youth in his teens, of truths held sacred by the wisest, most learned and best men, and I hold acts of insolent disrespect to the public rites and observances of a Christian Church, to be no common outrage. Your son's good character in general, and his faithful attention to his studies induced the Faculty to limit the censure to a public admonition. I have only to add, that while we claim no right to interfere with the private opinions of any student, we should feel it our duty to request the removal of any one who should undertake to undermine the faith of his associates. I hope you will caution your son upon this point, for any attempt to spread the mischievous opinions which he fancies he has established in his own mind, would lead to an instant communication to his guardian to take him away.

Yours with much respect,
C. C. Felton, President.

AN ADMONITION FOR MR. LINCOLN

Hon. Abraham Lincoln,
President of the United States,
Washington, D. C.

Cambridge, Mass. Dec. 9, 1862.

Dear Sir

The Faculty last evening voted "that Lincoln, Junior, be publicly admonished for smoking in Harvard Square after being privately admonished for the same offence." The word *"publicly"* simply makes it my duty to inform you of the admonition, and I trust, Sir, that you will impress upon him the necessity not only of attention to matters of decorum, but of giving heed to the private admonitions of his instructors.

Very respectfully yours,
Thomas Hill
President of Harvard College

Harvard University Archives.

Thomas Hill

A COLLECTING TRIP WITH LOUIS AGASSIZ

(1848)

In the stimulating Harvard community of the mid-nineteenth century few names shone so brightly as that of Louis Agassiz. The foreign visitor who quickly sought out Longfellow, Lowell, Holmes, or Emerson, just as quickly went to call on the great and popular Swiss naturalist who had awakened so many Americans of his time to a love and knowledge of science. Agassiz was a member of the Faculty for twenty-six years and he established the Museum of Comparative Zoology, which has since been supported to a large degree by the copper fortune of the Agassiz family. The following description of an expedition with Professor Agassiz was written by Thomas Hill, later president of Harvard. Hill reveals in this sympathetic sketch his friendship for Agassiz and his feeling for the unity of God and nature which char-

acterized his gentle approach to life—the same qualities which made him a
good teacher and a thoughtful educator; but a relatively poor administrator
and neither an entirely successful nor a happy president.

WHEN Mr. Samuel Felton was superintendent of the Fitchburg Railroad he used to take a party of friends, once or twice a year, to observe the progress in building the Cheshire, and afterward the Sullivan Road. One of the most delightful of these excursions was the last; when the line of rail had been extended up the valley of the Ammonoosuc, as far as Littleton, New Hampshire. The party included his two brothers, Mr. Cornelius Conway Felton, afterwards President of Harvard College; and Mr. John B. Felton who afterwards died in California; Professor Arnold Guyot, author of "Earth and Man," who died, a few years ago, at Princeton, New Jersey; Professor Peirce; Agassiz; his son, Alexander Agassiz, then a boy just arrived from Europe, and not knowing a word of English; and myself.

I was surprised, during the journey, to find that Agassiz knew the plants along the road as well as I did. I never knew him make any mistake in naming a wild plant, but once; and then it was a mere slip of the tongue, calling a Lespedeza a Hedysarum. His early intimacy with the great botanists Braun and Schimper had given him a far better knowledge of vegetable physiology, and of the classification of plants, and of the name of species, than I have sometimes found in so-called Professor of the Chair of Botany in colleges.

We started on this expedition in an accommodation train which had picked up one man at Charlestown, two or three others at Cambridge, and myself at Waltham. But at the end of the first twenty-five miles, all got out at South Acton and waited for an express train. While thus waiting we all utilized the time in hunting for specimens of animal life, for Agassiz. His son Alexander had a gauze net at the end of a pole with which to catch butterflies. Agassiz seeing a fine specimen on the wing called to the boy to come and catch it, "Alexe! Vite! Beau Papillon." A few moments after Mr. Samuel Felton turned over a log on the ground, and seeing a fine black beetle under it, repeated the cry, "Alexe! Vite! Beau Papillon." The boy ran up and seeing that his fine butterfly was a black beetle, burst into such a merry laugh, that none of us, not even Mr. Felton himself, could resist joining; and "Beau Papillon" became the watch-word of our party.

From Littleton we took stages for Franconia Notch. There was but one other passenger in the coach, an exceedingly solemn-looking man, and very silent. He was apparently shocked by the levity and gayety of our party; who, although on science bent, all had a cheerful mind. When we came to the foot of a long hill, we all got out and walked, except Professor Cornelius Felton who remained on the seat with the driver. As we were turning over stones and sticks, for hidden reptiles or insects; looking on the under side of leaves to discover butterflies, or snails; rapping the bushes, to start little moths, and occasionally shouting one to another "Beau Papillon"; the driver asked Professor Felton who these men were, that were with him. He replied "they are a set of naturalists, from an institution near Boston."

Our zoological pursuits retarded our movements up the hill so much that the coach had got far ahead of us, and our van was led by the solemn man, who had not taken any part in our performances. As we drew near the top of the hill, however, a remarkably beautiful butterfly went in front of him. The flush of his boyhood seemed instantly to return. He took off his hat, and made a sweep for it; and as the butterfly easily eluded him, he made a second and a third; growing more and more eager, till, at length, as the butterfly rose and soared over a high clump of bushes, our solemn man leaped into the air, made his last frantic swoop, and screamed, at the top of his voice, "Beau Papillon." At that moment, the stage in the opposite direction met ours, at the top of the hill. The drivers paused a moment to exchange salutations, and the other said to ours, "Why! You've a strange freight down there. Who are they?" Our driver, leaning toward him, said in a confidential whisper, "They are a set of naturals from that insane asylum near Boston. Their keeper just told me so."

The next day, Peirce and Agassiz were walking on the shores of Echo Lake. Agassiz saw a peculiar species of dragonfly, which he thought new, or at least rare. He had with him the muslin net on the pole, and set himself to work to catch them. Presently Peirce saw one and, in his eagerness to call Agassiz to it, gave it the name with which he had been familiar in his boyhood. "Here, Agassiz, here's one of those Devil's Needles." As Agassiz came up, Peirce turned, following the insect with his eye, and saw that the solemn man had been within hearing and was looking shocked at this semi-profanity. "Sir," said he solemnly to Peirce, "can you tell me the proper botanical designation of that insect?" The delicious absurdity of the botanical name of an insect made "Botanical Designation" remain with us, ever since, a synonym for the proper name of anything in either of the kingdoms.

I cannot tell the delight which the friendship of Agassiz gave to me in more serious hours. His own conscientious fidelity to duty and the resulting approval of his conscience lay among foundations of his perennial cheerfulness and hope. But deeper than this was his religious faith in God, on which his faith in special endowment and special obligation was based. Certain scientific men have spoken of that faith in God as a weakness; inherited by Agassiz from six generations of pious Huguenot ancestry. But a man who has sustained a searching examination in Plato's philosophy, studied in the original Greek; a man who has thoroughly studied the metaphysics of Germany as far down as Hegel; and who has accomplished results in zoological and geological inquiry which, on the lowest estimate that can be made of them, must be acknowledged to be of the very highest magnitude and importance, is not a man to be pitied for his intellectual weakness. If weakness is to be charged upon any one, in these premises, it would seem as likely that it is weakness of intellect which fails to recognize the demonstrative force of the inductive reasoning by which Agassiz shows that there is no intelligent understanding of the animal creation, unless that creation is intelligible, i.e. in the product of intellect.

Louis Agassiz and Joseph Henry were two of the largest and broadest minds, in all directions, that I have ever chanced to meet; they were both men of indefatigable scientific industry; and both men who accomplished exceedingly high results, each in his own department; and they agreed in regarding every scientific investigation, wisely conducted, as an intelligent questioning of the Creator; so that scientific discoveries they regarded as his intelligible answers. Agassiz's adoption of Theism in preference to either Atheism, Agnosticism or Pantheism, was the result of profound original thought, and original investigation; during which he distinctly saw, and weighed, all the considerations which have ever been brought against his conclusions; weighed them and found them wanting. He once mentioned to me half a dozen of the very strongest arguments, which have been recently brought forward by the advocates of evolution, through natural selection, and assured me that he had distinctly seen, and distinctly weighed them, and rejected them, ten or fifteen years before the publication of Darwin's "Origin of Species"; and, of course, before the publication of those arguments by which others have attempted to supplement Darwin's reasoning.

Agassiz's views, on the origin of species, have often been misunderstood, and caricatured, by enthusiastic advocates of Darwin's views. Yet as the matter lay in Agassiz's own mind it seems to me that his positions were absolutely impregnable. He thought that the origin of species in their diversity, and the origin of life on this planet, were problems not within the present range of human knowledge; and that we must, for the present, rest content with studying the plan, order and connection of the universe, as a revelation of the Divine Thought. It was to him an axiomatic truth, that Science has dignity and value only when it is regarded as a recognition and exposition of the *intellectual* harmonies of the universe; that is, as an interpretation of God's thought. With this strong, clear sight of the fundamental truth in theology; there was joined a purity of heart, and a warmth of emotion, which naturally led him to a devout frame of mind. He shrunk from any display of such sacred feelings. He was repelled from those who make a boast of their piety; but he always reverenced and loved the truly devout. I never was acquainted with a man who seemed to me of purer, more temperate, self-restrained, charitable and loving character; or one who more perfectly fulfilled the royal laws of loving God with all the heart, and loving his neighbor as himself. The attachment of his friends to him was founded incomparably more upon their love of his genial, affectionate, modest, truthful, character; than upon their admiration of his transcendent abilities and marvelous accomplishments . . .

In his twenty-second year, February 14th, 1829, Agassiz wrote to his father; and among other things said, "Here is my aim. I wish it may be said of Louis Agassiz that he was the first naturalist of his time, a good citizen, and a good son; beloved of those who knew him. I feel within myself the strength of a whole generation to work toward this end; and I will reach it if the means are not wanting." These remarkable words of the young man were most remarkably fulfilled in every particular for more than thirty years before his too early death. Before a will thus consecrated to a noble aim, consecrated to the search for truth, to the service of men, to the perfection of his own character, obstacles vanished. That will was *equivalent* to the strength of a whole generation. This sentence of the young student, read in the light of his subsequent scientific achievements, and of the personal love and veneration in which his name is held, on both sides of the Atlantic, seems almost like prophetic inspiration. He was a man who, always and everywhere, not only commanded high respect, but drew men toward him in warm affection. When in an assembly of scholars, July, 1858, he announced his intention of remaining permanently in this country, and added: "I am no longer a European," a vast assembly rose, by a sudden impulse, to their feet; and greeted the announcement with joyous and repeated cheering.

Harvard University Archives.

John T. Wheelwright and Frederic J. Stimson

HOW ROLLO CAME TO BE EXAMINED

(1880)

Rollo's Journey to Cambridge *was written by two of the editors of the* Harvard Lampoon *and first appeared in its pages in 1879–80. Since then it has gone through several editions, the latest of which appeared in 1926. Rollo is a Harvard classic. Of course, Rollo is dated today and probably would not seem funny to those who do not know Harvard, but it is a nice satire on the dangers which face a young innocent in an evil place such as Harvard. Yes, Rollo Holiday met an unhappy fate as the result of his trip to Cambridge with his Uncle George. The legend on his tombstone reads:*

ROLLO

Died Suddenly June 27th, 1879
"Those whom the gods love die hung"

[PRINCIPAL PERSONS OF THE STORY]

Rollo—*Fifteen years of age.*
Mr. and Mrs. Holiday—*Rollo's father and mother.*
Thanny—*Rollo's younger brother.*
Jane *or* Jinny—*Rollo's cousin, adopted by Mr. and Mrs. Holiday.*
Mr. George—*A young gentleman, Rollo's uncle.*

It was a bright June morning at about half past five. Rollo and Thanny were at play in the back yard. They had an half an hour back locked little Jinny, Rollo's cousin, in the wood-shed, and had been throwing empty tomato-cans and apple-cores through the window. Jinny had not been pleased at it, but, as Thanny said, Jinny was a girl.

Now, Thanny, who was a very ingenious boy, was cutting a willow stick into whistles with Mr. Holiday's razors, while Rollo, several years his senior, was smoking a paper cigarette which he had found in his Uncle George's pocket. Mr. George smoked for a cruel nervous disease, and therefore his smoking was no precedent for a boy to follow. Rollo knew this well, and therefore felt a little guilty when he heard Mr. George's voice over the fence.

"Rollo," said Mr. George.

"Yes," answered Rollo, hiding his cigarette behind his back.

"What are you about, Rollo?" asked Mr. George.

"About fifteen," answered Rollo.

"What!" inquired Mr. George, sharply, who was always very peremptory and decisive, though always just in his treatment of Rollo.

"Bunch! Uncle George," was Rollo's reply.

"Rollo," said Mr. George, waiving the repartee, "What are you going to do to-day?"

"To try to be good; Jonas has promised to make me a jack-a-lantern in the shed after tea, if I am a good boy all day."

"I have something far better for you to do to-day, Rollo," rejoined Mr. George.

Rollo was very much pleased, for Mr. George was a very thoughtful man, who had his nephew's interest very much at heart; so Rollo clambered briskly over the fence and went into the house.

He put on his cloth cap with a leather visor and a silken tassel, and brushed his green spencer; when his toilet* was made, he ran down into the "settin' room," where Mr. George was reading the Encyclopaedia.

* Toilet is a French word. It means dressing yourself so as to look as spruce as possible, using little or no soap and water.

Mr. George was reading this work through, and had advanced as far as Abyssinia.

"Uncle George," cried Rollo, "I am sorry to disturb you!"

"You are very polite, Rollo. See, I put a mark in my book that I may know where I left off. If I did not do so, I should have to begin over again. I once got as far as Xerxes, and, neglecting to put in the mark, was compelled to go back to Aaron."

It was very kind and thoughtful for Mr. George to tell Rollo this.

"What is your plan for to-day?" asked Rollo.

"I am going to drive with you, Jonas and Thanny to Cambridge. I had intended to take Jinny with me, but she is in the wood-shed and I have no authority to take her out."

"What are we to do there?" asked Rollo.

"You are to be examined for College, Rollo. You will be examined in twenty required subjects and five optional ones all at once."

"But," interrupted Rollo, "I have travelled so much that I have never been to school, and have never studied!"

"That may or may not be unfortunate," was Mr. George's reply. "As I understand it, an examination is to find out what you do not know rather than what you do. If, as you say, you know nothing, you must see the necessity of your being examined."

Rollo was convinced by the argument, and was glad when he heard the sound of wheels on the carriage road, and saw Jonas flicking a fly from old Dapple's flank.

"Come, Rollo," said Mr. George, putting on his dress-coat and patent-leather shoes. "I am prepared to go . . ."

"One of the greatest benefits of a course at Harvard, Rollo," said Uncle George, as they descended the steps, "is that derived from viewing the noble architecture specimens which are all around you."

Rollo had seen many beautiful things, both in his journey to Cambridge on that morning and in his European travels, but he had never seen anything which impressed him so much as the spacious building which Mr. George pointed out to him. It was built in the perpendicular style of architecture, its lines were straight, its roof slated, and it had many windows in it, which gave upon the green.

"What is it used for?" asked Rollo.

"It is called Thayer's Hall; and as, from its size, Mr. Thayer would not require it all for his residence, I suppose that some of the scholars live here also."

"I want to know!" said Rollo. "Perhaps I shall live here next year, Uncle George."

"Whether you do or not depends upon yourself, my boy. Jonas and Thanny have not appeared yet. Can it be that they are in trouble? I must look after them, and after information as to your examinations. For, although the Dean was a frank-spoken and affable gentleman, I did not get from his remarks a clear idea of the requirements for admission. Therefore I leave you to look around here by yourself. You will undoubtedly commit many blunders; but that is your own look-out. In no event must you look for help from me."

Saying this, Mr. George walked off across the path leading to a gate. Rollo watched him go across the street and finally disappear . . .

"Rollo," said his uncle, ". . . It is high time for you to go to your examination. Jonas will show you the way."

Jonas took a large box under his arm, and they walked along together.

"Did you ever go to college, Jonas?" said Rollo.

"Yes," said Jonas. "I went to the Bussey Institute. In fact, I may say, Le Bussey Institute, c'est moi."

"Don't you wish you could go now?"

"Yes," said Jonas, "I think I should like it better than you will."

"Better than I?" said Rollo, looking up with surprise; "why, I like it very much indeed."

"You haven't tried it yet," said Jonas.

"O, but I know I shall like it."

"They all like it the first day; but afterwards they find a great many things which they do not like very well."

"What things?" asked Rollo.

"Why, sometimes you will get to playing poker after tea, and when prayertime comes before breakfast you will not want to go. Then your studies will be hard sometimes, and the Dean will not be nice to you. And perhaps they will not elect you into the St. Paul's."

Rollo felt somewhat disappointed at hearing such an account of the business of going to college from Jonas. He had expected that it was to be all pleasure, and he could not help thinking that Jonas must be mistaken about it. However, he said nothing, but walked along slowly and silently.

"Please to tell me what have you in the box, Jonas," asked Rollo.

"O, that I call my examination apparatus," answered Jonas.

"An examination apparatus?" cried Rollo.

"An examination apparatus," answered Jonas.

Jonas set the box upon the ground and opened the lid, which was fastened with two hinges and a hook. Rollo saw therein many strange things.

"This," said Jonas, taking up a bundle of cigarette papers, "contains all Latin and Greek Grammar, Chinese I, Fine Arts III, Ancient and Modern Geography, Calisthenics, Andrew's Latin Lexicon, and Quackenbos's History of the United States. And this is a preparation for producing a sudden and violent nose-bleed. This is a certificate of good moral character, signed by the Superintendent of Police and the Treasurer of the Howard Athenaeum. This bank-note is counterfeit. On the back—which is blank—is written in invisible ink all irregular verbs, the equations of eccentric curves, and the obscure and disputed points in American history."

"But suppose they ask me the regular verbs?" said Rollo.

"They will not," said Jonas. "They only wish you to know the exceptions, because they prove the rules."

"But suppose they see me with the bank-note—"

"They will only think you are endowing the proctor: and a percentage of all bribes goes to the fund for pensioning good and faithful servants."

Rollo's Journey to Cambridge (Boston, 1880).

George Santayana

THE HARVARD YARD

(1882–1912)

George Santayana once described Harvard as a place where "much generous intellectual sincerity went with such spiritual penury and moral confusion as to offer nothing but a lottery ticket or a chance at the grab-bag to the orphan mind." Despite this disparagement, the Spanish-born Santayana remembered with tenderness; and he in turn is remembered with reverence. After graduating from Harvard in 1886, he took two years of graduate study at Berlin. He came back to Cambridge at the age of twenty-six as an instructor in philosophy, and during twenty-two years of teaching rose to the rank of full professor. He resigned in 1912 and until his death in 1952 lived a meditative life in Europe, his last years as the guest of a convent just outside Rome. Aside from his philosophical writings, the chief of which is The Life of Reason, *Santayana is known as a poet. He also published a three-volume autobiography* (Persons and Places, The Middle Span, *and* My Host the World) *as well as a "novel in the form of a memoir,"* The Last Puritan.

IF FORTUNE had been unkind to me in respect to my times—except that for the intellectual epicure the 1890's were enjoyable—in respect to places fortune has been most friendly, setting me down not in any one center, where things supposed to be important or exciting were happening, but in various quiet places from which cross-vistas opened into the world. Of these places the most familiar to me, after Avila, was the Harvard Yard. I lived there for eleven years, first as an undergraduate, later as an instructor and proctor. No place, no rooms, no mode of living could have been more suitable for a poor student and a free student, such as I was and as I wished to be. My first room, on the ground floor in the northeast corner of Hollis, was one of the cheapest to be had in Cambridge: the rent was forty-four dollars a year. I had put it first for that reason on my list of rooms, and I got my first choice. It was so cheap because it had no bedroom, no water, and no heating; also the ground floor seems to have been thought less desirable, perhaps because the cellar below might increase the cold or the dampness. I don't think I was ever cold there in a way to disturb me or affect my health. I kept the hard-coal fire banked and burning all night, except from Saturday to Monday, when I slept at my mother's at Roxbury. An undergraduate's room in any case is not a good place for study, unless it be at night, under pressure of some special task. At other times, there are constant interruptions, or temptations to interrupt oneself: recitations, lectures, meals, walks, meetings, and sports. I soon found the Library the best place to work in. It was not crowded; a particular alcove where there were philosophical books at hand, and foreign periodicals, soon became my regular place for reading. I could take my own books and notebooks there if necessary; but for the most part I browsed; and although my memory is not specific, and I hardly know what I read, except that I never missed *La Revue des Deux Mondes,* I don't think my time was wasted. A great deal stuck to me, without my knowing its source, and my mind became accustomed to large horizons and to cultivate judgments.

As to my lodging, I had to make up my sofa bed at night before getting into it; in the morning I left the bedding to be aired, and the "goody," whose services were included in the rent, put it away when she came to dust or to sweep. I also had to fetch my coal and water from the cellar, or the water in summer from the College pump that stood directly in front of my door. This was economy on my part, as I might have paid the janitor to do it for me; perhaps also to black my boots, which I always did myself, as I had done it at home. But my life was a miracle of economy. I had an allowance from my mother of $750 a year to cover all expenses. Tuition absorbed, $150; rent, $44; board at Memorial Hall, with a reduction for absence during the week-end, about $200; which left less than one dollar a day for clothes, books, fares, subscriptions, amusements, and pocket money. Sometimes, but very rarely, I received a money-prize or a money-present; I had no protection or encouragement from rich relations or persons of influence. The Sturgises were no longer affluent, and as yet they hardly knew of my existence. Later, when their natural generosity could (and did) express itself, it did so in other ways, because I was already independent and needed no help. Yet on my less than one dollar a day I managed to dress decently, to belong to minor societies like the Institute, the Pudding, and the O.K., where the fees were moderate, to buy all necessary books, and even, in my

Junior year, to stay at rich people's houses, and to travel. Robert had given me his old evening clothes, which fitted me well enough: otherwise the rich people's houses could not have been visited . . .

Life in the Yard for me, during my second period of residence there, 1890–1896, had a different quality. I hadn't a horse or a valet, but could count on enough pocket-money, a varied circle of friends, clubs, and ladies' society in Boston and Cambridge, and the foreglow and afterglow of holidays spent in Europe. The first year, when I had only one foot in the stirrup and was not yet in the saddle as a Harvard teacher, I lived in Thayer; graceless quarters and the insecure stammering beginnings of a lecturer. The only thing I remember is the acquaintance I then made with my next-door neighbor, Fletcher, who was afterwards a professor of Comparative Literature and made a translation of the *Divina Commedia*. He was also a football player; and I remember one day when I was violently sick at my stomach— my digestion in those days being imperfect—he thought to help me by holding my head (a common illusion among helpful people) and his grasp was like a ring of iron. He was a very good fellow, with a richer nature than most philologists, and firm morals. We had long talks and discovered common tastes in literature and the arts; but he didn't remain at Harvard, and I lost sight of him. Even if he had been at hand, we should hardly have seen each other often: there were things in us fundamentally inaccessible to one another. Besides, though I became a professor myself, I never had a real friend who was a professor. Is it jealousy, as among women, and a secret unwillingness to be wholly pleased? Or is it the consciousness that a professor or a woman has to be partly a sham; whence a mixture of contempt and pity for such a poor victim of necessity? In Fletcher, and in the nobler professors, the shamming is not an effect of the profession, but rather, as in inspired clergymen, the profession is an effect of an innate passion for shamming. Nobody feels that passion more than I have felt it in poetry and in religion; but I never felt it in academic society or academic philosophy, and I gave up being a professor as soon as I could.

The next year I again had my pick of rooms in the Yard, securing No. 7 Stoughton, in the southeast corner of the first floor, where I stayed for six winters. Here there was a bedroom, and my coal and water were brought up for me by the janitor; on the other hand I often made my own breakfast—tea, boiled eggs, and biscuits—and always my tea in the afternoon, for I had now lived in England and learned the comforts of a bachelor in lodgings. Only—what would not have happened in England—I washed my own dishes and ordered my tea, eggs, milk and sugar from the grocers: domestic cares that pleased me, and that preserved my nice china—a present from Howard Cushing—during all those years. There was a round bathtub under my cot, and my sister's crucifix on the wall above it: only cold water, but the contents of the kettle boiling on the hearth served to take off the chill. I had also acquired a taste for fresh air, and my window was always a little open.

One day a new goody left the bathtub full of slops, explaining that she hadn't known what to do with it; it was the only bathtub in her entry. I had myself taken only recently to a daily sponge bath. When I was an under-graduate few ever took in a bath in Cambridge; those who lodged in private houses might share one bathroom between them, and those who went to the Gymnasium might have a shower bath after exercise; but your pure "grind" never bathed, and I only when I went home for the week-end. In Little's Block I believe there was a bathroom on each floor; but Beck was the only luxurious dormitory where each room had its private bathroom. Habits, however, were rapidly changing. Violent exercise and fiercely contested sports were in the ascendant among the athletes; this involved baths, but not luxury. Yet luxury was in the ascendant too; and the polite ideal of one man one bathroom, and hot water always hot, was beginning to disguise luxury under the decent names of privacy and health . . .

Hollis and Stoughton were twin red-brick buildings of the eighteenth century, solid, simple, symmetrical and not unpleasing. No effort had been made by the builders towards picturesqueness or novelty; they knew what decent lodgings for scholars were, and that there was true economy in building them well. The rectangular wooden window frames divided into many squares, flush with the walls, and painted white, served for a modest and even gay decoration. There was a classic cornice, and the windows immediately under it were square instead of oblong and suggested metopes, while the slope of the roof also was that of a temple, though without pediments at the ends. On the whole, it was the architecture of sturdy poverty, looking through thrift in the direction of wealth. It well matched the learning of early New England, traditionally staunch and narrow, yet also thrifty and tending to positivism; a learning destined as it widened to be undermined and to become, like the architecture, flimsy and rich. It had been founded on accurate Latin and a spellbound constant reading of the Bible: but in the Harvard of my day we had heard a little of everything, and nobody really knew his Latin or knew his Bible. You might say that the professor of Hebrew did know his Bible, and the professors of Latin their Latin. No doubt, in the sense that they could write technical articles on the little points of controversy at the moment among philologists: but neither Latin nor the Bible flowed through them and made their spiritual lives; they were not vehicles for anything great. They were grains in a quicksand, agents and patients in an anonymous moral migration that had not yet written its classics.

In both these old buildings I occupied corner rooms, ample, low, originally lighted by four windows, with window seats in the thickness of the wall, which a cushion could make comfortable for reading. Between the side windows the deep chimney stack projected far into the room, and no doubt at first showed its rough or glazed bricks, as the low ceiling probably showed its great beams. But an "improvement" had spoiled the dignity of these chambers. The rage for "closets" invaded America, why I am not antiquary enough to know. Was it that wardrobes and chests, with or without drawers, had become too heavy and cumbrous for an unsettled population? Or was it that a feminine demand for a seemly "bed-sitting room" had insisted on a place of hiding for one's belongings? Anyhow, in 19 Hollis both the side windows had been hidden by oblique partitions, going from the edges of the chimney stack to the front and back walls and enclosing the desired closets, not large enough for a bed, but capable of containing a washstand, trunks, and garments hanging on pegs. Luckily in 7 Stoughton this operation had mutilated only one angle, and left me one pleasant side window open to the South, and affording a glimpse of Holden Chapel and the vista then open over the grass towards Cambridge Common.

Yet it was the outlook to the east, from both rooms, that was most characteristic. The old elms in the Yard were then in all their glory, and in summer formed a grove of green giants, with arching and drooping branches, that swung like garlands in the breeze. This type of elm, though graceful and lofty, has a frail air, like tall young women in consumption. The foliage is nowhere thick, too many thin ribs and sinews are visible: and this transparency was unfortunate in the Harvard Yard, where the full charm depended on not seeing the background. In winter the place was ungainly and forlorn, and not only to the eye. The uneven undrained ground would be flooded with rain and half-melted dirty snow one day, and another day strewn with foul ashes over the icy pavements. This was a theme for unending grumbling and old jokes; but we were young and presumably possessed snow-boots called "arctics" or thick fisherman's boots warranted watertight. Anyhow we survived; and as bad going for pedestrians is made inevitable during winter and spring by the New England climate, the Yard was not much worse in this respect than the surrounding places.

Holworthy in my day was still nominally the "Seniors' Paradise," but not in reality: in reality those who could afford it lived in private houses, in Little's Block, or in Beck. Holworthy preserved, as it has sometimes recovered, only the charm of tradition. The two bedrooms to each study favored the pleasant custom of chumming; but as yet Holworthy had no baths, not even shower baths, and no central heating. Modern improvements seem to me in almost everything to be a blessing. Electricity, vacuum cleaning, and ladies' kitchens render life simpler and more decent; but central heating, in banishing fireplaces, except as an occasional luxury or affectation, has helped to destroy the charm of home. I don't mean merely the ancient and rustic sanctity of the hearth; I mean also the home-comforts of the modern bachelor. An obligatory fire was a useful and blessed thing. In northern climates it made the poetry of indoor life. Round it you sat, into it you looked, by it you read, in it you made a holocaust of impertinent letters and rejected poems. On the hob your kettle simmered and the little leaping flames cheered your heart and ventilated your den. Your fire absolved you from half your dependence on restaurants, cafés, and servants; it also had the moralizing function of giving you a duty in life from which any distraction brought instant punishment, and taught you the feminine virtues of nurse, cook, and Vestal virgin. Sometimes, I confess, these cares became annoying; the fire kept you company, but like all company it sometimes interrupted better things. At its best, a wood fire is the most glorious; but unless the logs are of baronial dimensions, it dies down too quickly, the reader or the writer is never at peace; while a hard-coal fire (which also sometimes goes out) sleeps like a prisoner behind its iron bars, without the liveliness of varied flames. The ideal fire is soft coal, such as I had in England and also in America when I chose; like true beauty in woman, it combines brilliancy with lastingness. I congratulate myself that in the Harvard Yard I was never heated invisibly and willy-nilly by public prescription, but always by my own cheerful fire, that made solitude genial and brought many a genial friend who loved cheerfulness to sit by it with me, not rejecting in addition a drink and a little poetry; no tedious epic, but perhaps one of Shakespeare's sonnets or an ode of Keats, something fit to inspire conversation and not to replace it.

The quality of the Harvard Yard, both in its architecture and its manners, was then distinctly Bohemian: not of the Parisian description, since no *petite amie* or *grande amie* was in evidence, but of the red-brick lodging, tavern and stable-yard Bohemia of Dickens and Thackeray; yet being in a college, the arts and the intellect were not absent from it altogether . . .

Persons and Places (New York, 1944).

Richard C. Evarts

EXAMINATION FOR ALICE

(1913)

One cannot read Alice's Adventures in Cambridge, *by Richard Conover Evarts, A.B. 1913, without asking what else this gifted humorist wrote; for his Alice must rank high among the many parodies of Lewis Carroll's little girl. The answer is nothing—at least for publication. Evarts became a Boston lawyer and lived in Cambridge until his death in 1972. He was active in Cambridge politics and was for many years City Solicitor. "Harvard is all right, I guess," he remarked in the 25th anniversary report of his College*

Class. "The Harvard Law School gave me an excellent training. It was my own fault if Harvard College didn't too. I sometimes think the denizens of Harvard, and probably of every other college too, are liable to consider themselves too élite and of a different race from the ordinary unregenerate people who make up the rest of the world, and they're not."

ALICE was just about to enter one of the tempting little shops with purple socks and ties in the window, when she saw the White Rabbit hurrying across a mud puddle. She ran after him, and caught him just as he reached a curbstone.

"Please—" she began.

But the White Rabbit did not even turn his head.

"No, I haven't any pennies," he said.

"But I wanted to know—" said Alice.

"Oh, it's you, is it?" the White Rabbit said, turning round and blowing a huge cloud of smoke from his pipe into Alice's face. "Well, come on."

"Where?" asked Alice.

"To the Infection Meeting, of course," said the White Rabbit, starting off at a rapid pace.

"But I don't want to be infected," Alice said, as she ran after him, "I've had the mumps once, and the measles, and ever so many other things."

"Ah! But you haven't had probation yet," said the White Rabbit, "and you'll catch it sure if you don't go to your Infection Meetings. I'm a Sophomore and I ought to know. Come on."

"Who will give it to me?" asked Alice, feeling a little alarmed.

"The Queen, of course. Come on."

Alice didn't like being ordered about in this way, but she followed the White Rabbit, who led her to a room filled with animals of all kinds sitting on benches. At one end of the room was a platform where a large frog sat behind a desk. He was a very young-looking frog, Alice thought, but he looked so severe that she sat down quietly beside the White Rabbit.

The frog, after looking more severe than ever, suddenly began to write very fast on a blackboard behind him. Alice tried to make out what he was writing, but it seemed to be chiefly nonsense. It ran something like this:

"If, other things being equal, the level of prices should rise, and thus falling create a demand and supply with, and as which, would you consider this a division of labor? If so, when, and in what capacity? If not, why not, and under what circumstances?"

As soon as he had finished, all the other animals produced paper from nowhere in particular, and began to scribble as fast as they could. Alice noticed that the Lizard, who was sitting in the front row, was the only one who wrote anything original. All the others copied from his paper, and crowded round him so closely that Alice was afraid the poor little creature would be smothered. Meanwhile the frog looked at the ceiling. "He couldn't look anywhere else, poor thing," thought Alice; "his eyes are in the top of his head."

About two seconds had passed when the frog called out "Time!" and began to gather up the papers. When he had collected them all, he took them to his desk and began to mark them. He marked the first one A, the second one B, and so on down to F, when he began over again with A. All this time he kept his eyes tight shut. "So he will be sure to be impartial," the White Rabbit explained to Alice.

After the marking was finished, the frog handed the papers back to their owners. The White Rabbit, who had written nothing at all, had a large A on his paper. The Lizard, however, had an F marked on his.

"A," said the White Rabbit to Alice, "means that I wrote an excellent paper."

"But you wrote nothing," objected Alice.

"Nothing succeeds like success," said the White Rabbit, and hurried away, leaving Alice a little puzzled.

Meanwhile all the animals except the frog had disappeared.

"Would you mind telling me," began Alice, feeling that there ought to be some conversation, "why you—"

"Certainly not," said the frog, handing her a book. "I think you will find this a very able exposition of the subject."

Alice opened the book, and finding it to be poetry, she read the first piece through.

JABBERWOCKY

'T was taussig, and the bushnell hart
    Did byron hurlbut in the rand,
All barrett was the wendell (Bart.)
    And the charles t. cope-*land*.

Beware the Münsterberg, my son!
    'T will read your mind—you bet it can!
Beware the Grandgent bird, and shun
    The frisky Merriman.

He took his bursar sword in hand:
    Long time his neilson foe he sought—
So rested he by the bernbaum tree,
    And stood awhile in thought.

And as in coolidge thought he stood,
    The Münsterberg, with eyes of flame,
Came spalding through the perry wood,
    And babbit as it came!

One, two! One, two! And through and through
    The bursar blade went snicker-snack!
He left it dead, and with its head
    He santayanad back.

And hast thou slain the Münsterberg?
Come to my arms, my bierwirth boy!
O Kittredge day! Allard! Bôcher!
He schofield in his joy.

'T was taussig, and the bushnell hart
Did byron hurlbut in the rand,
All barrett was the wendell (Bart.)
And the charles t. cope-*land.*

"It's very interesting," said Alice, after she had finished, "but I don'
quite understand it."

"You will absorb it after awhile," said the frog, as he got up and walked
away, "if you have the faculty."

Alice's Adventures in Cambridge (Cambridge, 1913).

Theodore Pearson

PRESIDENT LOWELL BUILDS HIS HARVARD

(1925)

One spring day in his senior year, when the seniors still lived in the College Yard, Theodore Pearson glanced through his study window and saw President Lowell on an inspection tour of the new freshman dormitories rising to cloister the older buildings from the noise of Harvard Square. His description of the scene comes from Dean Yeoman's life of President Lowell.

I WAS LOOKING out of my window in Hollis yesterday afternoon at the piles of dirt, the outhouses, and the concrete forms, when round the corner a small brown spaniel came into the enclosure. He was followed, at a respectful distance, by President Lowell, and he, in turn, by Professor Yeomans. While the President was still on the path in front of Holden Chapel he was his usual self—the downcast head, the gloomy stoop of the shoulders, the plodding stride, and the inconsequential cane—but when he came in sight of the construction work, his aspect changed. His head became erect, his shoulders were thrown back, his pace was quickened, and his cane—here was the greatest difference—became the baton of a field marshal.

I was viewing the proceedings through a closed window, but the vigor of the pantomime told more clearly than words the subject of their conversation. President Lowell was expounding the system of paths within the quadrangle; the cane became positively voluble. It pointed, swept, darted, flourished, even commanded. It laid down gravel walks, covered the ground with green sod, planted shrubs . . . and perhaps a few "Keep off the Grass" signs. It spoke great volumes about its owner; it whispered that here, amid the lime barrels and the scaffolding, he daily found his happiness. Away from current cudgelings of press and alumni—albeit face to face with one of their favorite targets—the President dreamed and planned the Harvard that is to come.

Yet all this dumb-show was not really a conversation, but a monologue; Professor Yeomans had no cane, and was further gagged by having to carry an overcoat. He could do no more than tag along in polite acquiescence as the President stalked from one vantage point to the next. Only the spaniel took part in the comment; his tail was eloquent of approval. He clambered up the mounds of dirt, inspected the tool sheds, sniffed approbation at the lime barrels, and expressed satisfaction with odd corners of the lot. In fact, he continued his waddling appraisement some time after President Lowell had resumed his downcast carriage and reverted to the world of now.

Henry Aaron Yeomans, *Abbott Lawrence Lowell, 1856–1943* (Cambridge, 1948).

Nathan M. Pusey

AN ISLAND OF LIGHT
(1925)

Almost twenty-five years ago, at the time of the big push to raise money for Harvard College, Brooks Atkinson, A.B. 1917, asked a group of Harvard graduates, representative of various callings in life, to write brief "minutes" on the subject of what Harvard had meant to each of them. Following is what President Pusey considered particularly significant about his college experience. Pusey had come to Harvard from Abraham Lincoln High School in Council Bluffs, Iowa. Since his widowed mother was a school teacher only modestly paid, Pusey had always had to work to help the family, and if it had not been for a scholarship reserved for students who lived in the communities along the Burlington Railroad's main line, Harvard would have been out of the question. But he came, eager and expectant, and was not disappointed (as was Séan O'Faoláin; see page 74). As an undergraduate Pusey won high honors in English literature, played on the freshman basketball team, and earned undying fame as the leading scorer on that notable team from Harvard College that handily defeated Yale in an unrepeated, experimental "brain test" held in his senior year.

I CAME to Harvard in the autumn of 1924, an unintimidated freshman in an expectant and receptive mood. My first impression, as I suppose is true of most new students who come to Cambridge from the Midwest, was a sense of the history around me illustrated by Harvard's old buildings and other evidences of a notable past of which I was only vaguely conscious through my reading. But my second impression was of my classmates—or at least the first group of them I met.

The first time I entered the dining hall of Gore, which was then a freshman dormitory, I went to the nearest empty chair. As I sat down, I said hello to my two or three nearest neighbors. They must at least have looked in my direction; perhaps they may well have grunted a response to my greeting, as a minimum concession to etiquette. But my clear recollection is that with very little recognition of my presence they went right on talking animatedly among themselves.

What talk it seemed to be! Shaw, Ibsen, Nietzsche. Back and forth the conversation went, in the clever fragmented sentences of quick repartee. Before dessert they had gone on to Katherine Mansfield, and then in a postprandial few minutes they dealt, to their satisfaction and mine, with Cabell and Mencken.

This was not the kind of talk which experience with contemporaries back home had led me to expect. I was at once amazed, terrified, excited, and pleased. And so began my experience of Harvard.

The names of the authors discussed so confidently at that meal have remained in my memory, for though I may have heard of them before coming to Harvard, I certainly had not read them, and later, as I discovered them for myself, their names were driven into my memory. Each time I met one, I recalled the sick feeling I had had that first night when I came to Harvard alone—my first trip east of Chicago—and was confronted with the incredible, if perhaps—may I add this now?—slightly pretentious erudition of a select new group of Harvard undergraduates clearly much better prepared for what lay ahead than I. But may I also say that the great respect I acquired for Harvard undergraduates at that time, though it may since have changed character, has never been diminished in even slight degree by prolonged association with them.

Dare I admit that now my most vivid recollection of my first year's study is a phrase from a freshman German examination? The teacher of this course was a lively young German graduate student, a superb teacher, whose name, unfortunately, has long since left me. For our final examination in sight reading he had written in German a short, whimsical account of an American movie. Perhaps he had the senior Douglas Fairbanks in mind. At any rate in the first few sentences the hero was shown performing a series of incredible physical exploits. Next we were shown the heroine in peril, drowning in a mountain lake. As I recall, the text then ran something like this: "But don't worry, it is now nearly eleven o'clock, and since this is a movie all must soon end happily." At once the hero appeared from nowhere, dove into the lake, thrashed about madly, if ostentatiously, and finally pulled the heroine safe to shore. Immediately the camera came close to reveal her in his arms, dry, beautiful, and perfectly groomed, and then, at the end, moved from the handsome, happy couple, to show a little dog who looked on (the typical movie fade-out of the period) *"und wedelt mit dem Schwanze."*

I imagine we were supposed to be learning which cases followed which prepositions, but this particular teacher, like so many teachers at Harvard, was teaching a great deal more than the immediate matter in hand. It was his guiding idea, I suppose, that to get on in the world we should learn to be critical; but it was also salutary for us that in his practice criticism was always characterized by good humor.

A year or two later I had found my way into courses of John Livingston Lowes and Irving Babbitt. From that time each day was filled with what were to me fresh ideas and excited inspiration to read and go on learning. Professor Lowes' course in sixteenth- and seventeenth-century lyric poetry was one of the first at Harvard which for me seemed completely to break through the limitations of the containing course. It was not so much an exercise in learning as an experience of life itself. There was much in the course of interest and delight, but what chiefly remains now is an image of Lowes reading—one might almost say barking—an endless flood of lyric poetry with such delight that one could not fail to feel its enchantment.

> It was a lover and his lass,
> With a hey, and a ho, and a hey nonino.
>
>   o   o   o
>
> Tell me where is Fancy bred,
> Or in the heart or in the head?
>
>   o   o   o
>
> If she think not well of me,
> What care I how fair she be?

And there is Babbitt, rolling a pencil between his hands, looking over the tops of his glasses, saying of Tennyson's *Locksley Hall:* "This scientific belief in the far-off divine event is nothing other than a form of nostalgia, an offshoot of the Romantic imagination, illegitimately associated with the religious virtue Peace." It was heady stuff for a young student finding his way into the world of ideas. This and much more of the kind in endless profusion. Whatever one thought of Babbitt's point of view, there was never any mistaking that he had one, nor any reason to doubt that he was every day dealing with matters of immense and urgent importance. From him one learned more than ever that life and learning are not to be separated—

that what one thinks matters! He was a superlative pedagogue whose classes were full of import, broadly conceived as few would now dare—and never dull.

The intimate experiences of Harvard are, of course, as individual and as numerous as the students who come here. Today it may be that I am more aware of and impressed by the variety and range of intellectual interest represented in the great faculty of the whole University, and by the faculty's importance both for enriching the known and for keeping alive the possibility for learning, than I am perhaps by students. But fortunately there is no need to set these two groups against each other. They both belong; together they make Harvard.

In the complex and confused world in which we all find ourselves it is possible to think of Harvard as a kind of island of light in a very widespread darkness, and I must confess I sometimes do just this. But I also know that the figure is not really an apt one, for Harvard has never been an island severed from the broad concerns of men and is certainly not one now. Instead, it is rather intimately involved in the complex culture to which it belongs. Its distinction is that in it intellectual activity has an opportunity to come into sharper focus, and so becomes richer, more vivid, more convincing, and more captivating than in society at large.

As the freshman comes into this place he cannot fail to be impressed by the extraordinary liveliness, concentration and devotion with which learning long has been and is now pursued—nor can a President!

Brooks Atkinson, ed., *College in a Yard* (Cambridge, 1957).

Séan O'Faoláin

HARVARD—VINTAGE 1926— VERY DRY

(1926)

How many come to Harvard with a preconceived notion of what the university holds for him or her, and finds the expectations fall short? One was the Irish writer, Séan O'Faoláin, A.M. 1928. After a youth spent partly in the Irish Republican Army and partly getting a degree at University College, Cork, he came to the American Cambridge at the age of 26, on a Commonwealth Fellowship, still unsettled in mind as to a future profession. His unformed idea was to study literature at the graduate level for a possible teaching career, but the philological bent of the Harvard English department soon turned him away. Yet he loved the ambiance of Cambridge, and his untested literary inclinations found encouragement in association with Lincoln Kirstein, R. P. Blackmur, Varian Fry, and others associated with Hound & Horn, *the new quarterly that was setting Harvard's literary world afire from 1927 to 1934. O'Faoláin's story "Fugue" (his first major appearance in print) was in the second number (1928). "Maybe it wasn't the fault of the College, but I think it was," Kirstein said later, "that inside of two years they let Foster Damon, Conrad Aiken, and O'Faoláin slip through their by no means rich fingers."*

IT WAS quiet Cambridge and Harvard, however, that gave me the sharpest knuckle-rap. On every side, at every moment, by good example—or bad, according to your ideas?—I heard the puritan murmur of the eleventh American commandment:

> Then come home, close the door,
> And at your leisure
> Sweat some more,
> And call it pleasure.

In humble recognition thereof I took lodgings at Number 48 Irving Street, a quiet, dusty, undistinguished surburban side street, wholly devoted to students' lodging houses, as was plain to be seen every night by the number of green-shaded reading lamps staining the dusk of every window; every morning by the number of milk bottles deposited with a different jingle on every porch; and every Saturday and Sunday morning by the lines of exhausted-loooking jalopies waiting along the sidewalks ...

Within days my routine was in accord with my simple lodgings. The first thing I bought was an alarm clock, then a teapot, one cup, saucer, plate, spoon, knife and fork, tea towels and paper napkins from the five-and-ten, to make breakfast and afternoon tea and, if I had no lectures, or if it was snowing badly, a snack lunch. Every morning, including Sundays, my clock buzzed me awake at seven. After breakfast I worked until nine, went to my tiny carrel in Widener until dinner time. Each day I squeezed in a fast bout of exercise. I tried rowing on the Charles but found that it took too long. I tried swimming but found that it was not strenuous enough. Anyway—it may be a token of my prudery—I did not like the Harvard convention of swimming naked. In the end I found that I could lose the most sweat in the shortest time on the squash courts. After dinner, mostly in some steamy, noisy, students' cafeteria—we all loathed these places but could not afford better—I either went back once more to Widener or returned home to Number 48, there to add my green lamp to the thousands of other green lamps all about me, many of them burning, like green eyes, into the small hours of the morning.

I fell completely in love with this ascetic life, for a rather crass reason. It gave me the feeling that I was sharing Harvard's special and perhaps unique reflection of the New England puritan tradition—high-minded and self-denying, lean-limbed and stout-hearted, privileged yet responsible, hierarchical and leisured, sometimes boringly jaunty, but always chock-full of character, never vulgar, often fastidious, and if Harvard was not exactly a liberal institution (I cannot imagine any university in America being called, like Oxford, the Home of Lost Causes!) it was not bigoted, or mean, or parochial, or shut-minded. I felt I was imbibing the finest wine of old Boston's mandarinism as I had been induced to imagine it by such men as Emerson and Thoreau and William Dean Howells, but especially by those three great Harvardians, Henry Adams, William and Henry James.

This pleasant illusion faded only when I discovered that what I was really admiring in Harvard was not Boston but Berlin. I could not have known that all over America, from coast to coast, other students of the humanities were living very similar lives under the same Germanic academic influence; devotedly earnest, pedantically specialized, fanatically rationalist, emotionally arid, fundamentally anti-aesthetic. But I could have seen, and did gradually come to see, that whatever about other places, literature in Harvard at the graduate level chiefly meant philology; as all over America it now means critical analysis. I know no Harvard professor of the twenties, except Babbitt, who realized that plays, poetry, or novels had ever been written at a higher temperature than an icebox. If I am right in this it is not surprising that the book which then presented the ideal approach to literature was John Livingston Lowes's *The Road to Xanadu*, an exotic piece of scholarly bravura where every line of "Kubla Khan" is traced to its source, and all that wild wonder of the poem annihilated. ("Our most accomplished sleuth," Babbitt called Lowes.) Perhaps I came at a bad time; too late for Santayana, Whitey and Foster Damon, too soon for F. O. Matthiessen and Theodore Spencer (both in the graduate school with me in '26), for Harry Levin, Kenneth Murdock, and Archibald MacLeish; and Alfred North Whithead was not teaching while I was there; too soon, above all, to escape the powerful and, I now feel, baleful influence of that devouring old lion of the humanities in Harvard for some forty years, George Lyman Kittredge.

Like everybody else who sat under him, I never failed to be entranced by Kitty's lucid brain, and depressed to find him invariably remote from his students, to whom he always gave the impression that he regarded everybody under fifty as little better than a schoolboy. I do not doubt that among his colleagues he must often have expanded; I never once saw him do so in class, and as well as attending all his lectures in the Beowulf course—which were of a deadly dullness—I dropped as often as I could into his other classes simply for the joy of seeing that lovely brain and that faultless memory working as smoothly as a precious instrument. A student in his famous

English 2 course might, for example, shoot up his hand and say: "Sir, is there any reason for maintaining a parallel between the story of Hamlet and the story of Orestes?"

Kittredge would instantaneously reply: "No, sir, for the following six reasons. Number one. We do not know that the mother of Hamlet was privy to the death of Claudius. We do know that the mother of Orestes was privy to the murder of her husband. Number two. The madness of Orestes occurs *after* he has slain his father's murderer, whereas Hamlet . . ."

And so on, unhesitating, clear and orderly no matter what the question. Agreed that he had been doing this sort of thing for forty years!

I only wish I had been in his Beowulf class the day he irritably reproved my friend Moody Prior, later professor of English at Northwestern, for halting his translation with an occasional "Er . . ." (This was a common practice of Kitty's with all of us: he really was a testy old man!)

"But, sir!" Moody had the wit to retort. "To er is human?"

It would have been something to see Kittredge smile, however feebly.

I have often, since then, heard it proposed that the reason why Kittredge and his colleagues persisted in the grim Ph.D. regime that they imposed on their students—it meant at least two grueling years of linguistic or philological studies, and one, two, or more years on a thesis of the most pedantically concentrated nature—was not only because they had been trained that way themselves in Berlin, or Munich or Heidelberg, but because they felt that very few, if any, of their students had enough background or brains to be anything but useful language teachers. If there ever was any validity in this idea it could, surely, refer only to the sort of pioneer or backwoods America which they had known in their boyhood. Certainly, by the twenties, when Kitty's patriarchal beard and leonine mane were white as snow, this argument of despair was fast losing any such validity as it may ever have had. It was nothing but blind militarism to have subjected men like Matthiessen, or Spencer, or Ernest Simmons to this (for them pointless) discipline: men who were cut out to be, and proved themselves to be, perceptive and inspiring literary critics as well as sound scholars. I used to groan whenever I thought of Ernie Simmons toiling over his doctoral thesis on one single folktale at a time when he might have been laying the foundations for his three great later books on Tolstoy, Dostoyevsky and Chekhov. Instead, in search of variants of that single tale he had to travel all over Europe to satisfy the Kittredgian insistance on absolute completeness of detail irrespective of any other quality whatever. If Ernest Simmons were proposing to be a folklorist, yes. But had Kitty no perception of the young man's real potentialities?

Over the years I have canvassed the opinions of others who knew Kittredge. The general feeling is that his mind was assimilative rather than original; he had, that is, amassed an encyclopedic knowledge of a certain orthodox combination of subjects, and never forgotten one jot of it. All pay tribute to his domineering personality. He built up what Babbitt called the Philological Syndicate in Harvard, which he was also able to control indirectly in other universities throughout the United States. On the verbal precison of his mind everybody is admiringly agreed: as most are about his behavior as a crotchety martinet in the classroom. No present-day student, one feels, would put up with his petty despotism. His throne did not so much fall as crumble in the late thirties and forties; "toppled," says Harry Levin in his monograph on *Irving Babbitt and the Teaching of Literature,* "by the sheer unbalanced poundage of Germanized scholarship"; or undermined by the gradual shifts of emphasis of younger men like Matthiessen, Spencer, and Levin himself, though not without some tough hand-to-hand fighting from the old rearguard. And nobody who has ever taught in any university needs to be told just how tough these gentle recluses can be. Others may consult the reticent novels of Sir Charles Snow, and multiply by ten. A key date for the beginning of the changeover may be the appearance of T. S. Eliot in Harvard as Charles Eliot Norton Professor in 1932–1933.

Is it far-fetched of me to think that, long after Kittredge's era is over, his young-clerks-become-old-presbyters still carry on something of his pedantic tradition under other forms? Such as the lethally mechanical pedantic and dogmatic application of the so-called New Criticism; i.e., literary "criticism" by means of microscopic verbal analysis, and the bloodless sport of truffle-hunting under every literary oak tree not now for Sanskrit and Old High German word roots but for symbols and archetypes: like a certain, far from untypical, Ivy League professor of my acquaintance who always explains to his classes on Mark Twain that *Huck Finn* is not about the Mississippi River but about the River of Life, that the fog that descended on the runaways is not a real Mississippi fog but an archetypal soul-fog, that the island is not a real island, that the slave is not a real slave, and so on and on. To all of which, I have no reason to doubt, his young pupils sit enraptured, because it is, alas, true that the one thing all American youngsters love is a rational explanation of the otherwise vague, mysterious and troubling. In justice to Kittredge, this sort of thing would have driven him mad. In full justice to him, it was all inherent in his own refusal to treat the humanities as human. Or is it simply that there is some endemic demon in the academic nature that aches for machine control, even in the arts?

This, then, was what I really fell in love with that September of 1926, all unknowing, uncritical, happily deceived. Still, such after all is the way of love, and by the time I saw through my love, undeceived, I had learned at least one thing well worth the experience—the difference between imaginative and unimaginative scholarship.

The nature of the thing-in-itself, as a discipline or as an abstract virtue, I, apart from all question of its use and abuse, learned in my first fifteen seconds at Harvard. One single sentence did it, spoken by my adviser in studies, Fred Norris Robinson, whom we all affectionately called either Fritz or Robby, a distinguished Chaucerian with a sound knowledge of early English and Celtic philology. He uttered it after I had outlined to him the project I proposed to work on while at Harvard. This ingenious project was to have been "The Possible Influence of Old Irish Verse on Anglo-Saxon Metrics," which was exactly the sort of damn-fool project that young would-be scholars then loved to dream about o' nights—until somebody like Fritz Robinson taught them the elements of common sense.

Fritz, who over decades of study in medieval history, literature, and linguistics had gathered more than a few facts about the places and centuries I proposed to deal with, listened patiently, and I may now well think quizzically, as I eagerly told him all about Iona and Lindisfarne, about the Celtic missionaries who had founded them, and about their possible (I said probable) influence on Northumbrian letters; pointing out to him that Caedmon (whom I regret to say I called "The Father of English Song") had actually lived and worked in Whitby; which (I explained to Fritz) was a foundation, part hermitage, part monastery, that had grown up in the wake of those Irish missionaries. Having then given Fritz a little lecture on the nature of Irish metrics and of Anglo-Saxon metrics, and declared finally that "nothing would have been easier" than for the Irish verse mode to have influenced the Anglo-Saxon verse mode, I leaned back and awaited his approval.

For a few moments, Fritz, impassive as a bonze, breathing heavily, pipe-puffing, said nothing. Then, very slowly, in his pleasant double-bass, double-chinned, port-winey voice he uttered *the sentence.* "Well," he said, "it might be worth while. To spend two or three years on it. Just to see. If there is anything in it."

It is a sentence that every neophyte might well hang over his bed and look at long and ponderingly every time he feels himself about to give birth to a bright idea. I have timed the sentence many times, and if I speak it slowly and breathingly, as Fritz did, it always takes fifteen seconds. Each time it sinks into my bowels like a very, very cold drink. If you care to pour it out rapidly and stir it briskly you will get Instant Harvard; vintage 1926; *very* dry.

I do not pretend that on hearing those twenty-odd words I was converted instantly to the faith, but I did at once yearn to be a catechumen. If I never did become a member of the community it was because I was no more cut out to be any kind of scholar (whether with or without imagination), either by temperament or by natural endowments, than I had earlier been cut out to be a gunman. I think I might, with training and discipline, have developed at least some of the qualities of mind necessary for scholarship—coolness, detachment, a healthy modesty, a distrust of the flashy, and a terror of all emotionally attractive generalizations. I lacked utterly that most elementary scholarly requirement of all—a quick, capacious, accurate, and retentive memory, without which no scholar can move an inch. Still, like Saul about to be anointed by the prophet Samuel, I did see the darkness and the light. As from a little hilltop I could at least see henceforth the supreme beauty of accuracy in thought and word, even when actually hearing anything but accuracy balloon out of my mouth, quite effortlessly and indeed quite involuntarily—it is an ethnic gift—like conversations in a strip cartoon.

I became aware that Fritz was still talking in the same leisurely voice, gentle and authoritative, developed, no doubt, over years of dealing with other yearners for the true faith, who (he presumed, possibly quite wrongly) would never rise beyond the degree of married subdeacons with large families in some remote Baptist high school in Mississippi or Alabama. He was saying: "I think, perhaps, to begin with, you had better join my class in Old Irish. I know you have done some work on this in Cork. It will be no harm to polish it up a bit more. And you might also do some Middle Welsh with me. And I don't see why you should not take Professor Kittredge's course in Beowulf. And it might be no harm to do some Middle English as well. And then," he concluded pleasantly, "we will see."

I had no doubts. Eagerly I set to. Two or three years? Why not four or five? I saw myself going on to Gothic and Old High German with Francis Magoun; to Chaucer under Robby; to Old French under J. D. M. Ford. I thought of my old professor back in Cork, W. F. P. Stockley, who had only a smattering of Old English and Middle English, who never even mentioned O. H. G., who knew no Old Irish or Middle Welsh, whose finest gesture when dealing with Chaucer was to recite the first four lines of the Prologue in a rousing Harry Lauderish version of the Midland-Kentish dialect, after which all references to linguistics were firmly dropped. I thought how all this would impress my registrar at U.C.C. After three years at Harvard, and with its Ph.D. under my belt, I could see myself swishing into the quadrangle of U.C.C. in a low-slung, high-powered car, with a beard just like Stockley's.

I duly attended the classes recommended by Fritz. They were gruelers, especially his own since there were only two students at each, myself and Ernie Simmons. I got an A in my courses. I grew a small beard. I bought a Model T Ford second-hand. And I ultimately got an A.M. in what the authorities called, in kindness, Comparative Philology, which it was not. To achieve even this little I worked as I never worked before or since, and while it lasted I felt as happy and as immortal as a student; for Edward Thomas was right when he said of Oxford that to a student life is forever. My happiness lasted until I found about the middle of my second term that the factual stocks I had accumulated with so much effort during my first term were already disappearing as slowly and surely as whiskey in an uncorked bottle.

It is likely that, just as religious doubts often flower in the mind only after they have begun with a revolt in the body, my doubts about the vocation of scholarship began to proliferate only after I made this sad discovery of my physical inadequacy for it; though it has to be said, I have already as much as said it, that when I looked at the end results of scholarship among the Melchizedeks about me, their bleakness fed the flames of doubt like dry leaves in autumn. It would be only a matter of time before I would finally decide that while everything good, great and worthwhile that men think, dream, and do is based on our knowledge of the world as scientific fact, or is nonsense, so that without even philology a great part of the world of letters would be closed to us—its precise meaning, and craft, its technical forms, through which alone every subsequent creator (however, he may modify them) can express himself—I was not going to add one word to that eloquent tradition of words if I were to devote all my energies under Harvard's dry-as-dust antiquarians to the history of words alone.

Not that I expressed my decision to myself in this way, and not that there were not many other human influences working on me, other distracting considerations and reconsiderations—friendships, Ireland, love, and opening doors, and after a few months an insistent tapping in my attic every night after I had gone to bed, as of some spirit writer putting black on white.

Vive Moi (Boston, 1963).

Rollo Walter Brown

THE OLD DEAN

(1934)

No Harvard teacher or administrator was more beloved or better known by Harvard men during his lifetime than Le Baron Russell Briggs (1855–1934), Dean of Harvard College. He was the ideal teacher, a man of compassionate interest in his fellow men, a kindly administrator whose modest and delightful personality endeared him to thousands in the "golden age" of the Harvard Yard. Among Dean Briggs's graduate students near the beginning of the century was Rollo Walter Brown, whose admiration led him to write "the biography of a modest man" and to enjoy thirty years of close friendship with Dean Briggs. Mr. Brown was a well-known writer and lecturer known especially for his book The Creative Spirit, *but he also wrote many articles about Harvard and Harvard men; a novel,* The Hillikin, *about a hard-working undergraduate; an autobiography,* The Hills Are Strong; *and* Harvard Yard in the Golden Age, *a collection of sketches of Faculty personalities.*

IN THE EIGHT years of his life after the book was published, I saw more of him than before. He was busy much of the time as a member of committees of the Board of Overseers at Harvard, and he was active in many other groups that concerned themselves with semipublic enterprises. Yet he had greater freedom in using his time than he had ever before enjoyed. He had entered into an agreement with one of the large publishing houses to write his memoirs, but when he came face to face with the actual writing, he asked to be released from the agreement. "I saw," he explained to me one day in rejoicing over the still greater freedom that he hoped he was now to have, "that if I wrote those memoirs and did not conceal a part of the truth, I was going to cause pain to people whom I would not hurt for anything in the world—and get myself into a hornets' nest in the bargain. So I think I'll just concentrate on baseball for the rest of my life, and let it go at that."

He usually had supplies of tickets from the Boston Major League Clubs—he never got through explaining that while they were given to him he had not begged them—and he was always looking for somebody who could go to games with him. He liked to be there ahead of time. "It is never quite a whole game for me, you know," he always explained if he feared I might be late, "unless I can see the attendants make the white lines of the batter's box before play begins." Since my writing day is over rather early, it came to pass that we went much together—as often as two or three times a week. At seventy-seven he was the best-informed fan I have known. Constantly he set sports correspondents and baseball managers straight on college and league scores and players of ten, twenty, thirty, and forty years ago.

In his inside coat pocket he carried a leather case that served as a depository for unusual scores. But it served also as a depository for anecdotes from *Punch,* new poems that he liked, clippings about former students, photographs of his grandchildren, lists of groceries that he was to order, or take home with him, ideas that he thought worth jotting down. I never did see him get all the way through the contents of that case, and only on a few occasions did I ever see him find what he was looking for. But he invariably found something else that was interesting, something that started a train of stories, memories, observations. He did not repeat the same story to the same person after the manner of some old men. But he was always afraid that he might be doing so, and was constantly prefacing new stories with, "Did I ever tell you . . ." "Did I ever tell you how President Eliot said to me: 'No, don't say he is "low-down"; just say "less sensitive" '?" Or, "Have I ever said to you before . . ."

And on the subway train, in Fenway Park, at Soldiers Field, on Larz Anderson Bridge while we rested our elbows upon the coping and watched the crews on the river, his active mind was busy with all sorts of interesting oddments that he had remembered or thought upon. He was so free from guile that it never occurred to him to speak in veiled statements. With wholly untrammeled honesty he discussed men in public life—he remembered the grades they had made in college—he characterized colleagues, he commented upon changing conceptions of culture, he reflected upon new social practices. Sometimes he was caustic, as when he told me of a nationally known editor who bought an article from him and then "lifted" a certain section of it and published it as a part of one of his own signed editorials. "Of course, it was *his* after he bought it!" Sometimes he was distressed by the ethics of men in whom he had had confidence, as when he discussed a vice president of the United States who had proved in a magazine article that the Radcliffe undergraduates were a bolshevik lot, by showing that a debating team representing them had one evening argued for the closed shop, and by withholding the equally important information that another team representing them had on the same evening argued for the open shop. "I never can believe he wrote that article himself," the Dean declared. "He must have hired somebody to do it for him and then signed it without knowing what was in it. But let me see, that explanation would not help matters much, would it?" He made an effort to smile, as though he were trying to conceal the hurt of some great, inclusive soreness of body. "I'm afraid the terrors of the closed shop will remain as nothing compared with the terrors of the closed mind." Sometimes he became extremely grave and talked with the nervous, fading voice that troubled him much when he spoke in public. But more often he was swept by irrepressible humor and made his commentaries with invigorating saltiness. Once when the Harvard football team was having an unusually poor season, some players on their way to practice in a strikingly luxurious automobile nearly ran us down as they made the short trip from the north side of the Charles to Soldiers Field. "Perhaps I'm old-fashioned," the Dean observed as we walked on, "but I sometimes wonder"—and his voice became crackling and merry—"if Harvard may ever hope to win games unless we somehow find players who are equal to getting from one end of the Larz Anderson Bridge to the other under their own steam." On another occasion, while we stood by the Charles and surveyed the Graduate School of Business Administration, dazzling in its newness and much white paint, he remarked as a sly smile flitted across his closely checked pink face, "It reminds me of the Spotless Town in the old advertisement for Sapolio."

There were, to be sure, all sorts of occasions when baseball was not responsible for our being together. Often I met him along lower Brattle Street late in the afternoon when he was on his way home with a green bookbag full of provisions, and he half leaned, half hung like a grotesque question mark against the brick front of a grocery store and told me the latest anecdote he had liked—of the British lady, for instance, who had said, after heavy storms in the English Channel, "Just think, my dear, for two days the Continent has been completely isolated!" When he was shut in for several weeks of observation before he was taken to the hospital for an operation that his friends feared might not be successful, I sometimes sat with him in the bright room upstairs, while he lounged on the wide bed and read to me from the book of charades that he was writing. He seemed to be much more concerned over the way the charades were coming out than over any possible outcome of his period under observation. When finally it was decided that he must go to the hospital, he protested that they must hold off a little until he had finished the last of the charades. "I promised Pottinger that he was to have the manuscript, and he must have it." And after the operation—which turned out to have been unnecessary—just as before, he remained my final court of appeal whenever I was finishing a manuscript, or was reading proofs and had to contend with editors who believed the subjunctive mood ought to be eliminated from the English language. After he had tried a sentence out on himself—he had become eye-minded through a lifetime of theme reading and had to look at whatever he put to the test—he would relive a little of his experience as a teacher by digging from the leather case in his pocket, or from his memory, every sort of interesting specimen of idiomatic English, from Dryden's "He was a man stepped into years, and of great prudence" down to the instance he had just found in some recent volume written by a former student.

Yet through all this greater intimacy that grew from what I could not fail to see—and with a certain regret—was a habit of looking on me less as a youth and more as a near-contemporary, I never discovered in him anything that would lead me to revise my earlier interpretation of his life—save in this: the closer I came to him, the more genuine I found him. The high level on which he lived was his natural level. The irrepressible inclination to see the ridiculous in so many things was his natural appreciation of the vast chasm between what men pretend and what they achieve. The glow of good will which shone in his face was the natural expression of his own great humility and his own great beneficence. With Miguel de Unamuno he cried out through everything he did: "Warmth, warmth, more warmth! For men die of cold and not of darkness; it is not the night but the frost that kills."

This fundamental warmth of spirit infused every other quality of his character. No matter how his fellow beings chanced to come in contact with him, they discovered in him very soon something that was friendly to life. Colleagues said, "Yes, he's one of the fellows Briggs helped through college." Professors at Yale said, with the least trace of pleasure in their skepticism, "But do you think the Harvard of today produces men with the sympathies of Dean Briggs?" Harvard students far from home said, "We were feeling low last night and went over and spent an hour with the Dean—and his cat Joshua." Radcliffe graduates said, "We wouldn't for the world have had him a nice, sleek, impervious president in a morning coat." Policemen on the lower Brattle Street beat said, "And don't you suppose we could tell you about one or two ourselves that he kept from going plumb to hell?" The Irish housemaid who had long been with the family said, "And once in the country when he was taking me to ten-thirty Mass, and the door of the old machine came open a dozen times, he slammed it hard and said, 'Confound it!' And said I, 'Oh, Mr. Briggs! Now I've learned what I've been wanting to know all these years: you are no angel!' And then for days after, when he was in the house he'd say softly but so that I'd be sure to hear him, 'Well, confound it!' And I'd say, 'Oh, try to patch things up if you want to, but I don't believe you can ever get forgiven for anything as grievous as that!' " And Harvard men of all ages below fifty or sixty said when they saw him trudging along in front of the baseball stands with his big yellow blanket on his arm, "Why, there's the old Dean!" Then they gathered round him in such numbers that the policeman had to ask them—in the least obtrusive manner he could invent—not to block the way behind the catcher's net, and the Dean was unable to get to his accustomed seat along the third-base line until the first or second man at bat was out.

It was this warmth of spirit which resulted in such vast accumulations of renown and affection that to many he seems more like a legend than a man who took his departure only one morning in 1934. "He is not real!" "Men like that do not exist!" "He is too good to be true!" "He is somebody's creation!" And now that I never meet him in Harvard Square or in the Yard— though in some ineradicable way I am constantly expecting to do so—I sometimes wonder myself: Is it possible that I once walked in the full light of day in this matter-of-fact, turbulent world with such a man as that?

On Writing the Biography of a Modest Man (Cambridge, 1935).

John H. Finley, Jr.

A CAMBRIDGE HORATIAN

(1945)

In the art of short biography the reader's pleasure derives at least as much from the skill of the biographer as from an interest in the subject. Edward Kennard Rand, the subject of this sketch, walks briskly in spirit along the paths of the Yard, and his bright personality still shines for those who ante-date the Second World War. He was a lively scholar famous for his literary and historical work on Virgil, Horace, Ovid, and the founders of the Middle Ages. Cantabrigians recall the international enthusiasms of Mr. and Mrs. Rand, especially for things French, and the generous hospitality they dispensed to students at their house on Lake View Avenue. Yet the memory of Rand's lifetime of achievement and good works becomes especially real to later generations because of John Finley's brilliant evocation of Rand's personality. Eliot Professor of Greek, long Master of Eliot House, Finley was appointed after his normal retirement in 1974 to the unprecedented post of Senior Professor in the Faculty of Arts and Sciences. One of the College's most popular teachers, he is the author of critical studies of Thucydides *(1942) and Homer's* Odyssey *(1978), and much occasional writing and verse, including recent biographical sketches of Roger Bigelow Merriman and James Bryant Conant.*

EDWARD KENNARD RAND . . . tells in a Class Report how, as a last and desperate recourse, he presented himself armed with his school record at Mr. Eliot's front door early in the opening morning of the college year. That was a green, idyllic Harvard, innocent as yet of blanks and forms. The President saw him, read his record, and sent him to the Secretary of the University, Mr. Bolles, to whom, Rand later learned, he wrote a note in the course of the day. Thus simply began Rand's lifelong tie with Harvard, and the attachment may never quite have lost the glad surprise of that first morning. He lived first at home supporting himself by tutoring, then moved to college in scholarships, and few can have had happier undergraduate years. He was an editor of the *Monthly,* played the lead in a long-remembered production of *Phormio,* and began the association with the Signet which for him and others brightened many future years. He was graduated, as was usual with him, *summa cum laude,* made at his Commencement the first of what were to be his three Latin orations (the second was at the Tercentenary Celebration, the third at the Commencement following the Second World War), and he was elected Secretary of his class of 1894. In reply to one of his own later questionnaires, he wrote, "Amusements: a garden à deux, tennis, music, and class reports," and one may safely say that the last proved the chief or at least the most lasting diversion. He remained the Secretary of his Class for the fifty-one further years of his life, and to glance at the reports which he edited, at his Latin menus, complete with quotations, for class dinners (did any class ever continue compulsory Latin so long?), at his many happy speeches as toastmaster, and above all at his appreciations of classmates, living and dead, is to feel the depth of a duty that could thus mask itself as diversion. He had a way of transforming his loyalties into minor arts . . .

It is not easy to describe the fullness of Rand's Harvard life . . . Few lives more happily refuted the dour precept that a man will lose by following more than one track. Not that unity was lacking to his life, but it was a unity imparted by his own sympathy and knowledge. The Christian humanism which he held as an ideal found illustration in his life, and impressive as was his writing, his final work was, as by his creed it should have been, the man himself. "The crown of a professor's activities," he wrote for his fiftieth report in 1944, "is his teaching. Whatever his success in administration or scholarly research, these matter little if they are not caught up into character—*abeunt studia in mores*—and insensibly transmitted to students." Again, he said of students, "If the teacher gives himself to them, they furnish part of his education. While he is maturing them, they are keeping him young. He is also prompted by their varied interests not to stay too closely tethered to his subject." If these words express the teacher's code, they were in no conflict with the scholar's. In a volume of essays dedicated to him in 1935 by former students, the list of his writings includes more than a hundred and twenty-five articles, on subjects broad and narrow and ranging from Greek literature to the Renaissance. Of his dozen books, two, his chief palaeographical work, *Studies in the Script of Tours,* and the edition of the Virgilian commentator Servius in which he collaborated with several of his students, were works of scholarship in the exact sense, while others such as *The Magical Art of Virgil, The Building of Eternal Rome,* his admirable *Ovid and His Influence,* and the book that most fully reflects him, *The Founders of the Middle Ages,* were literary and historical. If one add his continuing interest in questions of education and service on University committees—he was not surprisingly an opponent of Mr. Eliot's elective system and a collaborator of Mr. Lowell in introducing more disciplined schemes of study—and add further the ties which took him for study and lecturing to Italy and France, and still further his presidency of the American Philological Association and first presidency of the Mediaeval Academy of America, of which he was a founder and leading spirit, something of the scope and sunny energy of his life is clear. It is worth remembering that in these years when the United States was emerging as a great power and many voices in American universities were asserting the novelty of our culture, the group of men at Harvard who concerned themselves with remoter origins and longer continuities was never stronger. By charm as well as knowledge Rand was a leading figure of this group, and his friendship with Haskins, Grandgent, G. F. Moore, Lowes, and Kittredge speaks in both his and their work.

But something escapes a mere catalogue of achievements, never more so than with one who shone in the sparkle of phrase, written or spoken, and in the exchanges of friendship. His friendships, one felt, included the ancient authors, and as Horace easily addressed Roman friends in poems which held echoes of the Greek authors, so Rand mingled present and past in the common light of cheerful fellowship, as if, compared to fellowship, time were irrelevant. Lightness was his code and signature; he by nature shunned the thunders of Cicero, even the gravity of Virgil, for Horace's smiling indirection and deceptive ease. Something may have been lost to his teaching and writing by this cast of mind. He did not like to deal with things massive and central, perhaps because they struck him as obvious. Moreover, he preferred not to speak ill, hence would calmly neglect dull pages of an author to fix with joy on a redeeming phrase. As the Middle Ages could see in Virgil an *anima naturaliter Christiana* and as Erasmus could speak of St. Socrates, Horace to Rand's fond eyes had most of the Christian virtues, and what he found to say of him seemed to apply to himself also.

> He wants to talk [Rand wrote] of life's comedies with us and of some of its deeper meanings. 'Come in,' he seems to say. 'Take that easy chair. What are we going to talk about today?' If tobacco had been discovered in Horace's day, he would have offered us a good cigar . . . 'What is the harm,' he says, 'in speaking the truth with a smile? *Ridentem dicere verum Quid vetat?*' These two principles—moderation and seriousness lightly borne— are a clue to everything that Horace thought and wrote. The method is to scrutinize a friend's defects and with a gentle push to tip them over into the contiguous virtues. If your friend is a bit near, call him economical. If he monopolizes the conversation, call him entertaining. If he is hot-tempered, call him high-spirited. If we try out this method it will do us no harm. Sometimes our first estimate may be wrong and our friend may be better than we thought. Sometimes a delicate irony underlies the courtesy. We do not blunt our perceptions by metamorphosing a villain into a comic character. We purge our own spirits of envy, hatred and malice.

Comedy thus understood has no conflict with Rand's charity. It was rather the tie, if one may put it so, between charity and history: the means by which history may be won over from its violence and sorrow into a bright and cheerful instruction. Rand understood such ancients as Plutarch who sought moral instruction from history.

> Horace [he goes on] is a pleasant counsellor, a perfect Freshman adviser, always at home, always at leisure, ever ready to pour out for us a glass of one of the mellower brands and to expound the comfortable doctrine of *nil admirari*, caught from Socratic irony and handed down to choice souls through the ages. The *sprezziatura* of the Renaissance, French wit in any period, Oxford reserve, and rightly understood, Harvard indifference, these are links in a golden chain. *Nil admirari* does not mean absence of enthusiasm or snobbishness or faded Puritanism but the spirit of comedy as George Meredith set it forth and urbane independence; it is the art of riding the waves of experience . . . The spirit of comedy is no foe of the imagination or romance or poetry or piety; only when the dreamer, the prophet, or the priest acts with a proud complacency in his part, does it look wonderingly at him with a 'slim, feasting smile' . . . A cynic is one who takes himself seriously but not his world; a Horatian is one who takes his world seriously but not himself.

If these quotations do less than justice to Rand's major works, they express a spirit which ran through his life and works alike. His massive palaeographic writings had their critics, and it may be that such a minutely specialized subject demands a concentration of life that he fortunately did not give it. The fame which was greeted by many invitations and degrees, including a posthumous degree that he would have valued most, from the Sorbonne, was at bottom the fame of the man himself, and it best survives in works such as his lectures on Horace, his *Ovid*, and his *Founders of the Middle Ages*, which breathe most of him. This spirit, at the same time ardent and playful, speaks in his enthusiasms. Early in the first war his love of France took him promptly but incongruously to Plattsburg in an undergraduate training corps, and he writes, "It did not take us long to find the level of a common lot. For me it was like going to college again; I would not change the experience for any that I have known . . . At present by one of the inscrutable turns of fate, one of my sergeants whom I most admired is taking the Freshman Latin course under me." Again after his exchange professorship at the Sorbonne in 1933–34, he writes, "No finer group of scholars and gentlemen exists than the colleagues I learned to know there. We enjoyed the hospitality of households rich and poor, with everywhere the same good dinner flowing with wit and wine, the same courteous cordiality and refinement of manners, and the same gay French spirit." Again, to accompany a photograph of three Italian peasant women and a wood-carrying donkey, from his little book *A Walk to Horace's Farm*, "We started off hopefully and on the bridge that spans the Fosso del Chiuse met Tyndaris again, with Phyllis and Chloe—or Galatea? or Lydia? or Cinara whom sober editors call the only *real* maiden that Horace loved? Perhaps it was merely rustic Phidyle and her friends—three merry Italians at any rate, along with the Italian's best friend." Again and somewhat more seriously, from a paper *On Going to College*, "As our studies proceed and the writers of old seem more and more like human beings, all of a sudden our perspective is reversed, as when the planetary system of Ptolemy changed to that of Copernicus; history no longer revolves about us but we know our place in the shifting panorama of time." Finally from his fiftieth Class Report, "Only a word on religion, the most important matter of all. Travel and study and above all residence in France have led me to believe that the Catholic Church of Rome may one day prove the normal fold of the wandering sheep of Christ." Yet, he adds, the Church of England "is to me home whether or not its line of continuity is quite clear. It is not for one form to despise another or to seek for the different forms a mechanical unity of procedure, when all of honest heart and soul are traveling the same road."

In 1935 he read a novel kind of Phi Beta Kappa poem, half in English, half in goliardic Latin, at the meeting during Commencement week in Cambridge, and the occasion conspires with the form and subject to give these verses some color of commentary.

Horace benignly saw my fear,
Drew his chair the hearth-stone near,
Sipped a vintage of some force,
And then pursued his high discourse.
"Think not our ancient world," said he,
"For us was in its infancy.
Culture was as complex then
As yours, and yours may be again
As wisely simple as of yore
If you but aggravate the store
Of inner wealth. Pray let alone
The world's disorders and reform your own . . ."

Picture the snowy hair, the rubicund cheek, the twinkling rimless glasses, the smooth parabola of the waistcoat, the head cocked on one side with pretended innocence just when the shaft was about to be let fly, then the gay peal of laughter, and on all except the most formal occasions the emphasis of a gently waved cigar. This was the inimitable Rand of Class and Signet dinners, of the Saturday Club, of the debates of the Harvard Faculty, and not least of his study in the Widener Library, where from behind sheaves of notes he waved friend or student to the easy-chair beside his own.

The Saturday Club: A Century Completed, 1920–1956 (Boston, 1958).

Jacob Loewenberg

EMERSON HALL REVISITED

(1948)

When Jacob Loewenberg, Professor of Philosophy at the University of California, came back to Cambridge in 1947–48 as Visiting Lecturer in Philosophy, he found himself teaching in Emerson Hall in the very rooms where he had listened forty years before to "the great masters—Palmer, James, Royce, Münsterberg, Santayana, et al." He wrote to the Secretary of his College Class: "These men who belonged to the 'golden age' of the Department of Philosophy . . . are not dead. The influence they exerted by their independent and constructive thinking is still a dominating force . . ." A graduate of the College in 1908, Professor Loewenberg also took the A.M. degree in 1909 and the Ph.D. in 1911. He taught at Berkeley for some forty years, the last of which were marred by the newly instituted loyalty oath required by the California Regents as a condition of employment. He and many other faculty refused to sign and were dismissed. When the oath was struck down by the California Supreme Court, Loewenberg, then past retirement age, was rein-

stated as Professor Emeritus. He died in 1969. He was the author of an edition of Royce's Lectures on Modern Idealism, *a volume of* Fugitive Essays, *and a text of selections from Hegel.*

THERE ARE many advantages in growing older. One is freedom to gratify with impunity a sense of humor. Another is freedom to indulge in reminiscences. After the lapse of so many years, the temptation to recall with natural piety the Harvard philosophers of the past is irresistible. For these philosophers shaped my mind and influenced my point of view.

Emerson Hall is the intellectual home of my youth, and in revisiting it I feel as if I were walking into a hallowed place, hallowed by unseen but living spirits. The great teachers who belonged to a sort of "golden age" of American philosophy are not dead: Their inspirations and aspirations, though forgotten by some, have not been completely ignored or neglected by all our contemporaries. There are of course modern rebels against philosophy in the grand manner (such as was taught here in my student days, its roots deep in tradition yet wide and broad in speculative sweep), but their rebellion strikes me as too *enragé* and extravagant, often without focus or direction or aim. Analysis and criticism, when not directly related to the "thick" and varied content of human experience, are in danger of becoming merely verbal, that is, concerned with words as signs or symbols, and with sentences having such words for their constituents.

The semantic method is important, and I am far from belittling it, but if carried to great lengths, esoterically and zealously, the risk is great that the depth and wealth of philosophic ideas will be lost sight of or will become so simplified and attenuated as to be virtually meaningless. And what is worse, our modern analysts and semanticists and positivists may be led by their passion for clarity to identify the principal task of philosophy with their favorite method of utterance, method thus ceasing to be ancillary to subject matter and acquiring instead the position of an autonomous discipline, universal in its quest, the quest for the method of method, the meaning of meaning, the language of language.

This is not the place to raise controversial issues. I have noted elsewhere that exclusive preoccupation with methodology, initially governed by the spirit of criticism, may end in dogmatism, taking the form of *methodolatry,* the worship of a single method, which breeds one phobia or another, the chief being ontophobia, the fear of metaphysic. The old masters, who taught at Harvard in my day, subordinated technology to fecundity of reflection, reflection about first and last things in life and the world, requiring not only analysis but synopsis, not only refinement of locution but creative thought.

To this old-fashioned view, if it be old-fashioned, I am not ashamed to confess that I still adhere. I have brought it back to Harvard where originally it received its inception and cultivation. The courses I [have given] here all show traces of what I learned from James and Perry, from Palmer and Santayana, from Münsterberg and Royce. It was my privilege to enjoy close associations with some of these men, and especially with Palmer and Santayana and Royce.

To Palmer and Santayana I owe my interest in literature, for its own sake as well as for the philosophic content it may be made to elicit. And to Santayana in particular I am beholden for the conviction that philosophic discourse need not be carried on in the bloodless categories of certain schools; philosophic diction may even be musical without forfeiting either lucidity or cogency. Imagery and eloquence have their place in a human philosophy which aspires also to be humane. There is after all no virtue in being artless. Those who disparage metaphor and rhetoric, affecting a jejune or graceless style, probably do so because of scruple either of method or doctrine. But there is no necessary connection between obscurity and euphony of expression. Palmer and Santayana, in different ways and from different standpoints, taught me never to be afraid of the felicitous and pregnant phrase—but to be master and not the slave of it.

What Josiah Royce taught me, who resorted to a passionate eloquence of his own, would take too long to recount. For with Royce my relations were peculiarly personal and intimate. I shall single out but one of the many ways in which he influenced my thinking and teaching. What I have in mind is his tolerance.

Royce proclaimed the truth volubly enough, but he always retained a genial indulgence of opinions opposed to his own. How was it that so stanch a believer could have harbored such a tolerant soul? His tolerance was not that of the sceptic, for whom one belief is as uncertain as another; his was the tolerance of the catholic mind eager to assimilate the insights vouchsafed to others. His doctrine was such as to permit him to include within its ample embrace the most antagonistic views. But his penchant for synthesis, which prompted him to justify as partial or fragmentary aspects of truth whatever ideas struggled for expression, explains only one side of his tolerant spirit.

Apart from doctrinal considerations, his vocation as teacher, a vocation in which his conscience was engaged, laid upon him the obligation to inculcate in his pupils freedom of thought and independence of belief. Acquiescence in his ideas, merely because they were his, he did not countenance. He welcomed vigorous opposition, for what he valued in his students was not docility but power.

He took delight in the exercise of dialectic, and thrusts aimed at his arguments, if serious and well-directed, gave him much satisfaction, not only because he rejoiced in parrying them, but also because he enjoyed the logical prowess and skill of his opponents. A dissenter himself in matters his reason could not commend, he sincerely respected those who dissented from him. And for those who were disposed to accept his teaching uncritically he had a feeling bordering on disdain.

I remember how on one occasion he humorously reproved me for too docile a conformity to his views. He was my examiner in metaphysics for the doctor's degree. The day before I was to be examined he called me to his study and suggested that, to enable him to test my acumen, I prepare a detailed table of contents for a systematic treatise I might perhaps be inclined to write at some future time. Well, I was no Aristotle, and even the young Stagirite might have required more than twenty-four hours for the planning of a work on metaphysics. It was natural, anxious as I was to pass the examination, that I should have freely availed myself of the ideas derived from my teacher. The safest thing, I foolishly thought, was to play the role of disciple. And, as it happened, I was then not altogether averse to the doctrine Royce had been maintaining.

At the appointed hour I presented the fatal document. For an interminable time he tormented me with questions, acting as a sort of devil's advocate for positions hostile to his own. I stoutly held my ground by reproducing faithfully his favorite arguments which I knew by heart. When it was all over, he looked at me quizzically, and a merry smile tempered his evident disappointment.

"Well," he said, "I do not know what to say about our examination. You know too much about Royce and not enough about metaphysics. I wonder if, instead of the Ph.D., you should not receive the degree of R.D. You are certainly qualified to hold the title 'Doctor of Royce.' "

I recall another occasion when Royce lauded a student for a trenchant attack upon his doctrine. For some years, as his assistant, it fell to my lot to read and appraise the essays written in connection with his course on metaphyics, known as "Philosophy G." His procedure was to let me select for his personal perusal and comment some of the essays worthy of his attention. Some papers, which frankly puzzled me, especially those with a slant towards the occult, he would interpret for my benefit, reading into them out of the goodness of his heart ideas and motives of which their authors were blissfully unconscious. Towards painstaking work, however obscure or mediocre, his attitude was charitable; he took seriously what import he could divine or find there. No earnest mind, though ungifted or confused, went from him discouraged. But he relished superior performance, and upon such performance, no matter how odd in method or result, he would lavish high praise.

One day I consulted him about a paper which contained a devastating criticism of his philosophy expressed in what seemed to me too light a vein. Comparing Royce's Absolute to a "purple cow," the writer contrasted its apotheosis with the worship of the "golden calf," and he candidly preferred the latter as being more useful in its greater promise of "cash-value."

The criticism was not without substance and it certainly had style, but somehow I did not like the "purple cow." I questioned the propriety of the image and I asked Royce whether I should not return the paper with the comment that it was too frivolous.

"I don't think you understand the man," was Royce's reply after reading the essay with ill-concealed pleasure. "He has wit, imagination, and understanding. How James would have liked his style! Give him an 'A,' and compliment him on his originality. I shall myself have something to say about his brilliant criticism in the course of my next lecture."

I shall never forget that lecture. He devoted it entirely to an analysis of the young man's ideas, and with his inimitable humor he expatiated on the far-reaching metaphysical implications the contrasted images entailed. To his class this was a welcome interlude; for what abstract exposition failed to impart, the "purple cow" and the "golden calf" made wonderfully luminous.

I could mention dozens of incidents to illustrate Royce's method of teaching. It was a method altogether free from proselytism. His tolerance and considerateness were almost excessive. He was not one of those who felt called upon to exorcise error to insure the triumph of truth. So robust was his faith in truth that he looked for the foundation of it in the very existence of error. He was willing to let the truth take care of itself. He did not think that to honor truth we must ruthlessly abolish differences of opinion. Fear of assailants of one's belief, he seemed to feel, was a dubious compliment to its truth; if true, no attack could damage it. And so he perpetually courted criticism on the part of his pupils and colleagues.

Very characteristic is an incident related by Professor Palmer. Once when Royce was to be absent for six weeks to lecture at Aberdeen, he asked Palmer to take charge of his advanced course.

"I told him," writes Palmer, "that there might be an objection to my doing so in that I dissented from everything he had been saying. He said he was aware of this and for that reason he had asked me. He thought my coming would enrich the course. I took it and devoted myself to pulling up all the plants which Royce had carefully set out. When he came home he ordered a thesis on the entire work of the half-year, and he told me it was the best thesis he had ever received."

Palmer recalls also how Royce and James, intimate friends but philosophic opponents, once combined in a course on metaphysics, Royce occupying the first half-year, and James exposing the fallacies of idealism during the second.

Cultivation of the critical spirit as belonging to the very essence of creative philosophy—this was what all of Royce's colleagues aimed at. It was exhilarating if bewildering to hear of their polemics and mutual respect. In such an atmosphere it was impossible not to delight in the free play of ideas. And no one contributed to its zest more fully than Royce. It was his habit, for instance, to invite to one of his seminars scholars from different departments who would discourse broadly on their respective fields of research.

One year, as I remember, his visitors included a geologist, an archaeologist, a historian, a philologist, a chemist, a bio-chemist, a psychiatrist; each of them expounded some theme relevant to his special corner of knowledge, dwelling particularly upon a crucial experiment or problem illustrative of the inductive method. The discussion which ensued consisted for the most part in an amicable altercation between Royce and his guests, the students picking up whatever crumbs of learning they could.

I can still see Royce sitting at the head of the table in Emerson C, a large notebook in front of him, in which he would record minutely the visitor's discourse and his replies to questions. It was a thrilling experience to watch the encounter of critical minds and to participate in a free trade of ideas. The trade was indeed a flourishing one, for Royce appropriated from the many scholars valuable material for interpretation and synthesis, and the scholars in their turn learned to appreciate the importance and relevance of philosophy. Some of them would return to the seminar year after year. And as for the students, the vistas gained into unsuspected worlds of knowledge loosened their dogmatism and deepened their understanding.

The method in Royce's case was well adapted to the content of his teaching. He exemplified in his person an uncommon consistency of theory and practice. His life was a superb illustration of his philosophy. His attitude towards his pupils and colleagues was a concrete expression of his ethics of loyalty. His devotion to the ideal of truth did not preclude perfect courtesy on his part in dealing with the devoted labors of those who radically disagreed with him. He honored unselfish devotion in whatever form it chanced to express itself. For in such devotion lay for him the secret of the good life. The values and virtues of the good life he derived from principles designed to justify the heterogeneous objects of men's rational allegiance. And these principles, to the formulation and defense of which he dedicated his efforts, governed unswervingly his daily conduct. What Royce preached he practiced. He walked by the light which his heart kindled and his mind sustained.

Although I have traveled very far from some of Royce's cherished beliefs, the influence his intellectual tolerance exerted upon my mind still dominates, after all these years, my thoughts and perspectives. I must of course walk by my own light; and if I find such light luminous, I am never tempted to mistake it for a divine revelation; consequently, it does not occur to me to impugn as dark what other philosophers declare to be the sources of their illumination.

There are now current everywhere too many expressions of dogmatism and authoritarianism, and in certain circles the Roycean conception of loyalty would be considered obsolescent, demanding as it does critical *and* sympathetic attention to the diversity of human beliefs. Yet what Royce emphasized belongs to the very essence of democracy. Democracy, like charity, begins at home; if democratic or tolerant hospitality of ideas and persuasions opposed to our own does not take root within the private precincts of our minds, it can take root nowhere else.

Harvard Alumni Bulletin, January 29, 1949.

John T. Bethell

LISTENING TO MUSIC WITH WOODY
(1969)

The collected works of John Torrey Bethell, A.B. 1954, encompass many volumes—a scrapbook full of clippings pertaining to energetic journalism with the Gloucester Times, *nine bound annuals as managing editor of the monthly* National Petroleum News, *and then fifteen fat tomes containing that familiar publication which under his skillful editorial direction (1966 to date) has metamorphosed from the* Harvard Alumni Bulletin *into* Harvard Magazine. *His observant eye, his dryly humorous and sympathetic observation of the Harvard scene, his enthusiasm for music, and his deep attachment to Harvard are encompassed in this lively word picture of Woody, the admired and beloved G. Wallace Woodworth, A.B. 1924, who taught at Harvard from 1925 until his death in 1969. Woody was the successor of his own master and teacher, Archibald T. (Doc) Davison, A.B. 1906, as James Edward Ditson Professor, as long-time conductor of the Harvard Glee Club, as University Organist, and as choirmaster.*

LISTENING to music, I keep hearing Woody's voice interrupting, warning me to be alert for an inverted theme or exulting over the tonal glories of the orchestration.

Serious music means a great deal to me, but I was almost unaware of it until my junior year at Harvard, when I started auditing Music 1 because a certain Radcliffe girl was taking it. Last April I came back for "Return to Harvard" Day, and at eleven o'clock I climbed to the Paine Hall balcony and took my old seat. Things hadn't changed at all. Same Woody, same grand piano, same blackboard, same disc jockey sitting at that little table, ready to play the recorded illustrations (the sound system did seem a bit better than it used to). Woody still played brief illustrations at the piano, standing up. He lectured on Stravinsky that day. Playing recorded sections of the *Sacre du printemps*, he kept interrupting to explain the ballet phraseology, the counterpoint, the polyharmony. "Listen to those *driving* monotonous rhythms! Accented! I*rregular!* What *discipline* there is in Stravinsky's music!" Pausing a moment for an aside: "Now that's the gospel for today." Some of the students hissed (it was the day before the occupation of University Hall). "Discipline," Woody went on, nodding amiably, "you'll get further with it than you ever will without it!" This brought scattered applause. Stravinsky honked, in fifths. "Now *that's* the beauty of vulgarity," Woody cackled. He moved on to *Petrouchka.* Transported by the fourth tableau, he stomped across the stage, impersonating a dancing bear with a ring through its nose. What joy he took in his work! What *brio* he brought to it! When I picture him now, I see that performing bear. I'm not at all sure they make them like Woody any more.

For years, Professor Woodworth's "rehearsal" of the coming Boston Symphony broadcast was a staple of station WGBH-FM's programming. It seemed fitting that his last program should be devoted to Erich Leinsdorf's farewell concert, which included the Beethoven Ninth. Woody's commentary ended—also fittingly—with a loving, excited appreciation of the choral movement that concludes the symphony. "Millions of people, in Elysium," were his final words: "Dancing! Dancing for joy!"

Harvard Bulletin, September 15, 1969.

Kevin Starr

MEMORIES AND REFLECTIONS ON THE OCCASION OF READING SAMUEL JOHNSON BY MY FORMER NEIGHBOR, MR. WALTER JACKSON BATE

(1978)

A native Californian, Kevin Starr came to Harvard in the tumultuous sixties to take his doctorate. He taught American literature as assistant and associate professor and served as Allston Burr Senior Tutor of Eliot House until 1973, when he resigned to become city librarian of San Francisco. His attachment to his native state is firmly evident in his distinguished study,

Americans and the California Dream, *and in a historical novel of San Francisco,* Lands End, *yet he reserves a large place in his heart for Harvard and in particular for his teacher, the distinguished scholar Walter Jackson Bate, now Arthur Kingsley Porter University Professor, who won his second Pulitzer Prize for biography in 1978 for his life of Samuel Johnson. His first, for John Keats, came in 1964.*

IN HIS monumental dictionary, Samuel Johnson defined *essay* as "a loose sally of the mind; an irregular undigested piece; not a regular and ordered composition." This, then, is an essay on Walter Jackson Bate and his heroic new biography, *Samuel Johnson.* Thirty years in the making, 600 pages in length, Bate's is the best life of Johnson since Boswell's. Its author may well be the finest literary biographer at work in English today—a ranking that will surely be seconded when the National Book Awards are announced in April.

Bate's research shows that during 21 years of friendship with Johnson, Boswell spent just 426 days in his company. As senior tutor of Eliot House, I lived for three years next to Bate, Harvard's Abbott Lawrence Lowell Professor of the Humanities. Our suites, J-11 and K-11, were joined by a fire door. Early in the morning, sitting at my desk, I could hear Jack humming, or knocking his pipe clean (a frequent task), or now and then speaking to himself—words or phrases, never sentences, and never quite intelligible on my side of the door. About six in the evening, before we had dinner with the undergraduates, I would often drop by J-11, and Jack would pour me "a bourb." Like Johnson, who playfully affixed diminutives to such intimates as Boswell ("Bozzy"), Goldsmith ("Goldy"), and Dodsley ("Doddy"), Jack Bate is fond of abbreviations ("abbreves"), which he uses with friends as a mark of affection. Sipping bourbon and water, we would sit in the softly lit room and talk. The conversation ranged from gossip to high discourse, but it was never dull, because Jack has a way of working back to certain essential themes: literature, human life, and the sustaining relationship that exists between them. Those hours, punctuated by the tapping of Jack's pipe and the tinkle of ice against glass, were among the happiest of my life.

My wife, Sheila, would cook up a storm when Jack came for dinner. My two daughters were crazy about him. Even hell-raising Jessica, the younger, calmed down when he visited. We have a photograph of Uncle Jack reading Dr. Seuss to Jessica, then four. It is the summer in which he wrote *The Burden of the Past and the English Poet,* and Jack wears a blue-and-white striped linen jacket. Jessica, supporting her head on one hand, stares at Jack's face, not the book.

As a graduate student, I had been excited by Jack Bate's lectures on the history of criticism and the Age of Johnson. At my doctoral orals, he was one of the interrogators. Later, he wrote generous letters of recommendation for me. But since 1973, when I resigned my three-year nontenured associate professorship to become city librarian of San Francisco, I have had little contact with Jack. When I picked up *Samuel Johnson*, the force and flavor of the man came flowing back.

I held the book, comforted by its elegance of design and production, its massivity of scale (646 pages, including notes and index), its sheer solidity. Big books can be frightening: so much to digest. Yet little books, little academic literary books especially, can be equally off-putting. For the past two decades, thousands of articles containing one good idea have been elaborated into hardbacked university-press books containing one good idea and 125 pages of tedious argument. By contrast, the most significant books of literary scholarship—at least among those emanating from Harvard—have been big books, conceived and executed on a scale commensurate with the sweep and grandeur of European, English, and American letters. What we hope for from Harvard, after all, is scholarship, passion, imagination, range, robustness—and literary grace.

We get all this, and much more, in *Samuel Johnson*, a work that restores belief in a "Harvard tradition" of literary scholarship—a tradition that stays above the nit-picking pedantry, bourgeois careerism, and splenetic ideological squabbles that make contemporary literary scholarship so irrelevant to the needs of students and the vitality of our civilization. Academic literary scholarship seems to suffer from a detached retina. Its eye compulsively focuses on this or that irrelevance of detail, but cannot keep in sight the shape of the whole, the central, accessible life of literature itself, which is Life Itself: the passions, confusions, hungers, and tragedies of men and women enduring time, struggling for meaning, order, and symbolic expression.

Bate's *Johnson*, however, is a book unembarrassed of its subject, a book that seeks wholeness of life and action, not fragmentation of explanation. Nearly forty years ago, Bate—then a Harvard graduate student—first thought of writing the life of Johnson. The book accreted, he says, like a coral reef, through decades of reading, note-gathering, thinking. Bate began his odyssey of research in 1947 at Lichfield, Johnson's birthplace, and at the British Museum. He was guided along the way by the great eighteenth-century scholar Geoffrey Tillotson, who died in 1969. "Forever, when I think of London," Bate writes in the preface to *Samuel Johnson*, "Geoffrey will be walking across Russell Square from Birkbeck College and I shall be hurrying to meet him."

Like most of Bate's work, *Samuel Johnson* was written in a ferocious bout of composition. Johnson worked in similar fashion: long preparation, rapid writing. Bate has other Johnsonian traits. Indeed, anyone who knows him cannot help being struck by the correspondences, the cross references of thought and behavior between the monarch of the London coffeehouses and his Cambridge annalist. Biography, after all, can be an act of self-definition. Forty years ago, something in Samuel Johnson spoke to something in young Jack Bate. The two have kept intimate company ever since. Bate the man of near-sixty, the accomplished scholar and astonishing lecturer, is what he now is partly because of his long friendship with Johnson. In its deepest dimension of existence and meaning, the conjunction of these two men is one of the mysteries of the human spirit. We can read its outer surfaces without violating anyone's privacy, however, for in *Samuel Johnson* Bate tells us by indirection, by celebrating another's pain and transcendence, what he himself most values, celebrates, and fears.

Take work habits, for example. One of the previously unexplored areas of Johnson's creativity, admirably explicated by Bate, is the way external adversity brought forth torrents of prose from Johnson's pen. For his imaginative reconstructions of Parliamentary debates, to take one instance, Johnson could write twelve thousand words between noon and early evening, with the printer's boy at the door to rush the unread, ink-wet pages to the typesetter. Miraculously, as Bate makes clear, those polished, exquisitely balanced phrases were forged in a tension between punishingly high self-expectation and enormous time pressure—not to mention the enormous economic pressure of being broke. Johnson wrote furiously, as if he wanted the job over and done with, which he did. He wrote for money, and to appease a superego that impelled him to struggle against the unformed and chaotic by imposing the order of fine prose.

Few academics have been so prolific as Jackson Bate. Many of his finest books, it appears, were written rapidly and in circumstances of self-imposed adversity. For the earlier books, this almost goes without saying. Every aspiring academic writes a book or two under the Damoclean sword of a tenure decision. Many are so undone by the experience that they seldom write again. Among the tribunes and stalwart centurions of literary scholarship are scores whose reputations rest upon the victories of their first and last campaign. They had a thing or two to say, they said it, and they now devote themselves to teaching and making tenure decisions on younger scholars. By contrast, the tenure-winning books of Jackson Bate—*Negative Capability* (1939), his senior honors thesis; *The Stylistic Development of Keats* (1945), his doctoral dissertation; and *From Classic to Romantic* (1946), the work of his assistant professorship—neither strain nor search for finality. They are writers' books, lucid and firmly structured, concerned with open-ended processes rather than final conclusions. They sketch out territories that the older Bate mapped with greater precision in later books: *John Keats* (1963), *The Achievement of Samuel Johnson* (1955), and, triumphantly, *Samuel Johnson* (1977).

Just as Johnson needed adversity to lash himself into creativity, Bate seems to have sought the pressures of a crowded schedule. He allowed him-

self scant sabbatical time, taught full loads, and tutored squads of undergraduates in both English and history and literature, long after his senior
status made such tutorial activity expendable. He has been chairman of history and literature, English (twice), and the English department's busy
committee on undergraduate instruction. He has served on numerous Uni-
versity-wide committees, including the recent committee on faculty retirement, which he chaired, and whose eloquent report he wrote. Meanwhile,
he lectured in crowded courses, wrote innumerable letters of recommendation, read and commented on hundreds of theses, and poured gallons of
bourb for members of Eliot House. Somehow, he also wrote. The magisterial biography of Keats was written early in the morning and on weekends,
and completed in eighteen months. *Samuel Johnson*, produced on the same
kind of schedule, took just three years.

These books were written against the clock, but not against the grain.
Like Johnson, whose *Preface to Shakespeare* was long delayed by a mysterious inner resistance as he rounded fifty, Bate cannot write against the grain.
As *he* rounded fifty, something went wrong with *Coleridge*, a brief, brilliant
biography that may have cost Bate more effort than all his previous work
together. Something in the tragically flawed personality of Samuel Taylor
Coleridge—his habit of delay, perhaps, before a self-induced overschedul-
ing, or his difficulties with middle age—struck a resistant, fearful chord in
Bate, and the writing of *Coleridge* dragged on in agony, though you would
not detect it from the book. In 1972, the bicentennial of Coleridge's birth,
Bate was invited to lecture at Jesus College, Cambridge, where Coleridge,
in his erratic fashion, had studied. Bate declined.

Like Samuel Johnson (b. Lichfield, Staffordshire, 1709), Walter Jackson
Bate (b. Mankato, Minnesota, 1918) is a boy from the provinces who made it
against adversity, and did not forget it. Overaged and underfinanced, Johnson improbably got to Oxford, but poverty forced his departure after a year.
For the rest of his life, even after he had conquered London, he lamented
Oxford like a lost first love. Bate wooed and won Harvard, gloriously; but
the early encounter was almost as perilous as Johnson's.

Bate entered Harvard with the notion of studying archaeology. As a
scholarship boy in the Depression, he paid his way by washing dishes in the
Freshman Union. He could not help noticing that in front of Eliot House,
Lowell House, the Fly Club, and the Porcellian, there were lines of cabs—
lemon colored, robin's-egg blue, as in *The Great Gatsby*—waiting to take
nice-smelling undergraduates into Boston for a night's entertainment. You
can resent such things at Harvard. Many have. Your resentment may propel
you into the get-even world of business, where you make a bundle. Many
have. But if scholarship calls, your resentment can be dangerous. You may
miss the point of Harvard—the scholarly point. You can become so obsessed

with the lemon-colored taxis that you forget Widener Library, and Alfred North Whitehead, and the fact that no one forced you to go to Harvard in the first place. You knew the risks, and took them because you wanted the Harvard beneath the shimmering Gatsby surface, so defiant of poor Depression America: the Harvard of midnight oil, the place that nourishes a belief in the transforming effects of the life of the mind.

Bate identified with that Harvard. It carried him through, personally and professionally. But just as Johnson clung to Lichfield, returning at odd moments of need, Bate incorporated the Midwest into his Harvard persona. Indiana, where he was raised, gives a twang to his speech, and fills his discourse with homey idioms. It persists in his footwear: Bate will show up for a formal portrait in a three-piece suit and clodhoppers. Long before Jimmy Carter wore Jimmy Carter boots, Jack Bate was wearing Jimmy Carter boots—the sort one wears to walk over cornfields and back-country roads. Indiana, too, anchors his politics in a bedrock belief in the ordinary citizen, and has nourished a lifelong love of Abraham Lincoln (whose moral imagination had its roots in Bate's beloved eighteenth century). In Bate's Eliot House study, a portrait of Lincoln shares the place of honor with a portrait of Samuel Johnson.

For some years—in addition to his teaching and research—Bate ran a working dairy farm in western Massachusetts. He now owns a farm in New Hampshire. Like Johnson, he is acquainted with the useful arts: brewing, tanning, planting, plowing, carpentry, cattle care. One side of his nature delights in the sophistications of Cambridge, but he purposely stays close to rural things. Next to T. S. Eliot, his favorite poet is Robert Frost.

Bate spends as much time as he can upcountry, working fields, chopping wood, fixing a barn, cooking generous country meals for his guests on a burnt-black wood stove. Then, after dinner, he will talk far into the night about literature, read Eliot or Frost aloud (he reads superbly, with an unearthly sense of rhythm and cadence), or play nineteenth-century songs and hymns on a venerable foot-pumped organ.

Still, Bate is a professor, not a farmer. Farming may be the road not taken; he chose instead the labyrinthine ways of a university. He has been at Harvard for 43 of his sixty years, and for decades now he has traced a path from Widener Library to Warren House, headquarters of the English department, to Eliot House, where he lives. He experiences, perhaps, occasional encounters with the ghosts of younger Jack Bates, met unexpectedly around a corner or reflected in a barbershop mirror. Jack Bate the Dunster House undergraduate, Class of '39 and a *summa*-to-be, hurrying to the Union to wash dishes. Jack Bate, new doctorate in hand, exultant over his election to Harvard's prestigious Society of Fellows (1942). Assistant Professor Bate (1946), starting up the slippery ladder from which so many promising scholars would fall. Associate Professor Bate (1949), given permanency at the unusually young age of 31. Professor Bate (1956), busy about the writing of books, the teaching of classes, the staffing of a department. And, finally, Walter Jackson Bate, Abbott Lawrence Lowell Professor of the Humanities (1962), a chair held previously by another polymath and welder of good prose, Howard Mumford Jones.

Bate has never accepted a visiting professorship, and his vacations grow shorter and shorter. Even his retirement plans are tied to Harvard: eventually, he intends to write a series of profiles on early Harvard figures.

Benjamin Jowett, long the master of Balliol College, Oxford, once remarked that there is a certain kind of greatness that comes from remaining at the heart of a great institution. Jack Bate partakes of this greatness. To hear him lecture is to come close to the moral and intellectual center of Harvard itself. In formal discourse, his Indiana twang is supplanted by a precise Anglo-American, BBC baritone, rich and resonant and hauntingly cadenced. As a student, Bate absorbed the art of lecturing and reading aloud from his English instructors: Robert Hillyer, Theodore Morrison, Theodore Spencer. His lectures in "The Age of Johnson" (English 140) are masterpieces of argument, anecdote, and pace. For thirty years, the Harvard and Radcliffe undergraduates in his courses have heard the rattle of teacups, port glasses, and good talk at the weekly meetings of Johnson's Club. They have experienced the eloquence of Edmund Burke in the Commons, and known the pathetic as rendered by Oliver Goldsmith. Finally, at the end of the course, they die with the 75-year-old Johnson, overcome by circulatory disease, rheumatoid arthritis, chronic bronchitis, emphysema, and congestive heart failure, but still struggling for life, and able to plunge a scissors into his dropsy-swollen legs after his physician had refused to act further. (Johnson: "Deeper, deeper; I want length of life, and you are afraid of giving me pain, which I do not value.") Generations of students—now Manhattan stockbrokers, Wyoming ranchers, Tucson engineers, Vermont weavers, members of Congress, perhaps even a convict or two—remember these moments, and in the remembering recall something precious about the time they were young and at Harvard.

Samuel Johnson was hungry for institutions, yet curiously disaffiliated from them. Religious, he attended church irregularly and declined to take holy orders when the chance presented itself. Loving the law, he felt himself excluded from legal practice for want of a university degree. Loving learning, he was forced from Oxford. Clubbable, loving good company, he could be needlessly pugnacious to his friends, as if to drive off the very associations he craved.

In time, however, he achieved three institutional or quasi-institutional relationships. Henry and Hester Thrale gave him a family. London gave him something even better than Oxford: an open university where he could research the human condition. Literature gave him a profession, albeit a reluctant one.

Had Johnson remained at Oxford, he might have distinguished himself as a don there. Then again, we might never have heard of him. After all, the great writer loathed the act of writing. Gibbon described mid-eighteenth-century Oxford as an Aeolian cave of sleep and port, and the modern university is also prey, if not to sleep and port, to promised projects long postponed, with conference calls, conventions, committee meetings, the fussy busyness that serves to mask laziness and procrastination. Grub Street had its risks for Johnson, but Oxford might have been even more dangerous.

The university liberated Jack Bate, man of letters, but not without cost. Bate accomplished much very early. He won tenure at an age when others were still finishing their Ph.D.'s. Even now, there is an essential youthfulness to Bate—a boyish energy, a persistent romanticism, an intermittent dreaminess. The Pulitzer Prize-winning *John Keats*, the life of an ever-young poet, rounded out the prodigious struggle and accomplishment of Bate's youth. Then, in his forties, came a terrible time: a time, to quote Bate on a similar crisis in the life of Johnson, haunted by "the sense of time passing, of the melting away of alternative choices, of the lessening of chances to make a fundamentally new start."

Bate was particularly vulnerable to a midlife crisis because he had burned up his youth in hard work. His father, an overworked high-school principal, had said on his deathbed, "I hope you'll be able to go through life free of what has always bothered me—a terrible sense of rush, of there never being enough time." By the midforties, Bate was gripped by the fear that for him as for his father, there would never be time to do all the things that needed to be done.

One can surmise that for Bate, as for all overachievers who experience a midlife reassessment, there were heavy doses of second-guessing. Had his gains been worth the effort and the sacrifices? Had one made a false god of books? Was one's Harvard life too restricted, too donnishly cenobitical? Such questions were the more tormenting because they came in a rush, after a clear line of youthful development and a brilliant and prodigiously busy period in the thirties and early forties.

No wonder, then, that Bate writes with such sympathetic insight into Sam Johnson's years of middle-aged stress. The moral drama of Johnson's middle age constitutes the bituminous center of Bate's biography. Johnson, Bate tells us, postponed his crisis (or at least its effects) by plunging into an orgy of work—the dictionary, the volumes of moral essays written for *The Rambler, The Idler, The Adventurer:* a storm of effort that blew him past crisis in his early forties, but shipwrecked him in his early fifties on the desolate shores of incipient insanity.

Bate is also splendid on Johnson's needs as a social being. Like Johnson, Bate loves solitude as an environment for work. Also like Johnson, he has need of friends and the convivial table. (Said Johnson: "I live in the crowd of jollity, not so much to enjoy company as to shun myself.") Bate is a superb dinner-table conversationalist, capable, even, of the most amusing small talk when he is on his best behavior—which is most of the time.

Samuel Johnson once surprised a dinner party by taking off across the lawn in a foot race with a young lady who had challenged all comers. Kicking off his slippers as he ran, the 53-year-old Johnson bested the girl in his bare feet. Bate, too, can exhibit such spontaneity. He is also a gifted mimic, as Johnson was, though he keeps that talent in reserve for pretentious bores and departmental enemies. The soul of courtesy, an avoider of open conflict, he now and then vents his ire through private invective that suggests Hieronymus Bosch in its fertility of fiendish invention and comic virtuosity.

As did Johnson, Bate loves the ambience of ordered domesticity. In *Samuel Johnson* he writes marvelously of women. He rescues the humanity of Mrs. Johnson from generations of hostile commentators who have seen poor Tetty as a comic, even repulsive figure—so much older than her husband, such a whimpering, complaining clinging vine; so ludicrous with her rouge, her wig, her trashy novels and afternoon gin-drinking. Bate shows us these things, for they are partly true, but he also shows us Elizabeth Jervis Porter Johnson's generosity and courage, her sound instincts, and her early, welcomed belief that the ungainly, twitching, shambling, half-blind fellow that some ridiculed "is the most sensible man that I ever saw in my life."

Radcliffe undergraduates and women graduate students have found in Jack Bate a perceptive teacher and tutor, and a number of women have found in him an excellent friend. It was for his friend and fellow Johnson scholar Mary Hyde that Jack Bate ventured into formal dress, a rare event, climbing into the Harry Levin Memorial Tuxedo (worn by the Irving Babbitt Professor of Comparative Literature in the midthirties, when Levin was a Junior Fellow; donated to Jack Bate sometime after World War II; and still sporting, on its left inside pocket, the proud eagle of the National Recovery Administration).

Unlike Sam Johnson, Bate evinces a distaste for travel. Nevertheless, he has retraced his subject's journey to the Hebrides, and, on a lesser scale, was once involved in a memorable English-department day trip from Marblehead to the Dry Salvages, a cluster of rocks off Cape Ann, notable mainly because they appear in Eliot's *Four Quartets*. A fishing trawler had been chartered for the occasion, which began promisingly but turned menacing as the seas began to build. Warmed by a colorfully striped Peruvian poncho, Harry Levin sat alone in the bow, lunching on Chablis and crab salad, as serenely aloof as a Byzantine envoy taking passage with a passel of Adriatic pirates. John Bullitt, for unknown reasons, wore a black neoprene wet suit (complete with scuba gear and underwater watch), as if he were understudying Sean Connery in a James Bond film. Robert Fitzgerald, handsome, gray-haired, with the look of the Irish Ascendancy in his face, intermittently answered the howling winds with defiant quotations from Homer, rendered in sonorous Greek. I scavenged the goodies from lunches abandoned by seasick colleagues. Alas, Jack Bate was among them. He, David Perkins, and John Paul Russo sat side by side, green with nausea. Jack looked woefully up at me. "Kevin," bellowed the distinguished scholar, "go ask the captain of this pitching scow when the hell we're going to get to those goddam rocks!"

Such a moment of homey realism says something about the paradox of Walter Jackson Bate, literary scholar and critic. Tolerant, sympathetic, capacious in mind and imagination, he still has his *bêtes noires* when it comes to current literary scholarship and critical practice. He cannot abide the modish, the mandarin-highbrow, the deliberately obscurantist. Artistic and critical gnosticism, he says, has arisen because of the gulf that separates the popular and sophisticated arts, in music, literature, and painting especially. The masters of Baroque and nineteenth-century music, he points out, composed for as large an audience as possible. The masters of prose fiction—Scott, Dickens, Stendhal, Hugo, Balzac, George Eliot, Cooper, Manzoni, Twain, James, Dostoyevsky, Tolstoy—wrote with mass audiences in mind. These artists saw no dichotomy between popularity (and financial success) and literary excellence. Critical and intellectual prose writers—like Johnson, Burke, Newman, Ruskin, Mill, Carlyle—also sought the widest possible area of influence and persuasion.

Bate's preferences, as far as I can judge, are for what he calls "the open idiom"—literature and criticism that is not overly formalistic or self-contemplating as to strategies and processes. Bate likes writing that shows ambition, sweep, and scale; that takes its central vitality not from symbolism for its own sake, or from a deliberate artiness, but from human life in all its bewildering variety. He is especially attracted to those moments of analysis or narrative when social event, psychological experience, and the shaping force of the imagination intersect; those high moments—in an essay by Johnson, a speech by Burke, a novel by George Eliot—when we feel the imagination, especially the moral imagination, working in its most intense mode: lifting up, shoring against deficiencies, completing the incomplete, forearming against disaster, accepting mystery, celebrating a transitory happiness, healing an abiding pain.

Some of his personal tastes are startling, at least in a day of fussy correctness about what's in and what's out. For instance, he loves the novels of H. Rider Haggard—*King Solomon's Mines* (1886), *She* (1887), *Allan Quatermain* (1887) among them—because of their action and narrative sweep, and because of the way Haggard conveys a sense of mystery, of dreamy romance, forearmed against real danger by imagination and moral resolve. Bate also likes the histories of Samuel Eliot Morison for many of the same reasons. Morison tells a good story, and he is unashamed of elemental moral drama.

Bate the scholar is working in a discernible Harvard tradition of literary study, a tradition that has sought appreciation and wholeness of insight when bringing a masterpiece to scrutiny. The most influential of his own teachers at Harvard were Alfred North Whitehead, John Livingston Lowes, Douglas Bush, and Abbott Lawrence Lowell. From Whitehead, the philosopher of wholeness, he absorbed a hunger for the discovery of organic relationships and a taste for broadly philosophical speculation. From Lowes, the scholarly detective *par excellence*, he learned just how complex the genesis of a masterpiece can be: how fragments of reading and experience can lie suspended in an artist's subconscious for years, until the creative impulse brings them forth in a meaningful pattern. Douglas Bush, that great Christian humanist, a man who breakfasts each morning on Latin and Greek, challenged Bate to catholicity of learning, respect for grand continuities, and concern for literature as moral statement. A. Lawrence Lowell studied government as a mode of humanistic expression; as president of Harvard (1909–1933), he founded the House system and the Society of Fellows. As a Junior Fellow, Bate came to know Lowell just before his death, and from him he took a conception of Harvard as resting its reputation on the quality of undergraduate life and instruction.

Bate turned naturally to the study of the late eighteenth century and the practice of biography. The Age of Johnson, he feels, has much in common with our own. A high formalist tradition, the neoclassicism spawned by the Renaissance, was giving way to a less formal, more open-ended idiom, known retrospectively as the Romantic Movement. Expository prose—the essays and oratory of Burke, Johnson's criticism and biography, the "Discourses" of Sir Joshua Reynolds—led the way in returning literature to its pre-neoclassical flexibility and range. Today's "high modernist mode" (the phrase is Professor David Perkins's) forced an astringent formalism on English and American writing: a dryness of utterance, a severity of subject matter, a rigidity of structure comparable to the Augustan mode of the mid-eighteenth century. Now, thinks Bate, prose is again leading the way to a more capacious, flexible, open-ended literature. The historical writing of Morison is one example, but so is the solid, vigorous prose of current biography, history, journalism, and public commentary. Like Sam Johnson, Jack Bate takes literature where and when he finds it—that is, where it is most vigorous, most catholic, and humane.

Above all else, Bate is attracted to biography—both the reading and the writing of it. In this, again, he resembles Johnson, who virtually invented the genre of literary biography that Bate's *Samuel Johnson* exemplifies. Biography, Bate points out, is by definition engaged with life, with inner realities, symbolic experience, and the externalities of the great and grand and terrifying world of social experience. Because great lives are circuitous and complex, biography keeps alive the range and variety of the big Victorian novel. Bate points to George Eliot's *Middlemarch* (1872) as a prototype for *Samuel Johnson:* panoramic, with room for both the big and little moments of life, bold and venturesome and unafraid of moral drama and the play of speculative ideas. Like the Victorian novel, biography contains worlds within worlds. It depends on no single explanation of experience. It can be psychological without being pedantically psychiatric. It can be philosophical without reducing life to the remorseless working out of a theoretical proposition, as if life were a set problem in symbolic logic. Biography seeks rational understanding, but is also at ease with mystery. The "action" of a life, its quality of (in the Greek root of the word) *antagonism,* is never a one-to-one calculation of cause and effect. Some things get done. Other things are left undone. Some longings are fulfilled, some go unassuaged to the grave. Never can the biographer say exactly why. He can suggest, but he always wrestles with the unknown and the absurd.

Subject and biographer could hardly be better matched than in *Samuel Johnson.* Although Bate uses the pronoun "I" only once or twice in 600 pages, two streams of life and thought, Johnson's and Bate's, converge in the book. In point after point of the narrative, we experience a certain warming of prose, a certain back-music behind the utterance, signaling to us that in the course of telling Johnson's story, Bate is telling us something precious about himself. The Indiana boy in Bate warms to the story of the struggling provincial. In 1737 Johnson walked from Lichfield to London; in 1935, young Jack Bate took the bus from Richmond, Indiana, to Harvard. Both learned to revere learning and hate cant. Both detested snobbery, yet in their ferociously antisnobbish ways became snobs of a sort. Both hoped initially for other things—Johnson the law, Bate archaeology—and then stumbled magnificently into letters; Johnson after running the risks of Grub Street, where writers wrote too much, and Bate after running the risks of the academy, where many would-be writers (Morison spoke of "gonna" historians) never write at all.

"I'll write my biography of Johnson," Jack Bate once told me, "just as soon as I feel satisfied that I understand his politics and his religion." I cannot say how Bate's own politics inform his comprehension of Johnson's, but his brilliant explanation of Johnson's Toryism dispels any suspicion that the man was a political reactionary. In politics, as in everything else, Johnson sought wholeness and balance. He distrusted the laissez-faire economics of the Whigs, but Toryism for him was neither moonlit castles nor a privileged aristocracy. Proud and independent, he was apt to grow testy in the company of privileged but unaccomplished aristocrats. For Johnson, Toryism was the organic enfoldment of an element of protection and stability in society. The crown, he believed, offered the lower orders their best protection against exploitation by either the aristocracy or the bourgeoisie. Sanctioned by religion, monarchy existed in a sphere beyond class. Its first function was the preservation of justice. Bate, in effect, rescues Johnson for both liberals and conservatives. As Bate presents him, he was something of a modern liberal in that he was protectionist, but something of a conservative in his reverence for organic relationships and the social order.

Johnson's Christianity always gave Bate a bit of trouble. Raised a Christian Scientist, Bate had not remained in the church of his youth. He seems to have flirted with Catholicism. For a time, certain Jesuit graduate students at Harvard fanned rumors of Bate's incipient conversion. Jack respected his Jesuit students for their enormous erudition and their excellent martinis, but remained quintessentially Protestant in character and mode of thought: a man, at least in religious matters, alone with his skepticism and his conscience, both of which are formidable.

Bate's treatment of Johnson's Christianity, however, is totally sympathetic. I suspect that one of the reasons for the persistent popularity of English 140 among Harvard and Radcliffe undergraduates is an old-fashioned, unappeased hunger for religious ideas and moral philosophy, presented in a nondenominational, nonproselytizing manner. Harvard's department of philosophy has long since abandoned the teaching of the lives of great philosophers, the drama of great philosophical ideas, presented, as Raphael Demos used to present them, with passion and clarity and a concern for their useful human context. In English 140, Jack Bate offers unembarrassed access to the primal questions of moral philosophy: what is human life, for example, and how and for what should one lead it?

This, after all, was what first attracted me to Walter Jackson Bate—my own desperate hope that what I was pursuing at Harvard, literary scholarship, might in the long run prove useful. I knew that literature does not offer salvation, but I did want it to provide some solid assistance for the journey. Jack Bate spoke to that hope. Like Samuel Johnson, he believed in the healing, reconciling effect that the humanities can have if properly studied and appreciated.

Bate's teaching, his scholarship, the stunning achievement of *Samuel Johnson* remind me of Horatius at the bridge, defending Rome from Etruscan invaders. Bate and a small band of scholars at Harvard and elsewhere have for two decades fought against that deliberately obscure, irrelevant gnosticism that threatens to make the profession of literary scholarship a laughingstock. "Autodeixis: Metatexts and Metaphors" was one of the papers given at the Modern Language Association's Chicago convention in December.

But while such as Jack Bate are around, there is always hope, Bate describes Johnson's autumnal masterpiece, *Preface to Shakespeare* (1765), and his Indian-summer *Lives of the Poets* (1781) as products of a life. Bate's *Samuel Johnson* is the same sort of lavish, ripe performance: autumnal in its richness of texture, pervaded by quiet joy over the completion of a long harvest. Let us wish Jack Bate a long-lasting autumn, for Harvard has need of him.

And so do I, in memory and in metaphor. My Harvard is past, but I want it to be useful, to liberate and exhilarate me as I struggle with my decidedly non-Harvardian present. Each of us has his own Harvard, including, for some, an imperial presence that wears no clothes, that postures in naked arrogance and sham. But humanistic Harvard does have clothes—preppy outfits from the Andover Shop, jerseys with numbers, crimson robes with slashed black velvet on the sleeves. I prefer to think of Harvard dressed in an unpretentious tweed jacket of the sort Jack Bate wears, and a pair of L. L. Bean boots to negotiate the soggy snow and treacherous ice between Widener Library and Eliot House.

Reading *Samuel Johnson,* remembering Bate at Eliot House, I gain possession of a metaphor beyond compromise or qualification. In the long run, people and institutions ought to be judged by their best, by their ideals. *Samuel Johnson* radiates a distinct, palpably Harvardian ideality: a conviction of transforming humanistic force in letters, a passion for high moral and imaginative apprehension, a humility before the infinitely complex edifice that mankind has wrought.

After nearly three and a half centuries, Harvard still manages to preserve some of its founding Puritan energy. The Puritans, after all, believed that virtue and good letters go hand in hand: that the life of the mind is essential to the life of the soul. They believed that learning should not make for pride, but for humility. So did Samuel Johnson. So does Jack Bate. And so, at its best, does Harvard.

Harvard Magazine, March–April, 1978.

III

TROUBLE UNDER THE ELMS

When I was asked to come to this university, I supposed I was to be at the head of the largest and most famous institution of learning in America. I have been disappointed. I find myself the sub-master of an ill-disciplined school.

EDWARD EVERETT (1847)

While these labours were in progress, I was becoming, of course, better acquainted with the history and character of the graduates. Several instances of strange experience in childhood, of brave struggles to obtain an education, of virtue and heroism under temptations of wealth and worldly honors, awakened hearty sympathy and admiration. Notwithstanding short-comings, and cases of iniquity which may have escaped punishment, I was convinced that the worth and influence of the graduates as a body had not been properly appreciated. More than two centuries have passed since the College was established, yet I found but one graduate who had been executed as a malefactor, and he was the victim of the witchcraft delusion; and but one who had been sent to a State penitentiary, and this was for passing counterfeit money . . .

JOHN LANGDON SIBLEY (1873)

Mistress Eaton

I OWN THE SHAME AND CONFESS MY SIN

(1639)

Complaints about the cooking have been characteristic since the establishment of the College. The Harvard Epic—"The Rebelliad" (1819)—was inspired by one of the many food riots in the College commons, but the first and nastiest complaint about Harvard food occurred in the second academic year of the College's existence. When the first master, Nathaniel Eaton, was haled into court for beating his assistant with a walnut tree cudgel, it was an occasion for a general ventilation of grievances against Eaton for the severity of his discipline, and against his wife for the quality of food and drink she served her boarders in the Peyntree House. As a result, the Eatons lost their jobs and have gone down in Harvard history as a pair of rogues. Here is Mrs. Eaton's apologia for her "loathsome catering," one of the few documents recording the unpleasantnesses of the College's first years.

FOR THEIR BREAKFAST, that it was not so well ordered, the flour not so fine as it might, nor so well boiled or stirred, at all times that it was so, it was my sin of neglect, and want of that care that ought to have been in one that the Lord had intrusted with such a work. Concerning their beef, that was allowed them, as they affirm, which, I confess, had been my duty to have seen they should have had it, and continued to have had it, because it was my husband's command; but truly I must confess, to my shame, I cannot remember that ever they had it, nor that ever it was taken from them. And that they had not so good or so much provision in my husband's absence as presence, I conceive it was, because he would call sometimes for butter or cheese, when I conceived there was no need of it; yet, forasmuch as the scholars did otherways apprehend, I desire to see the evil that was in the carriage of that as well as in the other, and to take shame to myself for it. And that they sent down for more, when they had not enough, and the maid should answer, if they had not, they should not, I must confess, that I have denied them cheese, when they have sent for it, and it have been in the house; for which I shall humbly beg pardon of them, and own the shame, and confess my sin. And for such provoking words, which my servants have given, I cannot own them, but am sorry any such should be given in my house. And for bad fish, that they had it brought to table, I am sorry there was that cause of offence given them. I acknowledge my sin in it. And for their mackerel, brought to them with their guts in them, and goat's dung in their hasty pudding, it's utterly unknown to me; but I am much ashamed it should be in the family, and not prevented by myself or servants, and I humbly acknowledge my negligence in it. And that they made their beds at any time, were my straits never so great, I am sorry they were ever put to it. For the Moor his lying in Sam. Hough's sheet and pillow-bier, it hath a truth in it: he did so one time, and it gave Sam. Hough just cause of offence; and that it was not prevented by my care and watchfulness, I desire [to] take the shame and sorrow for it. And that they eat the Moor's crusts, and the swine and they had share and share alike, and the Moor to have beer, and they denied it, and if they had not enough, for my maid to answer, they should not, I am an utter stranger to these things, and know not the least footsteps for them so to charge me; and if my servants were guilty of such miscarriages, had the boarders complained of it unto myself, I should have thought it my sin, if I had not sharply reproved my servants, and endeavored reform. And for bread made of heated, sour meal, although I know of but once that it was so, since I kept house, yet John Wilson affirms it was twice; and I am truly sorry, that any of it was spent amongst them. For beer and bread, that it was denied them by me betwixt meals, truly I do not remember, that ever I did deny it unto them; and John Wilson will affirm, that, generally, the bread and beer was free for the boarders to go unto. And that money was demanded of them for washing the linen, it's true it was propounded to them, but never imposed upon them. And for their pudding being given the last day of the week without butter or suet, and that I said, it was miln of Manchester in Old England, it's true that I did say so, and am sorry, they had any cause of offence given them by having it so. And for their wanting beer, betwixt brewings, a week or half a week together, I am sorry that it was so at any time, and should tremble to have it so, were it in my hands to do again.

Samuel E. Morison, *The Founding of Harvard College* (Cambridge, 1935).

Edward Holyoke

THE BURNING OF HARVARD HALL
(1764)

"The opening of the year 1764," wrote Josiah Quincy in his history, "had been distinguished by the completion of Hollis Hall, under the patronage of the legislature; but the bright sky, which thus dawned on Harvard, was early obscured by the heaviest cloud that ever burst on the head of our Alma Mater." In the midst of the bitter and snowy night of January 24, Harvard Hall, the oldest and most valuable college building, was burned to the ground. With it were destroyed the 5000-volume College library, the scientific equipment of the Apparatus Chamber, and other treasures accumulated since the early years of Harvard history. This account of the conflagration was prepared for the newspapers by President Holyoke himself, who though seventy-five years of age at the time had been present to direct the fire fighting. The president spent much of the remaining five and a half years of his life repairing the damage (the new Harvard Hall was completed in 1766) and arousing the sympathy and interest of friends of Harvard in replacing books and equipment.

LAST NIGHT Harvard College suffered the most ruinous loss it ever met with since its foundation. In the middle of a very tempestuous night, a severe cold storm of snow, attended with high wind, we were awaked by the alarm of fire. Harvard Hall, the only one of our ancient buildings which still remained, and the repository of our most valuable treasures, the public library and philosophical apparatus, was seen in flames. As it was a time of vacation, in which the students were all dispersed, not a single person was left in any of the Colleges, except two or three in that part of Massachusetts most distant from Harvard, where the fire could not be perceived till the whole surrounding air began to be illuminated by it. When it was discovered from the town, it had risen to a degree of violence that defied all opposition. It is conjectured to have begun in a beam under the hearth in the library, where a fire had been kept for the use of the General Court, now residing and sitting here, by reason of the small-pox at Boston: from thence it burst out into the library. The books easily submitted to the fury of the flame, which with a rapid and irresistible progress made its way into the Apparatus Chamber, and spread through the whole building. In a very short time, this venerable monument of the piety of our ancestors was turned into a heap of ruins. The other Colleges, Stoughton Hall and Massachusetts Hall, were in the utmost hazard of sharing the same fate. The wind driving the flaming cinders directly upon their roofs, they blazed out several times in different places; nor could they have been saved by all the help the town could afford, had it not been for the assistance of the gentlemen of the General Court, among whom his Excellency the Governor was very active; who, notwithstanding the extreme rigor of the season, exerted themselves in supplying the town engine with water, which they were obliged to fetch at last from a distance, two of the College pumps being then rendered useless. Even the new and beautiful Hollis Hall, though it was on the windward side, hardly escaped. It stood so near to Harvard, that the flames actually seized it, and, if they had not been immediately suppressed, must have carried it.

But by the blessing of God on the vigorous efforts of the assistants, the ruin was confined to Harvard Hall; and there, besides the destruction of the private property of those who had chambers in it, the public loss is very great, perhaps irreparable. The Library and the Apparatus, which for many years had been growing, and were now judged to be the best furnished in America, are annihilated.

Josiah Quincy, *The History of Harvard University* (Cambridge, 1840).

Samuel Chandler

A COLLEGE TRAGEDY

(1773)

Sam Chandler, the Gloucester minister's son, studied at Harvard during the exciting days before the outbreak of the Revolution. A favorite of his father, Sam was more attracted by music and magic than he was by such mundane subjects as spelling. Still, he kept a journal until just before his graduation in 1775, and from it is reprinted an account of an unhappy student accident. Chandler served on seacoast defense in the war, married a sea captain's daughter, and led the life of a teacher of mathematics until his death in 1786.

THURSDAY July 1. This forenoon at half after ten I saw Lovel Padock & Winslow a going through the last entry in Massachusetts in order to go in a swimming. I was in company with Hendley. We moved to go with them but by some cause or other did not. I got excused from reciting at eleven of clock. About ten minutes after the bell tolled, news came to the College Yard that Padock was drowned. Being struck with the news I ran down to the river where I imagined they went in, a place above the bridge near a creek, a place they commonly called the brick works, a place where there was no bank but descended gradually from high water to low, the tide running very strong which makes it very dangerous for those who can't swim. When I came to the place I find they have just got him out of the water. They were all but————at swimming and Padock and Lovel going off deep, Padock was suddenly carried off by the tide where it was over his head. He catched hold of Lovel and pulled him under water once or twice but Lovel disengaged himself and got clear, leaving Padock to drive from this world to the world of immortality. They gave without doubt all the assistance they were capable of with safety. There was an old man named Huse—a crazy part of a man—who being within sight ran for assistance, but never called to any man till he got to the College when the scholars flocked down in multitudes. I hear likewise that there was a man a raking hay on the meadow who came part of the way and seeing him a sinking returned to raking saying that he could not swim. It is my opinion that he might have saved him easy with his rake if he had gone for he was then within a few yards of the shore. The scholars soon got a diving to find him. Parker, a boy belonging to Welsh the painter, first felt him. Bliss first brought him off the bottom, and Peele who saved his life yesterday first brought him out of the water, when he was soon brought on shore, rolled and rubbed with salt etc . . . He was supposed to be under water near half an hour before they found him. They brought him ashore about half after eleven, tried all experiments such as rolling him, rubbing with salt, pouring spirits down his throat, blowing into his mouth with bellows etc. They tried to bleed him but could find no vein. There was not a quart of water in him which made the doctors think he was frighted into a fit. They worked on him at the side of the bank till near twelve when they carried him to Welsh's the painters where they wrapped him up in ashes and continued rubbing and applying hot cloths. Dr. Lord who came from Boston accidentally made out to bleed him in the jugular vein. He bled very freely but no life appeared. After dinner I went down again to see him when he was quite stiff and cold. His father got there a little after one but could not see him. The whole College and even all the town seem much affected as he was the prettiest and likeliest youth in his class about fifteen years of age. He was kept the afternoon wrapped up in salt all but his head. I continue with him likewise numbers of other scholars the chief of the afternoon. At night he was carried to Mr. Sewal's and put in a warm bed. The news was sent to his father about twelve and before one it was spread all about Boston, likewise all the other neighboring towns. At four we do not recite neither do I attend prayers.

Friday 2. This morning in at declaiming there was a sort of funeral oration offered by Maynard. At about ten of the clock the corpse was carried down in Welsh's boat to Boston, it being put in a coffin. After dinner I walk to Boston. Have some time at my sister's. I go about the wharves to inquire for an opportunity to send a letter to my father by my mother's desire as she has a mind to go home next week. I go to Bethune's store and drink punch with him there when finding Paston I spend some time very agreeable with him as he is going away next week for Philadelphia College. I walk by Major Padock's and incline to go in. I lay at my sister's at night.

Saturday 3. In the morning I rose early and got up to Cambridge before breakfast so as to wait. Mr. Wardsworth has got leave for the freshmen to wear black gowns and square hats at the funeral today. After dinner Hendley rode up in his father's chaise and carried me down to Charlestown. I go over the ferry and stay some time at my sister's when I go up to the factory in a room which is provided for the scholars where young Padock's picture is hung up for them to see. I go to see the button makers etc. in the factory. The freshmen several of them have walked about the town with their black gowns on, the inhabitants not knowing what it meant nor who they were. Gay, Gove, two Leverits, Lovel & Winslow were chosen bearers but afterwards Peele was chosen bearer in the room of Gay. They proceeded from Major Padock's about five of clock when the bells tolled, even the grammar school bell. The freshmen went in procession in their dress, then followed the corpse, then the mourners which were very numerous, then the governors of the college, then the scholars, and then followed a very numerous retinue of the inhabitants. The streets were crowded with spectators. They went down Prison Lane up School Street and into the Middle Burying Place where he was interred in a tomb where there was no other coffin. Near the Bridewell opposite his own house, when coming into the Burying Yard the freshmen opened to the right and left till the students had all passed through then waited upon the Major to his house, then to the factory, and then home. Numbers of the freshmen walked over the ferry with their gowns on. Seemed very grand in general. Thatcher sent a piece to Salem for the print, another he left at Edes & Gils and upon his returning back to give an account of the funeral found Mr. Eliot reading of it who did not very much approve of it. I drank coffee at my sister's. Went to Mr. Hendley's and rode up with Zech. I tried at Charlestown to get my watch but in vain. It has been a very warm day. I believe the proceedings in Boston were agreeable in general.

Monday 10. This morning very early the President and Tutors go out a fishing.

Harvard Graduates' Magazine, March and June, 1902.

Eliphalet Pearson

JOURNAL OF DISORDERS
(1788)

*The great Eliphalet—"big name, big frame, big voice and beetling brow"—
came to Harvard in 1786 as Hancock Professor of Hebrew after a period of
service as first principal of Phillips Academy, Andover, Massachusetts.
Those were the days when the "stiff and unbending" President Willard's
conduct of affairs encouraged disorder and disrespect among the students.
From 1788 until 1797 Professor Pearson kept a "journal of disorders" in
which the most lengthy and frequent entries occurred during December
1788 and January 1789. Pearson was elected a Fellow of Harvard College in
1800 and, after the death of Willard in 1804, acted for more than a year as
president. When Harvard began a swing toward Unitarianism, Pearson resigned (1806) and went back to Andover, where he founded the Andover
Theological Seminary.*

DEC. 4 [1788]. Exhibition A.M. before the immediate government.—P.M. A
large collection at the chamber of Vose & Whitwell. Present, the occupants,
Fay, 2 Sullivans, Trapier, Walker, Welles, Withers, & two strangers. A disorderly, riotous noise called up Mr. Webber who desired them to be still.
Immediately upon his leaving them, the noise became more violent, which
occasioned his return. He then ordered all to their chambers; but none
withdrew. He then ordered them individually & by name. The two Sullivans declined going, & James said he would go, when he pleased.—After
this the two Sullivans conducted improperly towards Mr. Smith, & diso-
beyed a positive order of Mr. James.—

Dec. 5. A snow ball was thrown at Mr. Webber, while he was in the desk
at evening prayers.

Upon complaint, a meeting was called 6 Dec. And, upon pleading, as
others had done before, that he was intoxicated, Sullivan 2d was admitted
to a public confession; which was exhibited at a meeting 8 Dec. At which
meeting the government had a talk with Sullivan 1.

Dec. 9. The President read the confession of Sullivan 2; but there was
such a scraping, especially in the junior class, that he could not be heard. He
commanded silence, but to no purpose. Disorders coming out of chapel.
Also in the hall at breakfast the same morning. Bisket, tea cups, saucers, & a
knife thrown at the tutors. At evening prayers the lights were all extin-
guished by powder & lead, except 2 or 3. Upon this a general laugh among
the juniors.—From this day to 13 Dec. disorders continued in hall &
Chapel, such as scraping, whispering &c. Lights were blown out one morn-

ing, & two evenings, the last time by Howard, as it is said, many scholars being present.—The disorders by this time had spread, in a degree, among the Sophomores and Freshmen.

Dec. 12. After prayers Sullivan 1 called a class meeting, in order to prevent disorders in the chapel among the juniors. After which there was less disorder in the chapel for several days. Many of the chapel windows also were broken.

N.B. On the evening of the 5 Dec. all the Sophomores, except Ward, were collected at Bayley's chamber in a disorderly manner, from which they were ordered to their chambers by Mr. James. Upon this they went to the chamber of King & Whitney; from which they sallied out, & ran thro' the entries of Massachusetts in a noisy and tumultuous manner. Three were caught by Mr. Abbot, viz. Ellery, Derby, & Hodge. Between 8 & 9 o'clock, same evening, Mr. Abbot had 6 squares of his study window broken. All the tutors' windows were also broken the same week Sullivan's confession was read.

Dec. 15. More disorders at my public lecture, than I ever knew before. The bible, cloth, candles, & branches, I found laid in confusion upon the seat of the desk. During lecture several pebbles were snapped, certain gutteral sounds were made on each side [of] the chapel, beside some whistling.

Dec. 16. Still greater disorders at Dr. Wigglesworth's public lecture. As he was passing up the alley, two volleys of stones, one from each side, were thrown at him, or just before him. Upon this the Doctor turned about & addressed the scholars. After which he proceeded; but, before he reached the pew, another volley of stones was discharged from the north side of the alley. During the first prayer there were disorders; after which the Doctor again addressed them more largely, & particularly cautioned them against disorders; but, notwithstanding this, they continued thro' the lecture; such as sending stones, making gutteral noises, whistling &c.—While the Doctr. & two tutors were walking down the alley, a stone was sent into the chapel thro' a window, the glass of which was driven against one of the gentlemen.

Dec. 20. The government were called together.

Dec. 22. Government met again, & voted that Bowman & Howard be removed from College for 6 months, & that Ellery be degraded to the bottom of his class.

Dec. 24. Dr. Howard took away his son.

Dec. 25. Ellery's sentence of degradation was read in the chapel. Upon which, instead of taking his place as ordered, Ellery withdrew several steps, & then turned about, & told the President that "he should leave a society, the government of which is actuated by *malice*, & whose decisions are founded in prejudice," or to this effect.—That evening, a few minutes before 11, a stone, weighing 8 lbs. 11 oz., was throw into Dr. Wigglesworth's sleeping room.—Previously to this, the same evening, there had been a very great noise, principally, as was said, at Rice's chamber, & partly at Thacher's.

Dec. 26. In the evening there was a firing of pistols between 8 & 11. This evening there was a collection at Rice's chambers till just after 12, without noise. After separating, candles were lighted at the chambers of Hodge, Harris & Phelps, King & Whitney.

Dec. 27. Bowman went off.—That night, between 1 & 2, two persons, in a violent & noisy manner ran up the stairs of the east entry in Massachusetts, & went into Rice's or Thacher's chamber.

Dec. 30. In the evening, about 10 o'clock, Messrs. Smith & Abbot caught a riotous company, which had been driving thro' town in a noisy & violent manner, some of which appeared to be very drunk.

Dec. 31. The government voted to accept Ellery's confession, which the next morning he read in the chapel.

Jan. 1 [1789]. Mr. Smith & Abbot took up the conduct of the rioters. In the evening Mr. Smith prayed. Several coppers were thrown at him, while in prayers, as was supposed by juniors on the north side of the chapel.— After which Mr. Smith sent down the punishments of the rioters, viz, Trapier 5/ for noise in town, 1/6 for not going to chamber when ordered, & 1/6 for intoxication; Welles 5/ for noise, 3/ for not going to chamber, when repeatedly ordered, & 1/6 for intoxication; Callender 5/ for noise, Hubbard Do., Thacher Do., Tilton Do., Withers Do. & Wragg Do.

Jan. 2. Mumbling noise & whispering at morning prayers, chiefly among the juniors on the north. Bible taken away at evening prayers.

Jan. 3. Bible taken away at morning prayers & concealed at evening prayers. In the evening, which was Saturday eveng., there was a large collection at Withers's room, which sallied out in a noisy manner, one of which, viz, Whitwell, was caught by Mr. Crosby in a cellar.

Jan. 4. Bible concealed at eveng. prayers, & several squares of glass found broken in the window of the desk.

Jan. 5. Government met A.M., & Dr. Waterhouse requested in writing that Rice, Harris, Phelps, Whitney, & Thacher, might be examined relative to the charge, brought against Ellery, of his throwing stones in the College yard. Meeting continued thro' the day.

Jan 6. Met by adjournment at 9 o'clock, & at 4 P.M. determined that nothing asserted by the above named persons invalidated the direct evidence against Ellery.

Jan. 7. Vacation commenced.

Harvard University Archives.

Augustus Peirce

OVERTURE TO THE RIOT
(1818)

*The great epic of Harvard history, "The Rebelliad," commemorating a food
riot in the College commons, was written "principally in the recitation
room" and delivered in July 1819 before the College Engine Club. The author, Augustus Peirce, of the Class of 1820 (founders of the famous "Med.
Fac."), was then only seventeen, but his comic and poetic senses were highly
developed. Peirce's method of composition was a daily stint undertaken immediately after he had completed his own recitation. After many months of
such installment invention, the work was completed. It was in such demand
that his classmates made their own personal handwritten copies, which were
widely circulated. (Such a manuscript, copied off by a Bowdoin student, was
recently offered for sale by a dealer in rare books.) The original manuscript,
however, was destroyed by Peirce's father, and the author had to reconstruct
a large portion of his classic from memory. The first printed edition did not
appear until 1842. Peirce studied medicine under Dr. George C. Shattuck of
Boston, practiced in Tyngsboro, Massachusetts, and died in 1849.*

PROLOGUE, OH! IN HARVARD!

Parody on Hohenlinden

I.

At Harvard, when the sun was low,
All bustling was the kitchen's glow,
And hot as tophet was the flow
    Of coffee, boiling rapidly.

II.

But Harvard saw another sight
When the bell rang at fall of night,
Commanding every appetite
    To snatch a supper hastily.

Everyone who ever attended Harvard should know that a goody (said to be a con-
traction of the word "Good-wife") was one of the college bedmakers, and the author
of "The Rebelliad" specially identifies his Goody Muse as "Miss Morse, the daughter
of her mother." Others of Peirce's allusions deserve a word of explanation. Lord Bibo
was President Kirkland; Dr. Pop was John Snelling Popkin, Professor of Greek; Sikes
was the Reverend Henry Ware, Professor of Divinity; Nathan was sophomore Robert W. Barnwell, later United States Senator from South Carolina; Abijah was "a
freshman." Carolus McIntire was a local shoemaker who was given a spurious honorary degree by the Med. Fac. in 1823.

III.

By mess and table fast arrayed,
Each Freshman drew his eating blade,
And furious every jaw-bone played,
    Devouring Cooley's cookery.

IV.

Then shook the Halls with racket riven,
Then rushed each Soph to battle driven,
And louder than the bolts of heaven,
    Round smashed the brittle crockery.

V.

And louder yet that noise shall grow;
And fiercer yet that strife shall glow;
And hotter yet shall be the flow
    Of coffee, boiling rapidly.

VI.

'T is night,—but scarce had Dr. Pop
Put half his supper in his crop,
When Freshman fierce and furious Soph
    Shout in their savory canopy.

VII.

The combat deepens. On, ye brave,
And let the cooks the pieces save!
Wave, Goodies, all your besoms wave!
    Inspire their souls with chivalry.

VIII.

Ah! few shall part where many meet
With anything but blows to eat,
And every dish beneath their feet
    Shall be a supper's sepulchre.

THE REBELLIAD

Canto I

THE ARGUMENT

Invocation.—Battle between the Sophomores and Freshmen in Commons Hall.—Doctor Pop endeavors to obtain a suspension of arms; goes to Lord Bibo's study; makes a speech.—Sikes also pours forth a torrent of eloquence.

TIME:—*Two hours on Sunday evening.*

OLD Goody Muse! on thee I call,
Pro more, (as do poets all,)
To string thy fiddle, wax thy bow,
And scrape a ditty, jig, or so.

Now don't wax wrathy, but excuse
My calling you old Goody Muse;
Because "Old Goody" is a name
Applied to ev'ry College dame.
        Aloft in pendent dignity,
            Astride her magic broom,
        And wrapt in dazzling majesty,
            See! see! the Goody come!
Riding sublime on billowy air,
She tun'd her instrument with care;
And that her voice and fiddle might
In mingling harmony unite,
She blow'd her nose and cried, ahem!
To throw off maccaboy and phlegm:
Then, with slow melancholy, sung
How for a witch her ma' was hung;
And with a doleful aspect blunder'd
Through half a stanza of "old hundred."
        She ceas'd, her misty mantle shook,
And from her magic pocket took
A box—not such as that in story,
A gift from Jove to Miss Pandora;
From which went forth as many ills,
As from a box of Conway's pills;
No: it was fill'd with vulgar stuff,
Call'd maccaboy, or headache snuff.
        Her pocket held another thing,
Which ancient dames do sometimes squeeze,
        A bottle of New England sling,
Or any other kind you please;
        (For't does not signify a pin,
            Whether 't was brandy, rum, or gin;)
Which, ever and anon, she'd kiss
        With smacking fondness and delight;
Until her fancy, full of bliss,
        Was fir'd to sing of deeds of might.
Her viol she attun'd anew;
To lofty themes her fingers flew.
Hark! the melodious sounds have ris'n!
        The spirits of the tuneful nine
            Delay their dewy car,
In which they cleave the arch of Heav'n,
        On their celestial harps recline,
            And listen from afar;
While thus she sung: One Sunday night
The Sophs and Freshmen had a fight.
'T was when the beam that linger'd last
Its farewell ray on Harvard cast,
Or Sol, with night-cap on his head,
Was just a creeping into bed,
When Cookum told a boy to tell
Another boy to toll the bell,
To call the students to their tea.

As when a brood of pigs, who see
Their feeder with a pail of swill,
With which their maws they're wont to fill,
Do squeal and grunt, and grunt and squeal,
In expectation of a meal;
So they to commons did repair
And scramble, each one for his share:
When Nathan threw a piece of bread,
And hit Abijah on the head.
The wrathful Freshman, in a trice,
Sent back another bigger slice;
Which, being butter'd pretty well,
Made greasy work where'er it fell.
And thus arose a fearful battle;
The coffee-cups and saucers rattle;
The bread-bowls fly at woful rate,
And break many a learned pate.
As when a troop of town-school boys
Fall out and make a plaguy noise,
On either side the boldest close,
And kick and cuff with furious blows;
While others, fearful of their bones,
Slink out of sight and fight with stones,
Although they now and then appear,
And rave heroic, curse and swear;
But, when the danger comes, quick flee
Behind a neighb'ring wall or tree;
Just so these learned sons of College
Did bruise their instruments of knowledge.
Regardless of their shins and pates,
The bravest seiz'd the butter plates,
And rushing headlong to the van,
Sustain'd the conflict—man to man.
There, in the thickest of the fight,
Did Nathan show such deeds of might,
As would have rais'd, in times of yore,
A statue o'er a tavern door;
And 'Bijah, fearless of his foes,
Help'd many to a bloody nose.
From right to left these heroes fly
Until they catch each other's eye.
As when two ram-cats, fierce for fight,
Do bristle up with vengeful spite,
And, as the combat dread they dare,
With caterwaulings rend the air;
So they, when each the other saw,
Their grinders grittingly did gnaw;
And grumly growl'd, with dire intent,
As at it terribly they went.
First each uprais'd his brawny fist,*
And aim'd a deadly blow, but—miss'd.

* Est mihi fist-ula.

Then 'Bijah seiz'd a coffee-pot,
Surcharg'd with liquid boiling hot,
And hurl'd it with such matchless force,
As smash'd two pitchers in its course;
But Nathan dodg'd the mighty blow,*
And, turning quickly on his foe,
Repaid the visit with his foot,
Cas'd in a McIntirian† boot.
Full drive it hit Abijah's bum
And keel'd him over; but his chum
Had wielded, in his just defence,
A bowl of vast circumference.
Ye Powers of Mud! no mortal tongue
Can tell how all the College rung,
How stars did shoot from eye to eye,
How suns and moons flew flashing by,
When Nathan's thick-bon'd jobbernowl
Did come in contact with the bowl!
The foemen, likewise, in the rear,
On both sides valiantly appear;
And fiercely brandishing on high
Their missiles, straightway let them fly;
Though some there were, oh! shame to say!
Who fled like cowards from the fray,
And slily sneak'd behind the door,
Where they might safely bawl and roar;
From whence they now and then did pop,
To throw a cup or tea-pot top . . .
Go on, dear Goody! and recite
The direful mishaps of the fight.
Alas! how many on that eve,
O'er suppers lost, were doom'd to grieve!
What daylights pummell'd black and blue!
What noddles smear'd with goreless hue!
How dishes did *not* float in blood,
As Noah's Ark did in the flood!
What heroes fell to bite the bricks,‡
O'erthrown by bowls! perchance by kicks!

* —: ille ictum venientem a vertice velox
Praevidit, celerique elapsus corpore cessit.—*Aeneid,* v. 444.
† Carolus McIntire, qui ocreas, quae Galoches necessitatem *supersedent*, facit, etc.
Vid. Cat. Fac. Med.
‡ The floor of Commons Hall is made of bricks.

Cleveland Amory

DR. PARKMAN TAKES A WALK
(1849)

When Dr. George Parkman disappeared from sight one day in late November 1849, it caused a convulsion in Cambridge and Boston, the spasms of which have even now hardly subsided. Edmund Pearson, A.B. 1902, has called the Parkman case "America's Classic Murder," and no one has reported the crime in so spirited and yet sympathetic a fashion as Cleveland Amory, A.B. 1939. Writer and champion of animals, Amory is the author of Home Town, *a novel, as well as* Who Killed Society?, The Last Resorts, *and* The Proper Bostonians, *from which the present chapter is an excerpt.*

TO THE STUDENT of American Society the year 1849 will always remain a red-letter one. In that year two events occurred at opposite ends of the country, both of which, in their own way, made social history. At one end, in Sutter's Creek, California, gold was discovered. At the other, in Boston, Massachusetts, Dr. George Parkman walked off the face of the earth.

The discovery of gold ushered in a new social era. It marked the first great rise of the western *nouveau riche*, the beginning of that wonderful time when a gentleman arriving in San Francisco and offering a boy fifty cents to carry his suitcase could receive the reply, "Here's a dollar, man— carry it yourself," and when a poor Irish prospector suddenly striking it rich in a vein near Central City, Colorado, could fling down his pick and exclaim, "Thank God, now my wife can be a lady!"

Dr. Parkman's little walk did no such thing as this. It must be remembered, however, that it occurred some three thousand miles away. Boston is not Sutter's Creek or Central City or even San Francisco. There has never been a "new" social era in the Western sense in Boston's rock-ribbed Society, and it remains very doubtful if there ever will be one. The best that could be expected of any one event in Boston would be to shake up the old. Dr. Parkman's walk did this; it shook Boston Society to the very bottom of its First Family foundations. Viewed almost a hundred years later it thus seems, in its restricted way, almost as wonderful as the Gold Rush and not undeserving of the accidental fact that it happened, in the great march of social history, in exactly the same year.

The date was Friday, November 23rd. It was warm for a Boston November, and Dr. Parkman needed no overcoat as he left his Beacon Hill home at 8 Walnut Street. He wore in the fashion of the day a black morning coat, purple silk vest, dark trousers, a dark-figured black tie, and a black silk top hat. He had breakfasted as usual, and he left his home to head downtown toward the Merchants Bank on State Street. Dr. Parkman was quite a figure as he moved along. His high hat and angular physique made him seem far taller than his actual five feet nine and a half inches. He was sixty years old and his head was almost bald, but his hat hid this fact also. To all outward appearances he was remarkably well-preserved, his most striking feature being a conspicuously protruding chin. Boston Parkmans have been noted for their chins the way Boston Adamses are noted for their foreheads or Boston Saltonstalls are noted for their noses, and the chin of old Dr. Parkman was especially formidable. His lower jaw jutted out so far it had made the fitting of a set of false teeth for him a very difficult job. The dentist who had had that job had never forgotten it. He was proud of the china-white teeth he had installed. He had even kept the mold to prove to people that he, little Dr. Nathan Keep, had made the teeth of the great Dr. George Parkman.

Although he had studied to be a physician and received his degree Dr. Parkman had rarely practiced medicine in his life. He was a merchant at heart, one of Boston's wealthiest men, and he spent his time in the Boston manner keeping sharp account of his money—and a sharp eye on his debtors. He had many of the traits of character peculiar to the Proper Bostonian breed. He was shrewd and hard, but he was Boston-honest, Boston-direct and Boston-dependable. Like so many other First Family men before his time and after Dr. Parkman was not popular but he was highly respected. It was hard to like a man like Dr. Parkman because his manners were curt and he had a way of glaring at people that made them uncomfortable. Without liking him, however, it was possible to look up to him. People knew him as a great philanthropist and it was said he had given away a hundred thousand dollars in his time. The phrase "wholesale charity and retail penury" as descriptive of the Proper Bostonian breed had not yet come into the Boston lingo, though the day was coming when Dr. Parkman might be regarded as the very personification of it. Certainly he had given away large sums of money with wholesale generosity—even anonymously—yet with small sums, with money on a retail basis, he was penny-punctilious. "The same rule," a biographer records, "governed Dr. Parkman in settling an account involving the balance of a cent as in transactions of thousands of dollars."

Children in the Boston streets pointed out Dr. Parkman to other children. "There goes Dr. Parkman," they would say. People always seemed to point him out after he had passed them. There was no use speaking to Dr. Parkman before he went by. If you weren't his friend, Dr. George Shattuck, or his brother-in-law, Robert Gould Shaw, Esq. or a Cabot or a Lowell, or perhaps a man who owed him money—and then, as someone said, God help you—the doctor would ignore you. Dr. Parkman had no need to court favor from anybody. The Parkmans cut a sizeable chunk of Boston's social ice in 1849, and they still do today. Like other merchant-blooded First Families they were of course economically self-sufficient. They hadn't yet made much of an intellectual mark on their city, but a nephew of the doctor, Francis Parkman, had just published his first book and was on his way to becoming what Van Wyck Brooks has called "the climax and crown" of the Boston historical school. The Parkmans were in the Boston fashion well-connected by marriages. Dr. Parkman's sister's marriage with Robert Gould Shaw, Boston's wealthiest merchant, was a typical First Family alliance. As for Dr. Parkman's own wealth, some idea of its extent may be gathered from the fact that his son, who never worked a day in his life, was able to leave a will which bequeathed, among other things, the sum of five million dollars for the care and improvement of the Boston Common.

On the morning of that Friday, November 23rd, Dr. Parkman was hurrying. He walked with the characteristic gait of the Proper Bostonian merchant—a gait still practiced by such notable present-day First Family footmen as Charles Francis Adams and Godfrey Lowell Cabot—measuring off distances with long, ground-consuming strides. Dr. Parkman always hurried. Once when riding a horse up Beacon Hill and unable to speed the animal to his satisfaction he had left the horse in the middle of the street and hurried ahead on foot. On that occasion he had been after money, a matter of debt collection.

This morning, too, Dr. Parkman was after money. He left the Merchants Bank and after making several other calls dropped into a grocery store at the corner of Blossom and Vine Streets. This stop, the only non-financial mission of his morning, was to buy a head of lettuce for his invalid sister. He left it in the store and said he would return for it on his way home. The time was half past one and Dr. Parkman presumably intended to be home at 2:30, then the fashionable hour for one's midday meal. Ten minutes later, at 1:40, Elias Fuller, a merchant standing outside his counting room at Fuller's Iron Foundry at the corner of Vine and North Grove Streets, observed Dr. Parkman passing him headed north on North Grove Street. Fuller was later to remember that the doctor seemed particularly annoyed about something and recalled that his cane beat a brisk tattoo on the pavement as he hurried along. What the merchant observed at 1:40 that day is of more than passing importance, for Elias Fuller was the last man who ever saw the doctor alive on the streets of Boston. Somewhere, last seen going north on North Grove Street, Dr. George Parkman walked off the face of the earth.

At 8 Walnut Street Mrs. Parkman, her daughter Harriet and Dr. Parkman's invalid sister sat down to their two-thirty dinner long after three o'clock. Their dinner was ruined and there was no lettuce, but Mrs. Parkman and the others did not mind. They were all worried about the master of the house. Dr. Parkman was not the sort of a man who was ever late for anything. Right after dinner they got in touch with Dr. Parkman's agent, Charles Kingsley. Kingsley was the man who looked after the doctor's business affairs, usually some time after the doctor had thoroughly looked after them himself. Almost at once Kingsley began to search for his employer. First Family men of the prominence of Dr. Parkman did not disappear in Boston—and they do not today—even for an afternoon. By night-fall Kingsley was ready to inform Robert Gould Shaw. Shaw, acting with the customary dispatch of the Proper Bostonian merchant, went at once to Boston's City Marshal, Mr. Tukey. Marshal Tukey did of course what Shaw told him to do, which was to instigate an all-night search.

The next morning the merchant Shaw placed advertisements in all the papers and had 28,000 handbills distributed. The advertisements and the handbills announced a reward of $3,000 for his brother-in-law alive and $1,000 for his brother-in-law dead. The prices, considering the times, were sky-high but Shaw knew what he was doing in Yankee Boston. Before long virtually every able-bodied man, woman and child in the city was looking for Dr. Parkman. They beat the bushes and they combed the streets. Slum areas were ransacked. All suspicious characters, all persons with known criminal records, were rounded up and held for questioning. Strangers in Boston were given a summary one-two treatment. An Irishman, it is recorded, attempting to change a twenty-dollar bill, was brought in to the police headquarters apparently solely on the assumption that no son of Erin, in the Boston of 1849, had any business with a bill of this size in his possession.

Every one of Dr. Parkman's actions on the previous day, up to 1:40, were checked. At that time, on North Grove Street, the trail always ended. Police had to sift all manner of wild reports. One had the doctor "beguiled to East Cambridge and done in." Another had him riding in a hansom cab, his head covered with blood, being driven at "breakneck speed" over a Charles River bridge. Of the papers only the Boston *Transcript* seems to have kept its head. Its reporter managed to learn from a servant in the Parkman home that the doctor had received a caller at 9:30 Friday reminding him of a 1:30 appointment later in the day. The servant could not remember what the man looked like, but the *Transcript* printed the story in its Saturday night edition along with the reward advertisements. Most people took the caller to be some sort of front man who had appeared to lead Dr. Parkman to a dastardly death. By Monday foul play was so thoroughly suspected that the shrewd merchant Shaw saw no reason to mention a sum as high as $1,000 for the body. Three thousand dollars was still the price for Dr. Parkman alive but only "a suitable reward" was mentioned in Shaw's Monday handbills for Dr. Parkman dead. Monday's handbills also noted the possibility of amnesia but the theory of a First Family man's mind wandering to this extent was regarded as highly doubtful. Dr. Parkman, it was stated, was "perfectly well" when he left his house.

All that the Parkman case now needed to make it a complete panorama of Boston's First Family Society was the active entry of Harvard College into the picture. This occurred on Sunday morning in the person of a caller to the home of Rev. Francis Parkman, the missing doctor's brother, where the entire Family Parkman in all its ramifications had gathered. The caller was a man named John White Webster, Harvard graduate and professor of chemistry at the Harvard Medical School. He was a short squat man, fifty-six years old, who had a mass of unruly black hair and always wore thick spectacles. He had had a most distinguished career. He had studied at Guy's Hospital, London, back in 1815, where among his fellow students had been the poet John Keats. He was a member of the London Geological Society, the American Academy of Arts and Sciences, and during his twenty-five years as a Harvard professor had published numerous nationally noted scientific works. His wife, a Hickling and aunt of the soon-to-be-recognized historian William Hickling Prescott, was "well-connected" with several of Boston's First Families.

The Rev. Parkman was glad to see Professor Webster and ushered him toward the parlor expecting that his desire would be to offer sympathy to the assorted Parkmans there assembled. But Webster, it seemed, did not want to go into the parlor. Instead he spoke abruptly to the minister. "I have come to tell you," he said, "that I saw your brother at half past one o'clock on Friday." The minister was glad to have this report. Since Webster also told him he had been the caller at the Parkman home earlier that day it cleared up the mystery of the strange appointment as recorded in the *Transcript*. Webster explained he should have come sooner but had been so busy he had not seen the notices of Dr. Parkman's disappearance until the previous night. The minister was also satisfied with this. Webster further declared that, at the appointment shortly after 1:30 which took place in his laboratory at the Medical School, he had paid Dr. Parkman the sum of $483.64 which he had owed him. This, of course, explained why the doctor had last been seen by the merchant Fuller in such a cane-tattooing hurry. It had indeed been a matter of a debt collection.

When Professor Webster had left, Robert Gould Shaw was advised of his visit. Shaw was intimate enough in his brother-in-law's affairs to know that Webster had been owing Dr. Parkman money for some time. He did not, however, know the full extent of Webster's misery. Few men have ever suffered from the retail penury side of the Proper Bostonian character as acutely as John White Webster.

The professor received a salary from Harvard of $1,200 a year. This, augmented by income from extra lectures he was able to give, might have sufficed for the average Harvard professor in those days. But Webster was not the average. His wife, for all her connections with Boston's First Families, was still a socially aspirant woman, particularly for her two daughters of debutante age. Mrs. Webster and the Misses Webster entertained lavishly at their charming home in Cambridge. Professor Webster went into debt. He borrowed money here and he borrowed money there. But mostly he borrowed from Dr. George Parkman.

Who better to borrow from? Dr. Parkman, man of wholesale charity, Proper Bostonian merchant philanthropist. He had given Harvard College the very ground on which at that time stood its Medical School. He had endowed the Parkman Chair of Anatomy, then being occupied by the great Dr. Oliver Wendell Holmes. He had himself been responsible for Webster's appointment as chemistry professor. There were no two ways about it. When Webster needed money the doctor was his obvious choice. As early as 1842 he had borrowed $400. He had then borrowed more. In 1847 he had borrowed from a group headed by Dr. Parkman the sum of $2000. For the latter he had been forced to give a mortgage on all his personal property. He knew he had little chance to pay the debt but he was banking on the generosity of the "good Dr. Parkman." A year later, in 1848, he even went to Dr. Parkman's brother-in-law, the merchant Shaw, and prevailed upon him to buy a mineral collection for $1,200. This was most unfortunate. The mineral collection, like the rest of Webster's property, in hock to Dr. Parkman and his group, was not Webster's to sell. By so doing he had made the doctor guilty of that cardinal sin of Yankeeism—the sin of being shown up as an easy mark. No longer was there for Webster any "good Dr. Parkman." "From that moment onward," says author Stewart Holbrook, "poor Professor Webster knew what it was like to have a Yankee bloodhound on his trail. His creditor was a punctilious man who paid his own obligations when due and he expected the same of everybody else, even a Harvard professor."[*]

Dr. Parkman dogged Professor Webster in the streets, outside his home, even to the classrooms. He would come in and take a front-row seat at Webster's lectures. He would not say anything; he would just sit and glare in that remarkable way of his. He wrote the professor notes, not just plain insulting notes but the awful, superior, skin-biting notes of the Yankee gentleman. He spoke sternly of legal processes. Meeting Webster he would never shout at him but instead address him in clipped Proper Bostonian accents. It was always the same question. When would the professor be "ready" for him?

Dr. Parkman even bearded Professor Webster in his den, in the inner recesses of the latter's laboratory at the Medical School. He had been there, in the professor's private back room—according to the janitor of the building—on Monday evening, November 19th, just four days before he had disappeared.

The janitor was a strange man, the grim New England village type, a small person with dark brooding eyes. His name was Ephraim Littlefield.

---

[*] "Murder at Harvard," by Stewart Holbrook, *The American Scholar*, 1945.

He watched with growing interest the goings-on around him. Following Webster's call on Rev. Francis Parkman, which established the farthest link yet on the trail of Dr. Parkman's walk, it had of course been necessary to search the Medical School. Littlefield wanted this done thoroughly, as thoroughly for example as they were dragging the Charles River outside. He personally led the investigators to Webter's laboratory. Everything was searched, all but the private back room and adjoining privy. One of the party of investigators, which also included Dr. Parkman's agent Kingsley, was a police officer named Derastus Clapp. Littlefield prevailed upon this officer to go into the back room, but just as Clapp opened the door Professor Webster solicitously called out for him to be careful. There were dangerous articles in there, he said. "Very well, then," said Officer Clapp, "I will not go in there and get blowed up." He backed out again.

The whole search was carried on to the satisfaction of even Robert Gould Shaw who, after all, knew at firsthand the story of Webster's duplicity via the mineral collection. And who was the little janitor Ephraim Littlefield to dispute the word of the great merchant Robert Shaw? As each day went by the theory of murder was becoming more and more generally accepted, but in a Boston Society eternally geared to the mesh of a Harvard A.B. degree the idea of pinning a homicide on a Harvard man—and a professor at that—was heresy itself. One might as well pry for the body of Dr. Parkman among the prayer cushions of the First Family pews in Trinity Church.

But Littlefield was not, in the socially sacrosanct meaning of the words, a "Harvard man." He was a Harvard janitor. Furthermore he was stubborn. He wanted the Medical School searched again. When it was, he was once more prodding the investigators to greater efforts. He told them they should visit the cellar of the building, down in the section where the Charles River water flowed in and carried off waste matter from the dissecting rooms and privies above. The agent Kingsley took one gentlemanly sniff from the head of the stairs and refused to accompany the janitor and the other investigators any farther. The others, however, went on. As they passed the wall under Webster's back room the janitor volunteered the information that it was now the only place in the building that hadn't been searched. Why not, the men wanted to know. The janitor explained that to get there it would be necessary to dig through the wall. The men had little stomach left for this sort of operation and soon rejoined Kingsley upstairs.

Littlefield, however, had plenty of stomach. He determined to dig into the wall himself. Whether he was by this time, Monday, already suspicious of Professor Webster has never been made clear. He had, it is true, heard the Webster-Parkman meeting of Monday night the week before. He had distinctly overheard the doctor say to the professor in that ever-insinuating way, "Something, Sir, must be accomplished." Just yesterday, Sunday, he had seen Professor Webster enter the Medical School around noontime, apparently shortly after he had made his call on Rev. Francis Parkman. Webster had spoken to him and had acted "very queerly." Come to think of it, Littlefield brooded, Sunday was a queer day for the professor to be hanging around the School anyway. "Ephraim," writes Richard Dempewolff, one of the Parkman case's most avid devotees, "was one of those shrewd New England conclusion-jumpers who, unfortunately for the people they victimize, are usually right. By putting two and two together, Mr. Littlefield achieved a nice round dozen."*

The janitor's wife was a practical woman. She thought little of her husband's determination to search the filthy old place under the private rooms of the Harvard professor she had always regarded as a fine gentleman. Her husband would lose his job, that would be what would happen. Just you wait and see, Mr. Littlefield.

Mr. Littlefield deferred to Mrs. Littlefield and did wait—until Tuesday, five days after Dr. Parkman's disppearance. On Tuesday something extraordinary happened. At four o'clock in the afternoon he heard Professor Webster's bell jangle, a signal that the janitor was wanted. He went to Webster's laboratory. The professor asked him if he had bought his Thanksgiving turkey yet. Littlefield did not know what to say. He replied he had thought some about going out Thanksgiving.

"Here," said Webster, "go and get yourself one." With that he handed the janitor an order for a turkey at a near-by grocery store.

John White Webster had here made a fatal error. The call he had paid on Rev. Francis Parkman had been bad enough. It had aroused the searching of the Medical School and had brought Littlefield actively into the case. But as Webster later admitted he had been afraid that sooner or later someone would have found out about his 1:30 Friday rendezvous with Dr. Parkman and felt that his best chance lay in making a clean breast of it. For this action in regard to the janitor's Thanksgiving turkey, however, there could be no such defense. If he hoped to win the janitor over to "his side," then he was a poor judge of human nature indeed. Harvard Janitor Ephraim Littlefield had worked for Harvard Professor John Webster for seven years—curiously the same length of time Professor John Webster had been borrowing from Dr. Parkman—without ever receiving a present of any kind. And now, a Thanksgiving turkey. Even the deferentially dormant suspicions of Mrs. Littlefield were thoroughly aroused.

Janitor Littlefield had no chance to begin his labors Wednesday. Professor Webster was in his laboratory most of the day. On Thanksgiving, however, while Mrs. Littlefield kept her eyes peeled for the professor or any other intruder, the janitor began the task of crow-barring his way through

---

* *Famous Old New England Murders,* by Richard Dempewolff (Brattleboro, Vt.: Stephen Daye Press, 1942).

the solid brick wall below the back room. It was slow work and even though the Littlefields took time off to enjoy their dinner—the janitor had characteristically not passed up the opportunity to procure a nine-pound bird—it was soon obvious he could not get through the wall in one day. That evening the Littlefields took time off again. They went to a dance given by the Sons of Temperance Division of the Boston Odd Fellows. They stayed until four o'clock in the morning. "There were twenty dances," Littlefield afterwards recalled, "and I danced eighteen out of the twenty."

Late Friday afternoon, after Professor Webster had left for the day, Littlefield was at his digging again. This time he had taken the precaution of advising two of the School's First Family doctors, Doctors Bigelow and Jackson, of what he was doing. They were surprised but told him since he had started he might as well continue. But they were against his idea of informing the dean of the School, Dr. Holmes, of the matter. It would, they felt, disturb the dean unnecessarily.

Even a half-hearted First Family blessing has always counted for something in Boston, and Janitor Littlefield now went to work with renewed vigor. Again his wife stood watch. At five-thirty he broke through the fifth of the five courses of brick in the wall. "I held my light forward," he afterwards declared, "and the first thing which I saw was the pelvis of a man, and two parts of a leg . . . It was no place for these things."

It was not indeed. Within fifteen minutes Doctors Bigelow and Jackson were on the scene. Later Dr. Holmes himself would view the remains. Meanwhile of course there was the matter of a little trip out to the Webster home in Cambridge.

To that same police officer who had been so loath to get himself "blowed up" in Webster's back room fell the honor of making the business trip to Cambridge and arresting the Harvard professor. Once bitten, Derastus Clapp was twice shy. There would be no more monkeyshines, Harvard or no Harvard. He had his cab halt some distance from the Webster Home and approached on foot. Opening the outer gate he started up the walk just as Webster himself appeared on the steps of his house, apparently showing a visitor out. The professor attempted to duck back inside. Officer Clapp hailed him. "We are about to search the Medical School again," he called, moving forward rapidly as he spoke, "and we wish you to be present." Webster feigned the traditional Harvard indifference. It was a waste of time; the School had already been searched twice. Clapp laid a stern hand on his shoulder. Webster, escorted outward and suddenly noting two other men in the waiting cab, wanted to go back for his keys. Officer Clapp was not unaware of the drama of the moment. "Professor Webster," he said, "we have keys enough to unlock the whole of Harvard College."

Boston was in an uproar. Dr. Parkman had not walked off the face of the earth. He had been pushed off—and by the authoritative hands of a Har-

vard professor! Even the *Transcript,* calm when there was still a hope the
Parkman case was merely a matter of disappearance, could restrain itself no
longer. It threw its genteel caution to the winds. There were two exclamation marks after its headline, and its editor called on Shakespeare himself to
sum up the situation:

> Since last evening, our whole population has been in a state of greatest pos-
> sible excitement in consequence of the astounding rumor that the body of
> Dr. Parkman has been discovered, and that Dr. John W. Webster, Professor
> of Chemistry in the Medical School of Harvard College, and a gentleman
> connected by marriage with some of our most distinguished families, has
> been arrested and imprisoned, on suspicion of being the murderer. Incredu-
> lity, then amazement, and then blank, unspeakable horror have been the
> emotions, which have agitated the public mind as the rumor has gone on,
> gathering countenance and confirmation. Never in the annals of crime in
> Massachusetts has such a sensation been produced.
>
> In the streets, in the market-place, at every turn, men greet each other
> with pale, eager looks and the inquiry, "Can it be true?" And then as the
> terrible reply, "the circumstances begin to gather weight against him," is
> wrung forth, the agitated listener can only vent his sickening sense of hor-
> ror, in some expression as that of Hamlet,—-
> "O, horrible! O, horrible! most horrible!"

There is irony in the fact that proud, staid Boston chose the time it did
to provide American Society with the nineteenth century's outstanding social circus. Boston was at the height of its cultural attainments in 1849. In
that year a scholarly but hardly earth-shaking book by a rather minor Boston author, *The History of Spanish Literature* by George Ticknor, was the
world literary event of the year and the only book recommended by Lord
Macaulay to Queen Victoria. Yet just three months later, on March 19,
1850, Boston put on a show which for pure social artistry Barnum himself
would have had difficulty matching. The Boston courtroom had everything.
It had one of Boston's greatest jurists, Judge Lemuel Shaw, on its bench; it
had the only Harvard professor ever to be tried for murder, John White
Webster, as its defendant; it had promised witnesses of national renown,
from Dr. Oliver Wendell Holmes on down; and in the offing, so to speak, it
had the shades of Dr. George Parkman, perhaps the most socially distinguished victim in the annals of American crime.

Nobody wanted to miss such a sight. Trains and stages from all parts of
the East brought people to Boston. They wanted tickets. Everybody in Boston wanted tickets, too. Consequences of revolutionary proportions were
feared if they could not be accommodated. Yet what to do? There was only
a small gallery to spare, it having been decreed in typical Boston fashion
that the main part of the courtroom would be reserved on an invitation
basis. Finally, Field Marshal Tukey hit on the only possible solution, which
was to effect a complete change of audience in the gallery every ten minutes during the proceedings. It took elaborate street barricades and door-

way defenses to do the job, but in the eleven days of the trial, to that little gallery holding hardly more than a hundred souls, came a recorded total of sixty thousand persons. Considering that the constabulary of Boston assigned to the job numbered just fifteen men, this feat ranks as a monumental milestone in police annals.

From the suspense angle the trial, which has been called a landmark in the history of criminal law, must have been something of a disappointment. By the time it began, despite Webster's protestations of innocence, there was little doubt in the minds of most of the spectators as to the guilt of the professor. A few days after his arrest a skeleton measuring 70½ inches had finally been assembled from the grisly remains found lying about under the professor's back room, and while the sum total of this was an inch taller than Dr. Parkman had been in happier days, there had been no question in the minds of the coroner's jury, of Dr. Holmes, and of a lot of other people, but that Dr. Parkman it was. The case against the professor was one of circumstantial evidence of course. No one had seen Webster and Parkman together at the time of the murder; indeed, during the trial the time of the murder was never satisfactorily established. But the strongest Webster adherents had to admit that it was evidence of a very powerful nature, as Chief Justice Shaw could not fail to point out in his famous charge to the jury, an address which lawyers today still consider one of the greatest expositions of the nature and use of circumstantial evidence ever delivered.

There were a number of pro-Websterites. Harvard professor though he may have been, he was still the underdog, up against the almighty forces of Boston's First Families. Many of the Websterites had undoubtedly had experiences of their own on the score of Proper Bostonian retail penury and were ready to recognize that Dr. Parkman had been so importunate a creditor that he had quite possibly driven the little professor first to distraction and then to the deed. They went to Rufus Choate, Boston's great First Family lawyer, and asked him to undertake the defense. After reading up on the case Choate was apparently willing to do so on the condition that Webster would admit the killing and plead manslaughter. Another First Family lawyer, old Judge Fay, with whom the Webster family regularly played whist, thought a verdict of manslaughter could be reached.

But Webster would not plead guilty. From the beginning he had made his defense an all but impossible task. He talked when he shouldn't have talked and he kept quiet when, at least by the light of hindsight, he should have come clean. On his first trip to the jail he immediately asked the officers about the finding of the body. "Have they found the *whole* body?" he wanted to know. This while certainly a reasonable question in view of the wide area over which the remains were found was hardly the thing for a man in his position to be asking. Then, while vehemently protesting his innocence, he took a strychnine pill out of his waistcoat pocket and attempted to kill himself, an attempt which was foiled only by the fact that, though the dose was a large one, he was in such a nervous condition it failed to take fatal effect. At the trial Webster maintained through his lawyers that the body he was proved to be so vigorously dismembering during his spare moments in the week following November 23rd had been a Medical School cadaver brought to him for that purpose. This was sheer folly, and the prosecution had but to call upon the little dentist, Nathan Keep, to prove it so. Tooth by tooth, during what was called one of the "tumultuous moments" of the trial, Dr. Keep fitted the fragments of the false teeth found in Webster's furnace into the mold he still had in his possession. Charred as they were there could be no doubt they had once been the china-white teeth of Dr. Parkman.

The spectators were treated to other memorable scenes. The great Dr. Holmes testified twice, once for the State on the matter of the identity of the reconstructed skeleton and once for the defense as a character witness for the accused. Professor Webster's character witnesses were a howitzer battery of First Family notables, among them Doctors Bigelow and Jackson, a Codman and a Lovering, the New England historian John Gorham Palfrey and Nathaniel Bowditch, son of the famed mathematician—even Harvard's president Jared Sparks took the stand for his errant employee. All seemed to agree that Webster, if occasionally irritable, was basically a kindhearted man, and President Sparks was thoughtful enough to add one gratuitous comment. "Our professors," he said, "do not often commit murder."

Credit was due Webster for his ability as a cadaver carver. He had done the job on Dr. Parkman, it was established, with no more formidable instrument than a jackknife. A Dr. Woodbridge Strong was especially emphatic on this point. He had dissected a good many bodies in his time, he recalled, including a rush job on a decaying pirate, but never one with just a jackknife. Ephraim Littlefield was of course star witness for the prosecution. The indefatigable little janitor talked for one whole day on the witness stand, a total of eight hours, five hours in the morning before recess for lunch and three hours in the afternoon. Only once did he falter and that on the occasion when, under cross-examination with the defense making a valiant attempt to throw suspicion on him, he was asked if he played "gambling cards" with friends in Webster's back room. Four times the defense had to ask the question and four times Littlefield refused to answer. Finally, his New England conscience stung to the quick, he replied in exasperation, "If you ask me if I played cards there *last winter,* I can truthfully say I did not."

In those days prisoners were not allowed to testify, but on the last day of the trial Professor Webster was asked if he wanted to say anything. Against the advice of his counsel he rose and spoke for fifteen minutes. He spent most of those precious moments denying the accusation that he had written the various anonymous notes which had been turning up from time to time in the City Marshal's office ever since the disappearance of Dr. Parkman. One of these had been signed CIVIS and Webster's last sentence was a pathetic plea for CIVIS to come forward if he was in the courtroom. CIVIS did not, and at eight o'clock on the evening of March 30th the trial was over.

Even the jury seems to have been overcome with pity for the professor. Before filing out of the courtroom the foreman, pointing a trembling finger at Webster, asked: "Is that all? Is that the end? Can nothing further be said in defense of the man?" Three hours later the foreman and his cohorts were back, having spent, it is recorded, the first two hours and fifty-five minutes in prayer "to put off the sorrowful duty." When the verdict was delivered, "an awful and unbroken silence ensued, in which the Court, the jury, the clerk, and the spectators seemed to be absorbed in their own reflections."

Webster's hanging, by the neck and until he was dead, proceeded without untoward incident in the courtyard of Boston's Leverett Street jail just five months to the day after he had been declared guilty. Before that time, however, the professor made a complete confession. He stated that Dr. Parkman had come into his laboratory on that fatal Friday and that, when he had been unable to produce the money he owed, the doctor had shown him a sheaf of papers proving that he had been responsible for getting him his professorship. The doctor then added, "I got you into your office, Sir, and now I will get you out of it." This, said Webster, so infuriated him that he seized a stick of wood off his laboratory bench and struck Dr. Parkman one blow on the head. Death was instantaneous and Webster declared, "I saw nothing but the alternative of a successful removal and concealment of the body, on the one hand, and of infamy and destruction on the other." He then related his week-long attempt to dismember and burn the body. Even the clergyman who regularly visited Webster in his cell during his last days was not able to extract from the professor the admission that the crime had been premeditated. He had done it in that one frenzy of rage. "I am irritable and passionate," the clergyman quoted Webster as saying, "and Dr. Parkman was the most provoking of men."

The late Edmund Pearson, recognized authority on nonfictional homicide here and abroad, has called the Webster-Parkman case America's classic murder and the one which has lived longest in books of reminiscences. Certainly in Boston's First Family Society the aftermath of the case has been hardly less distinguished than its actual occurrence. To this day no Proper Bostonian grandfather autobiography is complete without some reference to the case. The Beacon Hill house at 8 Walnut Street from which Dr. Parkman started out on his walk that Friday morning almost a hundred years ago is still standing, and its present occupant, a prominent Boston lawyer, is still on occasion plagued by the never-say-die curious.

Among Boston Parkmans the effect was a profound one. For years certain members of the Family shrank from Society altogether, embarrassed as they were by the grievous result of Dr. Parkman's financial punctiliousness and all too aware of the sympathy extended Professor Webster in his budgetary plight. In the doctor's immediate family it is noteworthy that his widow headed the subscription list of a fund taken up to care for Webster's wife and children. Dr. Parkman's son, George Francis Parkman, was five years out of Harvard in 1849. He had been, in contrast to his father, a rather gay blade as a youth and at college had taken part in Hasty Pudding Club theatricals; at the time of the murder he was enjoying himself in Paris. He returned to Boston a marred man. He moved his mother and sister from 8 Walnut Street and took a house at 33 Beacon Street. From the latter house he buried his mother and aunt, and there he and his sister lived on as Boston Society's most distinguished recluses. His solitary existence never included even the solace of a job. Describing him as he appeared a full fifty years after the crime a biographer records:

> Past the chain of the bolted door on Beacon Street no strangers, save those who came on easily recognized business, were ever allowed to enter. Here George Francis Parkman and his sister Harriet, neither of whom ever married, practised the utmost frugality, the master of the house going himself to the market every day to purchase their meager provisions, and invariably paying cash for the simple supplies he brought home.
>
> The windows of his house looked out upon the Common but he did not frequent it . . . He always walked slowly and alone, in a stately way, and attracted attention by his distinguished though retiring appearance . . . In cool weather he wore a heavy coat of dark cloth and his shoulders and neck were closely wrapped with a wide scarf, the ends of which were tucked into his coat or under folds. He sheltered himself against the east winds of Boston just as he seemed, by his manner, to shelter his inmost self from contact with the ordinary affairs of men.*

Tremors of the Parkman earthquake continued to be felt by Boston Society often at times when they were least desired. Twenty years later, when Boston was privileged to play proud host to Charles Dickens, there was a particularly intense tremor. Dickens was asked which one of the city's historic landmarks he would like to visit first. "The room where Dr. Parkman was murdered," he replied, and there being no doubt he meant what he said, nothing remained for a wry-faced group of Boston's best but to shepherd the distinguished novelist out to the chemistry laboratory of the Harvard Medical School.

A Webster-Parkman story, vintage of 1880, is still told today by Boston's distinguished author and teacher, Bliss Perry. He recalls that for a meeting of New England college officers at Williamstown, Massachusetts, his

---

* *Famous Families of Massachusetts*, by Mary Caroline Crawford (Boston: Little, Brown & Co., 1930).

mother had been asked to put up as a guest in her house Boston's First Family poet laureate, diplomat and first editor of the *Atlantic,* James Russell Lowell. Unfortunately Lowell was at that time teaching at Harvard and for all his other accomplishments Mrs. Perry would have none of him. He had to be quartered elsewhere.

"I could not sleep," Mrs. Perry said, "if one of those Harvard professors were in the house."

The Proper Bostonians (New York, 1947).

Ellery Sedgwick

JANE TOPPAN'S CASE
(1892)

Of the eight successive pilots of the Atlantic Monthly, Ellery Sedgwick, *said E. K. Rand in 1944, was "the quickest to catch the breeze"—a man who combined business ability with literary taste. During thirty years as editor, he built the modern* Atlantic *from a small, unprofitable, rather local magazine of 13,500 circulation into one of national importance with ten times that number of subscribers. "I have a great affection for Harvard College," he has written, "atavistic as well as personal ... but I do not look back on my own four years with any touch of nostalgia. The decades at Harvard have multiplied its opportunities by geometric progression, but it is my feeling that the elixir cultural or perhaps spiritual which is the essence of the educated man has been diluted with the years. We have thrown off the prejudices of our fathers, not realizing that the heart of intelligent prejudice is conviction."*

THE MOST IMPORTANT fact for a parent to know about Harvard or any other college for that matter is never mentioned in the catalogues. College walls are not high enough to shut out the larger life which flows about them. Education aims at segregated experience, but experience like all nature abhors a vacuum, and the influences to which young men are subject are beyond calculation. As an odd instance of this I will tell of a curious incident which happened to me during my sophomore year. In bitter weather, after a late party, I had driven out from Boston in one of those ancient sleighs known, I know not why, as "booby-hutches." The characteristic of these eccentric conveyances was their discomfort. They were shrouded in leather curtains which flapped wildly in the wind and had an inanimate genius for intensifying drafts. After the heat of the dance, this particular booby-hutch did for me. I caught a heavy cold, pneumonia followed, and within a day or two both my lungs were seriously involved. Harvard had no hospital in those days, and there I was; my big room in Holworthy Hall heated by the coals of a single grate, with running water three floors below and two trained nurses to assist such chances of life as sick students had in those days.

Now as it happened the attack had caught me just as I was wrestling with a thesis on the character of Jonathan Swift, and turbulent incidents in the life of the ferocious Dean of St. Patrick's swam about me in my delirium. One of my nurses, distinguished by red hair and an angular figure, I called Vanessa. The other was to me the dearer Stella. She was a comfortable body, pink, plump, and motherly, and between us the happiest of domestic relations were soon established, in spite of my whirling head and the desperate pain in my left side. When I tried to throw myself out of the big picture over the bed which I took to be a window, it was Stella who made me all snug again. She it was who watched me with a nurse's intentness as I fixed my own gaze on a tobacco jar standing on the mantel across the room, and said aloud (as she afterwards reported), "I am too tired. That jar holds the elixir of life in it. All I have to do is to struggle up, walk five steps, and drain life from it. But I am too tired. The road back is rougher and longer than the way ahead." Then she bathed my hot forehead, whispered that she would bring that draught of life to me, gave me my medicine, and slipped me off to sleep. Stella's American name was Jane Toppan, and as the crisis passed, the bond between Jane and me grew strong. Some weeks after the crisis, Vanessa left, but Stella stayed to see me through my convalescence and many a confidence we exchanged during the long days and nights. We laughed together about how I had christened her my "Star," and I gave her a deal of instruction about the savage Dean and his inscrutable affections, and translated for her, whether correctly or not I can't remember, the famous inscription on his tomb:—*Ubi saeva indignatio ulterius cor lacerare nequit.*

Then we would fall into more personal discourse. She asked me about my ambitions, and in return would tell me of the satisfactions of her own career, the passionate interest surrounding endless battles between life and death in the sick-room, and how it was in the nurse's lap that the destiny of the patient lay. As I grew stronger, I told her stories about the three: Clotho, Lachesis, and Atropos, who spin the thread, wind it, and cut it with shears. She listened eagerly and explained in return how it was not the doctor but the nurse who held the shears and how she was ever conscious that the fate of a human being rested upon her. On Sunday evenings it had been her custom to go to church, but she hated to leave me and said it was better fun to settle me in an armchair at one side of the grate, while she threw on another scuttle, poked the red coals below, and made all ready for a good talk. When the time came for saying goodbye, we promised always to be friends.

For years I heard nothing of Jane Toppan, and then a strange history appeared in the newspapers. Jane Toppan had been arrested and charged with murder, not the indiscretion of a single homicide, but the massacre of thirty-one patients. Thirty-one only were proved victims but the doctors believed that the holocaust numbered nearly one hundred. After all, thirty-one is a sufficient number of indictments for murder. It seemed unnecessary to pursue the gruesome trail to the end. Many families preferred to let their sisters and brothers rest quiet in their graves and not to open the gates of speculation as to whether their deaths had been owing to natural causes. It seemed, and later evidence bore it out, that my Stella had a homicidal mania on an imperial scale. For three or four deaths she had been responsible before she undertook to weigh my own fate, and skipping occasional patients, as she mercifully skipped me, she put away the rest in a succession that grew more rapid with practice. Her method and the fascination of it gave me a tiny peephole into the deeper abnormalities. Jane would fight hard for a patient's life, but when victory seemed within her grasp and the doctor, confident that vitality was mounting, had left for the night, Jane would stand by the lonely pillow holding two vials in her hand. One contained morphia, one atropin. She would give a dose of morphia and, stooping over the bed, scrutinize the dilation of the patient's pupils as they expanded into a wide and vacant stare. Then with a dose of atropin she would watch the drama of the pupils as they narrowed further and further till they became pin points of light. To such treatment there was an inevitable end. The extraneous and unexpected symptoms would puzzle the physician. They seemed to transcend his experience, and it was not until a long line of patients collapsed, one after another, just as they seemed destined for physical salvation, that suspicion turned upon Jane.

And just at that unfortunate moment Jane did an imprudent thing. She had been the devoted nurse of two sisters. One had just died and Jane, like a decent body, went to the funeral. As the coffin was lowered into the grave, to the consternation of the bereaved family some one thought she heard Jane mutter: "It won't be long now before the other goes." Vague suspicion gathered about her but Jane was known as the best nurse in Cambridge and any definite imputation was too dreadful to be spoken aloud. It was only when four members of a single family in which Jane had been the competent nurse followed each other to the grave within the unreasonable interval of forty-one days that action was taken. Jane was questioned and arrested. A series of bodies were exhumed, stomachs were analyzed. Finally the whole terrifying story came to light. The nurse's mania was diagnosed. Her fifteen years in the assiduous practice of murder were reviewed by the court. She was convicted, sent to Bridgewater, and incarcerated in a hospital for the criminal insane, where I trust she found nurses competent and considerate as she. There, for thirty-five years, till at the ripe age of eighty-one her own time came, Jane Toppan revolved the story of the Three Fates.

Much that was interesting was said of Jane Toppan's career. I quote a pungent paragraph from the unpublished papers of Dr. Charles F. Folsom, Professor of Mental Diseases at Harvard.

"In the pleasure and excitement of crime," he wrote, "Jane Toppan seemed to find the criminal enjoyment of doing aesthetic work to which danger appeared to add zest."

But perhaps Jane's attitude toward life can best be summed up in words of her own, uttered during her trial. She had paused to recall the circumstances surrounding the murder of one of her particular cronies who had come all the way up from Cataumet on the Cape for a sociable visit. The women dined together. The dinner was prepared by Jane. The visitor was taken violently ill and a few days later returned to Cataumet in her coffin. Jane, who never failed a friend, had journeyed to the Cape for the funeral and thus described her sensations as a mourner:—

"When the people came down to Cataumet from Cambridge with Mrs. Davis's body and brought flowers and other emblems of sorrow, I wanted to say to them: 'You had better wait, for in a little while I shall have another funeral for you. If you will only wait, I will save you the trouble of going back and forth.' "

How much better they order these things abroad. Here was a champion of American murder without an equal, yet she was permitted to die in obscurity. Jack the Ripper in London, Bluebeard in Paris; how much had they accomplished? Jack the Ripper may have had half a dozen or perhaps a dozen killings to his credit; Bluebeard, eight or ten wives, yet their names are blazoned in the majestic history of crime. But this New England spinster who could have taught both of them their trade from the ground up has left no biographer behind. This simple tribute of mine is her unique reward.

What ought a boy to carry away from college? Facts are convenient but of little value compared with knowledge of how to read shutting out every avenue of consciousness except the single road which he is traveling; to understand just why two and two make four; to know a man when he sees one—all these are cheap at cost of three or four years. But there is something else, which if the student understands it, and few do, is a possession of great price. The boy has lived in a community free from the grosser iniquities of the world, a society of scholars to whom learning is its own ample return, a republic where the crown of olive is the unmaterial reward. And if the young graduate is wise as well as knowledgeable, his diploma will tell him that in all this world there is no such fun as learning to understand.

The Happy Profession (Boston, 1946).

Victor O. Jones

WHEN RIOTS WERE RIOTS

(1928)

Victor Owen Jones, A.B. 1928, was one of Boston's leading newspapermen for forty years, all of them with the Boston Globe. *Undergraduate correspondent for the* Globe *while at Harvard, he took up sportswriting and became the* Globe's *sports editor in 1933, night editor in 1945, managing editor in 1955, and executive editor in 1962. For many years he reported football for the* Harvard Alumni Bulletin *and later served as a director of the Harvard Alumni Association and of the Harvard Bulletin, Inc., and as a trustee of the* Crimson. *The following account was one of his favorite anecdotes of college days, and suggests a later parallel with that morning a few days after the "bust" in 1969 when President Pusey sent Dean Watson to the Cambridge district court to ask for dismissal of criminal trespass charges made against the occupiers of University Hall.*

THIS being the spring season, nobody should be surprised that the country's campuses are over-running with saps. Spring fever takes different forms from year to year, but you can always count on its showing up among the school and college set about now.

It may be that, like everything else, modern campus capers are better than the old ones, but you'll have to go far to top the famous Harvard Square riot of 26 years ago.

Given the ingredients, that one could have been predicted with almost mathematical certainty.

In the first place, it was spring. Secondly, there had been scheduled the grand opening of the University Theater, right in Harvard Square. This opening wasn't set for noon or for 8:30 P.M., but for midnight.

Besides, Bob Lampoon had been engaged as an extra added attraction. Bob is dead now, but in those days he was the pint-sized janitor of the Lampoon building and a Yard character famous for playing the piccolo, if not well, at least shrilly.

Well, the Harvards, having no place in particular to go while waiting for the University Theater's midnight opening, naturally started tanking up for the great event. They also laid in copious supplies of overripe fruit and vegetables in honor of their pal, the piccolo player.

When the doors finally opened, there was a rush of exuberant undergraduates, feeling no pain, but with strange bulges popping out all over them.

Everything went reasonably well until Bob Lampoon was announced.

The minute he stepped on stage and blew his first toots, another added, but unplanned, attraction reigned. I mean good old pandemonium.

The show ended abruptly and the crowd sallied forth into the Square and immediately got out of hand. The blue coats, who perhaps justifiably are annoyed by all manifestations of spring fever, laid on the wood pretty good and grabbed everyone in sight. Among those accidentally incarcerated was Arthur Clement, the owner of Arthur's Smoke Shop and a very respectable citizen.

I forget how many were pinched and how many stitches were taken in various heads, but the dramatic point came the next day in East Cambridge court.

Judge Arthur Stone ['93, LL.B. '95] listened to the complaints and when almost every student indicated he'd appeal, he started to set bail.

At this point a distinguished-looking gentleman, who had been sitting unnoticed in the back of the room, stepped forward and addressed the court, saying that he would be responsible for the defendants' showing up. It was Dr. A. Lawrence Lowell, the Harvard president. Judge Stone released all hands in his custody.

Dr. Lowell was an aloof sort of man, but he had apparently convinced himself that the police were almost as much to blame as his students. In any case, besides putting himself in hock, he also hired a State St. counsel to defend them. The whole undergraduate body had a feeling of warmth for Dr. Lowell which wasn't matched until years later when they used to see him helping his blind spaniel across Massachusetts Ave. by hooking his umbrella through the dog's collar.

Reprinted in the *Harvard Alumni Bulletin*, March 29, 1954.

James B. Conant

I HADN'T THE STOMACH TO APOLOGIZE TO THE FACULTY

(1939)

When James B. Conant succeeded A. Lawrence Lowell as president of Harvard in 1933, the new Harvard leader found that one of his initial responsibilities was to stimulate reform in the Faculty of Arts and Sciences. He felt that the first need was to introduce a representative executive council to facilitate the faculty's legislative process, next to create a definite but flexible retirement policy, and then to insist on firmer criteria for pro-

motion and tenure. Because of muddled public understanding of what he was trying to accomplish in clarifying the faculty's tenure policies, President Conant was forced into appointing a committee of eight faculty leaders to help him formulate the conditions for promotion and tenure. Even so, as he tells here, he ran into bitter faculty rebellion and almost lost the battle.

AS SOON as I returned to Cambridge in September, I heard rumors that at the fall meeting of the faculty of arts and sciences one or more professors would air their discontent with the actions of the new dean and the policy of the president. According to the scheme which the faculty had adopted in 1934 at my suggestion, the major business of the faculty was generally conducted by an elected council and only one meeting of the full faculty was scheduled for each term. The latter had become perfunctory as the faculty council proved its effectiveness.

There was to be nothing perfunctory about the meeting of October 8, 1939. One hundred and thirty-five members were present. The actions taken the previous June were at once referred to by several speakers; sharp questions were directed to the dean, who was attending his first faculty meeting in that capacity. As president, I, of course, was in the chair. Dean Ferguson, who had been forewarned, read a memorandum of several pages in which he set forth the actions of his administration. He pointed out that all the decisions reached in the spring had been made jointly by the administration and each department concerned. Usually, he said, the department had been unanimous; in no department was there more than one dissenting opinion. The administration, he declared, was not open to the charge of having proceeded hastily or ruthlessly. All assistant professors who failed of appointment to the permanent staff were given at least a year's extension or a year's notice.

The challengers were not satisfied. On a motion by one of them, the meeting was adjourned to the next Tuesday. At the adjourned meeting 158 were present. The discussion of the application of the Committee of Eight recommendations continued. The meeting grew more and more into an attack on the president of the university for his failure to keep the faculty informed of the development of the new policy. The chairmen of the departments of English, government, and biology demanded a reversal of the decisions of the spring which affected adversely the young men in their departments. Finally, an old friend of mine moved that "further discussion of personnel administrative problems be deferred until the dean, after discussion with representatives of all departments, writes a report." The motion was adopted without debate.

By this time the debate had been picked up by the press. Dean Ferguson released his entire memorandum. The discontent focused on the recommendation of the Committee of Eight that the rank of assistant professor be abolished. I had noted in my report to the Overseers in May that while I had accepted this particular recommendation of the Committee of Eight as a guide to general policy, I had not agreed to it as a binding commitment. "In general the proposal seems to me wise," I wrote, "but any department of the faculty will be free to argue any particular case for the appointment of an assistant professor. In those cases in which it may seem best to make such appointments, I shall have no hesitation in recommending such action to the Governing Boards."

The dean was ready to report to a meeting of the faculty on November 7, 1939. The omens were not favorable. Members of the Committee of eight who were on the dean's side reported increasing hostility on the part of a number of departments, some of whom were in a bitter mood. It looked as if some compromises would have to be made in individual cases, which was done a few weeks later. What disturbed me and some of my advisers most was the announcement by a professor of government that he would move that the faculty elect a committee of ten to examine the role of the faculty in the government of the university and report back. Such a motion obviously was put forward by those who thought the president should have consulted the faculty from the start and who objected strongly to my attempt to make definite the limited power of the faculty in matters of appointments. Much of the unpleasantness in the last meeting had pointed in this direction.

I consulted with a number of persons, indicating that the dean and I were prepared for a knockdown fight if necessary. Dean Wallace B. Donham of the School of Business Administration, on hearing of our intent through mutual friends, came to see me in alarm. For the first time during the controversy, he said, he was deeply worried. The issue which was now being raised was at the heart of the Harvard system; I had lost the confidence of a majority of the faculty of arts and sciences; if I let this loss of confidence result in faculty action that jeopardized the long-standing faculty-governing boards relation, I would be doing Harvard a great and perhaps permanent disservice. "The only thing for you to do," he said, "is to admit frankly and openly at the faculty meeting that you have made mistakes (and you have made mistakes) and ask the faculty not to attempt a revolution in the Harvard constitution because of your own errors. In my experience," he added, "if one admits a mistake to a faculty group, they will usually rally in support."

I did not like the advice at all. I had no stomach for apologizing to the faculty, particularly when I was under violent attack. I had made mistakes, beginning with the unfortunate press release of April 1937—that I had to admit to myself at least. To follow the course Dean Donham suggested was another matter. Yet I agreed with him completely as to the consequences of the election of a faculty committee to examine the government of the university. After considerable soul-searching, I finally decided that the dean's advice was wise, and entered the faculty meeting determined to follow it if a suitable occasion arose.

The audience was the largest ever—223. In response to the speakers who had blamed the existence of the faculty council for the failure in communications, a motion was passed 140–6 abolishing the council. The action was certainly a slap in the face of the president but raised no constitutional issue. The council had been my own invention; in destroying it, the faculty might be in part giving vent to its collective resentment. The next item on the docket was quite different. This was the motion to elect a committee to examine the role of the faculty in the government of Harvard.

Before the debate on this second motion had started, I said that as president of the university I wished to make a statement. I pointed out the grave implications of the motion. I agreed that the situation which had arisen in regard to promotion and tenure had greatly disturbed the members of the faculty. That I had made errors which were largely responsible for the current tension, I admitted. I asked the faculty, however, not, on account of my mistakes, to take a hasty step which might affect Harvard adversely for years to come. When I had finished, there was silence. Someone moved the motion be laid on the table; by voice vote, which sounded unanimous, the tabling motion was carried. Dean Donham was proved to have been right.

The question of a shift in the appointive power from the governing boards to the faculty was never raised again during the remaining fourteen years of my administration. If I had argued against the disturbing motion, I have no doubt it would have passed; the mood of the faculty that afternoon was close to being vindictive. A profound change might have started; though it can be argued that conservative forces would eventually have regained control. But the moral of the story for all new college presidents is clear: when you receive sound advice, however unwelcome, make the most of it and do so as rapidly as you can.

My Several Lives (New York, 1970).

Steven Kelman

MEETING MR. McNAMARA
(1966)

During the fall of Steven Kelman's freshman year, while he was assembling impressions of the College and his classmates for the New York Times Magazine, *Kelman recorded in his journal the story of what happened when Secretary of Defense Robert McNamara came to Cambridge to participate in the program of the Institute of Politics of the John F. Kennedy School of Govern-*

*ment. The protest organized to interfere with this visit was the first of a series
that culminated almost three years later in the occupation of University
Hall and the subsequent strike. Kelman's account of this event comes from*
Push Comes to Shove, *which he published in 1970, now one of two or three
important basic texts on the developing tug of war among students, faculty,
administration, and alumni which began in the late sixties and continued
into the early seventies. Kelman is now Assistant Professor of Public Policy
in the Kennedy School.*

NOVEMBER 6, 1966

I'm going to go to the McNamara demonstration tomorrow to see what
happens. Mainly today I tried to find out from Mark Dyen what will happen
tomorrow. The outline is that there will be a rally outside Quincy House
while McNamara is inside talking with the fifty students. SDS has mimeoed
a series of questions about Vietnam for McNamara, which they're distribut-
ing around the school and especially to sympathetic ones among the fifty
who'll be inside.

Meanwhile, SDS will have commandos staged around all the exits to the
building, and they will signal when and if McNamara comes out of one of
them with the walkie-talkies that they will all be provided with. Then SDS
kids will block McNamara as he tries to leave, and a representative of SDS
will ask McNamara to answer some questions about Vietnam before they let
him go.

But obviously he'll refuse, and I can't get any answers on what will happen then. It's either a secret, or else they don't know.

At any rate, SDS is trying to call up today every one of the 1100 who
signed his registration interest card and ask him to come tomorrow. They
are so desperate for manpower that Mark Dyen even asked—I should say
bludgeoned—my roommate Mike into making ten phone calls for him.
Mike, unfortunately, is too good-natured to refuse anyone, even though he
opposes any potential disruption. But Mike finally stopped calling after the
fourth straight person on the list hadn't even remembered signing an SDS
interest sheet or else angrily told him that he had heard rumors that there
was going to be violence against the secretary of defense and that he was
strongly opposed to that.

November 7, 1966

Quincy is the most recently built of the Harvard houses. It is collo-
quially known as "the Harvard Hilton," I found out, because of its modern,
garden-apartment appearance. As if to fit the appearance of the house,
Quincy House "men" have a midwestern, suburban, conservative image.
Perhaps that explained the messages carefully painted on bed sheets and
draped out of the big picture windows to greet the demonstrators.

NAPALM SDS.

KILL THE CONG!

To be fair, there was also one that read, VIETNAM—ANOTHER EDSEL FOR MCNAMARA. Before the action started, someone near me playfully commented, "Gordon Linen is sure in for a big cleaning job next week." Harvard's collective sense of humor never leaves it.

When I arrived, McNamara was still inside, but the events had already started. Scheer was speaking, to the steady jeering of some tough-looking jock types. Their impoliteness went unnoticed by the press. They were counterjeered by antiwar people and at times it was impossible to hear Scheer and the other speakers over the loud monotone of the jocks and the shouting of the others.

"Shut up, you shitheads!" one person yelled out so loud that his voice boomed over the cacophony. The antiwar people cheered.

Around me was the unconcerned air of "after me, the deluge." There were several hundred people there, most of them anti-McNamara, and most everybody, on both sides, was eager for action. But nobody knew exactly what was going to happen.

"Get your copy of *New America*, America's democratic socialist newspaper! Only ten cents!" I yelled.

I saw one of the Trotskyists, burly and smiling, near me. "Beat that kid over there up, Jim," he indicated to the person next to him. I didn't think he was serious.

"Hey, don't you believe in freedom of speech?"

"Freedom of speech for counterrevolutionaries?" He chuckled and walked away through the thick crowd.

"We call Khrushchev the 'Butcher of Budapest' here in the United States," Scheer shouted into the microphone of the hastily prepared stand. "The United States Air Force has bombed the North Vietnamese city of Vinh out of existence. I think it's time to start calling LBJ the 'Butcher of Vinh!'"

Acting like Walter Cronkite, or some other anchorman at a political convention, David Loud of SDS took up the microphone every few minutes to say, "We have spies inside to tell us from what exit McNamara is leaving. As soon as we receive the word from inside, we'll tell you." Now back to the speeches.

The main entrance to Quincy House was locked up. We were demonstrating on Plympton Street, not inside the courtyard. The grass inside the courtyard was green. The pro-McNamara jocks were sitting in a row on the fence. I saw a helicopter fly overhead—I don't know if it had anything to do with us.

The Kennedy Institute had hoped that by keeping McNamara's exit point secret they could allow him to escape undetected. But actually they were merely increasing the chance of "trouble." Then there was the squad of student bodyguards selected by the Kennedy Institute to protect McNamara. Although the institute denies it, the guards claim they had gotten instructions to beat up any students who tried to block McNamara's path.

The SDS people got tired of talking. Mike Ansara took the microphone. "Will everyone please move from Plympton Street onto Mount Auburn," he ordered slowly. Mt. Auburn is just perpendicular to Plympton. "We've gotten word that McNamara will be coming out of there." The PA went dead for a minute, and nobody could hear him. By the time it came on again, the crowd was already moving, and Ansara was already off the platform, pushing his way over to Mt. Auburn Street so he could be at the center of the action.

I was right next to him. The PA came on again, but I heard him without it. "When McNamara comes out, everyone lock arms so he can't leave!" His voice projected through the microphone was an ominous echo of his unmagnified voice as I heard it. He was calmly angry, playing around with the mike.

He told the crowd to keep quiet so they could hear him. "When he comes, I'll say to him, 'Mr. McNamara, there are several questions we'd like to ask you.' Now I don't want any yelling or screaming when he comes. Everyone keep silent."

Since I was right up front, I was marked for the group to be locking arms, I inched myself away from the front.

But before the chain could get established, one of the SDS commandos at the back garage exit from Quincy House started yelling. The chain unchained, and everybody started running. Feeling like an Indian surrounding a wagon train, I ran along, arriving in time to see a car rushing out of the garage and a mob scene around the car.

"Holy shit, they're going to run over that kid!" I screamed out as someone seemed to be caught under the black limousine.

So here was McNamara.

Dyen had been the commando who had yelled. He's advancing fast in SDS. His hair was plastered down with sweat.

The kid escaped from the path of the car.

But suddenly people started running again, on around to Mill Street, almost completing the rectangle. What was going on? Shit! (Later I found out that the car from the garage was another decoy.) I kept running, outside the perimeter of the crowd. My copies of *New America* were still in my hands, getting sweated up. Hold on tightly.

When I got onto Mill Street, most of the crowd hadn't arrived yet. There was a limousine at the center of the street, and a group of twenty kids were sitting down in front of it. One kid from SDS was yelling, "Everybody sit down! Stop the car!"

But most people were simply surrounding the car, being pushed inexorably into the vacuum which had existed when I first arrived. The crowd was rushing to see the "real thing"; now it was forced into the middle of it. A few were screaming.

"Hey, let me get out!"

"Let me out of here. I don't want to block the fucking car!"

I almost felt like a newspaper reporter.

None of the circumstances leading up to the confrontation on Mill Street favored, to say the least, a peaceful demonstration. I didn't know at the time whether the sit-down had been originally planned by SDS; at any rate, it wasn't publicized. (Tonight Mark Dyen admitted to me that it had been a secret part of the plans.) But there was a lot of fighting going on, and screaming from both pro and anti kids. An older kid in front of me was yelling, "Down with American imperialism!" It seemed stridently out of place, even here.

I was about five feet from the car, but I couldn't see McNamara inside. There was no question about it: the car wouldn't be able to move. The noise crescendoed.

Then McNamara climbed, slowly, out of the car.

In all the plots I had imagined, the idea of McNamara giving in and coming out of the car was never considered. I still don't know exactly how he got out—the guy in front of me was too tall—but I could catch him finally as he jumped on top of the car, aided by Mike Ansara.

McNamara was smiling. I'm not sure whether he was more excited than I was. As people saw him, there was a cheer of victory on Mill Street. As if it were a cheer for him, McNamara held up his hands like an actor requesting the audience to stop the lengthy applause because he wants to get onto the next number.

He was still smiling.

The noise never died down enough so that I could hear what Ansara and David Loud were saying to McNamara. But soon Ansara grabbed the mike and yelled out, "Secretary McNamara has agreed to answer a few questions." Cheers. Victory. Again, I never expected that. I was sure he was getting out to politely ask everyone to disperse. And then, maybe, the fire hoses would come.

McNamara took the mike. He completed Ansara's sentence for him. ". . . for five minutes, and then I'll have to ask you to let me get on to my next appointment." His hair was perfectly in place, as always. Ansara told everyone to keep quiet, and for the first time there was silence. It came only slowly, but it came. The guy in front of me shouted, "Don't listen to him! He's killing the people of Vietnam! He doesn't even have the right to speak!" But for the time being he was a small minority.

Everyone was raising his hand to ask questions. The first question was about civililian casualties, the second about whether the war had really started as an invasion from the north. Afterward people claimed the questions were stupid. But the fact was that nobody expected ever to be able to ask any questions, so nobody was ready to pour on the rhetoric.

The audience didn't like the answers McNamara started to give.

"I'm afraid I don't know how many civilian casualties there have been in the Vietnam conflict."

"Don't you *care?*" someone shouted from the back, and that was the signal for the end of the silence. I could still hear McNamara talking, but people a little farther away said that McNamara's voice had become completely drowned out.

"The war in Vietnam didn't begin in nineteen fifty-seven, as you said in your question. It began earlier than that, in nineteen fifty-four when the North Vietnamese sent down cadres to infiltrate with the refugees who were leaving North Vietnam." That was the first time anybody had ever heard *that* argument from the government. Some people laughed above the noise. I heard one cry of "bullshit!"

Suddenly SuperMac broke.

He yelled out, pointing at one person who had said I don't know what, "Look, I went to school at Berkeley and spent four years there doing a lot of the same things you here are doing." I couldn't help thinking something unserious to myself: I wondered whether the Defense Department knew he had been a subversive at Berkeley when they hired him.

The shouting grew louder. Almost all of the kids with rooms overlooking Mill Street had opened their windows, looking over the proceedings with box seats. Strange, I thought, there didn't seem to be any policemen around.

McNamara continued, "I was doing the same things as you are, but there were two big differences." Pause. "I was *tougher,* and I was more *courteous.*" The computer had shattered. The man was fighting back.

The television cameras were taking it all down. Total confusion. McNamara pointed to another face. "And I'm *still* tougher!"

The play was over; after that it was downhill. McNamara asked, after a pause, without any noticeable sarcasm, "... you ladies and gentlemen to please let me get on to my next appointment." The press conference was over. Ansara conferred with David Loud a moment and then asked the crowd to leave. They did, rather quickly. I stayed around until almost everyone had gone.

Within the next two days, 2700 Harvard undergraduates—an amazing number, really—signed a petition apologizing to McNamara.

Push Comes to Shove (Boston, 1970).

IV

YOU CAN TELL A
HARVARDIAN . . .

Students of H[arvard] do not on all occasions appear much better than their less favored countrymen, either in point of gentlemanly and *distingué* appearance or in conversation.

FRANCIS PARKMAN (1844)

As I look back on my college days it strikes me that we were boys. Honest, energetic, square-trotting, manly boys, but still boys. The fault was not wholly ours; the apparent aim of the authorities was to keep us so.

ROBERT GRANT (1896)

Thoreau and Kennedy are just two of the uncounted alumni numbered among the great. But the great majority of us are, to speak plainly, mere worms hiding under the societal equivalent of flat stones on a barren hillside. Our conscious minds know that we are worms. But our subconscious minds, irradiated by glory, refuse to believe. It shows through, and that's why you can always tell a Harvard man.

KARL M. ELISH (1961)

You can tell a Harvard man almost anything you want to, but you can't get him to believe it just because you say it.

HOWARD MUMFORD JONES (1961)

It is really the undergraduate who makes a university, gives it its lasting character, smell, feel, quality, tradition. You can never know a university, or ever belong to it, by entering it as a graduate student; it may even be that no professor coming to it late from another university will ever know it as well as his newcome sophomores, juniors and seniors. It is these whose presence creates it and whose memories preserve it—its rakes, rapscallions and idlers, its rebels and its aberrants, no less than its scholars, sloggers and bright stars. It is to these that the first toast should be drunk at every university dinner: To every shade who here once was happy, because he was young. I think that it is in recognition of this truth and not from snobbery that your true Harvardian says, with just the faintest emphasis, that he went to Harvard *College.*

SÉAN O'FAOLÁIN (1964)

A Series of Excerpts

KEEP THOU THE COLLEGE LAWS
(1655–1790)

One of contemporary Harvard's proudest boasts is that of its encouragement of students' personal responsibility—responsibility toward society and toward self-education. Despite age-old arguments over parietal regulations, and other College requirements, there are really relatively few rules to hinder a student's development as a person. In the early years it was a different story. The College laws were intended to confine students to the Yard and the College twenty-four hours a day; the students could not go to the nearby pub, join a military company, or be seen in the company of those who "lead an ungirt and dissolute life." President Dunster formed the first law code for the College in 1642 and thereafter "the laws, liberties, and orders of Harvard College" were required to be copied by all entering students "for the perpetual preservation and government." From 1790 onward they were regularly revised and printed in English.

 EVERY undergraduate shall be called only by his surname unless he be the son of a nobleman, or a knight's eldest son or a fellow commoner. [1655]

All students shall be slow to speak, & eschew and (as much as in them lies) shall take care that others may avoid all swearing, lying, cursing, needless asseverations, foolish talking, scurrility, babbling, filthy speaking, chiding, strife, railing, reproaching, abusive jesting, uncomely noise, uncertain rumors, divulging secrets, & all manner of troublesome & offensive gestures, as being they who should shine before others in exemplary life. [1655]

No scholar shall go out of his chamber without coat, gown or cloak, & every one, every where shall wear modest & sober habit, without strange ruffianlike or new-fangled fashions, without all lavish dress, or excess of apparel whatsoever; nor shall any wear gold or silver, or such ornaments, except to whom upon just ground the president shall permit the same: neither shall it be lawful for any to wear long hair, locks or foretops, nor to use curling, crisping, parting or powdering their hair. [1655]

Candidates for admission into Harvard College, shall be examined by the President and two at least of the Tutors. No one shall be admitted, unless he can translate the Greek and Latin authors in common use, such as Tully, Virgil, The New-Testament, Xenophon &c understands the rules of grammar, can write Latin correctly, and hath a good moral character. [1767]

If any undergraduate shall lead an idle & dissipated life, after those in the government of the College shall have taken pains to reform him; or if he shall otherwise so offend against those rules and laws of the College, . . . they shall judge it most tending to the reformation of the delinquent (the honor of the College at the same time being secured) that he should, for a time, be taken from the College, and be put under the immediate inspection & instruction of some private gentleman in the country. [1767]

If any undergraduates shall be absent from, or carelessly perform their stated exercises with their respective tutors, or absent themselves from the private lectures of the professors, they shall be fined not exceeding two shillings; and if they do not speedily reform by such pecuniary mulcts, they shall be admonished, degraded, suspended, or rusticated, according as the nature and degree of the offence shall require. [1790]

To animate the students in the pursuit of literary merit and fame, and to excite in their breasts a noble spirit of emulation, there shall be annually a public examination, in the presence of a joint committee of the Corporation and Overseers, and such other gentlemen as may be inclined to attend it. [1790]

If any scholar shall associate with any person of dissolute morals, or, in the town of Cambridge, with one that is rusticated, or expelled, within three years after such rustication or expulsion, unless the rusticated person shall be restored within that space, he shall be fined not exceeding five shillings for the first offence; and if any Undergraduate shall persist therein, he shall be farther liable to admonition, degradation, suspension, or rustication, according to the circumstances of the offence. And if any undergraduate shall lead a life of dissipation, after those in the Government of the College shall have endeavored to reform him by admonition and the lesser punishments, he shall be degraded, suspended, or rusticated, as the degree of the offence may require. [1790]

If any scholar shall go into any tavern or victualling house in Cambridge, to eat and drink there, unless in the presence of his father or guardian, without leave from the President or one of the Tutors, he shall be fined not exceeding two shillings. [1790]

If any resident graduate shall play at cards or dice, after having been admonished by the President, he shall not be allowed to continue any longer at the College. [1790]

If any scholar or scholars, belonging to the College, shall be found guilty of making tumultuous or indecent noises, to the dishonour and disturbance of the College, or to the disturbance of the town or any of its inhabitants; or, without leave from the President, Professors and Tutors, shall make bonfires or illuminations, or play off fireworks, or be any way aiding or abetting of the same, every scholar, so offending, shall be liable to a fine not exceeding ten shillings, or to be publicly admonished, degraded, suspended, or rusticated, according to the degree and aggravation of the offence. [1790]

All the undergraduates shall be clothed in coats of blue gray, and with waistcoats and breeches of the same colour, or of a black, a nankeen, or an olive colour. The coats of the freshmen shall have plain button holes: The cuffs shall be without buttons. The coats of the sophomores shall have plain button holes like those of the freshmen; but the cuffs shall have buttons. The coats of the juniors shall have cheap frogs to the button holes, except the button holes of the cuffs. The coats of the seniors shall have frogs to the button holes of the cuffs. The buttons upon the coats of all the classes shall be as near the colour of the coats as they can be procured, or of a black colour. And no student shall appear, within the limits of the College, or town of Cambridge, in any other dress, than in the uniform belonging to his respective class, unless he shall have on a night gown, or such an outside garment, as may be necessary, over a coat: Except only, that the seniors and juniors are permitted to wear black gowns; and it is recommended that they appear in them on all public occasions: Nor shall any part of their garments be of silk; nor shall they wear gold or silver lace, cord or edging upon their hats, waistcoats, or any other parts of their clothing: And whosoever shall violate these regulations, shall be fined a sum not exceeding ten shillings for each offence. [1790]

From "College Laws and Customs," *Publications of the Colonial Society of Massachusetts*, XXXI, and from the official printing of "The Laws of Harvard College" (Boston, 1790).

Thomas Shepard, Jr.

THAT PRECIOUS TIME YOU NOW MISSPEND

(1672)

*Two famous letters of advice to seventeenth-century Harvard students have
come down to us. One was from Leonard Hoar, A.B. 1650, to his freshman
nephew Josiah Flynt, and principally concerned matters of the curriculum.
The other was from Rev. Thomas Shepard, Jr., A.B. 1653, to his son, Thomas,
who graduated from Harvard in 1676. President Hoar's letter was reproduced in full in Morison's* Harvard College in the Seventeenth Century.
*The Shepard letter is less well known, although written by one of the promi-
nent Harvard graduates of the seventeenth century. Thomas Shepard, Jr.,
was the son of the founder of the first permanent church in Cambridge, an
Overseer of the College, and a defender of the principles of religious toleration. His son, according to Cotton Mather, was "his Grandfather's and his
Father's genuine Off-Spring" who came "unto such Learning as gave him an
Early Admission into the College, and raised great Hopes in good Men concerning him." Unhappily he died in 1685, at the age of twenty-six, only
eight years after his father's death, and a brief ministerial career. Here is a
portion of the father's "Paper of Golden Instructions."*

REMEMBER that these are times and days of much light and knowledge and
that therefore you had as good be no scholar as not excel in knowledge and
learning. Abhor therefore one hour of idleness as you would be ashamed of
one hour of drunkenness. Look that you lose not your precious time by falling in with idle companions, or by growing weary of your studies, or by love
of any filthy lust; or by discouragement of heart that you shall never attain
to any excellency of knowledge, or by thinking too well of your self, that
you have got as much as is needful for you, when you have got as much as
your equals in the same year; no verily, the Spirit of God will not communicate much to you in a way of idleness, but will curse your soul, while this sin
is nourished, which hath spoiled so many hopeful youths in their first blos-
soming in the College. And therefore tho' I would not have you neglect
seasons of recreation a little before and after meals (and altho' I would not
have you study late in the night usually, yet look that you rise early and lose
not your morning thoughts, when your mind is most fresh, and fit for study)
but be no wicked example all the day to any of your fellows in spending
your time idly. And do not content yourself to do as much as your tutor sets
you about, but know that you will never excel in learning, unless you do
somewhat else in private hours, wherein his care cannot reach you: and do

not think that idling away your time is no great sin, if so be you think you can hide it from the eyes of others: but consider that God, who always sees you, and observes how you spend your time, will be provoked for every hour of that precious time you now misspend, which you are like never to find the like to this in the College, all your life after.

Publications of the Colonial Society of Massachusetts, XIV (Boston, 1913).

Richard Waldron

A FRESHMAN GUIDE

(1735)

One of the freshman's first duties in Harvard's early days was to procure a copy of the College laws. This document, signed by the President or one of the Fellows, was considered a certificate of admission. More than a score of these admittaturs *exist as examples of the laws of different periods, as early as 1683. Richard Waldron, who copied his on June 24, 1735 with his own immature hand and erratic orthography, was the son and namesake of the Secretary of the Province of New Hampshire, himself a graduate of Harvard (1712). Little is known about young Richard after his graduation in 1738. At the time he went into the wide world his father was engaged in a political life-and-death struggle which resulted in his removal from office. The younger Richard Waldron was lost at sea in 1745.*

1. No freshman shall wear his hat in the College yard except it rains, snows, or hails, or he be on horseback or hath both hands full.
2. No freshman shall wear his hat in his senior's chamber or in his own if his senior be there.
3. No freshman shall go by his senior, with out taking his hat off if it be on.
4. No freshman shall intrude into his senior's company.
5. No freshman shall laugh in his senior's face.
6. No freshman shall talk saucily to his senior or speak to him with his hat on.
7. No freshman shall ask his senior an impertinent question.
8. Freshmen are to take notice that a senior sophister can take a freshman from a sophomore, a middle bachelor from a junior sophister, a master from a senior sophister & a fellow from a master.
9. Freshmen are to find the rest of the scholars with bats, balls, and footballs.
10. Freshmen must pay three shillings apiece to the Butler to have their names set up in the Buttery.
11. No freshman shall loiter by the [way] when he is sent of an errand, but shall make haste and give a direct answer when he is asked who he is

going [for], no freshman shall use lying or equivocation to escape going of an errand.

12. No freshman shall tell who [he] is going [for], except he be asked, nor for what except he be asked by a fellow.

13. No freshman shall go away when he hath been sent of an errand before he be dismissed which may be understood by saying it is well I thank you, you may go or the like.

14. When a freshman knocks at his senior's door he shall tell [his] name if asked who.

15. When anybody knocks at a freshman's door he shall not ask who is there, but shall immediately open the door.

16. No freshman shall lean at prayers but shall stand upright.

17. No freshman shall call his class mate by the name of freshman.

18. No freshman shall call up or down to or from his senior's chamber or his own.

19. No freshman shall call or throw any thing across the college yard.

20. No freshman shall mingo against the College wall or go into the fellows' cuzjohn.

21. Freshmen may wear their hats at dinner and supper except when they go to receive their commons of bread and beer.

22. Freshmen are so to carry themselves to their seniors in all respects so as to be in no wise saucy to them and whosoever of the freshmen shall break any of these customs shall be severely punished.

Harvard University Archives.

Frederic West Holland

A FRESHMAN HAZING

(1827)

"Be ready in fine to cut, to drink, to smoke, to swear, to haze, to dead [i.e. be unprepared to recite], to spree,—in one word, to be a sophomore," so runs an early nineteenth-century epigram. The plight of the green freshman was perilous indeed. Early in Harvard history he became errand boy and unpaid servant to the sophs, and when he was not plagued with errands, he was plagued with tricks, some of them unusually disagreeable. The perils of being a freshman in 1827 were carefully recorded by Frederic West Holland, A.B. 1831, who later became a Unitarian clergyman. It did not take Holland and his friends long to discover that they were the victims of a series of labored jokes.

SEPTEMBER 1st 1827. I moved my goods & effects to Stoughton No. 4 & in the afternoon with my chum commenced housekeeping. But scarcely had the shades descended, when we were visited by a numerous company of Juniors, most of them my acquaintances, who smoked, talked, & laughed with us, and made a most tremendous noise. It was then after eight. In about ¼ of an hour, we were told some one wished to see us at No. 24 Stoughton. We went there; & were there admonished for disrespect, & a lesson of 5 pages of Grotius and 10 of Adams' Antiquities was set. The presiding personage was named Dr. Farmer; another one was named Mr. Van Bomb-shell; as I enter'd I mentioned to chum that I thought it was a hoax. The presiding personage was seated in an arm-chair at a table, a shade-lamp before him, around him were many persons seated without much order. After they had set the lesson, they dismissed me, but they kept my chum, & reproached him with lewdness and profane language; we could before hardly keep from laughing-out loud; when chum went out, he slammed the door after him like vengeance.

Well that concern having had enough of me, I returned to my room, and before my chum returned, I was summoned to appear before Tutor Lunt, the Proctor of our entry.

I followed my conductor to the 3rd story, corner room, Stoughton, he entered and made a low bow, I did the same; he (Lunt) bade me step in, & asked me if there had not been a great noise in my room. I told him there had; he then asked me if I did not know that it was contrary to the Laws; I told him I had not yet recd a copy of the Laws; he replied that then it was partly excusable, but that it was contrary to law to have a noise after study hours in our rooms; & that, in addition, Saturday night was sacred, he then sent me for my chum; after waiting a few moments chum came in, I informed him of the circumstances, & then showed him the room, told him to make his bow and departed: on his return I found out that he was treated pretty much as I was: Lunt told him he was sorry to be obliged to note him the first night, etc., etc. Whilst chum was yet absent, the door suddenly opened and a mean soph threw at me a large winter squash; this formidable & destructive weapon bounced powerless upon the floor at about ¾ of a yard from me, & the assailants immediately fled. My chum returned; and by the time he was informed of the foregoing event, our window suddenly flew open and a heavy shower of pieces of punkins proceeded. We were rather startled, I confess, at this strange visitant: but in a few moments down came the Junior Sophisters again; the instruments of attack still reclined in various positions on the floor. We informed them that we had been called up before Proctor Lunt, and noted; and requested them to be as still as possible; but they on the contrary, thumped the squash against the walls, & and made an awful racket. They shortly retired, and in an hour afterwards we were summoned before the Proctor of our entry. We were again asked with regard to the noise, confessed, were reprimanded; and he concluded with saying, that he would represent our affair to the Government in as favourable a light as possible.

After we had returned, the visiting sophs entered our rooms; we stated our case & requested them to make as little noise as possible, they soon peaceably retired. And we having bought lots of books, & having broken lots of laws, retired to bed.

Harvard Alumni Bulletin, September 29, 1927.

Oliver Wendell Holmes

OF CAMBRIDGE AND FEMALE SOCIETY

(1828-1830)

In his time, there was surely no more enthusiastic son of Harvard than Oliver Wendell Holmes, who entered College in 1825 and kept up an active interest in the College and in his classmates until his death in 1894 at the age of eighty-five. Holmes was the perennial toastmaster, the ready versifier for the suitable occasion, and he kept up the pace throughout his life, despite a busy medical practice and his teaching duties as Parkman Professor of Anatomy and Physiology. No reunion of the famous class of 1829 was complete without a word from the good doctor, and it was an annual event after 1851. The written record of Holmes's days at Harvard is unfortunately meager, but it is freshened by his desultory though sparkling correspondence with a boyhood friend, Phineas Barnes, then a student at Bowdoin ("a fine rosy-faced boy, not quite so free of speech as myself, perhaps, but with qualities that promised a noble manhood"). This was one of the two or three friendships which lasted all the doctor's life. The letters from Harvard—now in the Harvard Library—span part of his College days, his year at the Law School, and his venture into medicine.

August 15, 1828

I SUPPOSE I must begin with an apology for not writing sooner. I have been away from home about a month, or I would not have been guilty of such neglect. Your letter was the first token of remembrance that I have received from any of my old Andover friends or acquaintance, saving certain catalogues of the different colleges, in which article I have kept up quite a brisk correspondence . . . With regard to myself I am determined that you shall not be so much in the dark. I shall therefore describe myself as circumstantially as I would a runaway thief or apprentice. I, then, Oliver Wendell Holmes, Junior in Harvard University, am a plumeless biped of the height of exactly five feet three inches when standing in a pair of substantial boots made by Mr. Russell of this town, having eyes which I call blue, and hair which I do not know what to call,—in short, something such a looking kind of animal as I was at Andover, with the addition of some two or three inches to my stature. Secondly, with regard to my moral qualities, I am rather lazy than otherwise, and certainly do not study as hard as I ought to. I am not dissipated and I am not sedate, and when I last ascertained my college rank I stood in the humble situation of seventeenth scholar. You must excuse my egotism in saying all this about myself, but I wish to give you as good an idea as I can of your old friend, and I think now you may be able to form an idea of him from this. The class we belong to is rather a singular one, and I fear not much more united than yours. I am acquainted with a great many different fellows who do not speak to each other. Still I find pleasant companions and a few good friends among the jarring elements . . .

I am sorry you feel so sober for want of friends, but you need not be afraid that I shall think it silly in you to say so, for indeed I have had many such feelings myself. I have found new friends, but I have not forgotten my old ones, and I think I have had quite as pleasant walks within the solemn precincts of Andover as I have ever had amidst the classic shades of Cambridge. I should like to go over some of those places again in the same company . . .

October 23, 1828

It is Saturday afternoon—the wind is whistling around the old brick buildings, in one of which your humble servant is seated in the midst of literary disorder and philosophical negligence . . .

Wednesday . . . was our Exhibition; on the whole it was very poor; sometimes fellows will get high parts who cannot sustain them with credit. Our Exhibition days, however, are very pleasant; in defiance of, or rather evading, the injunctions of the government, we contrive to have what they call "festive entertainments" and we call "blows." A fine body of academic militia, denominated the "Harvard Washington Corps," parades before the ladies in the afternoon, and there is eating and drinking and smoking and making merry . . .

December 1828

I am going to answer part of the fifty questions, and I suspect I shall not have much room to ask anything in return. And so here I am, with your two last sheets before me, like a sheep about to be sheared, or a boy to be catechised.

Imprimis . . . "What do I do?" I read a little, study a little, smoke a little, and eat a good deal! "What do I think?" I think that's a deuced hard question. "What have I been doing these three years?" Why, I have been growing a little in body, and I hope in mind; I have been learning a little of almost everything, and a good deal of some things . . .

If you ever come to Boston you will, of course, come out to Cambridge. Our town has not much to boast of excepting the College . . . I have studied French and Italian, and some Spanish. We have been studying this year Astronomy, Good's *Book of Nature,* Brown's *Philosophy of the Mind,* and attended Dr. Ware's Lectures on the Scriptures. We have themes once a fortnight, forensics once a month, and declamation every week . . .

I will send you a catalogue of the officers and students, and one of the Medical Faculty. This will need some explanation. It is a mock society among the students, which meets twice a year in disguise, and, after admitting members from the junior class, distributes honorary degrees to distinguished men. The room where they meet is hung round with sheets and garnished with bones. They burn alcohol in their lamps, and examine very curiously and facetiously the candidates for admission. Every three years they publish a catalogue in exact imitation of the Triennial Catalogue published by the College. The degrees are given with all due solemnity to all the lions of the day. I thought it might afford you a little amusement, although it was not intended for wide circulation. Remember, it is only a private thing among the students . . .

September 1829

. . . I am settled once more at home in the midst of those miscellaneous articles which always cluster around me wherever I can do just as I please,—Blackstone and boots, law and lathe, Rawle and rasps, all intermingled in exquisite confusion. When you was here, I thought of going away to study my profession; but since Judge Story and Mr. Ashmun have come, the Law School is so flourishing that I thought it best to stay where I am. I have mislaid your last letter, and my not being able to find it has been one reason, in addition to my procrastinating disposition, why I have not written sooner. And now, young man, I have no more conception where you are, or how you are situated, than I have of the condition of the ear-tickler to his majesty the Emperor of China. I can imagine, however, that you are in some queer little outlandish Eastern town, with a meetinghouse the timbers of which bore acorns last autumn, that you live in the only painted house in the village, and that at this present time you are seated in magisterial dignity, holding the rod of empire over fourscore little vagabonds, who look up to you as the embodied essence of all earthly knowledge. I might go farther and fancy some houri of the forest welcoming you home from your daily labors with a kiss and a johnny-cake and all other sweet attentions that virgin solicitude can offer to the champion of education. Alas! I [fear] too much that, where you had fondly anticipated a blushing maiden of sixteen, you have a good-natured dowdy of forty, or an ill-natured walking polygon of fifty. You must write and tell me all about these things, if you have indeed persisted in your plan of school-keeping. As for Cambridge, nothing great has happened here, and even what seems great to us can have little interest for you. I will just tell you that the Law School has increased from one solitary individual to twenty-six . . .

January 13, 1830

. . . And now I suppose that you are brooding over your involuntary retirement, and thinking what a fine time I must have in this focus of literature and refinement. Nothing is easier than to make disadvantageous comparisons between ourselves and our neighbors. I will tell you honestly that I am sick at heart of this place and almost everything connected with it. I know not what the temple of the law may be to those who have entered it, but to me it seems very cold and cheerless about the threshold. And another thing too; I feel, what one of the most ill-begotten cubs that ever entered college when he was old enough to be a grandfather most feelingly lamented, "the want of female society." If there was a girl in the neighborhood whose blood ever rose above the freezing point, who ever dreamed of such a thing as opening her lips without having her father and her mother and all her little impish brothers and sisters for her audience,—nay if there was even a cherry-cheeked kitchen girl to romance with occasionally, it might possibly be endurable. Nothing but vinegar-faced old maids and drawing-room sentimentalists,—nothing that would do to write poetry to but the sylph of the confectioner's counter, and she—sweet little Fanny has left us to weep when we think of her departed smiles and her too fleeting icecreams. I do believe I never shall be contented till I get the undisputed mastery of a petticoat . . .

Houghton Library.

James Woodbury Boyden

EXAMINED FOR ENTRANCE

(1838)

When James Woodbury Boyden came down to Cambridge from Salem in late summer of 1838, the admission process was a far cry from this year of grace when a candidate applies to the several colleges of his or her choice and drills for months in preparation for the critical struggle for admission through a series of aptitude and "achievement" tests. Boyden came to Harvard after two years' teaching experience, and went through several long days of testing before he was adjudged fit for acceptance. After his college career, Boyden went on to Law School and later lived in Chicago.

Monday, August 27th 1838.

LAST NIGHT, I walked from Beverly to Salem, with Joseph and Charles, who carried my preparatory books. On arriving there, I went to Dr. Johnson's, who will carry me with his son [Samuel Johnson, 1842] to Cambridge for examination.

I was waked at three-o-clock by the Dr., and after drinking a cup of coffee, we all started in a carryall for Cambridge.

It was yet dark, the streets and houses were shrouded in the thick mantle of night, and all was silent and still, save the rattling of our carriage upon the stony pavements. A few stars would now and then show their dim faces in the heavens, but they were few and far between, for their light could not find a way through the clouded atmosphere.

Our course was over the Forest River road, & through Lynn;—when we reached the latter place, the sun had just risen and shone in all its splendor.

We reached Cambridge at 6¼ o'clock and carried our books to No. 13, Stoughton Hall, occupied by Edward B. Pearson [Peirson], who had kindly offered us the use of the room, during our examination. Thence we went to University Hall, were met at the door by President Quincy who took the certificates of good moral character and sent us in.

Entering a room to the right, we encountered old Dr. Ware, who took down our names and sent us to the Salem division, so called. In this room were fifty-seven young men, some standing, others sitting, in different postures—some full of dread and apprehension, half afraid to meet the eye of others, and shivering:—these are generally known as *Green-horns*. Some were full of confidence and bold,—full of self respect,—observing others,—laughing at the awkward or diffident,—all however were very orderly and quiet.

In a short time, each division was called, in order, into the two adjoining rooms, where we sat down at tables, upon which, were sheets of paper, inkstands, quills and a printed copy of some English sentences, which we were required to translate into Latin and commit to paper, sign our names & then hand it to the Tutor who occupied the "highest seat in the synagogue."

But first, each member of the several divisions gave his name—age—month in which he was born—name of his parent (father) and of the instructor who sent him, all which were duly recorded by the Tutors.

We were now dismissed till 7½-o-clock, that the Faculty and Students might take breakfast. In the meantime, Johnson and myself returned to Pearson's [Peirson's] room, where I translated the seventeenth section of the fourth book, containing the plan of Caesar's Bridge over the Rhine, into Germany.

At the appointed hour, we took our dictionaries and grammars, proceeded to our seats in University Hall, and commenced writing the translation of the English sentences into Latin.

Our division, the fifth, had been seated a few minutes only, when we were called out and directed to go to Professor Felton's room, to be examined in Greek Prosody and Syntax. I was asked two questions, viz:—what cases do verbs of admiring—despising etc. govern? Ans. the Genitive and Dative;—what cases do verbs of commanding and abounding govern; Ans. Genitive, Dative, or Accusative.

We resumed writing our translation, but shortly after were sent to Mr. Very, who examined us in the Etymology of the Greek Grammar. He asked me the formation of the first and second aorists active, and the synopsis of the verbs in -μ. At the expiration of two hours, we had finished our translations and were sent into the next room, where we were furnished with printed papers containing sentences to be translated into Greek.

Shortly after we were sent to Dr. Beck, who examined us in Latin Grammar. He asked me the several terminations of the futures in the different conjugations; together with the manner in which they are distinguished from each other. We then went down to the room and finished the Greek translation. A recess followed till eleven.

I saw Dr. Johnson, who had been looking for a room for his son:—he had found one in Divinity Hall, which he liked very much and which he engaged for Samuel. He told me that there was one more, which I had better endeavor to secure; we went down and examined the two and I thought I would like to have it, but concluded to wait till my father came up tomorrow.

At eleven, we resumed our seats, and remained till two. Our division was sent to Mr. Mason's room, where we were examined in scanning. Besides asking us some of the rules, he required us to scan several lines each in Virgil, and to give the rules.

Then (two-o-clock) we were dismissed till four.

From University Hall, I went to the Tavern, and took dinner. The table was laid tolerably well for a common tavern—among the "multa bona," were roast beef, mutton boiled into a stew—potatoes,—onions—applesauce—and other delicacies. The second table was graced by a large plumpudding, with sugar-sauce, followed by mince pies and water-melons. For this dinner, I paid fifty cents.

I then went to Peirson's room and talked over matters and things with Johnson till four.

At this hour, we adjourned to the University Hall. Here Mr. Peirce, Professor of Mathematics gave us some sums in Algebra. The first was to multiply a + b by a − b. The second was a long sum in Division. The third was to raise a + x to the 5th power by Binomials. The fourth was to solve an equation & the fifth was to find the distance between two signals etc. etc. rather difficult.

When we had finished these sums, we were sent to Mr. Wheeler to be examined in Ancient and Modern Geography. Here one or two questions were asked me; the ancient names of Scotland and Ireland which I could not answer, all the others I knew very well.

We then went to another room, where we were examined in like manner, in Arithmetic. Eight sums were given us, in vulgar fractions,—Compound Subtraction-Decimals—Double rule of Three and Compound Interest. These occupied us till six, when we were dismissed. I eat no supper, but studied a few sections in Caesar and retired at nine in Pierson's room.

Tuesday, August 28th.

The ringing of the Bell in the church opposite the College Buildings, at twenty minutes past five, waked me.

After dressing, I studied a few of the sections in the beginning of each of the last five books in Caesar.

Johnson and myself then went to a refreshment room and bought two mince pies and two ounces of lozenges, whole cost being eighteen cents, being nine cents apiece.

Thence we returned to Peirson's room, and took breakfast, eating pies & drinking good, cold water from the pumps in the yard.

At half past seven, we went to University Hall; and found on our tables a Latin extract, printed, which we were required to translate into English and commit to writing, one hour and a half being allowed us.

A half an hour afterward, our division was sent to Professor Felton's room, and examined in Greek Poetry, translating and scanning. None of us failed here, and we were all in good spirits as we descended to the lower room.

When we had finished the Latin Exercises, we were dismissed till ten & told to go to the next room, on our return at eleven. Till this hour, I was in Peirson's room, looking over a few of the Rules in Greek Grammar.

On taking our seats, we found a printed copy of an extract from some Latin Poet, which we translated into English Prose. Then we were presented with a printed page from Xenophon, and when that was written, with some Greek verse, copies of which, Greek and English, I have preserved.

We were sent to Mr. Very, who examined us in Greek Prose, our division had no difficulty, either in translation, parsing or giving the roots and themes.

We went also to Dr. Beck, and were examined in Caesar, and made no mistakes or *bulls.*

Mr. Mason examined us in Virgil, taking us up in the sixth book, seven hundred and third line. At two we were dismissed and directed to come to the University Hall door at four-o-clock whence each division would be called, in order, to the Faculty, and would receive from them certificates of admission.

Harvard Alumni Bulletin, September 24, 1949.

Thomas Hill

THERE IS NOTHING BUT MISCHIEF IN THEIR HEADS
(1839)

"My objections to Cambridge," wrote Thomas Hill, during the period when he was uncertain what college to attend, "are: its expenses are entirely beyond my means; its nearness to the sea shore I am afraid would injure my lungs . . . and its great and peculiar advantages are useless to me because my preparatory school studies have not been enough to enable me to enjoy them." Yet, Thomas Hill entered Harvard College at the age of twenty-one in 1839. His studious habits and his religious attitude made him a target for the unkind and the light-hearted members of his Class and the College; the early months of his freshman term were misery, but Hill made a mark for himself and he was regarded by Professor Benjamin Peirce as one of the ablest mathematicians to come under his tutelage. For many years a Unitarian clergyman, Hill became President of Antioch and was President of Harvard during the Civil War. The undergraduate letters to his family quoted here were written between August and December of Hill's first year in Cambridge.

HAVING become very near settled into College I thought I would begin another letter as no lessons have appointed, and thus I am at leisure. I suppose you would like to know where I am fixed. The room is on the north entry of Hollis Hall ground floor, south side west end . . . I board in Commons, where the table is very good indeed and victuals are furnished at cost. I wish they were more of them . . . It would please me better and cost them less. I suppose that many of the students however care nothing either for health or economy. There is nothing but mischief in their heads from morn till night. While I am writing some of the wise fools are amusing themselves by throwing shot into my open windows. I advised them not to waste their lead so, for it was silly to be so extravagant. They have now gone. Perhaps some of them may want the cost of the shot ere long, to buy a halter to hang themselves. I would however hope . . . better things of most of them. There is a scandalous degree of profanity and wine bibbing here, I don't care who says to the contrary. I've seen enough since I've been here to make me sick of the sight. I have a room mate from N. York city named Spear. As I have been in his company but an hour or two, I can tell you nothing of his character; but Phrenologicaly it is tolerable, rather much self conceit and obstinacy perhaps ... On looking at my floor I find that it was gravel that was thrown in my windows. This is the first time I have been troubled I hope twill be the last, for as they saw I neither moved nor raised my eyes from the paper they will think I care nothing for them and thus leave me ...

This evening at six we were called together for prayers and the freshmen had their places assigned. An old man who could hardly see even with his specs on officiated, and in a very feeling manner too. (Rev. Dr. Ware, father of H. W. Jr.) I do not know with whom I shall meet tomorrow to commemorate the love of the dying Saviour, but I trust it will be with brethren having their hearts filled with a sense of that love, and that we shall have a pleasant season together ...

I was surprised on coming here to find that furniture of every kind must be purchased by the student, and I have well nigh spent my money in buying a four years stock of furniture consisting of hair mattress and pillow, sheets pillow cases and comfortables, bedstead, chairs, table, table cover, lamp, lampfiller, oil, broom, shovel and tongs, wash stand, bowl & ewer, etc. etc. I shall have no more necessity for money till after next vacation, when the term bill is due for this term ...

The Freshman Class consists of 76 and is divided into three divisions; the first containing thirty seven or eight; the second twenty two or three, and the third sixteen. The divisions are made according to the scholarship and apparent talents of the scholars; the third division containing the best scholars and taking rather longer lessons than the second, and the second than the first. Our division recites in Livy (Latin historian) at 8, and in Herodotus (Greek historian) at 9. At two o'clock we recite in Geometry. Our lessons are pretty long and we spend a good deal of time in studying.

... One of our Tutors Robt Bartlett, has been two years in the Divinity School here, and is I believe now studying. He is a very kind man and has shown me marks of his good feelings. He says that the best condition to be in with respect to college is to be unknown & disregarded. The second best is to be hated by all hands. The worst is to be beloved and "popular." For if the whole class are hanging about you seeking assistance and counsel, or dragging you into sports & amusements, they waste your time and entirely prevent you from becoming any thing ...

... I confess I did wrong in not telling you what my trouble was, but I did not know whether it was yet over and I wanted to tell you of it altogether. Some little brats had gone into a closet and opening the window were firing out of this dark hole at the windows in Kingmans room. My own windows had just been stoned in and I thought these fellows were firing at mine too, Kingmans room adjoining mine. We went outside, found out who were firing, and told a college officer who came and scared the chaps by scolding them. This immediately gave us the character of spies and the next night, I unguardedly going to bed with the door unlocked, some ruffians came in, dragged the mattress from under me and emptied several pails of water on me. I immediately ran yelling out of doors and when I waked up I was dancing on the frosty grass in the bright moonlight, dripping with water. I ran back to my room and it was 15 or 20 minutes before I could think what was the matter. A young man lost his life in this way a few years ago, the shock and the chill bringing on a cold which soon killed him. I was half sick under it for four or five days, trembling and jumping at even the creaking of my own shoes.

In addition to this I was hissed and laughed at, had bottles thrown out of the windows at me etc. etc. Our windows were broken almost every night and at last we moved to the 3d story of Mass. Here we were in peace till last Friday night, when two or 3 more lights were broken. On Sunday night they were fired at again. On Monday night they were fired at again, and I complained of the boys to the Faculty and on Tuesday morning 2 of them were expelled. From this I suppose fresh trouble will arise, but I will be better prepared to meet it if it comes now.

I should not have been injured if most infamous lies had not been previously circulated, which had already made me hated. For instance such stories as these were circulated by two whom I had previously offended; vis that I had boasted that I was going to become the first scholar; that I had said I was about to reform the University and bring it into a state of good order; that I had thrown my door open and prayed aloud when folks were passing; and a parcel more ridiculous tales; told out of sheer malice by these two boys.

. . . In College commons the board is $2.25 a week. The boys are very unruly, yelling, throwing bread at each other, and firing boiled potatoes round the room. The board is a great part of it hot wheat flour bread and milk which makes me suffer very much from costiveness. I grew so fat living at commons that even my friends laughed at me and I was ashamed of myself . . .

. . . I am sorry you are grieved on account of my college troubles. They do not trouble me any more; I mean the past transactions do not trouble me; nor are the students making any fresh trouble with fresh insult. Mr. Stebbins passed through just such an ordeal at Amherst, and so must every one who prefers his idea of duty to a slavish compliance with wicked customs. Every year however this necessity is diminished for these customs are broken up gradually and it is hoped that in a few years this system of college honor and discipline will be put to rest with the laws of duelling and war.

Harvard University Archives.

William Tucker Washburn
A MEETING OF THE MED. FAC.
(c. 1858)

When the "Medical Faculty" was outlawed as a secret organization in 1905–06, the deeds and misdeeds of this reckless and mysterious group passed almost into oblivion. Founded in the early 1800's, the Med. Fac. was originally a society dedicated to relatively harmless undergraduate pranks, but it had many imitators and, when the hazing of freshmen became an accepted practice, some of the evening fun grew very rough indeed. We may assume the following description is a not-too-exaggerated account of the College in its adolescence. The scene is Harvard in the 1850's. The time is late in an autumn evening just after the freshman, Wentworth Saulsbury, hero of Fair Harvard, has left his friends in No. 1 Holworthy to return to his own lodgings. The author of this "story of American college life," William Tucker Washburn (1841–1916) of the Class of 1862, was a successful New York lawyer who published four novels and two volumes of poems in a busy lifetime. He has the distinction of having written the first Harvard novel. That he did not take his achievement too seriously is indicated in the preface where he remarks that, despite the adverse opinions of friends, "the author feels it to be a crime to keep his work longer from the Public."

"THAT'S THE FELLOW," whispered some one as Wentworth turned into Linden Street, and at the words, four men in masks sprang out upon him, from the doorway of the corner house. Saulsbury was no coward, but the darkness and the surprise for a moment unnerved him. He, however, struck one fair blow at the man just in front of him. The man stooped, the blow passed over his head, and the next moment Wentworth was seized around the waist, and thrown; two hands grasped his throat; his own were tied behind his back, his eyes bandaged, and his mouth gagged. Our hero exerted all his strength in a desperate struggle to gain his feet.

"How the child wriggles," muttered one of the masks, and gave Wentworth a blow with the flat of his hand, which made him writhe in a frenzy of rage.

"Lift him," now whispered one of the men, and Wentworth was placed in a vehicle which drove rapidly off.

He lay still, though burning with anger. "I'd give my life," he thought "for one blow at that coward who struck me." They drove rapidly for several minutes, until at length the carriage stopped, and Wentworth was taken out, turned round half a dozen times, and led up a flight of stairs into a room.

"Mr. President, we have brought you the culprit," said one of the men who held Saulsbury.

"Remove the band," commanded a voice resembling the angry mew of a cat. The band was removed and our hero glanced around him not without a feeling of terror. The walls of the room in which he found himself were painted with revolting figures, representing the growth of Disease. In the rear a table was placed, on the centre of which rested a large Bible presented to Harvard by the pious youth of Yale College in expectation of a similar gift in return. Behind the Bible stood a box of medical instruments with a letter from the Emperor Nicholas. The front of the table discovered bunches of skeleton keys; a few delicate Freshman moustaches, with the names of their former possessors; rich folds of hairs marked, "the wig of Tutor Jones, captured Oct. 3rd, 185–;" and a billet with cords twisted around its handle.

The Bible itself sustained a punch bowl of singular shape, adorned with the motto, "Satano duce, nil desperandum," and two huge clubs, rough with letters and figures. The words "Hell Fire Club" on the larger of these would have recalled to the antiquary the deeds of iniquity by which that society had justified its name. Carved upon this sole memorial of a famous brotherhood were the initials of men distinguished in the law and ministry, who in their youth had furnished employment to the professions which in their advanced years had supported them. On the smaller club was the mysterious name, "Thundering Bolus." This weapon, in former times swung by the arm of the bravest Senior in the College, for many years struck dismay into the hearts of hostile villagers, trusting in their numbers.

Little desire, however, had our hero to examine these or the other objects of interest which the chamber held. His eyes were fastened on the scene before him. Directly in front of him sat a hideous monster, with horns projecting from his forehead, and his dress ablaze with flames. Next the Devil to the right, was a creature whose features were nearly eaten off by a cancer, while on the left leered a withered hag. Flanking these three stood a dozen wretches, each incarnating some malady.

Between Wentworth and the "Leeches and Doctors," for such was the title these horrors wore on their breasts, was a table covered with a sheet, on one end of which stood a small brazier with scalpels, pincers, and other instruments around it. Above, at the centre of the wall, before Wentworth, was hung a strip of black cloth, on which were written in scarlet six letters. The sight of these at once riveted our hero's eyes, drove a cold iron rod down his spine, and made him tremble with fear. These six letters were M E D. F A C.

"Remove the gag," ordered the Devil, and Wentworth's tongue was set free.

"Where's that d—— coward who struck me?" he exclaimed. "I dare——"

"Burn the profane fellow! dissolve him, flay him, dissect him," and other suggestions interrupted his words.

"Gag the rebel!" screeched the Devil. "Delilah!" he added, "chasten the lawlessness of this young Samson."

At this, Wentworth was forced upon the table and the hag shuffled up to him, and slowly pulled from his head twenty-seven hairs and burnt them in the brazier.

"Remember," the Devil warned him, as the gag was again removed and Wentworth set on his feet, "that you are in the august presence of the Medical Faculty of Harvard University. You are charged," he continued solemnly, "with having spoken lightly of the godly society of the 'Med. Fac.' Is the accusation true?"

"I think you have done a great many mean acts," muttered Wentworth, losing all prudence in his anger.

"He blasphemes against the Med. Fac.!" shrieked a dozen voices, mingled with groans.

"Brother Plummer," commenced the Devil, "read the punishment decreed against one who offends against the majesty of the Med. Fac."

"Whoever," began a deep voice behind our hero, "shall speak evil against the Medical Faculty of Harvard University shall receive the punishment of air, fire, water, and earth, and the purification of assafœtida and brimstone." "Such are the words of holy writ," added the Devil. "Your own good compels us to punish you, with whatever pain to ourselves. Let the law be executed," he concluded, and waved his sceptre, at which sign each monster removed a leg or arm and brandished it over his head.

Wentworth was then blindfolded, led into the open air and placed in a blanket. Were we writing a romance, we should not allow our hero to be tossed in a blanket, but the spirit of truth, which rules all histories, compels us to set down the evil with the good.

"Are you ready?" cried one of the men, holding the blanket. "Now all together—one, two, three, toss!" and at the word our hero winged his way heavenward with such aid as ten stalwart devils could lend him.

Wentworth was now nearly exhausted with excitement and fatigue, yet he nerved himself to endure without flinching. Suddenly a device occurred to him. As he was descending from his third flight, feeling like Vulcan landing upon Lemnos he extended both his feet to the utmost. "Heavens!" cried one of his tormentors, "my head's broken," and Wentworth had the pleasure of feeling his heel strike a hard skull; this was, however, lessened at the same moment, by his falling heavily upon the ground.

"Let the punishment of fire be now inflicted," commanded the Devil, after Wentworth had been led back to his room. At this two bands, the ends of which were attached to hooks in the ceiling, were placed one round Wentworth's feet and the other round his chest. Again the boy broke out in execrations.

"Hush," whispered in his ear the voice of some one half relenting, "or they'll gag you," and with a sullen look of rage, Wentworth repressed his words.

The "Leeches and Doctors" then placed the brazier beneath him; some fluid was poured into it and lighted, and our hero swung to and fro over it several times, and then taken down.

"Let the punishment of water be inflicted," commanded the Devil. At this, Wentworth was placed in a coffin, and borne from the room. Soon he heard a noise as of the turning of a windlass, and felt himself sinking lower and lower. "What if the rope should break!" he thought, and derived little pleasure from the reflection. Suddenly the bottom of the coffin struck water, and Wentworth heard the men talking above him. "Pull him up!" "pull him up!" "No, bless him; give him a dowse; he nearly broke my head!" and the coffin sunk still lower. The water pours through the cracks: it covers the boy's ankle: it rises to his knee: the air grows dense: the water has reached his waist: his head seems bursting: his eyes start from their sockets; and with a cry of despair, he loses all remembrance.

"You oughtn't to have let him down so far." "Confound the fellow! Why doesn't he come to?" are the first words Wentworth hears on returning to consciousness, and at the same moment water is dashed in his face, and he feels some one chafing his hands.

The boy opens his eyes and looks languidly around him. "Where am I?" he asks, and shudders at the masks and figures.

"We've punished him enough." "There's game in the fellow." "We'll drive him home." Wentworth heard the men whisper to each other. A glass of brandy was then given him, his eyes were again bandaged, and he was placed in a carriage. After a drive of some minutes he was taken from the carriage and set upon the ground. He pulled off his bandage, and found himself by the familiar gate of Danforth's. Through this he passed, and groped his way to his room, where he was soon buried in sleep, not without strange dreams.

Fair Harvard: A Story of American College Life (New York, 1869).

Robert Nathan

PETER KINDRED'S FIRST DAYS

(1919)

Robert Nathan followed the steps of his Peter Kindred from Phillips Exeter Academy to Harvard, and Peter Kindred *became the first of his more than a score of books. In this early novel can be seen some of the characteristics of Nathan's later writing. An illusive, transitory thread slips through much of his work—a sense of place but not time. Whether his setting is Central Park or Truro near the "Cape end"—"There the old house, much loved, and cosily panelled, stands on its hill between the elms and the pine trees"—the poetry is there, and the fantasy, which have made Nathan one of the most appealing writers in contemporary American letters. Among his books are* One More Spring, Portrait of Jennie, Journey of Tapiola, But Gently Day, *and* Long After Summer.

IT SEEMED that Harvard had expected their coming, and when Peter registered, which he found to be a simple enough matter, no one told him that he had no right to do so, but a weary and patient man handed him a large pink card, and sent him in search of his faculty advisor. He was struck by the great number of such pink cards moving aimlessly about. Upper classmen carried different colors, and moved about more purposefully, much as the second year men had done at Exeter. Peter made his way to Warren House, and waited on his advisor, watching the small group of men about him curiously. There was an unkempt lad from some northern village, powerful, and mother fearing. There was a lean and wan-looking elderly man who clutched a couple of shabby books close to his coat, and asked questions of Peter humbly. There was a keen-faced youth in tweeds, who wore tremendous rimmed glasses which gave him an affable and owllike appearance, and an aristocratic-looking fellow with a delicately chiselled face, who carried himself delightfully, his shoulders back and his chin high, and whom the professor seemed very glad to see again. Peter thought he was very fine, and wondered who he was; he wished that he himself made so splendid an appearance, or that David did.

Men whose lives are given to the contemplation of letters and sciences, who do not spend their days bickering in the market place, but whose dens are chosen from among the choicest rooms in the house, dens that remain strewn and inviolate for years, attain a quiet and complacent dignity which creates a deeper impression upon the perplexed youth of our land than all the doughtiest and most profound lectures ever given. There is something about a serene and vigorous old age which constitutes a fairer promise of heaven than all the creeds and tenets of belief.

Peter's advisor was such a man, a stalwart and patriarchal figure, unhurried and resolute. Peter felt that he must know a vast deal, as indeed he did, but Peter did not give sufficient credit to the holy quiet of the man's den, and to the rows upon rows of friendly books between the ceiling and the floor. But, mind you, I would not advocate a den of that sort for any common man; he would do nothing in it at all.

For all his learning, the professor proved to be amazingly ignorant of the courses Peter had chosen to attend, and since there was therefore nothing to say one way or another about them, he signed Peter's card and dismissed him. Peter passed the Union with a warming sense of belonging finally to Harvard, and walked slowly down Massachusetts Avenue toward Harvard Square.

The street, with its small, well-appointed shops, hummed with the coming and going of students. They passed in groups or singly, alert, cheery, well-groomed men; and all with the same satisfied look on their faces. For a college is no more than an attitude toward life, and the kindly gentlemen of Oxford are as far removed from the contented moralists of Harvard, as the latter differ from the wistful youths of Yale, and the happy children of Princeton.

To Peter there was the same romance in the name Harvard as there had been in Exeter, and he was mightily beguiled by the small but venerable Yard and the enchanted flavor of the halls, which, like old men before a fireside, seemed in their silence to be forever considering themselves.

At Holyoke Street he turned down toward Mount Auburn and climbed the creaking steps of No. 26. He had chosen a room in a ramshackle frame house at the edge of the gold coast, opposite the yellow walls of the Institute.

Below his windows the men passed down the street, through the gate, and into the Institute. Peter watched them with a deal of wonder and a stir of envy at first. For the Institute is the solid basis of Harvard clubdom. It goes through Harvard with a coarse comb, separating the wheat from the chaff; all men who are socially possible are Institute men. Among these the exclusive clubs move with finer combs in varying degrees, but, on the whole, a man at Harvard is an Institute man, or he is not.

Peter's room was two dilapidated flights up, but he found, to his surprise, that such a place was considered very fine at Harvard, much more desirable, indeed, than the new brick houses far removed from the coast, or the dormitories in the Yard. But that was characteristic of Harvard, to put up splendid draperies in a tumbled down room, and glory in the result. Peter had no splendid draperies, but David envied him his room and his two sunny windows facing the south. David had chosen a modern brick building not far from the Square, where he had his own bath to delight him, but no sun at all. He had installed a grand piano, and was making a desk of a soap box.

Peter's room, at first in its barrenness, had depressed that gentleman almost to despair, but as he began to unpack his furniture, he saw some possibility in it, and when at last his rug was down, he haled David over to view it. David was impressed, but left at once for his soap box and some intricate figuring he had been doing, whereby he hoped to discover some way of also buying a bed.

Peter's desk chair had not come, and to ask advice, he tapped on his neighbor's door. A voice roared for the son-of-a-gun to come in, and he stepped into a scene of such boundless confusion that he could do nothing but stare. At first glance it looked as though some truckman had moved the belongings of one room into another, and had dumped them all pell mell on top of each other. Clothes and books competed with sofa cushions and pictures for the seats of chairs, and overflowed onto the floor. Where there were no books, there were shoes, and occasional beer mugs. In the midst of this chaos stood a dark-browed, rugged man, puffing at a long calabash pipe.

"Oh," he said, "come right in. Excuse me. I thought you were a friend of mine." He swept the vista of the room with his arm. "Find a place to sit down, and make yourself at home. I'm not usually so upset, but our amiable goody forgot me to-day."

He sat down himself and regarded Peter curiously. Before him, Peter was shy and confused; he explained the reason for his visit, and asked him if he could suggest anything to do about the chair. The dark-browed man regarded the ceiling somberly, puffed at his pipe, and shook his head, but suggested at last that the chair would probably turn up some day, and that a desk chair was a small matter at best, and that if Peter needed one, he could let him have several to choose from. Peter thanked him, and somewhat encouraged, asked him how one might unearth the bursar and pay him the fabled ninety dollars. The man directed him to Dana [Dane] Hall, and Peter asked him how he would know what to do when he got there.

"Trust to the Lord," said the big man, and lost himself in reverie. Peter stammered a thanks, and returned to the tidy primness of his own room. The advice, for all its absurdity, was soothing and Peter's troubles fell away. He no longer felt responsible for his affair with the bursar.

That night both he and David went to the freshman reception at Brooks House, hoping for much, but doubting that anything would befall them. They were given little tags on which they wrote their names. These they tied diffidently in their buttonholes, where they dangled unnoticed for the rest of the evening. With a vast mob of shoving and perspiring men they were herded into a large room where they sat on the floor at first, but later stood in a vain effort to hear some part of the speeches. On a low platform tall heroes appeared, bowed, were tremendously applauded, spoke, waved their arms, grinned, bowed, and sat down in the din. Mr. Molmf presented Mr. Smith of the Grmmpump, who in turn presented Mr. Xmymst. Tommy

Reilly, captain of the eleven, rose and received an ovation. Amid a dead silence, he started in.

"Well, fellows," he said. The applause was interminable. Through it he went on.

"Well, fellows, Percy Haughton here thinks we've got a pretty good team here this year, and I guess Yale will think so all right." Cheers, shrieks, whistles, and the prolonged stamping of feet. "Well, fellows, all I want to say is I want you fellows to stand back of the team and give us the right support and get some good, snappy cheering over this year when we go down to New Haven, and I guess we can leave the rest to Percy Haughton here." He bowed awkwardly and sat down, amid a bedlam. Peter and David fought their way to the door and emerged disheveled.

They walked back through the Yard together across the Autumn moonlight, under the looming, black shadows of the dormitories. Beyond the wall, a car jarred distantly around the curve of the street, and died away toward Boston. Occasional low voices reached them, and the twang of a mandolin. The sky was calm and luminous with stars, the light breeze redolent of earth. But Peter and David could find no words to gauge their thoughts, wherefore they left each other without discussing the event.

Again the greater freedom of the college aroused in Peter a sense of transformation, of gathering manhood, and for a while he, too, walked with his shoulders thrown back and his chin held high. Then lectures began, and he forgot everything in the rush to buy books, and the trouble of their expense. In the large classes he sat unnoticed, scribbling notes, and hearing for the first time new principles in unexplored fields of thought discussed and expounded. To each he reacted with a faint shock of appreciation, believing everything, his imagination powerfully exercised. David came with the same enthusiasm from his classes, and their discussions grew top heavy with the weight of their learning until they made no headway at all.

Peter Kindred (New York, 1919).

Burriss Young

SAGE WARNINGS TO FRESHMEN

(1980)

In the seventeenth century student rules were unilaterally imposed by administrative diktat (see pages 157–159). Three centuries later they come couched as an appeal to common sense, persuasively and lightheartedly. The author of the following injunctions (reminiscent of the elegant admonitions of Master Elliott Perkins of Lowell House) is Associate Freshman Dean

Burriss Young, who has been since 1963 a teacher, advisor, and mentor to freshmen. Aside from being expressed in "exemplary prose" as Primus IV of Harvard Magazine *has remarked, they "also provide a glimpse of the seamy underside of freshman life at Harvard ca. 1979–80."*

DID THE DISH RUN AWAY WITH THE SPOON???

Between September 8 and October 12, $1,185.12 worth of dishes and silverware disappeared from the Union. Twelve dozen soup bowls at $9.22 a dozen, fifty-nine dozen plastic cups at $10.01 a dozen, thirty-two dozen knives at $3.80 a dozen, forty-two dozen teaspoons at $1.45 a dozen, plus much more equaled a loss of $33.86 a day.

These things did not stray. They were carried off, most likely for use in student rooms. If you have any dining hall property, please return it to the Union. By helping Food Services save $33.86 a day, you may save yourself from countless servings of economical meatless meatloaf.

SNOW

In spite of evidence to the contrary, the Yard is often the setting for snowball fights. The only one this year was very costly in terms of broken windows. In case it snows again and the urge to throw snow comes on you, observe two rules. Do not throw snowballs at buildings. Do not throw snowballs where passing citizens might be hit. Some say that snow is a good thing. Injuries and broken windows are not goods things, so be careful and use common sense with your snow.

FOOD FIGHTS

In recent weeks there have been several "food fights" in the Union. There is a certain irony that a group that signs up for a symbolic fast against hunger should also indulge itself in symbolic tribute to our national proclivity to waste. Less speculative is the mess that food fights cause. This has to be cleaned up by the Union help who were not hired to be extras in a freshman aping of *Animal House.* So cut it out.

CLEAN ENOUGH?

Each week several bursar's cards turn up in the dishwashing machine in the Union. They are not particularly soiled. The reason they are there is that their owners showed them to the checker and then put them on their trays. The trays and dirty dishes, even the forgotten cards, are put on the conveyor and go together into the machine. Save yourself a lot of bother and don't put your card on your tray.

HE QUICKLY TURNED——

At about five on Sunday afternoon a student returned to her room on the third floor of a Yard dorm. Her roommates were not at home and there were very few other students in the building. A man she had never seen before came out of the bathroom. She asked him if he was visiting someone in the suite. He said no and asked if he was frightening her. He then quickly turned and left the room, taking his coat from a coat rack and a roommate's tape recorder from a desk top. The student then called the University Police, who report that the entry door was unbolted and that the suite door was unlocked. This student was lucky.

DON'T HELP STOCK THE PAWN SHOPS

Every day we get reports in the FDO of thefts of watches, cameras, calculators, jewelry, etc., stolen from student rooms. In the majority of cases these items were stolen from unlocked rooms or rooms in unlocked entries. One freshman woke up to hear a thief say, "We finally got something worth taking." It was his watch. Don't give such satisfaction to thieves. Lock your door and don't mess with the outside-door locking system. Challenge strangers and report suspicious ones to the University Police, 495-1212.

FIRE

Energy conservation is, of itself, not a very romantic thing. It can lead to the use of candles instead of harsh electric lights. This is a romantic thing, but a very dangerous thing. Candles have been responsible for a great many dormitory fires. The use of candles is prohibited in dormitory rooms or hallways. Don't let romance turn you to ashes.

FIRE ALARMS

Two weeks ago, there was a smoky fire in the basement of the Union. The alarms went off and several hundred freshmen went on eating their breakfast. Although this may be seen as a tribute to the Union kitchen, it is certainly an ill-advised one. Had the fire spread quickly there might not have been time for you to get out of the building. Fire alarms are set off to warn of real danger. When you hear one go off, get outside. It is better to eat cold toast than to be toasted.

FIRE-ESCAPE SAFETY

On Saturday evening one of your classmates fell through the fire escape of her dorm, landing on an air-conditioning unit two floors below. As of this writing she is still hospitalized. Freshmen have fallen through and off of fire escapes in the past, and their injuries have ranged from cuts and bruises to serious lacerations and broken bones. They have all been very lucky. The odds against luck are rapidly mounting. Stay off the fire escapes unless you must use one to escape a fire. Don't be the one that luck fails.

WHAT HAS FOUR LEGS AND APPARENTLY WALKS?

About forty director's chairs, colored canvas backs and seats with blond birch frames, have disappeared from the Expos. Office on the third floor of the Union. If you see one around your room, please help it back to the Union, where it belongs. Use cover of darkness if you wish.

Harvard Magazine, May-June 1980.

V

SPORTS AND SPORTING TYPES

The passage of horse-cars to and from Boston, nearly, if not quite, a hundred times a day, has rendered it practically impossible for the Government of the College to prevent our young men from being exposed to all the temptations of the city.

THOMAS HILL (1864)

I was talking with Schuman the other day concerning Harvard when he made the remark that the whole damned institution ought to be wiped out. I can hardly agree with him, although I think myself that it is the root of a world of unlicensed deviltry; but for that matter, who can name a place of any considerable size that is not? The matter seems to me something like this: the college is there with its corps of instructors, and the student has his choice as to improving the opportunities placed before him or not. If a fellow goes there and spends all his time raising the devil, it does not seem exactly a fair thing to lay the whole burden of blame upon the college.

EDWIN ARLINGTON ROBINSON (1891)

After the severe intellectual labors of the day it is a not infrequent custom of the ingenuous youth of Harvard to refresh the weary mind with convivial ale, the social oyster, jolly songs, and conversation upon topics of less profundity than those that usually occupy the thoughts of young truthseekers.

FAIR HARVARD (1869)

Jacob Rhett Motte

A SOUTHERN SPORT AT HARVARD

(1831)

*A delightfully complete record of the thoughts and emotions of a lively
young southerner is contained in the diary of Jacob Rhett Motte of Charleston, South Carolina, who spent the Cambridge summer of 1831 alternately
velocipeding and drinking soda water. Motte's comments are perhaps the
best of the many journals preserved in the Harvard archives. Motte followed
his Harvard course with study at the Medical College in South Carolina,
served ten years in the Army Medical Corps (including the Seminole War),
practiced medicine in Charleston, and died shortly after the close of the Civil
War.*

16th August. Tuesday. [1831]

GOT UP earlier than usual this morning—before breakfast bought
two dozen crackers and some hot rolls, which, with a pound of
fresh butter, were no insignificant additions to my larder;—while
enjoying this delectable breakfast, a knock is heard at the door;
the usual open sesame being given, in stalk Crafts and Gray, come by appointment to attend a furniture auction, at Mrs. Mellen's, in Cambridge.
Saw nothing there worthy of a bid—some old bottles, of all shapes and sizes,
and some old books, valuable only as antiquities. There was one very comfortable old-fashioned easy-chair, which I felt very much disposed to buy.
We left them at it about 5 o'clock to go and take a bathe, after which I went
for my velocipede, agreeing to meet the two fellows at the post-office; my
velocipede I found painted a neat light blue; but not so light was the price.
On my way to the post-office met brother, who had been waiting at my
room for me an hour. He came out for a dagger I had in my possession, he
being determined to walk the next day to Yarmouth, and therefore wished
some defence. After drinking a glass of soda water, which he *admired* (yan-
keeism), we started for Boston, I on my horse.—Of course, I got to the

bridge long before him, and amused myself by racing with the horses I met there until he came up.—Invited me to go on and drink tea at Mr. Loring's.—I called at Mrs. Wolcott's, where Crafts and Gray staid.—Was threatened by a man, whom I frightened, by running on his heel, with a fine for riding on the side-walk—disregarded him.—Went to Mr. L. where I found a Miss Sullivan, in whose company I took a hot cup of tea to cool me, philosophically.—After tea, gratified this lady by exhibiting my rosinante to her.—expressed great satisfaction at my condescension and benignity.—In riding back to Cambridge, through a back street in Boston—Pleasant street—anything but pleasant to me at this time—was in rather an unpleasant predicament. A mob of boys attracted by my strange horse, soon collected around me, and if a rolling stone gathers no moss, I can test, that a rolling velocipede will certainly gather more spectators than is agreeable to a modest rider. On I went, and on went the mob, shouting and hollowing, until I could bear it no longer, but stopt,—they stopt too; I hollowed at them; they hollowed in return at me, when I found that safety lay in flight, and on reaching the wooden side-walk by the Common, on I flew leaving my persecutors some distance in the rear. When I got to Beacon street, I found myself alone, much to my heart's content; and never shall I be found in such a situation again, if I can help it. I reached Cambridge in about an hour, having stopt some time to converse with a sociably disposed chap, whom I fell in with in Port. He wished to appear a great connoisseur in velocipedes, having been on one for about 5 seconds once; he said he once had some intention of making one for himself, having frequently to go on errands to the Point, but he gave up the idea after a while. He must be a cute chap, and deserves to have a leather medal awarded to him, for his judicious scheme; however, he was a well spoken fellow, and quite the reverse of the Boston chaps, and deserves a medal for his civility if nothing else; at least I would have given him one at the time.

17th August. Wednesday.

That I might recover from the fatigues of my last night's violent exercise, slept until 9 o'clock—debated within myself whether to go to Boston or not—came to the determination about 11 to go—shaved—dressed, and started for Boston—got there at 12 o'clock—called for Crafts and Gray—went to 24 Collonade Row, where an auction of Mr. Price's furniture was held—bought nothing, but put on a connoisseur-like look, and tried all the wines that were sold. Went to my brother's house—not a living thing visible—house all shut up—got in by means of my key—attempted to make a dinner on a half loaf of mouldy bread which I found and some butter, which, by long soaking in water, and proximity to some antiquated lobster, was not the sweetest I ever tasted. I was wrong when I said not a living thing was visible, for a piece of cheese, which I found, was nothing but life—I carefully left it to its merry gambols. After sitting an hour to digest my dinner, I directed my course to the Athenaeum gallery of pictures . . . Saw little company there, but many pictures, a few of last year's exhibition,—not a very splendid collection, notwithstanding the premiums offered. The portrait of my father, which he mentioned in his letter as having sent on, not there—I suppose not arrived. Returned to my brother's house, intending to sleep there; on my way, bought a loaf of rye bread, and a muskmelon, for my supper.—Was taken for a robber in the house by Mr. Richardson and Francis Alger; they having entered the house to shut a window, which I had opened, not knowing me to be there, heard me moving upstairs, which they supposed to be made by a thief, who had broken in; immediately retreating, Mr. Richardson ran for help, while Francis remained outside the house to watch; he saw me at a window, and hailed, I answered, and the whole stood disclosed; Mr. R. brought two stout men to catch the thief, but was disappointed, I know not whether agreeably or not, finding it was *only* unconscious me. One good consequence followed from this affair,—I got a light, by means of which I amused myself with a book—Mrs. Manley's novels—until near 12 o'clock; whereas, before, I was preparing to go to bed at 9 o'clock.

18th August. Thursday.

Rose at 7—read a little—breakfasted on bread and butter, and muskmelon—in the midst of my breakfast, startled by a knock at the door—an invitation for brother to the English school examination, and afterwards to dinner. Having finished my breakfast, started to my appointment, at the Julian Hall; auction of New England society held there today. Saw one or two things I was much in want of, such as a table and a desk, or a gentleman's writing table; but the one thing needful was also wanting. Gray bought a bed and washstand; the former half moss half hair, for $3; the latter for $1.25. Saw J. Sargent.—Went home to dinner, on the remains of my breakfast. In the afternoon read. Walked out to Cambridge, through the Common, where the Portland Rifle Corps were encamped. They presented a strange appearance on guard with pikes.—A warm walk to Cambridge.

19th August. Friday.

The heat being very oppressive to-day, instead of going to Boston as I intended, remained at my room.—Succeeded admirably in amusing myself with John Shipp's memoirs, and cooling myself with soda water.—I ought certainly to be in a perfect state of health, if abstinence and exercise conduce to it; my diet is that of Byron, crackers and soda water; my exercise riding on the velocipede in the evening . . .

20th August. Saturday.

Still too warm to walk to Boston;—feel more like lying on the sofa with a novel, than trudging through the abominable Cambridge Port, that abomination of all that is sweet-scented. Read John Shipp the whole morning—dined on herrings and crackers, with a dessert of crackers and honey. After dinner, and after bathing read, and after reading rode, and after riding supped, and after supping rode again. This afternoon tried the road to West Cambridge on my velocipede; find it very hard, and accommodating to my horse, but not quite long enough in its accommodations. Attract quite as much attention as a modest man may desire, ladies stopping to look at me, and furl up their pretty mouths in still prettier smiles. Read after my return until near 1 o'clock, then to bed.

Arthur H. Cole, ed., *Charleston Goes to Harvard, The Diary of a Harvard Student of 1831* (Cambridge, 1940).

Charles W. Eliot

WHAT A DAY FOR OUR RACE!
(1858)

President Eliot, a graduate of 1853, was Assistant Professor of Mathematics and Chemistry at Harvard and found recreation in rowing on the Charles. To use the president's own words: "In the season of 1857 the Harvard eight-oared crew had been very badly defeated by a crew organized by the Union Boat Club of Boston; and the undergraduates were so much discouraged as to Harvard's prospects in rowing that it turned out to be impossible to get together even a six-oared crew for the season of 1858. I had graduated in 1853 and Mr. Agassiz in 1855. Thus it came about that I rowed in two regattas on the Charles River Basin ... The crew ordered from St. John builders a new boat, which was the first shellboat to appear on the Charles. It was short and broad compared with the shells of today, but it was much lighter in construction and much more ticklish than Harvard crews had been accustomed to. It had long outriggers, but no sliding seats and no coxswain. The bow oar used the rudder by means of a yoke which was close to his feet. In both these races the Harvard crew carried off the first prize, a purse of money ..."

It was during the season of 1858 that crimson first was used as a Harvard color. President Eliot's account of the race is from two letters written to his fiancée, Ellen Peabody.

June 19 [1858]

VERY DEAR ELLEN,—... What a day for our race! just perfect—clear and bright, not hot, no wind. If it is like this at 6 oclk tonight, those Irishmen will have to pull about as hard as they conveniently can in order to beat the Harvard. Crowninshield is going to row stroke, so I get my old oar—No. 3—which I like better than any other. Everybody, as far as I have heard, thinks that the Harvard is to be beaten, and it certainly is very possible that she may be, but unless we meet with some accident, we shall make better time round the course than any American or Irish crew has ever made before, so that we shan't disgrace ourselves if we are beaten. I had rather win than not, but it is mighty little matter whether we beat or are beaten—rowing is not my profession, neither is it my love,—it is only recreation, fun, and health. I am going to remember your injunctions, and take the best possible care of myself, and row just as hard as I comfortably can, and not a bit harder. I have been rowing so much within three days that my fingers feel as stiff as any hodcarrier's,—hence certain eccentricities and irregularities in the form of my letters. I shall miss you this afternoon, *if* we win,—I had rather see you up in one of those windows, than see all the thousands of people that I suppose will be there. What do I care for them, and what don't I care for you! And I shall miss you tomorrow too—Sunday won't be Sunday without you. What a grind it was, bidding you good-bye in those cars, and letting you go off alone—I hope I shan't have to do that many times in our lives for I didn't relish it a bit—quite the contrary. Now I must stop, and when I go on that race will have been settled one way or the other.

Sunday morning 8½ *oclk.*

Hurra! Hurra!! Hurra!!! We've beaten the entire crowd tremendously— and made the quickest time ever made round the course. 19 min. 22 sec. was our time; 21 min. 20 the time of the next boat; we therefore beat by 1 m. 58 s. which is a very large difference. Ellen, it was perfectly splendid—we had the sympathy of the entire crowd, and what a crowd it was! The moment we appeared, the people began to clap and hurrah—we looked "flash," I tell you—and rowed mighty prettily up by the houses and back to our place which was on the outside, next the Judges boat. Then we saw the men we were to row against—great stout Irishmen, with awful muscles—as Crowninshield said, his heart was right in his mouth—in a moment Shimmin said "ready" and the pistol was fired. At the first stroke, Crowninshield bent his rowlock, we were too nervous, the boat rocked and we did not get ahead of all the boats as we hoped to. I saw two green boats shooting ahead of us, and felt decidedly scared. The girls [his sisters] were up at Dr. Hooper's, they saw that we were not ahead, and thought it was all up with us. If you had been there you would have been frightened. But in a moment we got steady, and pulled with a will, and the boat slipped along like a beauty,—we began to gain. How nice I felt! we left all the Irish boats but two in the first half mile, those two kept up, one nearly even with us, the other a little behind. At the end of the first mile we were rowing first, and we saw that we had the best chance of winning. The larboard side was a little too strong for the starboard (here Cooke came in to congratulate me, so I had to stop writing, and walk into town, to hear Mr. Huntington preach at the King's Chapel, and to go to church with my family for the last time in our old pew) so that I did not have to work as hard as I could by any means, and had time to see that we were ahead and likely to come first to the turning stake. Just as we had completely turned and started on the return, the next boat came so near us that her bow nearly hit our stern; but that boat had only half turned and we had wholly turned and we stretched away from them before they could turn around, making a long gap between the two boats. In the next half mile the Irish boat next behind us began to pull up; Crowninshield saw it, and said "Come, fellows, she [is] gaining! Give way!" so we all put in together, and left that green boat behind, just like walking by a post, as Agassiz expressed it. Oh, wasn't it jolly! The boys say that Eliot was excited, and I know I felt mighty pleasant, not an idea of being tired. Goodwin heard a Sophomore giving an account of the matter on the steps of Hollis, and said Sophomore stated that "Eliot got tremendously excited," called Caspar Crowninshield, "Cas," and told him to "go it, my boy"; all of which is true in the main, I believe. In the last half mile the people shouted and clapped, and cheered tremendously, which was a very nice thing to hear, and made us pull all the harder and better—we came in in beautiful style, ever so far ahead of the next boat. What an ovation we had—the paddies behaved beautifully,—shook hands and owned up handsomely— Everybody seemed to be in a state of ecstasy; the Cambridge boys did not think that we should beat, so they were doubly glad, and made a great row about it in Boston, and afterwards at Cambridge.

Profs. Peirce, Agassiz, and Huntington were all in Boston to see the race, and came out to Cambridge in a state of exaltation. Huntington cheered and shouted to such an extent that he was as hoarse as a crow today.

There were many other circumstances which you would like to hear about, but I must take this letter to the post-office in five minutes or it will not reach you on Monday, as I hope it may, and if I say anything more about that race, I shan't have time to tell you how dearly I love you, how much more I should have enjoyed our victory, if you had been there to see, or how much I long to hear something from you. Tell me how you do, what you are enjoying and when you are coming home to

Your affectionate   CHARLES W. E.

I have got lots more to say and shall write again very soon.

Henry James, *Charles W. Eliot* (Boston and New York, 1930).

Owen Wister

THE SEARCH FOR THE BIRD-IN-HAND

(1903)

If Harvard's good name had been threatened by the revelations of Flandrau's Harvard Episodes, *it was rescued from peril by the publication of a gay little volume,* Philosophy 4. *This tale recounted the adventures of Billy and Bertie, two of Harvard's gilded youth, who hired as a tutor a fellow student named Oscar and then proceeded to prove to the satisfaction of many that the best of a gentleman's education does not lie in books. To modern ears this has a jarring sound, but the story has long been one of the most popular in Harvard literature. To print only the latter half of this tale seems a little like coming in at the end of the picture, but we cannot have it all. The author, Owen Wister (1860–1938), was a member of the Class of 1882 at Harvard, a graduate of the Law School (1888), and an Overseer. Although he is best known for his novel* The Virginian *(1902), he also wrote* Red Men and White, Members of the Family, A Straight Deal, The Pentecost of Calamity, *and* Indispensable Information for Infants.

BILLY got up early. As he plunged into his cold bath he envied his roommate, who could remain at rest indefinitely, while his own hard lot was hurrying him to prayers and breakfast and Oscar's inexorable notes. He sighed once more as he looked at the beauty of the new morning and felt its air upon his cheeks. He and Bertie belonged to the same club-table, and they met there mournfully over the oatmeal. This very hour to-morrow would see them eating their last before the examination in Philosophy 4. And nothing pleasant was going to happen between,—nothing that they could dwell upon with the slightest satisfaction. Nor had their sleep entirely refreshed them. Their eyes were not quite right, and their hair, though it was brushed, showed fatigue of the nerves in a certain inclination to limpness and disorder.

> Epicharmos of Kos
> Was covered with moss,

remarked Billy.

> Thales and Zeno
> Were duffers at keno,

added Bertie.

In the hours of trial they would often express their education thus.

"Philosophers I have met," murmured Billy, with scorn. And they ate silently for some time.

"There's one thing that's valuable," said Bertie next. "When they spring those tricks on you about the flying arrow not moving, and all the rest, and prove it all right by logic, you learn what pure logic amounts to when it cuts loose from common sense. And Oscar thinks it's immense. We shocked him."

"He's found the Bird-in-Hand!" cried Billy, quite suddenly.

"Oscar?" said Bertie with an equal shout.

"No, John. John has. Came home last night and waked me up and told me." "Good for John," remarked Bertie, pensively.

Now, to the undergraduate mind of that day the Bird-in-Hand tavern was what the golden fleece used to be to the Greeks,—a sort of shining, remote, miraculous thing, difficult though not impossible to find, for which expeditions were fitted out. It was reported to be somewhere in the direction of Quincy, and in one respect it resembled a ghost: you never saw a man who had seen it himself; it was always his cousin, or his elder brother in '79. But for the successful explorer a dinner and wines were waiting at the Bird-in-Hand more delicious than anything outside of Paradise. You will realize, therefore, what a thing it was to have a room-mate who had attained. If Billy had not been so dog-tired last night, he would have sat up and made John tell him everything from beginning to end.

"Soft-shell crabs, broiled live lobster, salmon, grass-plover, doughbirds, and rum omelette," he was now reciting to Bertie.

"They say the rum there is old Jamaica brought in slave-ships," said Bertie, reverently.

"I've heard he has white port of 1820," said Billy; "and claret and champagne."

Bertie looked out of the window.

"This is the finest day there's been," said he. Then he looked at his watch. It was twenty-five minutes before Oscar. Then he looked Billy hard in the eye. "Have you any sand?" he inquired.

It was a challenge to Billy's manhood. "Sand!" he yelled, sitting up.

Both of them in an instant had left the table and bounded out of the house.

"I'll meet you at Pike's," said Billy to Bertie. "Make him give us the black gelding."

"Might as well bring our notes along," Bertie called after his rushing friend; "and get John to tell you the road."

To see their haste, as the two fled in opposite directions upon their errands, you would have supposed them under some crying call of obligation, or else to be escaping from justice.

Twenty minutes later they were seated behind the black gelding and bound on their journey in search of the Bird-in-Hand. Their notes in Philosophy 4 were stowed under the buggy-seat.

"Did Oscar see you?" Bertie inquired.

"Not he," cried Billy, joyously.

"Oscar will wonder," said Bertie; and he gave the black gelding a triumphant touch with the whip.

You see, it was Oscar that had made them run so; or, rather, it was Duty and Fate walking in Oscar's displeasing likeness. Nothing easier, nothing more reasonable, than to see the tutor and tell him they should not need him to-day. But that would have spoiled everything. They did not know it, but deep in their childlike hearts was a delicious sense that in thus unaccountably disappearing they had a won a great game, had got away ahead of Duty and Fate. After all, it did bear some resemblance to an escape from justice.

Could he have known this, Oscar would have felt more superior than ever. Punctually at the hour agreed, ten o'clock, he rapped at Billy's door and stood waiting, his leather wallet of notes nipped safe between elbow and ribs. Then he knocked again. Then he tried the door, and as it was open, he walked deferentially into the sitting room. Sonorous snores came from one of the bedrooms. Oscar peered in and saw John; but he saw no Billy in the other bed. Then, always deferential, he sat down in the sitting room and watched a couple of prettily striped coats hanging in a half-open closet.

At that moment the black gelding was flirtatiously crossing the drawbridge over the Charles on the Allston Road. The gelding knew the clank of those suspending chains and the slight unsteadiness of the meeting halves of the bridge as well as it knew oats. But it could not enjoy its own entirely premeditated surprise quite so much as Bertie and Billy were enjoying their entirely unpremeditated flight from Oscar. The wind rippled on the water; down at the boat-house Smith was helping some one embark in a single scull; they saw the green meadows toward Brighton; their foreheads felt cool and unvexed, and each new minute had the savor of fresh forbidden fruit.

"How do we go?" said Bertie.

"I forgot I had a bet with John until I had waked him," said Billy. "He bet me five last night I couldn't find it, and I took him. Of course, after that I had no right to ask him anything, and he thought I was funny. He said I couldn't find out if the landlady's hair was her own. I went him another five on that."

"How do you say we ought to go?" said Bertie, presently.

"Quincy, I'm sure."

They were now crossing the Albany tracks at Allston. "We're going to get there," said Bertie; and he turned the black gelding toward Brookline and Jamaica Plain.

The enchanting day surrounded them. The suburban houses, even the suburban street-cars, seemed part of one great universal plan of enjoyment.

Pleasantness so radiated from the boys' faces and from their general appearance of clean white flannel trousers and soft clean shirts of pink and blue that a driver on a passing car leaned to look after them with a smile and a butcher hailed them with loud brotherhood from his cart. They turned a corner, and from a long way off came the sight of the tower of Memorial Hall. Plain above all intervening tenements and foliage it rose. Over there beneath its shadow were examinations and Oscar. It caught Billy's roving eye, and he nudged Bertie, pointing silently to it. "Ha, ha!" sang Bertie. And beneath his light whip the gelding sprang forward into its stride.

The clocks of Massachusetts struck eleven. Oscar rose doubtfully from his chair in Billy's study. Again he looked into Billy's bedroom and at the empty bed. Then he went for a moment and watched the still forcibly sleeping John. He turned his eyes this way and that, and after standing for a while moved quietly back to his chair and sat down with the leather wallet of notes on his lap, his knees together, and his unblacked shoes touching. In due time the clocks of Massachusetts struck noon.

In a meadow where a brown amber stream ran, lay Bertie and Billy on the grass. Their summer coats were off, their belts loosened. They watched with eyes half closed the long waterweeds moving gently as the current waved and twined them. The black gelding, brought along a farm road and through a gate, waited at its ease in the field beside a stone wall. Now and then it stretched and cropped a young leaf from a vine that grew over the wall, and now and then the warm wind brought down the fruit blossoms all over the meadow. They fell from the tree where Bertie and Billy lay, and the boys brushed them from their faces. Not very far away was Blue Hill, softly shining; and crows high up in the air came from it occasionally across here.

By one o'clock a change had come in Billy's room. Oscar during that hour had opened his satchel of philosophy upon his lap and read his notes attentively. Being almost word perfect in many parts of them, he now spent his unexpected leisure in acquiring accurately the language of still further paragraphs. "The sharp line of demarcation which Descartes drew between consciousness and the material world," whispered Oscar with satisfaction, and knew that if Descartes were on the examination paper he could start with this and go on for nearly twenty lines before he would have to use any words of his own. As he memorized, the chambermaid, who had come to do the bedrooms three times already and had gone away again, now returned and no longer restrained her indignation. "Get up, Mr. Blake!" she vociferated to the sleeping John; "you ought to be ashamed!" And she shook the bedstead. Thus John had come to rise and discover Oscar. The patient tutor explained himself as John listened in his pyjamas.

"Why, I'm sorry," said he, "but I don't believe they'll get back very soon."

"They have gone away?" asked Oscar.

"Ah—yes," returned the reticent John. "An unexpected matter of importance."

"But, my dear sir, those gentlemen know nothing! Philosophy 4 is to-morrow, and they know nothing."

"They'll have to stand it, then," said John, with a grin.

"And my time. I am waiting here. I am engaged to teach them. I have been waiting here since ten. They engaged me all day and this evening."

"I don't believe there's the slightest use in your waiting now, you know. They'll probably let you know when they come back."

"Probably! But they have engaged my time. The girl knows I was here ready at ten. I call you to witness that you found me waiting, ready at any time."

John in his pyjamas stared at Oscar. "Why, of course they'll pay you the whole thing," said he, coldly; "stay here if you prefer." And he went into the bathroom and closed the door.

The tutor stood awhile, holding his notes and turning his little eyes this way and that. His young days had been dedicated to getting the better of his neighbor, because otherwise his neighbor would get the better of him. Oscar had never suspected the existence of boys like John and Bertie and Billy. He stood holding his notes, and then, buckling them up once more, he left the room with evidently reluctant steps. It was at this time that the clocks struck one.

In their field among the soft new grass sat Bertie and Billy some ten yards apart, each with his back against an apple tree. Each had his notes and took his turn at questioning the other. Thus the names of the Greek philosophers with their dates and doctrines were shouted gayly in the meadow. The foreheads of the boys were damp to-day, as they had been last night, and their shirts were opened to the air; but it was the sun that made them hot now, and no lamp or gas; and already they looked twice as alive as they had looked at breakfast. There they sat, while their memories gripped the summarized list of facts essential, facts to be known accurately; the simple, solid, raw facts, which, should they happen to come on the examination paper, no skill could evade nor any imagination supply. But this study was no longer dry and dreadful to them: they had turned it to a sporting event. "What about Heracleitos?" Billy as catechist would put at Bertie. "Eternal flux," Bertie would correctly snap back at Billy. Or, if he got it mixed up, and replied, "Everything is water," which was the doctrine of another Greek, then Billy would credit himself with twenty-five cents on a piece of paper. Each ran a memorandum of this kind; and you can readily see how spirited a character metaphysics would assume under such conditions.

"I'm going in," said Bertie, suddenly, as Billy was crediting himself with a fifty-cent gain. "What's your score?"

"Two seventy-five, counting your break on Parmenides. It'll be cold."

"No, it won't. Well, I'm only a quarter behind you." And Bertie pulled off his shoes. Soon he splashed into the stream where the bend made a hole of some depth.

"Cold?" inquired Billy on the bank.

Bertie closed his eyes dreamily. "Delicious," said he, and sank luxuriously beneath the surface with slow strokes.

Billy had his clothes off in a moment, and, taking the plunge, screamed loudly. "You liar!" he yelled, as he came up. And he made for Bertie.

Delight rendered Bertie weak and helpless; he was caught and ducked; and after some vigorous wrestling both came out of the icy water.

"Now we've got no towels, you fool," said Billy.

"Use your notes," said Bertie, and he rolled in the grass. Then they chased each other round the apple trees, and the black gelding watched them by the wall, its ears well forward.

While they were dressing they discovered it was half-past one, and became instantly famished. "We should have brought lunch along," they told each other. But they forgot that no such thing as lunch could have induced them to delay their escape from Cambridge for a moment this morning. "What do you suppose Oscar is doing now?" Billy inquired of Bertie, as they led the black gelding back to the road; and Bertie laughed like an infant. "Gentlemen," said he, in Oscar's manner, "we now approach the multiplicity of the ego." The black gelding must have thought it had humorists to deal with this day.

Oscar, as a matter of fact, was eating his cheap lunch away over in Cambridge. There was cold mutton, and boiled potatoes with hard brown spots in them, and large pickled cucumbers; and the salt was damp and would not shake out through the holes in the top of the bottle. But Oscar ate two helps of everything with a good appetite, and between whiles looked at his notes, which lay open beside him on the table. At the stroke of two he was again knocking at his pupils' door. But no answer came. John had gone away somewhere for indefinite hours and the door was locked. So Oscar wrote: "Called, two P.M.," on a scrap of envelope, signed his name, and put it through the letter-slit. It crossed his mind to hunt other pupils for his vacant time, but he decided against this at once, and returned to his own room. Three o'clock found him back at the door, knocking scrupulously. The idea of performing his side of the contract, of tendering his goods and standing ready at all times to deliver them, was in his commercially mature mind. This time he had brought a neat piece of paper with him, and wrote upon it, "Called, three P.M.," and signed it as before, and departed to his room with a sense of fulfilled obligations.

Bertie and Billy had lunched at Mattapan quite happily on cold ham, cold pie, and doughnuts. Mattapan, not being accustomed to such lilies of the field, stared at their clothes and general glory, but observed that they could eat the native bill-of-fare as well as anybody. They found some good, cool beer, moreover, and spoke to several people of the Bird-in-Hand, and got several answers: for instance, that the Bird-in-Hand was at Hingham; that it was at Nantasket; that they had better inquire for it at South Braintree; that they had passed it a mile back; and that there was no such place. If you would gauge the intelligence of our population, inquire your way in a rural neighborhood. With these directions they took up their journey after an hour and a half,—a halt made chiefly for the benefit of the black gelding, whom they looked after as much as they did themselves. For a while they discussed club matters seriously, as both of them were officers of certain organizations, chosen so on account of their recognized executive gifts. These questions settled, they resumed the lighter theme of philosophy, and made it (as Billy observed) a near thing for the Causal law. But as they drove along, their minds left this topic on the abrupt discovery that the sun was getting down out of the sky, and they asked each other where they were and what they should do. They pulled up at some cross-roads and debated this with growing uneasiness. Behind them lay the way to Cambridge,—not very clear, to be sure; but you could always go where you had come from, Billy seemed to think. He asked, "How about Cambridge and a little Oscar to finish off with?" Bertie frowned. This would be failure. Was Billy willing to go back and face John the successful?

"It would only cost me five dollars," said Billy.

"Ten," Bertie corrected. He recalled to Billy the matter about the landlady's hair.

"By Jove, that's so!" cried Billy, brightening. It seemed conclusive. But he grew cloudy again the next moment. He was of opinion that one could go too far in a thing.

"Where's your sand?" said Bertie.

Billy made an unseemly rejoinder, but even in the making was visited by inspiration. He saw the whole thing as it really was. "By Jove!" said he, "we couldn't get back in time for dinner."

"There's my bonny boy!" said Bertie, with pride; and he touched up the black gelding. Uneasiness had left both of them. Cambridge was manifestly impossible; an error in judgment; food compelled them to seek the Bird-in-Hand. "We'll try Quincy, anyhow," Bertie said. Billy suggested that they inquire of people on the road. This provided a new sporting event: they could bet upon the answers. Now, the roads, not populous at noon, had grown solitary in the sweetness of the long twilight. Voices of birds there were; and little, black, quick brooks, full to the margin grass, shot under the roadway through low bridges. Through the web of young foliage the sky shone saffron, and frogs piped in the meadow swamps. No cart or carriage appeared, however, and the bets languished. Bertie, driving with one hand, was buttoning his coat with the other, when the black gelding leaped from the middle of the road to the turf and took to backing. The buggy reeled; but the driver was skilful, and fifteen seconds of whip and presence of mind brought it out smoothly. Then the cause of all this spoke to them from a gate.

"Come as near spillin' as you boys wanted, I guess," remarked the cause.

They looked, and saw him in huge white shirt-sleeves, shaking with joviality. "If you kep' at it long enough, you might a-most learn to drive a horse," he continued, eying Bertie. This came as near direct praise as the true son of our soil—Northern or Southern—often thinks well of. Bertie was pleased, but made a modest observation, and "Are we near the tavern?" he asked. "Bird-in-Hand!" the son of the soil echoed; and he contemplated them from his gate. "That's me," he stated with complacence. "Bill Diggs of the Bird-in-Hand has been me since April '65." His massy hair had been yellow, his broad body must have weighed two hundred and fifty pounds, his wide face was canny, red, and somewhat clerical, resembling Henry Ward Beecher's.

"Trout," he said, pointing to a basket by the gate. "For your dinner." Then he climbed heavily but skilfully down and picked up the basket and a rod. "Folks round here say," said he, "that there ain't no more trout up them meadows. They've been a-sayin' that since '74; and I've been a-sayin' it myself, when judicious." Here he shook slightly and opened the basket. "Twelve," he said. "Sixteen yesterday. Now you go along and turn in the first right-hand turn, and I'll be up with you soon. Maybe you might make room for the trout." Room for him as well, they assured him; they were in luck to find him, they explained. "Well, I guess I'll trust my neck with you," he said to Bertie, the skilful driver; " 'tain't five minutes' risk." The buggy leaned, and its springs bent as he climbed in, wedging his mature bulk between their slim shapes. The gelding looked round the shaft at them. "Protestin', are you?" he said to it. "These lightweight stoodents spile you!" So the gelding went on, expressing, however, by every line of its body, a sense of outraged justice. The boys related their difficult search, and learned that any mention of the name of Diggs would have brought them straight. "Bill Diggs of the Bird-in-Hand was my father, and my grandf'ther, and his father; and has been me sence I come back from the war and took the business in '65. I'm not commonly to be met out this late. About fifteen minutes earlier is my time for gettin' back, unless I'm plannin' for a jamboree. But tonight I got to settin' and watchin' that sunset, and listenin' to a darned red-

winged blackbird, and I guess Mrs. Diggs has decided to expect me some-
wheres about noon to-morrow or Friday. Say, did Johnnie send you?" When
he found that John had in a measure been responsible for their journey, he
filled with gayety. "Oh, Johnnie's a bird!" said he. "He's that demure on
first appearance. Walked in last evening and wanted dinner. Did he tell you
what he ate? Guess he left out what he drank. Yes, he's demure."

You might suppose that upon their landlord's safe and sober return fifteen minutes late, instead of on the expected noon of Thursday or Friday,
their landlady would show signs of pleasure; but Mrs. Diggs from the porch
threw an uncordial eye at the three arriving in the buggy. Here were two
more like Johnnie of last night. She knew them by the clothes they wore and
by the confidential tones of her husband's voice as he chatted to them. He
had been old enough to know better for twenty years. But for twenty years
he had taken the same extreme joy in the company of Johnnies, and they
were bad for his health. Her final proof that they belonged to this hated
breed was when Mr. Diggs thumped the trout down on the porch, and after
briefly remarking, "Half of 'em boiled, and half broiled with bacon," himself led away the gelding to the stable instead of intrusting it to his man
Silas.

"You may set in the parlor," said Mrs. Diggs, and departed stiffly with
the basket of trout.

"It's false," said Billy, at once.

Bertie did not grasp his thought.

"Her hair," said Billy. And certainly it was an unusual-looking arrangement.

Presently, as they sat near a parlor organ in the presence of earnest family portraits, Bertie made a new poem for Billy,—

> Said Aristotle unto Plato,
> "Have another sweet potato?"

And Billy responded,—

> Said Plato unto Aristotle,
> "Thank you, I prefer the bottle."

"In here, are you?" said their beaming host at the door. "Now, I think
you'll find my department of the premises cosier, so to speak." He nudged
Bertie. "Do you boys guess it's too early in the season for a silver-fizz?"

We must not wholly forget Oscar in Cambridge. During the afternoon
he had not failed in his punctuality; two more neat witnesses to this lay on
the door-mat beneath the letter-slit of Billy's room. And at the appointed
hour after dinner a third joined them, making five. John found these cards
when he came home to go to bed, and picked them up and stuck them

ornamentally in Billy's looking-glass, as a greeting when Billy should return. The eight o'clock visit was the last that Oscar paid to the locked door. He remained through the evening in his own room, studious, contented, unventilated, indulging in his thick notes, and also in the thought of Billy's and Bertie's eleventh-hour scholarship. "Even with another day," he told himself, "those young men could not have got fifty per cent." In those times this was the passing mark. To-day I believe you get an A, or a B, or some other letter denoting your rank. In due time Oscar turned out his gas and got into his bed; and the clocks of Massachusetts struck midnight.

Mrs. Diggs of the Bird-in-Hand had retired at eleven, furious with rage, but firm in dignity in spite of a sudden misadventure. Her hair, being the subject of a sporting event, had remained steadily fixed in Billy's mind,— steadily fixed throughout an entertainment which began at an early hour to assume the features of a celebration. One silver-fizz before dinner is nothing; but dinner did not come at once, and the boys were thirsty. The hair of Mrs. Diggs had caught Billy's eye again immediately upon her entrance to inform them that the meal was ready; and whenever she reëntered with a new course from the kitchen, Billy's eye wandered back to it, although Mr. Diggs had become full of anecdotes about the Civil War. It was partly Grecian: a knot stood out behind to a considerable distance. But this was not the whole plan. From front to back ran a parting, clear and severe, and curls fell from this to the temples in a manner called, I believe, by the enlightened, *à l'Anne d'Autriche.* The color was gray, to be sure; but this propriety did not save the structure from Billy's increasing observation. As bottles came to stand on the table in greater numbers, the closer and the more solemnly did Billy continue to follow the movements of Mrs. Diggs. They would without doubt have noticed him and his foreboding gravity but for Mr. Diggs's experiences in the Civil War.

The repast was finished—so far as eating went. Mrs. Diggs with changeless dudgeon was removing and washing the dishes. At the revellers' elbows stood the 1820 port in its fine, fat, old, dingy bottle, going pretty fast. Mr. Diggs was nearing the end of Antietam. "That morning of the 18th, while McClellan was holdin' us squattin' and cussin'," he was saying to Bertie, when some sort of shuffling sound in the corner caught their attention. We can never know how it happened. Billy ought to know, but does not, and Mrs. Diggs allowed no subsequent reference to the casualty. But there she stood with her entire hair at right angles. The Grecian knot extended above her left ear, and her nose stuck through one set of Anne d'Autriche. Beside her Billy stood, solemn as a stone, yet with a sort of relief glazed upon his face.

Mr. Diggs sat straight up at the vision of his spouse. "Flouncing Florence!" was his exclamation. "Gee-whittaker, Mary, if you ain't the most unmitigated sight!" And wind then left him.

Mary's reply arrived in tones like a hornet stinging slowly and often. "Mr. Diggs, I have put up with many things, and am expecting to put up with many more. But you'd behave better if you consorted with gentlemen."

The door slammed and she was gone. Not a word to either of the boys, not even any notice of them. It was thorough, and silence consequently held them for a moment.

"He didn't mean anything," said Bertie, growing partially responsible.

"Didn't mean anything," repeated Billy, like a lesson.

"I'll take him and he'll apologize," Bertie pursued, walking over to Billy.

"He'll apologize," went Billy, like a cheerful piece of mechanism. Responsibility was still quite distant from him.

Mr. Diggs got his wind back. "Better not," he advised in something near a whisper. "Better not go after her. Her father was a fightin' preacher, and she's—well, begosh! she's a chip of the old pulpit." And he rolled his eye towards the door. Another door slammed somewhere above, and they gazed at each other, did Bertie and Mr. Diggs. Then Mr. Diggs, still gazing at Bertie, beckoned to him with a speaking eye and a crooked finger; and as he beckoned, Bertie approached like a conspirator and sat down close to him. "Begosh!" whispered Mr. Diggs. "Unmitigated." And at this he and Bertie laid their heads down on the table and rolled about in spasms.

Billy from his corner seemed to become aware of them. With his eye fixed upon them like a statue, he came across the room, and, sitting down near them with formal politeness, observed, "Was you ever to the battle of Antietam?" This sent them beyond the limit; and they rocked their heads on the table and wept as if they would expire.

Thus the three remained, during what space of time is not known: the two upon the table, convalescent with relapses, and Billy like a seated idol, unrelaxed at his vigil. The party was seen through the windows by Silas, coming from the stable to inquire if the gelding should not be harnessed. Silas leaned his face to the pane, and envy spoke plainly in it. "O my! O my!" he mentioned aloud to himself. So we have the whole household: Mrs. Diggs reposing scornfully in an upper chamber; all parts of the tavern darkened, save the one lighted room; the three inside that among their bottles, with the one outside looking covetously in at them; and the gelding stamping in the stable.

But Silas, since he could not share, was presently of opinion that this was enough for one sitting, and he tramped heavily upon the porch. This brought Bertie back to the world of reality, and word was given to fetch the gelding. The host was in no mood to part with them, and spoke of comfortable beds and breakfast as early as they liked; but Bertie had become entirely responsible. Billy was helped in, Silas was liberally thanked, and they drove away beneath the stars, leaving behind them golden opinions, and a host who decided not to disturb his helpmate by retiring to rest in their conjugal bed.

Bertie had forgotten, but the playful gelding had not. When they came abreast of that gate where Diggs of the Bird-in-Hand had met them at sunset, Bertie was only aware that a number of things had happened at once, and that he had stopped the horse after about twenty yards of battle. Pride filled him, but emptied away in the same instant, for a voice on the road behind him spoke inquiringly through the darkness.

"Did any one fall out?" said the voice. "Who fell out?"

"Billy!" shrieked Bertie, cold all over. "Billy, are you hurt?"

"Did Billy fall out?" said the voice, with plaintive cadence. "Poor Billy!"

"He can't be," muttered Bertie. "Are you?" he loudly repeated.

There was no answer; but steps came along the road as Bertie checked and pacified the gelding. Then Billy appeared by the wheel. "Poor Billy fell out," he said mildly. He held something up, which Bertie took. It had been Billy's straw hat, now a brimless fabric of ruin. Except for smirches and one inexpressible rent which dawn revealed to Bertie a little later, there were no further injuries, and Billy got in and took his seat quite competently.

Bertie drove the gelding with a firm hand after this. They passed through the cool of the unseen meadow swamps, and heard the sound of the hollow bridges as they crossed them, and now and then the gulp of some pouring brook. They went by the few lights of Mattapan, seeing from some points on their way the beacons of the harbor, and again the curving line of lamps that drew the outline of some village built upon a hill. Dawn showed them Jamaica Pond, smooth and breezeless, and encircled with green skeins of foliage, delicate and new. Here multitudinous birds were chirping their tiny, overwhelming chorus. When at length, across the flat suburban spaces, they again sighted Memorial tower, small in the distance, the sun was lighting it.

Confronted by this, thoughts of hitherto banished care, and of the morrow that was now to-day, and of Philosophy 4 coming in a very few hours, might naturally have arisen and darkened the end of their pleasant excursion. Not so, however. Memorial tower suggested another line of argument. It was Billy who spoke, as his eye first rested upon that eminent pinnacle of Academe.

"Well, John owes me five dollars."

"Ten, you mean."

"Ten? How?"

"Why, her hair. And it was easily worth twenty."

Billy turned his head and looked suspiciously at Bertie. "What did I do?"

"Do! Don't you know?"

Billy in all truth did not.

"Phew!" went Bertie. "Well, I don't, either. Didn't see it. Saw the consequences, though. Don't you remember being ready to apologize? What do you remember, anyhow?"

Billy consulted his recollections with care: they seemed to break off at the champagne. That was early. Bertie was astonished. Did not Billy remember singing "Brace up and dress the Countess," and "A noble lord the Earl of Leicester"? He had sung them quite in his usual manner, conversing freely between whiles. In fact, to see and hear him, no one would have suspected—"It must have been that extra silver-fizz you took before dinner," said Bertie. "Yes," said Billy; "that's what it must have been." Bertie supplied the gap in his memory,—a matter of several hours, it seemed. During most of this time Billy had met the demands of each moment quite like his usual agreeable self—a sleep-walking state. It was only when the hair incident was reached that his conduct had noticeably crossed the line. He listened to all this with interest intense.

"John does owe me ten, I think," said he.

"I say so," declared Bertie. "When do you begin to remember again?"

"After I got in again at the gate. Why did I get out?"

"You fell out, man."

Billy was incredulous.

"You did. You tore your clothes wide open."

Billy, looking at his trousers, did not see it.

"Rise, and I'll show you," said Bertie.

"Goodness gracious!" said Billy.

Thus discoursing, they reached Harvard Square. Not your Harvard Square, gentle reader, that place populous with careless youths and careful maidens and reticent persons with books, but one of sleeping windows and clear, cool air and few sounds; a Harvard Square of emptiness and conspicuous sparrows and milk wagons and early street-car conductors in long coats going to their breakfast; and over all this the sweetness of the arching elms.

As the gelding turned down toward Pike's, the thin old church clock struck.

"Always sounds," said Billy, "like cambric tea."

"Cambridge tea," said Bertie.

"Walk close behind me," said Billy, as they came away from the livery stable. "Then they won't see the hole."

Bertie did so; but the hole was seen by the street-car conductors and the milkmen, and these sympathetic hearts smiled at the sight of the marching boys, and loved them without knowing any more of them than this. They reached their building and separated.

One hour later they met. Shaving and a cold bath and summer flannels, not only clean but beautiful, invested them with the radiant innocence of flowers. It was still too early for their regular breakfast, and they sat down to eggs and coffee at the Holly Tree.

"I waked John up," said Billy. "He is satisfied."

"Let's have another order," said Bertie. "These eggs are delicious." Each of them accordingly ate four eggs and drank two cups of coffee.

"Oscar called five times," said Billy; and he threw down those cards which Oscar had so neatly written.

"There's multiplicity of the ego for you!" said Bertie.

Now, inspiration is a strange thing, and less obedient even than love to the will of man. It will decline to come when you prepare for it with the loftiest intentions, and, lo! at an accidental word it will suddenly fill you, as at this moment it filled Billy.

"By gum!" said he, laying his fork down. "Multiplicity of the ego. Look here. I fall out of a buggy and ask—"

"By gum!" said Bertie, now also visited by inspiration.

"Don't you see?" said Billy.

"I see a whole lot more," said Bertie, with excitement. "I had to tell you about your singing." And the two burst into a flare of talk.

To hear such words as cognition, attention, retention, entity, and identity, freely mingled with such words as silver-fizz and false hair, brought John, the egg-and-coffee man, as near surprise as his impregnable nature permitted. Thus they finished their large breakfast, and hastened to their notes for a last good bout at memorizing Epicharmos of Kos and his various brethren. The appointed hour found them crossing the college yard toward a door inside which Philosophy 4 awaited them: three hours of written examination! But they looked more roseate and healthy than most of the anxious band whose steps were converging to that same gate of judgment. Oscar, meeting them on the way, gave them his deferential "Good morning," and trusted that the gentlemen felt easy. Quite so, they told him, and bade him feel easy about his pay, for which they were, of course, responsible. Oscar wished them good luck and watched them go to their desks with his little eyes, smiling in his particular manner. Then he dismissed them from his mind, and sat with a faint remnant of his smile, fluently writing his perfectly accurate answer to the first question upon the examination paper.

Here is that paper. You will not be able to answer all the questions, probably, but you may be glad to know what such things are like.

PHILOSOPHY 4

1. Thales, Zeno, Parmenides, Heracleitos, Anaxagoras. State briefly the doctrine of each.

2. Phenomenon, noumenon. Discuss these terms. Name their modern descendants.

3. Thought = Being. Assuming this, state the difference, if any, between (1) memory and anticipation; (2) sleep and waking.

4. Democritus, Pythagoras, Bacon. State the relation between them. In what terms must the objective world ultimately be stated? Why?

5. Experience is the result of time and space being included in the nature of mind. Discuss this.

6. Nihil est in intellectu quod non prius fuerit in sensibus. Whose doctrine? Discuss it.

7. What is the inherent limitation in all ancient philosophy? Who first removed it?

8. Mind is expressed through what? Matter through what? Is speech the result or the cause of thought?

9. Discuss the nature of the ego.

10. According to Plato, Locke, Berkeley, where would the sweetness of a honeycomb reside? Where would its shape? its weight? Where do you think these properties reside?

Ten questions, and no Epicharmos of Kos. But no examination paper asks everything, and this one did ask a good deal. Bertie and Billy wrote the full time allotted, and found that they could have filled an hour more without coming to the end of their thoughts. Comparing notes at lunch, their information was discovered to have been lacking here and there. Nevertheless, it was no failure; their inner convictions were sure of fifty per cent at least, and this was all they asked of the gods. "I was ripping about the ego," said Bertie. "I was rather splendid myself," said Billy, "when I got going. And I gave him a huge steer about memory." After lunch both retired to their beds and fell into sweet oblivion until seven o'clock, when they rose and dined, and after playing a little poker went to bed again pretty early.

Some six mornings later, when the Professor returned their papers to them, their minds were washed almost as clear of Plato and Thales as were their bodies of yesterday's dust. The dates and doctrines, hastily memorized to rattle off upon the great occasion, lay only upon the surface of their minds, and after use they quickly evaporated. To their pleasure and most genuine astonishment, the Professor paid them high compliments. Bertie's discussion of the double personality had been the most intelligent which had come in from any of the class. The illustration of the intoxicated hack-driver who had fallen from his hack and inquired who it was that had fallen, and then had pitied himself, was, said the Professor, as original and perfect an illustration of our subjective-objectivity as he had met with in all his researches. And Billy's suggestions concerning the inherency of time and space in the mind the Professor had also found very striking and independent, particularly his reasoning based upon the well-known distortions of time and space which hashish and other drugs produced in us. This was the sort of thing which the Professor had wanted from his students: free comment and discussions, the *spirit* of the course, rather than any strict adherence to the letter. He had constructed his questions to elicit as much individual discussion as possible and had been somewhat disappointed in his hopes.

Yes, Bertie and Billy were astonished. But their astonishment did not equal that of Oscar, who had answered many of the questions in the Professor's own language. Oscar received seventy-five per cent for this achievement—a good mark. But Billy's mark was eighty-six and Bertie's ninety. "There is some mistake," said Oscar to them when they told him; and he hastened to the Professor with his tale. "There is no mistake," said the Professor. Oscar smiled with increased deference. "But," he urged, "I assure you, sir, those young men knew absolutely nothing. I was their tutor, and they knew nothing at all. I taught them all their information myself." "In that case," replied the Professor, not pleased with Oscar's tale-bearing, "you must have given them more than you could spare. Good morning."

Oscar never understood. But he graduated considerably higher than Bertie and Billy, who were not able to discover many other courses so favorable to "orriginal rresearch" as was Philosophy 4. That is twenty years ago. To-day Bertie is treasurer of the New Amsterdam Trust Company, in Wall Street; Billy is superintendent of passenger traffic of the New York and Chicago Air Line. Oscar is successful too. He has acquired a lot of information. His smile is unchanged. He has published a careful work entitled "The Minor Poets of Cinquecento," and he writes book reviews for the *Evening Post*.

Philosophy 4 (New York, 1903).

John Dos Passos

ADVENTURE AT NORUMBEGA

(1923)

This episode at the commencement of John Dos Passos' third novel, Streets of Night, *is in itself a short story, but the style shows few of the characteristics of the writer's later work. There is a rather pleasing immaturity about this little freshman adventure which would be lost in the larger canvas of the trilogy,* U. S. A. *Dos Passos is a superb reporter and his writing method has been much imitated by young, would-be authors, many of them from Harvard. For Harvard consumption (his 25th Anniversary Class Report) he listed only four books as published by him;* Streets of Night *was not among them, but this excerpt deserves recall from oblivion. "Harvard," wrote Dos Passos in* Nineteen Nineteen, *"stood for the broad a and those contacts so useful in later life and good English prose . . . if the hedgehog cant be cultured at Harvard the hedgehog cant . . ." Those who know today's Harvard with its generally comfortable relationship between the sexes may find Dos Passos's tale a little discordant, but it was a true reflection of the male naïveté of another era.*

BUT I don't think I want to, Cham." "Come along, Fanshaw, you've got to." "But I wouldn't know what to say to them." "They'll do the talking . . . Look, you've got to come, date's all made an' everything."

Cham Mason stood in his drawers in the middle of the floor, eagerly waving a shirt into which he was fitting cuff-links. He was a pudgy-faced boy with pink cheeks and wiry light hair like an Irish terrier's. He leaned forward with pouting lips towards Fanshaw, who sat, tall and skinny, by the window, with one finger scratching his neck under the high stiff collar from which dangled a narrow necktie, blue, the faded color of his eyes.

"But jeeze, man," Cham whined.

"Well, what did you go and make it for?"

"Hell, Fanshaw, I couldn't know that Al Winslow was going to get scarlet fever . . . Most fellers 'ld be glad of the chance. It isn't everybody Phoebe Sweeting'll go out with."

"But why don't you go alone?"

"What could I do with two girls in a canoe? And she's got to have her friend along. You don't realize how respectable chorus girls are."

"I never thought they were respectable at all."

"That shows how little you know about it."

Cham put on his shirt with peevish jerks and went into the next room. Fanshaw looked down at Bryce's *American Commonwealth* that lay spread out on his knees and tried to go on reading: This decision of the Supreme Court, however . . . But why shouldn't he? Fanshaw stretched himself yawning. The sunlight seeped through the brownish stenciled curtains and laid a heavy warm hand on his left shoulder. This decision of the Supreme . . . He looked down into Mount Auburn Street. It was June and dusty. From the room below came the singsong of somebody playing "Sweet and Low" on the mandolin. And mother needn't know, and I'm in college . . . see life. A man with white pants on ran across the street waving a tennis racket. Stoddard, on the *Lampoon,* knows all the chorines.

Cham, fully dressed in a tweed suit, stood before him with set lips, blinking his eyes to keep from crying.

"Fanshaw, I don't think you're any kind of a . . ."

"All right, I'll go, Cham, but I won't know what to say to them."

"Gee, that's great." Cham's face became cherubic with smiles. "Just act natural."

"Like when you have your photograph taken," said Fanshaw, laughing shrilly.

"Gee, you're a prince to do it . . . I think Phoebe likes me . . . It's just that I've never had a chance to get her alone."

Their eyes met suddenly. They both blushed and were silent. Fanshaw got to his feet and walked stiffly to the bookcase to put away his book.

"But Cham." He was hoarse; he cleared his throat. "I don't want to carry on with those girls. I don't . . . I don't do that sort of thing."

"Don't worry, they won't eat you. I tell you they are very respectable girls. They don't want to carry on with anybody. They like to have a good time, that's all."

"But all day seems so long."

"We won't start till eleven or so. Phoebe won't be up. Just time to get acquainted."

From far away dustily came the bored strokes of the college bell.

"Ah, there's my three-thirty," said Fanshaw.

It was hot in the room. There was a faint smell of stale sweat from some soiled clothes that made a heap in the center of the floor. The strokes of the bell beat on Fanshaw's ears with a dreary, accustomed weight.

"How about walking into town instead?"

Fanshaw picked up a notebook out of a patch of sun on the desk. The book was warm. The beam of sunlight was full of bright, lazy motes. Fanshaw put the book up to his mouth and yawned. Still yawning, he said:

"Gee, I'd like to but I can't."

"I don't see why you took a course that came at such a damn-fool time."

"Can't argue now," said Fanshaw going out the door and tramping down the scarred wooden stairs.

.   .   .   .   .

"You ask the clerk to call up and see if they're ready," said Cham. They stood outside the revolving door of the hotel, the way people linger shivering at the edge of a pool before diving in. Cham wore a straw hat and white flannel pants and carried a corded luncheon basket in one hand.

"But Cham, that's your business. You ought to do that." Fanshaw felt a stiff tremor in his voice. His hands were cold.

"Go ahead, Fanshaw, for crissake, we can't wait here all day," Cham whispered hoarsely.

Fanshaw found himself engaged in the revolving door with Cham pushing him from behind. From rocking chairs in the lobby he could see the moonfaces of two drummers, out of which eyes like oysters stared at him. He was blushing; he felt his forehead tingle under his new tweed cap. The clock over the desk said fifteen of eleven. He walked firmly over to the desk and stood leaning over the registry book full of blotted signatures and dates. He cleared his throat. He could feel the eyes of the drummers, of the green bellboy, of people passing along the street boring into his back. At last the clerk came to him, a greyfaced man with a triangular mouth and eyeglasses, and said in a squeaky voice:

"Yessir."

"Are Miss ... Is Miss .. ? Say, Cham, what are their names, Cham?" Guilty perspiration was trickling on Fanshaw's temples and behind his ears. He felt furiously angry at Cham for having got him into this, at Cham's back and straw hat tipped in the contemplation of the Selkirk Glacier over the fireplace. "Cham!"

"Miss Montmorency and Miss Sweeting," said Cham coolly in a businesslike voice.

The clerk had tipped up one corner of his mouth. Leaving Cham to talk to him, Fanshaw walked over to a rocker by the fireplace and hunched up in it sulkily. With relief he heard the clerk say:

"The young ladies will be down in a few minutes; would you please wait?"

Fanshaw stared straight ahead of him. He'd never speak to Cham again after this. When the bellboy leaned over the desk to say something to the clerk, the eight brass buttons on his coattails flashed in the light. The clerk laughed creakily. Fanshaw clenched his fists. Damn them, what had he let himself be inveigled into this for? He looked at the floor; balanced on the edge of a spittoon a cigar stub still gave off a little wisp of smoke. The temptations of college life; as he sat with his neatly polished oxfords side by side, making the chair rock by a slight movement of the muscles of his thin calves, he thought of the heart-to-heart talk Mr. Crownsterne had given the sixth form this time last year about the temptations of college life. The soapy flow of Mr. Crownsterne's voice booming in his ears: You are now engaged, fellows, in that perilous defile through which all of us have to pass to reach the serene uplands of adult life. You have put behind you the pleasant valleys and problems of boyhood, and before you can assume the duties and responsibilities of men you have to undergo—we all of us have had to undergo—the supreme test. You all know, fellows, the beautiful story of the Holy Grail ... Galahad ... purity and continence ... safest often the best course ... shun not the society of the lovely girls of our own class ... honest and healthy entertainment ... dances and the beautiful flow of freshness and youth ... but remember to beware in whatever circle of life the duties and responsibilities of your careers may call you to move, of those unfortunate women who have rendered themselves unworthy of the society of our mothers and sisters ... of those miserable and disinherited creatures who, although they do not rebuff and disgust us immediately with their loathsomeness as would common prostitutes, yet ... Remember that even Jesus Christ, our Saviour, prayed not to be led into temptation. O, fellows, when you go out from these walls I want you to keep the ideals you have learned and that you have taught by your example as sixth formers ... the spotless armor of Sir Galahad ...

The rocking chair creaked. The clock above the desk had ticked its way to eleven fifteen. Old Crowny's phrases certainly stayed in your mind. Suppose we met mother on the trolley? No, she'd be at church. Nonsense, and these were respectable girls anyway; they wouldn't lead into temptation. A heap lot more respectable than lots of the girls you met at dances. Why don't you come?

"Gee, I bet they weren't up yet," said Cham giggling.

"What, at eleven o'clock?"

"They don't usually get up till one or two."

"I suppose being up so late every night." Fanshaw could not get his voice above a mysterious whisper. He sat in the rocking chair without moving and stared at the clock. Eleven thirty-six. The bellboy stood in front of the desk, his eyes fixed on vacancy. The bellboy grinned and drew a red hand across his slick black hair.

"Did ye think we'd passed out up there?" came a gruff girl's voice behind him, interrupted by a giggle. He smelt perfume. Then he was on his feet, blushing.

They were shaking hands with Cham. One had curly brown hair and a doll's pink organdy dress and showed her teeth, even as the grains on an ear of sweet corn, in a continual smile. The other had a thin face and tow hair and wore the same dress in blue.

"I was coming up to help," shouted Cham.

"Ou, what's that?"

"It's a present." The blue dress hovered over the lunch basket.

"A case of Scotch!" They all shrieked with laughter.

"That's our eats," said Cham solemnly.

"And this is Mr. ——?"

"Beg pardon, this is my friend, Mr. Macdougan . . . answers to the name of Fanshaw."

Fanshaw shook their hands that they held up very high.

"This is Miss Phoebe Sweeting and this is Miss Elise Montmorency."

"We'll never be able to eat all that," said the blue girl tittering.

"We'll drink some of it," said Cham. "There's some Champagny water."

"My Gawd!"

"You carry it now, Fanshaw," said Cham in a hurried undertone, and pushed the pink girl out in front of him through the revolving door.

Fanshaw picked up the basket. It was heavy and rattled.

"O, I just do love canoeing," said the blue girl as they followed. "Don't you?"

.   .   .   .   .

They stood on the landing at Norumbega. A man in a seedy red sweater torn at the elbows was bringing a canoe out of the boathouse. A cool weedy smell teasing to the nostrils came up out of the river.

"Ou, isn't it deep?" said Elise, pressing her fluffy dress against Fanshaw's leg.

"Stop it, I tell you . . . You'll push me in the water . . . Ow!" Cham was brandishing a bullrush at the pink girl, tickling her with it. She was protesting in a gruff baby lisp full of titters. "If you spoil my dress . . ."

"I'm sure you paddle beautifully . . . D'you mind if I call you Fanshaw . . . It's a funny name like a stage name. Look at them!"

Phoebe had snatched the bullrush and was beating Cham over the head. The brown fluff fell about them bright in the streaming sunlight. Fanshaw found himself picking up Cham's straw hat, palping a dent in the rim with his finger. Cham's hair shone yellow; he grabbed the pink girl's hand. The bullrush broke off and the head fell into the river, floated in the middle of brown bright rings.

"Ow, damn it, you hurt," she cried shrilly. "There now, you made me say damn."

"Momma kiss it an' make it well."

Fanshaw found the blue girl's grey glance wriggling into his eyes.

"Silly, ain't they? Kids, are they not?"

The ain't stung in Fanshaw's ears. The girl was common. The thought made him blush.

"Come along, let's get started. Man the boats," cried Cham.

"I'm scared o' canoes. You can paddle all right, can't you, Fanshaw?" The blue girl pressed his hand tight as they stood irresolute a moment looking down into the canoe. The other canoe was off, upstream into the noon dazzle.

"Come along," shouted Cham. The sun flashed on his paddle. He began singing off key:

> I know a place where the sun is like gold
> And the cherryblooms burst with snow
> And down underneath . . .

"All right, Missy, step in," said the man in the red sweater who was holding the canoe to the landing with a paddle. "Easy now."

"Let m-m-me get in first," said Fanshaw stuttering a little. "I hope this isn't a tippy one."

"I'll help you in Missy," said the man in the red sweater. Fanshaw, from the stern seat he had plunked down in, saw the man's big red hand, like a bunch of sausages against the blue dress, clasp her arm, press against the slight curve of her breast as he let her down among the cushions. "Thanks," she said, as she tucked her dress in around her legs, giving the man a long look from under the brim of her hat.

"Ou, I'm scared to death," she said, leaning back gingerly. "If you tip me over . . ."

Fanshaw had pushed the canoe out from the landing. Over his shoulder he caught a glimpse of a grin on the face of the man with the red sweater. He paddled desperately. The other canoe was far ahead, black in the broad shimmering reach of the river. He was sweating. He splashed some water into the canoe.

"Ou you naughty . . . Don't. You've gotten me all wet."

"I think I'll take my coat off if you don't mind."

"Don't mind me, go as far as you like," giggled Elise.

Fanshaw took off his coat and rolled up his sleeves. He was trying not to look at the pink legs in stockings of thin black silk with clocks on them that stretched towards him in the canoe, ending in crossed ankles and bronze high heel slippers.

"Warm, isn't it?"

"Hot, I call it. I hope they don't go awfully far. I don't want to get sunburned . . . A boy swiped my parasol." Her grey eyes flashed in his. She was giggling with her lips apart.

"How was that?" How solemn I sound, thought Fanshaw.

"I dunno, one o' them souvenir hunters out at the Roadside Inn." She pulled down her babyish-looking hat that had blue and pink roses on it so that it shaded her eyes.

"Whew, smell that!" she cried.

"Must be a sewer, or marshgas."

"Clothespins! Clothespins!" Elise was holding her nose and wriggling in the bottom of the canoe. Then she burst into giggles again and cried: "Gee, this little girl loves the country, nit!"

"Now it's better, isn't it?"

"I want to eat. Cham's crazy to go so far."

"They've got the picnic basket, so I don't see what we can do but follow."

"Follow on, follow on," sang Elise derisively.

Upstream Cham's canoe had drawn up to the bank under a fringe of trees grey in the noon glare. Behind it a figure in white and a figure in pink, close together, were disappearing into the shadow.

"They'll have every single thing eaten up," wailed Elise.

"I'm afraid I'm not a very good paddler," said Fanshaw through clenched teeth.

"There you go again."

"Well, I didn't mean to. I'm sorry."

"You'll have to get me a new dress, that's all."

The canoe ran into the bank with a sliding thump.

Phoebe was looking at them from behind a clump of maples. She cooed at them in her most dollish voice.

"What have you kids been doing all by yourselves out in the river?"

"We saw you, don't you worry dearest," said Elise balancing to step out of the canoe. "O murder, I got my foot in it!"

"Bring the cushions, Fanshaw," shouted Cham, who was kneeling beside the open picnic basket with a bottle in his hand.

Fanshaw's hands were sticky. The warm champagne had made him feel a little sick. He sat with his back against a tree, his knees drawn up to his chin, looking across the gutted lunch basket at Cham and Phoebe, who lay on their backs and shrieked with laughter. Beside him he was conscious of the blue girl sitting stiff on a cushion, bored, afraid of spoiling her dress. Overhead the afternoon sun beat heavily on the broad maple leaves; patches of sunlight littered the ground like bright torn paper. Through the trees came the mud smell and the restless sheen of the river. Fanshaw was trying to think of something to say to the girl beside him; he daren't turn towards her until he had thought of something to say.

"Doggone it I've got an ant down my back," cried Cham, sitting up suddenly, his face pink.

"Momma catch it," spluttered Phoebe in the middle of a gust of laughter.

Cham was scratching himself all over, under his arm, round his neck, making an anxious monkey face till at last he ran his hand down the back of his neck.

"Yea, I got him."

"He's a case, he is," tittered Elise.

Cham was on his hands and knees whispering something in Phoebe's ear, his nose pressed into her frizzy chestnut hair.

"Stop blowin' in my ear," said the pink girl, pushing him away, "Wouldn't that jar you?"

"What we need is juss a lil more champagny water." Cham picked the two bottles out of the basket and tipped them up to the light. "There's juss a lil drop for everybody."

"Not for me . . . I think you're trying to get us silly," said the blue girl.

"God did that."

"Well, I never."

"Ou something's ticklin' me . . . Did you put that ant on me?" The pink girl scrambled to her feet and made for Cham.

"Honest, I didn't . . ." cried Cham, jumping out of her way and doubling up with glee: "Honest, I didn't. Cross my heart, hope I may die, I didn't."

"Cham, you're lyin' like a fish. I got an ant down my dress. Ou, it tickles!"

"I'll catch it, Phoebe."

"Boys, don't look now. I'm goin' fishin' . . . Ou . . . I got him. O it's just a leaf . . . O he looked. He's a cool one. I'm goin' to smack your face."

"Catch me first, Phoebe deary," cried Cham running off up a path. She lit out after him. "Look out for your dress on them bushes," cried Elise. "I should worry."

Fanshaw watched the pink dress disappear down the path, going bright and dull in the patches of sun and shadow among the maple trees. Their laughing rose to a shriek and stopped suddenly. Fanshaw and Elise looked at each other.

"Children must play," said Fanshaw stiffly.

"What time are we goin' home, d'you know?" said Elise yawning.

"You don't like—er—picnicking."

There was a silence. From down river came the splash of paddles and the sound of a phonograph playing "O Waltz Me Around Again Willie." Fanshaw sat still in the same position with his knees drawn up to his chin, as if paralyzed. With tightening throat he managed to say:

"What can they be doing . . . They don't seem to be coming back."

"Ask me something hard," said the blue girl jeeringly.

Fanshaw felt himself blushing. He clasped his hands tighter round his knees. He felt the sweat making little beads on his forehead. Ought he to kiss her? He didn't want to kiss her with her rouged lips and her blonde hair all fuzzy like that, peroxide probably. A fool to come along, anyway. What on earth shall I say to her?

She got to her feet.

"I'm goin' to walk around a bit . . . Ou, my foot's gone to sleep."

Fanshaw jumped up as if a spring had been released inside him.

"Which way shall we go?"

"I guess we'd better go the other way," said Elise tittering and smoothing out the back of her fluffy dress.

They walked beside the water; along the path were mashed cracker boxes, orange peel, banana skins. The river was full of canoes now. Above the sound of paddles occasionally splashing and the grinding undertone of phonographs came now and then a giggle or a man's voice shouting. Elise was humming "School Days," walking ahead of him with mincing steps. He saw a woodpecker run down the trunk of an oak.

"Look, there's a woodpecker." Elise walked ahead, still humming, now and then taking a little dance step. "It's a red-headed woodpecker." As she still paid no attention, he walked behind her without saying anything, listening to the tapping of the woodpecker in the distance, watching her narrow hips sway under the pleats of her dress as she walked. A rank, heavy smell came from the muddy banks. He looked at his watch. Only four o'clock. She caught sight of the watch and turned round.

"What time is it, please?"

"It's only four o'clock . . . We have lots of time yet."

"Don't I realize it? Say, what's the name of this old damn-fool park?"

"Norumbega."

"It's never again for me," she cried giggling. Then all at once she dropped down on the ground at the foot of a tree and began to sob with her dress all puffed up about her.

"But what's the matter?"

"Nothing . . . My God, shut up and go away!" she whined through her sobs.

"All right, I'll go and see nobody swipes the canoe."

Biting his lips, Fanshaw started slowly back along the path.

.   .   .   .

The air of the examination room was heavy and smelt of chalk. Through the open windows from the yard drifted the whir of lawnmowers and the fragrance of cut grass. Fanshaw had just finished three hundred words on "The Classical Subject in Racine." He found himself listening to the lawnmowers and breathing in the rifts of warm sweetness that came from the mashed grass. It almost made him cry. The spring of Freshman year, the end of Freshman year. The fragrance of years mown down by the whirring, singsong blades. He stared at the printed paper: Comparative Literature 1. Devote one hour to one of the following subjects . . . And the girl in the blue dress had plunked herself down under a tree and cried. What a fool I was to walk away like that. "What's that perfume?" "Mary Garden," she had said, and her grey glance had wriggled into his eyes and his hands had moved softly across the fluffy dress, feeling the whalebone corsets under the blue fluff. No, that's when I helped her back into the canoe. Elise Montmorency, the girl in the blue dress, had plunked herself down under a tree and cried because he hadn't kissed her. But he had kissed her; he had come back and lain on the grass beside her and kissed her till she wriggled in his arms under the blue fluff and the sunshine had lain a hot tingling coverlet over his back.

He sat stiff in his chair staring in front of him, his hands clasped tight under the desk. All his flesh was hot and tingling. He breathed deep of the smell of cut grass that drifted in through the window, under the smell of mashed grass and cloverblossoms, sweetness, heaviness, Mary Garden perfume. Gee, am I going to faint?

> And there on beds of violets blue
> And freshblown roses washed in dew,
> Filled her with thee a daughter fair
> So buxom blithe and debonair.

Fanshaw felt the blood suddenly rush to his face. If the proctor sees me blushing he'll think I've been cribbing. He hung his head over his paper again.

Devote one hour . . . She was common and said ain't. That was not the sort of girl. He was glad he hadn't kissed her . . . The spotless armor of Sir Galahad. Maybe that was temptation. Maybe he'd resisted temptation. And lastly, Mr. Crownsterne's voice was booming in his ears: And lastly, fellows, let me wish each one of you the best and loveliest and most flower-like girl in the world for your wife. A lot old Crowny knew about it. Marriage was for ordinary people, but for him, love, two souls pressed each to each, consumed with a single fire.

> Not the angels in heaven above
> Nor the demons down under the sea
> Can ever dissever my soul from the soul
> Of the beautiful Annabel Lee.

The moth's kiss, dearest. He was in a boat with red sails, in the stern of a boat with red lateen sails and she was in his arms and her hair was fluffy against his cheek, and the boat leapt on the waves and they were drenched in droning fragrance off the island to windward, wet rose gardens, clover fields, fresh-cut hay, tarry streets, Mary Garden perfume. That perfume was common like saying ain't.

Sudden panic seized him. The clock was at twenty-five past. Gosh, only thirty-five minutes for those two questions! The nib of his fountain pen was dry. He shook a drop out on the floor before he began to write.

Streets of Night (New York, 1923).

Lucius Beebe

NOTES ON A DRY GENERATION
(1927)

Lucius Beebe went to Harvard for a while (1924–25) and to Yale for a while (1926). He got his A.B. degree at Harvard (1927) and still later in life was elected an honorary member of Princeton's Triangle Club. These academic facts are cited to show Beebe's varied intellectual taste which ran to such things as poetry, criticism, food and drink, local history and legend, and railroading (with a camera). The comments following were written at the time of the Harvard Tercentenary when Beebe found Harvard little changed from his day. The gilded youth of Cambridge was still in possession of the Ritz, of Locke's, and of The Country Club.

AN EARLIER and wittier commentator once made the remark that "Harvard University was pleasantly and conveniently situated in the bar-room of

Parker's in School Street," and what was to all intents and purposes the
focal point of valor and the humanities as the class of 1927 went about absorbing the higher learning (through the agency of what always seemed a
sort of process of osmosis) was only a short distance down the line in Winter
Place. In other words, the University, ever aware of change and prompt to
keep abreast of the latest movement, contrived, in the interval between
Josh Billings* and Bob Benchley, to move precisely four city blocks, where,
of course, it again found itself in a saloon.

I refer, as you have surmised, to the most gracious and comforting tavern that ever survived an era of outrage, pillage and Federal barbarism,
Frank Locke's Winter Place Wine Rooms. It has been variously known as
the Dutchman's, as Winter Place Restaurant, as Locke's and as Locke-
Ober's, and even, to irreverent undergraduates, as the Nekked Lady, but by
any other name it smells the same; fragrant and holy in the souvenirs of
many discerning men of several generations.

Jack Wheelwright (the elder) once remarked that he had designed the
West Boston Bridge "so that he could get from State Street to the bar in the
Lampoon Building, get stiff and back to State Street again in half an hour."
The undergraduates of the middle twenties improved on this short sighted
formula. Being youths of vision, their design for living called for using the
West Boston Bridge to get to Winter Place, get crocked and get back to
Cambridge in four years. Once established in the shadow of the mahogany
bar beneath the cheerful aspect of the nude on the wall, they found themselves strangely persuaded by the philosophy of Dr. Holmes's Beacon Street
young lady who, when urged to go abroad, remarked "Why should I travel
when I'm already there?"

During the years of the Great Foolishness Locke's never sold a drop, although now and then a waiter maintained a private concession without the
knowledge of the management. Massachusetts, apparently subscribing to
the appalling bigotry of the times, was willing to place the citizens of the
Commonwealth in double jeopardy by maintaining a "Baby Volstead Act"
while in more patriotic New York posses of outraged burghers were gouging
the eyes out of Federal officers and throwing their carcasses into refuse barrels in Fifty-second Street. Bostonians wrote letters to the editor of the
Transcript and drank in the butler's pantry at home.

But if Locke's never violated the law, that is a far cry from saying nobody ever felt better after leaving the premises, and diners always seemed
to arrive burdened with parcels, brief cases, and even swag-bellied port-
manteaux, which were placed under the table, and for the rest of the evening caused any shifting of feet to be accompanied with the ginger precision of a cigar smoker in a powder mill.

* See page 435.

Locke's was (and for the matter of that, still is) a temple of robust and masculine good cheer, a resort of dining *au serviette au cou* where the menu is overwhelmed with Kansas City steaks, lobster thermidor, sweetbreads Eugénie, shad, mutton chops, Cape oysters, jack rabbit stews and pigeon pies. If you didn't order a full portion from every classification on the bill of fare, from shellfish, through turtle soup, flounder, rack of lamb and a fancy dessert, Nick Stuhl, the manager, knew there was something the matter with you. It took a lot of Jamaica rum to float what you were supposed to eat in Winter Place, and all the management, from Emil Camus, the urbane proprietor, to Charlie, Maurice and Eddie, the waiters, took an interest in what you ate. When you had placed your order Charlie would lay a knowing finger along his nose and say: "The chef, he works but very hard tonight," and you sent out a highball glass of straight rum for the chef and whoever else Charlie favored in the offices out back. And if it was a special occasion and you were drinking wine, you asked Mr. Camus to have a glass, but you hardly dared accost so august a personage as the proprietor with anything less than hock.

The undergraduate group which most favored Locke's was a gathering of chivalry known as the Michael Mullins Chowder and Marching Society which met at unstated but frequent intervals in a private room upstairs. Whatever secret ends the order may have served, they included neither marching nor the consumption of chowder. The members invariably arrived in top hats and evening tail coats, and a sort of self-limiting rule of the organization was that each new member provide a lavish champagne dinner for the already elected members. As the capacity of the adherents of Mullins was apparently unbounded, this served to keep membership within decently exclusive limits.

Next to the delights of Locke's on winter nights when the wind hastened down the Avenue in a tangible, gelid wall and the Arlington Street roundsman found it expedient to seek the shelter of the Sears's carriage house, was an ageless gaffer named Freddy. Freddy was the proprietor of the last of the town's horse drawn hacks, a valiant Jehu and a Bostonian of note whose origins antedated by a generation or so the brave days when Sam Shaw, miraculous in a white top hat and fawn paddock coat, was accustomed to tool a gleaming red and yellow coach to the Country Club races in Brookline, or when Tommy Taylor's "Whitechapel" hansom cab was a marvelous thing to behold. Freddy rolled up and down the Boulevards of Boston, ancient, blasphemous and trailing clouds of glory from Honest Parker Shannon's bar, an undismayed coda to the saga of horsecabs which had its origins two hundred years before in Jonathan Wardell, who held the town's first hackney license and kept his rig on the rank outside the Orange Tree Inn in Hanover Street. Freddy was a figure out of the past whose silver side lamps were an oriflamme of the night. He was, too, a caution.

Nobody ever saw Freddy in a condition even remotely approximating sobriety, but, within the definition of the Scotch magistrate, nobody ever saw him gone in wine. He could always wiggle a finger, and usually he contrived to mount the box of his herdic without the aid of more than a mere handful of assistants. He maintained three equipages: a victoria, a closed coach of the genus growler, and a magnificent arrangement, but rarely brought into service, a coupé on runners known as the "booby," and reserved for the most social snowstorms. To have been wafted home from a ball at the Somerset in the booby, amidst an early morning blizzard, your *chapeau claque* tilted over your nose to avoid smashing against the low roof, the fine snow drifting in over the buffalo robe through the chinks in the door, and your last measure of S. S. Pierce's overproof rum reserved as defense (for you and Freddy) against the elements while crossing the Harvard Bridge is a lyric memory not to be ranked with any of the other exquisite souvenirs of this world.

Nobody knew where Freddy made his headquarters or how he sensed party doings, but he never missed a debutante party along the reaches of the Avenue or a club dinner in Mount Auburn Street. When in the middle twenties the Iroquois Club burned up one night (and a very social fire it was, too, what with the pompiers waited on by a liveried club steward with glasses of chilled champagne), Freddy drove a fiacre load of top hatted youths through the firelines and to a point of vantage just as the roof fell in. "My patrons don't like the set pieces," he told bystanders as the cheering subsided, "so I allus get 'em there for the sky bombs and such!" There was a school of thought which maintained that Charlie Alexander, pontifical society editor of the *Transcript*, kept Freddy posted on major events of the Back Bay calendar.

Nobody ever learned, either, where or how Freddy lived. It was reported that he maintained housekeeping arrangements all the year round in the inner economy of the growler, tethering his horse to the trunk rack and sleeping with his feet out the window. He asserted that he had taught Theodore Roosevelt, while at Harvard, the essentials of boxing, and nobody would have batted an eye if he had claimed to have taught Grant the use of strong waters. For you could pay Freddy in cash or in trade, and six in the morning was entirely apt to find him seated, whip in hand, in your sitting room, his wicked white eyebrows working up and down with delight, as he put away the most amazing quantities of spirits. The fare from Boston to the vicinage of Harvard Square came to approximately a bottle of rye. Heart of oak and watchman of the night, undergraduates will not look upon his like again.

Utopia came to Harvard in 1924 through the agency of John Clement, Bradley Fisk and a dozen gallons of what was generally known as "Medford" rum. John was part proprietor, with Maurice Firuski, of the Dunster House Bookshop when it was located in Mount Auburn Street directly opposite the Phoenix-S. K. Club, and he lived in what then seemed Babylonish elegance in a three-room suite upstairs. Bradley was an undergraduate of some means, many clubs and a vast imagination, who lived round the corner in Apthorp House with Bydie Kilgour and John Rosecrans. The antecedents of the rum were never closely enquired into, but it was reputed to have been the fruit of a raid on a bonded warehouse in South Boston. Whether or not it was authentic Medford spirits nobody we knew was qualified to judge; certainly it was magnificent stuff, uncut, overproof, clear and with the bouquet of a great Cognac. It served the purpose.

The reordering nearer to our hearts' desire of an even then vaguely unsatisfactory world was planned nightly in John's rooms. John and Bradley smoked pipes, and the flue in the stove was a source of perpetual grief, with the result that Utopia was born in an atmosphere suggestive of nothing so much as the Burning of Rome. John was a Vermont Yankee with red hair and yellow Norseman's mustaches, and once it was agreed that he was to be supreme head of the wonderstate, a decision usually unanimously arrived at about midnight, there was nothing left but a few details before we went in town to the Lamb's Club for the night. Our principal thesis, if memory serves, held that central authority existed for maintaining an army, issuing currency against a reserve of proof spirits, and the collection and disposal of garbage. Beyond that we had little use for government, although occasionally Pierre LaRose, mystery man and Merlin of Harvard Yard and a herald of the Catholic Church, was consulted on problems of purely ritual significance. He knew, for instance, about the construction of Savannah Artillery Punch, and there was talk of making him chamberlain of the realm, but nothing much came of it. There were to have been three poet laureates, Barry Bingham, Robert Hillyer and Jack Wheelwright (the younger), but Wheelwright came back from Paris wearing a broad brimmed black hat and reading "transition" and was blackballed after an all night session in the course of which a window was broken and the stovepipe detached from the chimney. The Utopians nearly perished of asphyxiation.

Boston Herald, Harvard Tercentenary Supplement, September 13, 1936.

George Weller

ELEVEN O'CLOCK IN NOVEMBER

(1933)

The search for the great American college novel will always come back to George Weller's Not to Eat, Not for Love. *Its prestige has grown rather than dwindled with the years. In 1946 Richard C. Boys called it the "best of all our college novels" and fifteen years after publication Frederick L. Gwynn termed it "the very best of college fiction, and one of the most engaging and thoughtful novels of the interwar period." The author, a distinguished foreign correspondent and former Nieman Fellow, worked himself through Harvard College with the Class of 1929. He played a little football, waited on table at the Pi Eta Club and in Gore Hall, sold his blood, addressed envelopes for the Harvard University Press, worked afternoons as a tutor and playground supervisor, and even read proof for pay while serving as editorial chairman of the* Crimson. *The result is a remarkably broad picture of Harvard life in the early thirties, and yet character has not been neglected for the sake of the panoramic and historical purposes of the novel. Weller has described his book as an account of "one man's change against the period of Harvard's change."*

AT THE SIDEDOOR of the Lampoon the stink of the tenement beyond Central Square assaults the nose of circulation manager Waugh. In a smelly cloud above the unwashed boys hangs the rotten clothing smell of being poor, renewed each moment from those who wait, in sweatshirts and gray flannel skullcaps fantastically perforated, for Waugh to give out Lampoons. The Game Number lies piled high beside the door, red, blue, orange, green spluttered on slick white. He reads names. "Corcoran." A tall thin boy with rotten teeth, a baseball shirt with PELICANS showing under the unbuttoned sweater that just hangs on his shoulders, razors himself through the crowd. "What happened to your other four copies at the West Point game? You didn't come back." "I lost two." "Well?" "I say I lost them." "I know, but godammit, the other two?" "They got dirty when it rained." His excuse is amended anonymously by other salesmen. Alexander McCoomb, business manager of the Lampoon, comes suddenly out of the building. "How about a line here?" he says to the boys, grinning at them. They make him a line, and he brushes past circulation manager Waugh with a quick nod.

"What did you put for psycho-physical parallelism?" asks Abraham Eckstein, who lives in a Dorchester threedecker and whose father did piecework in Brooklyn but now owns his own little shop, of Harold Radman, whose father did piecework in the Bronx and now owns platoons of duplicate dwellings near Hell Gate Bridge and is building a skyscraper whose shadow lattices Brooklyn City Hall. Radman, anxious to be away, mumbles in the slurring accent of the Manhattan arriviste, "See you later. Forgot to get my tickets from the H. A. A." They leave the Saturday section in philosophy and part, the janitor locking Emerson Hall behind them.

A man in black about sixty or seventy years old enters Doctor Prentiss' Sever Hall section of first year Italian just as it begins, crosses the room and seats himself quietly at the end of the benches by the windows. Philip Hofstetter watches him, trying to remember what title has been underneath when he has seen the picture of that brown face, so wonderfully seamed with wrinkles. Briggs. Dean Briggs. There were two biographies on sale in the Coop. The new Briggs baseball cage. And before that the biggest dormitory at Radcliffe, Briggs Hall. But who was he, who was Dean Briggs? He was a man who was Dean under Eliot, wasn't he? And who was Eliot? A man who said: "The summer camp is America's greatest single contribution to education." But who was he? who were they?

At 11:17 traffic officer Joe Lang greets traffic officer Joe Doherty, tells him to watch the equipment on the broad driving a big blue boat when she comes out of the corner shoeshine parlor, picks from the traffic box floor the rolled morning paper that the guy in the new Ford about quarter past nine always passes him, and from a telephone booth in the bank calls his wife. "I'm handling the machine this aft for the captain. On the game squad. Harvard and somebody else. Some big one. It sounds like a real break to me, the captain being in the side car, because all the sergeants are pretty old and next year they'll be needing one that knows all the rules, nothing over the Anderson Bridge after 12:15 and all like that." Emerging through the greasy folding door he looks past the subway entrance islanded in the middle of the Square over toward Straus Hall, but the big blue boat has gone.

Bill Galt, down for the game, stomach feeling dried out from seven hours' dancing, remembers that in Cambridge they call the campus the Yard. Last night he dressed at the chapter house over at Boston Tech, but all the beds there are gone and to change from the wrinklearmed dinner coat in which he was found by a breakfast maid of the Boston Wellesley Club, caved in a wicker chair near the front door innocent and asleep, he now must discover Mower Hall, a fellow named Wells Fargo. He rests his suitcase to buy a feather for his derby. "Red?" "No," he says, and picks one to match his tie. "A quarter," says the vender, "and I hope you beat hell out of them. That's the way we feel about the Hahvad boys."

In an alley behind one of the big garages Teddy has propped up his big board covered with green felt against a hydrant. From a black rubberoid weekend case with the lock broken he takes two big kewpie dolls with lampshade skirts, the crimson and the green, and behind the frilly pink lining of the case he folds away the gray and yellow skirt that the West Point doll wore last week. In rows he pins to the board tin footballs hung on crimson silk, armbands thick-lettered in white felt, hatbands, handkerchiefs, and celluloid dogs with red ribbon plumply sashed. In the top left hand corner he affixes the fishtail banners with their slender reedy varnished standards and under it the wire holder for the bootleg programs. In his pockets he puts two pairs of opera glasses, the gold and the pearl. Through the broken half window of a cellar next the garage he reaches a bending explorative arm, feels around, scans the alley for enemies, then shoves the weekend case inside. Twelve cushions of straw covered with speckly butcher's paper go under one arm and holding the loaded board away from his shapeless blue serge knees he moves slowly out of the alley.

Wells Fargo, sent down from the lyke wake bridge game in the room of Farnsworth the tutor in economics to buy more lemons and a piece of ice in two paper bags, is addressed in the Square by a tall thin boy in a baseball shirt who tries to sell him a Lampoon and a football program. He is reminded that there is a football game, that he has not breakfasted except at four that morning, that he has not lunched, that none of the lyke wake bridge players is aware that flesh is soon to be torn asunder in the crimson name. He considers them: unbelieving, cynical, fractious, embittered, dubitative, rejective not reflective, subjunctive (the mood of doubt), deniers and repudiators all. Only in proof's august presence would their tongues, loose all night in the room of Timothy Farnsworth, cleave to their mouths. Seeing, they believe; unseeing, they heckle. His lips move: "I, Wells the winged, rainbowcolored messenger, manytongued, I saw the lemons pyramided beside the morning paper, I saw the lemons and I turned aside, and I bought of the football Lampoons two, and of the unofficial football programs two." Hymning through the Yard the merit of his deed he returns and first giving them gifts he breaks asunder that game of bridge, for he will sleep in his tent ere wardrums roll.

From a window of Claverly open on Linden Street pips a clarinet:

> Look where the crimson banners fly,
> Hark to the sound of tramping feet,
> There is a host approaching nigh,
> Harvard is marching up the street;

breathes a moment, and then begins:

> Hit the line for Harvard
> For Harvard wins today,
> And we'll show the sons of Eli
> That the crimson still holds sway.

A man in a white sailor hat, crimson sweater and white flannels comes to the window and cranes around the reddish cornice to ask the man in the next room the right time.

Two men stand on the edge of the Westmorly pool rubbing themselves dry. "Pretty lucky to be able to swim in your dormitory," says the visitor, watching the green waves grow calm. "I know," answered the host. "There's a story about Ann Pennington and this pool, but no one seems to tell it the same way."

Tex decides to wait until tomorrow to close his trunk. It's liable to be right cold in their big gray stadium, and he'd better tote his furcoat anyway, might have to wear it as far as Nashville. They and their hour examinations! Ought to give a boy a chance on a long pull, not bust him because he gets three Ds and a couple of Es the first time, before he's hardly got his parcels undone. Hope he doesn't meet Mr. Ogden from the Harvard Club of Dallas first off. Along about January-February he'll end up at State, just as he always thought. Anyway he met a lot of nice boys and that's something.

Of the two student waiters, Al and Wheatman, eating cream soup in the basement kitchen of the clubhouse while John the head student waiter hustles rice pudding with raisins to the last few members hastening gameward, Al the big redhead thinks about the members and Wheatman the sharpnosed blonde little Yankee thinks about the cream soup. They never talk while they eat. The redhead is always wondering whether the members think it is fresh for him to call some of them by their first names. The little Yankee watches for John's trips into the diningroom, because he does not like to blow healingly upon his soup spoon when John is around. And John, for the sixth time trying to drive the chef's cat out of the dark corners of the diningroom, is saying to himself: "The hardest thing I know is not to be a snob, either a snob downward, or a snob upward."

Six freshmen, two sophomores, three Business School and two Law School men are eating round mosqueshaped buns and drinking coffee inside the gates of Soldiers Field. Several wear the green pasteboard badges of head ushers. The sophomores are discussing whether it is better to see the game in full as a head usher or to earn a couple of dollars as ticket taker and miss the first half. Fallon, a law student who says he has been ticket taking for five years, tells them that all rainy day games and some others, all the big games anyway, begin with a kicking duel for the first quarter. Better take two dollars whenever they can get it for two hours' soft work.

In Mower Hall Mrs. Magillicuddy goes to the iron rail of the landing and sees that it is Mr. Fargo ascending, who lives in number 17.

Hat over his eyes, hands deep in the sagged pockets of his winter overcoat, the fifty yearold man is on the corner saying in a voice low, intimate and whining, "Tickets, boys? tickets?" Past him go all the twenty yearold men, luncheonbound before the game. They exchange stories of the blacklisted who, having sold their tickets to a speculator, will never again be able to see a Harvard game. But the fifty yearold man, safety razor salesman, shell and pea player, sideshow barker, dip, counterman, bum, concession artist, skating rink ticketman, hijacker, filling station handyman, shillaber, marathon dance timekeeper, gobetween, bookmaker, though it is almost too late for him to hope more from this day or more from this lifetime, goes on whining while he watches the traffic cop, "Tickets, boys? Tickets?"

And then as east in Boston harbor, in Kendall and Central Squares, in the Brighton stockyards the screaming wild white gnomes of steam dance around the sweatdrops on the whistles the sullen boom of Harvard's deep bell in the cupola of Harvard Hall, over all the hurriers in the restless Square, over all the walkers in the peaceful Yard, tolls down the cinder of the halfday, down into memory, down into forgetfulness.

Not to Eat, Not for Love (New York, 1933).

Alistair Cooke

A LESSON FOR YALE

(1951)

Despite Harvard's historical indebtedness to British tradition, cricket as played on Smith Field at the Harvard Business School and cricket as played at Lord's bear very little resemblance. Just to check this point the Manchester Guardian *sent its American correspondent to Cambridge one May afternoon, and he duly made his report under the heading "A Lesson for Yale . . . Magnificent Losers—by An Innings." Alistair Cooke, who briefly attended both Harvard and Yale, has been commentator on American affairs for the British Broadcasting Corporation since 1938 and, until 1972, Chief Correspondent in the United States for the* Guardian. *Before joining the* Guardian's *American staff in 1945, he was special correspondent on American Affairs for* The Times. *He is the author of* A Generation on Trial: U.S.A. v. Alger Hiss *(1950) and of* One Man's America *(1952),* Talk about America *(1968), and* Alistair Cooke's America *(1973). In the late 1950s Cooke was the host of the three-hour "Omnibus" television program devoted, totally "live," to Harvard, up to that point the most elaborate broadcast ever tried outside a central studio. He has since played host on some of public television's best dramatic programs, such as "Masterpiece Theater."*

THE RIVALRY of Yale and Harvard is going into its third century and has been bloodied down the years by many a student riot and pitched battle on each other's campus, to say nothing of the more routine muscle-matching of football games.

By the end of the last century the typical Yale man had evolved into a human type as recognisable as a Cossack or the Pitcairn skull, and there was a tense period in the late twenties and early thirties when Harvard could no longer bear close proximity with these well-developed anthropoids and primly refused to play them at anything. The football and chess fixtures were summarily cancelled. But by now even a Harvard man has heard of "one world," though of course he recognises no obligation to belong to it. So today, in a wild lunge of global goodwill, Harvard recalled the sons of Elihu Yale to their common heritage by suggesting a revival of the ancient joust known as cricket.

Not for 44 years have Yale and Harvard together attempted anything so whimsical. But a far-sighted alumnus lately gave $100 to revive the match and encouraged Harvard men to learn how the other half lives. Accordingly, with this bequest, pads and bats were fetched from Bermuda and Canada, and a roll of coconut matting was bought wholesale in Philadelphia. These props were assembled to-day on Smith Field, which is a dandelion enclosure lying west of the Harvard football stadium.

Here at 1:30 in the afternoon came ten of the visiting Yale men, various sets of white and grey gentlemen's pantings, a score-book and a couple of blazers for the sake of morale. Fifteen minutes later, and two hundred yards away, the Harvard team arrived in two old Chevrolets and a Cadillac. They carried the matting out to a weedy airstrip devoid of dandelions; stretched it out and pegged it down; made Indian signs at the glowering Yale men and, discovering that they understood English, formally challenged them to a match; spun a dime, won, and chose to go in first.

The eleventh Yale man was still missing and the Harvard captain, a mellifluous-spoken gentleman from Jamaica, offered to lend them a Harvard man. The Yale captain suspected a trap and said they would wait. Ten minutes later the eleventh man came puffing in, swinging from elm to elm. Everything was set. It was a cloudless day. It had been 92 the day before, but Providence obliged with a 35-degree drop overnight and we nestled down into a perfect English May day—sunny and green, with a brisk wind. The eleven spectators stomped and blew on their hands at the field's edge. And the game began.

Mr. Conboy and Mr. Cheek put on the purchased pads. Conboy took centre and faced the high lobbing off breaks of Mr. Foster, who delivered six of these nifties and was about to deliver a seventh but saw that Mr. Cheek had turned his back and was off on a stroll around the wicket. This mystery turned into a midfield conference at which it was found out that Yale expected to play an eight-ball over and Harvard a six. An Englishman on the Harvard side kindly acquainted the Yale men with the later history of cricket, and they settled for a six-ball over.

This shrewd act of gamesmanship effectively rattled the Harvard team for a while, and Conboy was soon out for three and Cheek for a duck. But Frank Davies, from Trinidad, knew a sophisticated play that shortly demoralized the Yale men. He came in slowly, hefted his pads, squinted at the coconut matting, patted it, rubbed his right shoulder, exercised his arm and, while the Yale men were still waiting for him to get set, started to cut and drive the Yale bowling all over the field.

Yale retorted by occasionally bowling an over of seven balls and once an over of five. It had no effect. They were now thoroughly cowed by Davies's professional air—once he cleverly feigned a muscle spasm and had the Yale side clustered round him terrified at the prospect of a doctor's bill. They were so trembly by now that they thought it only decent to drop any fly ball that came their way. Davies hooked a ball high to leg, but the Yale man obligingly stumbled, pawed the air, and gave a masterly—and entirely successful—performance of a man missing an easy catch.

Davies tried another hook with the same result, but the agreement was now so firmly understood that no Yale man would hold anything. Davies accordingly cut with flashing elbows, secure in the new-found knowledge that considered as a slip fielder a Yale man is a superlative bridge player. Davies went on to cut fine and cut square and drive the ball several times crack against the cement wall on which two mystified little boys were sitting. This, it was decided, was a boundary, and the scorer was told to put down four runs.

Davies did some more shrugs and lunges with his shoulder-blades, and, though there was a fairly constant trickle of bating partners at the other end, Davies had scored never less than two-thirds of the total. Suddenly he let go with a clean drive to mid-on for two and the astonished scorer discovered that the total was now 68 and Davies had reached his half-century.

There had been so far a regrettable absence of English spirit but Bruce Cheek, a civil servant, formerly of Peterhouse, Cambridge, was signed up to repair this omission by shouting "Well played, sir!"—an utterly alien sound to the two Boston small fry on the cement wall. This cued the growing crowd to rise and applaud the incomparable Davies. All fourteen of them joined in the ovation.

Ten minutes later the Rev. Bill Baker, a Baptist from Manchester, went in to receive his baptism of fire from Foster, who had suddenly found his off-break again. The result was that Mr. Baker was walking back right after walking out. Then Davies hit a short ball into a Yale man's hands. He failed to drop it in time. And the whole side was out. Harvard, 102—Davies, 70.

The two small fry dropped off the cement wall and came into the field to investigate the ritual. One of them stayed in the outfield and the tougher one came on and asked a question of the retreating umpire. It was a simple question. It was: "What game you playin', mister?" He was told, and turned round and bawled: "Cricket!" at his pal. The pal shrugged his little shoulders and went off and picked up two Boston terriers from somewhere, for no reason that anyone discovered then or since. They did manage to invade the field during the Yale innings and had to be shooed off.

Meanwhile we had taken tea, from a steel thermos about the size of a city gas tank. From nowhere a parson arrived, wearing an old straw caddie. It was a heart-warming sight, and I found myself mumbling through a tear the never-to-be-forgotten lines ". . . some corner of a foreign field that is forever Lipton's."

With a knightliness that cannot be too highly praised, Yale maintained the dogged pretense that they were playing cricket. It entitled their going out to the matting and back again in a slow though spasmodic procession. The continuity of this parade was assured by one Jehangir Mugaseth, a dark supple young man from Bombay, who had one of those long, beautiful, unwinding runs that would have petrified even the nonchalant Mr. Davies. At the other end was a thin, blond man with another long run, an American who distrusted breaks but managed a corkscrew baseball swerve in mid-air.

Between them the Yale team fell apart, and your reporter had no sooner looked down to mark "McIntosh caught" than he looked up to see Allen's middle stump sailing like a floating coffin past the wicketkeeper's right ear. Yale were suddenly all out—for 34. They followed on, more briskly this time—they were catching on to the essential tempo of the game—and were out the second time in record time for 24 runs. It was all over at 6.40.

No excuses were offered from the Yale team. They had fine English names—such as Grant, West, Allen, Foster, Parker, and Norton—and true to the Old Country traditions they lost magnificently. Nobody mentioned the mean Colonial skill recruited by the Harvard side. Nobody, that is, except a Yale man who dictated to me the exact tribal composition of the Harvard team: one Indian, one Jamaican, one Australian, one Egyptian, one Argentinian, one from Trinidad, one from Barbados, a Swiss New Yorker, two Englishmen, and a stranger from Connecticut.

But after all it's not the winning that matters, is it? Or is it? It's—to coin a word—the amenities that count: the smell of the dandelions, the puff of the pipe, the click of the bat (when Harvard are batting), the rain on the neck, the chill down the spine, the slow, exquisite coming on of sunset and dinner and rheumatism.

Manchester Guardian, May 21, 1951.

David Halberstam

THE GREATEST HOUSE CREW EVER

(1955)

A very long time ago, a quarter century or so before he had achieved na-
tional fame as a foreign correspondent and writer of books like The Making
of a Quagmire, The Best and the Brightest, *and* The Powers That Be, *David*
Halberstam was a Harvard undergraduate. He has described himself as a
"terrible student," somewhat careless about class attendance because of his
almost total dedication to the Crimson. *Yet, he consoles himself, "Now,*
sometimes, when I am around certifiably literary people and am a little em-
boldened by liquor, I mention almost slyly that Vladimir Nabokov taught
my freshman humanities class, on the novel . . . What I do not mention is
that I could not understand (no fault of his) a single word he said, that each
morning I would enter the lecture hall eager for his wisdom, anxious for
something tangible to write down in my notebook, only to depart some fifty
minutes later with a few scrawled half sentences, 'symbolism v. important,'
'epic has scope,' 'Quixote doomed to seek.'" Fortunately, despite the horrors
he has seen and the misuses of power he has observed in the world, Halber-
stam has retained his wonderful sense of humor, as the following remem-
brance of Harvard rowing attests.

THIS IS an untold sports epic. Leaf through the yellowed pages of the Boston
sports section or the *Crimson* and you will find nothing about it. Even in the
realm of word-to-mouth—where some of the greatest stories find their only
means of transportation—this story has no past. It is the story of the Greatest House Crew Ever. Nathan Pusey doesn't know about it; Tom Bolles and
Harvey Love don't know about it; indeed, and this is one of the most refreshing aspects, the members of the greatest crew themselves, now graduated and presumably educated men, don't know about it. Here then for
the first time is a short, slanted and inaccurate history of that crew.

The Great Crew occurred in the spring of 1955, which was not necessarily a vintage year on the River for Harvard. Dunster needed a crew. And
Dunster, for all its house athletic superiority, had never been noted for
crewmen—abundance of house basketball players, fine touch football team,
excellent squashers, yes. Crewmen? No. But according to the rules, even if
you don't have crewmen, you have to have a crew. That's where we came
in. We were the least traditional group in the most traditional of sports.

Even as an ordinary assembly of eight undergraduates we were pretty
unlikely; as an eight-man shell we were simply preposterous. Only one of

our men had rowed before going to college; two others had rowed as freshmen. We were all gloriously out of shape—our chief exercise stemmed from climbs to the third and fourth floors of Dunster House. We came from everywhere, Minnesota, Ohio, Massachusetts, Connecticut, Seattle, Washington, Illinois, and Manchester, England. About the only thing we had in common was considerably less rowing experience than our counterparts in the other House crews; that, and for some odd reasons, the desire to get out on the River.

The reasons behind that desire were as varied as the people. Paul Hewlett was a Knox fellow from England assigned to the House. Hewlett always wanted to see Americans in action. Someone assured him that if he went out on the River he would see plenty of both Americans and action. So he became our six man. Stan Katz, our coxswain and coach, had reportedly been chased out of his room by a temperamental roommate who preferred the company of a Radcliffe sophomore during the afternoons. Going out with us then allowed Katz to escape the roommate and also gave him a chance to yell at someone else for a change.

I had just finished a year as managing editor of the *Crimson* and suddenly found myself with some 65 additional hours a week, at least 35 of which I was reluctant to devote to Lamont. And this was the way it was: we were not athletes (an Army lieutenant has since confided in me that a giraffe on a bad day has superior coordination), we were instead grinds, and cynics, and premeds and playboys, and bright young men and fools. We were all at Harvard for different reasons and because of different influences—and the last place one would have expected to find us was on the Great Crew.

There was only one binding factor to the crew. This was a dark bespectacled Minnesotan named Dave Knutson. Knutson had never rowed before he came to Harvard, but he rowed second freshman heavies and he loved it. By junior year, he had to give up his place in the third varsity boat for a place in the Mallinckrodt chemistry labs. He has never forgiven science for this decision, and is this day, I am told, enlisting young businessmen for Proctor and Gamble advertising.

Knutson recruited the crew. It was not what you would call big-time pressure. He walked up to me and asked me if I could row.

I mumbled and admitted that I couldn't.

"Why not," he demanded, "you're 6'2", aren't you?"

I mumbled again. It was a little late to shrivel up, and after all, there were my feet. It is very hard to have size 12½ feet and not be willing to row.

"Would you like to row?" he asked.

Well I was pretty embarrassed by then, and I didn't dare give another negative answer so I said "Yes," and I became the number three man.

That was the way we became a crew. And we were terrible. You just don't take eight awkward, half-hearted, ill-conditioned undergraduates and make good oars out of them. I think if it was humanly possible we would have sunk the shell right at the beginning, and there would have been no Dunster crew.

But crew did to us what it had done to thousands before and what it will do to thousands after us; it caught us, hooked us and got into us. Even the week before Weld Boathouse opened, Knutson herded the group—all bitterly protesting of course—down to Newell where we used the varsity indoor tank. It was a painful experience. We had absolutely no form at all. What made it worse were the varsity oarsmen who watched us and roared with laughter.

This was very humiliating—I think we all felt a bond of sympathy with Knutson who knew them and therefore served as the brunt of their jokes. Instead of walking back to Dunster we double-timed. It was a faint stab at exercise—and probably made little impression on our bodies. But I think that's when we started to become a crew. At least no one complained about the exercise during the run.

But this didn't change us immediately. We could not row a quarter mile at a 15 stroke without becoming exhausted. We were awkward and jerky and all the terrible things a truly bad crew can be. Bruce McDonald, who rowed bow, complained bitterly about the lurching. It made it extremely difficult to get his oar into the water. "I'm not getting enough exercise," he said.

But in the face of this we continued to row. We enjoyed it and we were the first shell out and the last shell in. One week when it rained every day, unlike the other house shells, we rowed every day—and we even rowed on Saturday.

Knutson kept after us constantly—pushing us, demanding more, complaining about our style and our attitude. Finally we retaliated. One afternoon while we were taking a brief break Hewlett said:

"Ten thousand Swedes ran through the weeds . . ."

And Peter McKinney at five picked it up: ". . . Chased by one Norwegian!"

It helped. We roared—and from then on it became our byword. Whenever Katz wanted to put the stroke up he said: "The Norwegians are coming."

Somehow House crew started becoming important. Hewlett and I went to a pre-bachelor party for a friend and had one beer each; McKinney slipped out of a Glee Club rehearsal; and Katz started watching his weight. And we improved. Katz, who was a History and Lit major and could tell about these things, said that Hewlett rowed a mountain of water; Senkler, he said, had style; even Halberstam and Stimpson were improving. Perhaps they did go at their own beat, but at least when they went at the wrong beat they did it with far better form than three weeks ago.

But we were still a Dunster crew, and physically we looked like a Dunster crew, so no one expected much. There were, after all, four first-class crews that year—Eliot, the traditional scourge of the River, Leverett, with a light but skilled group composed almost entirely of former 150-pound oarsmen, Lowell, which as far back as three oar had a man who had rowed first boat varsity heavies, and Winthrop, which was experienced and heavy. Eliot was the favorite, but we felt Lowell was the crew to beat. Dunster, they said, should beat Dudley and might take Adams with a running start.

Eight crews were too many for one race and so they broke us down into two groups of four—with the top five—on the basis of time—to row for the championship.

Lowell and Winthrop were in our heat. We rowed down to the Basin kidding all the way. The last thing that disturbed us was the possibility of winning. That, after all, was the least of the reasons we were rowing.

We got a terrible start. A racing start is a delicate thing and we were not a delicate group. After about two minutes of a bumping, frustrating existence when no stroke was right, Knutson lowered the beat. We caught it and then slowly he brought it back up. And suddenly we were right. We were going as though the most natural thing in the world for us was to be out there on the Charles River moving backward at the rate of 31 pulls to the minute. It was smooth and strong. But of course, we were behind—or at least we thought so.

Then, just as we were about a quarter mile from the finish Katz suddenly yelled in utter amazement—as if he were sitting in the wrong shell:

"My God! You can win this race!"

A few seconds more he yelled even more incredulously:

"You're going to win this race!"

We did. I will never forget the Lowell people looking over at us, looking around at the other crews, then taking a second look and saying in utter amazement:

"Well rowed, Dunster House!"

We rowed back to the boathouse. The news of our victory had been relayed back to Dunster by the coaches' launch, so as we passed, half the House turned out to cheer. It was a momentous occasion.

We reached the boathouse and threw Katz into the water. Then because he was standing near the edge we threw Knutson in; then because he had always wanted to see Americans in action, we threw Hewlett in; then because I suggested Hewlett, they threw me in. A thing like that starts and it becomes very difficult to control . . .

The effect of the victory in the trials was immense upon the House. We were given three cheers as we walked in to dinner, and Stan Miles, the senior tutor, gave us Scotch instead of the usual sherry.

In the finals we again got a terrible start. This time we tried an authentic racing start, and by the time we got around to questioning its authenticity we were last, a very bad last.

"Not a pressure crew are you," said Katz over the megaphone. That eased things and we settled—and then picked up the beat. Leverett was way ahead, but Eliot, Lowell, and Winthrop were in a small group fighting for second, and they were all three lengths ahead of us.

Halfway through we passed Winthrop. Then we got Lowell.

"Eliot's loaded with Norwegians," Katz said, "lots of Norwegians."

Slowly we picked up on Eliot, stroke by stroke—until on the very last stroke of the race we caught and passed them. It was a case of our oars being in the water and theirs in the air. We were second, and not disappointed. Only with a running start could we have beaten Leverett—and our time in this race was even better than in the preliminary.

We laughed and kidded on the way back to the boathouse. Then, oddly, because Harvard after all is not for sentimentalists and we are consciously against a show of emotion—we sang *Auld Lang Syne* and then *Fair Harvard*. It is not easy to forget something like that. After all, we were upperclassmen, and we were not the singing type, or the kind that put Harvard stickers on windshields.

No one was thrown off the boathouse this time, which was just as well, since the Salk vaccine was then limited to little children and pregnant women. We stood around and talked. Someone asked Hewlett if he could get us into the Henleys. Hewlett said he had so little loyalty already he certainly didn't want to divide it in half. Then just like the singing, with no one actually saying anything, we went around and shook hands with each other. No one was going anywhere—we would all see each other at dinner that night and for the next few weeks. But we shook hands.

Harvard Today, May, 1958.

Roger Angell

HARVARD WINS, 29–29!
(*1968*)

There had to be a story about that 1968 football game with Yale. Even though there may be aficionados who maintain that some other football game with Yale was almost equally stupendous—the 1977 game, for example, which Harvard nearly won. Or a moment in some other sport like Izzy Zarakov's home run in the ninth inning of the 1927 baseball game, or that incredible team effort of 1962 that brought Harvard a one-point victory over

Yale and the Eastern intercollegiate swimming championship. Still the 29–29 tie "out-Dowlinged Dowling and out-Merriwelled Merriwell," as the Harvard Alumni Bulletin *commented. (The* Crimson *headlines read "Harvard Wins 29–29!") Although the* Bulletin *did a splendid job of reporting the moments of triumph, and James K. Glassman's account of the game will ever be memorable, it took the style and flair of Roger Angell, A.B. 1942, to set down what it all meant—ten years later. Angell, as all who read him know, is a great national treasure, and it is meet that he should have put his special imprint on the story of this high moment in Harvard's record.*

IT IS ONE of the prime sports memories in this undiscriminating collector's private gallery. Come into the inner room here, where the best few pieces are hung. Here's Lou Gehrig. That's Don Budge hitting a backhand to Fred Perry. There's Mickey Owen dropping the third strike at Ebbets Field. Here it is. Here we are. November 23, 1968, at Soldiers Field. The game has just ended—The Game, I mean—and both teams are still undefeated. I don't think *that* ever happened before. The picture's pretty dark, because it's the end of a long afternoon in November, but if you look over here, down at the closed end of the Stadium, you can make it all out. All the dark jerseys are jumping up and down—the whole Harvard squad seems to have both feet off the ground and both hands upraised. Some of the white jerseys are just beginning to walk slowly toward the Yale side of the field. No jumping over there. Now look back on this side, beyond the players and up the steep stands. This part of the picture is blurry, because the spectators there—all those thousands stuffed together, row on row, all the way up to the back of the colonnades—are dancing and crying and screaming and hugging and waving *their* arms in the air. If you look still higher, up above them and all the way around the topmost rim of the old stone battlements, you can see hundreds more waving, writhing watchers silhouetted against the evening sky—a frieze of exultation and disbelief.

The big Harvard player in the end zone, that Number 80, with the football held up in his right hand, is Pete Varney, the sophomore tight end. (Later on, he became a catcher with the White Sox.) He has just caught a pass from Frank Champi for a two-point conversion, and the game has just ended. No, that's not quite right. The clock actually ran out a few instants before that, during the play on which Champi found Vic Gatto in the corner of the end zone and threw to him for a touchdown; Varney's catch came after the gun (and after hundreds of spectators had been cleared from the field), because the conversion play is not timed. Two points and six points is eight points. Forty-two seconds earlier, Harvard had completed another eight-point play. Eight and eight is sixteen. Sixteen and thirteen is twenty-nine. Thirteen is what we had back when the score stood at 29–13, Yale—way back forty-two seconds ago. Now it's over. Twenty-nine to twenty-nine. Ten years ago. I'll never forget it.

More than forty thousand of us were there on that remarkable afternoon, and I imagine that everyone who stayed until the very end found himself exultantly or agonizingly thinking just that: "I'll never forget this." Not everyone stayed to the end, however. One of the early departees was Heywood Hale Broun, who was covering the game for CBS television news. He left in the middle of the fourth period and hopped into a waiting CBS limousine, which hurried him to a Boston studio, where he would tape his story in time for the national six o'clock news. He wrote on the way in town: undefeated Yale, behind its great senior pair, quarterback Brian Dowling and running back Calvin Hill, had utterly dominated the day, and by the second quarter Yale was ahead by 22–0. Dowling had rolled out for one touchdown, and had passed to Hill and to Del Marting for two more. As always, Dowling looked calm and commanding on the field, finding time and room to execute the killing play when it most mattered. In every football game in which Brian Dowling had started since the seventh grade in school, his team had emerged the winner. Undefeated Harvard, by contrast, had seen its two best runners, Vic Gatto and Ray Hornblower, hobble off the field with injuries, and its quarterback, George Lalich, who had performed valiantly all year, was so ineffective on this day that he had given way to a sub, Frank Champi. Just before the half, Champi threw a touchdown, to make it 22–6; early in the third period, he engineered another Crimson drive that brought things to 22–13. Yale, in spite of two fumbles (the visitors fumbled six times in all), took control again, and early in the fourth period, Dowling again rolled out for a touchdown. Yale chose to kick the point: 29–13 was safe enough.

Typing in the back seat, Woody Broun had encapsulated all this in his elegant polysyllables by the time his car delivered him to the studio. "I walked in there," he told me a few days later, "and found all the engineers watching the end of the game on a set over in the corner, and screaming. None of them were Harvard men, as far as I knew, but they were all in tears. That was when I realized I'd probably have to rewrite."

To tell the truth, time has blurred many of the details of the melodrama that began when Harvard captured a Yale fumble on its own fourteen yard-line, with three minutes and thirty-one seconds to go. Yale never got the ball back—I know that. I recall Champi being buried once for a frightful loss—and the play then reversed by a Yale penalty downfield. I recall Champi, again beleaguered by white jerseys, extemporizing a lateral to his big left tackle, Fritz Reed, who galloped heavily for many yards. I remember, of course, the predictable and critical onside kick after the first Harvard touchdown and two-pointer—a squibbler toward the Yale sideline, a frantic agglomeration of dirty white and crimson jerseys there, and then the Harvard players emerging exultantly from the scrum: a sophomore Harvard back named Bill Kelly had come up with the ball. And I recall—it was very late in the game now, and the green grass had gone almost black down there in the shadows—Vic Gatto, the captain, limping onto the field for the last couple of plays of his career, and his last touchdown.

The rest of it—the sudden gigantic party, the celebration of that tie as if it were a great Harvard victory, and its utterly downcast mourning by the shocked, murmurous, scattering Yalies—is more vivid to me than the game itself. Down all we Harvards came onto the field in an avalanche of noise and good feeling. The field, torn and lumpy and damp underfoot, was examined as if by historians at Thermopolae; here stood the fair-armed Champi, there uprose the Hephaestian Varney. We thickened, thousands of us, in front of the band, which was still in the stands, and sang and cheered and hugged each other, and then fell into an immense untidy parade behind the band, now haphazardly reformed on the field, as it boomed and tootled and trampled and danced down to one end of the Stadium and then back up to the other and off toward the fieldhouse. It was dark now, or almost dark, and as we came off the field everyone pointed up at the scoreboard, which now bore only the two illuminated twenty-nines.

The celebration went on for a long time, there in the mud in front of the fieldhouse. The players—heroes and footsoldiers—appeared in windows and doorways and up on the balcony and were cheered, and Coach John Yovicsin waved shyly to us through the darkness and noise. I can still feel the heavy thump of the drums in my stomach, and hear the chorus of one football song, "Yo-Ho," played again and again. Clustered and crowded around me are countless undergraduates in wild and wonderful clothes: serapes and parkas and kilts and beads and denims and coonskin caps and cowboy hats and straw skimmers (and one top hat) and scarves and tattered school sweatshirts. The young women with them are dressed exactly the same, and there are children here and there, staring up at the grownups gone mad with pleasure all about them, and a lot of old grads, of course—men my age and men much older, with their wives—in their old football-game overcoats and carrying their football-game steamer rugs and wearing, some of them, beat-up football-game fedoras that have survived thirty or forty famous November Saturdays, but none so famous as this one. The faces of the young people are beautiful, of course, but the geezers look wonderful, too; their cheeks are pink with excitement and their eyes are watery with cold or emotion. A lot of people here have been crying.

Why did it matter so much? Why did I care so much then, and why does it give me such pleasure to think again about that exaggerated afternoon and its unforeseen, impossible ending? Two reasons suggest themselves. The year of that game, 1968, was in most respects the most awful of this entire century in this country. Two national leaders had been assassinated, an incumbent president had declined to run for reelection because he had lost the trust of the people, campuses across the country had become the scene of intergenerational sieges and rioting. The war in Vietnam had torn us asunder. A tie in the Harvard-Yale game that year meant absolutely nothing to the nation, but to those of us who were there that day and in on that celebration, the game may have suggested, just for an instant, that things were not quite as bad as we had suspected. We were not utterly undone, after all, if some hundreds of thousands of us, of all ages, could forget our deep anxieties and apprehensions for a single afternoon and give our attention and then our joy to this suddenly illuminated ancient party. I think it may have been the first time that year that so many old people and so many young people had met anywhere and ended up smiling at each other.

The other reason, for me, is connected to the first. I come back to the Game, year after year, not so much for the sport as for a feeling of renewal. It has become a rite, and its capacity to move me does not have much to do with the final score or even with the pleasures of meeting old friends there, before the kick-off and after. It has something to do with the turn of the seasons; winter begins here, every year, when the gun goes off and the last cries and songs are exchanged across the field. It seems to mean something to be at the same place (in Cambridge or New Haven, it doesn't matter; they are the same) at exactly the same time each year. Each time, I have grown a year older, but each year the undergraduates there are exactly the same age. The whole crowd, in fact—all forty or fifty thousand of us—is always the same yet each of us inside that crowd is growing older. The Game picks us up each November and holds us for two hours and then releases us into the early darkness of winter, and all of us, homeward bound, sense that we are different yet still the same. It is magic. The football doesn't matter; no great championship is at stake here, thank God. Yet ritual requires its own special memories and celebratory fires, at least from time to time. For those of us on the right side of the field that day, the 29–29 tie in 1968 was the first game ever to live up to The Game.

Harvard Football News, November 18, 1978.

Erich Segal

LOVE AND VIOLENCE ON THE ICE

(1970)

Though Erich Segal is a scholar of repute, author of works on Euripides, Plautus, and Aristophanes, his public fame stems from more popular productions, such as the screenplay of the Beatles' Yellow Submarine *and the novel and motion picture* Love Story. *He is also an accomplished marathon runner who spent "a happy decade . . . mostly in Dunster House," first as an undergraduate and then as a resident tutor. He departed to teach classics at Yale. In his immensely popular novel of 1970, Segal portrayed the undergraduate love affair between a fairly normal Radcliffe woman of humble background and a fairly normal Harvard man of assured family and fortune, depicting a kind of Harvard life which had immediate appeal to millions of readers, seeking escape from news of undergraduate protests and college disorders. The scene below describes a Dartmouth hockey game with Oliver on the ice and Jenny in the stands.*

Oliver Barrett IV   Senior
Ipswich, Mass.   Phillips Exeter
Age: 20   5'11", 185 lbs.
Major: Social Studies
Dean's List: '61, '62, '63
All-Ivy First Team: '62, '63
Career Aim: Law

BY NOW Jenny had read my bio in the program. I made triple sure that Vic Claman, the manager, saw that she got one.

"For Christ's sake, Barrett, is this your first date?"

"Shut up, Vic, or you'll be chewing your teeth."

As we warmed up on the ice, I didn't wave to her (how uncool!) or even look her way. And yet I think she *thought* I was glancing at her. I mean, did she remove her glasses during the National Anthem out of respect for the flag?

By the middle of the second period, we were beating Dartmouth 0–0. That is, Davey Johnston and I were about to perforate their nets. The Green bastards sensed this, and began to play rougher. Maybe they could break a bone or two before we broke them open. The fans were already screaming for blood. And in hockey this literally means blood or, failing that, a goal. As a kind of noblesse oblige, I have never denied them either.

Al Redding, Dartmouth center, charged across our blue line and I slammed into him, stole the puck and started down-ice. The fans were roaring. I could see Davey Johnston on my left, but I thought I would take it all the way, their goalie being a slightly chicken type I had terrorized since he played for Deerfield. Before I could get off a shot, both their defensemen were on me, and I had to skate around their nets to keep hold of the puck. There were three of us, flailing away against the boards and each other. It had always been my policy, in pile-ups like this, to lash mightily at anything wearing enemy colors. Somewhere beneath our skates was the puck, but for the moment we were concentrating on beating the shit out of each other.

A ref blew his whistle.

"You—two minutes in the box!"

I looked up. He was pointing at me. Me? What had I done to deserve a penalty?

"Come on, ref, what'd I do?"

Somehow he wasn't interested in further dialogue. He was calling to the officials' desk—"Number seven, two minutes"—and signaling with his arms.

I remonstrated a bit, but that's de rigueur. The crowd expects a protest, no matter how flagrant the offense. The ref waved me off. Seething with frustration, I skated toward the penalty box. As I climbed in, listening to the click of my skate blades on the wood of the floor, I heard the bark of the PA system:

"Penalty. Barrett of Harvard. Two minutes. Holding."

The crowd booed; several Harvards impugned the vision and integrity of the referees. I sat, trying to catch my breath, not looking up or even out onto the ice, where Dartmouth outmanned us.

"Why are you sitting here when all your friends are out playing?"

The voice was Jenny's. I ignored her, and exhorted my teammates instead.

"C'mon, Harvard, get that puck!"

"What did you do wrong?"

I turned and answered her. She was my date, after all.

"I tried too hard."

And I went back to watching my teammates try to hold off Al Redding's determined efforts to score.

"Is this a big disgrace?"

"Jenny, please, I'm trying to concentrate!"

"On what?"

"On how I'm gonna total that bastard Al Redding!" I looked out onto the ice to give moral support to my colleagues.

"Are you a dirty player?"

My eyes were riveted on our goal, now swarming with Green bastards. I couldn't wait to get out there again. Jenny persisted.

"Would you ever 'total' me?"

I answered her without turning.

"I will right now if you don't shut up."

"I'm leaving. Good-bye."

By the time I turned, she had disappeared. As I stood up to look further, I was informed that my two-minute sentence was up. I leaped the barrier, back onto the ice.

The crowd welcomed my return. Barrett's on wing, all's right with the team. Wherever she was hiding, Jenny would hear the big enthusiasm for my presence. So who cares where she is.

Where is she?

Al Redding slapped a murderous shot, which our goalie deflected off toward Gene Kennaway, who then passed it down-ice in my vicinity. As I skated after the puck, I thought I had a split second to glance up at the stands to search for Jenny. I did. I saw her. She was there.

The next thing I knew I was on my ass.

Two Green bastards had slammed into me, my ass was on the ice, and I was—Christ!—embarrassed beyond belief. Barrett dumped! I could hear the loyal Harvard fans groaning for me as I skidded. I could hear the blood-thirsty Dartmouth fans chanting.

"Hit 'em again! Hit 'em again!"

What would Jenny think?

Dartmouth had the puck around our goal again, and again our goalie deflected their shot. Kennaway pushed it at Johnston, who rifled it down to me (I had stood up by this time). Now the crowd was wild. This had to be a score. I took the puck and sped all out across Dartmouth's blue line. Two Dartmouth defensemen were coming straight at me.

"Go, Oliver, go! Knock their heads off!"

I heard Jenny's shrill scream above the crowd. It was exquisitely violent. I faked out one defenseman, slammed the other so hard he lost his breath and then—instead of shooting off balance—I passed off to Davey Johnston, who had come up the right side. Davey slapped it into the nets. Harvard score!

In an instant, we were hugging and kissing. Me and Davey Johnston and the other guys. Hugging and kissing and back slapping and jumping up and down (on skates). The crowd was screaming. And the Dartmouth guy I hit was still on his ass. The fans threw programs onto the ice. This really broke Dartmouth's back. (That's a metaphor; the defenseman got up when he caught his breath.) We creamed them 7–0.

If I were a sentimentalist, and cared enough about Harvard to hang a photograph on the wall, it would not be of Winthrop House, or Mem Church, but of Dillon. Dillon Field House. If I had a spiritual home at Harvard, this was it. Nate Pusey may revoke my diploma for saying this, but Widener Library means far less to me than Dillon. Every afternoon of my college life I walked into that place, greeted my buddies with friendly obscenities, shed the trappings of civilization and turned into a jock. How great to put on the pads and the good old number 7 shirt (I had dreams of them retiring the number; they didn't), to take the skates and walk out toward the Watson Rink.

Love Story (New York, 1970).

John Updike

THE FOLLY ON BOW STREET

(1973)

Were The Harvard Book *not a prose anthology, John Updike, A.B. 1954, would surely be represented here by his "Apologies to Harvard"—"dear, drear Harvard, crown of the pilgrim mind"—the Phi Beta Kappa poem of 1973, which Updike considers the best thing he ever wrote about his alma mater. He has also dealt with the Harvard scene in fictional form in a lengthy short story, "The Christian Roommates," to be found in his collection* The Music School.

Probably the cleverest cartoonist and sharpest satirist of his time at Harvard, Updike became president of the Lampoon in his junior year and often stepped into the breach, almost alone, when contributors were short. Now known as one of the great prose stylists of American letters, Updike treats mature and difficult themes in his fiction and criticism, but we are fortunate to have evidence that Updike still thinks back fondly on his Harvard years, particularly on his adventures with the Lampoon. Has the Lampoon ever been characterized more lovingly than in this fragment from Updike's introduction to the magazine's centennial anthology?

THERE IT STANDS, in the shadow of Adams House, where Mt. Auburn Street unaccountably branches into Bow, an unaccountable little flatiron building with Amsterdam gables and a face—two round windows that look cross-eyed, a red lantern for a nose, and, above the bright bow-tie of its door, an exclamatory mouth of which the upper lip is so complex it might be a mustache. A copper hardhat tasseled with a cage completes the apparition. This is the Lampoon building. One's first impression is of an extravagance and even in the 1950s, before the national-parody money shored up the subsiding foundations and restored luster to the furnishings, this impression was confirmed by entering the tiled, worn, odorous, festooned interior. The gorgeous playful thing was put up, as a civilized prank, by American wealth when it was untaxed and unconscience-stricken: it is a folly and a toy and a bastion, an outcropping, like the brick mass of Harvard itself, of that awful seismic force which has displaced nine-tenths of the world: WASP Power. The Lampoon is a club and, as do all clubs, feeds on the delicious immensity of the excluded. Robert Lampoon, born Robert H. Stewart, like a lay brother gratefully turned apologist and promulgator, lucidly advances the doctrine usually left unspoken: college men are the "highest type in the world," Harvard men are "the best of all," and Poonsters are "the cream of Harvard men" . . . And with him we travel to an enchanted realm where young Lord Byrons, garbed as monks and nuns, are served roast pigs on platters and sit each "with a bottle of imported sherry between his knees." In 1973, sipping our bitter domestic sherry, we feel, even without John Reed and Granville Hicks to remind us, that there is a shadow side to this "Harvard of the chosen few," the underworld of callow snobbishness . . . The Lampoon, though a flower of the Establishment, is a twisted flower, stemmed from the Establishment's wise instinct to grant itself license —license to be idle and (hence) open, license to mock and hence (symbolically) to destroy. Of my uneasy year as president, I remember fondly certain moments of ecstatic, probably revolutionary confusion. Trying to deliver stern speeches about impending deadliness, I was pelted with buttered rolls. A born follower, I found myself leading a bellowed medley of preposterously obscene songs, waving my potent baton, the presidental jester's stick . . . donated, as I remember, by the beneficent Sadri Khan. Where is it now? Not stolen, I hope, as was my engraved mug, and my youth.

The Lampoon is saved from mere sociable fatuity by being also *The Lampoon*, a magazine. Month after month, through thin seasons and thick, it insists on coming out, even though it contain naught but hastily hustled ads and snippets of past issues scrambled together through a haze of beer and boisterous kibitzing. Along with the anarchic camaraderie of Thursday nights, I cherish those groggy Monday-morning subway rides down to the South Station stop and thence to the emporium (up several flights in a quivering elevator of art-nouveau tracery) of Best Print, Inc., where a mild, mustached, and unblinking craftsman called Harold (Harold o' Bestprint, he was invariably called in the Common Books) relieved me of my raggedy pasted-up dummy and, unless his lawyer advised him otherwise, turned it into 1200 (more or less) shiny magazines, with real staples, on real paper— or "stock," as we learned to term it, amid a richness of resonant professional terms such as "pica" and "ital" and "halftone" and "mortise" and "bleed." An undergraduate magazine loses its maturest contributors every June, a fact which, combined with the distracted condition of the average collegiate head, creates a wonderfully ongoing vacuum for those few who want to fill it. Fop though it pretends to be, the Lampoon has apprenticed a sturdy number of professional writers and artists. It was the editorial aspect, presumably, that weighed so heavily on the young Robert Benchley as he wrote to his mother of his election as president, "It will mean a lot of work and a lot of worry and responsibility, for it is a responsible position" . . . George Santayana, a half-century earlier, even more solemnly felt the invisible pressure of the "fortnightly editor," conjured up in "an atmosphere of respect for holy things," by young men with "literary tastes, leaning toward the sentimental and nobly moral" . . . The vocabulary surprises but the reverent tone is right. Raising a smile is a delicate piece of artistic engineering that may well prepare one for higher things. "It's all in the execution," we used to say of some particularly lame cartoon idea hatched in a Sanctum gag session. That is to say, there *was* such a thing as execution; no humor is so broad it cannot be relayed badly or ably . . .

The Harvard Lampoon Centennial Celebration, 1876–1976, ed. Martin Kaplan (Boston, 1973).

VI

HER SOLITARY CHILDREN

At the age of sixteen I turned my steps towards these venerable halls, bearing in mind, as I have ever since done, that I had two ears and but one tongue . . . Suffice it to say, that though bodily I had been a member of Harvard University, heart and soul I have been far away among the scenes of my boyhood. Those hours that should have been devoted to study have been spent in roaming the woods, and exploring the lakes and streams of my native village.

HENRY D. THOREAU (1837)

Henry Adams

THE EDUCATION OF A HARVARD MAN

(1856 and 1907)

Until the publication of Ernest Samuels' The Young Henry Adams in 1948, those who had read the autobiographical Education of Henry Adams only knew that the bitter and disappointed author looked back on his life at Harvard with no dislike but little enthusiasm. It was not ever thus, for the undergraduate Henry Adams showed himself to be as properly sentimental and youthful in his enthusiasm as the older Henry Adams pictured himself failing and intellectually misplaced. Adams—the grandson and great grandson of an American president—was the son of Charles Francis Adams. He was for seven years Assistant Professor of History at Harvard (1870–1877), and his historical contribution was the History of the United States of America [1801 to 1817]. His reflections on his college room come from The Harvard Magazine (1856); his mature conclusions about Harvard from his Education, completed in 1905 and first published in a limited edition in 1907.

MY OLD ROOM

IT IS DUSTY and dirty and dingy. Spiders have spun their webs on the ceiling. The paper is faded with age, and discolored with stains of many hues. Long experience in Cambridge has taken away from my furniture all that was breakable, and my chairs are marked deeply with the initials of half my classmates and a host of friends. Queer odors linger about the closets and the bedrooms, as though their former contents had been embalmed and laid on the shelves, like the urns in the old Roman tombs.

In winter the winds howl around me, and rush over my head, without the slightest regard to the walls which should keep them away. No amount of heat yet attained will prevent the water which stands in my pitcher from freezing inches deep in the cold weather of the winter term. In short, my room is the coldest, the dirtiest, and the gloomiest in Cambridge.

But what do I care for the cold, so long as a good fire burns in the grate? Or what do I care for the dust that whitens my pictures and hats and books, or the stains that mark my walls, or the cracks that run through the ceiling, so long as they stay on the walls and ceiling, and give no discomfort to me? Or what do I care for the darkness and gloom, when, in the long December evenings, the cannel snaps and blazes in the fireplace, and shines merrily on the gilded books that line my shelves? . . .

My room is in an old house which seems to have witnessed guest after guest come within its doors when Freshmen, full of ambition and hope, and leave them at last when Seniors, downcast and disappointed . . .

In this old room, have I lived while years have passed by. In the winter I have set up my household gods upon this hearth, and many a time when in the bright, frosty forenoons the sun has cheerfully shone into my room, and the fire blazed warmly in the grate, I have asked myself whether life here is not as full of enjoyment as life can be, and whether negative happiness, the absence of all real discomfort, is not, after all, the best that is granted to man . . .

The philosophy of College rooms! How many misunderstand it! How many take their degrees, and depart, without having such an idea enter their heads! Yet few satires would be more bitter than a history of the thoughts of the inhabitants of these rooms, of their actions, and of their failures or successes, as the case may be. How great a proportion of those who have left their names on the catalogues should we find acknowledging that here they have wasted their time, have thrown away their opportunities and have disappointed their friends? Not that they have done wrong. No. They have simply done nothing.

But College has been very much abused; much more so than it deserves. Stories of the past—told by fathers and grandfathers over their walnuts and wine, or handed down in venerable manuscripts, or laughed at in the works of brilliant and famous writers for centuries back—have cast a shade of doubt upon the respectability of College life. Visions of midnight suppers and Deipnosophoi Clubs, spectres of irreligion and blasphemy, of utter and irretrievable corruption, of sensuality and brutalizing debauchery, in the imaginations of very many who live near and among us, would rightly be the only recollections that a College room could call up. They insist upon condemning the whole upon the testimony against a few, and must have it that I am thoughtless and extravagant, because such may have been the vices of my predecessors.

All students know that these ideas are mistaken ones. We all know that dissipation is the exception, and not the rule. Here and there a person may be led away, or lead himself away. The bright air-castle that his friends built for him may be undermined. That great column of fire and cloud that led him forward always, when he first trod these College paths, the vast outline of his hopes filled in by his boyish ambition, may be overthrown and vanish for ever. But was a rational system ever invented that admitted of no failure? Did ever the most earnest enthusiast, even in his wildest conceptions of universal happiness, imagine a world where temptation should exist, and yet no sin? With such a system Paradise would indeed be regained.

One of the common systems of education is little better than another. If the College is dangerous and hurtful, the store or the counting-room is as bad, or worse. Fortune does not favor alone their occupants, but her cornucopia showers its gifts equally upon all men. The standard of morality, which some say is so low among us, is not raised by confinement to the counter and the ledger. Temptation and vice are citizens of the world, and wander at will,—no more confined within College walls than shut away from monks and nuns by their deep vows, or by the bolts and bars of their cloisters.

I am about leaving my old room to seek another resting-place, and I hope a better one. It has been very pleasant to me, however, and I am very sorry to go. To me it will always be haunted by my companions who have been there, by the books that I have read there, by the pleasure and the pain that I have felt there, and by a laughing group of bright, fresh faces, that have rendered it sunny in my eyes for ever. I have learned there what College really is. I have learned there one part of the great secret of life. I have learned, too, however late, that College rank is *not* a humbug, as some pretend; also, that nothing can be done without study, though some suppose that "smartness" is sufficient. If a boy appreciated all this before he entered College, his life there might be a success, and not, what it usually is, a failure.

And so I have bidden my room good-bye. I have spent my last evening there. I have studied my last lesson there. I have seen the pictures taken down from the walls, and the carpet torn up from the floor. Since I entered it, the world has not stood still. Many of the greatest events of the century will be associated in my mind with my old room . . .

The Harvard Magazine, September, 1856.

THE GRADUATE HAD FEW STRONG PREJUDICES

The next regular step was Harvard College. He was more than glad to go. For generation after generation, Adamses and Brookses and Boylstons and Gorhams had gone to Harvard College, and although none of them, as far as known, had ever done any good there, or thought himself the better for it, custom, social ties, convenience, and, above all, economy, kept each generation in the track. Any other education would have required a serious effort, but no one took Harvard College seriously. All went there because their friends went there, and the College was their ideal of social self-respect.

Harvard College, as far as it educated at all, was a mild and liberal school, which sent young men into the world with all they needed to make respectable citizens, and something of what they wanted to make useful ones. Leaders of men it never tried to make. Its ideals were altogether different. The Unitarian clergy had given to the College a character of moderation, balance, judgment, restraint, what the French called *mesure;* excellent traits, which the College attained with singular success, so that its graduates could commonly be recognized by the stamp, but such a type of character rarely lent itself to autobiography. In effect, the school created a type but not a will. Four years of Harvard College, if successful, resulted in an autobiographical blank, a mind on which only a water-mark had been stamped.

The stamp, as such things went, was a good one. The chief wonder of education is that it does not ruin everybody concerned in it, teachers and taught. Sometimes in after life, Adams debated whether in fact it had not ruined him and most of his companions, but, disappointment apart, Harvard College was probably less hurtful than any other university then in existence. It taught little, and that little ill, but it left the mind open, free from bias, ignorant of facts, but docile. The graduate had few strong prejudices. He knew little, but his mind remained supple, ready to receive knowledge.

The Education of Henry Adams (Boston and New York, 1918).

W. E. Burghardt Du Bois

THAT OUTER WHITER WORLD OF HARVARD

(c. 1890)

One of Harvard's most famous black alumni is W. E. B. Du Bois, who graduated from the College in 1890 and received the doctorate of philosophy in political science in 1895. Until his death in 1963, Dr. Du Bois, a noted teacher of economics and history, was a convinced disciple of Marxian socialism and insisted on unity of racial action in carrying out the social reforms which he felt were necessary before the Negro could ever attain full freedom. From 1910 to 1933 Dr. Du Bois edited The Crisis, *a magazine de-*

voted to the social betterment of the Negro. He also served as director of pub-
licity and research for the American Association for the Advancement of
Colored People but resigned in disagreement in 1933 over the direction
which he felt the Association's policies should take. From 1933 to 1944 he
was head of the sociology department at Atlanta University. He was the au-
thor of many books, largely scholarly interpretations of various Negro prob-
lems, but they include his "essay toward an autobiography of a race con-
cept," Dusk of Dawn *(1940), which outlines his radical philosophy. "I was*
not and am not a communist," Dr. Du Bois asserted. "I do not believe in the
dogma of inevitable revolution in order to right economic wrong. I think war
is worse than hell, and that it seldom or never forwards the advance of the
world."

I WAS HAPPY at Harvard, but for unusual reasons. One of these unusual circumstances was my acceptance of racial segregation. Had I gone from
Great Barrington high school directly to Harvard I would have sought
companionship with my white fellows and been dissappointed and embittered by a discovery of social limitations to which I had not been used. But I
came by way of Fisk and the South and there I had accepted and embraced
eagerly the companionship of those of my own color. It was, of course, no
final end. Eventually with them and in mass assault, led by culture, we were
going to break down the boundaries of race; but at present we were banded
together in a great crusade and happily so. Indeed, I suspect that the joy of
full human intercourse without reservations and annoying distinctions,
made me all too willing to consort with mine own and to disdain and forget
as far as was possible that outer, whiter world.

Naturally it could not be entirely forgotten, so that now and then I
plunged into it, joined its currents and rose or fell with it. The joining was
sometimes a matter of social contact. I escorted colored girls, and as pretty
ones as I could find, to the vesper exercises and the class day and commencement social functions. Naturally we attracted attention and sometimes the shadow of insult as when in one case a lady seemed determined to
mistake me for a waiter. A few times I attempted to enter student organizations, but was not greatly disappointed when the expected refusals came.
My voice, for instance, was better than the average. The glee club listened
to it but I was not chosen a member. It posed the recurring problem of a
"nigger" on the team.

In general, I asked nothing of Harvard but the tutelage of teachers and
the freedom of the library. I was quite voluntarily and willingly outside its
social life. I knew nothing and cared nothing for fraternities and clubs. Most
of those which dominated the Harvard life of my day were unknown to me
even by name. I asked no fellowship of my fellow students. I found friends
and most interesting and inspiring friends among the colored folk of Boston
and surrounding places. With them I carried on lively social intercourse,

but one which involved little expenditure of money. I called at their homes and ate at their tables. We danced at private parties. We went on excursions down the Bay. Once, with a group of colored students gathered from surrounding institutions, we gave Aristophanes' "The Birds" in a colored church.

So that of the general social intercourse on the campus I consciously missed nothing. Some white students made themselves known to me and a few, a very few, became life-long friends. Most of them, even of my own more than three hundred classmates, I knew neither by sight nor name. Among my Harvard classmates many made their mark in life: Norman Hapgood, Robert Herrick, Herbert Croly, George A. Dorsey, Homer Folks, Augustus Hand, James Brown Scott, and others. I knew practically none of these. For the most part I do not doubt that I was voted a somewhat selfish and self-centered "grind" with a chip on my shoulder and a sharp tongue.

Something of a certain inferiority complex was possibly present: I was desperately afraid of not being wanted; of intruding without invitation; of appearing to desire the company of those who had no desire for me. I should have been pleased if most of my fellow students had desired to associate with me; if I had been popular and envied. But the absence of this made me neither unhappy nor morose. I had my "island within" and it was a fair country.

Only once or twice did I come to the surface of college life. First, by careful calculation, I found that I needed the cash of one of the Boylston prizes to piece out my year's expenses. I got it through winning a second oratorical prize. The occasion was noteworthy by the fact that the first prize went to a black classmate of mine, Clement Morgan. He and I became fast friends and spent a summer giving readings along the North Shore to help our college costs. Later Morgan became the center of a revolt within the college. By unwritten rule, all of the honorary offices of the class went to Bostonians of Back Bay. No Westerner, Southerner, Jew, nor Irishman, much less a Negro, had thought of aspiring to the honor of being class day official. But in 1890, after the oratorial contest, the students of the class staged an unexpected revolt and elected Morgan as class orator. There was national surprise and discussion and later several smaller Northern colleges elected colored class orators.

This cutting of myself off from my fellows did not mean unhappiness nor resentment. I was in my early young manhood, unusually full of high spirits and humor. I thoroughly enjoyed life. I was conscious of understanding and power, and conceited enough still to think, as in high school, that they who did not know me were the losers, not I. On the other hand, I do not think that my classmates found in me anything personally objectionable. I was clean, not well-dressed but decently clothed. Manners I regarded as more or less superfluous and deliberately cultivated a certain brusquerie. Personal adornment I regarded as pleasing but not important. I was in Harvard but not of it and realized all the irony of "Fair Harvard." I sang it because I liked the music.

The Harvard of 1888 was an extraordinary aggregation of great men. Not often since that day have so many distinguished teachers been together in one place and at one time in America. There were William James, the psychologist; Palmer in ethics; Royce and Santayana in philosophy; Shaler in geology; and Hart in history. There were Francis Child, Charles Eliot Norton, Justin Winsor, and John Trowbridge; Goodwin, Taussig, and Kittredge. The president was the cold, precise but exceedingly just and efficient Charles William Eliot, while Oliver Wendell Holmes and James Russell Lowell were still alive and emeriti.

By good fortune, I was thrown into direct contact with many of these men. I was repeatedly a guest in the house of William James; he was my friend and guide to clear thinking; I was a member of the Philosophical Club and talked with Royce and Palmer; I sat in an upper room and read Kant's *Critique* with Santayana; Shaler invited a Southerner, who objected to sitting by me, out of his class; I became one of Hart's favorite pupils and was afterwards guided by him through my graduate course and started on my work in Germany.

It was a great opportunity for a young man and a young American Negro, and I realized it. I formed habits of work rather different from those of most of the other students. I burned no midnight oil. I did my studying in the daytime and had my day parceled out almost to the minute. I spent a great deal of time in the library and did my assignments with thoroughness and with prevision of the kind of work I wanted to do later. I have before me a theme which I wrote October 3, 1890, for Barrett Wendell, then the great pundit of Harvard English. I said:

> Spurred by my circumstances, I have always been given to systematically planning my future, not indeed without many mistakes and frequent alterations, but always with what I now conceive to have been a strangely early and deep appreciation of the fact that to live is a serious thing. I determined while in the high school to go to college—partly because other men went, partly because I foresaw that such discipline would best fit me for life . . . I believe foolishly perhaps, but sincerely, that I have something to say to the world, and I have taken English 12 in order to say it well.

Barrett Wendell rather liked that last sentence. He read it out to the class.

It was at Harvard that my education, turning from philosophy, centered in history and then gradually in economics and social problems. Today my course of study would have been called sociology; but in that day Harvard did not recognize any such science. I had taken in high school and at Fisk the old classical course with Latin and Greek, philosophy and some history. At Harvard I started in with philosophy and then turned toward United

States history and social problems. The turning was due to William James. He said to me, "If you must study philosophy, you will; but if you can turn aside into something else, do so. It is hard to earn a living with philosophy."

So I turned toward history and social science. But there the way was difficult. Harvard had in the social sciences no such leadership of thought and breadth of learning as in philosophy, literature, and physical science. She was then groping and is still groping toward a scientific treatment of human action. She was facing at the end of the century a tremendous economic era. In the United States, finance was succeeding in monopolizing transportation, and raw materials like sugar, coal, and oil. The power of the trust and combine was so great that the Sherman Act was passed in 1890. On the other hand, the tariff at the demand of manufacturers continued to rise in height from the McKinley to the indefensible Wilson tariff of 1894. A financial crisis shook the land in 1893 and popular discontent showed itself in the Populist movement and Coxey's Army. The whole question of the burden of taxation began to be discussed and England barred an income tax in 1894.

These things were discussed with some clearness and factual understanding at Harvard. The tendency was toward English free trade and against the American tariff policy. We reverenced Ricardo and wasted long hours on the "Wages-fund." The trusts and monopolies were viewed frankly as dangerous enemies of democracies, but at the same time as inevitable methods of industry. We were strong for the gold standard and fearful of silver. On the other hand, the attitude of Harvard toward labor was on the whole contemptuous and condemnatory. Strikes like that of the anarchists in Chicago, the railway strikes of 1886; the terrible Homestead strike of 1892 and Coxey's Army of 1894 were pictured as ignorant lawlessness, lurching against conditions largely inevitable. Karl Marx was hardly mentioned and Henry George given but tolerant notice. The anarchists of Spain, the Nihilists of Russia, the British miners—all these were viewed not as part of the political development and the tremendous economic organization but as sporadic evil. This was natural. Harvard was the child of its era. The intellectual freedom and flowering of the late eighteenth and early nineteenth centuries were yielding to the deadening economic pressure which made Harvard rich but reactionary. This defender of wealth and capital, already half ashamed of Sumner and Phillips, was willing finally to replace an Eliot with a Lowell. The social community that mobbed Garrison, easily hanged Sacco and Vanzetti.

Dusk of Dawn (New York, 1940).

Edwin Arlington Robinson

BEGINNING TO FEEL AT HOME

(1891)

A small-town boy from Gardiner, Maine, Edwin Arlington Robinson came to Harvard in the autumn of 1891 for two years as a special student. He was lonely and blue; his finances worried him; and he was handicapped by poor eyesight and painful ear trouble. Yet at Harvard the shy and discriminating Robinson found friends, those who would sit and smoke a pipeful or two in stimulating conversation, those who liked to share a bottle over some good talk about recent books. To him this was satisfaction. "I have two more examinations yet to take, French and English, and then my Harvard career will be at an end," he wrote his friend, Harry de Forest Smith, in 1893. "I have no particular desire to come another year, but I would hate to part with the experience of the past two. I have lived, upon the whole, a very quiet life, but for all that I have seen things that I could not possibly see at any other place, and have a different conception of what is good and bad in life. From the standpoint of marks, my course here has been a failure, as I knew well enough it would be; but that is the last thing in the world I came here for." And later, he reflected, "I wonder more and more just where I might have come out if I had never seen Harvard Square as I did . . . There was something in the place that changed my way of looking at things." The record of this change is contained in his long and faithful correspondence with Harry Smith—then a student at Bowdoin but later Professor of Greek at Amherst—from which these excerpts are taken.

November 15, 1891

I AM beginning to feel at home and am in a better frame of mind than when I wrote you that half lugubrious epistle telling you of my woes and uncertainties. Of course there is some uncertainty now, and will be until after the mid-years, but I am not going to trouble myself any more about it. "Sufficient unto the day, etc."

.   .   .   .

Last evening I went into town to see the Russell Comedy Co. in the *City Directory*. I think it is a little the flattest thing I ever witnessed on any stage. I cannot understand how the Athenians can support such stuff. Cheap farce-comedy is undermining the whole dramatic scheme and God only knows what we shall have in a few years to come. Richard Mansfield plays *Dr. Jeckyll and Mr. Hyde* next Sat. evening and if nothing happens I shall be on hand to see it.

Last Wednesday, Dr. Schuman came to see me and I went to see him in the evening. Beer, oysters, pipes, cigars, and literary conversation were in order. It was the most thoroughly Bohemian evening I ever passed and one of the most satisfactory. The Doctor "uttered nothing base" during the whole time. I wished you were with us more than once; you would have enjoyed it.

For some reason or other I cannot take any particular interest in Harvard athletics, though I am as much a member of the University as any Senior. And I will say here that there is remarkably little feeling between the students of different grades. I am on comparatively good terms with a Senior, a Soph and two or three Specials. They are all alike, and all seem to be fellows of good common-sense. The "fast set" we hear so much about is not a fictitious body, but they keep themselves severely away from the common herd. I can generally tell one when I see him, and he is not much to see either.

The Professors are gentlemen; but when some upper-class man is temporarily promoted to some petty office like superintendent of exams, or assistant registrar, then authority is agonizing. They are harmless, however, and I rather enjoy watching them after I get used to their ways. I might do the same thing myself, unconsciously, should the opportunity present itself. But it will not.

There are eight bowling courts in the gym, and I am quite a fiend for that rather antiquated sport. As to the other appliances, I have not touched them. I fear I am not an enthusiast on the subject of physical culture, though I am an excellent subject to [be] experimented with. My stooping shoulders are disfiguring, but I cannot bring myself to a regular course of training. In fact, I cannot find the time . . .

November 22, 1891

The banners of Harvard are still crimson, but the air is blue—in a double sense. You could not well picture a more melancholy gang than came home from Springfield Saturday night. There was no enthusiasm, no yelling, and practically no drinking. Sorrow was drowned in thought rather than in booze. I am drowning mine in self-hatred, for this reason:

I was fool enough to sacrifice the Springfield game for *Dr. Jeckyll and Mr. Hyde.* It was Mansfield's only performance of the play in Boston this season and I was determined to take it in. *Hinc illae,* etc. The play was totally disappointing. Beyond the transformation scenes it does not amount to much anyway; and much to my surprise and disgust, the stage was in total darkness whenever they took place, and all the time that Hyde was personated. It might as well have been performed by an usher, as far as scenic effect was concerned. Of course we had the voice, but that was hardly satisfactory.

Just now, as I am writing, the Sabbath stillness is broken by a gang of four fellows riding by in a carriole yelling "Ya-a-ale! Ya-a-a-le!" It seems surprising that a Yale man should be in Cambridge today and perhaps they are only friends of the New Haven boys. They are making noise enough, whoever they are. If I could have the money that has changed hands through the game I should invite you down for a year or two. It would have done your soul good to see the scramble for tickets. As high as twenty and twenty-five dollars was paid for seats on the Harvard Side. I might have bought a seat in the centre section for three dollars Saturday morning, but I was set on *Dr. Jeckyll*. In consequence, I am now in a fierce humor for having made such an unconscionable fool of myself. Read the Sunday *Herald* and judge for yourself what I missed, while I might have taken it in as well as not. Experience is no doubt a good thing but I hate to think of spending a whole life in acquiring it.

I am beginning to feel blue already, thinking that I have but one year in Cambridge. And yet it is a little strange that I should feel so. I have made no intimate friends, in fact I have not yet met a single soul to whom I have been in any manner drawn. Literature is at a discount here, but I may find some damned fool yet who will read and smoke with me. The satisfaction I derive is doubtless due to the absolute change and the college atmosphere, which is enormous. I think of the old gray-headed buffers who have climbed the stairs of Massachusetts and Harvard Halls, and dream of a room in classic Holworthy. This is foolishness, but there is no great harm in it . . .

December 8, 1891

I suppose about this time you are wondering where in the devil my letter is; and in view of this state of things I will explain. Last Sunday I was (to use a worldly expression) sick enough to kill. I did nothing but lie around my room and feel blue and nasty. If I had written a letter I should probably [have] put the pessimism of our friend Omar Khayyam completely in the shade; so I concluded to let it go till I was in a better humor. I trust I am now and will try to make up for my failure to keep up the agreement.

This is the first opportunity this evening I have had a chance [*sic*] to write, though I have been intending to do so since I came out of Memorial from dinner at six o'clock. As soon as I got settled for a ruminative smoke in walked Mr. H. A. Cutler, business manager for the *Advocate*, and a rattling good fellow. He had the proof of my latest poetical (?) effusion,—a rondeau entitled "In Harvard 5." The subject is Shakespeare and you will see it in due time. I have not sent the last number containing the "Villanelle of Change," as I was hoping to send you a copy of the *Monthly* with one of my productions; but in this my hopes were blasted. After Cutler left, my cousins from Cambridgeport came and staid till nine o'clock. Then came a knock at the door; and at my yell of "Come!" in stepped Robert Morss Eliott [Lovett], perhaps the leading spirit of Harvard outside of athletics. Of course Capt. Trafford and his crew are with the immortals, Eliott [Lovett] is a Senior and in many respects a remarkable man. Without any "gushing," I actually felt honored to receive a call from him, being a Special and a first year man at that. He is editor in chief of the *Monthly* and brought back the manuscript of my sonnet on Thomas Hood. At a meeting of the board of editors it was weighed in the balance and found wanting. (Perhaps I have some foolish opinions of my own, but they are of no value in this case). We talked of college papers and kindred matters for about half an hour, when he left with a request for another contribution—which I have decided to make—and an urgent request to call on him. If I succeed in getting in with such fellows as that, college life will prove most agreeable. I think the best way to do it will be to keep silence on the matter of contributions. I may change my mind but these are my feelings at present. I was sailing along in such elegant shape, putting whatever I chose into the *Advocate*, that I must confess this declination put a slight "damper" on me; but Mr. Lovett (I wrote Eliott before by mistake—must have been thinking of the President)—showed himself to be such a gentleman and "white man" that I could not feel offended. If I am a little foxy I may get in with the whole gang, which will be rather more pleasant than my present situation. Of course I have found some good fellows—but you will understand precisely what I mean. I will send you the *Advocate* with Villanelle tomorrow with this letter. Perhaps I have tired you with talk of my own affairs, but you know that I am prone to enter into confidence with now and then a fellow spirit. Of course I need not ask you not to mention anything that I have written.

Our blue books in French came due today, and as I was badly prepared I shall get a low mark. But will work up in the review and ought not to get into trouble. The courses here in elementary French are conducted in a rather peculiar manner, and in my own poor opinion call for much unnecessary work on the part of the student; but I foresee good results in the future if I half do myself justice. My rank on the last bluebook was 9—, scale same as G.H.S. That was not bad, but quite a number got 10. The exams go by letters—A-B-C, etc. I have not yet heard from my English 9 exams. At last I am through with that most estimable lady, Jane Austen. Next week we go to work on the essayists—Hazlitt first, then Lamb and Leigh Hunt. When De Quincey and Carlyle come, there will be trouble. They are two writers of whom I am absolutely ignorant. I have read *Sartor Resartus*, but should hate to be called upon to write a review of it.

I am afraid that this letter will prove rather dry picking. I am sure it would to anyone *but* you, and feel a little guilty as it is. Rec'd a letter from Gledhill today. He is going on swimmingly and is apparently one of the "big guns" of St. L. University. That is one advantage, as I have said before, of a small college. For the leaders it is clover, but for the others it cannot be so pleasant if they are at all sensitive. Here at Harvard there is less of the real college spirit, but there is more equality. I have been treated first rate by everyone I have seen and have tried to do the same myself. Lovett said that my sonnet was about the first contribution on record by a first year man to the *Monthly.* I have an idea that that fact was instrumental in its restoration to its "inventor."

I have been writing for three quarters of an hour, and begin to feel sleepy. Will have a little smoke and turn in. Wish you were here with me.

December 13, 1891

This time I will endeavor to be prompt in my weekly letter and give you a page or two of my usual drool so that it may reach you the first of the week. I also hope to hear from you, as usual. Your letters form no inconsiderable item in my college existence. A letter from a human being who realizes the fact that there is some breadth to human sympathy, and that all men are in a way themselves, is a matter not to be disregarded. I think you give me much credit when you tell me that I know a different Smith from that popularly regarded as "Smithy"—at least that was the former title you bore. At present you are Mr. Smith, of Rockland, and as such I send you greeting. By your permission, or I suppose more properly "with your permission," I shall make you a Christmas present in the form of Wm. Hazlitt's essays. Some of them will please you—if they don't you need not read them. You may be amused at my freedom in this announcement, but you must remember that Robinson is writing and Robinson sometimes says strange things . . .

Last night I went to the "Globe" with Barnard to see Agnes Huntington in *Captain Thérèse.* Agnes was well enough but the opera was painful in its vacuity, if I may use the word. We left at the end of the second act, and repaired to Herr Engelhart's beer shop where [we] spent the remainder of the evening quite pleasantly and I think profitably. If you could come up here for a week or so this spring I should be more than happy; and I think you would manage to enjoy yourself too. Harvard University is a great place to set a man's thoughts going. Yesterday I watched two able-bodied men spreading fragrant New England dung on the campus. I began to wonder if they were not deriving quite as much benefit from Harvard as some of its more scholarly inmates. I think they were, and I have an idea that I felt a kind of envy for their lot. There is a kind of poetry in scattering dung—if the dung is good—that must needs awaken a fine sentiment in the mind of a man of any imagination. The excrement gives the increment to the emerald grass, etc., and when the spring zephyrs begin to blow the transformation becomes apparent. It is great stuff, and the faculty are obviously poets. They use no prepared fertilizer whatever, but cling to the mushy manure of our, and their, ancestors. And shades of Cincinnatus, doesn't it stink! The odor made me homesick, I think; never before have I realized what a real countryman I am. No man of feeling can smell the odors of his native land two hundred miles from home without experiencing a tender surge of emotion within his breast . . .

Denham Sutcliffe, ed., *Untriangulated Stars: Letters of Edwin Arlington Robinson to Harry de Forest Smith, 1890–1905* (Cambridge, 1947).

Charles Macomb Flandrau

A DEAD ISSUE

(1897)

Few books so much annoyed the 100 percent Harvard men of the nineties as Charles M. Flandrau's Harvard Episodes *(1897). The trouble was that it hit home, and loyal Harvard men did not like to think that readers outside Cambridge might get the wrong picture of Harvard life. No good Harvard man, commented the* Graduates' *Magazine, "would wish . . . to hear it quoted from unfriendly lips." And even Dean Briggs, as late as 1912, was saying that he thought it would have been much better if Flandrau had never written his broad condemnation of college snobs and butterflies. To modern eyes and ears Flandrau's book has the universal ring that approaches truth. Despite the fact that he retrieved some of his lost repute among his contemporaries with his later books, his lasting literary monument will probably be* Harvard Episodes, *from which comes this sharp story of a lonely and inexperienced teacher and his relations with his undergraduate club.*

MARCUS THORN, instructor in Harvard University, was thirty-two years old on the twentieth of June. He looked thirty-five, and felt about a hundred. When he got out of bed on his birthday morning, and pattered into the vestibule for his mail, the date at the top of the *Crimson* recalled the first of these unpleasant truths to him. His mirror—it was one of those detestable folding mirrors in three sections—enabled him to examine his bald spot with pitiless ease, reproduced his profile some forty-five times in quick succession, and made it possible for him to see all the way round himself several times at once. It was this devilish invention that revealed fact number two to Mr. Thorn, while he was brushing his hair and tying his necktie. One plus two equalled three, as usual, and Thorn felt old and unhappy. But he didn't linger over his dressing to philosophise on the evanescence of youth; he didn't even murmur,—

> Alas for hourly change! Alas for all
> The loves that from his hand proud youth lets fall,
> Even as the beads of a told rosary.

He could do that sort of thing very well; he had been doing it steadily for five months. But this morning, the reality of the situation—impressed upon him by the date of his birth—led him to adopt more practical measures. What he actually did, was to disarrange his hair a little on top,—fluff it up to make it look more,—and press it down toward his temples to remove the appearance of having too much complexion for the size of his head. Then he went out to breakfast.

Thorn's birthday had fallen, ironically, on one of those rainwashed, blue-and-gold days when "all nature rejoices." The whitest of clouds were drifting across the bluest of skies when the instructor walked out into the Yard; the elms rustled gently in the delicate June haze, and the robins hopped across the yellow paths, freshly sanded, and screamed in the sparkling grass. All nature rejoiced, and in so doing got very much on Thorn's nerves. When he reached his club, he was a most excellent person not to breakfast with.

It was early—half-past eight—and no one except Prescott, a sophomore, and Wynne, a junior, had dropped in as yet. Wynne, with his spectacles on, was sitting in the chair he always sat in at that hour, reading the morning paper. Thorn knew that he would read it through from beginning to end, carefully put his spectacles back in their case, and then go to the piano and play the "Blue Danube." By that time his eggs and coffee would be served. Wynne did this every morning, and the instructor, who at the beginning of the year had regarded the boy's methodical habits at the club as "quaint,"—suggestive, somehow, of the first chapter of "Pendennis,"—felt this morning that the "Blue Danube" before breakfast would be in the nature of a last straw. Prescott, looking as fresh and clean as the morning, was laughing over an illustrated funny paper. He merely nodded to Thorn, although the instructor hadn't breakfasted there for many months, and called him across to enjoy something. Thorn glanced at the paper and smiled feebly.

"I don't see how you can do it at this hour," he said; "I would as soon drink flat champagne." Prescott understood but vaguely what the man was talking about, yet he didn't appear disturbed or anxious for enlightenment.

"I'll have my breakfast on the piazza," Thorn said to the steward who answered his ring. Then he walked nervously out of the room.

From the piazza he could look over a tangled barrier of lilac bushes and trellised grapevines into an old-fashioned garden. A slim lady in a white dress and a broad brimmed hat that hid her face was cutting nasturtiums and humming placidly to herself. Thorn thought she was a young girl, until she turned and revealed the fact that she was not a young girl—that she was about his own age. This seemed to annoy him in much the same way that the robins and Wynne and the funny paper had, for he threw himself into a low steamer-chair where he wouldn't have to look at the woman, and gave himself up to a sort of luxurious melancholy.

In October, nine months before, Thorn had appeared one evening in the doorway of the club dining-room after a more or less continuous absence of eight years from Cambridge. It was the night before college opened, and the dining-room was crowded. For an instant there was an uproar of confused greetings; then Haydock and Ellis and Sears Wolcott and Wynne— the only ones Thorn knew—pushed back from the table and went forward to shake hands with him. Of the nine or ten boys still left at the table by this proceeding, those whose backs were turned to the new arrival stopped eating and waited without looking around, to be introduced to the owner of the unfamiliar voice. Their companions opposite paused too; some of them laid their napkins on the table. They, however, could glance up and see that the newcomer was a dark man of thirty years or more. They supposed, correctly, that he was an "old graduate" and a member of the club.

"You don't know any of these people, do you?" said Haydock, taking him by the arm; "what a devil of a time you've been away from this place."

"I know that that's a Prescott," laughed the graduate. In his quick survey of the table, while the others had been welcoming him back, his eyes had rested a moment on a big fellow with light hair. Everybody laughed, because it really was a Prescott and all Prescotts were simply more or less happy replicas of all other Prescotts. "I know your brothers," said the graduate, shaking hands with the boy, who had risen.

"It's Mr. Thorn." Haydock made this announcement loud enough to be heard by the crowd. He introduced every one, prefixing "Mr." to the names of the first few, but changing to given and even nicknames before completing the circuit of the table. The humour of some of these last,—"Dink," "Pink," and "Mary," for instance,—lost sight of in long established usage, suggested itself anew; and the fellows laughed again as they made a place for Thorn at the crowded table.

"It's six years, isn't it?" Haydock asked politely. The others had begun to babble cheerfully again of their own affairs.

"Six! I wish it were; it's eight," answered Thorn. "Eight since I left college. But of course I've been here two or three times since,—just long enough to make me unhappy at having to go back to Europe again."

"And now you're a great, haughty Ph.D. person, an 'Officer of Instruction and Government,' announced in the prospectus to teach in two courses," mused Ellis, admiringly. "How do you like the idea?"

"It's very good to be back," said Thorn. He looked about the familiar room with a contented smile, while the steward bustled in and out to supply him with the apparatus of dining.

It was, indeed, good to be back. The satisfaction deepened and broadened with every moment. It was good to be again in the town, the house, the room that, during his life abroad, he had grown to look upon more as "home" than any place in the world; good to come back and find that the place had changed so little; good, for instance, when he ordered a bottle of beer, to have it brought to him in his own mug, with his name and class cut in the pewter,—just as if he had never been away at all. This was but one of innumerable little things that made Thorn feel that at last he was where he belonged; that he had stepped into his old background; that it still fitted. The fellows, of course, were recent acquisitions—all of them. Even his four acquaintances had entered college long since his own time. But the crowd, except that it seemed to him a gathering decidedly younger than his contemporaries had been at the same age, was in no way strange to him. There were the same general types of young men up and down the table, and at both ends, that he had known in his day. They were discussing the same topics, in the same tones and inflections that had made the dinner-table lively in the eighties,—which was not surprising when he considered that certain families belong to certain clubs at Harvard almost as a matter of course, and that some of the boys at the table were the brothers and cousins of his own classmates. He realized, with a glow of sentiment, that he had returned to his own people after years of absence in foreign lands; a performance whose emotional value was not decreased for Thorn by the conviction, just then, that his own people were better bred, and better looking, and better dressed than any he had met elsewhere. As he looked about at his civilised surroundings, and took in, from the general chatter, fragments of talk,—breezy and cosmopolitan with incidents of the vacation just ended,— he considered his gratification worth the time he had been spending among the fuzzy young gentlemen of a German university.

Thorn, like many another college antiquity, might have been the occasion of a mutual feeling of constraint had he descended upon this undergraduate meal in the indefinite capacity of "an old graduate." The ease with which he filled his place at the table, and the effortless civility that acknowledged his presence there, were largely due to his never having allowed his interest in the life of the club to wane during his years away from it. He knew the sort of men the place had gone in for, and, in many instances, their names as well. Some of his own classmates—glad, no doubt, of so congenial an item for their occasional European letters—had never failed to write him, in diverting detail, of the great Christmas and spring dinners. And they, in turn, had often read extracts from Thorn's letters to them, when called on to speak at these festivities. More than once the graduate had sent, from the other side of the world, some doggerel verses, a sketch to be used as a dinner-card, or a trifling addition to the club's library or dining-room. Haydock and Ellis and Wolcott and Wynne he had met at various times abroad. He had made a point of hunting them up and getting to know them, with the result that his interest had succeeded in preserving his identity; he was not unknown to the youngest member of the club. If they didn't actually know him, they at least knew of him. Even this crust is sweet to the returned graduate whose age is just far enough removed from either end of life's measure to make it intrinsically unimportant.

"What courses do you give?" It was the big Prescott, sitting opposite, who asked this. The effort involved a change of colour.

"You'd better look out, or you'll have Pink in your class the first thing you know," some one called, in a voice of warning, from the other end of the table.

"Yes; he's on the lookout for snaps," said some one else.

"Then he'd better stay away from my lectures," answered Thorn, smiling across at Prescott, who blushed some more at this sudden convergence of attention on himself. "They say that new instructors always mark hard— just to show off."

"I had you on my list before I knew who you were," announced another. "I thought the course looked interesting; you'll have to let me through."

"Swipe! swipe!" came in a chorus from around the table. This bantering attitude toward his official position pleased Thorn, perhaps, more than anything else. It flattered and reassured him as to the impression his personality made on younger—much younger—men. He almost saw in himself the solution of the perennial problem of "How to bring about a closer sympathy between instructor and student."

After dinner Haydock and Ellis took him from room to room, and showed him the new table, the new rugs, the new books, *ex dono* this, that, and the other member. In the library he came across one of his own sketches, prettily framed. Some of his verses had been carefully pasted into the club scrap-book. Ellis and Haydock turned to his class photograph in the album, and laughed. It was not until long afterwards that he wondered if they had done so because the picture had not yet begun to lose its hair. When they had seen everything from the kitchen to the attic, they went back to the big room where the fellows were drinking their coffee and smoking. Others had come in in the interval; they were condoling gaily with those already arrived, on the hard luck of having to be in Cambridge once more. Thorn stood with his back to the fireplace, and observed them.

It was anything but a representative collection of college men. There were athletes, it was true,—Prescott was one,—and men who helped edit the college papers, and men who stood high in their studies, and others who didn't stand anywhere, talking and chaffing in that room. But it was characteristic of the life of the college that these varied distinctions had in no way served to bring the fellows together there. That Ellis would, without doubt, graduate with a *magna*, perhaps a *summa cum laude*, was a matter of interest to no one but Ellis. That Prescott had played admirable foot-ball on Soldiers' Field the year before, and would shortly do it again, made Prescott indispensable to the Eleven, perhaps, but it didn't in the least enhance his value to the club. In fact, it kept him away so much, and sent him to bed so early, that his skill at the game was, at times, almost deplored. That Haydock once in a while contributed verses of more than ordinary merit to the "Monthly" and "Advocate" had nearly kept him out of the club altogether. It was the one thing against him,—he had to live it down. On the whole, the club, like all of the five small clubs at Harvard whose influence is the most powerful, the farthest reaching influence in the undergraduate life of the place, rather prided itself in not being a reward for either the meritorious or the energetic. It was composed of young men drawn from the same station in life, the similarity of whose past associations and experience, in addition to whatever natural attractions they possessed, rendered them mutually agreeable. The system was scarcely broadening, but it was very delightful. And as the graduate stood there watching the fellows—brown and exuberant after the long vacation—come and go, discussing, comparing, or simply fooling, but always frankly absorbed in themselves and one another, he could not help thinking that however much such institutions had helped to enfeeble the class spirit of days gone by, they had a rather exquisite, if less diffusive spirit of their own. He liked the liveliness of the place, the broad, simple terms of intimacy on which every one seemed to be with every one else, the freedom of speech and action. Not that he had any desire to bombard people with sofa-cushions, as Sears Wolcott happened to be doing at that instant, or even to lie on his back in the middle of the centre-table with his head under the lamp, and read the "Transcript," as some one else had done most of the evening; but he enjoyed the environment that made such things possible and unobjectionable.

"I must make a point of coming here a great deal," reflected Thorn.

The next day college opened. More men enrolled in Thorn's class that afternoon than he thought would be attracted by the subject he was announced to lecture in on that day of the week. Among all the students who straggled, during the hour, into the bare recitation-room at the top of Sever, the only ones whose individualities were distinct enough to impress themselves on Thorn's unpractised memory, were a Negro, a stained ivory statuette of a creature from Japan, a middle-aged gentleman with a misplaced trust in the efficacy of a flowing sandy beard for concealing an absence of collar and necktie, Prescott, and Haydock. Prescott surprised him. There was a crowd around the desk when he appeared, and Thorn didn't get a chance to speak to him; but he was pleased to have the boy enroll in his course,—more pleased somehow than if there had been any known intellectual reason for his having done such a thing; more pleased, for instance, than he was when Haydock strolled in a moment or two later, although he knew that the senior would get from his teachings whatever there was in them. Haydock was the last to arrive before the hour ended. Thorn gathered up his pack of enrollment cards, and the two left the noisy building together.

"Prescott enrolled just a minute or two before you did," said Thorn, as they walked across the Yard. He was a vain man in a quiet way.

"Yes," answered Haydock drily, "he said your course came at a convenient hour"; he didn't add that, from what he knew of Prescott, complications might, under the circumstances, be looked for.

"Shall I see you at dinner?" Thorn asked before they separated.

"Oh, are you going to eat at the club?" Haydock had wondered the night before how much the man would frequent the place.

"Why, yes, I thought I would—for a time at least." No other arrangement had ever occurred to Thorn.

"That's good—I'm glad," said the senior; he asked himself, as he walked away, why truthful people managed to lie so easily and so often in the course of a day. As a matter of fact, he was vaguely sorry for what Thorn had just told him. Haydock didn't object to the instructor. Had his opinion been asked, he would have said, with truth, that he liked the man. For Thorn was intelligent, and what Haydock called "house broken," and the two had once spent a pleasant week together in Germany. It was not inhospitality, but a disturbed sense of the fitness of things that made Haydock regret Thorn's apparent intention of becoming so intimate with his juniors. The instructor's place, Haydock told himself, was with his academic colleagues, at the Colonial Club—or wherever it was that they ate.

Thorn did dine with the undergraduates that night, and on many nights following. It was a privilege he enjoyed for a time exceedingly. It amused him, and, after the first few weeks of his new life in Cambridge, he craved amusement. For in spite of the work he did for the college—the preparing and delivering of lectures, the reading and marking of various written tasks, and the enlightening, during consultation hours, of long haired, long winded seekers after truth, whose cold, insistent passion for the literal almost crazed him—he was often profoundly bored. He had not been away from Cambridge long enough to outlive the conviction, acquired in his Freshman year, that the residents of that suburb would prove unexhilarating if in a moment of inadvertence he should ever chance to meet any of them. But he had been too long an exile to retain a very satisfactory grasp on contemporary Boston. Of course he hunted up some of his classmates he had known well. Most of them were men of affairs in a way that was as yet small enough to make them seem to Thorn aggressively full of purpose. They were all glad to see him. Some of them asked him to luncheon in town at hours that proved inconvenient to one living in Cambridge; some of them had wives, and asked him to call on them. He did so, and found them to be nice women. But this he had suspected before. Two of his classmates were rich beyond the dreams of industry. They toiled not, and might have been diverting if they hadn't—both of them—happened to be unspeakably dull men. For one reason or another, he found it impossible to see his friends often enough to get into any but a very lame sort of step with their lives.

Thorn's occasional meetings with them left him melancholy, sceptical as to the depth of their natures and his own, cynical as to the worth of college friendships—friendships that had depended, for their warmth, so entirely on propinquity—on the occasion. His most absorbing topics of conversation with the men he had once known—his closest ties—were after all issues very trivial and very dead. Dinner with a classmate he grew to look on as either suicide, or a post mortem.

It was the club with its fifteen or twenty undergraduate members that went far at first toward satisfying his idle moments. Dead issues, other than the personal traditions that added colour and atmosphere to the every day life of the place, were given no welcome there. The thrill of the fleeting present was enough. The life Thorn saw there was, as far as he could tell, more than complete with the healthy joy of eating and drinking, of going to the play, of getting hot and dirty and tired over athletics, and cold and clean and hungry again afterwards. The instructor was entranced by its innocence—its unconscious contentment. It was so unlike his own life of recent years, he told himself; it was so "physical." He liked to stop at the club late in the winter afternoons, after a brisk walk on Brattle Street. There was always a crowd around the fire at that hour, and no room that he could remember had ever seemed so full of warmth and sympathy as the big room where the fellows sat, at five o'clock on a winter's day, with the curtains drawn and the light of the fire flickering up the dark walls and across the ceiling. He often dropped in at midnight, or even later. The place was rarely quite deserted. Returned "theatre bees" came there to scramble eggs and drink beer, instead of tarrying with the mob at the Victoria or the Adams House. In the chill of the small hours, a herdic load of boys from some dance in town would often stream in to gossip and get warm, or to give the driver a drink after the long cold drive across the bridge. And Thorn, who had not been disposed to gather up and cling to the dropped threads of his old interests, who was not wedded to his work, who was not sufficient unto himself, enjoyed it all thoroughly, unreservedly—for a time.

For a time only. For as the winter wore on, the inevitable happened— or rather the expected didn't happen, which is pretty much the same thing after all. Thorn, observant, analytical, and—where he himself was not concerned—clever, grew to know the fellows better than they knew themselves. Before he had lived among them three months, he had appreciated their respective temperaments, he had taken the measure of their ambitions and limitations, he had catalogued their likes and dislikes, he had pigeonholed their weaknesses and illuminated their virtues. Day after day, night after night, consciously and unconsciously, he had observed them in what was probably the frankest, simplest intercourse of their lives. And he knew them.

But they didn't know him. Nor did it ever occur to them that they wanted to or could. They were not seeking the maturer companionship Thorn had to give; they were not seeking much of anything. They took life as they found it near at hand, and Thorn was far, very far away. For them, the niche he occupied could have been filled by any gentleman of thirty-two with a kind interest in them and an affection for the club. To him, they were everything that made the world, as he knew it just then, interesting and beautiful. Youth, energy, cleanliness were the trinity Thorn worshipped. And they were young, strong, and undefiled. Yet, after the first pleasure at being back had left him, Thorn was not a happy man, although he had not then begun to tell himself so.

The seemingly unimportant question presented by his own name began to worry him a little as the weeks passed into months. First names and the absurd sounds men had answered to from babyhood were naturally in common use at the club. Thorn dropped into the way of them easily, as a matter of course. Not to have done so would, in time, have become impossible. The fellows would have thought it strange—formal. Yet the name of "Marcus" was rarely heard there. Haydock, once in a while, called him that, after due premeditation. Sears Wolcott occasionally used it by way of a joke—as if he were taking an impertinent liberty, and rather enjoyed doing it. But none of the other men ever did. On no occasion had any one said "Marcus" absentmindedly, and then looked embarrassed, as Thorn had hoped might happen. It hurt him a little always to be called "Thorn"; to be appealed to in the capacity of "Mr. Thorn," as he sometimes was by the younger members, positively annoyed him. Prescott was the most incorrigible in this respect. He had come from one of those fitting schools where all speech between master and pupil is carried on to a monotonous chant of "Yes, sir," "No, sir," and "I think so, sir." He had ideas, or rather habits,—for Prescott's ideas were few,—of deference to those whose mission it was to assist in his education that Thorn found almost impossible to displace. For a long time—until the graduate laughed and asked him not to—he prefixed the distasteful "Mr." to Thorn's name. Then, for as long again, he refrained markedly from calling him anything. One afternoon he came into the club where the instructor was alone, writing a letter, and after fussing for a time among the magazines on the table, he managed to say,—

"Thorn, do you know whether Sears has been here since luncheon?"

Thorn didn't know and he didn't care, but had Prescott handed him an appointment to an assistant professor's chair, instead of having robbed him a little of what dignity he possessed, he would not have been so elated by half. Prescott continued to call him "Thorn" after that, but always with apparent effort,—as if aware that in doing it he was not living quite up to his principles. This trouble with his name might have served Thorn as an indication of what his position actually was in the tiny world he longed so much to be part of once more. But he was not a clever man where he himself was concerned.

Little things hurt him constantly without opening his eyes. For instance, it rarely occurred to the fellows that the instructor might care to join them in any of their hastily planned expeditions to town after dinner. Not that he was ostracised; he was simply overlooked. When he did go to the theatre, he bought the tickets himself, and asked Prescott or Sears, or some of them, to go with him. The occasion invariably lacked the charm of spontaneity. When he invited any of them to dine with him in town, as he often did, they went, if they hadn't anything else to do, and seemed to enjoy their dinner. But to Thorn these feasts were a series of disappointments. He always got up from the table with a sense of having failed in something. What? He didn't know—he couldn't have told. He was like a man who shoots carefully at nothing, and then feels badly because he hits it. He persisted in loitering along sunny lanes, and growing melancholy because they led nowhere. It was Sears Wolcott who took even the zest of anticipation out of Thorn's little dinners in town, by saying to the graduate one evening,—

"What's the point of going to the Victoria for dinner? It's less trouble, and a damned sight livelier, to eat out here." Sears had what Haydock called, "that disagreeable habit of hitting promiscuously from the shoulder." The reaction on Thorn of all this was at last a dawning suspicion of his own unimportance. By the time the midyear examinations came, he felt somehow as if he were "losing ground"; he hadn't reached the point yet of realising that he never had had any. He used to throw down his work in a fit of depression and consult his three-sided mirror apprehensively.

The big Prescott, however, became the real problem, around which the others were as mere corollaries. It was he who managed, in his "artless Japanese way," as the fellows used to call it, to crystallise the situation, to bring it to a pass where Thorn's rather unmanly sentimentality found itself confronted by something more definite and disturbing than merely the vanishing point of youth. Prescott accomplished this very simply, by doing the poorest kind of work—no work at all, in fact—in the course he was taking from Thorn. Barely, and by the grace of the instructor, had he scraped through the first examination in November. Since then he had rested calmly, like a great monolith, on his laurels. He went to Thorn's lectures only after intervals of absence that made his going at all a farce. He ignored the written work of the course, and the reports on outside reading, with magnificent completeness. Altogether, he behaved as he wouldn't have behaved had he ever for a moment considered Thorn in any light other than that of an instructor, an officer of the college, a creature to whom deference—servility, almost—was due when he was compelled to talk to him, but to whom all obligation ended there. His attitude was not an unusual one among college "men" who have not outgrown the school idea, but the attendant circumstances were. For Thorn's concern over Prescott's indifference to the course was aroused by a strong personal attachment, one in which an ordinary professorial interest had nothing to do. He smarted at this failure to attract the boy sufficiently to draw him to his lectures; yet he looked with a sort of panic toward the approaching day when he should be obliged, in all conscience, to flunk him in the midyear examination. He admired Prescott, as little, intelligent men sometimes do admire big, stupid ones. He idealised him, and even went the length, one afternoon when taking a walk with Haydock, of telling the senior that under Prescott's restful, olympic exterior he thought there lurked a soul. To which Haydock answered with asperity, "Well, I hope so, I'm sure," and let the subject drop. Later in the walk, Haydock announced, irrelevantly, and with a good deal of vigour, that if he ever made or inherited millions, he would establish a chair in the university, call it the "Haydock Professorship of Common Sense," and respectfully suggest to the President and Faculty that the course be made compulsory.

Thorn would have spoken to the soulful Prescott,—told him gently that he didn't seem to be quite in sympathy with the work of the course,—if Prescott had condescended to go to his lectures in the six or seven weeks between the end of the Christmas recess and the examination period. But Prescott cut Tuesday, Thursday, and Saturday, at half-past two o'clock, with a regularity that, considered as regularity, was admirable. Toward the last, he did drop in every now and then, sit near the door, and slip out again before the hour was ended. This was just after he had been summoned by the Recorder to the Office for "cutting." Thorn never got a chance to speak to him. He might have approached the boy at the club; but the instructor shrank from taking advantage of his connection with that place to make a delicate official duty possible. He had all along avoided "shop" there so elaborately,—had made so light of it when the subject had come up,—that he couldn't bring himself at that late day to arise, viper like, from the hearthstone and smite. A note of warning would have had to be light, facetious, and consequently without value, in order not to prove a very false and uncalled for note indeed. The ready coöperation of the Dean, Thorn refrained from calling on; he was far from wishing to get Prescott into difficulties.

By the time the examination day arrived, the instructor was in a state of turmoil that in ordinary circumstances would have been excessive and absurd. In the case of Thorn, it was half pathetic, half contemptible. He knew that in spite of Prescott's soul (a superabundance of soul is, as a matter of fact, a positive hindrance in passing examinations), the boy would do wretchedly. To give him an E—the lowest possible mark, always excepting, of course, the jocose and sarcastic F—would be to bring upon himself Prescott's everlasting anger and "despision." Of this Thorn was sure. Furthermore, the mark would not tend to make the instructor wildly popular at the club; for although everybody was willing to concede that Prescott was not a person of brilliant mental attainments, he was very much beloved. One hears a good deal about the "rough justice of boys." Thorn knew that such a thing existed, and did not doubt but that, in theory, he would be upheld by the members of the club if he gave Prescott an E, and brought the heavy hand of the Office down on him. But the justice of boys, he reflected, was, after all, rough; it would acknowledge his right to flunk Prescott, perhaps, and, without doubt, hate him cordially for doing it. Thorn's aversion to being hated was almost morbid.

If, on the other hand, he let the boy through,—gave him, say, the unde-served and highly respectable mark of C,—well, that would be tampering dishonestly with the standards of the college, gross injustice to the rest of the students, injurious to the self-respect of the instructor, and a great many other objectionable things, too numerous to mention. Altogether, Thorn was in a "state of mind." He began to understand something of the fine line that separates instructor from instructed, on whose other side neither may trespass.

When at length the morning of the examination had come and gone, and Thorn was in his own room at his desk with the neat bundle of blue-covered books before him, in which the examinations are written, it was easy enough to make up his mind. He knew that the question of flunking or pass-ing Prescott admitted of no arguments whatever. The boy's work in the course failed to present the tiniest loophole in the way of "extenuating cir-cumstances," and Prescott had capped the climax of his past record that morning by staying in the examination-room just an hour and a quarter of the three hours he was supposed to be there. That alone was equivalent to failure in a man of Prescott's denseness. Not to give Prescott a simple and unadorned E would be holding the pettiest of personal interests higher than one's duty to the college. There was no other way of looking at it. And Thorn, whose mind was perfectly clear on this point, deliberately extricated Prescott's book from the blue pile on his desk, dropped it carelessly—with-out opening it—into the glowing coals of his fireplace, and entered the boy's midyear mark in the records as C.

No lectures are given in the college during the midyears. Men who are fortunate enough to finish their examinations early in the period can run away to New York, to the country, to Old Point Comfort, to almost any-where that isn't Cambridge, and recuperate. Haydock went South. Ellis and Wynne tried a walking trip in the Berkshire Hills, and, after two days' floundering in the mud, waded to the nearest train for a city. Boston men went to Boston—except Sears Wolcott and Prescott, who disappeared to some wild and inaccessible New England hamlet to snowshoe or spear fish or shoot rabbits; no one could with authority say which, as the two had veiled their preparations in mystery. So it happened that Thorn didn't see Prescott for more than a week after he had marked his book. In the mean time he had become used to the idea of having done it according to a some-what unconventional system—to put it charitably. He passed much of the time in which the fellows were away, alone; for the few who went to the club, went there with note-books under their arms and preoccupied expressions in their eyes. They kept a sharp lookout for unexpected maneuvres on the part of the clock, and had a general air of having to be in some place else very soon. Thorn, thrown on his own resources, had a mild experience of what Cambridge can be without a crowd to play with, and came to the conclusion that, for his own interest and pleasure in life, he had done wisely in not incurring Prescott's ill-will and startling the club in the new role of hard-hearted, uncompromising pedagogue. The insignificant part he played in the lives of the undergraduates was far from satisfying; but it was the sort of half a loaf one doesn't willingly throw away. By the time Prescott came back, Thorn had so wholly accepted his own view of the case that he was totally unprepared for the way in which the boy took the news of his mark. He met Prescott in the Yard the morning college opened again, and stopped to speak to him. He wouldn't have referred to the examination—it was enough to know that the little crisis had passed—had not Prescott, blushing uneasily, and looking over Thorn's shoulder at something across the Yard, said,—

"I don't suppose you were very much surprised at the way I did in the exam, were you?"

"It might have been better," answered Thorn, seriously. "I hope you will do better the second half year. But then, it might have been worse; your mark was C."

Prescott looked at him, a quizzical, startled look; and then realising that Thorn was serious, that there had been nothing of the sarcastic in his tone or manner, he laughed rudely in the instructor's face.

"I beg your pardon," he said, as politely as he could, with his eyes still full of wonder and laughter; "I had no idea I did so well." He turned abruptly and walked away. Thorn would have felt offended, if he hadn't all at once been exceedingly scared. Prescott's manner was extraordinary for one who, as a rule, took everything as it came, calmly, unquestioningly. His face and his laugh had expressed anything but ordinary satisfaction at not having failed. There was something behind that unwonted astonishment, something more than mere surprise at having received what was, after all, a mediocre mark. Thorn had mixed enough with human kind to be aware that no man living is ever very much surprised in his heart of hearts to have his humble efforts in any direction given grade C. Men like Prescott, who know but little of the subjects they are examined in, usually try to compose vague answers that may, like the oracles, be interpreted according to the mood of him who reads them. No matter how general or how few Prescott's answers had been—Thorn stopped suddenly in the middle of the path. The explanation that had come to him took hold of him, and like a tightened rein drew him up short. Prescott had written nothing. The pages of his blue book had left the examination-room as virgin white as when they had been brought in and placed on the desk by the proctor. There was no other explanation possible, and the instructor tingled all over with the horrid sensation of being an unspeakable fool. He turned quickly to go to University Hall; he meant to have Prescott's mark changed at once. But Prescott, at that moment, was bounding up the steps of University, two at a time. He was undoubtedly on his way to the Office to verify what Thorn had just told him. Thorn walked rapidly to his entry in Holworthy, although he had just come from there. Then, with short, nervous steps, he turned back again, left the Yard, and hurried in aimless haste up North Avenue. He had been an ass,—a bungling, awful ass,—he told himself over and over again. And that was about as coherent a meditation as Mr. Thorn was able to indulge in for some time. Once the idea of pretending that he had made a mistake did suggest itself for a moment; but that struck him as wild, impossible. It would have merely resulted in forcing the Office to regard him as stupid and careless, and, should embarrassing questions arise, he no longer had Prescott's book with which to clear himself. More than that, it would give Prescott reason to believe him an underhand trickster. The boy now knew him to be an example of brazen partiality; there was no point in incurring even harsher criticism. Thorn tried to convince himself, as he hurried along the straight, hideous highway, that perhaps he was wrong,—that Prescott hadn't handed in a perfectly blank book. If only he could have been sure of that, he would have risked the bland assertion that the boy had stumbled on more or less intelligent answers to the examination questions, without perhaps knowing it himself. This, practically, was the tone he had meant to adopt all along. But he couldn't be sure, and, unfortunately, the only person who could give information as to what was or wasn't in the book, was Prescott. But Prescott had given information of the most direct and convincing kind. That astounded look and impertinent laugh had as much as said:—

"Well, old swipe, what's your little game? What do you expect to get by giving a good mark to a man who wasn't able to answer a single question?" And Thorn knew it. At first he was alarmed at what he had done. He could easily see how such a performance, if known, might stand in the light of his reappointment to teach in the college, even if it didn't eject him at once. But before he returned to his room, after walking miles, he scarcely knew where, fear had entirely given way to shame,—an over-powering shame that actually made the man sick at his stomach. It wasn't as if he had committed a man's fault in a world of men where he would be comfortably judged and damned by a tribunal he respected about as much as he respected himself. He had turned himself inside out before the clear eyes of a lot of boys, whose dealings with themselves and one another were like so many shafts of white light in an unrefracting medium. He had let them know what a weak, characterless, poor thing he was, by holding himself open to a bribe, showing himself willing to exchange, for the leavings of their friendships, something he was bound in honour to give only when earned, prostituting his profession that they might continue to like him a little, tolerate his presence among them. And he was one whom the college had honoured by judging worthy to stand up before young men and teach them. It was really very sickening.

Thorn couldn't bring himself to go near the club for some days. He knew, however, as well as if he had been present, what had probably happened there in the meanwhile. Prescott had told Haydock and Wolcott, and very likely some of the others, the story of his examination. They had laughed at first, as if it had been a good joke in which Prescott had come out decidedly ahead; then Haydock had said something—Thorn could hear him saying it—that put the matter in a pitilessly true light, and the others had agreed with him. They usually did in the end. It took all the "nerve" Thorn had to show himself again.

But when he had summoned up enough courage to drop in at the club late one evening, he found every one's manner toward him pretty much as it always had been; yet he could tell instinctively as he sat there, who had and who hadn't heard Prescott's little anecdote. Wolcott knew; he called Thorn, "Marcus," with unnecessary gusto, and once or twice laughed his peculiarly irritating laugh when there was nothing, as far as Thorn could see, to laugh at. Haydock knew; Thorn winced under the cool speculative stare of the senior's grey eyes. Wynne knew; although Thorn had no more specific reason for believing so, than that the boy seemed rather more formidably bespectacled than usual. Several of the younger fellows also knew; Thorn knew that they knew; he couldn't stand it. When the front door slammed after him on his way back to his room, he told himself that, as far as he was concerned, it had slammed for the last time.

He was very nearly right. He would have had to be a pachyderm compared to which the "blood sweating behemoth of Holy Writ" is a mere satin-skinned invalid, in order to have brazened out the rest of the year on the old basis. He couldn't go to the club and converse on base-ball and the "musical glasses," knowing that the fellows with whom he was talking were probably weighing the pros and cons of taking his courses next year, and getting creditable marks in them, without doing a stroke of work. He couldn't face that "rough justice of boys" that would sanction the fellows making use of him, and considering him a pretty poor thing, at the same time. So he stayed away; he didn't go near the place through March and April and May. When his work didn't call him elsewhere, he stayed in his room and attempted to live the life of a scholar, —an existence for which he was in every conceivable way unfitted. For a time he studied hard out of books; but the most profitable knowledge he acquired in his solitude was the great deal he learned about himself. He tried to write. He had always thought it in him to "write something," if he ever should find the necessary leisure. But the play he began amounted to no more than a harmless pretext for discoursing in a disillusioned strain on Life and Art in many letters he wrote to people he had known abroad,—people, for whom, all at once, he conceived a feeling of intimacy that no doubt surprised them when they received his letters. His volume of essays was never actually written, but the fact that he was hard at work on it served well as an answer to:—

"Why the devil don't we ever see you at the club nowadays?"

For the fellows asked him that, of course, when he met them in the Yard or in the electric cars; and Haydock tarried once or twice after his lecture and hoped politely that he was coming to the next club dinner. He wasn't at the next club dinner, however, nor the next, nor the next. Haydock stopped reminding him of them. The club had gradually ceased to have any but a spectacular interest for Thorn. His part at a dinner there would be—and, since his return, always had been—that of decorous audience in the stalls, watching a sprightly farce. The club didn't insist on an audience, so Thorn's meetings with its members were few. He saw Haydock and Prescott, in a purely official way, more than any of them. Strangely enough, Prescott seemed to be trying to do better in Thorn's course. He came to the lectures as regularly as he had avoided them before the midyears. He handed in written work of such ingenious unintelligence that there was no question in Thorn's mind as to the boy's having conscientiously evolved it unaided. The instructor liked the spirit of Prescott's efforts, although it was a perpetual "rubbing in," of the memory of his own indiscretion; it displayed a pretty understanding of *noblesse oblige.*

The second half year was long and dreary and good for Thorn. It set him down hard,—so hard that when he collected himself and began to look about him once more, he knew precisely where he was—which was something he hadn't known until then. He was thirty-two years old; he looked thirty-five, and he felt a hundred, to begin with. He wasn't an undergraduate, and he hadn't been one for a good many years. He still felt that he loved youth and sympathised with its every phase,—from its mindless gambolings to its preposterous maturity. But he knew now that it was with the love and sympathy of one who had lost it. He had learned, too, that when it goes, it bids one a cavalier adieu, and takes with it what one has come to regard as one's rights,—like a saucy house-maid departing with the spoons. He knew that he had no rights; he had forfeited them by losing some of his hair. He wouldn't get any of them back again until he had lost all of it. He was the merest speck on the horizon of the fellows whom he had, earlier in the year, tried to know on a basis of equality,—a speck too far away, too microscopic even to annoy them. If he had only known it all along, he told himself, how different his year might have been. He wouldn't have squandered the first four months of it, for one thing, in a stupid insistence on a relation that must of necessity be artificial—unsatisfying. He wouldn't have spent the last five of it coming to his senses. He wouldn't have misused all of it in burning—or at least in allowing to fall into a precarious state of unrepair—the bridges that led back to the friends of his own age and time.

"I have learned more than I have taught, this year," thought Thorn.

To-day was Thorn's birthday. Impelled by a tender, tepid feeling of self-pity the instructor had come once more to the club to look at it and say good-bye before leaving Cambridge. He would have liked to breakfast on the piazza and suffer luxuriously alone. But just at the moment he was beginning to feel most deeply, Sears Wolcott appeared at the open French window, and said he was "Going to eat out there in the landscape too." So, Thorn, in spite of himself, had to revive.

"What did you think of the Pudding show last night?" began Sears. Talk with him usually meant leading questions and their simplest answers.

"It was very amusing—very well done," said Thorn. What was the use, he asked himself, of drawing a cow-eyed stare from Wolcott by saying what he really thought—that Strawberry Night at the Pudding had been "exuberant," "noisy," "intensely young."

"I saw you after it was over," Sears went on; "why didn't you buck up with the old grads around the piano? You looked lonely."

"I was lonely," answered Thorn, truthfully this time.

"Where were your classmates? There was a big crowd out."

"My classmates? Oh, they were there, I suppose. I haven't seen much of them this year."

Wolcott's next question was:—

"Why the devil can't we have better strawberries at this club, I wonder? Where's the granulated sugar? They know I never eat this damned face powder on anything." He called loudly for the steward, and Thorn went on with his breakfast in silence. After Sears had been appeased with granulated sugar, he asked:—

"Going to be here next year?"

"I've been reappointed; but I think I shall live in town. Why do you ask?"

"Oh, nothing—I was thinking I might take your courses. What mark is Prescott going to get for the year?"

Thorn looked up to meet Wolcott's eyes unflinchingly; but the boy was deeply absorbed in studying the little air bubbles on the surface of his coffee.

"I don't know what mark he'll get. I haven't looked at his book yet," said Thorn. Sears remarked "Oh!" and laughed as he submerged the bubbles with a spoon. It was unlike him not to have said, "You do go through the formality of reading his books then?"

Prescott and Wynne joined them. They chattered gaily with Wolcott about nothing out there on the piazza, and watched the slim lady on the other side of the nodding lilac bushes cut nasturtiums. Thorn listened to them, and looked at them, and liked them; but he couldn't be one of them, even for the moment. He couldn't babble unpremeditatedly about nothing, because he had forgotten how it was done. So, in a little while, he got up to leave them. He had to mark some examination books and pack his trunks and go abroad, he told them. He said good-bye to Prescott and Wolcott and Wynne and some others who had come in while they were at breakfast, and hoped they would have "a good summer." They hoped the same to him.

As he strolled back to his room with the sounds of their voices in his ears, but with no memory of what they had been saying, he wondered if, after all, they hadn't from the very first bored him just a little; if his unhappiness— his sense of failure when he talked to young people—didn't come from the fact that they commended themselves to his affections rather than to his intellect. Thorn was a vain man in a quiet way.

Prescott's final examination book certainly didn't commend itself to his intellect. It was long, and conscientious, and quite incorrect from cover to cover. The instructor left it until the last. He almost missed his train in deciding upon its mark.

Harvard Episodes (Boston, 1897).

Lee Simonson

MY COLLEGE LIFE WAS AN INNER ONE

(c. 1908)

Lee Simonson, a founder and for more than twenty years a director of the Theater Guild, was one of America's foremost designers for the stage. His autobiography, Part of a Lifetime, *is a sensitive chronicle of the development of an artistic personality, for Simonson could write as well as paint and build. Of him it has been said "no other artist of our time can surpass him in making the technical details of a production fit the play so accurately and harmonize with the ideas of the author and director." At Harvard he was one of the founders of the Dramatic Club, won the Bowdoin Prize, and graduated magna cum laude in philosophy. Through his own testimony he is revealed as one of those highly individual personalities which the Harvard atmosphere occasionally nurtures. He was the author of* The Stage is Set *(1932).*

WILLIAM JAMES, George Santayana, Josiah Royce, George Herbert Palmer, Hugo Münsterberg, Ralph Barton Perry, William Allan Neilson, Charles Townsend Copeland, George Pierce Baker—this Olympian roster evokes a Harvard that in retrospect seems to be a Harvard of a golden age, or rather a golden afternoon, for the college seemed like some well-kept orchard, cooled by the first lengthening shadows and warmed by the sun of a benign enlightenment, where the fruits of knowledge and culture hung ripe, waiting to be plucked for the asking. A kind of peace of infinite intellectual plenty seemed to lie even over the dingiest of our academic halls, though Emerson Hall, the center of philosophy, was, as Münsterberg reminded us, "new and insofar esthetically satisfying." Of William James I had only a glimpse when he gave the opening lecture of an introductory course, Philosophy 1. But the largest lecture hall was packed when Münsterberg asked those of us "who had fountain pens not to ejaculate any ink upon the floor." The excitement of new knowledge was in the air and pervaded us even as we imbibed his more mechanical version of the mind's processes and followed as best we could his buzzing accent and rolling r's—"ze zenz zenzationz zemzelvez . . . ze nerf imbulses fr-r-rom ze ber-r-ipher-r-ry to ze occz-zipital zenter of ze brr-rain, gendlemen . . ." It seemed important that, according to a rumor, there was an elevator large enough to hoist cows to the laboratory. Royce appeared to be a formidable legal mind retained as *amicus curiae* in the interests of the Deity. Since the New England heart no longer panted along the water brooks of theological injunction, Royce's "system" could be relied upon to demonstrate that God and the Absolute were metaphysical necessities. If neither had existed it would have had to be invented. The intellectual apparatus employed was formidable. I still get slightly dizzy recalling that as part of a final examination I regurgitated the proof that two infinities could be equal—or unequal. I can no longer remember which. But the realization of what it meant to live in the mind came from George Santayana.

When I am asked where I went to college, I am always inclined to reply, "I went to Santayana." He was a foreign presence, with the punctiliousness and the elegance of a courtier in his speech, his manner, his gait, elegant even in a sack suit, small and neat-footed, his cane and gloves hung in one hand as he made his exit from the lecture room. His face with its pointed beard, full, sensuous lips, and the dark humid eyes, so dark that the pupil and the iris were indistinguishable, was a portrait of a Spanish grandee by Velasquez incarnated. His speech was exactly like his printed prose, exquisitely articulated, balanced and modulated, without an instant's blur of casual conversation. (It was Walter Lippmann, I think, who later complained that Santayana wrote English as though it were a learned language.) He seemed a prince marooned among savages, whiling away his exile in attempting to civilize them, his eyes never clearly focused on us, gazing slightly above our heads as if looking for the sail that was to bear him home. But the warmth and the clarity of gift as an expositor held every one of us under a spell. Here Reason was no stern daughter-in-law of the Absolute, no frigid instrument, but an organic part of our faculties of apprehension, the dominating factor in the functioning of human personality. Truth might not be beauty, but as one apprehended it, it had the appropriateness of a beautiful object, and there was an almost sensuous satisfaction to the process of learning. One garnered the wisdom and culture of the past as one might live with a being one loved. There was a warmth, a glow and a living pulse, to Santayana's expositions, whether of Plato, Lucretius, Dante, or Goethe, that sets them apart in my memory from the form of exegesis known as philosophic discourse. I reminded him of this twenty years later in Paris over a table d'hôte. He was deprecatory of his career as a teacher at Cambridge. "There, my dear Simonson, I was a mere young lady, practicing the pianoforte." His metaphysical system, the Realm of Essence, had already claimed him and alone seemed to him of any importance.

These days, whenever I stay on a university campus for even an afternoon I have a sense that each faculty member, particularly every younger one, is a timid and intimidated intelligence, hunched in his mental coat collar, looking over his shoulder furtively for fear that a Board of Regents or a Board of Overseers will put the evil eye on him, unless the teacher is already a full professor; then, as the dean of one Middle Western faculty once remarked to me, "They can't get us out at any price except on statutory charges of rape." In the Harvard of my time academic freedom seemed part of the very air of the place. "Opinion in good men," as Milton said, "is but knowledge in the making." Knowledge and wisdom seemed coextensive. No doubt the patina of retrospect lends a possibly false glow and mellowness to the scene, as successive coats of varnish do to a painting which they are intended to preserve. It seemed a stable world. No philosophic heresy could flutter the pulses of State Street, let alone its strongboxes. In the department of economics, the Economic Man, the Charley McCarthy of the day, performed dutifully on every professor's knee. And Lawrence Lowell in his course on government failed to discern anywhere any possible pattern of a revolution.

The sense of security was such that Harvard of that day, as it no longer seems able to do, could tolerate a heretic: George Pierce Baker. The critical analysis of contemporary plays is now so much the order of the day, an opinion of O'Neill, Shaw, Sherwood, or Odets seems so much more important than a revaluation of *A New Way to Pay Old Debts* or *The Way of the World,* that it is difficult to convey what it meant to an undergraduate to be told that it was important to study Henry Arthur Jones and Arthur Wing Pinero even though none of their work might eventually qualify as literature or possibly ever be a seasoned strut in the ceiling of permanent literary values that crowned an academic Pantheon. What Baker reminded us of, not once, but insistently was that Jones, Pinero, Shaw, Barrie, and Clyde Fitch were important to study, whatever their ultimate shortcomings might prove to be from the point of view of dramatic history, because they were the best we had. This was our theater in the making, ours to make by a critical understanding of it. We could go on only from where we were. We were not the assenters to historic achievements or partisans of lost causes but, as potential audiences, critics, playwrights, the arbiters of living issues. The immense influence that Baker had on so many generations of students was not due primarily to his taste or to his particular opinions as to what was good play-writing and what was not, for much of which some of us had scant respect, but to the sense of our effective importance that he instilled in us. We were living intelligences who could affect actual issues before they were irrevocably decided one way or the other. We mattered. He cultivated consistently and successfully the sense of alternatives that William James had evoked.

No doubt the amount of time we spent analyzing the progress in structure and characterization displayed in *The Second Mrs. Tanqueray* compared with *The Profligate,* or *Michael and His Lost Angel* in contrast to *Mrs. Dane's Defense,* now seems ludicrous. I remember trying unsuccessfully to convince him that Shaw was worth more than two lectures. But the particular instances mattered less than the method of approach. Baker had the air less of a professor than of a celebrated actor, or rather an actor-manager who had been knighted. He was something of a snob as well, and his gift for discovering talent and imagination was often less than he was credited with. Robert Edmond Jones, who was later exhibited at testimonial banquets as one of Baker's prize products, was almost completely ignored and never admitted to the immediate circle of his disciples known as Baker's Dozen. But in Baker's presence the theater became a living art and remained so, I think, for everyone who ever sat under him.

Within sight of Sever Hall where I studied the dramatizations of sex and society, across Harvard Square another realm began. At the "Co-op" I found first editions of the Abbey Theatre and the Celtic revival, the dirge and wonder of Synge's *Riders to the Sea,* the miracle of *The Well of the Saints,* and drifted with Yeats upon *The Shadowy Waters* . . . At the same time I came upon a volume of Paul Verlaine, whose lyrics I literally took to my bosom, learning them by heart—*Clair de Lune, Streets, Chanson d'Automne, Sagesse.* I apostrophized myself more than once in my shaving mirror with:

> Qu-as-tu fait, ô toi que voilà
> Pleurant sans cesse,
> Dis, qu'as-tu fait, toi que voilà
> De ta jeunesse?

Having a romantic notion of what round-table camaraderie of college intellectuals should be like and being, by Harvard standards, socially a complete failure, I solaced myself with the wind that blew out of the gates of the day, fountains in polished marble basins that sobbed with ecstasy, and the violins of autumn wounding my heart with a languorous monotone, as I took my solitary walks under russet elms or through winter slush along Brattle Street to the reservoir and back again. My college life was largely an inner and introspective one . . .

Part of a Lifetime (New York, 1943).

John Reed

COLLEGE IS LIKE THE WORLD

(c. 1910)

John Reed caught typhus and died in Moscow in October 1920. It is worth recalling the personal sketch which Reed's classmate, Edward E. Hunt, wrote about him in 1935: "None of his Classmates can ever forget John Reed. He came bursting on the scene at Harvard with a noise and a grin that could not be ignored. Large, athletic, exuberant and humorous, he seemed to be on earth for the motion he got out of it . . . Nothing he did could be taken quite seriously for there was always a strain of the grotesque in his undertakings. He laughed at himself and the rest of us laughed with him." But after the war came Ten Days That Shook the World. *A new John Reed was born, died in Moscow, and was buried beside the Kremlin wall. The amazing story of John Reed the Soviet saint, and the symbol of attacks on the social order, seems all the more amazing after reading Reed's account of his College days at Harvard written in 1917 shortly before sailing for Russia.*

IN 1906 I went up to Harvard almost alone, knowing hardly a soul in the University. My college class entered over seven hundred strong, and for the first three months it seemed to me, going around to lectures and meetings, as if every one of the seven hundred had friends but me. I was thrilled with the immensity of Harvard, its infinite opportunities, its august history and traditions—but desperately lonely. I didn't know which way to turn, how to meet people. Fellows passed me in the Yard, shouting gayly to one another; I saw parties off to Boston Saturday night, whooping and yelling on the back platform of the street car, and they passed hilariously singing under my window in the early dawn. Athletes and musicians and writers and statesmen were emerging from the ranks of the class. The freshman clubs were forming.

And I was out of it all. I "went out" for the college papers, and tried to make the freshman crew, even staying in Cambridge vacations to go down to the empty boat-house and plug away at the machines—and was the last man kicked off the squad before they went to New London. I got to know many fellows to nod to, and a very few intimately; but most of my friends were whirled off and up into prominence, and came to see me no more. One of them said he'd room with me sophomore year—but he was tipped off that I wasn't "the right sort" and openly drew away from me. And I, too, hurt a boy who was my friend. He was a Jew, a shy, rather melancholy person. We were always together, we two outsiders. I became irritated and morbid about it—it seemed I would never be part of the rich splendor of college life with him around—so I drew away from him . . . It hurt him very much, and it taught me better. Since then he has forgiven it, and done wonderful things for me, and we are friends.

My second year was better. I was elected an editor of two of the papers, and knew more fellows. The fortunate and splendid youths, the aristocrats who filled the clubs and dominated college society, didn't seem so attractive. In two open contests, the trial for editor of the college daily paper and that for assistant manager of the varsity crew, I qualified easily for election; but the aristocrats blackballed me. However, that mattered less. During my freshman year I used to *pray* to be liked, to have friends, to be popular with the crowd. Now I had friends, plenty of them; and I have found that when I am working hard at something I love, friends come without my trying, and stay; and fear goes, and that sense of being lost which is so horrible.

From that time on I never felt out of it. I was never popular with the aristocrats; I was never elected to any clubs but one, and that one largely because of a dearth of members who could write lyrics for the annual show. But I was on the papers, was elected president of the Cosmopolitan Club, where forty-three nationalities met, became manager of the Musical Clubs, captain of the water-polo team, and an officer in many undergraduate activities. As song-leader of the cheering section, I had the supreme blissful sensation of swaying two thousand voices in great crashing choruses during the big football games. The more I met the college aristocrats, the more their cold, cruel stupidity repelled me. I began to pity them for their lack of imagination, and the narrowness of their glittering lives—clubs, athletics, society. College is like the world; outside there is the same class of people, dull and sated and blind.

Harvard University under President Eliot was unique. Individualism was carried to the point where a man who came for a good time could get through and graduate without having learned anything; but on the other hand, anyone could find there anything he wanted from all the world's store of learning. The undergraduates were practically free from control; they could live pretty much where they pleased, and do as they pleased—so long as they attended lectures. There was no attempt made by the authorities to weld the student body together, or to enforce any kind of uniformity. Some men came with allowances of fifteen thousand dollars a year pocket money, with automobiles and servants, living in gorgeous suites in palatial apartment houses; others in the same class starved in attic bedrooms.

All sorts of strange characters, of every race and mind, poets, philosophers, cranks of every twist, were in our class. The very hugeness of it prevented any one man from knowing more than a few of his classmates, though I managed to make the acquaintance of about five hundred of them. The aristocrats controlled the places of pride and power, except when a democratic revolution, such as occurred in my senior year, swept them off their feet; but they were so exclusive that most of the real life went on outside their ranks—and all the intellectual life of the student body. So many fine men were outside the charmed circle that, unlike most colleges, there was no disgrace in not being a "club man." What is known as "college spirit" was not very powerful; no odium attached to those who didn't go to football games and cheer. There was talk of the world, and daring thought, and intellectual insurgency; heresy has always been a Harvard and a New England tradition. Students themselves criticized the faculty for not educating them, attacked the sacred institution of intercollegiate athletics, sneered at undergraduate clubs so holy that no one dared mention their names. No matter what you were or what you did—at Harvard you could find your kind. It wasn't a breeder for masses of mediocrely educated young men equipped with "business" psychology; out of each class came a few creative minds, a few scholars, a few "gentlemen" with insolent manners, and a ruck of nobodies . . . Things have changed now. I liked Harvard better then.

Toward the end of my college course two influences came into my life, which had a good deal to do with shaping me. One was contact with Professor Copeland, who, under the pretense of teaching English composition, has stimulated generations of men to find color and strength and beauty in books and in the world, and to express it again. The other was what I call, for lack of a better name, the manifestations of the modern spirit. Some men, notably Walter Lippmann, had been reading and thinking and talking about politics and economics, not as dry theoretical studies, but as live forces acting on the world, on the University even. They formed the Socialist Club, to study and discuss all modern social and economic theories, and began to experiment with the community in which they lived.

Under their stimulus the college political clubs, which had formerly been quadrennial mushroom growths for the purpose of drinking beer, parading and burning red fire, took on a new significance. The Club drew up a platform for the Socialist Party in the city elections. It had social legislation introduced into the Massachusetts Legislature. Its members wrote articles in the college papers challenging undergraduate ideals, and muckraked the University for not paying its servants living wages, and so forth. Out of the agitation sprang the Harvard Men's League for Women's Suffrage, the Single Tax Club, an Anarchist group. The faculty was petitioned for a course in socialism. Prominent radicals were invited to Cambridge to lecture. An open forum was started, to debate college matters and the issues of the day. The result of this movement upon the undergraduate world was potent. All over the place radicals sprang up, in music, painting, poetry, the theatre. The more serious college papers took a socialistic, or at least progressive tinge. Of course all this made no ostensible difference in the look of Harvard society, and probably the clubmen and the athletes, who represented us to the world, never even heard of it. But it made me, and many others, realize that there was something going on in the dull outside world more thrilling than college activities, and turned our attention to the writings of men like H. G. Wells and Graham Wallas, wrenching us away from the Oscar Wildean dilettantism that had possessed undergraduate littérateurs for generations.

"Almost Thirty," *The New Republic*, April 29, 1936.

Thomas Wolfe

EUGENE GANT'S HARVARD

(c. 1923)

In the Houghton Library at Harvard there is a cheap ruled notebook containing jottings made by Thomas Wolfe in planning Of Time and the River. They are simply rough phrases separated by dashes: "My bewilderment and my despair—I close up suddenly—the lust for knowledge and for recognition—the feeling of impotence—the books in the Widener Library—the hordes of people on the pavements—to know all things and to try all places—the recourse to poetry—the vulgar definition of the Workshop people into creator and critic ... My enormous feats of reading—the ceaseless questing everywhere—the impact of loneliness—the ineradicable stain of solitude upon my spirit—the wild eyes—the flowing hair—utter rebellion from the group—sullen resentment for the group ..." In a few words these thoughts sum up Wolfe's feelings about Harvard when he studied here as a graduate student between 1920 and 1923, and the impressions and discouragements which pressed down upon an artistic conscience ever striving to burst out of control. Eugene Gant is, of course, Wolfe himself, and much of the novel Of Time and the River (1935) concerns Gant's experiences in Cambridge and Boston, particularly with the 47 Workshop of George Pierce

Baker. Wolfe was a member of that group, and three plays remain as examples of Wolfe's writing in this period. Wolfe has also left a manuscript fragment, "The River People," a portion of a projected work which has as its initial setting the steps of Widener.

THE TRAIN rushed on across the brown autumnal land, by wink of water and the rocky coasts, the small white towns and flaming colors and the lonely, tragic and eternal beauty of New England. It was the country of his heart's desire, the dark Helen in his blood forever burning—and now the fast approach across October land, the engine smoke that streaked back on the sharp gray air that day!

The coming on of the great earth, the new lands, the enchanted city, the approach, so smoky, blind and stifled, to the ancient web, the old grimed thrilling barricades of Boston. The streets and buildings that slid past that day with such a haunting strange familiarity, the mighty engine steaming to its halt, and the great train-shed dense with smoke and acrid with its smell and full of the slow pantings of a dozen engines, now passive as great cats, the mighty station with the ceaseless throngings of its illimitable life, and all of the murmurous, remote and mighty sounds of time forever held there in the station, together with a tart and nasal voice, a hand's breadth off that said: "There's hahdly time, but try it if you want."

He saw the narrow, twisted, age-browned streets of Boston, then, with their sultry fragrance of fresh-roasted coffee, the sight of the man-swarm passing in its million-footed weft, the distant drone and murmur of the great mysterious city all about him, the shining water of the Basin, and the murmur of the harbor and its ships, the promise of glory and of a thousand secret, lovely and mysterious women that were waiting somewhere in the city's web.

He saw the furious streets of life with their unending flood-tide of a million faces, the enormous library with its million books; or was it just one moment in the flood-tide of the city, at five o'clock, a voice, a face, a brawny lusty girl with smiling mouth who passed him in an instant at the Park Street station, stood printed in the strong October wind a moment—breast, belly, arm, and thigh, and all her brawny lustihood—and then had gone into the man-swarm, lost forever, never found?

Was it at such a moment—engine-smoke, a station, a street, the sound of time, a face that came and passed and vanished, could not be forgotten *here* or *here* or *here*, at such a moment of man's unrecorded memory, that he breathed fury from the air, that fury came?

He never knew; but now mad fury gripped his life, and he was haunted by the dream of time. Ten years must come and go without a moment's rest from fury, ten years of fury, hunger, all of the wandering in a young man's life. And for what? For what?

What is the fury which this youth will feel, which will lash him on against the great earth forever? It is the brain that maddens with its own excess, the heart that breaks from the anguish of its own frustration. It is the hunger that grows from everything it feeds upon, the thirst that gulps down rivers and remains insatiate. It is to see a million men, a million faces and to be a stranger and an alien to them always. It is to prowl the stacks of an enormous library at night, to tear the books out of a thousand shelves, to read in them with the mad hunger of the youth of man.

It is to have the old unquiet mind, the famished heart, the restless soul; it is to lose hope, heart, and all joy utterly, and then to have them wake again, to have the old feeling return with overwhelming force that he is about to find the thing for which his life obscurely and desperately is groping—for which all men on this earth have sought—one face out of the million faces, a wall, a door, a place of certitude and peace and wandering no more. For what is it that we Americans are seeking always on this earth? Why is it we have crossed the stormy seas so many times alone, lain in a thousand alien rooms at night hearing the sounds of time, dark time, and thought until heart, brain, flesh and spirit were sick and weary with the thought of it; "Where shall I go now? What shall I do?"

He did not know the moment that it came, but it came instantly, at once. And from that moment on mad fury seized him, from that moment on, his life, more than the life of any one that he would ever know, was to be spent in solitude and wandering. Why this was true, or how it happened, he would never know; yet it was so. From this time on—save for two intervals in his life—he was to live about as solitary a life as a modern man can have. And it is meant by this that the number of hours, days, months, and years—the actual time he spent alone—would be immense and extraordinary.

And this fact was all the more astonishing because he never seemed to seek out solitude, nor did he shrink from life, or seek to build himself into a wall away from all the fury and the turmoil of the earth. Rather, he loved life so dearly that he was driven mad by the thirst and hunger which he felt for it. Of this fury, which was to lash and drive him on for fifteen years, the thousandth part could not be told, and what is told may seem unbelievable, but it is true. He was driven by a hunger so literal, cruel and physical that it wanted to devour the earth and all the things and people in it, and when it failed in this attempt, his spirit would drown in an ocean of horror and desolation, smothered below the overwhelming tides of this great earth, sickened and made sterile, hopeless, dead by the stupefying weight of men and objects in the world, the everlasting flock and floodings of the crowd.

Now he would prowl the stacks of the library at night, pulling books out of a thousand shelves and reading in them like a madman. The thought of these vast stacks of books would drive him mad: the more he read, the less he seemed to know—the greater the number of the books he read, the greater the immense uncountable number of those which he could never read would seem to be. Within a period of ten years he read at least 20,000 volumes—deliberately the number is set low—and opened the pages and looked through many times that number. This may seem unbelievable, but it happened. Dryden said this about Ben Jonson: "Other men read books but he read libraries"—and so now was it with this boy. Yet this terrific orgy of the books brought him no comfort, peace, or wisdom of the mind and heart. Instead, his fury and despair increased from what they fed upon, his hunger mounted with the food it ate.

He read insanely, by the hundreds, the thousands, the ten thousands, yet he had no desire to be bookish; no one could describe this mad assault upon print as scholarly: a ravening appetite in him demanded that he read everything that had ever been written about human experience. He read no more from pleasure—the thought that other books were waiting for him tore at his heart forever. He pictured himself as tearing the entrails from a book as from a fowl. At first, hovering over book stalls, or walking at night among the vast piled shelves of the library, he would read, watch in hand, muttering to himself in triumph or anger at the timing of each page: "Fifty seconds to do that one. Damn you, we'll see! You will, will you?"—and he would tear through the next page in twenty seconds.

This fury which drove him on to read so many books had nothing to do with scholarship, nothing to do with academic honors, nothing to do with formal learning. He was not in any way a scholar and did not want to be one. He simply wanted to know about everything on earth; he wanted to devour the earth, and it drove him mad when he saw he could not do this. And it was the same with everything he did. In the midst of a furious burst of reading in the enormous library, the thought of the streets outside and the great city all around him would drive through his body like a sword. It would now seem to him that every second that he passed among the books was being wasted—that at this moment something priceless, irrecoverable was happening in the streets, and that if he could only get to it in time and see it, he would somehow get the knowledge of the whole thing in him—the source, the well, the spring from which all men and words and actions, and every design upon this earth proceeds.

And he would rush out in the streets to find it, be hurled through the tunnel into Boston and then spend hours in driving himself savagely through a hundred streets, looking into the faces of a million people, trying to get an instant and conclusive picture of all they did and said and were, of all their million destinies, and of the great city and the everlasting earth, and the immense and lonely skies that bent above them. And he would search the furious streets until bone and brain and blood could stand no more—

until every sinew of his life and spirit was wrung, trembling, and exhausted, and his heart sank down beneath its weight of desolation and despair.

Yet a furious hope, a wild extravagant belief, was burning in him all the time. He would write down enormous charts and plans and projects of all that he proposed to do in life—a program of work and living which would have exhausted the energies of 10,000 men. He would get up in the middle of the night to scrawl down insane catalogs of all that he had seen and done:—the number of books he had read, the number of miles he had travelled, the number of people he had known, the number of women he had slept with, the number of meals he had eaten, the number of towns he had visited, the number of states he had been in.

And at one moment he would gloat and chuckle over these stupendous lists like a miser gloating over his hoard, only to groan bitterly with despair the next moment, and to beat his head against the wall, as he remembered the overwhelming amount of all he had not seen or done, or known. Then he would begin another list filled with enormous catalogs of all the books he had not read, all the food he had not eaten, all the women that he had not slept with, all the states he had not been in, all the towns he had not visited. Then he would write down plans and programs whereby all these things must be accomplished, how many years it would take to do it all, and how old he would be when he had finished. An enormous wave of hope and joy would surge up in him, because it now looked easy, and he had no doubt at all that he could do it.

He never asked himself in any practical way how he was going to live while this was going on, where he was going to get the money for this gigantic adventure, and what he was going to do to make it possible. If he thought about it, it seemed to have no importance or reality whatever—he just dismissed it impatiently, or with a conviction that some old man would die and leave him a fortune, that he was going to pick up a purse containing hundreds of thousands of dollars while walking in the Fenway, and that the reward would be enough to keep him going, or that a beautiful and rich young widow, true-hearted, tender, loving, and voluptuous, who had carrot-colored hair, little freckles on her face, a snub nose and luminous gray-green eyes with something wicked, yet loving and faithful in them, and one gold filling in her solid little teeth, was going to fall in love with him, marry him, and be forever true and faithful to him while he went reading, eating, drinking, whoring, and devouring his way around the world; or finally that he would write a book or play every year or so, which would be a great success, and yield him fifteen or twenty thousand dollars at a crack. Thus, he went storming away at the whole earth about him, sometimes mad with despair, weariness, and bewilderment; and sometimes wild with jubilant and exultant joy and certitude as the conviction came to him that everything would happen as he wished. Then at night he would hear the vast sounds and silence of the earth and of the city, he would begin to think of the dark sleeping earth and of the continent of night, until it seemed to him it all was spread before him like a map—rivers, plains, and mountains and 10,000 sleeping towns; it seemed to him that he saw everything at once.

Of Time and the River (New York, 1935).

Theodore H. White

HARVARD LIES AT THE END OF THE SUBWAY

(1938)

Each of his friends and acquaintances will have their favorite memory of Teddy White—White the war correspondent living always on the edge of danger somewhere near the Mongolian border, White the courtier mingling easily with the retinue of Madame Chiang, White the boulevardier sipping coffee on the Rue de la Paix and thinking up a line of approach to the tall general in the Elysée Palace, White the tireless campaigner following his presidential candidates Kennedy and Johnson and Nixon from dawn to dusk, and White the Harvard Overseer stripped to his shirt and galluses pounding out on an office typewriter a draft statement that might help bring reason and peace in the spring of 1969 to a bitterly divided Harvard community. White has apparently been everywhere, done everything, but his memories of his intellectual awakening at Harvard are keen and clear and laced with humor.

AND THEN, in the fall of 1934, when I was two years out of Latin School, confused, angry, and on my way to nowhere, two things happened. Harvard College gave me a scholarship of $220 and the Burroughs Newsboys Foundation gave me a college grant of $180 (I still ran a newspaper route). Two-twenty and one-eighty came to four hundred dollars—which was the exact fee for a year's tuition at Harvard, and so I could try that for a year. Harvard then required a bond that a freshman would do no property damage there, and luckily, our neighbor, Mrs. Goldman, who owned a house down the street, was willing to sign such a bond. So in September of 1934, cutting a corner here and amplifying a hope there, I took the subway into Harvard Square to enroll.

I have, in the years since, served as an overseer of that majestic institution Harvard University, a member of the Honorable and Reverend Board of the most ancient corporation in the Western world, the chosen thirty who tip their silk hats as they file, two by two, past the statue of John Harvard on Commencement Day in the Yard. But it was a better Harvard I entered in the 1930s than it was later, when I sat on its Board of Overseers, or than it is today.

One emerged, as one still does, from the subway exit in the Square and faced an old red-brick wall behind which stretched, to my fond eye, what remains still the most beautiful campus in America, the Harvard Yard. If there is any one place in all America that mirrors better all American history, I do not know of it.

The signature building of the Harvard Yard was the Widener Library, its gray façade and pillars dominating all the open inner space. Widener was the crownpiece of the largest university library in the world and its architecture made a flat statement: that books and learning were what a school was all about. But the rest of the Yard spoke history. Across the green was the chapel built to commemorate Harvard men fallen in the First World War, which would, in time, have carved on its tablets the names of thirty-two of my classmates who were to fall in World War II. Across the street from the Yard, on the edge of Cambridge Common, stood the Washington Elm, where, legend claims, George Washington took command of the Continental Army in 1775. Beyond rose the gorgeous romanesque bulk of "Mem" Hall—the memorial for the veterans of the Civil War. To the north were acres and acres of a university no one person has ever fully explored—law school, graduate schools, museums, laboratories. To the south the residential houses rose along the Charles and there, beneath their turrets of red and blue and yellow, one could lie on the grass beside the slow-flowing Charles River with a friend and gaze at the Harvard Business School across the river. The business school, though few knew it, had its roots in history, too. It had sprung out of the Spanish-American War, when a few public-spirited alumni decided that America, for its new empire, needed a colonial school of administration to match Britain's imperial and colonial civil services. The school they envisioned became, in the course of time, the Harvard Graduate School of Business Administration, eventually fulfilling the imperial dreams of its sponsors by staffing the multinational corporations of the twentieth century.

Revolutionary War, Civil War, Spanish-American War, World War I, had all left marks behind at Harvard. World War II was on its way; and Harvard was in change under the leadership of James Bryant Conant, who was to leave to head a secret project called the "uranium bomb." Harvard had entered the modern world of learning in 1869, under the leadership of Charles William Eliot, who presided until 1909; it had passed through twenty-four years of the presidency of Abbott Lawrence Lowell, an aristocrat of great personal wealth who had candied Harvard's overwhelmingly New England student body with a top layer of the wealthiest adolescents of the Eastern seaboard. And then came Conant, the greatest of them all. Conant was of New England lineage as ancient as Lowell's or Eliot's, and was, like Eliot, a chemist of extraordinary creativity. Conant wanted to make Harvard something more than a New England school; he wanted its faculty to be more than a gentlemen's club of courtly learned men, wanted its student body to be national in origin. Excellence was his goal as he began shaking up both faculty and student body, and in the end, twenty years later, when he left in 1953, his insistence on excellence had made Harvard the most competitive school in American scholarship, a meritocracy in which students and professors vied for honors with little mercy or kindness.

But then, at the beginning of Conant's regime in the thirties, Harvard combined the best of the old warmth and the new strivings. Conant himself would address the freshman class. We all squatted on the floor of the Freshman Union, and he told us what a university was: a place for free minds. "If you call everyone to the right of you a Bourbon and everyone to the left of you a communist, you'll get nothing out of Harvard," he said to us. And went on to explain that what we would get out of Harvard was what we could take from it ourselves; Harvard was open, so—go seek.

Students divide themselves by their own discriminations in every generation, and the group I ran with had a neat system of classification. Harvard, my own group held, was divided into three groups—white men, gray men, and meatballs. I belonged to the meatballs, by self-classification. White men were youngsters of great name; my own class held a Boston Saltonstall, a New York Straus, a Chicago Marshall Field, two Roosevelts (John and Kermit), a Joseph P. Kennedy, Jr. The upper classes had another Roosevelt (Franklin, Jr.), a Rockefeller (David, with whom I shared a tutor in my sophomore year), a Morgan, and New York and Boston names of a dozen different fashionable pedigrees. Students of such names had automobiles; they went to Boston deb parties, football games, the June crew race against Yale; they belonged to clubs. At Harvard today, they are called "preppies," the private-school boys of mythical "St. Grottlesex."

Between white men above and meatballs at the bottom came the gray men. The gray men were mostly public-high-school boys, sturdy sons of America's middle class. They went out for football and baseball, manned the *Crimson* and the *Lampoon,* ran for class committees and, later in life, for school committees and political office. They came neither of the aristocracy nor of the deserving poor, as did most meatballs and scholarship boys. Caspar Weinberger, of my class of 1938, for example, was president of the *Crimson* and graduated magna cum laude; he later became Secretary of Health, Education, and Welfare, but as an undergraduate was a gray man from California. John King, of the same class of 1938, was another gray man; he became governor of New Hampshire. Wiley Mayne, an earnest student of history, who graduated with us, was a gray man from Iowa, later becoming congressman from Sioux City. He served on the House Judiciary Committee that voted to impeach Richard Nixon—with Wiley Mayne voting to support the President. The most brilliant member of the class was probably Arthur M. Schlesinger, Jr., who defied categorization. Definitely no meatball, Schlesinger lacked then either the wealth or the savoir-faire of the white men. Indeed, Schlesinger, who was to go on to a fame surpassing that of his scholar father, was one who could apparently mingle with both white men *and* meatballs. In his youth, Schlesinger was a boy of extraordinary sweetness and generosity, one of the few on campus who would be friendly to a Jewish meatball, not only a liberal by heredity, but a liberal in practice. Since Wiley Mayne, Arthur Schlesinger, and I were all rivals, in an indistinct way, in the undergraduate rivalry of the History Department, I followed their careers with some interest. Mayne was a conservative, tart-tongued and stiff. I remember on the night of our Class Day dance, as we were all about to leave, he unburdened himself to me on "Eastern liberals who look down their long snob noses on people like me from the Midwest." Over the years Mayne grew into a milder, gentler, warmer person until in his agony over Nixon, wrestling with his conscience on whether to impeach or not, he seemed to be perhaps the most sensitive and human member of the Judiciary Committee. Schlesinger, by contrast, developed a certainty about affairs, a public tartness of manner associated with the general liberal rigidity of the late sixties that offended many—and yet, for all that, he remained as kind and gentle to old friends like myself, with whose politics he came profoundly to disagree, as he had been in boyhood. Both Schlesinger and Mayne, the liberal and the conservative, were always absolutely firm in their opinions. I, in the years starting at Harvard, and continuing in later life, wandered all through the political spectrum, and envied them both for their certainties.

I find some difficulty in describing what a "meatball" was. Meatballs were usually day students or scholarship students. We were at Harvard not to enjoy the games, the girls, the burlesque shows of the Old Howard, the companionship, the elms, the turning leaves of fall, the grassy banks of the Charles. We had come to get the Harvard badge, which says "Veritas," but really means a job somewhere in the future, in some bureaucracy, in some institution, in some school, laboratory, university, or law firm.

Conant was the first president to recognize that meatballs were Harvard men, too, and so he set apart a ground floor room at Dudley Hall where we could bring our lunches in brown paper bags and eat at a table, or lounge in easy chairs between classes. The master of this strange enclave of commuting Irish, Jewish, and Italian youngsters from Greater Boston was a young historian named Charles Duhig, whose argument was that the most revolutionary force in history was the middle class. Duhig had contempt for the working class ("slobs"), disdain for the upper class. His theory held that modern history is carried forward chiefly by the middle class, their children, and what moves them to the future. In us, his wards, he had a zoo of specimens of the mobile lower middle class and he enjoyed watching us resist communist penetration.

Dudley Hall was plowed regularly by Harvard's intellectual upper-class communists, who felt that we were of the oppressed. Occasionally such well-bred, rich, or élite communist youngsters from the resident houses would bring a neat brown-paper-bag lunch and join us at the round tables to persuade us, as companions, of the inevitable proletarian revolution. Duhig, our custodian, welcomed their visits because he knew his scholarship boys could take care of such communists in debate as easily as they could take care of the Republican youngsters who staffed the *Crimson.* We were Duhig's own middle class in the flesh—hungry and ambitious. Most of us, largely Boston Latin School graduates, knew more about poverty than anyone from Beacon Hill or the fashionable East Side of New York. We hated poverty; and meant to have no share in it. We had come to Harvard not to help the working classes, but to get out of the working classes. We were on the make. And in my own case, the approach to Harvard and its riches was that of a looter. Harvard had the keys to the gates; what lay behind the gates I could not guess, but all that lay there was to be looted. Not only were there required courses to be attended, but there were courses given by famous men, lectures open to all, where no one guarded the entry. I could listen. There were museums to be seen, libraries and poetry rooms of all kinds to tarry in—and stacks and stacks and stacks of books. It was a place to grab at ideas and facts, and I grabbed at history.

One had a choice, in one's freshman year, of taking either one of two required courses—History 1 or Government 1. Government 1 was a "gut" course, and the student underground passed the word that no one ever failed in Government 1. History 1 had the reputation of being a nutcracker; no one ever got an A in History 1 except by luck. But History 1 was the course most freshmen took because its professor, "Frisky" Merriman, was perhaps the most colorful character on Harvard's then vivid faculty of characters. He believed history was story—thus, entertainment.

In History 1, Roger Bigelow Merriman stretched the story from the Age of the Antonines right down to the Treaty of Versailles—all 1800 years from the breakup of the Roman Empire to the breakup of Western Europe in 1914–1918. He is now considered a primitive by Harvard's present more elegant and austere masters of history—an academic histrionic who made his course in Western civilization a vaudeville sequence of thirty-six acts. Merriman could entertain a hall of six hundred students and hold them spellbound; he paced the platform from end to end, roaring, wheedling, stage-whispering, occasionally screeching in falsetto and earning fairly his nickname. We raced through the Antonines, enjoyed the Middle Ages, saluted Caliph Harun al-Rashid, thrilled with the struggle of Moors and Catholics in Spain, mourned for Boabdil, last sultan of the Moors. But the course was like an express train, pausing only at major stops on the track of history, and always, at every turning point, there would be "Frisky" Merriman, like a conductor calling the next stop and ultimate arrival, closing his lectures with "Unity, gentlemen, unity!"

Europe, he held, had sought the long-lost unity Rome had given it two thousand years ago as a man seeks to recapture a dream. Noted professors came from their own history courses to give a guest lecture or a week of lectures on their favorite subject, all falling into Merriman's mood as vaudevillians who try not to disappoint their producer. The last of these was the best, a young professor called James Phinney Baxter III, later to become president of Williams College and deputy director of the OSS. Baxter had observed World War I and thought that the machine gun was the instrument that ended the Age of Wars: he would crouch and go *hup-hup-hup* with an imaginary machine gun on the lecture platform explaining just what that machine gun had done to warfare and history between 1914 and 1918. I would have enjoyed hearing Baxter, twenty years later, on the nuclear bomb. But after Baxter, as after every other lecturer or turning point, Merriman would bring the course back on track: "Unity, gentlemen, unity!" he would roar. Charlemagne, Napoleon, Bismarck, the Hohenstaufen emperors, the Popes, the Hapsburgs, the Versailles Treaty—all had sought to give unity to Europe. It was a theme that would echo all the rest of my life; and resound again when I came to Europe to report the Marshall Plan, the Common Market, and the dreams of Jean Monnet, who had never heard of "Frisky" Merriman but held exactly the same view of Europe.

History 1 led in two directions, both of them luring me from my past without my knowing it.

The first direction in which History 1 led, as I romanticize the beginning, came by mechanical accident. It led across a corridor in Boylston Hall—to China.

It happened this way: A reading room on the ground floor of Boylston Hall was set aside for the hundreds of students who took Merriman's course, and it would become crowded, sweaty, and steamy on weekends as we crammed for the next week's sections. But across the corridor in the same building was the library of the Harvard–Yenching Institute—the library which would grow over the next forty years into the greatest collection of Oriental volumes outside Asia. It was easier to study in the empty library of the Harvard–Yenching Institute than in the History 1 reading room, so I would surreptitiously cross the corridor on Saturday afternoons. And if

I was bleary with reading about medieval trade, or the Reformation, or the Age of Imperialism, I could get up and pick Chinese volumes off the shelves—volumes on fine rice paper, blue-bound, bamboo-hooked volumes with strange characters, volumes with their own particular odor, an Oriental mustiness different from the mustiness of Western books. As I became more and more accustomed to the Oriental atmosphere, and my eyes rested on the scrolls of calligraphy on the walls, I began to feel at home. The Boston Latin School had given me reading knowledge of Latin, German, and French. Yiddish I understood from home. Hebrew was the language I knew I spoke best after my native English. Why not, then, take a giant step, and add Chinese to my languages—and find out what the blue-bound volumes said. And my father had told me to pay attention to China. The choice, then, at the end of my freshman year, as I had to choose a field of concentration for my sophomore year, became Chinese history and language.

And a more dangerous choice I never made.

Chinese is one of the simplest languages to speak, but the most difficult to read. The Chinese Department at Harvard, in those days, had the standards of the Emperor Ch'ien-lung laced with a dash of sadism. Their theory, entirely wrong, was that no youngster in his teens, no undergraduate, could possibly master the Chinese language. Conant had overruled such desiccated scholarship in his second year as president, and in my sophomore year the study of the Chinese language was thrown open to undergraduates for the first time. Chinese 1, the introductory course, was conducted by one of the most brutal men I have ever met. The class had five students, three graduate students and two undergraduates; but our professor was determined to prove his point (that undergraduates could *not* learn Chinese) by trying to flunk both of us immediately. The other undergraduate collapsed quickly. I, however, was at Harvard on scholarship, and if I flunked, I would lose my scholarship and thus my dreams would end. The professor taught the language by main force—simple visual memorization. We were never taught that almost all Chinese characters have a phonetic element which gives the sound, and an idea element which gives the meaning. Chinese should be taught to children while young—while their minds are elastic enough to associate vision and meaning. Graduates of American high schools now learn Chinese with far greater ease than graduates of Harvard in the old days. In those days at Boylston Hall one pounded each character into the mind by sheer force of recall, as one pounds nails into a board. I was put on notice of dismissal within six weeks of joining the course; and since my survival depended on staying at Harvard, I must not flunk, I must study—until one and two and three in the morning, forcing my memory to inscribe and retrieve Chinese characters. As the professor increased the burden in each session, the entire class, even graduate students, began to wilt. He relented, finally, and I survived, to get an A.

What we learned in Chinese was almost entirely useless. By the time I graduated from Harvard, I had memorized and could recognize by sight three thousand individual Chinese ideograms and as many more combinations of ideograms; I still have the memory cards on which each is written. But I can no longer recognize more than a hundred of the characters I once mastered, and can no longer read any kind of Chinese. All the characters and all the literature I was taught came from the Chinese classics: we read and translated Confucius and Mencius, histories and ancient odes. None of the spectacular Chinese novels of tradition (and the Chinese invented the novel form almost two thousand years ago), none of the lyric poems of the Tang or the nostalgic poems of the Sung were taught to us. We were taught the classics as if we were training for examinations in the Manchu civil service—and the classics were rules, regulations, moralities, history. And war. Those who think of the Chinese as a sublimely philosophical and peaceful people should be steeped in such Chinese classics. The Chinese tradition seeks order, discipline, moral behavior at all times; and when this order in the mind is affronted, the Chinese system reaches, as their tradition records, paroxysms of violence and ferocity.

Parallel to the path across Boylston Hall was the second direction in which I was invited—to the History Department. And history as it was taught in my four years at Harvard is, in retrospect, a wonder. Quite simply, history was not yet considered a science but was still thought more noble than a craft. The professors were a colony of storytellers, held together by the belief that in their many stories they might find a truth. They still cared about students and lingered after class for conversations. No better preparation for what was to come to me in life could have been planned than what came to me at Harvard, by accident and timing and osmosis of curiosity.

The best course in American history was given by Arthur Schlesinger, Sr., and Paul Buck. Schlesinger, a magnificent teacher, opened the course by telling us that American history was singularly poor in ideas, deficient in political theory, in philosophic system, in abstractions of all sorts. He insisted that American history swung in regular cycles of sixteen years, from hope to fear, from liberalism to conservatism. He concluded his masterly introductory lecture by saying: "The American people have not been governed by political theory, but purely by opportunism ... because of this plasticity we have been spared violent and bloody convulsions ..."

At Harvard, thus, I made the third round in American history: Miss Fuller had guided me the first time around, the Latin School the second, and at Harvard a large covey of professors gave me the final tour. But Schlesinger and Buck had set the tone: proud and patriotic as Miss Fuller had been, they saw American history as a struggle from which the good usually emerged triumphant. I was thus early bent to this patriotic view, and confirmed in it by higher learning, before I went out to see the story myself.

Yet Harvard's History Department offered more than American history. It offered a banquet of invitations to the past, of famous courses, of byways and coves and special delights of learning. Professor Crane Brinton, an urbane and aloof man, offered a course in the French Revolution. Cynical, caustic, disdainful of all morals, Brinton claimed as his own particular hero Talleyrand; but he lectured on Marat, Danton, Robespierre with an insight into character that would now be called, by fashionable scholars, psychohistory. Forced by the syllabus to devote one lecture to the financial policies of the revolutionaries, the inflation and the *assignats*, he read his notes from cards, and halfway through the lecture, he paused, yawning, and said, "Gentlemen, I don't see how you can stay awake listening to this, I'm falling asleep myself, but money is always important"—and went on.

A magnificent teacher, whose importance in historiography was unknown to me, was a man named Abbott Payson Usher. Usher taught economic history, but with such infectious enthusiasm, with such a waggle of his jaw, with such salivating eloquence, that he shook all my adolescent Marxism. Here, ran the story of Usher's course, was the way men made things and traded things; and history rests on how they manage the manufacture and exchange of goods. He took the Connecticut valley and explained how the Yankee tinkerers there invented mass production, interchangeable parts, and the American system of production. He traced on a map the coal beds that undervein Europe from England's Midlands, to France's North Country, to Germany's Ruhr and Silesia, demonstrating how one could track the development of political power in Europe by following the veins of energy and the times when coaling was first developed in each country. He taught about rivers, and how all the great cities of the world grew up at the mouths or fording places of rivers—London, New York, Paris, Rome. His course was basic introductory material for any reporter who would later write about the Marshall Plan. And in *Fire in the Ashes*, a book I wrote on European recovery, many years later, I plagiarized what I remembered of Abbott Payson Usher's lectures shamelessly. His course simply took all my previous ideas, shook them apart gently, then taught me how facts and large affairs arrange themselves in connections that made history seem like intellectual detective work.

Yet the teacher who, more than any other, spun me off into history as a life calling was a young man who arrived at Harvard only at the beginning of my junior year: John King Fairbank, later to become the greatest historian of America's relations with China. Fairbank was then only twenty-nine—tall, burly, sandy-haired, a prairie boy from South Dakota; soft-spoken, with an unsettling conversational gift of delayed-action humor; and a painstaking drillmaster. He had himself graduated from Harvard in 1929, but on his way back to the Yard had made a circuitous route via Oxford and Peking to become a specialist in modern Chinese history. He had a freshly minted Ph.D. and was on trial at Harvard both as a tutor and Orientalist; since I was the only undergraduate majoring in Chinese history and studies, I was assigned to him as tutee. No two young people could have come of more different backgrounds. The tutorial system at Harvard was then in its early years, exploring the idea that each young mind needs an older mind to guide it. Tutors at Harvard now are usually embittered graduate students, rarely, if ever, emotionally committed to the undergraduates they guide. But Fairbank approached me as if he were an apprentice Pygmalion, assigned a raw piece of ghetto stone to carve, sculpt, shape, and polish. He yearned that I do well.

It was not only that I was invited to my first tea party at his home, learning to balance a teacup properly; nor that, by observation, I learned proper table manners at a properly set breakfast table in the little yellow cottage where he lived with his beautiful young wife, Wilma. It was his absolute devotion to forcing my mind to think that speeded the change in me. We would talk about China and he would tell me tales of life in Peking as chatter—but only after our work was done. He was insistent that I read. I spent six weeks plowing through St. Thomas Aquinas, which, he agreed, was useless, yet necessary for a professional historian's understanding. He would make the hardest work a joy, and his monthly assignments were written with a skill and personal attention that no tutor at Harvard, or anywhere else, today gives to his students. One of his assignment memos, which I still treasure, shows how a great teacher goes about his calling.

> WHEREAS [read his communication] it is not possible to live (long) without thinking, and not possible to live well without thinking well; and
>
> It is not possible to think well without making *distinctions* between this and that, or heredity and environment, or cause and effect, or the group and the individual, or the law and the facts, or tactics and strategy, or rights and duties, or man and woman, or nominalism and realism, or communism and fascism, or collectivism and individualism, to say nothing of up and down, or backwards and forwards; and whereas
>
> It is not possible to go very far in making distinctions without making use of *categories of thought,* such as a category of laws and a category of events, or a category of noumena and a category of phenomena, or a category of spirit and a category of matter; and whereas
>
> It is not possible to think with critical power without being *critical* of the categories with which one is thinking; and
>
> It is not possible to avoid receiving certain categories at an early age from the contemporary intellectual environment;—
>
> THEREFORE—
>
> Philosophy is a most *necessary* and *admirable* subject, and
>
> You are cordially invited to be present at a meeting on Friday, January 8, 1937, at which there will be a discussion of Whitehead's volume *Science and the Modern World* (entire) conducted by none other than Mr. Theodore H. White.

Thus I was introduced to Whitehead's philosophy as to myriad other ideas by Fairbank's loving and disciplined tutelage.

Yet, though he molded me, he was pursuing his own cause, too—which was understanding the revolution in Asia in our time. The fossil sinologists of Harvard's Oriental Department felt that all Oriental history ended with the end of the Ch'ien-lung dynasty, in 1799. Professor Elisséeff, the department chief, insisted that everything after that date was journalism. Fairbank held otherwise—that history was happening now. He was probably the only man in all Cambridge who recognized that the Long March of Mao Tse-tung, the year before he himself joined Harvard's faculty, was epoch-making. Thus, then, in my senior year, young John Fairbank was allowed to teach a course—History 83b—on China from the death of Ch'ien-lung down to our times. It was a magnificent series of lectures, ground-breaking in intellectual patterns, and those few students who attended it caught the swell of what was happening in China and Asia from his wry, caustic, surgical stripping of myth from fact, noumena from phenomena, his separating Dr. Fu Manchu and *The Bitter Tea of General Yen* from what was really going on in China. His course reinforced what my father had told me of China and what I felt by instinct. It inflamed my itch to be off, away and out—to China, where the story lay.

We differed, Fairbank and I, in an affectionate quarrel, over my senior thesis. I was shooting for fellowships and highest honors and I wanted to write about the delicate interaction of force and order. I wanted to take as my thesis subject the war lords of modern China and their brutalities over the thirty-year span of collapse of China's civil order. Fairbank insisted it was too broad a matter for a college senior to write about. I had become obsessed with force as the engine of history: who gathers the guns together at what point to hammer at the state or the enemy. Fairbank wrote back to my remonstrance a long letter on the causes of human action in man, saying that "force forces them at times, fear of force more often—and ideals still more often." He insisted that I display my knowledge of Chinese historiography by writing about the Twenty-One Demands of Japan on China in 1915 from Chinese bibliographical sources. This kind of scholarly paper, he pointed out, might get me a fellowship in the Harvard–Yenching Institute as a candidate for a doctorate. I set out to pursue this thesis in my senior year; and did so. This study of Japanese imperialism may have been, in a tiny way, useful to scholarship. But already, in my senior year, after two years with Fairbank, I knew I was leaving home.

I had come to Harvard as an adolescent socialist and Zionist. I had helped organize the student Zionist activists on the New England campuses in what was called the Avukah (Torch) Society. I had helped organize a boycott of German goods in Boston, and been driven off by the cops for picketing Woolworth's. But somewhere between my junior and senior years, I had been lured to other interests. Harvard and History had intervened. So many other things were happening: The Japanese had begun their war on China in the summer of 1937, and were shattering Chinese resistance everywhere. Hitler was persecuting Jews. The Spanish Civil War was in its second year, and campus liberals were all engaged. What upset me most, the proximate cause of changed orientation, as Fairbank would have called it, was the siege of Toledo. Loyalists there outnumbered the Fascists; they had more men, but they were badly commanded. The Fascists held on to the Alcázar; Toledo had been lost; and men of good will had been defeated because they did not know *how* to fight. If we were to face fascism—and we could sense a war coming—all of us should know *how* to fight.

Thus, very consciously, I knew I was separating from my socialist and Zionist friends on the Harvard campus when I went into the yellow frame building, which now houses the Harvard Alumni Association, to apply to Colonel Harris of the Reserve Officers' Training Corps and ask whether I could, as a senior, join the ROTC. Colonel Harris was stern. I was a minor campus radical. Such radicals had rolled toilet paper down the steps of Widener Library when the West Point cadets came to visit, had brandished signs calling for "Scholarships Not Battleships" to protest Roosevelt's naval rearmament program. But I explained to Harris how I had changed my mind and wanted to learn how to be an officer. The colonel said that it was impossible to join the ROTC in the senior year and qualify for a commission. But he would let me audit the course, without credit; and he also let me join the unit in exercises.

The Harvard unit was a field artillery unit, which drilled with its horses in the armory in Boston. I had never touched a horse in my life, except for peddlers' cart horses on Erie Street. At my first muster in the armory, they presented me with a huge horse and played the Hoot Gibson comic Western trick on me. I stood at the right side of the horse, put my left foot in the stirrup, swung myself up to the saddle—and found myself facing the horse's tail. The ROTC students howled with laughter, and I was humiliated looking out at their laughing faces over a horse's behind. But then they did teach me how to mount correctly, and I attended the lectures on military strategy. What I most retained of my one year with the ROTC was this knowlededge of how to mount, speed, or slow a horse—which, when I was riding with communist guerrilla units behind Japanese lines in China two years later, proved to be the most valuable practical skill I learned at Harvard. Some forty years later, as an Overseer at Harvard, I vehemently and fruitlessly protested the abolition of Harvard's ROTC unit as authority yielded to campus violence. Then, with only one other Overseer, I presented myself for the commissioning of the last of Harvard's contribution to the ROTC. All wars, by 1969, had become abhorrent to Harvard's undergraduates. We, in 1937, lived in a different time and knew we would have to learn to fight.

But that is to get ahead of the story. My senior year passed pleasantly enough. I was reading Chinese, steeping myself in history, writing about the Twenty-One Demands, slowly swinging in my politics from socialist to hushed approval of Roosevelt's New Deal, concealing from friends that I was participating in ROTC exercises.

Graduation in 1938 was a pleasant June day. My mother and my sister came in by streetcar and subway to watch me graduate, and found nothing at all noteworthy in the program's statement that I had graduated summa cum laude under the rubric *"Qui adsecuti sunt summos honores."* That was what they had expected since I had entered the Boston Latin School. I left at noon, not staying to hear the commencement address by John Buchan, Baron Tweedsmuir. I was very hastily off that afternoon—by bus to Ann Arbor, Michigan, where they were giving a special summer course in reading Chinese newspapers, then back to Boston, then in a hurry to go to China.

Everything had come together in those last few months at Harvard.

In my own mind I was a revolutionary; but in reality I was the creature of other people, of another past, beneficiary of all the Establishment had packed into the Harvard processing system. My summa cum laude degree had won me a $1,200 fellowship from the Harvard–Yenching Institute. I could take that up, when I chose, and start on the long run of becoming a professor of Oriental history. But there was another surprise gift from the Establishment, which came in my last month at Harvard, something called the Frederick Sheldon Traveling Fellowship.

The Frederick Sheldon Traveling Fellowship was most important. Sheldon was a childless New England bibliophile who had graduated Harvard almost a hundred years before. When his widow died in 1908, she had bequeathed in his name half a million dollars for fellowships to let "students of promise" travel for a year as fancy took them. As it was explained to me, it was an invitation to spend a year traveling outside the United States, with no obligation either to study or work in the year of wandering.

The grant was $1,500—a fortune. For $600 (actually $595.27), I found, I could buy a series of tickets that would take me around the world: by U.S. President Lines to London, thence to Paris, thence to Marseilles; by Messageries Maritimes to Palestine, thence from Port Said to Hong Kong, then an economy passage from Hong Kong to San Francisco, and bus fare from San Francisco to Boston. This would leave $900 from the total. I could leave $600 of that behind for the family, as my contribution to the budget my mother and I had worked out—twenty dollars a week for eight months. There would still be $300 for me to eat, sleep, and live on as I moved around the world to China. If I could not earn a living in China, if I could not earn enough to help my sister keep the family going back in Boston, I would have to come back and take up the route to my Oriental professorship.

A new thought had also crept in in my senior year—the thought that I could, conceivably, write of history as a newspaperman. Both Charlie Duhig and John Fairbank thought I was not really and truly of the stuff of scholarship. Without being specific, both implied that I had the manners, lust, and ego of someone who might be a journalist. Fairbank had known Edgar Snow in China; and he thought I should try to do what Snow was doing.

So, then, with Establishment money in my pocket, and Harvard advice in my mind, I had begun to feel around the approaches to reporting. The Boston *Globe* was not then, as it is now, the best newspaper in Boston. But I was urged to try there before I went overseas. The name on the masthead that indicated "boss" was that of the managing editor, Laurence Winship, the father of its present editor, Thomas Winship. Larry Winship was a gruff man, but not frightening. In retrospect, he was the best of the old open-door newspaper editors. In his office on Boston's newspaper row, the Fleet Street of New England, he would, apparently, receive almost anyone—politicians, "cause" people, cranks, strangers, and Harvard seniors like myself. He gave me a brisk ten-minute hearing. I told him I was going to China, wanted to be a foreign correspondent and write for the Boston *Globe*. He listened, then said abruptly: All right. He could promise nothing except that he would read what I wrote if I mailed the copy to him personally; and if he liked what I wrote, he'd print it and pay for it. That was all, but he turned out to be as good as his word.

In the fall of 1938, then, I set out. I had a letter on stiff white Harvard stationery signed by James Bryant Conant, president of Harvard, recommending me to the good graces of the entire world as a Frederick Sheldon Traveling Fellow of the university. Charles Duhig, custodian of the meatballs at Dudley Hall, had always been upset by my vulgarity of manners and had given me a stern lecture about the graces of the world I was entering ("You've got to learn to clean your fingernails, White!"); then, as a gift, he also gave me his father-in-law's worn-out tuxedo. If I wanted to be a foreign correspondent, he said, I would have to go to diplomatic receptions and I would need a black-tie suit. John Fairbank's gift was more practical—a secondhand typewriter. My relatives gave me secondhand clothes. I bought a new suitcase and I had two hundred dollars in traveler's checks plus one hundred dollars in greenbacks in my wallet to get me to China.

I left Boston on the weekend of the great New England hurricane of September 1938, and my mother and sister cried seeing me off at the old South Station. All the way down to New York on the New Haven Railroad, the shoreline was littered with the wreckage of the hurricane; at New London, a huge ship's prow, blown on shore, hung within inches of the coach I was riding. It was a dramatic night. The next day I spent at the YMCA in New York and then boarded the SS *President Roosevelt* where, deep in the hold, above the throbbing engines, I shared a bunk with a young man whose name I still remember—Serafin Aliaga, a Spanish anarchist returning to fight Franco. Since the cause of the Republic was now hopeless, he said, he must therefore go back.

His sense of history was drawing him back to what must have been his death. My sense of history was drawing me outward, with no particular purpose of political passion. I hoped eventually to come back to Harvard. But first I must satisfy curiosity, my absolute lust to see what was happening in the China I had studied. How *did* history actually happen?

In Search of History (New York, 1978).

Lee A. Daniels

I'M A HARVARD MAN NOW

(1969)

Like Theodore White, Lee Arthur Daniels came to the College from Boston Latin School and could scarcely have picked a more critical period in which to find his place. Spurred by the temper of the times, the admissions offices of Radcliffe and Harvard were making an intense effort—some felt not enough—to bring to Cambridge an increasing number of minority students, particularly those of Afro-American background. Deeply conscious of a racial responsibility in following the path of Du Bois, Locke, and a line of distinguished Harvard black graduates, Daniels writes feelingly of his reactions to his Harvard experience in this excerpt from a manuscript in progress. As an undergraduate Daniels was managing editor of the Harvard Journal of Afro-American Affairs, *a government concentrator active in the* Crimson *and WHRB. He is currently a reporter for the* New York Times.

TEN MINUTES after Harvard's freshman dormitories were opened to the Class of 1971 on Friday, September 15, 1967, I was exultantly bounding up three flights of stairs in Weld Hall to room 36. Unlocking the door to the four-bedroom suite, I saw that one of my four roommates had already arrived (he wasn't there then) and had chosen the corner single which afforded a panoramic view of Tercentenary Theater. So I chose the single which, by facing the side of University Hall fifty feet away, offered views of both the Theater and the freshman quadrangle. I stepped to the window and, as I sensed more than saw the mosaic of color and movement across the expanse—for I was looking inward, savoring the realization of a two-year quest—I said to myself, "I'm a Harvard man now."

But that was not quite true then. For although my social comfort and academic success at the Boston Latin School, my reverence for history, tradition, and achievement, and my sense of being marked for distinction led me at times to think that my admission had been predestined as well as earned, I knew that in one singular way I did not fit the popular image of the Harvard man: I was black.

I entered Harvard during a period when American society had again begun, fitfully, debating how to apply its democratic ideals across the "Color Line," and, although I was deeply grateful to be at Harvard, I was determined that ignoring the struggle for racial justice would not be the price of my admission. As one who in adolescence had watched and read news accounts of the civil rights demonstrations in the South, who had read Baldwin's *The Fire Next Time* and Silberman's *Crisis in Black and White* and Stampp's *The Peculiar Institution* and Du Bois's *Black Reconstruction*, and who had marched and sung and spoken against school segregation in Boston, I saw myself as both an individual who dreamed dreams of achievement that are perhaps characteristic of Harvard freshmen and as the "representative" of an oppressed people with an obligation to work in their behalf.

I expected my activist bent to be fully engaged at Harvard, for I enrolled knowing that, though its graduate schools had trained several outstanding black scholars, it wasn't until the mid-1960s that the College admitted significant numbers of black students; that its workforce was nearly as lily-white as the most segregated Southern universities; and that its curriculum took scant notice of the presence of blacks in the New or Old World and paid even less heed to what they themselves had to say about it. In short, I entered Harvard in awe of the institution, yet, because of its past racial policies, unsure of what my relationship to Harvard would be. It was this ambivalence, heightened by events at the College and in the world beyond, which, despite the ambition and values I shared with my white classmates, produced in me sometimes a sense of pride and exhilaration, sometimes a sense of anxiety and estrangement, but always an awareness of the duality W. E. B. Du Bois—a Harvard man—had long ago poignantly identified as part of any black American's heritage.

"One ever feels his twoness—an American, a Negro," Du Bois wrote eighty years ago in *The Souls of Black Folk*, "two souls, two thoughts, two unreconciled strivings; two warring ideals in one dark body" . . . I had felt but not understood this sense of double-consciousness, of thinking in two colors, if you will, in secondary school. I could, and did avoid confronting it then because, despite my school's predominantly white student body and faculty, I lived in an environment peopled predominantly by blacks.

At Harvard, however, I could no longer avoid grappling with my "twoness," nor avoid trying to resolve the more urgent pressure I felt of being forced to choose between "white" and "black" worlds. This pressure, which, largely, was self-generated, was a consequence of my learning more about America's racial past, of my believing that many whites willfully refused to look upon black people as human beings, and of specific events such as the murder of Martin Luther King, Jr., and of the American government's prosecution of the war in Indochina and its persecution within the country of black and white activists.

I doubt if my ambivalence was readily apparent to most of my peers, black or white. My involvement in the efforts of the Association of African and Afro-American Students to change Harvard did not prevent me from participating in such extracurricular activities as the *Crimson* and WHRB, nor from accepting an invitation to join a final club. My sojourn in Cambridge, even during those necessarily fractious years, was far from being one long continual walk along the picket line, or a continuous struggle with angst. Yet I was baffled at how I, a black boy who knew what color and race have meant in America, could so enjoy being at Harvard and could choose whites as well as blacks as friends and role models. I would not begin to resolve this internal debate over my seemingly contradictory actions and aspirations for several years—not until I understood that, no matter what others thought, race for me was not a boundary circumscribing my thoughts, actions, and accomplishments, but a foundation for them. It was then that I came to accept and even to celebrate the duality Du Bois wrote of, and to integrate the man who keeps alive the racial memory of black people in America with the one who has an abiding but not uncritical affection for Harvard and for what it, at its best, stands for. It was then I could truly say, "I'm a Harvard man now."

VII

THE OTHER SIDE

The Corporation will not receive women as students into the College proper, nor into any school whose discipline requires residence near the school. The difficulties involved in a common residence of hundreds of young men and women of immature character and marriageable age are very grave.

CHARLES W. ELIOT (1869)

Whatever be its attitude in the future—whatever its relation to the University— whatever name it may bear, I hope it will always be respected for the genuineness of its work, for the quiet dignity of its bearing, for its adherence to the noblest ends of scholarship.

ELIZABETH CARY AGASSIZ (1892)

> Just on the other side
> Is a place which has sprung into fame,
> Tho I never go near for its learning I fear,
> Radcliffe I think is the name.

SOPHIA MORRIS AND MARY M. GIBSON (1917)

By terms of the contract, it may be ended with due notice at the will of either party. I believe, however, that it will never give place to the old loose association. It brings about an adjustment of fundamental importance in the development of Radcliffe; and President Conant and Dean Buck should always be counted with President Eliot as layers of foundations in the service which, through Radcliffe, Harvard gives to the education of women.

ADA LOUISE COMSTOCK (1943)

I am, as you might say, the first swallow of the summer, and I hope that there are dozens of other swallows coming along quite soon.

HELEN MAUD CAM (1948)

"It makes you feel so old to have gone to a college that doesn't exist anymore," a very recent Radcliffe graduate remarked very recently. But, in a sense, the old Radcliffe—and consequently, the old Harvard—have been slowly vanishing over the last few years, leaving like Alice's Cheshire cat, only a wide, wistful smile.

KERRY GRUSON (1969)

LUX

I DO NOT BELIEVE THAT WE CAN JUSTLY CALL AN INSTITUTION A UNIVERSITY WHICH IS CONFINED TO ONE-HALF OF MANKIND

(1866)

The name "Read '68" is neatly penciled in a bound copy of the December 1866 issue of the Harvard Advocate, *at the foot of an article arguing pleasantly for the admission of women to Harvard. There was no "Read '68" spelt that way, but there was a "Reed '68"—Milton Reed, if the unknown witness recorded the college class correctly. It is a great temptation to jump to the conclusion that "Lux" was Milton Reed, for the background of his life, his college preparation, all point to the conclusion, with no real evidence to support the argument. Reed had been the leading scholar at the Cambridge Latin School and had had as his room teacher Miss Lucy Elizabeth Shepard, who became in the summer of 1866 the second wife of President Thomas Hill of Harvard, her former teacher at Antioch College. A brilliant and dedicated teacher of the classics, she cannot have failed to serve Reed as an example of the benefit of higher education to women, and Reed's mention of "a young lady" who had to leave New England to "seek the doubtful advantages of Antioch" while her five male high-school classmates went to Harvard strongly suggests the young lady might be Miss Shepard, who graduated from Dorchester High School and went to Antioch.*

MESSRS EDITORS,—I cannot praise too heartily the various articles upon University Reform which have appeared in your magazine; and Dr. Hedge's most excellent address upon the same subject (which I had the pleasure of hearing) receives entire approval from me: but there is one branch of reform which, I believe, has not as yet been touched upon in your magazine,—a reform of paramount importance, and in regard to which, I will ask your attention to a few words from me.

I mean that advance upon our present state of civilization which will no longer exclude one-half of the human race from the walls of our college; which will no longer tolerate the barbarous idea that our sisters have not as good a right to a liberal education as ourselves.

Said a young lady to me on a certain occasion, "I would have given all that I could earn in five years, if I could have been allowed to be graduated from Harvard College. I went through a high school with five young men as classmates: these entered Harvard; but I, who had stood at the head of the class, was compelled to leave New England, and seek the doubtful advantages of Antioch College." I felt ashamed for my College, and blushed for the inconsistency of New-England civilization which tolerates such a manifest injustice in its pet colleges.

When our College was founded, the state of things was far different from what it is now. School-teaching then was confined almost entirely to men; now a great majority of our teachers are women; a large number of our students are prepared for college chiefly by women; and are we to set the same standard now for women's education as then?

I confess that I am unable to see what possible harm can result from throwing our College open to every person, male or female, who is desirous of entering it; on the contrary, I think that great good would be the result. It has been suggested by one of your contributors, that, if the expenses at Harvard were reduced, she would no longer be compelled to depend upon the immediate neighborhood for a supply of students: but I can inform him of a way by which a much more satisfactory result could be attained without half the difficulty attending his suggestion.

At the next examination for admission, let a notice be circulated throughout the country, that young ladies as well as young gentlemen will be received as candidates; and, if I am not mistaken, the result will be that in five years' time our number of students will be doubled. Then our expenses can be reduced to one-half the present amount, and we can properly say that we belong to a University; for I do not believe that we can justly call an institution *a University* which is confined to one-half of mankind.

It is often urged as an objection against receiving women into our larger colleges, that several colleges have been established exclusively for females, and several others are open both to males and females; and that women ought to be contented with these colleges, and not aspire to the dignity of becoming students of Harvard or Yale. This trifling argument is as applicable to men as women.

Why do so many young men leave their Western homes, and come all the way to New England for an education, ignoring the hundreds of little colleges, so called, which are struggling into existence on their boundless prairies? The simple reason is, that they are attracted by the superior advantages which our Eastern institutions afford; and, for the same reason, our sisters, who desire a collegiate education, cannot but feel disappointed to see us entering a first-class college, while they must put up with an Antioch or Oberlin. What a disgraceful sight!—an Eastern girl forced to leave her home in New England, so famous for its educational advantages, and seek the State of Ohio, as a place where she can enjoy even tolerable advantages!

If sectionalism is dangerous in government, it certainly must be so in education. Nature has placed boys and girls together in families, that they may mutually benefit each other; but, at the very age in which they are in the greatest need of each other's assistance, they are ruthlessly separated. What a glorious era it will be in American civilization, when a brother and sister, after attending school together during their younger days, can finally be received under the classic shades of Harvard, hand in hand, and continue here together for four happy years! A blessed day, too, will it be for the morals of our College, when the young men have the restraining influence of woman's society before them during their college course.

Alumni, the task is yours! See that this criminal exclusiveness be eradicated. Open the doors of your Alma Mater to all who desire and deserve her maternal care. Do away with this false distinction between the two sexes; and let the blessed light of civilization permeate the barriers of bigotry and injustice.   Lux.

The Advocate, December 11, 1866.

Elizabeth Cary Agassiz

A LETTER TO MY DEAR GIRLS

(1893)

Throughout most of his career President Eliot took a very cautious line on the question of women and higher education. In 1869 he clearly believed that the capacity of women to profit from the university experience needed proving. Yet, when the proposal for a Harvard "Annex," and later a Radcliffe College, came along, Mr. Eliot gave the new institution hearty support and testified before the State Committee of Education that "if Harvard College takes up the education of women, is there any reason to suppose that it will ever renounce it?" By the time of Mr. Eliot's retirement he was fully persuaded of the importance of higher education for women, although he thought most women's future careers would rarely lie outside education or homemaking.

If there was one individual in Cambridge responsible for Mr. Eliot's changed views, it was Elizabeth Cary Agassiz, who, as Radcliffe's first presi-

dent, demonstrated on home ground just how much able women students could benefit from their exposure to Harvard's teaching and influence. The widow of Louis Agassiz, the natural scientist, Mrs. Agassiz had founded and administered from 1855 to 1863 a very successful informal school for about eighty girls of high-school age, many of them faculty daughters. When Mr. and Mrs. Arthur Gilman proposed their idea of "private collegiate instruction for women" in 1878, Mrs. Agassiz became one of the original seven students selected. Five years later, after the incorporation of the Society for the Collegiate Instruction for Women, Mrs. Agassiz was elected president. This "Harvard Annex" received its state charter as Radcliffe College in 1894, with full recognition by the Harvard Corporation. In the following letter, Mrs. Agassiz responds to a group of graduates of the "Annex" who were suspicious of the wisdom of the new closer connection with Harvard.

MY DEAR GIRLS: . . . A year has been spent in the most careful deliberation and earnest discussion between the Harvard Corporation, the College faculty, and our own Society as to the means of bringing about a closer relation between the Annex and the University.

. . . We began the Annex as an experiment. We did it in the hope that Harvard would finally take us in some way under her protection. She has now made the first step in that direction. She has asssumed the whole responsibility of our education, and I confess it has never occurred to me that a degree given under her signature and seal would not be equivalent to a Harvard degree. It seems to me a distinction without a difference. What can any institution give more sacred than its signature and its seal? A pledge so guaranteed cannot be broken by any honorable body. To make this guarantee valid Harvard must keep our education up to the level of that of the Harvard student. She cannot set her hand and seal to an inferior degree. But I do her injustice in even hinting at such a possibility—the offer is made in perfect good faith and with the purpose of enlarging our education as fast and as fully as possible.

It seems to me unreasonable to expect the Corporation of Harvard to declare to the public between today and tomorrow everything they intend to do in a new departure which must be experimental for them as it has been for us. You may say that our experiment should suffice for them; on the contrary theirs is far more complicated, and has intricacies upon which ours did not touch. In saying this I allude to the governing boards, not to the professors. It would have delighted you to see the enthusiasm and earnestness with which the professors pursued the discussion in the faculty meetings, the confidence they showed in us, their readiness to do all and more than they have done for us. The fact that this body of teachers acquiesced in the final arrangement should satisfy you that it was one which was not intended to limit or retard our development.

But there are technical difficulties in the way of the governing boards which do not belong to the Faculty, and which touch upon a trust which they (the governing boards) have held for two hundred and fifty years and more. They must in loyalty to that older trust move cautiously and smooth over these difficulties gradually.

I do not believe in forcing the hand of the Harvard Corporation either by the weight of outside opinion or of individual remonstrances. I do not believe in an aggressive policy. I do believe in making the governing boards of Harvard our allies,—in showing them that all we ask can be granted without incurring any change of policy in the general government of the University or trenching in any way upon its original rights.

We have doubted (I mean we of the Annex) what part we should take in the sudden and startling protest against Radcliffe, which has taken us by surprise, because at first the air seemed full of congratulations. We decided not to enter into the newspaper lists. Patience and silence after all seemed best. We must go on with our work, keep our standard as high as possible, and let the results prove that we have not been mistaken in trusting ourselves to the guardianship of the University. This is always supposing that our act passes the Legislature, and that we really become Radcliffe College. Otherwise I am afraid there would be great depression in our ranks and we should find it hard to keep up our courage.

Believe me always

Your old and affectionate friend,
ELIZABETH C. AGASSIZ

Lucy Allen Paton, *Elizabeth Cary Agassiz: A Biography* (Boston, 1919).

Grace Hollingsworth Tucker

RADCLIFFE IN BLOOMERS
(1899)

Under the picture of Grace Hollingsworth in the 1903 Radcliffe yearbook is the phrase, "will discourse most eloquent music," and no one who has discovered Mrs. Tucker's charming reminiscence of Radcliffe life during the period between 1899 and 1903 will fail to catch some of the open-eyed enthusiasm for her college experience that she still carried with her thirty or more years later. After teaching in a New York City school for girls for a dozen years following graduation, she married a New York banker, raised a son, and continued to be interested in drama and music. She firmly believed in the economic emancipation of women but felt that careers for women could not be successfully mixed with marriage during the time of child-rearing.

All her life she valued "the rare scholastic privilege" of going to Radcliffe "because it is a part of Harvard University and ... not a 'female academy.' "

ONE September morning, more than thirty years ago, I stood at the foot of the old steps at Fay House, in the yard of Radcliffe College. I felt very much alone, thoroughly awed, tremulously expectant. In appearance I typified the "gay nineties." High, brown, laced shoes barely showed beneath my "reversible golf skirt," demurely plain without, colorfully plaided within; no asset to the playing of the game which had become so popular, merely a tribute to its existence. A long golf cape, also plaided beneath its sober exterior, wrapped me about, and a soft, gray felt hat with one long menacing quill and a dangerously extended hatpin, crowned my ratted pompadour.

There were a few such costumes in the groups that hurried past me, but they marked the newcomer. It soon became evident that most of the old-timers had turned their academic backs on the habiliments of the formal world outside, and were almost indifferent to appearance. Long skirts trailed across the grass and over the dusty paths, sometimes accompanied by the rustle of silk flounces beneath. Here and there a hem was down or a missing belt-pin left a white gap between the stiff grosgrain belt and a sagging skirtband. On the front of every shirtwaist a watch hung from an ornate watch-pin, and a fountain pen was clipped to a starched front band, or, sheathed in a leather case with a companion pencil, was fastened by a safety-pin device on chest or belt. In many cases, long academic gowns billowed open behind hurrying students, though obviously intended to conceal voluminous bloomers that were on their way to gym.

These same bloomers were, I soon learned, important factors in college life, and were taken to indicate either moral stability or moral laxity, according to the occasion in which they figured. During the college year we were frequently rounded up and admonished by the Dean, Miss Agnes Irwin, and "ill-concealed bloomers" headed one chapter of her theme. But unless they had been very much in evidence in all our theatricals, the history of the delightful, long-ago period of "The Idler," our dearly-loved dramatic society, would never have been written. It required a fine judgment to satisfy our mentors, and we sailed perilously between the Scylla and Charybdis of inconsistent standards.

One day the Dean stopped a very well-dressed girl whose attire was conspicuously fashionable, and asked her how her work was progressing, "I had fine marks on my hour-exams, Miss Irwin," was the answer. "I'm glad to hear it," said the Dean, "You give so much attention to your dress, I wondered if you were devoting enough time to your studies." The world, the flesh, and the devil were clearly out of place in cloistered halls of learning during the late nineties.

Miss Irwin was my first real contact with college. In time I came to know her as a remarkable woman and to value her as a dear friend. In the beginning she seemed Inhibition Incarnate. In those days the college was personally conducted along the lines of a large boarding school. The Dean showed a marvelous capacity for mothering the students, and an unusually keen perception in judging them. Her views were reflective of her time. If, from the vantage point of changed standards, we are critical of her straight-laced opinions, her inelastic views, we feel that she, too, would have adapted herself to the new world, had she lived to study its merits.

I saw her first standing in the door of an examination room where I was making up an entrance condition. She picked up an examination paper from the proctor's desk and lifted it close to her near-sighted eyes, with a quick, characteristic movement. Then she looked piercingly at each of the bent heads before her. As we left the room she stopped me, addressing me by name. "I knew you were to take this examination," she said, "and it was not hard to pick you out of a group of twenty. I'll send for you in a few days to talk over your program with you."

In the succeeding weeks and months and years she often sent for me. A note on the primitive letter-board behind the water cooler informed me that I was to see Miss Irwin, and at the appointed time I knocked fearfully on the great walnut doors of the Dean's room, Mrs. Agassiz's parlor. It was a beautiful room, rich in architectural beauty and old New England furnishings, richer still in the atmosphere and traditions of the old Fay House. I always fixed my gaze on the lovely portrait of Mrs. Agassiz over the mantel, awaiting the moment when Miss Irwin would raise her bent head from close contemplation of the papers on her desk, and tell me what I had done. Each interview brought new evidence of her perspicacity. Her admonitions were kindly, her decisions firm and immutable.

"You have signed up for English 7. At seventeen you are too young to study Fielding and Smollett. The best in them would pass you by; the worst in them would be magnified. Wait another year or two."

Again: "You are applying for Tannhäuser tickets for Saturday night. You are too young to come out from Boston after the opera with another under-graduate."

Or: "Your review of 'Tommy and Grizel' has been commended by Mr. Copeland. You are now eligible for the English Club. I wanted to have the pleasure of telling you."

So it was again and again, and I was only one of perhaps five hundred under her care. As the months passed by, I often dined at her house. I heard her clever analyses of matters political, international, her clear résumés of papers from both sides of the ocean, and her gay humor over anecdotes of the coffee hour. It was student gossip that she had frowned on Professor Barrett Wendell and his brilliant English course because he could not or would not refrain from swearing in his lectures at Radcliffe. The "Don'ts" of thirty years ago were proscriptions born of Victorian standards, and the end

of the Victorian Era was at hand. With Miss Irwin's passing came also the
passing of her day.

Radcliffe had no dormitories when I entered college, only one when I
left. Students who lived at too great a distance for commuting, boarded in
groups at student boarding houses in Cambridge or lived in Cambridge families, whose desirability was duly passed upon by the college office, and
listed for the consideration of parents. Because of the dangers lurking in an
unattached male (Miss Irwin remembered her Pamela!), it was college ruling that no student could reside where there was a son in the household. If
he existed, he was obliged to find outside quarters, so that the family income
might be properly augmented. It was my very good fortune to be a paying
guest in a delightful Cambridge home where there was one other student.
For some reason which we were never able to discover, the son remained in
spite of our presence, the only exception to the rule that I have ever known.
We frequently pointed out to him that the exemption in his case was un-
flattering to his charms. He merely suggested that he could be safely
counted on to be impervious to ours.

Many of the outstanding figures in the University life were frequent visitors and dinner guests during our stay there, and University topics were the
order of the day. We met also a number of charming Cambridge people
who had only an indirect connection with college life. We went every
Thursday evening to the Boston Symphony Concerts in Sanders Theatre,
with Mr. Gericke conducting, and sometimes to the Kneisel Quartet. We
saw all the Cambridge Dramatic Club plays in Brattle Hall, the little play-
house off Harvard Square. We journeyed to Jamaica Plain for the talented
amateur productions of The Footlights. Mrs. Ole Bull showed us her great
husband's treasures, Miss Alice Longfellow let us sit at her father's desk by
the Brattle Street window and lay reverent fingers on his pen. We wandered
in Lowell's garden at Elmwood. We went out to Concord and Lexington for
closer communion with Emerson and Thoreau, Hawthorne and Louisa Al-
cott. In Emerson's woods on Walden Pond we were indeed impelled to
hitch our wagon to a star, although with the inconsequential philosophy of
youth, we often rumbled contentedly along muddy roads thereafter.

We went no great distance from Cambridge, because the day of the
"horseless carriage" had not yet arrived. I do not remember seeing a single
automobile during my four undergraduate years, and even some time afterward we gaped at the few people who did own a car, even as we now com-
miserate with the few who do not. Transportation was very primitive.
Sawin's Express did all carting and provided a few one-horse, two-passenger
cabs for inclement weather or for lone women venturing out at night. The
fare within the limits of Cambridge was twenty-five cents, regardless of distance; but careful manipulating and a real social instinct increased Sawin's
receipts. When you sent for him he ascertained your destination, and from

his order list he paired you off with a suitable companion, for whom he stopped en route. If necessary, he made the proper introductions before climbing back to his seat. One trip, therefore, brought him two fares. I remember that I arrived in Cambridge with a large, new, gray trunk. Sawin put it down in my new home, remarking pleasantly, "They may call this a trunk in New York. In Boston we'd call it a Summer cottage."

Bicycles were in great favor. President and Mrs. Eliot were familiar figures riding on Brattle Street. Professor Morris Hicky Morgan always rode down to college. Our Ecclesiastical Prince, Bishop Lawrence, drove with Mrs. Lawrence in a victoria, a type of carriage that truly symbolized the dignity and formality of the age. A few undergraduates drove high carts, occasionally tandem, and many men rode horseback. Walking, however, was the most delightful and popular pastime of all. Everyone, young and old, great and small, walked. We walked up Brattle Street which led to the Elysian Fields of an undeveloped Fresh Pond. We walked out Mt. Auburn Street to the Watertown Arsenal, to Oakley, Newton, Waverley and over the Wellesley Hills, across country and along highways unmarred by motor sirens and honking horns. We walked to Belmont, and through the woods at Middlesex Fells. In early Spring we picked violets in great quantities and jumped agilely over Cambridge mud. In Autumn we waded ankle-deep through the leaves that carpeted all the walks, and thrilled to the rustle beneath our feet. In the long, white Cambridge winters we hitched our sleds to the delivery wagons that put on runners for the season.

On late Spring days we went canoeing up the Charles River. We drifted in under overhanging branches, piled up red cushions, and settled down to the Medea or floundered in The Fragments. If books had been left behind, an unusual occurrence, we remembered the relentless demands of English 2, and the approaching examinations, and refreshing our memories, we called out to the blue sky,

> "Once more into the breach, dear friends, once more,
> Or close the wall up with our English dead!"

All through June when the hour was late and Finals threatened, we lighted our student lamp—there was no electric light—and sat over our books far into the hot nights. Sometimes the bell of an ice-cream wagon broke the utter silence, and seizing a pocketbook, we dashed down the stairs and out into the deserted streets to purchase little packages of sweet frozen milk and cornstarch in various colors. Then back to the lexicon and the atlas, and again silence. Occasionally the Dickey song echoed in the distance, or a few Harvard undergraduates, returning from Strawberry Night at The Pudding, carolled out the important historical fact that "Harvard was old Harvard when Yale was but a pup."

Always, of course, we were under college regulations in manners and conduct. We could not go to Harvard Square bareheaded. Hair, being the crowning glory of woman, was undoubtedly a sex advertisement, and propriety demanded a covering for it. Shorn of our tresses today, are we, I wonder, less dangerous, or is the lipstick our substitute signal?

The feelings of our adopted family were outraged when they saw a Radcliffe girl hold a match to a Harvard cigarette. They were blissfully ignorant of the oncoming social débâcle from which she was to emerge lighting her own. Women, they said, should not telephone to men. It savored of pursuit. They were outspoken in disapproval when a young woman called their "exempted" son on the phone and asked him to dinner. The ensuing discussion at the home table was heated. Her act gave him, they insisted, no chance to decline. If he could not think up an excuse on the instant, he accepted because she had made an acceptance compulsory . . .

There were no "movies," nor even "nickelodeons," though in street car waiting-rooms we did have a chance to put a penny in the slot and turn a crank. This usually revealed a forbidden romance between a bewhiskered employer and an overdressed stenographer, with an irate wife in stiff sailor hat, mannish shirtwaist and long feather boa completing the triangle drama. Of course, we had an attraction much more wholesome than movies; football games in the Autumn and baseball in the Spring, so our Saturday afternoons were well provided for.

Occasionally, in the evening, we went to a Welsh rarebit party in a Harvard dormitory, chaperoned by a Cambridge matron. The proctors, notified of the occasion, had the privilege of attending but rarely exercised it. There was always a piano, always someone who could play it, and we sang songs from "The Burgomaster," "The Geisha," "The Runaway Girl," Weber and Fields and the Rogers Brothers, did close harmony on "The Little Old Red Shawl," roared out "Up the Street" and "Our Director" and "Down with Yale," and went home at ten o'clock.

I record, without any possible explanation and with great astonishment, the fact that we were allowed to have beer at these feasts. It troubled my parents when they heard it, but it left our Cambridge guardians quite undisturbed. I never saw wine or liquor served at any party while I was in college. Cambridge had "local option" and was dry during the years I was there, but Boston was a convenient source of supply. No Eighteenth Amendment was needed to keep us in line. We scorned one of the best soda fountains in Harvard Square because it was generally understood that "drinks" were served across the counter to the initiated. We drank a great many cups of tea and cocoa, and we had cocoa served to us during all three-hour examinations. Chocolate and Educator crackers revived many a Radcliffe student and sustained many a flagging spirit.

I have mentioned the moral stability we gained from gymnasium bloomers. I am sure more material went into them than the amount required today for a gown. They were baggy, voluminous garments, heavily pleated at the waist, longer than the sport skirts of today; but since they were actually, if not apparently bisected, we could not wear them around the college. They were, however, not only permitted but actually prescribed for all male characters in the productions of The Idler, which sponsored all our dramatics. Brothers and friends furnished immaculate dress coats, dinner coats, waistcoats, shirts, collars and ties for finished performances. No better dressed man ever stepped from Bond Street, London—that is, if you judged him from the waist up. His trousers were gymnasium bloomers!

In our Senior year we presented a musical comedy, "An Island Idyll" in Brattle Hall, open to the public and running for four nights. It was to be a gay affair, but what could we do about costuming our female men? We consulted the Dean. Could they, we pleaded, wear real trousers under the long Paddock overcoats of that day? The trouser legs would appear for ten inches only, we promised. The Dean was kindness itself. She wanted to help. She was prepared to be almost radical, but she had a moral duty to perform. Suppose the overcoats should open during a performance? She consented to a compromise. We might cut trouser legs off at the knee and sew them to these symbols of theatrical modesty—our gymnasium bloomers. And we did. Miss Irwin came to the dress rehearsal with a yardstick. The girls' skirts were seven inches from the floor; the overcoats, ten inches. This was satisfactory. The show went on.

Harvard Graduates' Magazine, June, 1933.

Le Baron Russell Briggs

TO WORK FOR RADCLIFFE IS AN ANXIOUS PLEASURE AND A HIGH ONE

(1924)

Le Baron Russell Briggs, Radcliffe's second president, once described his campus as "composed chiefly of a few back yards and an undersized apple tree." Agassiz House had just been completed when Mr. Briggs (who also served as Dean of Harvard's Faculty of Arts and Sciences) took office in 1903, and during his regime were added the library building, three dormitories and new endowment of $1 million to a total of $4 million. Dean

Briggs was a kindly, sensible, gentle man, enormously popular on both sides of the Common and among graduates of both sexes. He was no innovator but, though a part-time leader, he gave Radcliffe a strengthened position in relation to the University. Today his idea of education for women sounds paternalistic and old-fashioned. For him women's colleges existed "not for the competition of women with men, but for the ennobling of women as women." Yet he was a significant bridging figure in an era when higher education for women was becoming a solidly accomplished fact, and he did much to help broaden Radcliffe's curriculum. President Briggs spoke the following in 1924, addressing "friends and lovers of Radcliffe" at the dedication of the new residence hall named for him, which was already occupied by the time the cornerstone was laid.

IN CORNER STONES, my experience is limited; my ignorance is not. When I was young, the building was built on the corner stone; the corner stone was not shoved under the building with all the people living in it. The new order reminds one of "Sentence first, verdict afterwards" in the trial of the Knave of Hearts.

And I am even less experienced in corner stone oratory. My friend, Professor Edwin Hall, has favored me with a sample in the complete speech of an engineer on an occasion resembling this. "Ladies and gentlemen," he said, "when in the course of human events it becomes necessary to lay a corner stone, we lay it." Why say more? This tells the whole story.

Yet not the whole, either. In a certain sense this inverted process of construction symbolizes the rise of the Harvard Annex, whence came Radcliffe College. The Harvard Annex was in full swing before it had any building at all or a penny to build one. As with this hall, so with the Annex, the preposterous chronological sequence was apparent rather than real. The Annex stood fast: for the corner stone of the Annex was faith; and faith, you know, is the substance of things hoped for.

This building is a Radcliffe building through and through. It is built by Radcliffe herself; every commemorative part of it commemorates some friend of Radcliffe; even the architects got into Radcliffe as far as they could by marrying Radcliffe women—and Radcliffe women of the dyed-in-the-wool variety. If anything is Radcliffe a hundred per cent pure, it is this hall. Our architects have done well. The hall is good to look at and good to live in. As architects they know; as husbands of Radcliffe they care.

How to thank people who name a building after you is another strain on experience. I have rarely felt more grateful—or less competent. My heart expands; and my head shrinks. To work for Radcliffe is an anxious pleasure and a high one. Though by no means identical with virtue, it is like virtue in being its own reward. To work for Radcliffe through twenty years and then to lay the corner stone of your own monument, already erected, is not merely a *memento mori;* it is a cordial to warm the heart and a challenge to search it. The search reveals imperishable faith. Less than fifty years ago, even the Annex was a dream of Arthur Gilman and his wife. To-day Radcliffe College is a solid reality.

Radcliffe Quarterly, January, 1925.

Ada Louise Comstock

TWENTY YEARS AT RADCLIFFE

(1943)

It was Radcliffe's good fortune that Ada Louise Comstock never was elected president of Smith College. As Dean of Smith she came close, for she took over the administration of the College for a year in 1917 when Marion LeRoy Burton (a man by the way) stepped down as president. The trustees failed to give Miss Comstock even the title "acting," but she served loyally under the new president, William Allan Neilson, until her election as Radcliffe's first full-time head in 1923, and he was always one of her fast academic friends. The Comstock era at Radcliffe was a difficult time but crowned in triumph with the accomplishment of the 1943 agreement with Harvard. Although public speeches do not always make the best essays, it seems appropriate to reprint a brief talk to the alumnae by Ada Comstock at the Commencement of 1943, reflecting on her twenty Radcliffe years. It is a record of how her College prospered under her wise, good-humored, discreet, and patient leadership, and at the same time it shows how cautious were these new steps in the slow evolutions of the Harvard-Radcliffe relationship.

OF COURSE, I knew about Radcliffe. My sister had been a graduate student here. My successor at the University of Minnesota was Margaret Sweeney, a graduate of Radcliffe; but I learned first of the changes which were going to take place here when Marian Blackall Miller came to Northampton in the spring or the fall of 1922 and told me what was proposed in the way of electing a full-time president. She made an exceedingly interesting story of it all; and afterwards I thought it was a fortunate person who would hold that post—but of one thing I was sure, that it would never be offered to me.

On the twentieth of January, 1923, in my line-a-day book, I wrote about a meeting with "Radcliffe people" at Mrs. Wolbach's, in the house on Beacon Street; and I can see that room in my mind's eye now, and Mr. Moors talking about the "vat" of Harvard instruction on which Radcliffe could draw, and Mrs. Parkman sitting beside the fire and looking into it and saying never a word until the very end. Then there was a silence; and I expected no more from that quarter; but on the ninth of February I had a letter from

Mrs. Wolbach suggesting that we have an interview on the neutral ground of New York City. On February twelfth I met her at Miss Dean's apartment. Miss Park had been summoned up from Bryn Mawr, to tell me, as a kind of outside person—although she had been dean here for a year—what a wonderful place Cambridge was and what an extraordinary college Radcliffe was. At the end of the interview I was offered the presidency of the College.

Soon after that I received visitors, distinguished visitors. Mr. Briggs came for lunch, and Judge Cabot gave up a beautiful Sunday to call on me; and on February twenty-fourth I came to Boston, where I remember talking with Mr. Kenneth Webster, Mr. Robinson, and Miss Humphrey of the relationship between Harvard and Radcliffe, and with Mr. Ezra Baker, then our treasurer. There was tea at Greenleaf House, with Mr. and Mrs. Briggs and Dr. and Mrs. Cabot. That was my first glimpse of Greenleaf.

On February twenty-sixth I did a most unseemly thing. The committee which had invited me to come to Radcliffe to be nominated for the presidency had given me a month in which to reach a decision. Only two weeks of that month had passed, but on that day I sat down and wrote to Mrs. Wolbach that I should like to be president of Radcliffe College. You remember the old saying, "Don't marry the girl who is hard to get; marry the girl who comes a-running." Certainly I came a-running, and I was elected on March fourteenth. Then, on March thirty-first I had a talk with Bernice Brown, whose name had been suggested to the nominating committee as the dean of Radcliffe College; and from that day began one of the happiest associations of my life.

There have been outstanding events in these twenty years. There was the Semi-Centennial, in 1929. I have never ceased to be grateful that we had it in the spring instead of in the fall, when the crash came. We had high hopes up to that time for the development of the College. Longfellow Hall was already going up, and it seemed to us not impossible that within a very few years we should have realized the whole of our scheme. Of course, much of it is still unrealized.

Our campaigns have proved to be nothing short of electrical. The first one of them started with the Great Depression. The second one coincided with the beginning of the Second World War. Either we have a sinister effect on cosmic forces, or our timing is bad to the point of genius. However, both the campaigns have brought to Radcliffe, on the whole, surprising returns. We have had strokes of good fortune almost out of the blue. One morning, I can't remember how long ago—fifteen or sixteen years perhaps—we saw in the paper that Mr. Edmund Dana Barbour's will provided for the distribution of the residue of his estate among Harvard, the Massachusetts Institute of Technology, and Radcliffe; and nearly $798,000 has already come to us from that estate, and there will be, eventually, more.

Then there was Byerly Hall, given us by the General Education Board.

After some negotiations, it came very quickly and very easily, with a telephone call from New York, making a completely unrestricted gift to us for the purpose of building a science building. There was also a splendid bequest recently from Mrs. Georgine Holmes Thomas of something more than $350,000 . . .

And then there was a hard period of four years about which very little could be said to the alumnae, about which nothing could be printed in our publications, but of which those of us on the Board of Trustees and on the staff here were well aware. President Lowell saw the defects of the relationship between Harvard and Radcliffe, as they have been seen recently, but the cure that was proposed, that of splitting Radcliffe off completely from Harvard, would, I think, have been fatal to Radcliffe—fatal at any rate to Radcliffe as we know it and as we believe it should be. Mr. Lowell was a resourceful and determined man; and the struggle, for those four years, was pretty nearly incessant and at times gave us all great anxiety. In the long run I think that struggle did us good. It gave us champions and friends whom we otherwise might have lacked.

We have had gains in these twenty years. You know the new buildings we have added—Longfellow, Byerly, Cabot, the Health Center, as well as the Wall, the Sunken Garden, and many improvements in the plant. Altogether we have expended in these twenty years nearly $1,600,000 on the academic plant alone. We have added in real estate what I think real estate people call "parcels"—ten parcels, on Garden Street, Farwell Place, Appian Way, and Hilliard Street—and have spent $264,000 approximately for them. In spite of the fact that we lost a good deal at the time of the depression, our endowment is more than $3,000,000 larger than it was twenty years ago; and, though we have not tried to increase our enrollment—in fact we have limited it—we have averaged about two hundred more students a year than in earlier days.

There has been recognition of the College. Our association with the group of seven colleges was, I am sure, of advantage in making Radcliffe as an undergraduate college better known in all parts of the county. The Graduate School always drew from a wide area. You will soon be hearing about a scheme for national scholarships which the same seven colleges hope soon to launch, with the same intention of making friends and bringing to us students of a fine quality from quarters in which we might otherwise not have had them. I smiled to myself—and I do not know whether or not you will call it a distinction—when Radcliffe was described in a committee meeting in Congress not long ago as a "richly endowed college." I felt like the man who was asked for a loan of ten dollars and thanked the asker for the compliment.

Our greatest promise, I think, at the present time, is in our new relationship with Harvard University. It got off to a rather bad start from the point of view of publicity; and the headlines and some of the comments gave an emphasis and interpretation which was false, or, at any rate, misleading. When the story first appeared in the *Globe* headlines on the front page, it said that "Harvard goes coed"; other papers announced that Radcliffe was "surrendering its independence." Neither is true. What the new arrangement signifies is something quite different. It is the first assumption of responsibility on the part of the Harvard boards and of the Faculty of Arts and Sciences for supplying Radcliffe with instruction. When those seven ladies—our seven ladies—wished to establish here in Cambridge some means by which Harvard instruction could be given to women, Mr. Gilman sought President Eliot's permission to approach members of the Harvard faculty to ask them to repeat their courses for young ladies. President Eliot *gave* consent, and that consent has persisted to this day. When Radcliffe applied for a charter to be a college and to grant degrees, there was some doubt whether an institution which had no faculty of its own and no fixed endowment should receive such permission. Someone had the bright idea of trying to give assurance that Radcliffe would never drop from its high standards by asking Harvard to endorse all of its degrees. According to the charter, Radcliffe is at liberty to grant any degrees to which Harvard will certify as the equivalent of the same degrees when given at Harvard. Obviously, Harvard assumed a great responsibility in permitting itself so to become the certifying body of Radcliffe. In all these years, however, Harvard has never taken any responsibility for enabling Radcliffe to meet the conditions. If we managed to achieve equivalence, well and good; but, according to the theory, Harvard had no obligation to help us to do it. Under the new plan, of course, the situation is quite different.

The plan operates in this way. Instead of making individual payments to members of the Harvard faculty for teaching at Radcliffe, we shall pay a percentage* of our tuition to Harvard University, in a lump sum; and that sum will be applied to the improvement of Harvard faculty salaries. Each instructor is thus under obligation to teach at Radcliffe, if the department so decides. The addition to his Harvard program will be not more, on an average, than one half-course a year, though in one individual year he may undertake a whole course. It becomes the duty of the Harvard departments to supply us with an adequate program for the attainment of degrees. It is the duty of the faculty as a whole to determine the Radcliffe educational policy, and that is the point at which a good many people have thought we were losing our independence.

I find that people think that educational policy is determined by the administrative officers of a college. I should like you to recall the fact that it took Mr. Lowell fifteen years to get the Harvard faculty to accept the tuto-

---

* Since the 1977 agreement with Harvard, Radcliffe now pays all its tuition to Harvard.

rial system; and President Hutchins is known to be having his difficulties. It is the right of the faculty of an educational institution to determine the educational policy of that institution. The Harvard faculty has never before been empowered to consider Radcliffe educational policy as such. It has determined Harvard educational policy; and we have followed that policy, willy-nilly. You may call that independence if you like! Now it becomes the duty of the Harvard faculty, before putting any change into effect, to consider whether it should also be put into effect at Radcliffe. It must consider Radcliffe policy separately. If you believe that educational wisdom resides in Harvard's faculty, I think you will grant this provision is a great gain for us; and certainly it means no loss of independence, but a gain in independence under the law.

As to coeducation, I want to say just a word, because that subject has been misunderstood. It is true, provision is made for some slight extension of the opening of small, advanced middle-group courses which have heretofore been regarded as sacred. It can be done only by permission; and, as carried into effect this year, I believe it affected only seven courses. At the present time, however, because of the war emergency, and not as a part of this new plan, a great many course are being merged for the coming year. That process would have gone on whether we had this plan or not.

The new plan is going to make administration, which had become extremely cumbersome and difficult, much easier. We have had to keep in constant touch with Harvard in order to make up our schedule of payments to members of the Harvard faculty. The whole thing now will be handled with much greater ease. The terms given us in this arrangement insure instruction adequate for the attainment of degrees at Radcliffe of the same quality and standard as that given in Harvard College and the Graduate School of Arts and Sciences; and that is our present charter. If the plan works well—and I think it cannot fail to work well—it will be a permanent thing. The avowed purpose with which Radcliffe was founded is accepted and implemented by the Faculty of Arts and Sciences, by the Corporation, and by the Overseers of Harvard University.

I have given myself the pleasure of going over all this because I now have something to tell you which is not news to a good many of you. Last June I asked the trustees if they would release me as president a year hence, and I now am expecting to retire on September first. I shall be sixty-seven years old on my next birthday, and I have been here for twenty years; and I am perfectly certain the time has come for the direction of the College to be put into younger and stronger hands. When Mr. Lowell retired at Harvard, I heard him speak to the Alumni Association there. These were his words: "Gentlemen, you have been good to me"; and he asked that the same goodness be shown to his successor. I paraphrase his words: "Ladies, you have been good to me." There was no coldness in your welcome to me twenty years ago. You seemed to show no resentment of this "outlander," with strange ideas, who was coming into Radcliffe. You gave me every help in learning the character and philosophy of the College, a philosophy with strongly marked characteristics; and I want you to know that everything I have learned in these twenty years about Radcliffe has convinced me afresh of its value and distinction in the world of education and of the fact that it has much greater promise for the future than has yet been realized.

Radcliffe Quarterly, August, 1943.

Barklie Henry

LADIES IN THE YARD: AN ALUMNI REPORT

(1954)

When the famous Dr. Alice Hamilton decided in 1919 to accept an invitation of the Harvard Medical School to join the faculty as a teacher of industrial medicine, she was warned by her backers that some people were worried she might want to use the all-male Harvard Club of Boston or demand her quota of football tickets or insist on marching in the Commencement procession. By the 1950s most of the bastions of Harvard's male exclusiveness had begun to topple. A visiting professor of law simply plunked herself down, unchallenged, in the main diningroom of the Faculty Club. Miss Helen Maud Cam quietly and regularly took her place in Appleton Chapel. And a Harvard Alumni committee solemnly recommended that male and female degree holders should have equal status at Commencement. The report was signed by Leo F. Daley, A.B. 1927, Clement K. Stodder, A.B. 1917, and the chairman, Barklie McKee Henry, A.B. 1924, who presumably wrote it. A wise and witty man, Henry early entered a career in publishing and banking but eventually abandoned this for family and charitable interests, principally in New York City. For many years he was president or chairman of the New York Hospital. He also served as trustee of the Rockefeller Institute, Vincent Astor Foundation, John Hay Whitney Foundation, and the Pierpont Morgan Library.

THE COMMITTEE was appointed at the meeting of the Directors of the Harvard Alumni Association on October 24, 1953. Following the meeting, the members were shown a letter dated September 29, 1953, from Miss Marie Munk, an attorney, of 25 Eustis Street, Cambridge, an alumna of the Graduate School. The letter, which was thoughtful and carefully considered, raised questions concerning the status of women who hold Harvard degrees.

To what extent is a female entitled to the rights and privileges of the Harvard Alumni Association? Are they "full-fledged" or "by sufferance"? Should they feel free to attend any meeting of the Alumni Association or any reception? May they make use of Harvard Clubs? May they enter at Commencement that part of the Yard hitherto preserved for Harvard men, and may they partake of refreshments?

Miss Munk pointed out that women now hold degrees from the Harvard Law School, Graduate School of Education, the Medical School, School of Public Health, and also receive the degree of Adjunct in Arts, an equivalent of the A.B. degree. We believe that there are already approximately 1,800 ladies who hold Harvard degrees. We must emphasize that these are exclusively degrees from graduate schools, and that the problem which Miss Munk's letter raises does not involve the Harvard undergraduate body.

Miss Munk concluded her letter with the statement: "As the number of women who receive degrees from Harvard is steadily increasing, a clarification of their status seems desirable and eventually inevitable." It was the phrase "eventually inevitable" which filled your Committee with an indefinable sense of foreboding, and spurred them to a frenzy of action. To coin a phrase, your Committee has taken the dilemma by the horns, and has sought to throw the bull in a direction it has never been thrown before, at least not in the Harvard Alumni Association.

Accordingly, the Committee submits the following recommendations:

(1) All female holders of Harvard degrees may become members of the Harvard Alumni Association, in the same status as the male holders of the same degrees, and in the future, they should be informed of this privilege at the time of their graduation.

(2) As members of the Harvard Alumni Association, they shall be entitled to the same rights and privileges as the male holders of the same degrees.

(3) Since the Harvard Clubs organized by alumni groups in various communities are private bodies having no official connection with the Harvard Alumni Association and operate according to the individual constitution of each such club, the Harvard Alumni Association would be outside the bounds of its prerogatives to dictate to the Harvard Clubs concerning their membership policies, and therefore, if any female holders of Harvard degrees believe that any alumni Harvard Club in their community provides facilities in which they desire to participate, they should make known their request to the proper officials in each club concerned.

(4) If the Harvard Alumni Association endorses the above recommendations, they should be conveyed to the Committee on the Happy Observance of Commencement, with the request that female holders of Harvard degrees be provided at Commencement with all the rights and privileges accruing to the male holders of the same degrees. Your Committee is reluc-

tant to offer any detailed recommendations concerning the best manner in which this policy can be implemented at the time of Commencement, but offers the following suggestions for consideration, fully realizing that they can be improved.

It might be desirable for female degree holders, in order that they not be confused with the female *entourages* of male degree holders and degree recipients, to be identified by some less ascetic ornament than the academic gown and mortarboard. Of course academic apparel would distinguish them from the lady guests, but it would fail to distinguish them from the lady degree recipients. We therefore suggest that perhaps they should wear a crimson badge, plainly marked "ALUMNA." We admit the inconsistency of this notion, inasmuch as male alumni do not wear a badge marked "ALUMNUS." But our desire, in the process of transition to the new custom of giving lady degree holders full privileges, would be to make the problem of identification at the spread, in the parade, and so on, as simple for them as possible.

If they wore such a badge, the wearing of it would admit them, without further identification, to all the ceremonies and social occasions to which male degree holders are now entitled.

Female degree holders, your Committee believes, should have the privilege of marching with their appropriate graduate school groups in the Alumni Parade, in the usual order of precedence, without segregation from their male classmates.

We repeat: all these are merely suggestions concerning the conduct of Commencement, and we do not propose them dogmatically, but defer to the Committee on Observance, under whose wise and experienced guidance these detailed decisions should be evolved.

Harvard Alumni Bulletin, February 2, 1954.

Sallie Bingham

WINTER TERM

(1957)

It is quite a leap from the well-chaperoned times of Grace Hollingsworth Tucker to the more relaxed standards of the 1950s. Radcliffe's manners changed much with the years, as did Harvard's. And even though there were some in each Yard who boasted that they had never consorted with those on the opposite side of the Common in their entire four years in Cambridge, the statistics on Harvard-Radcliffe marriages annually argued otherwise. The year 1943 brought the famous agreement between the two colleges that began the slow process of transforming coordinate education into coeducation. "The last thing in the world that I desired when I took office," President Emeritus Conant recalled, "was to open Harvard College to 'young ladies.' " Yet, as time passed, Mr. Conant "became slowly convinced that administrative awkwardness was too high a price to pay for the continuation of the prejudices of those who, like myself, wished Harvard to remain strictly a man's college." So we move on to 1957 and Sallie Bingham's touching story of the painful Harvard-Radcliffe love affair between Hal and Ellie. At the time of its publication the story caused some consternation among college officialdom, but its reputation endures for its sensitivity and maturity and its impressive use of setting.

Sallie Bingham took her degree magna cum laude in English and now lives in Louisville, where she is raising a family of three boys and teaching creative writing at the University of Louisville. She is the author of a novel After Such Knowledge (1960) *and two volumes of short stories,* The Touching Hand (1967) *and* The Way It Is Now (1972). *In the last decade she has turned from the short story form to drama and has written four full-length plays and three one-act pieces.* Milk of Paradise *was produced in New York in March 1980 by the Women's Project of the American Place Theater, and a second play,* Paducah, *is scheduled for presentation in either New York or Louisville. Her stories have appeared in* Mademoiselle, The Atlantic Monthly, Harper's Bazaar, Redbook, Ms., Audience, *and other magazines.* "Winter Term" *was selected for inclusion in* The Best American Short Stories 1959.

IT WAS inconvenient. And worse: Hal watched the woman behind the desk ruffle through filing cards and wondered if she had noticed that he came to the library every evening. She must have noticed, for during the past month he had looked at her so often that he had begun to recognize her dresses and the two ways she fixed her hair. He often felt that she was watching him and Ellie and feeling surprised that they came every night. During the day Hal sometimes planned a new kind of evening, in the library still, for the dancing-and-movie Saturday nights he spent with Ellie were even more stereotyped. Sometimes he imagined that Eleanor would be there when he came, or that she would not be wearing lipstick, as when he had first seen her. He knew that the small change in details could not alter the whole evening. And so in the past week he had begun to imagine the only possible change: that Eleanor would not come at all. Hal planned to wait at the library until a quarter past seven, and then if she had not come he would leave, not pausing to button his coat and turning at once onto the street.

"Why don't you take off your coat?" the librarian asked him. He had never heard her voice before. It was pleasantly colorless, and he was surprised that with such a voice she had spoken to him at all.

"Oh, that's all right," he said vaguely. "I may have to leave in a few minutes." She pulled out another drawer of filing cards and began to go through them from the back. As he watched her Hal became more and more surprised that she had spoken to him. It reminded him that he was still an intruder, even after a month; there were usually only one or two other boys in the library, so few that the girls stared openly. He walked over to the reading room door and looked in; the red-haired boy whom he had begun to speak to on the street was studying with his girl. Eleanor said they were engaged, although Hal pointed out that the girl was not wearing a ring. Eleanor said that it did not really matter: they never went out except with each other, and on Saturdays and Sundays she had seen them having breakfast together in the Waldorf. Hal remembered asking her what they had been eating; it was a new way he had of testing Ellie, to see how long it would be before she laughed; he knew that if he teased her for a certain amount of time she would more probably cry. "French toast," she had answered promptly, "three orders, with maple syrup," and then she had asked him why he had laughed, and when he shook his head and went on laughing her mouth had begun to quiver in the way that made him tighten, and she had asked: "Why do you always laugh at me?" They had had a bad evening. The tightening had started it, Hal knew; he granted that to her in the careless objectivity of his remembering. He wondered if he would ever be able to prevent himself from feeling like that when she didn't laugh with him, or when she was inexplicably depressed, or when she asked him: "What are you thinking?"

He looked at the clock. She was already seven minutes late. It happened every night; he imagined her dawdling over combing her hair, watching the clock and planning not to leave in time. She often warned him against taking her for granted. Surprised by his own bitterness, he thought, Oh, God, why do I always have to be so hard on her; lately she can't do anything right. He remembered the way he used to feel when she came toward him, running because she was late, or to get in out of the rain; she would shake the rain out of her hair (too vain to wear a scarf), and her face would be flecked with drops. Then her coming had canceled his irritation.

Eleanor came in the door before he could decide when the change had begun. She started toward him, red-faced from the wind she had fought for four blocks. "Hello!" she said, and he knew that if he had looked permissive she would have kissed him, in spite of the librarian. It was one of the things that he first liked about her: she was willing to kiss him even on the Saturday night subway, when the whole row of people on the other side of the car was watching them. Hal remembered how surprised he had been when they first danced together and she had pulled close; the action did not suit the mild, high-necked dress she was wearing, or even the coolness of her cheek.

She was peeling off her coat and sweater, and he noticed how limberly she bent to unfasten her boots because he was watching. Her figure had improved since she gave up sweets. He remembered proudly that she had started to diet because he had told her once that a dress was too tight; he never had to tell her again. Now her hips were straight under her skirt, and he knew from looking at them how they would feel, very firm as she clenched the big muscles and smooth through her slippery underpants.

They went into the reading room. Hal had grown accustomed to the people who looked up as they walked down the corridor between the tables, but he knew from the way Ellie was smiling they still made her uncomfortable. When they sat down she whispered to him fiercely, "You'd think they'd learn not to stare every night!" and he whispered back, leaning so close her hair touched his mouth, "It's just because you're beautiful."

"You've said that before," she told him, mocking and pleased, but he had already realized it; it did not matter how often he repeated the compliment, for each time the situation was the same, until the lie had become as familiar as the library room. He did not think he would tell Ellie that she was beautiful if they were in a new place, a city or a green park. He looked at the clock.

"Bored?" she asked quickly.

"No." He tried not to frown. She made a little face at him and bent over her notebook.

Hal wished that he had not learned to translate her expressions; when he first met her he had been charmed by her good-humored pout or her wide-eyed expression after they kissed. But now he knew that the pout was made to conceal the quiver in her mouth, and if he watched her he would see that she was not reading; she was staring at the page and trying not to look at him. And as for her expression after they kissed—it always seemed to Hal that he was watching her rise through deep water—he did not know what it meant but it irritated him. It reminded him of the way she acted after they made love. She went into it as exuberantly as she jumped up to dance, she left it to him to make sure that his roommates were out and that the shades were down. By the time he had checked she would have pulled her dress over her head, rumpling her hair in bangs like a little boy's. He began to undress, folding his clothes on the chair—"Ellie, won't you hang up your dress?"—but when he turned around and saw her waiting, naked under her slip, he went to her and forgot what he had been about to say.

But afterward, if she did not cry, she would not let him go. She clenched him in her arms when he tried to get up, and he had to hurt her in order to break away. When she clung to him with her fingernails pricking his back he tried to force himself out of his sleepiness, to smooth her hair and kiss her. But her mouth tasted stale when he was so tired and he was afraid she might think he wanted to do it again.

"I'm sorry I was late," she said, not looking up from her book, and he realized that for the last five minutes she had been trying to decide why he seemed irritated.

"I thought we said we wouldn't apologize anymore." He wanted to sound gay, but he noticed at once that she was still raw to the subject; she said softly: "I wish you could forget that." She was bending down the corner of a page and he wanted to tell her to stop; the little mechanical action irritated him out of all proportion, and he wondered if he was so tense because they hadn't made love for four days. How did she feel about tonight? He knew that his roommates were out. He looked at her, but he could tell from the way she was hunched over her book that she was not thinking about making love but about the evening a week before when they had quarreled and then made a list of resolutions over coffee in The Grill. One of them had been not to apologize to each other any more for they had agreed it was hypocritical: apologies were only dog-in-the-manger ways of saying, I was right all along but I'll give in for the sake of peace. It had been a terrible evening and he wished that they had not gone to The Grill, for before they had both associated it with one of their first evenings together, when had held her hand between the salt and pepper.

"Oh, I forgot to ask you about the exam." She had not whispered, and the girl at the next table glanced up, frowning. "How was it?"

"Terrible!" The word did not relieve him; he had come back in the winter darkness, coffee-nerved, fingering the three pencils in his pocket whose points were worn flat. He remembered cursing himself for not reviewing more, and he wondered if he could have written at the end of the thin, scratched-out bluebook, "Circumstances beyond my control . . ."

"But I thought you were so well prepared; you've been reviewing for practically a week."

He tried not to say it, but the words promised too much relief: "Yes, but I can't really study here." He knew before he looked at her that she was hurt. As soon as he saw her mouth he felt the tightening; he wanted to laugh out loud and throw his head back and yell with laughter, and at the same time he wanted to pull her into his arms and fold her so tightly that her breath came in gasps and she groaned, Hal, Hal, you're hurting me . . .

"You never told me you couldn't study here," she said, and he knew how carefully she had weeded the hurt out of her voice.

"Well, I mean, what do you expect? How can I concentrate with you around?" He had meant it to be a compliment—he wanted to see her smile, flushing a little and looking up at him—but it sounded like an accusation. As she turned her face sharply away he thought, Oh, God, not another scene! And then he noticed abruptly how thin she had grown; he could see the point of her collarbone through her sweater, and her little breasts stood out almost too sharply.

Ellie had bent down the corner of the page so often that it broke off in her hand. She turned to Hal, smiling brightly. "You should have seen the dormitory tonight." In spite of the new-paint smile, Hal wanted to kiss her for changing the subject. He thought that afterward he would buy her an ice cream cone at the drugstore on the way back to her dormitory. She loved sweets, and she hadn't had any for at least two weeks; he remembered her inexpensive salad dinners, even on Saturdays. And she was really almost too thin.

"You know Wednesday night's usually bad anyway," she was saying. The girl at the next table looked up again, annoyed, and Ellie put her hand to her mouth. She would not have gone on if Hal had not asked, "Well, what happened?" and then she turned to him and whispered so softly, hesitantly that he could hardly hear. "You know Wednesday night is boy night, and they have candles and ice cream for dessert. Just because we eat at a quarter past six instead of six! Tonight I sat at a table with three other girls and their dates and I literally didn't say a word!" Hal had heard it often before; he looked around the room, trying to distract his attention from his own irritation. Why was she proud of not talking for a whole meal? He noticed the pretty girl who was in his humanities class; she was winding a shank of hair around her finger as she studied. Pretty hair. But she looked even more tense than the rest of them. During exam period you could cut the atmosphere in the reading room with a knife. Most of the girls looked overtired and ugly, and they had not bothered to comb their hair. Hal remembered that the library was the one place they had not expected to see any boys. But Eleanor hated the men's library. She said she felt too stared-at when there were so few girls. Hal had seen some of the looks boys gave her when they walked down the corridor, and he agreed. She had such a damn good figure.

"You're not listening," she said. "I know—don't apologize; I shouldn't be bothering you." As though her rigidly calm tone really expressed her feelings, Eleanor neatly wrote the date at the top of a notebook page and began to read.

"I am interested!" he lied, feeling her hurt. "It's just that I'm interested in this place too." She did not answer, and he slammed his book open and turned the pages roughly, looking for his place. They sat for ten minutes in silence. Hal tried to read but he was too conscious of the tip of her elbow, almost touching his; it looked a little chapped, and he remembered how hard the winter weather was on her blond skin. Then he wondered how he had known that—he had been through no other winter with her, or even a spring or summer—and inconsequentially he wondered what she looked like in a bathing suit. He hunched his shoulders and bent closer to the book, trying to force the words into his attention. There were long, ruler-straight lines under some of the sentences, and minute notes were printed in the margins. He had written them in October, when for a week he had devoted himself to Schopenhauer, reading each page passionately, proud of the learned comments he wrote in the margins. He had even found time to go into town to visit the museum, where there was a portrait of the philosopher, and he remembered how his head had pounded as he climbed the long steps and hurried down the corridor to the door of the room where the portrait hung. It had been a disappointment: an old, placid gentleman in conventional black. Did pessimism embodied look like that, he remembered wondering, like your own grandfather? But he had come back with a feeling of accomplishment.

Now he could not read his own notes. When Ellie was hurt the consciousness of it ticked like a clock at the back of his mind and he could not concentrate on anything. He gave up trying to ignore the point of her elbow. He wondered if she would move first, as she often did, slipping her hand into his or turning into his arms as soon as they were alone. He noticed how rigidly she was sitting; why did they both keep on pretending to study? He looked at the clock. Already half an hour wasted. God, I wish we'd had a chance to so I wouldn't feel like I'm going crazy! Exams—we couldn't afford the time. He remembered how self-righteously they had avoided his room, knowing that once they were there, where they had first told each other that they were in love, their resolution would dissolve in a panic of desire. Their coming together was always too violent, he thought, like the too big lunch you ate after missing breakfast, snatching and tearing at the food if no one was watching. But I bet she needs it now, he thought, that's why she's so quivery, close to tears, and maybe that's why I loused up that exam. He knew it was not an excuse, and he felt his resentment heating as he wondered why he had not really reviewed. But she's right: I spent all last week on it, he thought, and then he added, enjoying his own bitterness, Yes, but you know what studying here means, jockeying for position for three hours with our knees about to touch or our hands, and she's always looking up or else I'm looking at her until finally we give up and hold hands though that means I can't write or else she can't. Why didn't I have sense enough to tell her I had to study, two evenings would have done it . . . but I knew she'd cry. Not over the phone but in the booth after I hung up, so she couldn't go back to her room without the other girls seeing she'd been crying. He wanted to turn to her and break the thin, unreal wall of her concentration by asking, Why does everything hurt you too much? And why do I always have to know? Although he knew the last, at least, was not her fault.

He heard eight strike in silver, feminine notes from the clock over the girl's gym. That clock would never let him forget the amount of time he was wasting; all evening he would have to listen to its reproachful chiming. The thought drove him to the peak of his irritation and he slammed his books closed and began to stack them together. Eleanor looked up and he saw the terror in her eyes that he had seen once before when he told her that he would have to go home for the weekend. She had said: "You know that means three days without talking to anyone." And he had answered, trying to laugh: "But there must be someone—all those girls."

"I'm not a girl's girl; I don't really know how to talk to them. And anyway I haven't been spending my extra time in the smoker, so they hardly even know my name." He had understood what she had been unwilling to say, that he had taken up the evenings she might have spent padding herself with girl acquaintances against the time when she would be alone. In the end he had left without telling her goodbye and the weekend had been spoiled because he had known how she was feeling.

He stood up, although he had not decided what he was going to do; only, no more waste. "You want to leave?" she asked hurriedly gathering up her books, and Hal knew that she thought he was going to walk out without her. If she began to cry he would be more than ashamed; he would feel that his hands were as clumsy as trays as he tried to soothe her, and when he struggled to think of something gentle to say he would begin to go mad with irritation. He started toward the reading room door before she was ready, and he heard the almost hysterical ruffling of pages as she closed her books. He waited for her on the other side of the door, and when she came, almost running, he saw her face become young again as she smiled with relief.

"I agree with you; let's get out of this dreary place," she said, and Hal wished that she had been angry.

"Look, I'm going to walk you back now," he said as they went out into the sudden coldness. She began to fumble awkwardly with her scarf, adjusting it inside her coat collar.

"Right now?" Her voice was carefully casual.

"Look, Eleanor, I've got to get something done tonight. Friday's the Phil 101 exam."

"Oh, I understand." They began to walk, conscious of not holding hands. The quadrangle was dark except for the library windows and the illumined clock over the gym. It was always five minutes fast, on purpose, Hal knew, so that the girls who were late starting would still get to class on time. In spite of the clock Ellie was always coming in late; she would drop into the seat beside him, panting, and snatch off her gloves.

"You taking our history class next term?" Ellie asked. He wished that she would not keep her voice cheerful.

"I guess so. You can't divide it." He was ashamed of his grudging tone, although it was easy to justify it; even if he broke with her now (it was incredible, the idea of pushing off her hands and running without hearing her calling), he would still have to see her every Monday, Wednesday, and Friday at ten in the history class where they tried not to look at each other.

Her dormitory was full of lights. "At last they've taken down the wreath!" he said.

"And high time!"

Her voice had revived with his cheerfulness—real, this time, although he knew it was ridiculous that the tarnished wreath should have depressed him. It had been a soiled reminder of the Christmas vacation they had spent straining to be together, through long-distance calls, which they spent saying goodbye, and too many letters.

They stood under the porch light and she held out her hands. He took them and slipped his fingers inside her gloves. Her palms were soft and lined.

"Look at the bikes," he said, "you'd think they'd give up in this bad weather," and they both looked out at the heaped, stone snow. He remembered that he had a long walk back, but as he bent hurriedly to kiss her she slipped her arms around him and he had to pull back hard in order to get away. She let go at last and, no longer smiling, she whispered: "Hal, don't go." He hesitated. "Please. Don't go. Please." She was rigidly controlling her voice, but he knew the limit of her endurance and he wanted to be away before she began to cry, for then he would never be able to leave. He would have to stay until she was calm, rocking her in his arms and kissing her hair. Afterward when he walked back to his dormitory he would avoid looking at clocks. But when he was in his room he would see the tin alarm clock that was already set for the morning and then he would throw his books violently into a chair. He would go out and buy coffee so that with luck he could study until three. By that time nearly all of the lights across the courtyard would have gone out, and often it would have begun to snow.

Eleanor was watching him. "About tomorrow," she said lightly, wiping a fleck off one of her books, "I know we both have a lot of work. I'll call you in the morning and we can decide then. Maybe we ought to study by ourselves tomorrow night." Her voice was so matter-of-fact that if he had not known the pattern Hal would not have believed that next day, when they came to the deciding, she would plead with him to study with her— "Really, I promise we'll get something done"—and offer to sign a pledge that she would not speak to him for three hours. Now she was looking down and running her fingers along the edges of her books. "Hal," she said, "I'm sorry about tonight. You know how I get sometimes." He put his arms around her, trying not to tell her how sorry he was, trying to choke back his softness. "Oh, God, Ellie," he said, and he heard the almost-tears in his own voice, the rawness that was both tenderness and irritation. She strained up to kiss him and when she opened her mouth he felt tricked, for if he put his tongue between her lips he would not be able to leave. He kissed her, beginning half consciously to forget that he should go. She dropped her books and they tumbled over their feet. He was only vaguely conscious of the porch and the staring light as he pulled her against him, hearing her moan with pain and excitement. Then he drew back and said, his voice already labored: "Isn't there anywhere we can go?" Her face was flushed, reminding him in a twisted way of a child waking up, damp and fresh. She was trying to think of somewhere to go and holding his hands tightly as though she could brace his desire.

"It's too late to have you in the dormitory," she said, and they silently checked their short list of private places. It was too cold for the park—they had been nervous there, on the bench behind the thin screen of shrubbery—and it was too late to go to his room. Parietal rules! He wondered how many people they had forced into marriage. They had talked now and then of renting a room but Hal knew they would never do it; they were still too aware of the connotations. And although they prided themselves on their indifference to surroundings, Ellie's face seemed to reflect the gray walls when they lay together on his bed.

"At least let's get out of this porch light," he said, and they went down the steps and stood hesitating on the sidewalk. She was looking around eagerly and hopefully, and he wondered again how much of her desire was passion and how much grasping; girls used sex to get a hold on you, he knew—it was so easy for them to pretend to be excited.

They wandered down the sidewalk. As they passed the parking lot Eleanor hesitated. "Look, we could—" She did not go on but Hal knew that she meant the cars, the college-girl cars with boxes of tissues and clean seat covers that were parked in the lot behind the dormitories. "All right," he said, knowing that the whole time they would be afraid of someone coming, listening for steps. They walked around the lot, comparing cars, and Ellie was laughing so he would not think it was sordid. Hal wondered why it had become so easy to accept the back seats of cars and student beds with broken springs. Finally she chose a station wagon, and he felt himself growing more excited as she climbed into the back. He followed her and she turned to him and they sank together down onto the seat. For a moment her willing softness seemed to cancel the whole tense evening. He began to unbutton her blouse, feeling her stiffen and gasp as he traced her breast. Across the quadrangle the gymnasium clock chimed. Nine o'clock. Suddenly violent, he tore her blouse open, and as she whimpered, terrified, and tried to push him off, he pulled at her slip. "Stop it, Eleanor, God, stop it," he said when she tried to hold his hands, and as he dragged the straps off her shoulders she began to cry.

The Touching Hand (Boston, 1967).

Janet King

SOME THOUGHTS OF THE FIFTIES FOR A DAUGHTER OF THE SEVENTIES

(c. 1960)

Janet King's Radcliffe experience was that of being an undergraduate wife and mother, and her account of how she attained her educational goals in the face of her other obligations lends a familiar but poignant emphasis to the counterclaims of home and career in the lives of many women. At the same time this memoir is a vivid description of Radcliffe life only a few years before the profound changes that accompanied the inevitable union with Harvard. Janet King, A.B. 1961, Ph.D. 1978, did her graduate work in Slavic languages and literatures and wrote her doctoral thesis on "Marina Tsvetaeva's Mythobiographical Childhood." A teacher, translator, and freelance writer, she contributes to various scholarly journals and has continued her interest in Tsvetaeva. In 1980 she published an annotated translation of the Russian writer's prose works of the 1930s, under the title A Captive Spirit.

DEAREST ANNE,

I was so proud of you when you were admitted to Radcliffe last spring. First proud and then suddenly jolted—where were all those years between 1957 when I entered Radcliffe and now? That started me thinking about the things that had changed and wondering whether your years at college would be totally different from mine. I hoped they would be—I didn't like Radcliffe very much. But it wasn't the college's fault as much as the times, and that's what I want to write you about to give you some perspective on the Radcliffe of your generation. Here are two Radcliffes I knew: the "quaint" ladylike Radcliffe of the '50s and the "part-time" Radcliffe of the early '60s, "part-time" because even though I was officially a regular, re-turned, full-schedule student, I was very busy being your mother.

Radcliffe of the '50s was not only the stimulating, competitive, at times inspiring, intellectual community that still attracts good students like yourself. It was also a rather tightly knit set of women's dorms. You spent a lot of your time there and that meant obeying rules and conforming to standards that, although they seemed liberal (dangerously liberal, my mother thought) compared to other women's colleges in that permanent-waved, long-skirted decade, will seem positively prudish to you. I was aware of the rules because I always seemed to be breaking them. I had gone to a strictly regimented Catholic girls' boarding school. Maybe it was the disorientation produced by so many new and seductive freedoms that led me to the brink of lawlessness. Or maybe I resented any restrictions at all and was rebelling in the name of the nearly total freedom you will probably have and enjoy. But mostly, I think, I was already as absentminded as I still am.

Each dormitory required a set number of hours of work from each student. Work was either "bells," that is answering the central dorm phone and passing the call up to the student phone on the right floor (room phones were a private investment), writing messages on pink slips, corralling visitors in the front hall (no men above first floor), or else "waiting on" at the nightly sit-down dinners. Dinner was calm and genteel, and Harvard boy-friends gladly deserted noisy House dining rooms, plastic trays, and lines to come to Radcliffe. The housemother led the way through the living room where the assembled population was waiting, we all sat down together, bowed our heads for a silent minute, and dinner was served. Waitresses were usually freshmen because upper classwomen preferred "bells," and they had first choice on work. You wore a curl-and-ponytail-repressing hairnet, a scallop-edged white apron, and you obeyed the irascible, fiery-tempered Irish women regulars in the dorm kitchen. It was not Professor Levin or I. B. Cohen but a red-haired terror named Sadie in the Eliot Hall kitchen who put me down into my proper humble place that first year. After dinner you went back into the living room where the housemother served demitasse cups of coffee out of a silver urn. Then some of the women moved to the card table for a few rounds of bridge. Another group—this will sound *hopelessly* corny, I know—gathered around the piano and sang tunes by Gershwin and Rodgers and Hart from a songbook or listened to the various dorm pianists.

If you defaulted more than once on a work hour you got a "pro." A "pro" meant you had to stay in your room on the following Saturday night from 7 o'clock on. And in the '50s as you, my dear, probably know from the movies, people "dated" mainly or only on Saturday nights, so a "pro" was a real penalty. Men were friends or dates. More serious relationships were engagements sanctified by rings. An A - - - - r was not discussed, although I was *sure* the girl across the hall, in all other respects studious, sneaker-shod, and normal, was having one.

Radcliffe's reputation among southern high-school girls like myself for scandalous leniency was only partly justified. Radcliffe had—and there's no point in trying to circumlocute the ugly word—a dress code. You were not allowed outside the dormitory wearing trousers unless you had first covered them with a long (below the knee) coat. If they ever put that rule into effect again both I and the Levi's Company would be bankrupt overnight. You were given a key to the dormitory front door but, except for special permissions, you were expected to be back in the dorm by 1 A.M. And when you went out after 9, you wrote your name and destination in the sign-out book. There were traditional hieroglyphs for popular destinations: ☐ —"to the Square" or ∟—to the corner, where the drugstore sold pints of ice cream. Another institutional record book was the "Charred Body Book." If you had a (girl) friend in to stay the night or lent your room to a guest while you were away, her name was recorded in the book. Then, if the rescue squad happened to uncover extra or unfamiliar bones in the postignic rubble of a fire-swept dorm, they'd at least have an idea of *who* they hadn't managed to rescue.

I took a leave of absence after my freshman year, and that Radcliffe disappeared for good. It disappeared because the '50s were over, and because my life and expectations and no less so the commitments and pressures at the college had begun to change. But institutions move more slowly than individuals, and Radcliffe had no way as yet of adapting to the new kinds of students that are much more common now in the '70s. I was an undergraduate with a family. You, dear daughter, were well under two when I came back as a sophomore in the early '60s. Your brother Philip was due to arrive in time for final exams. There was no day care at the college or anywhere else in Cambridge. And there was little tolerance for a noisy toddler following or carried by a harried mother going through the library in search of a book. There were no exceptions to the rules. I had to make up the one-quarter of obligatory physical education I had missed freshman year. That sounds like nothing, but to find and pay for another babysitter when I could hardly manage even to attend lectures was a real blow. The people at the Radcliffe gym, who are still the most wonderful and accommodating people around, gave me the one official helping hand ever extended to me, when a woman in the sports office offered to watch and entertain you while I worked out upstairs. When Radcliffe's first day-care group moved into that gym it was no surprise at all to *me:* you had been the one-baby pilot program ten years earlier.

I had money for tuition from my parents, a book allowance, and nothing more. But I was grateful for that. I wonder how the college would have responded if I had asked for some financial support. The few people I talked to at 10 Garden Street were dubious about my ability to carry on and for good reason, since they offered no help or even good advice of any sort. My mother-in-law agreed to watch the baby (that was you until Philip came along) three mornings a week. That meant I had to choose my courses, fulfill my various distribution and concentration requirements, see the department tutor, find sections et cetera, all between 8 A.M. and 1 P.M. on Monday, Wednesday, or Friday. When your brother was born, I had also to work around his nursing schedule, although I took a semester off at the beginning when he was most capriciously hungry.

I was almost always late, always breathless, always shoving pages of notes hastily together into a pile and tearing off home after my five hours of college were up. Then there was housework, washing and cooking in the afternoons and early evenings. There was really no time for work in the library, and I almost never made it to sophomore tutorial. I studied my Russian vocabulary from a stenographer's notebook propped up above the kitchen sink. You look at a word, then repeat it once each time you shave off a piece of potato skin. When the potatoes are all peeled, you've done that assignment. Having to write a paper was a catastrophic event, an overwhelming task.

The hardest thing was feeling so isolated. I had no time to do more than exchange a few words with the other students, but as I dashed in and out of classes I imagined them and me in a kind of race with all of *them* running easily and gracefully way out in front, while I hopped along in the rear with one leg tied up and useless. I was always terribly overtired, and in the first months I was nauseous with morning sickness. I would drop in to the lavatory between classes and throw up. I sometimes fell asleep in lectures. Once sitting in the back row I even dozed off and slumped down against the section man's shoulder without being aware of it. At some point, feeling a Harris tweed roughness against my cheek, I opened one dazed eye and got a glimpse of his reddened face looking the other way, pretending not to notice anything unusual.

That particular episode was, in a way, symbolic. I never encountered hostile attitudes at Radcliffe or Harvard, not even plain curiosity. I was simply not noticed. It would have been unpleasant to notice me: I carried an aura of desperation and sour milk wherever I went. But I think just that was the greatest obstacle: not getting any encouragement, having no sense of support or fellow feeling. My fellow mothers, if there were any, were equally as invisible to me as I was to everyone else. We sat alone reading in laundromats. And so when I look back on that time I realize and want to let you know how foolish it is for any woman, and maybe any man too, to suppose they are independent of commonly held attitudes, even gross prejudices. The approval and sympathy that studying mothers can get today, the feminist climate that encourages and even expects a woman to have a career and a family simultaneously would have buoyed me up and given me the energy I needed as much as any practical help. Now, in the middle '70s, having a double life can mean a doubly rich experience. Then, the double life of a student-mother was just that—being split in two, having warring inner loyalties and conflicting practical commitments. It is indicative of my total insecurity that I was always torn between wanting to explain my circumstances and difficulties and wanting to hide them at any cost for fear I would cease to even be considered a real student of any kind.

So I think it is quite a different Radcliffe, Anne, that you will be starting this fall. Thank heavens. But I started by congratulating you and now I end by hoping that this letter gives you a better idea of why I am so proud of you, proud that you chose Radcliffe in spite of everything. You were exposed from the very first to a college experience (and then of course, all those years when I was at graduate school) that was far from idyllic, a process of education that seemed to lead to exhaustion and the grumps as much as to a degree. But you had bright eyes and a clear vision. You saw through it all to the one thing that kept me and other students like me going: the desire to know something, to be competent at something, the satisfaction of achieving something even if it wasn't always just perfect. All that is part of Radcliffe too and I hope you find it faster and more easily than I did.

Radcliffe Quarterly, December, 1976.

Faye Levine

THE GIRLS WHO GO TO HARVARD
(1965)

Among Harvard people of both sexes who go back to the mid-60s, Faye Levine is famed for three things. She was the first woman executive editor of the Harvard Crimson, *she wrote a much quoted article on "the three flavors of Radcliffe," and she ran a bold, spectacular, unsuccessful campaign for marshal of the Harvard Class of 1965. Less well known is her retrospective essay on her college years prepared in 1965 for the Harvard and Radcliffe yearbook, the first combined Harvard and Radcliffe yearbook. Since graduation Faye Levine has earned a Harvard master's degee in education, been a Fellow of the Bunting Institute, written articles for such magazines as* The New Yorker, Atlantic, Rolling Stone, Radcliffe Quarterly, *and published three books,* The Strange World of the Hare Krishnas *(1974),* Culture Barons *(1976), and a novel,* Solomon and Sheba *(1980). She was also consulting editor and contributor to the anthology* Feminist Revolution *(1979).*

THE CLIFFIE: many faces, one soul. Beneath years of straight hair, behind pale lips and eyes, she smiles an eternally self-satisfied secret smile. She is sure of herself even in railroad stations. She walks loudly and firmly on polished floors. She is a Cliffie.

The Cliffie was never virginal. Somewhere in her dim past she discovered the sexual Roots of Her Being, and her mother could never communicate with her thereafter. She is her mother's mother, her father's dream and despair.

All the resources of Harvard go into making her more beautiful. Music, incense, poetry, and human sacrifices she offers to her new boy-god. Among other Cliffies, she speaks not a word about sex; they recognize each other as coreligionists.

The Cliffie sifts through books with an unobtrusive mind. The less she studies, the better her grades. In four years she has whittled her working hours to a fine minimum, so that studying hardly ever interferes with the things she is really interested in. She swings with lectures, taking notes only on what she likes. She debunks Jesus Christ and Sigmund Freud in the same dispassionate breath. Long ago she gave up reading and took up movies. She has seen her favorite films countless times.

But she cannot discuss them. She feels she has lived, experienced, embodied the movies too much to be able to analyze them; she feels she doesn't know enough to judge them. And so she listens fascinated as her men discuss *Marienbad,* putting into words what she has felt, deeply, intuitively.

The Cliffie has a lust for wisdom, but no patience for facts. She wants to be accomplished, but hates work. And so she turns from book to book, from activity to activity, wanting to learn and do and see everything at once. Yet all the while she has a dread of being overconscientious, a fear of getting her nails dirty. She withholds something serious and vulnerable of herself. And so it all slips by.

The Cliffie has become cultivated in four years. She runs her fingers over the books in Widener's stacks, stands in awe on the hill between Lamont and Houghton, praises the quiet beauty of Radcliffe Yard at night. She has learned that there is no truth, that all life is ambiguous, many-sided, complex. She knows only the moment and the particular: she can be sure of nothing. She smiles scornfully at a statement that is not demonstrable enough to be science, not mysterious enough to be poetry. For the rest of her life people will hate her for this smile, the unloving smile of a cultivated ignoramus.

Being at Radcliffe means nothing more than being a girl at Harvard. It is a tricky business, since everyone knows that there are no girls at Harvard. Just when you are beginning to forget, to enjoy the myriad resources of this exciting community, Pow! somebody triumphantly points out that you are just a girl and makes you go back to the start.

Take the first woman professor at the Medical School, for instance, who was given the post in 1918 with the provisos that she would not a) enter the Harvard Club of Boston, b) march in the graduation procession, or c) ask for football tickets. Now really. Haven't we made any progress at all since 1918? They still put up elaborate displays of the emancipation of women in Lamont and forbid girls to see them. The woman professor agreed to the Humpty Dumpty-like stipulations in 1918, and we agree to them now, but the day is coming when women will simply not put up with them any longer.

We are no longer content with only some equality, Harvard. We have been poor relations, little sisters, grateful recipients of charity for just so long. We want football tickets, traveling fellowships, representation on educational policy committees. We share Harvard's hour exams; now we want to share its amusements, its benefits, its government.

We want a graduation ceremony that is part of Harvard's. Every school in this University graduates on the same day, in the same place, with so much pomp that you could die; except Radcliffe, which has a little oversightful ceremony next door. Why deny us this? Are we unclean?

We want to be studied as part of projects as ambitious as the Harvard Student Study. You have tried so hard to get a perfect cross section of the classes of 1964 and '65, with every variety of background, birth, and personality represented. Why, then, are there no females? Aren't you interested in what the college experience is for young women? Maybe if you were, you'd find something new besides Sophomore Slump. Are only boys people? Suppose some other big group had been excluded, on the grounds that it would have introduced too many new variables. Suppose Negroes had been excluded. My my.

We want to share Harvard's libraries, its dining halls. They are fine institutions, far outshining their meager Radcliffe counterparts, and should not be denied to people on the basis of race, creed, House membership, or sex. So long as there is room, let everyone come. It is the only just way. There will always be opportunity for men or women to escape into private retreats when they don't want company of the opposite sex. But to deny it to all, always, is unnatural. Studying and dining should be activities for both sexes, meeting as equals, not only as dates. The students desire this overwhelmingly. It is only the anachronistic pretentions of the adults in control which stand in the way. Let them reconsider, while there is still chance to do so peacefully.

And Radcliffe, oh Radcliffe, how long will you hang onto sign-out books, cards, warnings, pros, estimateds, permissions, one-o'clocks? Give your girls the dignity that Harvard boys have: let us out into the world to win or lose, to kill ourselves or find ourselves. Young married couples do not know more than we do about how we should spend our evenings. A time is coming in which young women will no longer have to be kept in padded cells. Face up to it, Radcliffe: it is happening under your nose.

It is certainly true that the iniquity Harvard and Radcliffe practice toward females is scarcely an eyelash in the eye of God. Compared to the situation of women in Uttar Pradesh, Radcliffe girls are fully of the ruling class. We have been given privileges and opportunities our grandmothers never imagined even for their sons.

But the human race is like that: give them a Harvard diploma and they want a Harvard graduation. You have opened the door of Shangri-La to us; do not be surprised when we stick our foot in it. The old world of our silent, contented acquiescence is gone forever. Feminism is its own punishment.

A girl hears that James Reston is speaking in Eliot House, and in all innocence asks her coffee date, who happens to live in that House, to take her. He informs her coldly that no girls are allowed. Taken aback, she declares that she really would like to hear Reston speak, and thinks it unfair that she be *a priori* prohibited.

A friendly dispute ensues, in which the girl pronounces Eliot House to be antifeminist. Whereupon the Eliot House man proclaims that her militancy has forfeited her the right ever to have her doors opened, her coat helped on, or her checks paid. Flushed with the heat of battle, she agrees, and that particular coffee date relationship is forever changed.

But of course she still doesn't get to go hear James Reston.

Cliffies are funny things. Al Capp says they are the only girls in the world to de-emphasize their bosoms and emphasize their feet. Jules Feiffer says the only way to impress them is to talk dirty.

When a strange man accosts a Radcliffe girl repeatedly on Garden Street as she walks home alone at midnight, she is careful to say, "No, thank you," to his offers.

When a tearful sophomore tells an upperclassman she has just been attacked by her tutor as part of his driving her home, the upperclassman says, "Oh, sure, tutors are like that."

When a policeman calls to see who's in the Yearbook darkroom long after parietals have ended, the Radcliffe girl answers back in a deep voice. She answers the telephone of her Dunster House boyfriend's room in a deep voice. She admires her father more than her mother. She came to Radcliffe because someone told her not to.

When she sees a striking worker, a Cliffie feels a social obligation to stop and talk to him, to force him to justify his cause, to take away his placard, if need be.

Ever since the disappearance of the bulk of curfew rules at Radcliffe, control of the situation has passed to a new group: the Cleaning Ladies. On the scene every morning from seven until noon, they are in the best position to know exactly who is staying out too late how often. The other girls in the dormitory are too busy with their own problems to really care. The head residents, though they're interested, have much less first-hand evidence.

"Haven't seen you around much, Cassandra," the middle-aged Irish lady will comment. If Cassandra, a degenerate Loeb type, can produce a convincing excuse quickly, for instance that her mother is sick and she has had to nurse her for the last twelve weekends, the matter may be closed. Failing that, however, the Cliffie is likely to get daily checks from the Cleaning Lady as she brushes her teeth, climaxing finally in a lecture about the good manners of the Cleaning Lady's sixteen-year-old daughter, a senior in high school, who never stays out later than 10 P.M.

Sometimes a Cliffie may try to hedge, defend herself, or even snub the cheerful inquisitor, but these practices are invariably unsuccessful. The Cleaning Lady's Ajax and omnipresence make her an invincible foe, and the only thing for a Cliffie to do who values her bathroom is shape up.

In Erik Erikson's course, Soc Sci 139, we learned how boys are different from girls. One day in class they read aloud the names of all the students who had not shown up for their section for the entire semester. Now, the enrollment was about half and half, but the list contained 25 boys and only a single girl. These scoffers were greeted by the class at large with affectionate amusement and a grudging respect.

It is no accident that the males far outdid the females in this upside-down achievement. It is always boys who are night people, wasting the hours between 2 and 6 A.M. in crummy cafeterias and sleeping through their classes. It is boys who take up pool, gin rummy, liquor, marijuana. For many boys, exams are to cram, notes are to copy from someone else, Harvard is to be beaten. From Thomas Wolfe to Teddy Kennedy, boys have flaunted this great university and made good.

But girls would not dream of such a thing. They take the legible notes boys will copy. They attend every lecture. They remember the date of their Graduate Record Exam. Even when they make a token gesture of rebellion, they stay neat, clean, and stylish. Girls, particularly Radcliffe girls, are the pillars of civilization, the rock without which the destructive male force would undermine society. In short, they are finks.

Praise us, oh high-school teachers of the world, for being good pupils. Train our handwriting. Reward our citizenship. Get us to internalize the all-important values of punctuality and tidyness.

But until females learn to chuck the whole business out the window, don't expect anything great from us.

Where is Radcliffe? Visiting high-school seniors look for it in vain among the cobbled puddles of Garden Street. Harvard freshmen look for it in vain at Jolly Ups. Even the Radcliffe Government Association calls out to it in vain from the mimeographed weekly newsletter tucked in mailboxes. Radcliffe is to be found in none of these places.

Old Radcliffe alumnae do not think back to certain trees, certain bricks, certain dining halls. The halls of Radcliffe have none of the special magic that graces Harvard. Radcliffe alumnae do not greet each other like reunited countrymen; more likely they smile ironically.

Radcliffe is nowhere. Its essence is its own nonexistence. Besides the spiritual shells that are desks and dressers, there is nothing. The piano music in the dormitories speaks sadly, nostalgically, of a Radcliffe that perhaps once was, but is no more.

The ceremony at the beginning of each year reminds Radcliffe of its own ambiguity. Maybe a third of the school gathers in Christ Church for Formal Opening: procession, robes, speeches, choir, alma mater. Even those singing never learn the words of their school song; many go through four years without ever hearing it. Yet for one moment there is a shiver of community. On the high notes of the alma mater the girls look around and think to themselves, "Yes, other girls, Radcliffe." It fades immediately, and is never recaptured.

We were never part of something. It just was, here, inorganic, like a great hulk without beginning or end. We passed it by, we touched it like home base for four years, but we didn't dwell in it. It was nothing, blank, dumb. Harvard was reality, the beginning and the end, everything: but for us, always a dream. Harvard was reality, but through a glass.

When they ask us where we were these four years, what can we say? We were nowhere.

329: The Yearbook of Harvard and Radcliffe (Cambridge, 1965).

Anne Fadiman

WHERE IS THE GRACE OF YESTERYEAR?

(1972)

Anne Fadiman survived the early seventies at Harvard apparently un-scathed, and many readers of Harvard Magazine *will remember her percep-tive articles on Harvard life, particularly those relating to the changed status of women in the College. Required reading for anyone interested in this pe-riod of Harvard history is her "Stages in the Early Manhood of the Future Dr. David Brachman," which covers at greater length and in somewhat more detail than the excerpt below the issues of Harvard and Radcliffe readjust-ment. She is currently on the staff of* Life, *but her articles have appeared in a variety of magazines, including* Esquire, Holiday, Reader's Digest, Country Journal, Saturday Review, *and* The New York Times.

THREE YEARS AGO, when I was a senior in high school, I spent Thanksgiving vacation with my brother, who was a freshman here. I returned to Califor-nia with two distinct impressions of Harvard life: it was terribly elegant, and it operated on social principles that utterly baffled me.

Little did I know that Mower B-12 was an artifact from Harvard's past, specially designed to shelter visiting little sisters from the grim realities of the modern university. I'd assumed that the habitués of the Square—beggars, Hare Krishna devotees, teeny-boppers, and a vast number of long-haired people whose age and sex I could not determine—were all Harvard students, and though I was glad to know that my brother lived in such a lively place, I wondered how well I'd fit in myself. What joy, then, to stagger into Mower Hall, throw my suitcase on the floor, and look around at four well-scrubbed boys, a fire, antique prints, a rickety table with a bowl of eggnog and the sort of cookies grandmothers make, and even a music stand holding a 1916 hymnal! Clearly the Square was the exception, and this was the rule. The Real Harvard consisted of lying on the floor listening to Mozart, singing "Come, Ye Thankful People, Come" in five-part harmony, and eating cookies by candlelight.

I was, in fact, eating cookies by candlelight when a knock on the door elicited from my brother this melodramatic hiss: "Hide! Hide! Hide or we're dead!" Feeling like a character in a Marx Brothers movie, I dashed into the bedroom, slammed the door, and spied through the keyhole at four boys explaining to the dorm proctor that no, there was no girl here, despite the open suitcase that was spilling a flannel nightgown onto the living-room floor. The proctor left, I emerged from my hideout, and my brother told me not to worry. "It's only parietals," he explained. Parietals, apparently, were the rules that prohibited boys from having girls in their rooms except during certain hours. Everyone except me agreed that a sister is not a Girl, but that, nonetheless, the letter of the law must be obeyed. Females at Harvard—possibly excluding grandmothers and maiden aunts—belonged to the same category as liquor and marijuana: fun, but not to be used in public.

When I came to Radcliffe the next year, I couldn't find the Harvard I thought I'd visited. When I had dinner with my brother, who now lived in Lowell House, I ate from compartmented plastic trays designed by Gropius to make food look like nuts and bolts. Old buildings were being torn down and new ones were going up. I weaved among hundreds of honking cars as I bicycled to class. I had to show my numbered identification card in order to study at the Radcliffe library. Where was elegance? Where was gentility? Where was tradition? Perhaps they resided in the Final Clubs, or in classes taught by professors over the age of sixty, or in the cupboards in the Radcliffe kitchen where old tea sets were kept.

Though I felt that the place had been mysteriously transformed in a single year, I told myself that *real* elegance hadn't been around Harvard for a long time—not since the eras of the Gold Coast (now Pizza Pad and the Gold Coast Student Valeteria), or of Professor James' little soirées, or of butterfly collars. But I think some interest in amenities really did disappear just before my class arrived. Harvard could no longer afford them, and students no longer seemed to care. The strikes of 1969 and 1970 awakened political consciousness in many people who became ashamed of their wealth and insularity, and of Harvard's. Some of them turned to social work in communities around Cambridge. They were still stuck with the Harvard image, though: one student returned from a nearby factory to say, "I've spent the whole day talking to the working classes, and you know what? The working classes *hate* students!" Of what use were decorum and ceremony? As one illogical but sincere girl cried out at a 1970 strike meeting, "How can you talk about Robert's Rules of Order when there are children dying in Cambodia?"

My class missed the strikes. We missed the big years of hard drugs, patched blue jeans, uncombed hair, and student politics. Apathy was closing in again when we arrived. Students retired to their rooms to study. No one talked any more about skipping exams, as they'd done in 1970. Most of the gates to the Houses and the Yard were locked to prevent theft, and few Cambridge people walked through the campus. Dining halls all over Harvard and Radcliffe started to serve identical food, to dispense bread out of identical plastic bread dispensers, to use identical cellophane packets of honey and mustard. Harvard was turning inward and becoming homogeneous.

My class was the first to enter a Harvard with co-residential housing and no parietals. Both students and faculty had been ignoring the rules for years anyway. In fact, my brother may well have been the only freshman left at Harvard who would have hidden his sister from the dorm proctor. A few years before, when boys started to wear T-shirts under their ties, everyone had known that dining-hall dress requirements wouldn't last long. Similarly, when officials began to look the other way in cases of parietal disobedience, the old rules were already on their way out. It is said that once, on his way to breakfast, the master of Adams House saw a boy and a girl coming out of the boy's room, and without skipping a beat, said, "Good morning, gentlemen." At that point, I think, co-residential housing was inevitable.

It is remarkable how quickly all this was taken as a matter of course. Just the year before I came to Radcliffe, the most elaborate machinations and subterfuges were required if a boy and a girl wished to live together. I have a friend, now a senior, who spent most of her freshman year trying to uncoil the red tape that bound up her social life. She was living with her boyfriend at Leverett House, but since she was not allowed to eat there, she had to bicycle up to Radcliffe for lunch, and hide in a corner of the Leverett dining hall at dinner, eating from her friend's tray. She was also required to do "bells" each week—to answer the telephone at her Radcliffe dorm, although she never received any calls there. At that time, Cliffies had to sign out for a specific length of time when they left the dorm, and to sign in when they returned. My friend started signing out every few days, then for a week, and finally for three months. When she failed to sign in at the appointed hour after three months, she was given extra bells duty. The point of signing out, ostensibly, was to be available in an emergency. But since her boyfriend's telephone number was posted on the bulletin board, she was clearly going through the motions of a system that no longer made very much sense.

My class arrived at a university where formal dating was frowned on and either a love affair or an Intense Platonic Relationship was *de rigueur.* A few years before, when Harvard students were forced to prowl outside their own environment in search of girls, it took several hours to "get ready for a date," and it was quite likely that after all that painstaking preparation, the date would consist of rejection at a girls' college mixer. Those rituals are still observed, but less often. The University's social community has become far more self-contained, and now that the Yard is co-residential, even the freshmen can be part of it.

The Harvard I saw three years ago was like an imaginary character one makes up as a child: it was pretty, it was quaint, and it was easy to feel nostalgic about later. Just as a university can seal its students from experience by enforcing senseless rules, so one can seal one's own doors from the outside world and create a new (or in this case an old) world inside. But Harvard, it appears, cannot be big and modern and gracious all at once. I dream about the time when truly civilized people sat up late in tasteful rooms, drinking port and discussing Shakespeare—but then I realize that, unless they were breaking parietal rules, none of these people could have been me.

Harvard Alumni Bulletin, December, 1972.

An Official View
WHAT IS RADCLIFFE?
(1981)

We cannot leave the unsuspecting reader with the somewhat puzzled conclusions of Faye Levine and Anne Fadiman, regarding the Radcliffe of 1965 and 1972. The suddenness with which Radcliffe joyfully rushed into its essentially happy marriage with Harvard was also a surprise to the respective "in-laws," Mary Bunting and Nathan Pusey. Since that time the college administrations of Matina Horner and Derek Bok have negotiated an agreement (1977) that continues to govern the relationship and has brought

such improvements as "equal access" to admissions, and equivalent ameni-
ties on playing fields and in locker rooms. The old Radcliffe and the old
Harvard are fading, as Kerry Gruson noted, like the smile of Alice's Cheshire
cat. While we await the next episode, readers should note the official current
description of Radcliffe's role.

IN THE BEGINNING Radcliffe College was *not* created like any other college
. . . It never had its own faculty and furthermore it never intended to do so.
Radcliffe College was established to give women the opportunity to have an
education equal to that of men at Harvard. Since Harvard did not admit
women, women had to create a separate institution . . . Radcliffe College, in
the beginning, made private arrangements with members of the Harvard
faculty to teach Radcliffe students. Thus, enrollment in the new college
gave women access to instruction on the same level as that provided at
Harvard.

Radcliffe was not designed to be a self-contained women's college with a
faculty of its own. Its founders envisioned that there would always be an in-
terdependence between Radcliffe and Harvard. This fact sometimes becomes obscured, and outsiders often assume that over the years Radcliffe
has somehow drifted away from being a fully autonomous and independent
institution. In actuality the college has moved steadily toward the fulfill-
ment of its founders' vision.

The Commonwealth's charter that officially established Radcliffe as a
college in 1894 stated that Radcliffe College was "authorized generally to
furnish instruction and the opportunities of collegiate life to women and to
promote their higher education." Today, Radcliffe continues to carry out
the purpose for which it was founded: to give women access to a Harvard
education and to promote the higher education of women in general. As it
did 103 years ago, it delegates to Harvard the academic instruction of
Radcliffe students. Now, it also delegates to Harvard the responsibility
for such aspects of undergraduate life as housing, athletics, advising, and
discipline . . .

Fulfilling the second purpose stated in its charter, Radcliffe continues to
be an advocate for women's higher education. It independently manages
and finances a number of divisions and programs concerned with promoting
women's higher education, as well as with supporting the scholarly search
for new knowledge.

While Radcliffe's purposes have remained the same over the past 103
years, the mechanics of educating and supervising its students have
changed. Opportunities open to women students within the university have
steadily expanded and are now equal to those available to men.

The Radcliffe Guide, 1981–82.

VIII

THESE FESTIVAL RITES

In the hot sultry month that's called July,
(Forever famous to posterity)
A day is yearly kept, no doubt with zeal
By some, who to New England's common weal
Wish well, in these apostatizing days,
Wherein religion sensibly decays.
No doubt for noble ends this day's observed
By some, who have to learning just regard;
Whose souls (bright as the light) would grieve to see
These regions buried in obscurity.

A SATYRICAL DESCRIPTION OF COMMENCEMENT (1718)

Maria Sophia Quincy

I NEVER SAW SUCH A SPLENDID SCENE

(1829)

The Quincy girls were the five daughters of Josiah Quincy, Member of Congress, State Senator, Mayor of Boston, and President of Harvard. They were the "articulate sisters"—as their editor, M. A. DeWolfe Howe, has called them—and between 1814 and 1834 they kept "profuse" journals which described for their own delectation (especially if one of them was absent from home) the doings of the Quincy family. Because of their close connection with Harvard College during the term of their father's presidency, it has been thought fitting to include in this anthology documentary evidence that the woman's influence in Harvard writing was present long before the advent of Radcliffe. The author of this excerpt, Sophia, was the third of the sisters; she was twenty-four years old when she described the events of her father's first Commencement as President and the lively doings in Wadsworth House.

Friday, 28th August, 1829.

WE HAVE ENJOYED a great deal of pleasure during the three last days and so constantly has the time been occupied that I have not been able to continue my regular journal. I shall now give a sketch of what we have been seeing and doing . . .

On Wednesday the weather was delightful for the occasion [Commencement], as cool as in October. We were all arrayed at an early hour. I wore blue [word illegible] blonde gauze handkerchief, and cameo comb. Abbey wore white and her hat, Susan a beautiful yellow dress made for this day—Mama in black with her blonde lace cap new trimmed with broad white ribbon. I never saw her look so handsome before. Ladies Margy and Anna preferred to stay at home. We were scarcely drest when a cry was heard through the mansion from the President and daughters, to us to assemble and tie up the degrees with blue ribbon, and write the names on them. It was now half past eight, and at nine the doors were to open. We surrounded Susan's bed on which were strewn a heap of degrees, Abby wrote the names, I held the scrolls, while Susan, Anna, and Margy tied them with ribbon. The hurrying exceeded all former experiences. The Corporation waited in the library. Papa flew in every other minute to snatch the rolls from our hands as soon as finished. The two pair of scissors perversely hid themselves among the papers, and the pieces of blue ribbon that came flying from Mrs. Farwell's were speedily exhausted. A fit of laughter assailed some of the ti-ers, while the impatience of others (who shall be nameless) retarded instead of forwarding the work. However, just in time all was finished and deposited in the library, and at that moment we were summoned to the parlour.

Margy and I descended and were soon followed by Mama, Susan, and Abby. Col. and Mrs. Morse, "Edward," and Mrs. Ford were therein seated. The ladies and the Colonel were introduced in due form to us. Mrs. Morse is a very plain but genteel, ladylike woman. Mrs. Ford in deep black, rather interesting. The Colonel a fine-looking man. The ladies said they would take off their bonnets if we thought best, and had bro't headdresses. We advised them certainly to do it, and upstairs we all ran, as there was no time to be lost. Mrs. Morse placed on her head a yellow toque, and Mrs. Ford a pretty, fashionable cap trimmed with black.

As soon as they were ready, attended by the gentlemen, and preceded by Horace, we all went through our back stable yard and stationed ourselves at a side door, at which was already planted Mrs. Farrar, and Mrs. Ripley. The other doors were thronged with ladies. Here we waited for a few minutes and as soon as the doors opened "caught up our frocks and ran." The rush of ladies was very great, and as they uplifted their voices and screamed as they ran, it was really frightful. I got into the gallery among the first and flew into the "King's Box," as Uncle Morton denominated our pew. Our party followed me like lightning, and if I had only shut the door as soon as they were all in, we should have been delightfully accommodated; but I was so confused and frightened with the noise and running that before I was aware two other ladies had packed in. We were very much crowded, but beckoning one of the Constables, we sent him to our house for a music-stool, which we placed at the foot of the pew, and on which I was perched in the most conspicuous place possible. It was an excellent seat, however, and I found my two neighbors (who had inserted themselves much against our wish) very agreeable people. One was Miss Ward from Salem, whose only brother had a part on this occasion, the other a Mrs. Fay from Alabama, a relation of the Hedge family. I had a great deal of pleasant conversation with them and with Nancy Perkins, Anna Higginson, and Mrs. Clarke. The three last-mentioned ladies were standing at the outside of our pew, and a happy thought came into my head, and when Mr. Chamberlain bro't the music-stool, I conveyed to him a request that he would furnish these ladies with chairs. Four chairs soon appeared and they were comfortably seated, and many were their acknowledgements to me for my kindness.

The galleries were filled from the lowest to the highest seat with ladies. I never saw such a splendid scene. It surpassed even the Inauguration. There were a greater number of beautiful women collected together than I ever saw before, and dressed with great elegance, and in the most shewy style. The house below equally filled with the lords of the Creation. We waited some time before the welcome sounds of the full band announced the approach of the procession, and soon the President in full costume sailed up the aisle, followed by the Governor [Levi Lincoln] and his aids in full uniform (Josiah looked elegantly), and all the dignitaries, civil and ecclesiastical, of the land, and strangers filled the house in a fine style. Mrs. Morse was delighted with the scene, and said she had never imagined such a crowd before, nor such a splendid spectacle.

Dr. [Eliphalet] Porter opened the services with a very fine prayer, which affected Mrs. Morse to tears. Papa then took his seat in the pulpit and the young men commenced speaking. Charles Fay was the first, and went through a Latin address with a very good air and graceful manner. Sixteen or seventeen young men spoke in succession with various degrees of merit—Wm. Channing and young Robbins the best. Mr. Storrow had the first part and of course spoke the last, and in truth everybody was excessively fatigued. I did not hear much of the first part of the oration, and the latter part I lost entirely, for poor Mrs. Fay, our new acquaintance, began to feel very faint, grew paler and paler. Miss Ward supported her, the Miss Hills wafted smelling bottles from behind us, while Abby and I fanned on each side, and soon the attention of the multitude was fixed on our pew. The poor lady grew worse and worse however. Luckily her husband beheld her from below and hastened upstairs, and reached the door just as she was going off entirely. The crowd was so great that we could scarcely get the door open. However, the people were very accommodating, and Mr. Colman and her husband with some other gentlemen bore her from our sight after we had played our parts before the audience for some ten or fifteen minutes.

When the oration was finished Papa took his seat in the antiquated arm chair before the pulpit with the degrees of hurried memories by his side, and the class came up on the stage in sixes and sevens. He addressed them in Latin, presented them to the Governor, and gave them their degrees in a very graceful style. A year from this day I was seated in the Library at Quincy penning a letter to Sophia Morton while all the rest of the family had come over here to Copley Greene's Commencement. What would we have thought if the curtain of Fate had been raised, and we had beheld the splendid scene exhibited on this day, and Papa seated on the stage in the costume of President of the University!

The degrees having been given, we had some delightful music from the band which had played at intervals during the morning, and then Mr. Walker from Northampton delivered the English Oration. It was a very fine one, but his style of speaking so exactly resembled Josiah's burlesquing different orators, that Abby and I were entirely overset, and laughed rather indecorously. A Latin Address closed the performances, spoken very well by Mr. Page, and at four o'clock the Assembly broke up. The procession formed and departed to the Dinner Hall, and as soon as possible our party left the church and entered our delightful residence. The crowd around the doors, the groups of carriages and rows of chaises really surpassed what I had seen before . . .

We found Margy, Anna and Mary Jane in the parlour, Margy arrayed in Anna's pink Battiste, and blonde gauze handkerchief, Anna in Margy's beautiful sheer muslin, and Mary Jane in black with carved comb and ornaments, and blonde gauze mantle—all three ladies looking very handsome. Mr. Greene and Edmund had met us at the door.

They were, as well may be imagined, half famished, and declared they thought we never were coming out; it was then half past four. Dinner was soon on the table, and added to our family were Mrs. Morse and her son, and Mrs. Ford. We went into the Freshmen's room, where York and another black attendant had spread the table with great elegance. The dinner was beautiful, dessert ornamented with flowers and all in the best style. Conversation during the repast turned on the pleasures of the morning. Anna and Margy had had a variety of people flitting in and out. Mr. Robbins, the father of the young man who spoke, was brought fainting from the church and comfortably put to bed up in our room. He had just recovered sufficiently to be carried off in his chaise as we came home.

We were at table till half past five, and had just got into the drawing room, which together with the dining room was beautifully decorated with flowers, when gentlemen and ladies began to pour in. One room was crowded, and a number of walkers in the entry and opposite room. The band were stationed in the back parlour, and animated the company with their delightful strains. The Governor and his train of course paid their respects. Eight or nine foreigners, among whom were Mr. Santag and Mr. Wallenstein, Sir Isaac Coffin, &c. &c. &c. Mrs. Derby and her two pretty nieces, all very much drest, the Miss Whites and Miss Silsbee, very handsome, and Miss Sumner and Miss Griffith, very genteel, sailed in and out. Marie Upham, who really looked beautiful, and of course drest with the best taste in the world in an elegant black dress, blonde gauze scarf and pearl ornaments, her hair put up with an ornamental comb, and a beautiful blonde gauze toque trimmed with blonde lace on her head. A great many

gentlemen, young and old. I conversed with Messrs. Santag and Wellen-
stein, Stackpole, Mr. Bethune, Wm. Payne, Mr. Adams, the Editor of the
Centinel, Col. Merrick (who declared I was the only lady in the whole
church whom he recognized) &c. &c. Mr. Stackpole introduced me to Miss
Silsbee, who in her turn introduced to me a youth whose name I have forgotten and then I presented her to Mary Jane. Mrs. Gorham Parsons and
Mary Ann Lee also came from Brighton, and a number of others whom I
cannot enumerate. Mrs. Morse and her friend seemed to enjoy the scene
very much.

The company were arriving and departing till half past seven, ice-
creams and coffee circulating all the time. The Governor took leave early,
and was escorted off by the troop of horse in a tempest of drums and dust,
and by half after seven almost all had departed. A pretty Spanish Lady drest
in black with a black toque on her head staid till the last, and by Mama's
request played a beautiful piece on the piano. Old Mr. Hedge and I were
conversing, and so interesting was our converse that we prosed on long
after the Lady had begun and thereby excited various shakes of the head,
and warning looks from many of the auditors. The piece was very long,
but well executed, and soon after the conclusion the lady and her husband,
and another light-haired unknown departed. Mr. Coit, Mr. Pickering,
Mr. Robinson (the tenant of No. 1. Hamilton Place) and Eliot Dwight
came after all the rest had departed, and we had a very pleasant evening,
as usual.

On Thursday morning at the breakfast table the party was formed for
the church. Margy had not intended going, but on the whole thought she
would, and prepared accordingly—Anna the only one who remained, and
she said she would wait till twelve and then try to get in with Josiah. I wore
green silk, pointed skirt, handkerchief, and white scarf, nothing on my
head,—Abby and Margy their hats. We all repaired to the same door. No
one was there but the Miss Hills and others soon joined us. The other doors
very much crowded. We stood some time, Mama on the upper step holding
an umbrella over our heads, and all conversing pleasantly. The moment the
bolt was pushed, the umbrella was thrown afar off, and we all rushed in.
There was more strife than yesterday, but pale and trembling, we all found
ourselves in our accustomed pew. It was really suprising to see the ladies
leap over the tops of the pews. A number of female forms were seen rushing
through our pew, and leaping over the highest side of it to those adjoining.
They were headed by Mrs. Abbott Lawrence, who certainly deserved to
have a degree given her for her powers of jumping. Mrs. Bigelow (the sister
or aunt of Mrs. L.) was the last of the train, and she was just half over the
pew when Mama entered, and catching her round the waist, pulled her
back and insisted on her keeping her place with us. The poor lady was so
agitated and frightened that she could scarcely speak, but appeared very

much obliged for the permission to remain with us. They seemed to have no idea of remaining in our seat, imagining it was reserved particularly for us. The two Miss Hills again sat with us, and we again sent for the music stool on which Abby sat at the foot of the pew. There was not nearly as many ladies as were collected on Commencement day, but still the galleries were well filled, and all the intervening spaces filled with gentlemen. Margy and I sat together and had a great deal of amusement in looking at the various figures in the opposite gallery and chatting with each other.

The prize speaking commenced at ten, Papa and seven or eight other gentlemen as Judges occupied the seat in front of the organ. Ten youths spoke in succession, all very respectable, but young Simmons the best. He spoke admirably an extract from "Ringan Gilhaize" and carried off the first prize, a medal of twenty dollars. I think his speaking gave us as much pleasure as anything of the kind I ever heard. He spoke very finely at the last Exhibition. Papa announced the distribution of Prizes from the stage when the speaking was over. The second prizes were awarded to others of the orators. They concluded speaking at half past eleven, and the Phi Beta Society were not to enter till twelve, so we conversed with a variety, Mr. Merriam among the rest, and listened to music during the intermission. Josiah brought Anna in with some difficulty and got her down to our pew, and then went for another music stool, on which I was enthroned at the head of the pew.

At twelve the Society entered. An unusual number turned out on this occasion, and the stage and pews on the broad aisle were filled with them, while the rest of the church was completely filled with the people in general. It was a fine scene, and the stage presented a striking assemblage of gentlemen of every age, from Dr. Prince of Salem (who has attended on these occasions for nearly sixty years) to the Marshals of the day, Mr. Tower and Mr. Andrews, two handsome young men who were very elegantly dressed and ornamented with their pink and blue ribbons and medals, and sat at the foot of the antiquated old chair, which has seen so many equally interesting groups around it, now passed from the stage of Life forever.

Mr. [Convers] Francis commenced speaking at twelve and never concluded till a quarter past *two*. His oration was a fine one, but so unconscionably and unwarrantably long that of course the whole audience were wearied out. Their impatience was so great that I believe they would have left the house, had not their desire to hear Mr. Sprague overbalanced their wish to leave Mr. Francis. At length he did conclude, and we had some music while we rose and got rid of some of our fatigue before Mr. [Charles] Sprague commenced. He pronounced an excellent Poem on "Curiosity," combining the severity of well merited censure and the drollery of ludicrous description in a very happy manner. It was curious to observe the faces of this crowded audience, now laughing and expressing great delight and clapping with might and main, and then silent, grave and thoughtful as the orator changed the picture from a gay to a grave subject. He spoke an hour, and closed with an elegant compliment to Papa, and when he concluded received a thunder of applause. It was indeed a gratifying moment for the Quincy family. Papa sat concealing his face with his hand, as he fronted the whole audience and must have felt somewhat embarrassed. The whole was concluded by half past three o'clock, and all the audience left the Church with expedition, the Society and orators of the day to dine at the University Hall, and the Judges of the prize speaking and other dignitaries adjourning to the President's House.

We waited till the crowd was gone, and received the compliments and congratulations of the surrounding ladies and from Mr. Bigelow and Mr. Cranch from the stage below. The latter was at our house the preceding evening, and seemed to have highly enjoyed these days, said he had now seen the glory of New England, and seemed to understand "what was what" (to use an elegant expression) perfectly well. He has been travelling about since he took leave of us six weeks since, and returned here to be present on these occasions. He goes to-morrow. I like him very much.

We received the thanks of Mrs. Bigelow and the Misses Hill for all our politeness, and returned to our mansion just after all the dinner party had assembled in the drawing room.

York and his co-partner had spread an elegant table in the dining room for two and twenty, and so only Susan could join the party. It was quite an amalgamation dinner and, as Susan said, composed of curious contrasts. There was Mr. Coit and Dr. Holmes, Isaac P. Davis and Mr. Bowditch, Daniel Davis and Dr. Porter, contrasted in the inward man certainly, and Mr. Harding and Mr. Coit presented a singular diversity in outward appearance. Besides these there were Judge Story, who talks all the time, and Dr. Popkin who never says a word; Mr. John Pickering and Mr. Callender, Mr. Francis and Mr. Willis, Frank Gray and Mr. Farrar, and Mr. Ritchie.

We ladies retired to our room during the dinner, and listened to Sarah's account of Miss Goldsboro' and Miss Coolidge being brought in here after fainting in the church—accompanied by six gentlemen and four ladies. We saw them carried out of the gallery, but little thought of their being deposited in our beds. However, they were recovered and departed before our return. Josiah came up to our room, saying he could get no seat at the Society's dinner, nor at the President's either, so came to us. We had a table spread in the little back parlour, and a great deal of amusement with our flying repast. The gentlemen in the dining room made a great noise laughing and talking, and all seemed to be going very well. We then retired to our room and Margy laid down while Abby prepared a dress for Mrs. Derby's this evening. I was dreadfully fatigued, body and mind.

The dinner party broke up at half past six, and we all ran down to hear accounts and regale on the ice-creams and fruits left on the table. Mr. Callender came in while we were in the height of conversation, upon which Margy [Mrs. Greene] cried out, "Mr. Callender, I am invisible," and he returned with his accustomed readiness, "My dear *Miss Quincy*, I am very happy to see you." He is very droll and added greatly to the brilliancy of the party. They had a delightful dinner, the entertainment elegantly got up, and the company extremely animated and agreeable.

As soon as all had departed the carriage was ordered, and Margy, Susan and Abby with their evening costumes whirled off to the city and Mrs. Derby's. The chaise bore away Josiah and Edmund to the metropolis and York and John in our *gig* followed in the rear. Mamma, Anna and I spent the evening in talking over the various events of the day, and the pleasure we had enjoyed during this week. The gentlemen declared today that these were "three of the proudest days old Harvard had ever seen," and they have certainly been "highly gratifying" to the Quincy family.

The girls remained in town all night—Anna recounted the visitors she had received while we were in church this morning. Mr. Pollard, Mr. Haydn, Mr. McCleary, and Mr. Sprague, the poet, among the rest. The first entertainment given by the President went off in the best style possible in every respect.

M. A. Dewolfe Howe, ed., *The Articulate Sisters* (Cambridge, 1946).

Josiah Quincy, Jr.

PRESIDENT JACKSON GIVES 'EM A LITTLE LATIN

(1833)

When President Andrew Jackson made his triumphal tour of New England in 1833, his aide-de-camp in Massachusetts was Josiah Quincy, Jr., son of the President of Harvard and later Mayor of Boston. Young Quincy well remembered General Lafayette's enthusiastic reception at Harvard in 1824, for Quincy had had to deliver a Latin greeting in honor of the great Frenchman; he had also served as Lafayette's aide-de-camp during the official welcome of the Commonwealth. The visit of General Jackson and Vice-President Van Buren was different; it was deplored by Brahmin Boston, and it was something of a shock for the Old Guard, like John Quincy Adams, to have Harvard give an honorary degree to Old Hickory, who was never noted for his erudition. The details of the visit were humorously revealed by "Major Jack Downing" (Seba Smith of the Portland Courier) *and many of Smith's imitators, among them Charles Augustus Davis of the New York Advertiser who made Major Jack tell in a fictitious report the now famous story of the Harvard ceremony. When Jackson acknowledged Harvard's honor, Jack Downing recorded, "the General was going to stop, but I says in his ear, 'You must give 'em a little Latin, Doctor!' . . . 'E pluribus unum,' says he, 'my friends, sine qua non.' "*

THE MORNING of Wednesday, the 25th, was chilly and overcast, not at all the sort of day for an invalid to encounter the fatigues of travel and reception. At ten o'clock, nevertheless, the President appeared, and took his seat in the barouche, and was greeted with the acclamations which will always be forthcoming when democratic sovereignty is seen embodied in flesh and blood. Very little flesh in this case, however, and only such trifle of blood as the doctors had thought not worth appropriating. But the spirit in Jackson was resolute to conquer physical infirmity. His eye seemed brighter than ever, and all aglow with the mighty will which can compel the body to execute its behests. He was full of conversation, as we drove to Cambridge, to get that doctorate whose bestowal occasioned many qualms to the high-toned friends of Harvard. College degrees were then supposed to have a meaning which has long ago gone out of them; and to many excellent persons it seemed a degrading mummery to dub a man Doctor of Laws who was credited with caring for no laws whatever which conflicted with his personal will. John Quincy Adams, I remember, was especially disturbed at this academic recognition of Jackson and actually asked my father, who was then president of the College, whether there was no way of avoiding it. "Why, no," was the reply. "As the people have twice decided that this man knows law enough to be their ruler, it is not for Harvard College to maintain that they are mistaken." But Mr. Adams was not satisfied, and the bitter generalization of his diary that "time-serving and sycophancy are the qualities of all learned and scientific institutions" was certainly not to be modified by his successor's visit to Cambridge. It did not require Jack Downing's fun to show the delicious absurdity of giving Jackson a literary degree; but the principle that wandering magistrates, whether of state or nation, might claim this distinction had been firmly established, and there were difficulties in limiting its application.

There is a familiar expression by which newspaper reporters denote the strong current of feeling which sometimes runs through an assembly, and yet reaches no audible sound of applause or censure. It has been decided that the word [*sensation*], put in brackets as it is here printed, shall convey those tremors of apprehension or criticism which cannot be exhibited with definiteness. Nobody who knows anything about Harvard College can doubt that there will be *sensation* whenever the people decide that Governor B. F. Butler shall appear upon the stage of Sanders Theatre to receive the compliment of the highest degree which can there be offered; but I will venture to say that an emotion much stronger than this was felt by the throng which filled the College Chapel when Andrew Jackson, leaning upon the arm of my father, entered the building from which he was to depart a Doctor of Laws. Fifty years have taught sensible men to estimate college training at its true worth. It is now clear that it does not furnish the exclusive entrance to paths of the highest honor. The career of Abraham Lincoln has made impossible a certain academic priggishness which belonged to an earlier period of our national existence. Jackson's ignorance of books was perhaps exaggerated, and his more useful knowledge of things and human relations was not apparent to his political opponents to whom the man was but a dangerous bundle of chimeras and prejudices; but I do not need the testimony of a diary now before me to confirm the statement that his appearance before that Cambridge audience instantly produced a toleration which quickly merged into something like admiration and respect. The name of Andrew Jackson was, indeed, one to frighten naughty children with; but the person who went by it wrought a mysterious charm upon old and young. Beacon Street had been undemonstrative as we passed down that Brahmin thoroughfare on our way to Cambridge; but a few days later I heard an incident characteristic enough to be worth telling. Mr. Daniel P. Parker, a well-known Boston merchant, had come to his window to catch a glimpse of the guest of the State, regarding him very much as he might have done some dangerous monster which was being led captive past his house. But the sight of the dignified figure of Jackson challenged a respect which the good merchant felt he must pay by proxy, if not in person. "Do some one come here and salute the old man!" he suddenly exclaimed. And a little daughter of Mr. Parker was thrust forward to wave her handkerchief to the terrible personage whose doings had been so offensive to her elders.

The exercises in the Chapel were for the most part in Latin. My father addressed the President in that language, repeating a composition upon which he somewhat prided himself, for Dr. Beck, after making two verbal corrections in his manuscript, had declared it to be as good Latin as a man need write. Then we had some more Latin from young Mr. Francis Bowen, of the senior class, a gentleman whose name has since been associated with so much fine and weighty English. There were also a few modest words presumably in the vernacular, though scarcely audible, from the recipient of the doctorate.

But it has already been intimated that there were two Jacksons who were at that time making the tour of New England. One was the person who I have endeavored to describe; the other may be called the Jackson of comic myth, whose adventures were minutely set forth by Mr. Jack Downing and his brother humorists. The Harvard degree, as bestowed upon this latter personage, offered a situation which the chroniclers of the grotesque could in no wise resist. A hint of Downing was seized upon and expanded as it flew from mouth to mouth until, at last, it has actually been met skulking near the back door of history in a form something like this. General Jackson, upon being harangued in Latin, found himself in a position of immense perplexity. It was simply decent for him to reply in the learned language in which he was addressed; but, alas! the Shakespearian modicum of "small Latin" was all that Old Hickory possessed, and what he must do was clearly to rise to the situation and make the most of it. There were those college fellows, chuckling over his supposed humiliation; but they were to meet a man who was not to be caught in the classical trap they had set for him. Rising to his feet just at the proper moment, the new Doctor of Laws astonished the assembly with a Latin address, in which Dr. Beck himself was unable to discover a single error. A brief quotation from this eloquent production will be sufficient to exhibit its character: "Caveat emptor: corpus delicti: ex post facto: dies irae: e pluribus unum: usque ad nauseam: Ursa Major: sic semper tyrannis: quid pro quo: requiescat in pace."

Now this foolery was immensely taking in the day of it; and mimics were accustomed to throw social assemblies into paroxysms of delight by imitating Jackson in the delivery of his Latin speech. The story was, on the whole, so good, as showing how the man of the people could triumph over the crafts and subtleties of classical pundits, that all Philistia wanted to believe it. And so it came to pass that, as time went on, part of Philistia did believe it, for I have heard it mentioned as an actual occurrence by persons who may not shrink from a competitive examination in history whenever government offices are to be entered through that portal . . .

To return to the real Jackson, who held what Dickens says Americans call a le-vee, after the exercises in the chapel. He stood at one end of the low parlor of the President's house, and bowed to the students as they passed him. "I am most happy to see you, gentlemen," he said; "I wish you all much happiness"; "Gentlemen, I heartily wish you success in life"; and so on, constantly varying the phrase, which was always full of feeling. The President had begun his reception by offering his hand to all who approached; but he found that this would soon drain the small strength which must carry him through the day. He afterward made an exception in favor of two pretty children, daughters of Dr. Palfrey. He took the hands of these little maidens, and then lifted them up and kissed them. It was a pleasant sight,—one not to be omitted when the events of the day were put upon paper. This rough soldier, exposed all his life to those temptations which have conquered public men whom we still call good, could kiss little children with lips as pure as their own.

Figures of the Past (Boston, 1884).

Josiah Quincy

THE CENTENNIAL CELEBRATION
(1836)

Lawyer by profession, former Congressman and later Mayor of Boston, Josiah Quincy became President of Harvard in 1829 at the age of fifty-seven. An able administrator who materially strengthened the growing University, he was less successful in his relations with students than in making current teaching methods more attractive. Morison called him "the most unpopular President in Harvard history since Hoar." Yet "brave 'old Quin' " was a stanch advocate of academic freedom and under his administration progress was made toward allowing students a choice of subjects. One of the big events of the Quincy period was the bicentennial celebration of September 8, 1836. On this occasion President Quincy delivered a two-hour address which was later expanded into his two-volume history of the University, from which the following official account is taken.

AS THE DAY of the Celebration approached, extensive and tasteful arrangements were . . . made by the Undergraduates for the decoration of the college edifices. The entrance to Harvard Hall, and the porticos of Dane and University Halls, were wreathed with evergreens and flowers; and arches decorated in the same manner were erected over the three principal entrances to the College grounds. The name of HARVARD was placed over the centre arch, between Massachusetts and Harvard Halls, while those of DUNSTER and CHAUNCY, the first two Presidents of the University, surmounted respectively the two side arches. Arrangements were also made for a general illumination of the College buildings.

On the morning of the 8th of September, 1836, a white banner, on which the device of the first seal of the University was emblazoned, was raised on the summit of the pavilion. At an early hour all the avenues leading from the city of Boston and its environs to Cambridge were thronged; and by nine o'clock the Alumni and invited guests, to the number of more than fifteen hundred, assembled in University Hall.

There were venerable and reverend divines,—grave and dignified judges,—statesmen and lawyers,—learned, intellectual, and eminent men of other professions and pursuits in life,—exchanging cordial salutations after years of separation. There were the young and ardent, looking forward in imagination to a brilliant future, and men of maturer age pleased with the retrospection of the past. The greetings of companions of early days, the efforts at recognition, the fond and fervent recollections not untinged with melancholy, which the meeting occasioned, the inquiries more implied than uttered after the absent, the inquisitive glances, rather than words, by which each seemed to ask of the other's welfare, constituted a scene not to be forgotten by any individual who witnessed it . . .

When the Chief Marshal named the classes of the Alumni, it was deeply interesting to mark the result. The class of 1759 was called, but their only representative, and the eldest surviving Alumnus, Judge Wingate, of New Hampshire, being ninety-six years of age, was unable to attend. The classes from 1763 to 1773 were successively named, but solemn pauses succeeded; they had all joined the great company of the departed, or, sunk in the vale of years, were unable to attend the high festival of their Alma Mater. At length, when the class of 1774 was named, Mr. Samuel Emery came forward; a venerable old man, a native of Chatham, Barnstable County, Massachusetts, who, at the age of eighty-six, after an absence of sixty years from the Halls of Harvard, had come from his residence in Philadelphia to attend this celebration. The Rev. Dr. Ripley, of Concord, of the class of 1776, and the Rev. Dr. Homer, of Newton, of the class of 1777, were followed by the Rev. Dr. Bancroft, of Worcester, and the Rev. Mr. Willis, of Kingston, of the class of 1778; and, as modern times were approached, instead of solitary individuals, twenty or thirty members of a class appeared at the summons.

On leaving University Hall, the procession moved along the principal avenues within the College grounds, through the gateway between Massachusetts and Harvard Halls, and, passing through the lines of the escort formed by the Undergraduates, entered the Congregational Church. The galleries of the edifice had been reserved for the ladies, and, after the entrance of the procession, every part of the building was filled by a crowded audience. After a voluntary on the organ, the Rev. Dr. Ripley offered a solemn and fervent prayer. Although more than eighty years of age, he spoke in a clear and powerful voice. Like the Jewish leader, "his eye was not dim, nor his natural force abated."

An Occasional Ode, written by the Rev. Samuel Gilman, of Charleston, S.C., was then sung.

> FAIR HARVARD! thy sons to thy Jubilee throng,
>   And with blessings surrender thee o'er
> By these festival-rites, from the Age that is past,
>   To the Age that is waiting before.
> O Relic and Type of our ancestors' worth,
>   That hast long kept their memory warm!
> First flower of their wilderness! Star of their night,
>   Calm rising through change and through storm!
>
> To thy bowers we were led in the bloom of our youth,
>   From the home of our free-roving years,
> When our fathers had warned, and our mothers had prayed,
>   And our sisters had blest, through their tears.

Thou then wert our parent,—the nurse of our souls,—
    We were moulded to manhood by thee,
Till, freighted with treasure-thoughts, friendships, and hopes,
    Thou didst launch us on Destiny's sea.

When, as pilgrims, we come to revisit thy halls,
    To what kindlings the season gives birth!
Thy shades are more soothing, thy sunlight more dear,
    Than descend on less privileged earth:
For the Good and the Great, in their beautiful prime,
    Through thy precincts have musingly trod,
As they girded their spirits, or deepened the streams
    That make glad the fair City of God.

Farewell! be thy destinies onward and bright!
    To thy children the lesson still give,
With freedom to think, and with patience to bear,
    And for Right ever bravely to live.
Let not moss-covered Error moor *thee* at its side,
    As the world on Truth's current glides by;
Be the herald of Light, and the bearer of Love,
    Till the stock of the Puritans die.

The touching allusions of this beautiful Ode excited a deep and solemn enthusiasm, and the Address of President Quincy commanded, during two hours, the attention of the audience. A prayer was afterwards offered by the Rev. Dr. Homer, and then the whole congregation united their voices in the solemn strains of "Old Hundred."

From all that dwell below the skies,
Let the Creator's praise arise;
Let the Redeemer's name be sung
Through every land, by every tongue.

Eternal are thy mercies, Lord;
Eternal truth attends thy word;
Thy praise shall sound from shore to shore,
Till suns shall rise and set no more.

No one could look around at this moment, without thrilling emotions, on this crowded assembly of educated and intelligent men, convened on the high festival of this ancient literary institution, and soon to be separated never to meet again.

The benediction was given by the Rev. Dr. Ripley; and, on leaving the church, the procession was formed in the same order as when it entered. The classes of the Alumni were again summoned, and solemn pauses again succeeded, until Mr. Emery walked down the aisle alone, and was greeted by testimonies of applause from his younger brethren. On leaving the church, the procession, including more than fifteen hundred individuals, proceeded to the left across the Common, and then, turning to the right, passed in front of the College edifices. By this arrangement, the graduates of the various classes passed in review before each other. After passing Dane Hall, the procession turned to the left, proceeded through Harvard Street, in front of the President's House, and entered the College grounds opposite the pavilion . . .

The tables were prepared to accommodate about fifteen hundred persons, and they were completely filled by the Alumni and their invited guests, except a division on the left of the President's chair, reserved for, and occupied by, the Undergraduates.

It was extraordinary to see how soon and how quietly fifteen hundred persons found places, each one seated and duly provided for the feast. On the left of the chair, the Undergraduates of the University were seated, and thence to the extreme right extended row above row, and class after class of Alumni, embracing every period of life, from the youth fresh from the studious hall, to the octogenarian, who seemed to live again in the memories of the distant past. When all were seated, a prayer was offered by the Rev. President Humphrey, of Amherst College. For a time the dining quietly proceeded; but soon the busy hum of many voices, the laugh, the joke, animated the scene. All were again hushed, as if by magic, when Mr. Everett, the President of the Day, rose to address them. To say that he was most happy, is feeble praise. He was eloquent, brilliant, touching;—and as he read, in the sea of intelligent faces around him, the effect of his own unrivalled declamation, his fancy seemed to burst away on freshened pinion, and to pour forth lavishly the riches of his well-fraught mind . . .

The History of Harvard University (Boston, 1840).

Horace Howard Furness

PRESIDENT WALKER TAKES THE HELM

(1853)

One of the world's great Shakespearean scholars, Horace Howard Furness is known to our time for the compilation of the New Variorum Edition *of the plays of William Shakespeare. In addition, however, he was a man of wide knowledge and interests, a correspondent par excellence. Of him, H. H. F. Jayne, the collector of his letters, has written: "The letters . . . beginning as they do with Furness's years at Harvard preserve sufficient continuity to mark the events of his crowded life . . . they reveal the expansion of his mind, the subtleties of his nature . . . his rare good humor and his kindly sympathy. He devoted much time to his correspondence, especially in his later years, and he always looked upon letter-writing as an art. He infused the merest note of acknowledgment with a twinkle of wit or a beguiling touch of his personality. His longer letters . . . are veritable mines for sparkling gems of observation and reflection." Furness entered Harvard at sixteen and came self-prepared in every subject except mathematics. He earned part of his way by tutoring and teaching school. The following letter was written to his sister at home, after the inauguration of President Walker following the resignation of President Sparks because of ill health.*

Cambridge, May 29, 1853

THIS WEEK has passed most delightfully. I felt perfectly free, & mingled study & recreation in the most delicious confusion. As time by no means hung heavy on my hands I was under no sort of obligations to teach the orphan girl to read or the orphan boy to sew. I read, wrote, slept, and smoked to my heart's content. Yesterday afternoon I read a "History of the Inquisition" & gradually dreamed off & awoke maintaining that some one or other, I couldn't remember the name, would make a most capital General Inquisitor. The event of the week, however, was the Inauguration of Pres't Walker. There was none of the pomp and magnificence of preceding years, yet it was still quite imposing. The first ceremony was the planting of a young tree, which ever after bears Dr. Walker's name. This is a time-honored custom and is performed as follows. In the morning about ten o'clock the Senior class marched in a body to Pres't Sparks' & presented a handsome bouquet to Lady S.; thence to Dr. Walker's & gave a similar bouquet to Lady W. Retiring from Dr. Walker's, the President-elect accompanied them and was escorted into the College yard to where a hole had been dug, into which was placed a fine young pine tree; the Chief Marshal then steps forward and addresses a flowery, spooney speech to Dr. Walker, who replies somewhat similarly, about children's children (i.e., grandchildren) sitting under the shade of it & reflecting with pleasure upon its planting. (Now if there are the same laws in force then, as now, they will be very quickly dispersed as a "parietal group.") Dr. Walker then advances & throws in the first shovelful of earth, & is followed by each member of the class, doing the same in turn; "and now," said the Doctor as he threw down the shovel, "where are your 'digs'?" What hand-clapping and what laughter! (But between you and me, I think it was a joke that he heard among the bystanders at President Sparks' or Everett's Inauguration.) The worthy Doctor was then accompanied home and the crowd dispersed to celebrate the day in uproarious carousals. And upon my word, I never saw such almost universal, what shall I call it—intoxication is too gross a term to apply to such good fellows & yet it was nothing more nor less. One of my classmates was not far from the truth, when he said that "there was not more than fifteen fellows out of our class, who were not 'tight' that day"; and what was true of our class was true of the other three also. You know my penchant for such scenes, & I assure you that that day I saw some rich ones. I hate to have any one get "tight," but if he must & will do so, why, pray let me see him, & when he is getting over it I will administer soda water & good advice to his heart's content. On the day in question, at about eleven o'clock I was lying reading on my sofa, now and then interrupted by bursts of merriment, when a real good friend of mine, who is, however rather fond of getting elevated semioccasionally & then comes & confesses to me, so to speak, rushed into my room, bawling out: "Furness, you old fool you! get up! come round to D.'s; you must come; all the fellows are round there & we're having a glorious time!" This speech was interspersed with adjectives "immentionable to ears perlite." I complied, & truly it was the most ludicrous sight I ever witnessed. There were about fifteen or twenty fellows scarcely conscious of what they were about, & in shaking hands with them I was obliged to dodge the wine & punch which they would otherwise have spilt over me. I could fill sheets with description of the ridiculous scenes; one, however, will suffice. One of the company happening to find himself in front of a looking-glass inquired "who was that spooney fellow looking at him"; receiving no reply he aimed a blow & shivered the glass to atoms, & turning around with a satisfied look said, he "thought *that* rather knocked him!"

So much for the forenoon; in the afternoon we were marshalled class by class & joined in the grand procession which escorted Dr. Walker to the church. Here the Governor (Clifford) made a very neat speech & delivered to Dr. W. the old Charter & seal & large silver keys of the College. Dr. W. replied, & there was an oration in Latin by Carroll, the first scholar of the Senior class. After that followed Dr. Walker's address, & a splendid one it was; it answered all the charges which of late have been brought against colleges. Its length was its only fault; it will be printed & will I think make quite a sensation. After the address followed the Doxology. And you'd better believe I put in vigorously. Every one joined & it did sound grandly. After that we again marched round Cambridge & finally dispersed, & night & carousals began to thicken. In the eve'g W. & myself went up to H. P. C. room and he read the last number of "Bleak House" to me, & we came to the conclusion that it was a fine one—*splenndid* . . .

My desire to see you all is inexpressible . . . Oceans of love to Father & Mother, & continents for yourself, & believe me, darling sister,

Yours
HORACE

H. H. F. J., ed., *The Letters of Horace Howard Furness* (Boston, 1922).

William Lawrence

BRET HARTE AND THE GREEN
GLOVES

(1871)

*William Lawrence, "the great alumnus of his Harvard generation" (as the
Harvard Alumni Bulletin referred to him), found time in his life of a busy
and distinguished churchman to serve his University with devotion and with
skill. He was successively Preacher to the University, Overseer, and Fellow
of Harvard College. At various times he was a one-man fund-raising committee and he twice played a leading part in large fund-raising campaigns in
behalf of the University. This retrospective and amusing account of another
Phi Beta Kappa Day was written in 1940 when he was ninety years of age.*

CAMBRIDGE can be hot and, if ever there was a hottest day in Cambridge,
that day was Thursday, June 29, 1871, Phi Beta Kappa Day. It was as hot
perhaps as that July day in 1775 when General Washington unsheathed his
sword in command of the American Army. You may recall that the prudent
George—just from sunny Virginia—retired to the shade of his great elm
while his future army, the "embattled farmers" of Lexington, Concord, and
other parts of Middlesex County, sweltered in the sun upon the treeless
plain called "Cambridge Common."

The Phi Beta Kappa exercises were to be held in the Unitarian Church,
as was usual before the erection of Memorial Hall. The program as announced was of exceptional interest; everybody in Cambridge was on the
tiptoe of expectation.

The President of Alpha Chapter was the author and hero of perhaps the
most widely read book of the seas, *Two Years Before the Mast*, Richard
Henry Dana, Jr., 1837, whose ancestors, by the way, rested in the graveyard
hard by. The orator, Dr. Noah Porter, was Professor, later President, of Yale
University and was thought to be the leading philosopher in the country.
Then and finally, to top off this feast of reason and flow of soul, the poet was
to be Bret Harte, who was in the heyday of his popularity. After some fifteen years in the West, he had just returned from San Francisco. His journey across the country was a veritable triumphal progress. The press hailed
him as he passed from city to city. Everyone was familiar with *The Luck of
Roaring Camp*. Men, women, and even children chuckled at *The Heathen
Chinee*. And now, as the guest in Cambridge of William Dean Howells,
editor of the *Atlantic*, he was welcomed by Longfellow, Emerson, Norton,
and Agassiz. He dined with the Saturday Club and was the center of interest

to all the literary groups of Cambridge and Boston. It was a queer mixture. Scholars, scientists, editors, and judges were intrigued and amused. So was Bret Harte—and also somewhat bored. What would be the topic of the poem, what its style, was the question of the members of Chapter A of the P.B.K. Would he attempt a classic or would his atmosphere savor of Hell's Kitchen? Cambridge was agog.

At eleven o'clock the exercises began. At noon I was to be at Christ Church in attendance upon the marriage of my classmate, Henry Cabot Lodge, to Nannie, daughter of Admiral Davis. They had been engaged since our sophomore winter vacation, two years and a half. Undergraduates were forbidden to marry in those days, and Cabot, determined to lose no time, was to be married within 24 hours of the time that he received his diploma at the hands of Harvard's young President, Charles Eliot.

I went with the crowd and at eleven o'clock was packed in the rear of the Unitarian Church. Richard Henry Dana, Jr., who was always most precise in his manner, opened the ceremonies and introduced Dr. Noah Porter, who announced his subject, "The Sciences of Nature or the Science of Man." His personality was so solemn and his voice so deep that, as he repeated the weighty subject, the air became unbearably oppressive. However, he went on. I believe that the scholars thought it a great oration. My impressions were those of dullness, confusion, and length. But that was my fault.

Twelve o'clock was approaching, and I slipped out for the wedding in Christ Church. The sun blazed as I passed by the graveyard; the marriage service with the wedding march was as usual. Cabot and his bride walked down the aisle and out through the porch and drove off. How little we realized that in forty and then fifty years I should be reading the burial service in the same church, first over Nannie and then over Cabot, and their bodies be carried out through the same porch.

Time, however, was precious. I must hear Bret Harte and then hurry on to the reception at the bride's house. So back to the Unitarian Church I went and, to my dismay, found Noah Porter still discussing the Sciences of Nature and Man. Soon he finished; and now the audience bristled with anticipation.

The Poet stood up and placed his manuscript upon the desk; Bret Harte at last! Of medium height, 35 years of age, to quote Mr. Howells, "He was then, as always, a child of extreme fashion as to his clothes and the cut of his beard, which he wore in a moustache with the dropping side whiskers of the day, and his joyful physiognomy was as winning as his voice" ... He was frightened, doubtless, for his voice was so weak that few heard it; being in the rear of the church, I heard almost nothing. But as Bret Harte went on, I could feel the dismay, the shock, the amusement, and the wrath of the several groups in the audience.

Newspaper accounts of the day only complicate the question of just what the Poet read. From the report in the Boston *Daily Advertiser* of June 30, it appears that Harte's poem was similar to one included in the same year in *East and West Poems* (James R. Osgood, Boston, 1871). Now called "The Aspiring Miss De Laine: A Chemical Narrative," the poem is part of the accepted works of Harte . . . Whatever the variance in the first lines, the tale is the same, and the finished work concludes:

> . . . For Miss Addie was gone! . . .
> Gone without parting farewell; and alas!
> Gone with a flavor of Hydrogen Gas.
>
> When the weather is pleasant you frequently meet
> A white-headed man slowly pacing the street;
> His trembling hand shading his lack-lustre eye,
> Half blind with continually scanning the sky.
> Rumor points him as some astronomical sage,
> Reperusing by day the celestial page;
> But the reader, sagacious, will recognize Brown,
> Trying vainly to conjure his lost sweetheart down,
> And learn the stern moral this story must teach,
> That Genius may lift its love out of its reach.

One of the best comments about the occasion is that contained in *Bret Harte, Argonaut and Exile*, by George R. Stewart, Jr. (Houghton Mifflin, 1931):

> Harte had been asked to compose and read the Phi Beta Kappa poem at the Harvard Commencement—a real honor undoubtedly and to Bostonians probably the highest honor which an American poet could receive. But Harte was fatally careless about the whole matter, and proceeded throughout with bad taste. In the first place, with foolish temerity he decided to be humorous. Now a second *Heathen Chinee* would undoubtedly have been successful even at a Harvard Commencement, but rather than anything less uproarious he should have taken refuge in the usual pompous windiness of Phi Beta Kappa poems. And Harte, apparently confident that people would eulogize anything which he happened to give them, did not even go to the trouble to write a new poem. Instead, he took some old verses in the style of Tom Hood which he had written and published nine years before[*] during his salad days with the *Era* [*The Golden Era*. December 28, 1862, a San Francisco literary magazine]. These he refurbished without improving greatly, and renamed *Aspiring Miss De Laine*. Then on Commencement Day he dressed himself somewhat more glaringly even than usual and took his seat on the platform. When he rose and began to read, all Boston's and Cambridge's asssembled social and intellectual leaders grew, according to individual temperament, cold with vicarious embarrassment and hot with choler. His *green* gloves! His poem—flippant and silly without being really funny! His manner, too, was unfortunate. He placed both green-gloved hands on the table and spoke in so low a voice as to be heard only with difficulty.

[*] This poem was entitled "The Lost Beauty," as was the Phi Beta Kappa version, and signed "Bret."

Whatever the true story, Harte was so imperfectly heard that there was no applause at the end. My interpretation of the incident was then and still is that Bret Harte was so bored by the scholastic atmosphere that he reacted and sprang what he thought was a joke upon his solemn audience, with the result that, shocked, amazed and angry, the members of Harvard Chapter Alpha of the P. B. Kappa departed to their homes in silence, uttering in an undertone language that was not fit to print.

Meanwhile I slipped off to the wedding reception on Quincy Street; joined with the guests in covering the bridal couple with rice as they drove off. Cabot was at the opening of his career of over half a century as historian, statesman, and United States Senator.

Harvard Alumni Bulletin, December 14, 1940.

James Russell Lowell

WHAT A GLORIOUS OBJECT IS A SENIOR!

(1875)

Poet, essayist, editor, diplomat, James Russell Lowell had a distinguished career that brought him international repute. Yet Lowell, with his Cambridge connections, was never very far, spiritually or physically, from Cambridge and his home "Elmwood." For more than thirty years he was a member of the Faculty, and he held the Smith Professorship of French and Spanish Languages and Literatures, a chair occupied before him by Ticknor and Longfellow. His "Commemoration Ode" was delivered at the memorial services honoring the Harvard students and graduates who gave their lives in the Civil War; and his oration at the 250th anniversary of the College in 1886 became a notable part of his collected works. Among his minor writings is this description of the Class Day revels around the tree in Holden Quadrangle.

THE COLLEGE YARD is cheery with music and gay with a quietly moving throng. The windows from groundsill to eaves bloom thick with young and happy faces. At half past four the sound of marching music in quick time is heard, passing at longer or shorter intervals for the *rah-rah-rah* with which the class bid good-bye to the buildings, and the waiting crowd are consoled by knowing that the last great show of the day is drawing nigh. At five o'clock comes the dance round the Liberty Tree, but long before that every inch of vantage-ground whence even a glimpse at this frenzy of muscular sentiment may be hoped for has been taken up. The trees are garlanded with wriggling boys, who here apply the skill won by long practice in neighboring orchards and gardens, while every post becomes the pedestal of an unsteady group. In the street a huddled drove of carriages bristle with more luxurious gazers. The Senior class are distinguished by the various shapes of eccentric ruin displayed in their hats, as if the wildest nightmares of the maddest of hatters had suddenly taken form and substance. First, the Seniors whirl hand in hand about the tree with the energy of excitement gathered through the day; class after class is taken in, till all College is swaying in the unwieldy ring, which at last breaks to pieces of its own weight. Then come the frantic leaping and struggling for a bit of the wreath of flowers that circles the tree at a fairly difficult height. Here trained muscle tells; but sometimes mere agility and lightness, which know how to climb on others' shoulders, win the richest trophy . . .

Perhaps the prettiest part of the day is its close. The College yard, hung with varicolored Chinese lanterns, looks (to borrow old Gayton's word) *festivously* picturesque, while the alternating swells and falls of vocal and instrumental music impregnate the cooler evening air with sentiment and revery. Youths and maidens, secluded by the very throng, wander together in a golden atmosphere of assured anticipation. Life is so easy in the prospect when a pair of loving eyes hold all of it that is worth seeing, and are at once both prophecy and fulfilment! Fame and fortune are so lightly won (in that momentary transfiguration of commonest things into the very elements of poetry and passion) by the simple jugglery of taking everything for granted! And what a glorious object is a Senior on Class Day to the maiden of sixteen!

F. O. Vaille and H. A. Clark, eds., *The Harvard Book* (Cambridge, 1875).

David McCord

ENTER A FORMER NAVAL PERSON
(1943)

In the decade of the forties the most famous visitor to the Harvard Yard was Prime Minister Winston Churchill. Tremendous secrecy surrounded his coming, but of course the inevitable rumors about the famous guest did leak through the official censorship. This is how the Harvard Alumni Bulletin *described the event, in the words of its editor, David McCord.*

With the suddenness of the coming of autumn leaves, there returned to the Yard on September 6 much of the color and excitement of three historic

Harvard events: the Tercentenary celebration of 1936, the memorable Oxford Convocation of June, 1941, and the great military Commencement of last May. A blend of these three festivals marked the dignified and delightful ceremony at which . . . the Harvard degree of Doctor of Laws was conferred on the Right Honorable Winston Leonard Spencer Churchill, Great Britain's Prime Minister, and man of the hour. Indeed, the surprise of the occasion brought it sharply into focus; and the time of the year—when the Yard is poised for first flight into fall days—enhanced the sense and feel of adventure. To learn overnight that within a few hours one might see and hear the man whose character and eloquence have been the inspiration of the free world in its darkest hour, brought professors home from vacations, and cheerfully cancelled hundreds of family plans for spending Labor Day away from Cambridge.

Early Monday morning those fortunate enough to hold one of the limited number of Yard tickets began to filter through the main gates. They were still not too sure as to just what was about to happen, for Mr. Churchill's name had so far appeared in print only in a brief announcement in the national press to the effect that he was to broadcast at noon from an unnamed American city. No official word of him had escaped in Cambridge. But the heavy ropes which marked off the large area of the Yard now known as the Tercentenary Theatre, and the battery of microphones on the steps of the Memorial Church, more than confirmed the suspected probability of the impending event. By 11 A.M., Harvard military units were gathering in formations in the old part of the Yard; Overseers and other dignitaries in morning dress were hurrying across diagonal paths, silk hats shining in the sun. Crowds of civilians—mostly women—were finding places on the steps of the Widener Library, members of the Navy Band began to assemble near the west porch of the Church; police were in view. At a quarter to twelve the specially and hurriedly invited to the academic exercises had entered Sanders Theatre; a few moments later began the exercises themselves, in which—now no surprise—the Prime Minister, in the brilliant red of his Oxford gown, played to great applause the leading part. Then the principals emerged from the south door of Memorial Hall, hurried across to the Church, and a minute later from the south steps President Conant was introducing to Harvard's six or seven thousand military, and five or six thousand students, Faculty, alumni, guests, and employees, the man who recently told the world that we have reached "the end of the beginning."

Up to the very last the secret had been well kept. Even those in the next-but-one of the University's inner circles knew nothing whatever of the event until a week before it occurred; and in many cases then there was indication only that an honorary degree was to be conferred. So, in fact, the invitations read to Overseers, alumni officials, the military, and distinguished guests. They were doubly marked *confidential.* The tickets which followed indicated Sanders Theatre, a time, a seat—no more. Yard passes were not generally thought to exist until the Saturday previous. There was suspicion; there were ultimate hints in the public press, such as that of Mr. Churchill's broadcast and something about his keeping "a long-standing engagement." Secrecy extended even to running off the programs late at night. The University Printing Office recalls that when copy was submitted, it appeared that only a Mr. X was to be honored; his name would come later. But at the end of the copy stood the text for *God Save the King!* By and large, one can now half believe that the potential audience *willed* that it prove to be the Prime Minister who was coming to the Yard.

He came. It was a long-standing invitation, to be accepted when opportunity offered. The opportunity had arrived, but there was no time for the University to invite an audience remote from Cambridge. It is remarkable, rather, that the staff in Massachusetts Hall was able to notify the immediate Harvard family to carry through so many complicated details—from secret service to broadcasting arrangements—in so short a time. But it was done, and here now at a little before noon in familiar Sanders Theatre sat and stood more than 1,200 people in what one man described as "the most exciting fever of a lifetime."

On the platform ranged the empty seats for 118 members of the academic procession. On the floor were set aside seats for the remainder of the procession—the Faculty and the Board of Overseers. At the right and left of the stage, underneath the balcony, sat the higher ranking members of the Army and Navy units at the University. At the back of the Theatre in semicircle stood a group of undergraduates. (Students were permitted to apply for a limited block of tickets, filled in the order of request.) Three or four WAVE officers took seats with the Navy. A number of ladies—wives of members of the Governing Boards and administrative officers—occupied the center balcony. In this group were Mrs. Conant, Mrs. Churchill, and Subaltern Mary Churchill.

A bugle sounded. Three minutes later, to the *Second Connecticut March*, the academic procession entered the Theatre—the Faculty by the south entry, the Overseers and dignitaries by the north. Ascending the platform, the Deans took places in the front row left, facing the House Masters. Robe after robe scattered a rainbow over the stage. Some of the most brilliant were those of the *Emeriti*, among them Professors Merriman and Rand.

At noon sounded the fanfare* from the balcony overlooking the transept. This was indeed the moment. The now standing audience broke into prolonged applause and cheers as the Prime Minister, with President Conant, preceded by the Secretary to the University and members of the Corporation, and followed by Jerome D. Greene, '96, LL.D. '37, Honorary Keeper of the Corporation Records, the Governor of the Commonwealth,

---

* Written by Walter H. Piston, '24, Walter W. Naumburg Professor of Music, first played at the Oxford Convocation in 1941.

Commander C. R. Thompson of the Royal Navy, and Brigadier General William J. Keville, the Governor's aide, entered the Theatre and ascended the center steps. From the press bank at the right flashed the camera bulbs. The applause continued. The President and Fellows took seats at the back center underneath the three crimson shields; the Prime Minister found his place at the left between the Governor (on his right) and George H. Chase, Dean of the University. Principals, Faculty, and audience then were seated. Throughout the exercises, six Secret Service men stood inflexible at strategic positions at the back of, and in front of, the stage.

The University Marshal, Dr. Reginald Fitz, said: "Mr. Sheriff, pray give us order"; and the Sheriff of Middlesex County, top-hatted and gold-braided, arose, thrice pounded the stage with his sword-in-scabbard, and said in the tradition: "The meeting will be in order." The Rev. Henry Bradford Washburn, '91, S.T.D.. '30, offered prayer:

> . . . and we most heartily beseech Thee, with Thy favour to behold and bless Thy servants the President of the United States, the gracious sovereign King George, his First Minister, and all to whom Thou hast entrusted the destinies of the United States of America and the British Commonwealth of Nations . . .

The University Choir, in black gowns with broad red facing, seated at the extreme left under the balcony, sang the anthem—the final chorus from Handel's *Samson,* with the magnificent words by Milton:

> Let their celestial concerts all unite,
> Ever to sound his praise in endless morn of light.

Twenty members of the Boston Symphony Orchestra accompanied them, under the direction of Associate Professor G. Wallace Woodworth, Organist and Choirmaster. The Orchestra also played the fanfare and played for the subsequent Seventy-Eighth Psalm and Paine's Commencement Hymn. This was the Orchestra's first participation in a Harvard ceremony since the Tercentenary, and many of those present returned from their vacations just for the one day. Mr. Churchill, it was noted, turned far around in his chair to observe and hear the music.

Leverett Saltonstall, '14, LL.D. '42, Governor of the Commonwealth, gave the brief address of welcome. When he had finished and resumed his seat, the Prime Minister turned and laid his hand on the Governor's arm. One could see his lips move. "Very good," he said. The Governor had concluded:

> Mr. Churchill: You are an inspiring example of the motto of our great President, Thomas Jefferson:
>
> Ye shall know the truth, and the truth shall make you free.*

* John 8:32.

The audience rose and joined in the singing of the Psalm. When all were again seated, the President stood up in his place and called Mr. Churchill by name. The Prime Minister also arose, and the President conferred on him the degree of Doctor of Laws, reading the citation.

WINSTON LEONARD SPENCER CHURCHILL

An historian who has written a glorious page of British history; a statesman and warrior whose tenacity and courage turned back the tide of tyranny in freedom's darkest hour.

When the University Marshal had handed Dr. Churchill his diploma, applause broke out in new strength. It is doubtful if anything in Sanders Theatre ever surpassed it. Again bulbs flashed. Mr. Churchill bowed and smiled, and bowed again. He was visibly touched by the reception.

Taking his manuscript from his pocket, he moved forward to the lectern and the battery of five microphones. On either side of him towered the white marble statues of President Quincy and the Colonial patriot, James Otis. He searched for his glasses with hands that reach more happily for a cigar. He looked constantly right and left. His mobile face and restless arms gave fluid emphasis to what he said. Chancellor of Bristol University, honorary Alumnus of Oxford and Harvard, his dramatic address nonetheless led out unerringly from academic groves to Anglo-American relations. There is no need to summarize. The radio and the press of the Nation have already done that and more. But beyond the objective, fraternal point of his speech, we may quote this paragraph:

And here let me say how proud we ought to be, young and old, to be living in a tremendous, thrilling, formative epoch in the human story, and how fortunate it was for the world that when these great trials came upon us there was a generation that terror could not conquer and brutal violence could not enslave.

He was cheered to the echo of the old Theatre. The power of his words had found a mark. He looked pleased.

There followed the Commencement Hymn and the Benediction. To more applause, the Prime Minister, the dignitaries, and Faculty left the platform and the audience immediately followed.

Most of the audience hastened at once across to the Yard and arrived there to find President Conant on the south steps of the Memorial Church introducing the man for whom the massed crowds had patiently waited. The sun was fainting hot. Our visitor saw the whole Tercentenary Theatre filled, the Army and Navy in the center, a large group of WAVES among them. On the steps of Widener stood hundreds. Nearly ten thousand voices cheered him. The Prime Minister, now, robe discarded—in short black jacket, gray trousers, gray unmatching waistcoat, black bow tie with dots, a black Homburg, and a light cane in his hand. This was the familiar figure;

no gown to hide his British squareness, no black velvet cap to shield his eyes. The crowd was delighted. Soldier, to soldiers and sailors. The veteran of older wars and this war spoke briefly to young men who had yet to go out. Cameras clicked and whirred. He rapped with his cane to drive home a point. He looked fiercely into the sun. He looked down and smiled. In his talk he was optimistic, but he emphasized that the end of the war is not yet round any visible corner. Closing, he made the sign of the V twice with the first two fingers of his right hand. The crowd voiced mighty concurrence, and V's appeared everywhere in answer.

From there the President escorted Mr. Churchill to the Fogg Museum to attend a small luncheon given by the University. Here he met members of the governing boards, administrative officers, and their wives, and members of the official party. In honor of the occasion, Harvard's 17th-century state silverware was used for service. President Conant made some brief remarks:

> Today Harvard welcomes the Prime Minister of Great Britain. We also welcome the Chancellor of Bristol University, a fellow academician. But most significant of all, we welcome a man whose inspiring leadership of a gallant people has preserved for us and our children that liberty without which no university can survive.
>
> Those of us of the Harvard family who are gathered here this afternoon have the special pleasure and high honor of greeting Mr. and Mrs. Churchill and the members of their official party. I trust our guests realize how deeply we appreciate this visit. It is no simple matter for a man who carries Mr. Churchill's burdens to find the time to attend an academic festival. This day will be long remembered in Harvard history. I am sure that I am speaking on behalf of all of you . . . when I express deep gratitude to the Prime Minister for the honor he has done us.
>
> Mr. Churchill has already spoken twice today. I shall not therefore trouble him by a request to make another speech. I am venturing, however, to take the liberty of asking him to propose the toast to the President of the United States.
>
> Ladies and gentlemen—Mr. Churchill.

A toast and some unrecorded words and a witticism followed.

Crowds trailed to the west entrance of the Museum, and waited patiently back of circulating police until the Prime Minister and President Conant—each now with a long Churchill cigar—emerged. In final response to final cheers, Harvard's newest Alumnus made the familiar sign and hoisted on his stick the familar black hat.

In the little while that he was long with us—to turn about a poet's phrase—the dominant impression of Mr. Churchill is the kindliness and brightness in his great vitality. It is true that he probably carried in his head that day the knowledge that the first of the Axis partners had given up. But that need not be counted. In a wearied world there was no weariness in that face. He smiled often. He caused his guardians great uneasiness by insisting twice on saluting the crowd through an open window of Memorial Hall before the academic procession had gathered. His informality was continually evident. On the platform he would hitch up the folds of his red gown, and his hands appeared frequently to stray through invisible slits to his pockets. He sat comfortably. When his wife and daughter lingered on the steps of the Museum before entering, he turned around and came out unaffectedly after them. There was no pose to anything that he said or did. He stood equally and foursquare among us, and we shall not forget him.

Harvard Alumni Bulletin, September 18, 1943.

Barbara Ward

A DAY FULL OF SINCERE EMOTION
(1957)

Ever cautious in changing university policy, the Governing Boards voted in 1955 with total agreement—and safety—the first Harvard honorary degree to a woman, the distinguished Radcliffe alumna, Helen Keller. Two years later, with growing confidence, they honored the energetic and perceptive editor of The Economist, *Barbara Ward (Lady Jackson, 1914–1981), whose brains combined with beauty made her a popular choice as the first feminine speaker to the Harvard alumni on Commencement Day. Here is Lady Jackson's chronicle of the day from a family letter recording her delight in breaking an old tradition.*

AT 5:45 in the afternoon of the day before Commencement, the Treasurer of Harvard, Paul Cabot, and his wife, Virginia, came to fetch me. Whether the original seafaring Cabot blood still flows in Paul's veins, I don't know, but I do know he is the nearest to a sea salt a proper Bostonian can be, with an open, tanned, shrewd face made from old hickory, and a loud voice with all the gales of the ocean roaring in it; a nice man, too, with an open mind and liberal convictions and great simplicity. The Cabots live about twelve miles outside Boston in a comfortable old house, and there we drove. It was still hot after a sultry day, but not unbearably so, and it grew cooler as dinner hour approached.

The drive in was a little uncomfortable, for Paul—in keeping with his old salt air—is a chain smoker of cigars, and my fine, fine dress got to smell like a smokeroom. But when we reached the Puseys it hardly mattered, for with forty people crowding in talk, what's a whiff of tobacco more or less?

The first person I saw was Chris Herter, whom I hadn't seen since 1947 when he came over with Win Riefler to look into the possibilities of the Marshall Plan. I talked to a number of old friends, the Lamonts, Erwin Griswold, Dean of the Law School, and to new ones including George Whitney, the president of the Harvard alumni.

By this time you will have had Joe Alsop's *Saturday Evening Post* account of the Commencement ceremonies. The only thing he missed is the part played by the alumni. They come back year by year, and each year has a headquarters somewhere where they can foregather. But the biggest year of all is the twenty-fifth reunion. Then they arrange things on a lavish scale. Wives are urged to come, a nursery school is organized for children, and for four and one-half days joy is unconfined. The alumni elect a president each year who presides over the afternoon celebrations, and all the marshals and honour guards are provided from the twenty-fifth year. They—along with the five Fellows who make up the Corporation (Paul Cabot and Tommy Lamont are Fellows) and the thirty Overseers—wear top hats and cutaways, a fine if funereal sight.

We dined in state with tables decked with Paul Revere silver in the ballroom at the Puseys' house. I sat beside Nate Pusey with Arthur Goodhart on the other side at the head of a square with the fourth end open, and I had a very good talk. That evening Nate was really on fire because Arthur Goodhart had suggested in a lunchtime speech that culture could be preserved only by keeping it for an elite, and this outraged Nate's soul and he declared his passionate belief that this was defeatism and you had to go right on trying to reach the masses. There was general conversation after dinner, first among the ladies—I talked to Ellie Lamont—and then all together, when my lot was the charming new young President of Princeton—Goheen —and a very quiet Dutch astronomer. Since this was an academic occasion, we were not late to bed and drove back to Needham by full moonlight.

Next day—the great day—was by a crowning mercy so cool that it was almost cold. Last year on the contrary, the heat reached 105° in the shade, and one distinguished guest, who injudiciously wore a hat decorated with wax strawberries, had them melt slowly down her neck. All day long the wind rustled through the trees with almost no gleam of sun, and since the oldest alumnus must have been ninety-eight, the cold was merciful.

When I arrived at the Harvard Yard I stood about with other degree getters and a vast assembly of professors wonderfully and colourfully clad. There I became aware of something which was a most attractive feature of the day—a mixture of ceremonial and informality. Everything, in fact, was carefully planned according to a century-old ritual, but since dons were doing the arranging, at any moment, you felt, something might go irretrievably wrong. In short, there was a lot of room for divine or human intervention.

About ten, the academic watchdogs had got their straying sheep into line. In front of me was Dag Hammarskjöld in a neat blue suit, behind me Professor Panofsky of Princeton wearing not only the Tudor bonnet but the Tudor ruff of some great German university. (I trust I looked as though I were a graduate of Balmain or Dior.) The Classes of alumni fell in ahead of us, with Fellows and Overseers, the Governor of Massachusetts and a brass band; the Faculty, and the graduates taking degrees behind us; and we set off on a slow procession through the first quadrangle round in front of John Harvard's statue—where all academic bonnets and Overseers' top hats were raised—past the steps of the Widener Library and then straight down the middle of Harvard Yard to the chapel, where a platform and an awning had been set up. All the way the senior class (about to get their B.A.'s) lined the route, and behind them alumni and wives and children stared and clapped and took innumerable photographs. The men had their year prominently displayed—on peaked caps, on breast buttons, on hat bands. Some at least had clearly had a night out, but the mood was decorous and gay.

We took our seats on the dais where Chris Herter joined us, and I found myself in the front row beside him and Hammarskjöld. The seniors filed in—about 900 of them—and then the Sheriff of Middlesex County (in top hat, blue frock coat, brass buttons, epaulettes, and sword) called the meeting to order as he has done for 300 years and more. Before the degrees, we had one Latin and two English orations, from seniors (fourth-year students). The Latin orator was superb, worthy of Cicero who, I am certain, was nowhere near as eloquent and dramatic and, judging by the giggles of the Latinists, amusing too. The second English disquisition made history by being the first time in forty years that religion had been mentioned at a Harvard Commencement, and one could hear secularists grinding their teeth in the audience.

There followed the conferring of degrees, interspersed with loud, joyful singing from the Harvard Glee Club. This was rather a long process, but Chris, Hammarskjöld, and I diverted ourselves by picking out unlikely subjects from among the theses of the new D.Phils. I found "Tooth Replacement in Reptiles," Hammarskjöld picked out "Sex Differentiation in the Embryology of the Reptilian Nose," and we were all nonplussed by Chris's choice—for a Doctorate in Theology—"The Use of Electric Computers in the Study of the Greek Text of the New Testament." Had science and religion met and kissed?

When the time came for the honorary degrees, the Marshal in red robes took from Dr. Pusey the scroll and citation in a flat red folder while Pusey read out the citation and each of us stood up. Mine was: "A charming lady whose respected voice and clear mind calls the West to freedom through faith." (Harvard is noted for the brevity of its citations—for instance, Goheen got: "We salute the chosen one of a favourite sister.")

The whole procedure lasted about five minutes and then the Sheriff of Middlesex County dismissed us. We processed out again down the middle of the Yard and up the steps to Widener where the photographers were massed. There they took us *verbatim et seriatim* and we moistened our lips and did our best, and nothing disturbed the equanimity of our good Nate. At this point, a new escort took me over, a splendid top-hatted Marshal of the class of '32—the 25th year—who, beneath the exterior magnificence, was a good-looking, very prosperous Boston banker. Then we began to make history, for although Helen Keller was the first woman to receive an honorary degree (last year), she took no further part in the celebrations. At lunchtime, ladies are taken off and entertained by Anne Pusey and Faculty wives, while the men are the guests of the officials of the Class of the year at a "spread" in the Fogg Museum. The question was: was I or was I not a woman, and the Class of '32 decided I was not! So I was escorted to the Fogg Museum, and there waiting were a host of friends and a most, most welcome glass of champagne.

In welcoming the gathering, our host, the Chief Marshal, introduced me as the first lady guest in history, and they all stood up and clapped and stamped and I felt like a little girl allowed downstairs for dessert—or Dr. Johnson's woman on her hind legs (or do I mean dog?). But the table flowed with champagne, my companions were most gallant, and, in fact, I had a beautiful time.

At two, we returned to the Yard and formed again into a procession. This time, Pusey, the Fellows and Overseers and honorary doctors led the way and took up stations on the steps of Widener in front of a great arc of "honour guards" (Class of '32 in morning dress). A good deal of chaff passed back and forth, and at one point the escort in charge of Arthur Goodhart looked round at his distinguished classmates and remarked in a ringing voice "Honour guard? Dem's a bunch of bums."

What followed was perhaps the most touching part of a day full of sincere emotion—the marchpast of the alumni, year by year, beginning, by Golly, with a member of the Class of '84. The very ancient fathers had each an escort, and as they made their way by—the feeble, the halt, and the game—one had a sudden sense of the continuity of a great institution and, wider than that, of the passing of the generations and the torch passed on from mind to mind and man to man and so of the continuity of the human family. When the Class of '32 marched in, brave with banners, the insults flowing back and forth from honour guard to marchers were unceasing, and the nobility and the ribaldry mixed in nice proportions.

When the parade had gone forward and filled the seats in the Yard—I wonder how many there were—5,000?—8,000?—along, of course, with sisters and cousins and aunts—we processed up to the dais on which long tables had been placed, and took our places. Then the speechmaking began among the green trees and the cold afternoon breezes. First the Governor of Massachusetts extended his greetings into a longish speech made with an eye on a national audience (but then, *all* Democratic Governors now have presidential aspirations), then Dr. Panofsky made a delicious, erudite, and witty speech in defence of the Ivory Tower which no one enjoyed more than he. Then I spoke, and it really did go well, for at the end—which has not happened in many long years—the entire audience rose to their feet and gave me what is known as a "standing ovation." And Geoffrey [Crowther] (who'd never heard me speak before) was sufficiently overcome to kiss me four times and say he was proud of me. We all went off helter-skelter to the Puseys, and there in the drawing room was Nate, looking solemn and relieved. We were given hot tea, and the mood was one of happy relief—Oh, specially for me, for there are few pleasures to equal the end of speeches.

The day closed with a dinner given by Paul Cabot at a Boston club to the Puseys, the Lamonts, the Archibald MacLeishes, Geoffrey, and a couple of other Harvard officials. It was a quiet and pleasant occasion during which Geoffrey disputed with the Treasurer of Harvard on degrees of permissible inflation, and Nate told me he thought my speech would have more effect than might seem to be immediately possible. We parted about eleven and I went back to Needham with my kind Cabots and to a long, long sleep.

Harvard Alumni Bulletin, December 14, 1957.

Peter J. Gomes

OUR SECULAR SACRAMENT

(1979)

The powerful invocations and benedictions of Peter Gomes have begun or ended the Commencement ceremonies in Harvard's Tercentenary Theater since 1972, and Mr. Gomes has come to have a deep affection and respect for the traditions of this special day in Harvard life. A graduate of Bates College and of Harvard Divinity School, Mr. Gomes began his ministry at Harvard as Assistant Minister in the Memorial Church in 1970, became Acting Minister in 1972, and Plummer Professor of Christian Morals and Minister in 1974. Occupying this central point in the university's life, Mr. Gomes takes his Harvard citizenship very seriously, in both his calling outside the univer-

sity as preacher and public speaker and within the institution as teacher, counselor to students, and as a member of committees concerned with student problems and aspirations. Mr. Gomes has taught the history of the early church, the development of Puritanism, and New England historiography and has recently chaired a committee of faculty and students that developed a proposal for improving relations among racial and ethnic groups at Harvard. Among personal historical interests, he avidly pursues the history of the Plymouth Colony, where he was born, the history of Harvard, and the background of his spiritual forebears.

COMMENCEMENT is not an event, but is rather, as it is so frequently said of Harvard itself, a state of mind. And it is a state of mind that consumes the waking hours of many in the last weeks of May and the first week of June. In this secular age, a sacramental metaphor may be thought to be both too particular and anachronistic to describe those "festival rites" on a sunny Thursday in June, but if a true sacrament is "an outward and visible sign of an inward and spiritual grace," then with that liberty of analogy that characterizes the academic mind, commencement is probably the only authentic secular sacrament we have in the University, if not in the nation, and, like a sacrament, it becomes different things to different people. Perhaps the genius of commencement is its chameleon-like character, and because it is seldom at the same time appreciated in the same manner by its many constituents, it belongs to and has a mysterious claim upon everybody.

Undergraduates, for whom their own commencement is frequently the first one to be witnessed, tend to be surprised to find others present in the Yard at "their" commencement, and wonder sometimes disagreeably who these "other people" are who are cluttering up the platform before their own debut into the society of educated men and women. In a peculiar way, the day belongs to the faculties of the University, the "eruditi professores," who in mothballed plumage saunter at the direction of their harried marshals into the seats of honor on the commencement platform. In a place noted for its decentralized style of government and community, Harvard has only the academic show of commencement to demonstrate its corporate scholarly enterprise. The alumni provide the most vivid contribution to the day: its singular continuity with the age that is past and the age that is waiting before. For generations, candidates for the degrees at commencement have formed a gowned corridor through which has passed the alumni procession led by the oldest ambulatory graduate of the college, followed in hale succession by the classes in descending order.

Impressive as it always is to see the "ancients and honorables" pass amidst the serried ranks assembled of the young, it is even more impressive to consider that he and his colleagues in their time assembled along these same walks as candidates and watched a similar procession led by some worthy of, say, the Class of 1847, and that succession of processions extends back in the memory's eye to that first modest commencement of 1642 under the proud and steady hand of the Reverend President and "Second Founder" of the College, Henry Dunster! Surely, the day belongs to the alumni, not only those present, but those before them, and those yet to come, that silent and universal fellowship in whose presence we who are present serve but as their trustees. It is such tradition that G. K. Chesterton calls "the democracy of the dead." Of it he writes, "Tradition refuses to submit to the small and arrogant oligarchy of those who merely happen to be walking around."

Among those "who merely happen to be walking around," however, are the parents, those men and women who by the sweat of their brow have probably made it possible for their sons and daughters to stand before the President and be admitted by him to their well-earned degrees. Most of these parents are strangers to Harvard: perhaps they delivered their child to the college four or more years before, and perhaps they were invited to return in between and were entertained from time to time. But most make but two trips to Cambridge: the first and the last, and it is this last which vindicates the first. The ceremonies of the day are designed to persuade the parents that they did the right thing.

And most leave Cambridge confident in that fact. Students often suggest that had they their own way, they wouldn't have anything to do with these silly exercises: "I'm doing it for my parents," they say. And so the parents are willing captives of a medieval spectacle, deliberately out of touch with the world from which they have come and to which they shall soon return. And it is the very unreality of the day that has so much appeal: grand processions, squealing bagpipes, a Latin address replete with in-jokes made available to the graduates in translation, the Sheriff of Middlesex, the Harvard Band and its inexhaustible supply of football songs, the man who rings by hand the "joyous peal" on the bell in the tower of Memorial Church, the primitive presidential chair of Edward Holyoke, it is all of a fantastic piece called "Commencement," and, once again like the University of which it is a sign, runs rather than is run.

Someone, observing the rather casual dignity of the day, remarked that commencement is more like a lawn party than a ballet, and a less charitable but more astute observer suggested that the vast assemblage in formation in the old Yard was very much like that wonderfully chaotic game of croquet with flamingos and hedgehogs in *Alice in Wonderland.* First-time visitors to the scene are rather horrified at what appears to be rank confusion, but then they remember that this is, after all, Harvard where conformity, even for self-preservation, has been elevated to the rank of an original sin. That it works at all is a tribute to patience and good will and the general sense that, come what may, the day is to be enjoyed. When the caller has finished his barking chores in the old Yard, he reports, with a bow to the President, that the audience is seated. Whereupon the University Marshal, William G. Anderson, gives the first line in the day's best received dialogue: "Mr. Sheriff, pray give us order." And the Sheriff of Middlesex County rises, removes his silk hat, and with tones perfected over the years for this day, responds "The meeting will be in order." The students yell and cheer, the audience applauds, and the exercises are off. Calling for order in the midst of chaos is a heroic act: neither the morning nor a career could have a more auspicious beginning than this.

It is a relatively easy task to describe the events of the day, to record the wisdom dispensed and the good humor enjoyed. There is a very tangible quality to the occasion with its colorful garb, its archaic speech, the exuberance of youth, and the sentiment of age. Certainly, we can see it all from our particular corner of the canvas and appropriate what we will of it to our peculiar needs and desires. And yet there is something more than these tangible realities—realities that we cannot see but which are equally very much a part of this rare and special day. We have long been citizens of a climate where it has become fashionable to define every mystery and strip every mystique of its veil in order the better to "understand" and "see." And in doing so, we frequently know more and understand less, see more and perceive less. Rituals, sacred and secular, are subject to this scrutiny, largely because rituals not thus "understood" and thereby controlled, intimidate us, suggesting that we are in the power of something beyond our powers to manage or control. We prefer statistics to symbols and meaning to metaphor—or so we say and are told.

But that within us and within our community that longs for wholeness beyond ourselves will not be satisfied with that analytical bill of goods for long. There is a point when the message of the myth exceeds its own meaning, and we with it are both willing and anxious to be caught up in something beyond the realm of mere measure, something that suggests in a world of fragmentation and specialization a whole that is larger than the sum of its parts, participation, as it were, in a primitive past and an expectant future. Willa Cather's epitaph, taken from *My Ántonia*, describes such as true happiness: "That is happiness: to be dissolved into something complete and great."

That sense of participation, belonging, if only for an instant, to the ages, sharing in the succession of learning from Moses and Plato through the academies of Europe and the Universities of Oxford and Cambridge, the fears they addressed, the hopes they represented—in a magical moment all of these and more are ours, a transaction that defies analysis and is yet as real as the shining sun and the falling rain. Much of what happens here can be translated to a somewhat indifferent public by the press with a combination of the epochal (so many thousands listening to the German Chancellor) or the mundane (the number of boiled chickens it takes to make the unbiquitous chicken salad to feed such a multitude).

But few can report or even record what is in essence the spell of the occasion; it is the challenge of continuity that is summoned forth as it has been for over 300 years—the longest running show in America. It is a day for the poets, to whom professors, preachers, and politicians must yield, for they know a rite when they see one, and they know both when to speak and when to keep silent. From their number comes one of our own, T. S. Eliot '10, whose sense of the paradox of ritual, while addressed to realms far beyond our own, is not unhelpful to us as we grope here for secret sense:

> What we call the beginning is often the end
> And to make an end is to make a beginning.
> The end is where we start from.

That is why "they" call it commencement: for it is scarcely a conclusion and barely a beginning, but, for better or worse, it is all that we have got. And so it is that the young go forth, the old return, the line continues, and we fall into place. Fearful, happy, arrogant, sad, sentimental, brave, uncertain and yet confident, alone and yet together,

> We shall not cease from exploration
> And the end of all our exploring
> Will be to arrive where we started
> And know the place for the first time.

Harvard University Gazette, June 7, 1979.

IX

THE ALUMNI

I have not much cause, I sometimes think, to wish my Alma Mater well, personally; I was not often highly flattered by success, and was every day mortified by my own ill fate or ill conduct. Still, when I went today to the ground where I had had the brightest thoughts of my little life and filled up the little measure of my knowledge, and had felt sentimental for a time, and poetical for a time, and had seen many fine faces, and traversed many fine walks, and enjoyed much pleasant, learned, or friendly society,—I felt a crowd of pleasant thoughts, as I went posting about from place to place, and room to chapel.

RALPH WALDO EMERSON (1822)

Why has this throng come up, out of the bustle and strife of the forum and the market-place, to our academic seat? What spirit stirs this multitude today? You have come to pay homage to the University of your love, and through it to all universities.

CHARLES W. ELIOT (1886)

"This," said Mr. George, "you will learn to know as your Alma Mater—which are two Greek words, meaning 'Go as you please.' "

ROLLO'S JOURNEY TO CAMBRIDGE (1880)

It is very pleasant to do you a kindness, and every one is glad of a chance to serve the dear old College. She needs help, and thought, and devotion, and gratitude from us all, for she has given us and our land more than any one of us will give back. She will keep on giving.

HENRY LEE HIGGINSON (1890)

Charles Francis Adams

THE ALUMNI MEET

(1857)

The son and grandson of a president of the United States, Charles Francis Adams (1807–1886) was one of the most distinguished public servants of his time. After an unusual childhood spent partly in Russia and England, he went through the Boston Latin School and graduated from Harvard in 1825 at the age of eighteen. He was trained in the law by Daniel Webster and admitted to practice in Boston four years later. Thereafter he was never out of the public eye. He served as a Whig in the Massachusetts House and Senate, edited the multi-volume works and memoirs of his grandfather and father, wrote articles on American history, ran for vice-president on the Free Soil ticket, managed a Boston daily paper, helped organize the Republican party, and served as American minister to Britain during the Civil War. Throughout his life he showed himself to be a citizen of conviction whose public career was above party and politics. In his detailed journals he recorded his many trips from Quincy to Cambridge on matters connected with the University and its Alumni. He spoke frequently of making the journey not so much because he wanted to as because he felt he ought to. For years active in the Alumni Association, he also served as Overseer and President of the Board from 1869 to 1881.

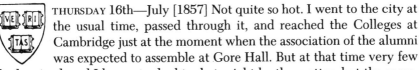 THURSDAY 16th—July [1857] Not quite so hot. I went to the city at the usual time, passed through it, and reached the Colleges at Cambridge just at the moment when the association of the alumni was expected to assemble at Gore Hall. But at that time very few had arrived, and I began to doubt what might be the matter, but the members soon filed in until the library was filled. Among the members however I saw but very few familiar faces. Only five or six of my Class, and a sprinkling of acquaintance, independently of official people. There was a formal meeting at which the process was gone through of an election of officers, but it was only a form. The old set was continued for another year. And it will be continued just so long as Mr. Winthrop fancies the place; when he

does not another sweep will be made, just like the last, so that I may be got rid of in the same way that Sumner was. For such distinctions I have no ambitions, so that it makes no difference to me—and I should never attend such exhibitions, but for the feeling that sometimes I ought to do so, if for no other reason, as representative of opinion. It was this that brought me here today.

At eleven o'clock the procession was formed and we marched to the church which was very soon filled up, though it struck me with a very small proportion of men. Of the alumni I think there could not have been more than eight-hundred. Of others it seemed as if there could not be more than a quarter as many. The galleries and remaining pews below swarmed with women. After a brief prayer by Mr. Mason, Mr. Everett made his speech. The main topic was college culture, which he undertook to defend on its three most disputed divisions, the dead languages, mathematics and metaphysics. But it was not so much a logical argument, as a brilliant series of illustrations rhetorically presented with all the gorgeousness of an oriental imagination. As an Orator for this species of labor Mr. Everett stands at the head of his class in this age. He has all the requisites for producing effects *ad libitum.* But after all it is not the highest species of eloquence. It wants depth of convictions, and earnestness of heart, and force of will. I witnessed this exhibition with just as much satisfaction as I should a very fine display of pyrotechnics, warm and brilliant and dazzling to the *eye,* but productive of not a single internal emotion. And as Mr. Everett grows older his imagination gains upon his reasoning powers, so that what he produces is more effective for a temporary purpose, and less valuable for permanent use. As a defence of the higher walks of education I do not think this will add a feather weight to the present opinion.

The ceremonies finished at half past one. Fifteen minutes later the alumni were once more called together at Gore Hall and marched to the philosophy rooms, (as they used to be called), where we dined. Here was Mr. Winthrop's turn, and he did very well. His own introduction was happy, and his mode of drawing out others would have been equally so, but for the drawback of extravagant compliment showered upon all around. This drew out in succession, the Governor, President Walker, Lord Napier, the British Minister, President Quincy, who was most vociferously cheered, President King of Columbia College, and Mr. Everett. He ended by introducing a gentleman from St. Louis. Mr. Winthrop had warned me that I was next in order. But I saw that the serious and grave thoughts which I had in my mind to present were not at all in harmony with all this, and that perhaps they might imply an invidious and very unwelcome lecture, which I did not mean. My wish was to say a single word in behalf of enthusiasm as a colaborer with knowledge in the support of high education against the inroads of materialism. This is the element the College wants. It has never had it since the decline of the Puritan fervor which founded it. In the last half century it has been in the cold embrace of commercial conservatism, which has piled up wealth on it but has taught it incredulity in all the earnest movements of the country. The representatives of it are such men as Mr. Everett and Mr. Winthrop, fine "chevaux de bataille" for a parade field day, but utterly incompetent to cope with the great moral struggles of the world. Had I touched such a thing as this, it would only have been discordant noise, jangling and out of tune, at best not understood; and if I did not touch that, I was little disposed to join in the race of compliments, so I made up my mind to depart in season, to escape the alternative. I sent a line to Mr. Winthrop telling him not to call me, and went off. This may be a little cowardice on my part too, for I am not ashamed to confess my utter aversion to this species of display, as foreign as possible from all my habits and feelings. I can speak when my mind and heart are full of a subject, and I have had too many proofs of the effect produced at such times to be distrustful of my power—but in cases like these I feel no confidence and therefore never accomplish any success. I took the car to the city and from thence after whiling away an hour at the Athenaeum, to Quincy at seven o'clock.

Massachusetts Historical Society.

Edward A. Weeks, Jr.

REUNIONS IMPROVE WITH AGE

(1933)

While editing the "Graduates' Window," a column in the Harvard Graduates' Magazine, *Edward Weeks turned one June to the thoughts rising in the mind of an alumnus who returned to Harvard for the festivities of Class Day and Commencement. The result, said only as Weeks could say it, appears below. One of the most versatile of his time in the field of American letters, Weeks was editor of the* Atlantic Monthly *from 1938 to 1966.He describes here a once familiar feature of Class Day, the alumni gathering for the Yale baseball game.*

FROM a seat high in the bleachers—those bleachers which were seemingly designed for a legless generation—gazing down at the assembly of the homecoming classes, the Graduate (whose class this year had not come home to roost) let his thoughts ruminate on Commencement. The turf of Soldiers Field stretched away to the furthest extremity of a home run. The sharp regular thud of the pitch was now and again broken by a hit, when the murmur of the crowd would break into a shout. Bands blared and the skirling of bagpipes opposite first base indicated the youngest graduates preparing to give every assistance to the Yale pitcher when the inevitable blow-up should occur. Nearer the plate sat the ten- and fifteen-year veterans, a little thinner on top, a little fuller at the bottom, a little less excited by the ball game, a little more interested in each other. Beyond the Yale bench rose the family phalanx of the twenty-fifth reunion and beyond them clustered the Old Guard. In the intervals of play the eye traversed the Charles to the green boundary of the trees, and above, Memorial and the towers of new Harvard.

The prospect of beating Yale is always inviting but, thought the Graduate, it certainly needs a deeper persuasion than this to fetch these people together. The meeting of friends long separated can be, and too often is, an embarrassing affair: the reunion of war veterans demonstrates how painfully self-conscious such things may be. College friendships are more homogeneous and less compulsory than those of 1917, yet up to the occasion of the twenty-fifth reunion it is an exceptional class that can call back more than one man in every seven. Of the delinquent six some—an unhappily high proportion these days—stay at home for the sake of economy; others because of a constitutional aversion to the "glad hand"; others, a few perhaps, being disappointed in their expectation of a career, prefer to avoid their contemporaries; and still others are too careless or too remote to make the effort.

Reunion begins as a network of small independent intimacies but as glasses are filled and emptied a feeling of cordiality extends from group to group. The glass that cheers is surely the most valuable means of banishing shyness and of obliterating those superficial partitions which college erects between its undergraduates. John Barleycorn is an Honorary Member of every good class.

The Graduate still relishes the remembrance of how the "spark" of 19— resolutely unwound the fire hose and with it washed a mercenary hotel manager out of his own lobby. He remembers a once-famous stroke rowing a dinghy around and around and around Marblehead harbor *with one oar* while the class on the lawn of the Rockmere performed as a coxswain should. Why this was so unspeakably funny is hard to say, but it was. Yet on soberer reflection the Graduate takes some satisfaction in the thought that the breaking and entering which seemed to characterize so many reunions directly after the war (and for which the hard stuff of Prohibition was no little responsible) has calmed down. It is no longer necessary to break three hundred glasses and fifteen windowpanes in order to prove that you've been college graduates for six years. Amen! Amen! sigh the hotel proprietors on the Cape.

It requires, of course, something more than equal parts of gin and sentiment to make a reunion attractive. It requires in the first place a good Class Secretary, a man with a friendly memory and an indefatigable grasp of detail. It requires a Class Bible, a *Who's Who* which whether its entries be reticent or fulsome has the singular virtue of being honest. It requires an old *Lampoon* editor to point up the publicity. It requires a brass band and a soiled Roman toga and the chance of beating Yale. But most of all it requires a man (some classes have more than one) with a genius for loyalty—"one of those individuals" as Carroll Perry says

> who fall in love with an *institution* and never get over it: one of those to whom Alma Mater means also wife and children ... He knew every man who had graduated and all the sometime members of the class as well. These last he managed to fetch back to the reunions in equal proportions to the graduates. He knew just who had died in the quarter-century and how it all happened, and in what condition they had left their families.

Mr. Perry was writing of Williams College but his words fit an occasional Harvard man in our memory.

Judging from what he hears of the Old Guard and from what he has experienced in his own time the Graduate concludes that reunions improve with age. The forced conviviality, the almost ostentatious exclusiveness of certain individuals, the shy reticence of others fade from the scene as time goes on. This is not because we learn the secret of Rotarians as we grow older. It is simply the mellow effect of an evolutionary process. In the process of maturity talents latent in college are discovered. Integrity and unswerving purpose that were once suspected by the few are now recognized by the many. Men have emerged, as it were, from the hidden recesses of their ambition, the doors of social indifference no longer shut them apart, they are, as the saying goes, ready "to take off their hats and tell their right names."

This evolution of a Class, this slow appraisal of the other fellow, is hardly complete before middle life. Some Classes attain a quicker perception than others but not till men have been twenty—twenty-five—years "out" do they come back to Cambridge eagerly and with that mingling of affection, respect—and tolerance!—which is best to be seen in the midst of the Old Guard. From that time forward professional entertainers are no longer necessary to top off the banquet; the class would rather hear from its own members especially those who "have done things." And even though this may result in such plain speaking as Mr. Sinclair Lewis indulged in at New Haven, the effect, once the shock has subsided, is for the good. In college we saw as through a glass darkly, but now face to face.

It is habitual for young men to gauge their efforts by the past and to put complete confidence in the future. Thus a young writer may say to himself "when Keats was my age he had written *Hyperion*" or "a year from now I shall be as old as Dickens when he wrote *Pickwick*" and spur himself on accordingly. But by mid-life the future has ceased to beckon with such sure promise; it is the present which holds us fast. "Getting and spending we lay waste our powers." And what a relief it is to shake off the traces, to rest in the green shade and chew the cud of experience. A wife of '07, Mrs. Helen Garnsey Haring, attending her first Harvard reunion, the twenty-fifth, saw this instantaneously, and wrote it down for others to remember. "The men of our generation" she wrote,

> twenty-five years out of College have borne the major weight of the late War and of the economic débâcle. We have become accustomed to weary and tense faces. But those June days of holiday-making, of relaxing in inti-mate companionship with others whose hopes, experiences, and fears had exactly paralleled theirs through the years, gradually eased the intolerable strain. There must have been more than one wife who knew that "it was months since she'd heard her husband laugh like that."

To recognize as we do at reunions that we have kept step with our con-temporaries is a fine and heartening thing, yet there is more to the Cam-bridge return than mere personal gratification. To the Old Guard, to those who have gone thirty—forty—fifty years onwards, there is a special signifi-cance in Commencement Day. The class dinners, of course, are more than dinners, for as the members decrease and the ranks close up there is more occasion than ever to revive the days of the past and the names that are memories. But on Commencement Day itself, as one passes down between the ranks of the Seniors, as one listens to President Lowell (more impressive than ever on this, his last appearance) confer the degrees, as one "spreads" on the perennial salad and then goes marching past the dignitaries on the steps of Widener, the feeling arises that we are part of something bigger than ourselves, of something more durable than the trees in the yard or the bricks of the buildings. In these days of shaken confidence and little faith it is good to come back to a firm foundation . . .

Harvard Graduates' Magazine, September, 1933.

Henry Richards

SENIOR IN THE LONG PROCESSION
(1936)

Eighty-eight years old at the time of the Harvard Tercentenary, Henry Rich-ards, A.B. 1869, lived on to reach the age of 101, but ironically, for one so devoted and loyal to the College, he never achieved the honor of "oldest liv-ing graduate." For some years he trailed Theodore Parker Adams, A.B. 1867, two years his elder, and from his bed sent confidential inquiries via family

members to the Harvard alumni office as to "how Adams is getting along."
Richards was a lifelong resident of Gardiner, Maine, the son-in-law of that
formidable couple Samuel Gridley and Julia Ward Howe. For years Rich-
ards operated a highly successful summer camp and sent an impressive
band of descendants and a still more numerous flock of former campers to
the College. This account of the Tercentenary was written for his classmate
the Reverend Francis G. Peabody.

Gardiner, Maine

DEAR FRANK:

When I found but three members of the Class of '69—beside myself—
lined up at our flag station in front of University Hall for the opening march
of the Tercentenary ceremonial, thoughts of absent friends, especially of
you, threatened to becloud the great day for me. And the shadows length-
ened when I found myself the senior Class Marshal in the long procession—the flags of classes from '60 to '68 being borne by "representatives."

Present and on time for '69 were Browne, Fay, and Fox—poor Browne
afflicted with heart trouble so serious that he could do no more than greet us
all round before his son took him away to rest, Fox with mind so beclouded
that it wrung one's heart to see him, but Fay "all there" and occupied entirely with the story of the small flag he had carried every year since 1929,
young Austen Fox accompanying his father, and my Hal—appointed to
provide eyes for me—swelled our ranks to four, marching by twos behind
me.

Next but one to the rear was Bishop Lawrence, flag marshal of '71,
much perturbed because he had to hand the flag over to his substitute, William Chatfield (no classmate being present) and don his gown in Widener to
appear with the dignitaries.

The interval during which the long line was falling in in marching order
brought many friends across the Yard for a handshake and a pleasant word.
Then came the successive bugle calls, and the memorable pageant was on.
Nothing could have been more tastefully designed, better ordered, or more
perfectly carried out. The march of the classes, the long double line of marshals down the center aisle of the "Theater," each holding his flag at "order
arms," the decoration of the dais and banks of seats in front of the College
Church, made a setting worthy of the procession of "dignitaries" (840 of
them) from Widener to their seats.

And when the Chimes of Southwark Cathedral rang out, sweet and
clear, one could feel, almost sensibly, the community of spirit all round the
world which animated the whole great gathering on the great day.

The music—admirably selected and beautifully performed by the band
and the Tercentenary Chorus—contributed greatly to the impressiveness of
the occasion, to which most of the speakers rose most adequately. Conant's

citations of the recipients of honorary degrees were well up to the high standard set by Eliot.

There were present representatives of 325 universities and colleges in the United States and Canada, delegates from the universities and learned societies of 45 countries in Europe, Asia, and Africa—yes, and Australia.

And the morning proceedings ended with a march in reverse order, just as the rain began to pour. We were all fairly well soaked, and the authorities—to avert pneumonia—provided several cases of "Scotch" which were well patronized by the dignitaries.

After the Chief Marshal's luncheon, in Memorial Hall, because of the downpour, the Alumni meeting in the afternoon was held in Sanders Theater, with President Lowell presiding.

He was admirable—needless to say. Franklin Roosevelt was adequate enough . . . I am happy to say that he was received with a good round of applause, which he needed—poor man—to help him face an audience almost unanimously opposed to him and all his works.

The highlight of the afternoon, to my mind, was the address of the Master of Balliol. Lowell introduced Conant to move the adjournment in a beautiful impromptu, and Conant hit a high note in his motion to adjourn to 2036.

Singing by the chorus and audience was most impressive, and there was a fine example of care in planning and timing when Lowell introduced Stanley Baldwin, and Baldwin responded—snap—just as promptly as if he had been standing by Lowell.

So it all ended, and I doubt if the world has ever before seen such a gathering of the great company of scholars, black, white, and yellow, male and female, all united in one spirit and one purpose.

Affectionately yours,
HENRY RICHARDS

Harvard Alumni Bulletin, April 23, 1955.

John P. Marquand

MR. HILLIARD TELLS ALL

(1941)

It seems superfluous to introduce John Phillips Marquand, A.B. 1915, to a Harvard audience or any audience. His preoccupation with the foibles of a certain stratum of our American society is so widely known that no remarks are necessary, save to say that he seems to have the matter well in hand. "Harvard is a subject that I still face with mixed emotions," he wrote to his

Class secretary in 1940. "I brought away from it a number of frustrations and illusions which have handicapped me through most of my life. Yet, on the other hand, Harvard taught me the value of intellectual enthusiasm. In spite of the efforts of Drs. Lowell and Conant, I still observe that one of its best known products is a type with which I find myself identified that has difficulty in surviving or making itself understood west of the Appalachians or south of New Jersey. This, I think, is as it should be. All institutions of learning, even the greatest, should have a local flavor." Here then is a little of the local flavor as a group of Marquand's characters, Mr. Harry Pulham included, go about planning their 25th anniversary celebration.

THE PRIVATE dining room contained an oval table. There was a picture of the Grand Canyon on one wall and a yellowed photograph of Boston after the fire of 1872 on the other.

"All right, boys," Bo-jo said. "Sit down anywhere. And get the soup on. We're all hungry."

First there was oxtail soup, and then came breaded veal cutlets, and then came a choice of blueberry pie or ice cream—a heavy lunch, more than I was used to eating, more than any of us wanted to eat—except Chris Evans, who looked hungry. The conversation was scattered as though we had come to realize that we were not there to talk. Curtis was telling me about his boat. Bo-jo was talking to Charley Roberts at the end of the table.

"Charley," he said, "what do you do for exercise these days?"

"I think about it mostly," Charley said.

"That's the way it is," said Bo-jo. "Doctors never take care of themselves."

"There isn't any time," Charley answered.

"Now, don't pull that on me," Bo-jo said. "Every doctor I know is always on a cruise or amusing himself whenever someone is having a baby. You doctors always consider yourselves as a class apart."

"We don't," Charley said.

"You doctors," Bo-jo told him, "always pretend you know everything. Now, actually, there are just as many boneheads in the medical profession as there are in business. Why, I damned near went to the medical school myself."

"That ought to bear your statement out," said Charley.

"I'm just saying," Bo-jo said, "that doctors don't know everything."

"Well, they don't," Charley said.

"They either assume they know everything," said Bo-jo, "or else they take the other tack. They say they just don't know."

"Well, what do you want us to do?" Charley asked.

"Now, that's begging the question," Bo-jo said. "And you've got plenty of time to exercise if you want to. Look at me. Sometimes I don't get home till ten o'clock, but I always have time for exercise. If I can't do anything else I get on the rowing machine."

"Whose rowing machine?" Charley asked.

"My rowing machine," Bo-jo said. "I have one in my dressing room in town and one out in the country. If all you boys had rowing machines you'd be better off. Every morning of my life I get on it for half an hour before breakfast, and when I get home I get on it and get up a good sweat before I change, and frankly I'm just as fit as I ever was. Do you know what I did last night?"

Faces turned toward him. No one knew what he had done.

"I was up at Joe Royce's for dinner, and I don't know how it came up, but somehow he bet me that I couldn't walk downstairs on my hands. I walked down two flights of stairs on my hands."

"Did you get corns on them?" Charley asked. Bo-jo began to laugh, and he beckoned to the waiter.

"You can pass around the Scotch-and-soda now," he said. "We'll have brandy with the coffee."

Curtis Cole had stopped talking about the boats, and Bob Ridge leaned across the table.

"Curtis, before we forget it we might make an appointment."

"What for?" Curtis asked.

"What we were talking about, Curtis. It's just a formality. What time do you get up in the morning?"

Curtis Cole's eyes opened wider.

"Now, look here, Bob," he said. "I know you've got to make a living—"

"You just tell me what time you get up in the morning," Bob said, "and I'll be right there."

"What the deuce are you boys talking about?" Bo-jo asked.

"Nothing," said Bob. "It's just a business matter, Bo-jo."

"Well, what are you going to do to Curtis in the morning?"

Curtis Cole pushed back his chair.

"He isn't going to do one damned thing to me in the morning."

"It's just a matter of business, Bo-jo," Bob said.

"Now, we're not here to talk business," Bo-jo said.

"I'm glad to hear you say it," Curtis said.

"What are you so sore about?" Bo-jo asked. "What's the matter with you, Curtis?"

"We'd better skip it," Curtis said. "But I'm just tired of having my classmates try to sell me things."

"Now, listen, boys," said Bo-jo, "let's not talk about business."

After the dessert was taken away we had coffee and brandy and cigars. I looked at my watch. It was two o'clock.

"Bo-jo," I said, "this has been perfectly swell, but I ought be be getting back."

"Now, listen," said Bo-jo, "no one has to go back for a while, anywhere.

If you boys just relax and lean back and listen, I've got something to say that's important. We've got to put aside personal matters. We've all got to do something for the Class."

Bo-jo leaned his elbow on the table. He passed one of his hands over his close-cropped head and his eyebrows drew together.

"I don't know how it is," Bo-jo said, and he gave a quick short laugh, "that I always get things put over on me. I'm always the one who has to do all the work. Now when we have to get ready for the Twenty-fifth here I am and everybody comes around to me and says, Well, go ahead, get it started, you're elected. Well, all right. I'm going to get it started. There'll be a lot of committees before we get through—entertainment committees and God knows what; but in the end it's going to come down to the graduates who live around here. It's up to us whether or not our Twenty-fifth is going to be something to remember, and when I thought it over I wondered how it would be if we started with just a small, informal committee, made up of people who didn't want to blow their own horns, but who are loyal to the Class, and who aren't afraid to work. That's why I picked you men. We're just our own little committee and by God we're going to take off our coats and pitch in." No one said anything.

"Now, don't look so blank," Bo-jo said. "It isn't going to be tough when we get started. We're all going to get right behind this and push it through, and we're all going to have a damned good time. Of course the whole system is pretty well worked out. The classmates and their wives and kids arrive and we put them into dormitories. But then the wives have to be entertained, and the kids have to be entertained, and we have to be entertained. Someone's got to see that the kids don't all get mixed up. Well, the wives can do that. But the thing that's bothering me is the big final entertainment, the one the whole class takes part in, the wives and kids and everybody. Now, last year they had a band playing popular tunes and the kids sang the old songs. Everybody had a good time except some of the kids got lost. Now, has anybody got suggestions about an entertainment?"

There was another silence.

"Come on—come on," Bo-jo said. "Naturally there'll be a ball game and a men's dinner and an outing at some country club or else at someone's place at Brookline, if anyone at Brookline has a place big enough. But what worries me is what about the entertainment. How about it, boys?"

"Someone might write a show," Curtis said. "I hear they did that once."

"All right," said Bo-jo. "Who can write a show? Can anyone here write one?"

No one seemed able to write one. Bo-jo's glance, level and confident, turned diagonally across the table toward Chris Evans.

"How about it, Chris?" he asked. "Can't you write a show?"

Chris put both his elbows on the table.

"I don't know how, and besides I haven't got the time."

"Well, go ahead and try," Bo-jo said. "That's the least anyone can do."

"I haven't got the inclination," Chris said, and his voice grew edgy. "And I haven't got the time because I work for my living."

"Well, we've all got to take a little time out and work for this," said Bo-jo, "and it's going to be like a vacation. We're all going to recapture something of the old days. Frankly, now, doesn't everyone agree that the happiest time he ever spent was those four years back at Harvard?"

No one replied, and it was hard to tell whether the silence meant agreement or not.

"And there's one thing more," Bo-jo said, "that I know you'll agree with. Our Class is the best damned class that ever came out of Harvard, and the reason is that we've always pulled together. Now, it's been suggested that someone in the class write a show. Well, that's a good suggestion, and that's what we're here for. Well, who can write it—someone who was in the Lampoon or the Pudding or something? We had one of the best damned Pudding shows I ever saw. Do you remember Spotty Graves doing the tight-rope act? We've got to have Spotty in the show."

"Spotty Graves has passed on," Bob Ridge said.

"Passed on where?" said Bo-jo.

"He passed on the year before last," Bob Ridge said. "He left a wife and four children, and only five thousand dollars in insurance. Not enough to clean up with."

"Oh, yes," said Bo-jo. "That's right. I remember now, but that's beside the point. Now, we certainly have a lot of literary birds in the Class if we try to think of them, a lot of quiet birds who didn't distinguish themselves much. That's one of the things that gripes me about Yale. The Elis are always wheeling out the Yale poets and the Yale literary group. Why, hell, we have a lot of the same thing in the Class, except we don't shout about them. Now, who is there who can write a show?"

"There's Bill King," I said. "Bill always has a lot of ideas."

"It's my personal opinion," Bo-jo said, "that Bill King's a bastard. I wouldn't be surprised if he were a Communist, and we don't want any smart, unconstructive cracks. What we want is something full of pep and good nature. Who else is there?"

Bo-jo looked around the table.

"Well," he said, "can't anybody think of anybody else? All right. I'll tell you what we'll do. We'll let Chris think about it for us. Chris, you think up the names of five people who can write a show and let me know the first of the week."

"All right," said Chris.

"And now we've got to keep our minds open," said Bo-jo. "Are there any other suggestions?"

"How about getting one of those professionals," Curtis Cole asked, "who organize song and dance shows?"

"All right," said Bo-jo. "Now we're talking. You make it a business to look it up, Curt. Send me in a memorandum of five of those professionals the first of the week. And now I've got an idea."

"Go ahead," said Charley. "It must be good."

Bo-jo glanced at the ceiling and flicked his cigar ash into his coffee cup.

"The main problem as I see it," he said, "is to get everyone in the proper spirit. Now, I don't know anything that makes people more happy than a good fight."

"A fight?" Bob Ridge asked. "What sort of a fight?"

"Boxing," said Bo-jo. "Two good game, fast lightweights, to fight ten exhibition rounds. We ought to get them cheap just for the publicity."

Charley Roberts looked at Bo-jo with interest. "Are you serious about that?" he asked.

"It surprises you, doesn't it?" Bo-jo inquired. "Well, it did me too when I thought of it first, but the more you think of it the better you'll like it. Two good game boys, right on a platform in the Harvard Yard, pasting each other. Why, it'll drive everybody crazy! It'll take them out of themselves. They won't remember where they are."

"But I thought the whole object of this thing was for everyone to remember where he was," Chris Evans said.

"That's beside the point," said Bo-jo.

"If you're going to get them," Charley Roberts said, "why not pick heavyweights?"

"Now you've got the spirit," said Bo-jo. "I've thought of that. They're too expensive, Charley."

"Well, why not get ten niggers in a battle royal?" Charley asked. "That ought to take the boys and girls out of themselves."

Bo-jo Brown wrinkled up his forehead.

"Now, look here, boys," he said, "we didn't come here to throw water on good ideas. There's nothing easier than knocking. Bob, I want you to go down to Mike's Gymnasium on Scollay Square. Just go and see Mike personally and ask Mike for the names of some good boys who want publicity, and let me know what you find first thing next week. Got it, Bob?"

"All right," Bob said, "if you really want me to, Bo-jo."

"Now we're getting somewhere," Bo-jo said. "Now, suppose we don't have boxing. That gets us back to song and dance stuff, doesn't it? Charley, you haven't got a job yet. Suppose you get busy and ask around about talent in the class—boys, girls, everybody—tap dancers, saxophones, stunts— We've got to have a lot of stunts—people who can do card tricks or impersonations."

"I haven't got much time," said Charley.

"You told us that before," Bo-jo said. "Just get off your fanny and get busy."

Bo-jo pushed back his chair and rose.

"Well," he said, "I've got to be getting back to the office now. We're all started—set to go. There's nothing like a talk around a table to get ideas. I've had a swell time and I hope you all have, and we'll get together sometime soon. Oh, Harry—"

"Yes," I said.

Bo-jo slapped me on the back and took a firm hold on my arm.

Harry, here, thought he was going to get off easy. Well, I haven't forgotten Harry. You're coming right down to the office with me now."

"Now, listen, Bo-jo," I said. "It's three o'clock."

"Don't I know it's three o'clock?" Bo-jo asked me. "I'm not crabbing about the time, am I? Besides, it won't take long—your job hasn't really started yet. All right, boys, is everything all straight? All right. Let's go."

The club was nearly deserted when Bo-jo and I got our hats from the checkroom. The only members left in the newspaper room were four old gentlemen who would have been my father's age if my father had been living. They sat in black leather armchairs rustling the papers, and I heard one of them speaking querulously.

"You can blame it all on Wilson," he said, "and the League of Nations."

Outside on the sidewalk Bo-jo took me by the arm again.

"Well," Bo-jo said, "it's a great life, isn't it?"

"How do you mean it's a great life?" I asked.

"Exactly what I say," Bo-jo answered, "a great life. What's the matter? Are you sore about something?"

"I was just thinking," I said. "I never realized that I'd been alive so long."

"What the hell's the matter with you?" Bo-jo asked. "What got that idea into your head?"

"Up there at lunch," I said. "I'd never realized that we were all so old."

"Now, that's a hell of a way to talk," Bo-jo said. "We're not old."

"We're in our middle forties," I said.

"That isn't old," Bo-jo said. "You're just as old as you feel. I'm just as good as I ever was, and so are you, but I see what you mean. Those other people up there looked terrible. It's because they don't take care of themselves. Not enough exercise. Too much worry."

"Maybe they have to worry," I said.

"No one has to worry. Look at me. I never worry."

His grip on my arm tightened. He began walking faster with the swift, elastic step of youth, drawing deep breaths of the humid spring air. There was still a crowd in front of the subway station, sailors talking to girls in tight silk dresses, two or three newsboys, a blindman and the old lady feeding the pigeons bread crumbs out of a brown paper bag.

"There's one thing I can always do," Bo-jo said. "I can always get people to work."

"I know you can," I said. "It's a gift, Bo-jo."

"It's just knowing how to handle them," Bo-jo went on. "Now, those boys are going to wear their fingers off. There's nothing like class spirit. It gets you out of yourself. If you want to be happy, get out of yourself."

On Washington Street in front of the news bulletins the paper boys were shouting. Their voices rose above the scuffling of shoe leather on the pavements.

"London Cabinet in session," they were shouting. "All about it. Braintree woman burned to death. All about it."

"It would be funny," I said, "wouldn't it, if it started all over again? It's about the same time of year."

"Forget it," Bo-jo said. "Get it out of your mind."

Bo-jo's offices were large and newly decorated. There was a rail with a boy sitting behind a table. Bo-jo pushed me in front of him.

"Come on," he said. "Come on."

"All right," I said, "but I can't stay long, really."

"Come on," said Bo-jo. "It won't take a minute. It's about the lives."

"You mean about the lives of the Class," I asked, "the biographies?"

"What's the matter with you?" Bo-jo asked. "Do you think I'm talking French? Come inside here and look."

Bo-jo opened the door of a long room. There were two large tables against the walls heaped with papers and form letters and two girls were seated at desks typing.

"Look here," I said. "This anniversary of ours is more than a year off, isn't it?"

Bo-jo slapped me on the shoulder.

"Now you're talking," he answered. "But we're not going to get caught out. It's time we began organizing."

I still could not understand him.

"All these papers," I said, "all these pictures—they haven't got anything to do with our Class, have they?"

"Now you're getting it," Bo-jo answered. "Of course it isn't *our* Class. This is the year ahead of us, this year's Twenty-fifth. Their Class Secretary works right in this office—you know him, Jake Meek—this is his staff and we're using the same girls for our book. This is Miss Ferncroft, Mr. Pulham. This is Miss Josephs, Mr. Pulham."

The girls turned around in their swivel chairs and smiled.

"Where do I come in?" I asked.

Bo-jo slapped me on the shoulder again and nearly threw me off balance.

"Why," he answered, "you're the one who's going to chase everybody and get their lives. You're going to have general oversight of the book—all the paper work, all the editing—someone's got to do it."

"Why doesn't our Class Secretary do it?" I asked. "That's what he's meant for."

Bo-jo frowned.

"Now, that isn't the right way to look at it, Harry," he said. "You know Sam Green. Sam's the best damned secretary any class has ever had, but he's got to have help, hasn't he? Now, let's get this straight. Are you going to let the Class down, or aren't you?"

"But look here, Bo-jo," I said. "I'm not accustomed to doing anything like this, and besides I haven't got the time."

Bo-jo gave my chest a playful push, causing me to take two steps backward.

"Now you're talking," he said. "I knew you'd get into the spirit of it. Time—why, the job doesn't really begin until next autumn. All you have to do now is to go over the general organization with Miss Ferncroft."

"But look here," I said. "This will take hours and hours."

"And when you take off your coat and start pitching in," Bo-jo went on as though he had not heard me, "you're going to be fascinated by it, and we're all going to have a swell time working together. I'm busy now and I've got to duck out. It's great to have seen you, Harry. I haven't had such a good time in years."

"Wait a minute, Bo-jo," I said.

Bo-jo pulled the door open and waved his other hand.

"It's a big meeting down the street," he said. "I'll see you later, boy"— and then the door closed, and I was on one side of it and Bo-jo was on the other.

I looked at the papers for a moment and then I looked at Miss Ferncroft. It was only right that someone should do this for the Class, but I did not see why it was put to me particularly; and yet I did not want to be disagreeable.

I picked up some of the typewritten sheets which were clipped together. They began with a printed form, dealing with the life of someone in college just about my time.

"And then there are the photographs," Miss Ferncroft said. "We're having a great deal of trouble collecting the photographs of before and after."

They would be the pictures of young men in high collars taken from the first Class Report, and then there would be the pictures of the way we were today, bald-headed, gray-headed, weary—and what had it all been about?

"So you can see," Miss Ferncroft said, "why Mr. Brown needs help."

"Yes, I can see," I said.

Then I began to read the manuscript which I was holding. It was written by someone whom I had never known. The name was Charles Mason Hilliard.

BORN: Ridgely, Illinois, March 23rd, 1893; son of Joseph, Gertrude (Jessup) Hilliard.

PREPARED AT: Ridgely High School and Brock Academy.

COLLEGE DEGREES: A.B., LL.B.

MARRIED: Martha Gooding, New York City.

CHILDREN: Mary Gooding, Roger, Thomas.

OCCUPATION: Lawyer.

ADDRESS: (*Business*) Mortgage Building, New York.
(*Home*) Mamaroneck, New York.

"He doesn't give any dates," I said.

"That's the trouble," said Miss Ferncroft. "No one ever follows instructions."

I continued reading John Mason Hilliard's personal history.

After leaving Law School I joined the firm of Jessup and Goodrich in New York. Five years later I was employed by the firm of Jones and Jones. I am now a partner in the firm of Watkins, Lord, Watkins, Bondage, Green, Smith and Hilliard. I have been very busy all this time practising corporation law and trying to raise a family. My work at Law School was interrupted by the war in which I served as a First Lieutenant, Engineer Corps. This seems to me a strange interlude, unrelated to my other activities. I still like to go to the football games and cheer for Harvard. My chief avocation is watching my children grow up. I am an Episcopalian, and I bowl occasionally and sometimes play golf. In politics I am a Republican, hoping that the day will come when Mr. Roosevelt leaves the White House. Ten years ago it was my good fortune to be sent on business to the Pacific Coast. I made the most of this opportunity for travel and still hope sometime, if I ever have a long enough vacation, to take the family to see the Grand Canyon. Harvard has always seemed to me the best educational institution in the world, and I can hope for nothing better than that my sons will follow my footsteps (which I trust they will do, if we can get Mr. Roosevelt out of the White House) and gain from our old Alma Mater what I have gained, both in experience and peace of mind. I have not had the time which I have wished for reading good books. On leaving college I started Gibbon's *Decline and Fall of the Roman Empire* and Nicolay and Hay's *Lincoln*. I am still working on them in my spare time and hope to report to those who are interested at the reunion that I have finished this self-imposed stint.

"Is this characteristic?" I asked Miss Ferncroft.

"Well, they all seem to be pretty much like that," Miss Ferncroft answered. "It's funny. Most of them have been so busy working that they haven't had time to do anything."

"Would you give me a sheet of note paper, please, Miss Ferncroft," I asked her, "and have you a fountain pen?" She handed me a sheet of note paper, and I sat down in front of it. I did not like what I was going to do, because in a sense it was disloyal to the Class. Nevertheless, I had been making up my mind. It was an imposition.

Dear Bo-jo [I wrote],
It was perfectly swell seeing you at lunch, and as you say, the idea of working on our Class Book is fascinating. I can't tell you how much I wish I could go ahead the way you ask me, but, as a matter of fact, I am going to be very busy, especially toward autumn, and I do not feel I am quite the person to undertake the responsibility. I can't tell you how flattered I am that you feel I am up to it.

What I had written sounded weak. I tore the paper up and put it in the wastebasket and started out again.

Dear Bo-jo,
You shoved this job off on me, because you thought I'd be flattered and because you think I am easily imposed upon. Though I accept you and eat your lunch, I can see that you are a fathead. What do I care what happens to the Class Report?

This was more what I wanted to say, but somehow you can't say things like that. I tore the paper up and tried another sheet.

Dear Bo-jo,
I forgot to tell you that it looks as though I shall have to take a long business trip to New York and Kay and I have been talking about going out to the Pacific Coast next autumn and next winter. Fascinating as all this work will be, I am sure you can see how I can't readily undertake it, but thanks ever so much for asking me.

I was aware that none of this was true. It might be possible that I could suggest to Kay that we go away somewhere, but if I did so it was doubtful whether she would do it, with bills coming in the way they were. I tore the letter up and threw it in the wastebasket.

Dear Bo-jo [I wrote again],
Before I really start out on this perhaps we'd better talk about it a little more.

Yours,
HARRY

I folded the letter and placed it in an envelope and handed it to Miss Ferncroft.

"Will you please give this to Mr. Brown?" I said. "Sometime when he isn't too busy. And I'm afraid I'll have to be going now."

"But you'll be back, won't you?" Miss Ferncroft asked.

H. M. Pulham, Esquire (Boston, 1941).

Willard L. Sperry

THE ALUMNUS

(1947)

Familiarity with English university life (he was a Rhodes scholar at Oxford) gave Willard L. Sperry the proper perspective to comment on the Alumnus as a phenomenon of the American educational scene. Dean Sperry could boast a universality of alumni experience with which few are blessed, since in addition to Oxford he had academic ties with Olivet College, Yale, Amherst, Brown, Williams, and Boston University, as well as Harvard. For thirty-one years Dean of the Harvard Divinity School, he was Plummer Professor of Christian Morals at Harvard from 1929 to 1953. Among his fifteen books is a delightful volume of reminiscent sketches, Summer Yesterdays in Maine, *which established him as a master in the art of the familiar essay.*

I

I SUPPOSE the real trouble was that I was coming down with a bad cold. I knew that I was already running a temperature. What is more I was some hundreds of miles from home. I had written the local Pullman office weeks earlier asking for a lower berth on that night. I had gone to the station that afternoon to pick up my reservation. After inching along in line for half an hour, I had been told that there was nothing for me. My protest that I had applied some time ago elicited only the threadbare liturgical response, "My God! Haven't you heard there's a war on?"

I then made the round of hotels near the station. Nothing doing. The lobbies were filled with men in uniform, and the desk clerk used the same liturgy as the man at the Pullman window. *In extremis* I called up a friend of other years and asked could he possibly get me in at his University Club? After ten minutes the answer came back: Yes, there would be a room for me.

This welcome news mitigated the mood of self-pity though it did not entirely dispel it. These colds; one never knows. It might be some sort of galloping pneumonia of which one dies within 36 hours. But at any rate I should not be found dead on a bench in the park. If I were to die, it would be decently in bed at the Club. A stubborn residual childishness did not prevent me from picturing my wife arriving too late to receive my whispered benediction and having to deal only with the cheerless business of hunting up the nearest mortician and getting "the remains" shipped home.

However, the first glimpse of the Club lobby was reassuring. I realized that I was a privileged person in being admitted at all, and I tried to rise to the occasion. The lounges lying beyond the lobby, lined with intimate nooks like the apsidal chapels of a cathedral, had an air of high seriousness. Architecturally they were in the best Tudor tradition, matching the fabric of the institution they served. Plainly, it is increasingly improbable that any American can hope to get an education hereafter in any building other than Perpendicular Gothic.

Elderly club servants in somewhat moth-eaten vestments—these too in the best English baronial tradition—were shuffling about with trays of ritual cocktails being served to what President Eliot once called—and his successors still call—"the society of educated men." Even the olives and cherries, the orange peel, and toothpicks in the glasses seemed to have taken on moral dignities and a sense of mission which they can never hope to attain in the outer illiterate world where they are at the best the unashamed symbols of candid self-indulgence.

The desk clerk handed me my guest card, and I found that I was assigned to "The 1894 Room"; he mentioned the assignment to the porter with a kind of reverent awe. This aged lackey delivered me there in due time and seemed not unwilling to honor the usual club rule about no tips in its breach rather than its observance. So there I was for the night, if not longer—indeed until the end.

I had forgotten the '90s. At that time I was not much concerned with aesthetics, being in the Philistine years of adolescence. But somehow the initial view of the room rang a far-off bell. The bed was larger than these straitened years now allow; it was a shameless out-size double bed. It was made of rosewood and had lush curlicues on the headboard and footboard. A poke at the mattress suggested honest horsehair, but the apparatus beneath the mattress plainly antedated the years of beauty rest. There were two Morris chairs, pseudo-mahogany, to match the rosewood; the bars at the back of both were in the nearest slots, suggesting decorum rather than abandon. A rather fragile writing table bespoke a feminine hand, presumably the gift of some devoted wife, intended to add a light home touch to the otherwise heavy masculine air of the room.

Then there was a period bookcase, made of built-up units with tilting glass doors. I forget the name of the firm that used to make those things. It was something like "Globe Wobberke." They were "period" pieces. The shelves had not been dusted for some time, but then, had I forgotten that there is a man-power shortage; "My God, haven't you heard . . . !" A glimpse through the dusty glass discovered a few imperfectly correlated objects, by no means all bookish. Item, a class flag of '94 tacked against a back wall; item, two steins with the college arms surmounted by the mystical figures " '94"; item, framed menus of the dinners at the tenth, twenty-fifth, and fortieth reunions; item, several books cowering apologetically in the left-hand corner of the lowest shelf.

There was a history of the University up to 1908 as written by the then President; a history of the Civil War, written by himself and donated by a professor who had been made an honorary member of the Class; then three sober-looking volumes by members of the Class who had gone on to take their doctorates, dealing variously with "The Mating Habits of the Lower Lepidoptera," "The Active Properties of the Trihydrobenzocarbonates and Their Derivatives," and "The Influence of the Pre-Dionysiac Orgies upon the Art of the Later Sumerians." There was something very reassuring about those volumes. They ballasted that bookcase. The flag and the mugs and the menus had suggested a society riding high, not down to a proper Plimsoll line.

But the striking thing about the room was the pictures. There were 39 of them. I counted them twice to be sure. They covered the entire wall space. They were all photographs, a kind of fifty-year family album of the Class in its totality, or in groups. My first view of them was a tremendous personal relief, like water on parched ground. I had come out of college with a precious freight of just such photographs: the college, the class, the crew, the debating society, the dinner club. They seemed to me to humanize my sheepskin, which assured me that the college had honored itself in honoring me, a generous bit of overstatement about which, by the way, I have never been quite certain. My wife, who is a disciple of Clive Bell and who believes in "significant form," will have none of them. They have been wrested from me, one by one, and relegated to the attic. So the '94 room was, at first glance, a kind of lost Eden given back again. I could imagine members of the Class escaping from home, where at the most a discreet copy of Picasso or Van Gogh hangs on the walls, to have their uninhibited hour of reminiscent self-indulgence here.

However, truth is a hard mistress, and if the truth be told, this gallery was not of itself, objectively viewed, a thing of unutterable beauty. Some of the photographs were very large and had been assembled plate by plate to cover an entire scene. They were coming unglued at the abutting edges. Some had been taken by a revolving camera, and prompted a feeling of dizziness as the right and left wings seemed to be closing in upon one— these wings were like tanks by-passing one. The earliest were "glossy prints" which had been light-struck here and there in developing, or else the fixing bath had been weak. Most of them had originally been brown— and what could be more appropriate, since Spengler says that brown is the "historical" color—but many had faded to a kind of jaundiced yellow. No, they were not loveliness incarnate.

However, the scenes and the persons could still be distinguished. There was the Class in its entirety as first gathered in front of Founders' Hall on a

September day in 1890, patently callow and self-conscious. There were the Class teams over four years: football, baseball, tennis, track; there were the crews—and in a world which prides itself upon improvement of its models year by year, how little an eight-oared shell has changed. There was the Class on graduation; in sailor straw hats, blue coats, and white flannels. And then the sequence of reunion pictures, with the successful few beginning to emerge from the ruck, seated always somewhere near the center of the group, or snap-shotted by select two's and three's: a Senator, a judge, the founder of the Whalebone Corporation, the president of a bank, and the cheery fellow who was always "the life and soul of the party." At the tenth reunion this group had been caught by the camera on a golf green, armed with prehistoric implements, putting across a terrain not unlike the Himalayas. The twentieth reunion seemed to have taken place by some lakeside; members of one-time crews were stripping again for action in rival barges; but their bags no longer buttoned at the top. The twenty-fifth must have been a great occasion. It convened at a country club, and the bank president had stood the crowd a clambake. The clams and lobsters and seaweed had been shipped from very far. Somehow those clams suggested intimations of mortality;

> Hence in a season of calm weather
> Though inland far we be . . .

One wondered whether they had really been fresh. In any case, there was the druidical stone circle required by a clambake, a chef in a high white cap, and the hungry crowd gathering around with plates.

As the sequence began to wear thin with the years, the numbers fell away, until finally a handful were convened for the fiftieth; bald, urbane, inscrutable, indomitable. But one could feel the spell of man's brief span over the scene; '94 was under sentence of death. Looking at this final picture, as the late Mr. Browning has it, "I felt chilly and grown old." I suspected the chills of being bodily as well as spiritual and I was right; my temperature was now 102° (there is always a clinical thermometer in my travelling case), I found myself wishing that there had been a room in the local Statler, where the art gallery is less likely to prompt morbid reflections; where the unfailing pair of pictures by Greuze hang over the bed, "La jeune fille à l'agneau" and "La jeune fille qui pleurt son oiseau mort"—with the omnipresent prints of Amiens and Beauvais cathedrals matching them on the opposite wall. At least Greuze's young ladies have life ahead of them, not behind them; and the French cathedrals have at any rate lasted longer than the members of '94. I put out the light and went to bed, to meditate through a white night upon the mystery of the alumnus. What sort of a person is he after all, what is his place in the cosmos? At least I lived to tell the tale.

II

Well, at any rate he is indubitably American. There is nothing like him in any other land. In the older English universities you are dated as of the year of your entrance, not of your graduation. Over there '94 would have been '90. But that means little or nothing; it is simply a bookkeeping entry on the ledgers, to show when you opened your account with higher learning. Indeed neither the university as a whole, nor a college in particular, seems to mean as much to an Englishman as does his school. His heart beats faster at the memory of Eton or Winchester, than at that of Christ Church or King's. In the continental universities nothing of the sort, either first or last, obtains. The class of 1194 at Bologna, or that of 1394 at Paris, is perished as though it had never been. Insofar as it ever existed by the calendar it did not become corporately self-conscious; it never "jelled."

No, '94 is as American as a Hopi dance or a ten-gallon hat. As was said of Lincoln, so one can say of '94, "Nothing is here of Europe." One wonders why the Class, even more than the college itself, should have become here the core around which the affections and memories of academic life have crystallized. Is it because members of a class usually lived together, moving en bloc from less favored to more favored quarters over the four years? In any case we accept the member of 1894, indeed for all his affectation we like him, because he is a creature of our culture, not a would-be copy of some outworn Old World model.

As for himself, over the on-going years, there is no doubt what his reunions mean to him. They are his instinctive protest against the way in which the world inevitably depersonalizes him, as it either invests him with dignities and public functions or takes the heart out of him on some treadmill. In a little Scottish cemetery there is a headstone which says, "Here lies the body of Tammas Jones who was born a man and died a grocer." One is prepared to rewrite that epitaph in countless other terms. There was once some warm humanity to him; but he died a banker or a surgeon, a parson or a lawyer. Against this stain and slow contagion of the trades and professions—particularly under the hard driving pressure of modern life—his reunion is his one best chance to reassert his authentic human self, if it is not gone beyond recall.

The reunion is just a bit pathetic and always rather liable to be ludicrous. George Meredith tells us that we make a mistake when "our hearts hold longings for the buried day"; the wisdom of the ages tells you that you cannot recover '94 as it originally was. "The moving finger writes, and having writ moves on." After fifty years, or even twenty-five, the bodily machine won't take it. The sober aftermath of the reunion proves it to you when you are back home; indigestion, a twinge of rheumatism in some new spot, an inordinate sunburn, perhaps even an ominous oppression across the chest. It was too high a price to pay for one day's fun. And yet there was something right in the intention, an instinctive hunger to be, even at this late date, one's unofficial authentic self.

Indeed, there may have been a strain of masochism in the decision to attend the reunion in the first place, a perverse determination to know how far one had allowed the machinery of the world to get one hopelessly enmeshed in its gears. Has one anything left to talk about save one's professional shop? Can one escape from the lock-step of one's vocational chain gang? The fear that this may not be so is a devastating emotion. The willingness to put oneself to the test in the presence of one's classmates of years gone by is in itself an ascetic exercise. We all dimly realize that the motives behind our homecoming to the college town are mixed and its transactions subtle. Beneath the surface festivities lie some of our darkest fears and dearest hopes.

Thus, there is the need of reassuring oneself from time to time as to one's identity, as well as one's independence. Has there been over the years a consecutive and reasonably consistent self? Why we should bother our heads over such a question is a riddle, but we do. We do so, probably, because we know that divided selves, disrupted selves, are the prelude to madness. There is no known subjective device by which we can gain any such assurance. Introspection, so far from reassuring us, only tends to alarm us. You have to take the self you now are back into the presence of some objective fact which is itself enduring, which you have known well and loved over a lifetime. You have to go back, for example, to some bit of external nature that has long been your mental second nature. That was what Wordsworth did when he went back to Grasmere in 1799. He had had an orphaned and homeless childhood, a desultory youth, alarms and excursions and an inconclusive amour in France during the days of the Revolution. He had returned to England a man of divided loyalties and for the moment a man without a country. Before he could settle down to work he had to satisfy himself as to his integrity and identity. This he did by putting himself in the presence of the bit of earth he knew best, the Lake District. The ten lines to the Rainbow (1802) are proof of his need and of the answer to his urgent self-imposed question. For this is not a poem about a rainbow at all—it rather is a poem like Emily Dickinson's "Single Hound"—concerned with the soul's "own identity." The danger, as Emily knew, is that the hound may slip its leash. When Wordsworth saw the rainbow over Helvellyn he knew that he was all right; he could honestly say that his days were "bound each to each by natural piety";

> So was it when my life began;
> So is it now I am a man;
> So be it when I shall grow old.

The other way of getting this reassurance is to go back to the enduring societies of which one has been a part. For this purpose such a society must be concrete, intimate, manageable by the human heart. The state is always there, but save in times of national emergency it is too complex or too abstract. The church and the college serve us better. You go to your reunion, prompted by the same imperious necessity which sent Wordsworth to Cumberland and Westmoreland. If all is well, you come away able to say, "So was it . . . so is it . . . so shall it be."

III

Then there is the problem of repaying a debt. No man, even the unscholarshipped and economically self-sufficient man, ever pays for the cost of his education. He goes out owing about half the bill to those shadowy figures known as "the founders and benefactors of this institution." One of my friends says that we begin life wondering whether the world is worthy of us and we go on humbly to wonder whether we are worthy of the world. We go to college wondering whether it is good enough for us; we look back on it wondering if we were good enough for it. Therefore very few of us, who have any conscience in these matters, can go through later years without trying to repay at least something of the balance of the account still standing against us.

If the truth be told, all the skills of American business, its ingenuity in advertising, and its shameless appeal to sentiment as well, are employed by the institution in building up its endowments from living alumni. The thing has become a vocation by itself, a recognized and necessary part of the life of the privately endowed American college and university. At its worst the procedure borders dangerously on something like blackmail or a professional racket. We resent the day when in the order of nature it becomes our duty to hand over a bigger check than we think we can at the moment afford, in response to the high-powered salesmanship of some classmate, who is insistent that "good old '94" shall not fall behind the gift of '93 and shall set the bar a bit higher for '95. It is, however, the method that irks us, not the cause. For unless we are wayward and thankless sons of the alma mater, we know that the homestead has this claim on us. This temper, too, is indigenous and wholly American. There is nothing like it in the Old World. The colleges and universities in England hark back to the days when the properties of despoiled abbeys were handed over to them. Their endowments still live on in the terms of ancient feudal lands, rather than as railroad bonds in the bank. The supposition is that the income from these lands still suffices. The suggestion that any living person should give anything to his university or his college has been, within the last few years, little short of a revolution in the mores of that people. We Americans have had to teach them how to do it. Yet in the twanging of this iron string of economic self-reliance we have achieved, even with our slick and streamlined methods of solicitation, a certain vigor and virtue which we identify as our very own.

IV

Then there is finally the more difficult problem of the attitude which the alumnus will take toward the ongoing and maturing apparatus for education in the institution. It is here, of course, that the alumnus, unless he is more than common generous, is apt to be a liability rather than an asset. The very reasons that endear the place to him and bring him back to his reunions make him cherish the college as it was in his time, not as he finds it now. There were great teachers in those days; he delights to remember them and to tell the well-worn tales about them. Today there are only pedants and specialists. The place has deteriorated. He does not understand the price which has now to be paid in the terms of strict specialization for the steady increment of sound knowledge, which must be the constant backlog for the pleasant hearth fire of a living culture. In want of that backlog the fire dies.

The president of one of our greatest universities once said,

> I could run this university if I had only the trustees and the faculty and the students and the general public to deal with. It is the alumni that make the job hard. There is at the entrance of the campus a pair of iron gates. Those gates swing a little in the wind. For years they have given off a rusty squeak, and no one has done anything about it. So the other day I took an oil can and went down and oiled the hinges myself. But I know what is going to happen at the next Commencement. The alumni are going to come back and say, "The dear old college isn't what it used to be; the gates to the campus don't squeak the way they did in our time."

When it comes to oiling the academic machinery, or what is worse, replacing it altogether by new devices when the old methods have served their day, the protest becomes more vocal and more serious. The people who are running the place now are trying to spoil it. They don't understand what a college is for. They are making dry-as-dust prigs out of the students; they have gone off after false gods of their own devising. The more the drink flows at the reunion, the more lachrymose this plaint. We were the people, and, alas, wisdom is perishing with us. This muddled mood of self-congratulation and self-pity is very pleasant for the romantic and anachronistic alumnus. What he fails to understand is that, in colleges, as in industries and as in war, skills have been immeasurably tempered and sharpened since he left college, that we live in an age of precision instruments and that mental sloppiness is not enough. It's all very like the pious deacon who makes unthinking use of every latest physical device for his comfort and then goes to church on Sunday to sing that "the good old time religion," which was good enough for all the generations gone, is good enough for him. He has no sense of incongruity between the plane reservation he holds for tomorrow's thousand-mile hop and his horse-and-buggy piety. Upon these matters the alumnus will do well to ponder, when he is corporately gathered for his next reunion. He can afford to deny himself too much conviviality for the sake of a sobriety of mind, to be intelligently addressed to the question of what the dear old place is trying to do for the needy present and the vastly perplexing future. It is no longer '94.

In the year 1790 Edmund Burke indulged in certain "Reflections on the Revolution in France." In the course of these reflections he says,

> To be attached to the subdivision, to live in the little platoon we belong to in society, is the first principle (the germs as it were) of publick affections. It is the first link in the series by which we proceed towards a love to our country and to mankind. The interest of that portion of social arrangement is a trust in the hands of all those who compose it; and as none but bad men would justify it in abuse, none but traitors would barter it away for their own personal advantage.

The alumnus in his more sober moments knows that this is so. The little academic platoon, in which he first learned what the "public affections" are, is dear and necessary to him for what it taught him about life and the world. Burke did not let the case rest there. He went on to describe the nature and structure of society in its entirety. What he said of "society" may be said with equal truth of all our serious institutions of learning, our colleges and universities:

> Society is indeed a contract. Subordinate contracts for objects of mere occasional interest may be dissolved at pleasure—but the state (and likewise the college) ought not to be considered as nothing better than a partnership agreement in a trade of pepper and coffee, callico or tobacco, or some other such low concern, to be taken up for a little temporary interest and to be dissolved by the fancy of the parties. It is to be looked upon with reverence; because it is not a partnership in things subservient only to the gross animal existence of a temporary and perishable nature. It is a partnership in all science; a partnership in all art; a partnership in every virtue, and in all perfection. As the ends of such a partnership cannot be obtained in many generations, it becomes a partnership not only between those who are living, but between those who are living, those who are dead, and those who are to be born. Each contract of each particular state is but a clause in the great primeval contract of eternal society, linking the lower with the higher natures, connecting the visible and invisible worlds.

Harvard Alumni Bulletin, April 26, 1947.

Alan Gregg

FORTY YEARS AFTER

(1951)

Alan Gregg was a scientist who never lost sight of the humanities, a physician whose first concern was the person treated rather than the disease. After twenty years' concentrating on "the methods and problems of medical education and research," Dr. Gregg retired as Director for the Medical Sciences of the Rockefeller Foundation. He also served as Chairman of the Advisory Committee for Biology and Medicine of the Atomic Energy Commission. At the time of his fortieth anniversary of graduation from Harvard College, Dr. Gregg told his Classmates: "All streets crossed without injuries or death to self or others. No parking tickets or arrests for my style of driving. Blood pressure still normal. Stopped cigarette smoking several times. Amazed and amused to reach my sixtieth birthday . . . intact, having survived both the agony of my family's illnesses and the exhaustion of their well being. Insurance paid up and prepared to meet inflation by decreasing my needs."

REMEMBER? There you were a little boy of eight, standing at the side of a broad sandy avenue in a Colorado town watching a parade. Not a circus parade, nor a military parade, but the parade of the Society Circus, a sort of summer horse show. In August 1898, or thereabouts.

Your beautiful eldest sister was going to be riding in the Harvard carriage. So many people you knew seemed to be actually in the parade. Lots of floats. A detachment of police, some G.A.R.'s led by Captain John Potter, then the Elks, the Modern Woodmen, the Daughters of Rebekah, and the Colorado Midland Band. And right after the Band came suddenly the Yale carriage, wheels and spokes wrapped with blue bachelors' buttons, with one side draped in a big blue Yale banner. The Yale boys of the town with bright blue hat bands and blue neckties and the girls carrying huge bouquets of violets. Cheers and laughter and smiles from the people on the sidewalk as the carriage proceeded.

Then you spied a much warmer color coming along, a carriage hardly visible as a carriage, so covered it was with red hollyhocks, crimson streamers, and ribbons, and—why there she was! Your own sister in it, carrying red American Beauty roses, laughing and happy with her friends. Such a warm color, red. And then something quite astonishing happened. Your whole family burst into cheers! You had never seen them so noisily happy and carefree—Mother smiling and clapping. Even Father took off his hat and cheered—which is a very unusual thing for a Congregational minister to do. This was the Harvard carriage.

It was your first experience of allegiance, acknowledged and expressed, open and unashamed—unadulterated and unqualified. Even you could feel you belonged! Then and there, for the rest of your life, the letter H became the naturally balanced symbol of dependability, of beauty and steadfast romance. The letter Y was like an arrow's tip, swift, neat, intense—but untrustworthy, all but dangerous. You even resented the Y in Y.M.C.A. Y—a symbol to put you on guard! And you could think, with deepest satisfaction, after the Harvard carriage had passed, that home and happy and heart and Heaven all began with H, too.

You were the youngest in a family of seven, and your brothers one by one "went East"—to Harvard. You were going, too. That was why you were going to school—to get to Harvard. Very sober business. You were going to leave everything else behind—Colorado and Pike's Peak and all your friends . . . everything. Twenty-six points required for entrance, but your school's schedule didn't allow for French as well as Latin, Greek, and German. So for three years your father read French with you every afternoon at 5:30 for an hour.

On Sunday afternoons, out of fascination with what your three older brothers seemed to know about Harvard, you pored over the *Harvard University Catalogue*, forwards and backwards. There were lots of strange and impressive things in it. There were "courses primarily for graduates." There was a Professor of French named de Sumichrast. It was clear that President Charles William Eliot had graduated in 1853, even earlier than your father's Class of 1866. It was stated that you could get entrance credit for a course in Chipping, Filing, and Fitting. Also there was a professor named Louis Grandgent—what an elegant name! And there were courses even in Sanskrit, given by Charles R. Lanman, who had translated from Sanskrit books you'd never seen mentioned anywhere. It was hard to believe, but the gymnasium was in charge of a man whose first name was Dudley. No cowboy in Colorado would have admitted to such a name—ever. But there it was! Dudley Allen Sargent . . . Sargent, of course, suggested something military and manly and that helped a little bit. It still was hard to believe the Dudley part. But, after all, Harvard was a place for Great Minds. Father kept talking about James and Royce and George Herbert Palmer—though a man named Santayana sounded more mysterious and alluring. From the excitement of these names you could return to reality via George Washington Cram, the Recorder, a title that carried more than the overtones of factual finality.

One day you learned that your oldest brother had been elected to Phi Beta Kappa—a piece of intelligence obviously justifying your father's kissing your mother in sheer gratitude almost before the postman had left the front porch. A few years later your next oldest brother's letter referred to "going to the Pudding"—incomprehensible but evidently a very sweet privilege indeed. You soon learned that it was a Club, and an ineffable wonder crept into your mind despite the disquiet it brought you—could there be gradations of Perfection? Could there be a quintessence of Harvard itself—the Hasty Pudding Club?

Sneers at "Easterner" and tenderfoot were the rule in those days in the West. All through the Academy you were teased by your classmates in the name of "Hahvud." "Thweee wowsing cheahs for deah old Hahvud"! A martyrdom borne in the silent loyalty of determined and Spartan conviction. "Veritas" could still count on defenders even when they were sadly outnumbered. Even your friends would have to go their ways, while you went yours, to Harvard—pronounced as it is written—Harvard.

Then one bitterly cold winter's night at 10:45—when you thought your father was going to tell you to go to bed, he gave you a letter that had come from the East addressed to "Dean Le Baron Russell Briggs," and told you to go down to the Santa Fé station, where Dean Briggs was to arrive at the wild hour of 11:55, and deliver that letter to him. It was important, and you knew you were just a kid. You got on Father's Hartford Columbia chainless bicycle and rode at top speed, almost bursting with a sense of consecration and your own first service to Harvard University. You delivered that letter to an almost disconcertingly genial man in a huge yellow-brown overcoat. You said "My Father wants you to have this now." It was done. To your speechless embarrassment you were thanked by Dean Le Baron Russell Briggs of Harvard. My! He had a lot of wrinkles in his face, and they all worked when he smiled.

There was a good deal of worry at home about finances. Father wore his winter suit all one hot summer because that would save $35. The Christmas of 1903, when you went into Mother's and Father's room to say Merry Christmas, they opened their presents from the children, and it was soberly happy and tender. Then Mother gave Father an envelope from the East. He began reading the letter and suddenly, to your utter consternation and anguish, he gasped loudly, threw himself on the bed and lay there—your own Father—sobbing and sobbing—with relief. It was a check from an admirer. You never knew how much it was for, but it would clear the mortgage, Mother said, as she patted him on the shoulder and said, "There! there! Bartlett, don't cry." You never knew there had been a mortgage to send the boys to Harvard and one of the girls to Radcliffe—and what exactly was a mortgage—did it mean a deadly promise? Of all wonders your own father sobbing without control and your mother in perfect control of herself! All that Christmas day you wondered if you had not come pretty near missing Harvard. Of course you wouldn't have not gone to Harvard . . . but, you knew you might not have been actually able to *get* there. What then? Gosh!

September 1907 finally came. At seventeen and two months you were being called a Harvard man. Do you remember the first meeting of the freshman class in Upper Massachusetts Hall? What an extraordinarily shabby building! How much longer could it last? All those fellows milling around, some of them so extremely well dressed in clothes that had been bought for them—not hand-me-downs from older brothers. Such self-assured dignity. It made you feel gawky. Then one asked you, holding out a registration form, "Say, what does this mean, 'Mother's maiden name'?" With a reassurring upsurge of maturity you told him. Oh infinite aplomb! You became a Harvard man.

Do you remember the excitement of having the chance to choose your courses? And of having men teachers in every single course! It was exhilarating. Names you had read a hundred times in the dog-eared catalogue at home in Colorado. These were they! This was it! Think of making your own choice of Abbott Lawrence Lowell, Charles Homer Haskins, Bliss Perry, William Morton Wheeler, George Santayana, T. W. Richards, Josiah Royce, Charles Townsend Copeland, William Morris Davis, George Lyman Kittredge—and many many more. It was like choosing from a tray of jewels. But these were men—all men—and expecting you to be grown up, too.

But in your Class—well, there you hardly knew anybody. Some of them behaved as though their friends were already made. So formal. Not at all like Colorado where everybody would be more likely to admit they were greenhorns and start from scratch. No—not here—not warm or casual but distant and cool. But of course you couldn't expect Olympians to chatter or be unbuttoned. In the Yard, on the street, in Gore Hall, at Boston dances, in classes, everybody seemed to know just what to do, just how to behave. When they were introduced they said "How do you do?" but never "Pleased to meet you" or just "Hello." They all seemed to have their friends—or maybe they didn't want to be bothered. Remember the sophomore you rowed behind on a scrub crew who just stared blankly at you when you said "Hello" to him on Massachusetts Ave.? It never occurred to you that he, too, might be toughing it out, a long way from, say, the Springfield High School and people he could be at ease with.

And the garret room at Miss Dudley's at 53 Dunster St., on the fourth floor. Forty-five dollars for the year. Perfectly comfortable, and if not more . . . well, after all, it helped in letting you go to Harvard. In the center of the room you could stand up. A cot, a chair, and a table—with which to receive the visit of Robert DeCourcy Ward, your Freshman Adviser, whose subject, meteorology, you were so interested in you didn't dare mention it for fear he might think you were pretending.

You went out for freshman football but all the others were so big that, with the overpowering sense of shame that only an adolescent can experience, you suddenly thought you had gotten into the varsity dressing room by a horrible mistake. You asked an enormous man named Maguire. No, you were in the freshman locker room and thence you betook your 119 pounds out to the field, glad to be tackled, for the earth at least had a somewhat familiar feel, though it was moist and soft as no Colorado football field had ever been.

Then there was the first day you saw President Eliot. He was crossing the Yard, and you had to pass him—close. Father had said once that President Eliot had a birthmark on his face. But this was stupendous. It flashed into your mind that this was another proof that Harvard was as great in what it ignored as in what it stood for. Meanwhile, on he came toward you. Off came your hat in bewildered reverence that increased as you passed such a demigod of dignity and fortitude.

Do you remember the Freshman night at Brooks House when you asked Professor Royce what his idea of Heaven was? He replied: "It would be my idea of Heaven to understand the full meaning of anything I was doing." Thereupon, you had that strange conviction that here was something you didn't in the least understand, but nonetheless it was probably overwhelmingly important. You thought about it, and thought about it, and, at long last you understand it—on your fortieth anniversary.

Harvard Alumni Bulletin, April 7, 1951.

John Lord O'Brian

THE SHINING MOMENTS
(1957)

Among the many illustrious figures who have found a place in Harvard's pantheon, none is more deserving than John Lord O'Brian. Few in this century can have loved Harvard more dearly or served the University more selflessly and faithfully than this wise, good-humored, keen-minded, and utterly devoted Harvardian. Graduated from the College and the Law School in the days of Eliot, he grew to be the valued and influential friend of Eliot's four successors, and by the end of his life, at the ripe age of ninety-nine, had become a figure of veneration among the alumni at large, who had honored him with election as President of the Harvard Alumni Association and as a Harvard Overseer. He received a Harvard honorary degree in 1946. A deeply religious man, O'Brian was an active lay leader in his church, and the Harvard professorship named in his honor bears witness to the all-important part he played in helping to secure endowment and advance the new program of the Harvard Divinity School in the 1950s. But he was no less faithful to the legal profession, to Harvard College and the Law School, and to the public service. The essay following is taken from O'Brian's brief remarks made to a national meeting of Harvard alumni in 1957, when O'Brian was in his late eighties.

IN OUR TIME there are, as there always are in every era, elements in our society that carry with them disintegrating influences. In our time I think the
chief one is that of the development of mass thinking, the impact that it has
upon the sense of responsibility of the individual, which has always been a
cherished belief in the Harvard tradition. The search for security is in reality a search for an escape from responsibility, and as President Kirk of Columbia said the other day, one of the most striking phenomena in modern
America is this great growth of mass attitudes which generate the divisive
influences which we recognize as intolerance and bigotry in certain parts of
our country. But it is the significance of Harvard that I have in mind.

James had many sayings. My favorite one, because I sympathized with
it, was that algebra was a peculiarly low form of cunning. James had a saying that he used to repeat: "What is it that makes life significant?" I would
like to paraphrase that: What is it that makes Harvard significant?

We have no monopoly on learning or brains or leadership or opportunities. There are many others that are our equals. But what is it about Harvard that is distinctive? What is the quality that men think of first in connection with Harvard?

I think it is the adherence over the centuries to that phase of the Puritan
tradition which John Milton summed up when he said that the right to
think and the right to utter—that is a quaint phrase, "the right to utter"—
was the first condition of personal rectitude and national progress. To that
tradition we have adhered. The shining moments of Harvard history can't
be dug out of old catalogues, musty and going back as far as they may go.
The shining moments of Harvard history have been the moments of sacrifice. But in our time, due to this mass thinking and mass communication
that prevails at present, it has become peculiarly disagreeable, not to say
difficult or impossible, for the individual to stand up against the tide of
public opinion expressed as it is in mass form with constant emphasis upon
conformity.

In Harvard history it is the sacrifices that made Harvard. The transept of
Memorial Hall is one memorial of extreme sacrifice, with those beautiful
Latin mottoes away up near the roof that nobody ever reads, reciting that
these men gave all to save the Republic—and the similar memorial in the
Harvard Memorial Church. When I was a boy and we showed our family
through that transept, or our friends, the boys always paused in front of the
tablet for Robert Gould Shaw, and the boys took off their hats as they went
by. You see, in those far-off days which seem so unregenerate to many of
you, boys did occasionally have glimpses into the sanctuaries of the heart
that so enriched Harvard's life in past years.

But the golden moments, the moments that count, have been the moments when men did stand up. Way back at the time of the Boston police
strike, when Professor Laski brashly made public utterances that offended
nearly all of us, it was President Lowell who spoke out and defended aca-

demic freedom, defended Laski, and prevented a demand for his resignation.

After the first World War, when Zechariah Chafee, who was the greatest liberal at Harvard in our day—and I use "liberal" there in the highest sense, the most sacred sense—brought out his book on freedom of speech, a committee of the alumni presented formal charges and asked that he be discharged because of certain statements that he made. A hearing was held, a formal hearing, and who appeared at the hearing but President Lowell as chief counsel for Zechariah Chafee.

And so in the years when hysteria was growing in Conant's time it was Conant who stood out in front and opposed the legislative attempts at restriction of utterance on the part of the teachers in the state.

And most dramatic of all was the appearance of President Pusey, when he with quiet courage stood out in defiance against the attacks made on the integrity of Harvard by politicians and evil-minded men.

To use Emerson's phrase, these are the incidents that we recall with "light in the memory" because they illuminate the Harvard history. The Puritan tradition of defending the freedom of the individual is a Harvard tradition. Those rights of the individual are frequently abused, and that makes their defense all the more difficult. But that is the price that we pay, and I submit that the significance of Harvard today in this country and throughout the world is derived from the fact that Harvard, generation after generation, has been and still is interested in defending the freedom of the individual and the right of free inquiry . . .

Harvard Alumni Bulletin, May 25, 1957.

E. J. Kahn, Jr.

THE HARVARDIZATION OF
E. J. KAHN

(1969)

In the fall of 1967, while his sons were undergraduates, E. J. Kahn, A.B. 1937, decided to take some time off from The New Yorker *to write a book about Harvard. It was to be "an impressionistic study of what Harvard has become, with emphasis on those aspects of Harvard's past and present that had nothing necessarily in common beyond that I found them interesting." In this article Kahn tells something about his experiences writing the book, in particular about his need to rewrite it after the events of the spring of*

1969 disproved earlier optimism concerning Harvard's ability to avoid a large-scale disruption. Among Kahn's recent publications are the autobiographical About The New Yorker and Me, Far-flung and Footloose, *and a newly completed biography of John Hay Whitney.*

I SOMETIMES think of myself as an ordinary Harvard alumnus, but then I wonder. The first time I took all three of my sons to a Harvard-Yale game, Yale won 54–0. The first time I ever attended a reunion of my class—our twenty-fifth, as it happened—several hundred of my contemporaries and their wives were laid low by chicken salad. Can that sort of repeated trauma be normal? The reunion was otherwise a festive occasion. Late one night, one of my classmates, during a prolonged bout of merriment, tripped over something and fell. Two other classmates dropped everything, rushed to his side, bent over him solicitously, and said, "He'll live."

"How would *they* know?" snarled the supine man's outraged wife. "How would any of you know?"

She had done our class, and especially the two samaritans, a grave injustice, for they happened to be the Dean of Admissions of the Harvard Medical School and the chief medical officer of the University Health Services. They are not the only luminaries we have contributed to the contemporary Harvard scene. Without bumping into a member of my class, one can hardly hope to make much headway, nowadays, in Massachusetts Hall, University Hall, the Botanical Museum, or Filene's. We even spawned the Treasurer of Radcliffe, which may partially explain why, as a group, we have been comparatively laggard about contributing to Harvard College.

I bask in this reflected glory by way of pointing out that when I moved to Cambridge in the fall of 1967 to do some research for a book about Harvard, I came not as a stranger. By then, I even had two sons in the College. Somewhere along their adolescence, evidently, they had concluded that any college that could survive a 54–0 shellacking in what to their father and his cronies was clearly the most significant confrontation of each year must have an inner resilience that made it worth cultivating. I stayed in Cambridge throughout that academic year. In a way, it was like attending a big class reunion all over again, but without the hijinks. But my interests this time went far beyond my class and indeed beyond the College. Now that I look back on it, I realize, somewhat embarrassedly, that I behaved much like a self-constituted one-man visiting committee to the entire University.

At first, I moved into a guest room at Eliot House, but after a couple of days I felt too old for the place. (John Finley, who hadn't yet become Master when I was in undergraduate residence there, had just completed a quarter of a century *as* Master.) So I transferred to the Hotel Continental. It was a brilliant tactical stroke. The average age of the other more-or-less-permanent tenants seemed, if they will forgive me, to be about ninety. I felt coltish by comparison and once or twice ventured a smile at the Radcliffe girls who also lived in the neighborhood. But as everybody knows Radcliffe girls never smile back. I wasn't really fooling anyone, though, except myself. I felt almost senile when I attended an Allen Ginsberg poetry reading one night at the Lowell Lecture Hall. During the intermission, Ginsberg was chatting informally, near the door, with some students. I drew near, hoping to ingratiate myself with these swingers. Ginsberg happened to look up and meet my eye. "Good evening, Sir," the poet said respectfully. It sounded like me talking to a companion in the elevator at my hotel, and I betook myself there directly.

I attended as many events as I could, even when it hurt. I sat in on classes and seminars. (Sometimes I would have trouble catching up with a professor whose lectures I particularly wanted to audit; there seemed to be no rational explanation for where or when classes met.) I had a library card. I could take out books and use the stacks; I could be a *scholar*. I had a Coop card. (What a thrill to get one's first Coop refund in more than thirty years! It is almost as good as watching an old Alice Faye movie.) I was granted an honorary membership in the Dunster House Senior Common Room; among other gratifying perquisites, that entitled me to free sherry before lunch every Wednesday. I watched the trees bud at the Arnold Arboretum and played tennis with a professor of Chinese law. I chatted with the Senior Fellow of the Corporation in that body's stately meeting room, and with Professor Samuel Eliot Morison in his riding togs. I visited the Cambridge electron accelerator (there was an explosion, but the director assured me it was nothing serious), and the top floor of the *Lampoon* building (which remained steady), and dined spendidly in their paneled chambers with the Society of Fellows. I got on the mailing list of the University News Office and may never get off it as long as I live, which will be fine with me. I had drinks at the Puseys' (he makes an excellent martini) and with the SDS (I treated). I broke bread one night with an undergraduate who wore a dark grey suit, with a matching vest, and who thought the defeat of Barry Goldwater was a modern American tragedy. I had signing privileges at the Faculty Club, where on one memorable occasion, at a time when an undergraduate thus uniquely named was working there, I was waited on by John Harvard. In some respects, the single high moment of my whole stay may have been when I tried to get a table at lunch at the Chez Dreyfus. The restaurant was crowded, and the head-waiter said, "I'm afraid you'll have to wait a few minutes, Professor."

Perhaps my most extraordinary discovery at Harvard—a place where everybody was supposed to be wrapped up in his own work and further protected against outsiders by his own sense of self-importance—was that just about everybody was ready, and often even eager, to be helpful. After I had collapsed into bed at midnight, for instance, following one day's harrowing stint of research, an undergraduate phoned me at 2 A.M. so I'd be sure to know about a rally he was helping to organize the following day. I skipped the rally. Maybe I should have gone, because as the first discarded draft of my book on Harvard accusingly attests, I guessed wrong about the events of the spring of 1969. I was convinced, by my own observations as well as by relayed thoughts of those whose eyes and ears were far more attuned to Harvard harmonies than mine, that Harvard would be spared most of the torment to which other campuses, in the year of my return to the academic scene, were increasingly being exposed.

Late in the afternoon of April 9, a friend in Cambridge called me in New York. Some students had occupied University Hall, he said, and if I was writing about Harvard I probably ought to come up. I had an important dinner date that night and an important dentist's appointment the first thing the next morning, so I stayed in New York. I had been through the Dow incident at Cambridge and I didn't think that the University Hall situation would get out of hand. The dinner was at the home of Stanley Kunitz, and Robert Lowell was another guest. I recall assuring those two distinguished Harvard poets, with all the myopia at my command, that there was no need for any of us to be unduly alarmed at the events at Cambridge; Harvard was Harvard; everything would turn out all right. I was sitting in the dentist's chair the following morning when, over his radio, came my first inkling that police had been summoned to the Yard. I left the dentist with his mouth open and flew to Boston. By the time I got to the Yard, outward calm prevailed. A student meeting was under way inside Memorial Church. I hadn't been there five minutes when my oldest son—whom Harvard had manifestly taught, if nothing else, clairvoyance—tapped me on the shoulder. "Hi, Dad," he began matter-of-factly. "I figured you'd be here. I went into University Hall last night and jotted down some notes for you." The notes were invaluable, and so was my subsequent reflection that the generation gap may yet be bridgeable.

Harvard is more settled now than it was that morning, though it is evident that a lot of people are still thinking along state-of-emergency lines. I was invited the other day by the Friends of the Harvard School of Dental Medicine (nobody asked me to such affairs before I went back to Harvard) to a black-tie dinner meeting on "The Crisis in Oral Health Care and Harvard's Obligation." But the University will obviously never settle back into its old habits, and neither, I suppose, will I. You can't hang around undergraduates for the better part of a year without having some of their spiritedness and their independence rub off on you. A few weeks ago, for instance, the head of the firm that is publishing my Harvard book phoned me and cordially invited me to join a weekly tennis foursome he was getting together. It was a critical time for the book. The publishers were holding meetings to decide how much money and time to devote to advertising and promoting it. For an author, that tennis invitation was analogous to a Harvard freshman's being invited by J. K. Galbraith to dine à trois with Mrs. Aristotle Onassis. I was tempted, naturally, to accept the invitation. But then I wondered what the Harvard undergraduates I had come to know and admire would have thought of it. Deciding, reluctantly, that if I besought their advice they would tell me not to fall for any of that crap, I told the publisher that he didn't play a good enough game for me and hung up on him. Now, whatever happens to the book, I can return to Cambridge with a clear conscience.

Harvard Bulletin, December 8, 1969.

Barbara Tuchman

I DIDN'T KNOW THAT TO BE A WOMAN WAS A TERRIBLE FATE

(1975)

At the time she received the Radcliffe Alumnae Recognition Award in 1975, Barbara Tuchman made some ironic remarks about the role of women in Harvard's world, which fortunately for posterity were recorded and later published in Radcliffe Quarterly. *Even though oral in tone, this excerpt still bears some of the same brilliance of style that has brought Mrs. Tuchman two Pulitzer Prizes and the admiration of countless readers for her literary and historical talents. Among her books are* The Zimmerman Telegram, The Guns of August, The Proud Tower, Stilwell and the American Experience in China, 1911–1945, *and* A Distant Mirror. *An ever helpful and generous alumna, she was for twelve years a trustee of Radcliffe and serves on the visiting committee for the Harvard University Library.*

AGASSIZ HOUSE, where the Choral Society used to practice, takes me back vividly to my undergraduate years, and thinking back to that time I realize how ignorant I was because I didn't know then, when I was here, that I was oppressed. I had no idea that growing up female in America was a position of slavery. Not that I was always happy; I often was very unhappy, even miserable. But I always thought that that was due to personal failings. If a boy didn't invite me to dance or to go on a date, I thought that was my own fault, not society's. I didn't know that to be a woman was really a very terrible fate. In fact, I thought we had an advantage. I thought that the capacity to recreate life, to create another life, which was what the Bible gave to God and Nature gave to women, gave us a superiority over men. I don't know why; I just grew up with that idea. I thought it was fine to be a woman. As you can see, I was ignorant.

And I didn't know that it was un-American or very reprehensible to refer to or even think of the word "elite." Between you and me, I thought that that's what the university *was* and that's what we were here for. I thought that to be at this institution and take advantage of the extraordinary riches and resources that the generations and the centuries had built up to offer to people like myself was a marvelous opportunity and that my purpose would be to make use of it in some way that would return to society something useful. I thought that that's what being an elite was. I didn't know it was something shameful or to be ashamed of.

I didn't feel that anyone was repressing my potential. It's true that I had the good fortune to be economically comfortable, but what I did with it, I did alone; nobody helped me. I never asked for help; it just never occurred to me that someone ought to help me. I didn't need a role model, whatever that is.

I always wonder when I read in the papers and magazines, especially this year, International Women's Year, why young women feel their capacities have been repressed and that "they," some unnamed "they," have prevented them from fulfilling their potential. What's to prevent it? If you have energy and the drive, you're going to do something with it. Obviously there have been great gains made by the women's movement, especially in the economic aspect of women's employment. The only thing that worries me is the wailing and the self-pity that goes on and the desire to see femininity as something to be discarded. It seems to me, maybe because I'm over 60, the more femininity the better, and the greater the difference between the sexes the better, too.

Radcliffe Quarterly, September, 1975.

X

SOME VISITORS FROM AFAR

It is a very great advantage you have above other provinces, that your youth are not put to travel for learning, but have the Muses at their doors.

RICHARD COOTE, EARL OF BELLOMONT (1699)

Cambridge is situated about 2 miles west of Boston. It is a large and handsome town, but derives its principal importance from Harvard University, which is located here, and is one of the oldest and most celebrated literary institutions in the United States.

THE FASHIONABLE TOUR IN 1825

Harvard College: This celebrated institootion of learnin' is pleasantly situated in the Bar-room of Parker's, in School street, and has poopils from all over the country.

ARTEMUS WARD; HIS TRAVELS (1865)

Cambridge, one of the two most renowned of academic cities lies about 3 miles W. of Boston (horse-cars from Bowdoin Square and Park Square) . . . Its greatest attraction is Harvard University, the oldest and most richly endowed institution of learning in America.

APPLETON'S GENERAL GUIDE TO THE UNITED STATES AND CANADA (1886)

Cambridge (no good hotels), an academic city with 70,028 inhab., lies on the N. bank of the Charles River, opposite Boston, with which it is connected by several bridges traversed by electric and other tramways. Its interest centres in the fact that it is the seat of Harvard University, the oldest, richest, and most famous of American seats of learning.

BAEDEKER'S UNITED STATES (1893)

Edward Johnson

OF THE FIRST PROMOTION OF
LEARNING IN NEW ENGLAND

(c. 1654)

*Edward Johnson (1598–1672) captain of militia, colonial historian, and
stalwart Puritan founder of Woburn, Massachusetts, chronicled some of the
early history of New England in an anonymous work* The Wonder-Working
Providence of Sions Saviour in New England *(1654). This homely but vigorous narrative describes in straightforward fashion the major happenings of
the author's time interpreted as the struggle of the faithful against the satanic forces of the new world exemplified in the wilderness of the country.
The work abounds with the author's own particular brand of "rustical rime"
and is full of printer's errors, the result of publication without the author's
revisions. Some of the nice phrases in his comments about Harvard have
been attributed to the unknown author of* Good News from New England
*(1648). Yet despite these apparent defects the work has a strength and direct-
ness of approach which is especially appealing to the reader in view of the
fact that Captain Johnson was much more a man of action than a man of
letters.*

 THE SITUATION of this College* is very pleasant, at the end of a
spacious plain, more like a bowling green, than a wilderness, near
a fair navigable river, environed with many neighbouring towns
of note, being so near, that their houses join with her suburbs. The
building [is] thought by some to be too gorgeous for a wilderness, and yet
too mean in others' apprehensions for a College. It is at present enlarging
by purchase of the neighbour houses; it hath the conveniences of a fair hall,
comfortable studies, and a good library, given by the liberal hand of some
magistrates and ministers, with others. The chief gift towards the founding

* The "College" referred to was Harvard's first academic structure built in 1642 as a
hall and dormitory but abandoned when Old Harvard Hall was erected in 1677.

of this College was by Mr. John Harnes [Harvard], a reverend minister; the country being very weak in their public treasury, expended about £500 towards it, and for the maintenance thereof gave the yearly revenue of a ferry passage between Boston and Charles Town, which amounts to about £40 or £50 per annum. The commissioners of the four united colonies also taking into consideration (of what common concernment this work would be, not only to the whole plantations in general, but also to all our English Nation), they endeavoured to stir up all the people in the several colonies to make a yearly contribution toward it, which by some is observed, but by the most very much neglected; the Government hath endeavoured to grant them all the privileges fit for a College, and accordingly the Governour and magistrates, together with the President of the College, for the time being, have a continual care of ordering all matters for the good of the whole: This College hath brought forth, and nursed up very hopeful plants, to the supplying some churches here, as the gracious and godly Mr. Wilson, son to the grave and zealous servant of Christ, Mr. John Wilson, this young man is Pastor to the Church of Christ at Dorchester; as also Mr. Buckly, son to the reverend M. Buckly of Concord; as also a second son of his, whom our native country hath now at present help in the ministry, and the other is over a people of Christ in one of these colonies, and if I mistake not, England hath I hope not only this young man of N. E. nurturing up in learning, but many more, as M. Sam. and Nathanael Mathers, Mr. Wells, Mr. Downing, Mr. Barnard, Mr. Allin, Mr. Bruster, Mr. William Ames, Mr. Jones. Another of the first fruits of this College is employed in these western parts in Mevis, one of the summer islands; beside these named, some help hath been had from hence in the study of physick, as also the godly Mr. Sam. Danforth, who hath not only studied divinity, but also astronomy; he put forth many almanacks, and is now called to the office of a teaching elder in the Church of Christ at Roxbury, who was one of the fellows of this College; the number of students is much increased of late, so that the present year 1651 on the twelfth of the sixth month, ten of them took the degree of Bachelors of Art, among whom the sea-born son of Mr. John Cotton was one. Some gentlemen have sent their sons hither from England, who are to be commended for their care of them, as the judicious and godly Doctor Ames, and divers others. This hath been a place certainly more free from temptations to lewdness than ordinarily England hath been, yet if men shall presume upon this to send their most exorbitant children intending them more especially for God's service, the justice of God doth sometimes meet with them, and the means doth more harden them in their way, or of late the godly Governors of this College have been forced to expel some, for fear of corrupting the fountain . . .

Mr. Henry Dunster is now President of this College, fitted from the Lord for the work, and by those that have skill that way, reported to be an able proficient, in both Hebrew, Greek, and Latin languages, an orthodox preacher of the truths of Christ, very powerful through his blessing to move the affection; and besides he having a good inspection into the well-ordering of things for the students' maintenance (whose commons hath been very short hitherto) by his frugal providence hath continued them longer at their studies than otherwsie they could have done; and verily it's great pity such ripe heads as many of them be, should want means to further them in learning. But seeing the Lord hath been pleased to raise up so worthy an instrument for their good, he shall not want for encouragement to go on with the work . . .

Wonder-Working Providence of Sions Saviour in New England (London, 1654).

Jasper Danckaerts

THEY KNEW HARDLY A WORD OF LATIN

(1680)

During the year 1679–80 two Dutch Labadists, the followers of the French Protestant theologian and preacher, Jean de Labadie, came to North America in search of a suitable location for a colony of their sect. They found the place they desired in Delaware and on their way home visited Boston. Their names were Jasper Danckaerts (1639–c.1704) and Peter Sluyter (1645–1722). Bartlett B. James, who edited Danckaerts' journal of the trip, commented that the Dutchman "viewed his surroundings through the eyes of a fanatical self-satisfaction. For this reason his criticisms or strictures upon persons and conditions are to be received with much discount. But he was an intelligent man, and a keen-eyed and assiduous note-taker."

WE STARTED OUT to go out to Cambridge, lying to the northeast of Boston, in order to see their college and printing office. We left about six o'clock in the morning, and were set across the river at Charlestown. We followed a road which we supposed was the right one, but went full half an hour out of the way, and would have gone still further, had not a Negro who met us, and of whom we inquired, disabused us of our mistake. We went back to the right road, which is a very pleasant one. We reached Cambridge about eight o'clock. It is not a large village, and the houses stand very much apart. The college building is the most conspicuous among them. We went to it, expecting to see something unusual, as it is the only college, or would-be academy of the Protestants in all America, but we found ourselves mistaken. In approaching the house we neither heard nor saw anything mentionable; but, going to the other side of the building, we heard noise enough in an upper room to lead my comrade to say, "I believe they are engaged in disputation." We entered and went up stairs, when a person met us, and requested us to walk in, which we did. We found there eight or ten young fellows, sitting around, smoking tobacco, with the smoke of which the room was so full, that you could hardly see; and the whole house smelt so strong of it that when I was going up stairs I said, "It certainly must be also a tavern." We excused ourselves, that we could speak English only a little, but understood Dutch or French well, which they did not. However, we spoke as well as we could. We inquired how many professors there were, and they replied not one, that there was not enough money to support one. We asked how many students there were. They said at first thirty, and then came down to twenty; I afterwards understood there are probably not ten. They knew hardly a word of Latin, not one of them, so that my comrade could not converse with them. They took us to the library where there was nothing particular. We looked over it a little. They presented us with a glass of wine. This is all we ascertained there. The minister of the place goes there morning and evening to make prayer, and has charge over them; besides him, the students are under tutors or masters. Our visit was soon over, and we left them to go and look at the land about there. We found the place beauitifully situated on a large plain, more than eight miles square with a fine stream in the middle of it, capable of bearing heavily laden vessels. As regards the fertility of the soil, we consider the poorest in New York superior to the best here. As we were tired, we took a mouthful to eat, and left. We passed by the printing office, but there was nobody in it; the paper sash however being broken, we looked in, and saw two presses with six or eight cases of type. There is not much work done there. Our printing office is well worth two of it, and even more. We went back to Charlestown, where, after waiting a little we crossed over about three o'clock.

Bartlett Burleigh James and J. Franklin Jameson, eds., *Journal of Jasper Danckaerts, 1679–1680* (New York, 1952).

J. P. Brissot de Warville

THE AIR OF CAMBRIDGE IS PURE
(1788)

J. P. Brissot de Warville (1754–1793), journalist, pamphleteer, and French revolutionist, disciple of Rousseau and Voltaire, visited the United States through his interest in the abolitionist movement and wrote one of the most penetrating of the early commentaries on the new nation. The author of two books on the philosophy of law, Brissot edited the Patriote française *during the French Revolution and took a leading part in public affairs. He served successively as a member of the municipality of Paris, of the legislative assembly, and then of the convention. As a member of the diplomatic committee, he is held to have been largely responsible for France's foreign policy of the time. When his party fell, he was executed on the guillotine.*

BOSTON has the glory of having given the first college or university to the new world. It is placed on an extensive plain, four miles from Boston, at a place called Cambridge; the origin of this useful institution was in 1636. The imagination could not fix on a place that could better unite all the conditions essential to a seat of education; sufficiently near to Boston to enjoy all the advantages of a communication with Europe and the rest of the world, and sufficiently distant not to expose the students to the contagion of licentious manners common in commercial towns.

The air of Cambridge is pure, and the environs charming, offering a vast space for the exercise of the youth.

The buildings are large, numerous, and well distributed. But, as the number of the students augments every day, it will be necessary soon to augment the buildings. The library, and the cabinet of philosophy, do honour to the institution. The first contains 13,000 volumes. The heart of a Frenchman palpitates on finding the works of Racine, of Montesquieu, and the Encyclopaedia, where, 150 years ago, rose the smoke of the savage calumet.

The regulation of the course of studies here is nearly the same as that at the university of Oxford. I think it impossible but that the last revolution must introduce a great reform. Free men ought to strip themselves of their prejudices, and to perceive, that, above all, it is necessary to be a man and a citizen; and that the study of the dead languages, of a fastidious philosophy and theology, ought to occupy few of the moments of a life which might be usefully employed in studies more advantageous to the great family of the human race . . .

But to return to the university of Cambridge, superintended by the respectable president Willard. Among the associates in the direction of the studies are distinguished Dr. Wigglesworth and Dr. Dexter. The latter is professor of natural philosophy, chemistry, and medicine; a man of extensive knowledge, and great modesty. He told me, to my great satisfaction, that he gave lectures on the experiments of our schools of chemistry. The excellent work of my respectable master, Dr. Fourcroy, was in his hands, which taught him the rapid strides that this science has lately made in Europe.

In a free country everything ought to bear the stamp of patriotism. This patriotism, so happily displayed in the foundation, endowment, and encouragement of this university, appears every year in a solemn feast celebrated at Cambridge in honour of the sciences. This feast, which takes place once a year in all the colleges of America, is called the *commencement:* it resembles the exercises and distribution of prizes in our colleges. It is a day of joy for Boston; almost all its inhabitants assemble in Cambridge. The most distinguished of the students display their talents in the presence of the public; and these exercises, which are generally on patriotic subjects, are terminated by a feast, where reign the freest gaiety, and the most cordial fraternity.

It is remarked, that in countries chiefly devoted to commerce the sciences are not carried to any high degree. This remark applies to Boston. The university certainly contains men of worth and learning; but science is not diffused among the inhabitants of the town. Commerce occupies all their ideas, turns all their heads, and absorbs all their speculations. Thus you find few estimable works, and few authors ... The arts, except those that respect navigation, do not receive much encouragement here.

New Travels in the United States of America (London, 1794).

Harriet Martineau

THE STATE OF THE UNIVERSITY WAS A SUBJECT OF GREAT MOURNING

(1838)

The English writer, Harriet Martineau (1802–1876), produced two books as a result of her visit to the United States in 1834–1836. The first was Society in America *(1837), an economic, political, and social critique of the United States, and the second* Retrospect of Western Travel *(1838), a series of descriptive sketches recording personal impressions of her experiences. While she was widely attacked, especially by southern critics, for her views on slavery and the south,* Retrospect of Western Travel, *from which the follow-ing selection is taken, was a popular success. In her comments on Harvard, wisely and sometimes amusingly stated, may be seen the underlying devel-opment of the political and ethical ideas which made her an important influ-ence on the intellectual life of the Victorian era.*

IF HARVARD is ever to recover her supremacy, to resume her station in use-fulness and in the affections of the people, it must be by a renovation of her management, and a change in some of the principles recognized by her. Every one is eager to acknowledge her past services. All American citizens are proud of the array of great men whom she has sent forth to serve and grace the country; but, like some other universities, she is falling behind the age. Her glory is declining, even in its external manifestations; and it must decline as long as the choicest youth of the community are no longer sent to study within her walls.

The politics of the managers of Harvard University are opposed to those of the great body of the American people. She is the aristocratic college of the United States. Her pride of antiquity, her vanity of preeminence and wealth, are likely to prevent her renovating her principles and manage-ment, so as to suit the wants of the period; and she will probably receive a sufficient patronage from the aristocracy, for a considerable time to come, to encourage her in all her faults. She has a great name; and the education she affords is very expensive, in comparison with all other colleges. The sons of the wealthy will therefore flock to her. The attainments usually made within her walls are inferior to those achieved elsewhere; her professors (poorly salaried, when the expenses of living are considered), being accus-tomed to lecture and examine the students, and do nothing more. The indo-lent and the careless will therefore flock to her. But, meantime, more and more new colleges are rising up, and are filled as fast as they rise, whose principles and practices are better suited to the wants of the time. In them living is cheaper; and the professors are therefore richer with the same or smaller salaries; the sons of the yeomanry and mechanic classes resort to them; and, where it is the practice of the tutors to work with their pupils, as well as lecture to them, a proficiency is made which shames the attainments of the Harvard students. The middle and lower classes are usually neither Unitarian nor Episcopalian, but "orthodox," as their distinctive term is: and these, the strength and hope of the nation, avoid Harvard, and fill to over-flowing the oldest orthodox colleges; and when these will hold no more, es-tablish new ones.

When I was at Boston, the state of the University was a subject of great mourning among its friends. Attempts had been made to obtain the services of three gentlemen of some eminence as professors; but in vain. The salaries offered were insufficient to maintain the families of these gentlemen in comfort, in such a place as Cambridge; though, at that very time, the managers of the affairs of the institution were purchasing lands in Maine. The Moral Philosophy chair had been vacant for eight years. Two of the professors were at the time laid by in tedious illnesses; a third was absent on a long journey; and the young men of the senior class were left almost unemployed. The unpopularity of the president among the young men was extreme; and the disfavour was not confined to them. The students had, at different times within a few years, risen against the authorities; and the last disturbances in 1834, had been of a very serious character. Everyone was questioning what was to be done next, and anticipating a further vacating of chairs which it would be difficult to fill. I heard one merry lady advise that the professors should strike for higher wages, and thus force the council and supporters of the university into a thorough and serious consideration of its condition and prospects in relation to present and future times.

The salary of the president is above 2000 dollars. The salaries of the professors vary from 1500 dollars to 500; that is, from £375 to £125. Upon this sum they are expected to live like gentlemen, and to keep up the aristocratic character of the institution. I knew of one case where a jealousy was shown when a diligent professor, with a large family, made an attempt by a literary venture to increase his means. Yet Harvard college is in buildings, library, and apparatus, in its lands and money, richer than any other in the Union.

The number of undergraduates, in the year 1833–4 was two hundred and sixteen. They cannot live at Harvard for less than 200 dollars a-year, independently of personal expenses. Seventy-five dollars must be contributed by each to the current expenses; fuel is dear; fifteen dollars are charged for lodging within the college walls, and eighty are paid for board by those who use their option of living in the college commons. The fact is, I believe, generally acknowledged, that the comparative expensiveness of living is a cause of the depression of Harvard in comparison with its former standing among other colleges; but this leads to a supposition which does not to all appear a just one, that if the expenses of poor students could be defrayed by a public fund, to be raised for the purpose, the sons of the yeomanry would repair once more to Harvard.

It may be doubted whether, if a gratis education to poor students were to be dispensed from Harvard tomorrow, it would rival in real respectability and proficiency the orthodox colleges which have already surpassed her. Her management and population are too aristocratic, her movement too indolent, to attract young men of that class; and young men of that class prefer paying for the benefits they receive; they prefer a good education, economically provided, so as to be within reach of their means, to an equally good education furnished to them at the cost of their pride of independence. The best friends of Harvard believe that it is not by additional contrivances that her prosperity can be restored; but by such a renovation of the whole scheme of her management as shall bring her once more into accordance with the wants of the majority, the spirit of the country and of the time.

Retrospect of Western Travel (London, 1838).

Charles Dickens

THE QUIET INFLUENCE OF CAMBRIDGE

(1842)

Charles Dickens' triumphant tour of the United States took place when he was but twenty-nine years old, and he celebrated his thirtieth birthday while in the States. He was the author of a half-dozen successful books, including Pickwick Papers, Oliver Twist, *and* Nicholas Nickleby. *The enthusiasm which greeted him knew no bounds. He met the President and all the most important people; tickets for the public receptions in his honor sold for fabulous prices. It was partly the warmth of his welcome and the resulting public idolization which caused the swift adverse reaction to his perfectly justified criticisms of America contained in the* American Notes, *published on his return to England. There was little, however, about Boston and New England that did not appeal to him, including his glimpse of Harvard.*

THERE is no doubt that much of the intellectual refinement and superiority of Boston, is referable to the quiet influence of the University of Cambridge, which is within three or four miles of the city. The resident professors at that university are gentlemen of learning and varied attainments; and are, without one exception that I can call to mind, men who would shed a grace upon, and do honor to, any society in the civilised world. Many of the resident gentry in Boston and its neighborhood, and I think I am not mistaken in adding, a large majority of those who are attached to the liberal professions there, have been educated at this same school. Whatever the defects of American universities may be, they disseminate no prejudices; rear no bigots; dig up the buried ashes of no old superstitions; never interpose between the people and their improvement; exclude no man because of his religious opinions; above all, in their whole course of study and instruction, recognise a world, and a broad one too, lying beyond the college walls.

It was a source of inexpressible pleasure to me to observe the almost imperceptible, but not less certain effect, wrought by this institution among the small community of Boston; and to note at every turn the humanising tastes and desires it has engendered; the affectionate friendships to which it has given rise; the amount of vanity and prejudice it has dispelled. The golden calf they worship at Boston is a pigmy compared with the giant effigies set up in other parts of that vast countinghouse which lies beyond the Atlantic; and the almighty dollar sinks into something comparatively insignificant, amidst a whole Pantheon of better gods.

American Notes (London, 1842).

Anthony Trollope

I DID NOT VISIT THE MUSEUM
(1861)

In the midst of the chaotic Civil War period Anthony Trollope came to these shores. His North America, *published in England and the United States, contains the result of his impressions—neutral toward the "irrepressible conflict" but reservedly realistic on matters of the traveler's experiences in America. Trollope's own self-criticism of his report was confirmed in the judgment of later critics. The novelist wrote of* North America: *"It was tedious and confused, and will hardly, I think, be of future value to those who wish to make themselves acquainted with the United States." Trollope was genuinely fond of America, however, and his book enabled him to repair many of the wounds left by his mother's sharp criticism as a result of her stay in the United States from 1827 until 1831. Trollope's comment about Harvard are among the most interesting passages in the book.*

CAMBRIDGE is not above three or four miles from Boston. Indeed, the town of Cambridge properly so called begins where Boston ceases. The Harvard College—that is its name, taken from one of its original founders—is reached by horsecars in twenty minutes from the city. An Englishman feels inclined to regard the place as a suburb of Boston; but if he so expresses himself, he will not find favor in the eyes of the men of Cambridge.

The University is not so large as I had expected to find it. It consists of Harvard College, as the undergraduates' department, and of professional schools of law, medicine, divinity, and science. In the few words that I will say about it I will confine myself to Harvard College proper, conceiving that the professional schools connected with it have not in themselves any special interest. The average number of undergraduates does not exceed 450, and these are divided into four classes. The average number of degrees taken annually by bachelors of art is something under 100. Four years' residence is required for a degree, and at the end of that period a degree is given as a matter of course if the candidate's conduct has been satisfactory. When a young man has pursued his studies for that period, going through the required examinations and lectures, he is not subjected to any final examination as is the case with a candidate for a degree of Oxford and Cambridge. It is, perhaps, in this respect that the greatest difference exists between the English Universities and Harvard College. With us a young man may, I take it, still go through his three or four years with a small amount of study. But his doing so does not insure him his degree. If he have utterly wasted his time he is plucked, and late but heavy punishment comes upon him. At Cambridge in Massachusetts the daily work of the men is made more obligatory; but if this be gone through with such diligence as to enable the student to hold his own during the four years, he has his degree as a matter of course. There are no degrees conferring special honour. A man cannot go out "in honours" as he does with us. There are no "firsts" or "double firsts"; no "wranglers"; no "senior opts" or "junior opts." Nor are there prizes of fellowships and livings to be obtained. It is, I think, evident from this that the greatest incentives to high excellence are wanting at Harvard College. There is neither the reward of honour nor of money. There is none of that great competition which exists at our Cambridge for the high place of Senior Wrangler; and, consequently, the degree of excellence attained is no doubt lower than with us. But I conceive that the general level of the University education is higher there than with us; that a young man is more sure of getting his education, and that a smaller percentage of men leaves Harvard College utterly uneducated than goes in that condition out of Oxford or Cambridge. The education at Harvard College is more diversified in its nature, and study is more absolutely the business of the place than it is at our Universities.

The expense of education at Harvard College is not much lower than at our colleges; with us there are, no doubt, more men who are absolutely extravagant than at Cambridge, Massachusetts. The actual authorized expenditure in accordance with the rules is only £50 per annum, *i.e.*, 249 dollars; but this does not, by any means, include everything. Some of the richer young men may spend as much as £300 per annum, but the largest number vary their expenditure from £100 to £180 per annum; and I take it the same thing may be said of our Universities. There are many young men at Harvard College of very small means. They will live on £70 per annum, and will earn a great portion of that by teaching in the vacations. There are thirty-six scholarships attached to the University varying in value from £20 to £60 per annum; and there is also a beneficiary fund for supplying poor scholars with assistance during their collegiate education. Many are thus brought up at Cambridge who have no means of their own, and I think I may say that the consideration in which they are held among their brother students is in no degree affected by their position. I doubt whether we can say so much of the sizars and bible clerks at our Universities.

At Harvard College there is, of course, none of that old-fashioned, time-honoured, delicious, mediaeval life which lends so much grace and beauty to our colleges. There are no gates, no porter's lodges, no butteries, no halls, no battels, and no common rooms. There are no proctors, no bulldogs, no bursers, no deans, no morning and evening chapel, no quads, no surplices, no caps and gowns. I have already said that there are no examinations for degrees and no honours; and I can easily conceive that in the absence of all these essentials many an Englishman will ask what right Harvard College has to call itself a University.

I have said that there are no honours,—and in our sense there are none. But I should give offence to my American friends if I did not explain that there are prizes given—I think, all in money, and that they vary from 50 to 10 dollars. These are called *deturs*. The degrees are given on Commencement Day, at which occasion certain of the expectant graduates are selected to take parts in a public literary exhibition. To be so selected seems to be tantamount to taking a degree in honours. There is also a dinner on Commencement Day,—at which, however, "no wine or other intoxicating drink shall be served."

It is required that every student shall attend some place of Christian worship on Sundays; but he, or his parents for him, may elect what denomination of church he shall attend. There is a University chapel on the University grounds which belongs, if I remember right, to the Episcopalian Church. The young men for the most part live in College, having rooms in the College buildings; but they do not board in those rooms. There are establishments in the town under the patronage of the University, at which dinner, breakfast, and supper are provided; and the young men frequent one of these houses or another as they, or their friends for them, may arrange. Every young man not belonging to a family resident within a hundred miles of Cambridge, and whose parents are desirous to obtain the protection thus provided, is placed, as regards his pecuniary management, under the care of a patron, and this patron acts by him as a father does in England by a boy at school. He pays out his money for him and keeps him out of debt. The arrangement will not recommend itself to young men at Oxford quite so powerfully as it may do to the fathers of some young men who have been there. The rules with regard to the lodging and boarding houses are very stringent. Any festive entertainment is to be reported to the President. No wine or spirituous liquors may be used, &c. It is not a picturesque system, this; but it has its advantages.

There is a handsome library attached to the College, which the young men can use; but it is not as extensive as I had expected. The University is not well off for funds by which to increase it. The new museum in the College is also a handsome building. The edifices used for the undergraduates' Chambers and for the lecture-rooms are by no means handsome. They are very ugly red-brick houses standing here and there without order. There are seven such, and they are called Brattle House, College House, Divinity Hall, Hollis Hall, Holsworthy [sic] Hall, Massachusetts Hall, and Stoughton Hall. It is almost astonishing that buildings so ugly should have been erected for such a purpose. These, together with the library, the museum, and the chapel, stand on a large green, which might be made pretty enough if it were kept well mown like the gardens of our Cambridge colleges; but it is much neglected. Here, again, the want of funds—the *res angusta domi*—must be pleaded as an excuse. On the same green, but at some little distance from any other building, stands the President's pleasant house.

The immediate direction of the College is of course mainly in the hands of the President, who is supreme. But for the general management of the Institution there is a Corporation, of which he is one. It is stated in the laws of the University that the Corporation of the University and its Overseers constitute the Government of the University. The Corporation consists of the President, five Fellows, so called, and a Treasurer. These Fellows are chosen, as vacancies occur, by themselves, subject to the concurrence of the Overseers. But these Fellows are in nowise like to the Fellows of our colleges, having no salaries attached to their offices. The Board of Overseers consists of the State Governor, other State officers, the President and Treasurer of Harvard College, and thirty other persons,—men of note, chosen by vote. The Faculty of the College, in which is vested the immediate care and government of the undergraduates, is composed of the President and the Professors. The Professors answer to the tutors of our colleges, and upon them the education of the place depends. I cannot complete this short notice of Harvard College without saying that it is happy in the possession of that distinguished natural philosopher, Professor Agassiz. M. Agassiz has collected at Cambridge a museum of such things as natural philosophers delight to show, which I am told is all but invaluable. As my ignorance on such matters is of a depth which the Professor can hardly imagine, and which it would have shocked him to behold, I did not visit the museum. Taking the University of Harvard College as a whole, I should say that it is most remarkable in this,—that it does really give to its pupils that education which it professes to give. Of our own Universities other good things may be said, but that one special good thing cannot always be said.

North America (London and New York, 1862).

Henry James

VERENA'S GUIDED TOUR
(1886)

*If Henry James could be said to have had an American home it was certainly
Cambridge. Brought up in "deliberate cosmopolitanism," he did not take a
formal college course but attended the Harvard Law School, beginning in
1862, and in Cambridge came under the influence of Norton and Howells. It
was in Cambridge that he began his role as a spectator of life, about 1866.
His novel, The Bostonians, written in England, is among the best and most
ambitious of his early books. It satirizes the cause of Feminism and makes
fun of reformers and philanthropists. Unpopular when first published because of its realistic treatment of polite society, it has since received more
favorable critical appraisal. In the tour of the Harvard Yard the protagonists
are Verena Tarrant (convinced disciple of the Feminist leader, Olive Chancellor) and Basil Ransom, a lank, good-humored Mississippian who is
James's satiric foil throughout this scene.*

THEY presently reached the irregular group of heterogeneous buildings—
chapels, dormitories, libraries, halls, which, scattered among slender trees,
over a space reserved by means of a low rustic fence, rather than enclosed
(for Harvard knows nothing either of the jealousy or the dignity of high
walls and guarded gateways), constitutes the great university of Massachusetts. The yard, or college-precinct, is traversed by a number of straight little paths, over which, at certain hours of the day, a thousand undergraduates, with books under their arm and youth in their step, flit from one school
to another. Verena Tarrant knew her way round, as she said to her companion; it was not the first time she had taken an admiring visitor to see the
local monuments. Basil Ransom, walking with her from point to point, admired them all, and thought several of them exceedingly quaint and venerable. The rectangular structures of old red brick especially gratified his eye;
the afternoon sun was yellow on their homely faces; their windows showed
a peep of flowerpots and bright-coloured curtains; they wore an expression
of scholastic quietude, and exhaled for the young Mississippian a tradition,
an antiquity. "This is the place where I ought to have been," he said to his
charming guide. "I should have had a good time if I had been able to study
here."

"Yes; I presume you feel yourself drawn to any place where ancient
prejudices are garnered up," she answered, not without archness. "I know
by the stand you take about our cause that you share the superstitions of the
old bookmen. You ought to have been at one of those really mediaeval uni-

versities that we saw on the other side, at Oxford, or Göttingen, or Padua. You would have been in perfect sympathy with their spirit."

"Well, I don't know much about those old haunts," Ransom rejoined. "I reckon this is good enough for me. And then it would have had the advantage that your residence isn't far, you know."

"Oh, I guess we shouldn't have seen you much at my residence! As you live in New York, you come, but here you wouldn't; that is always the way." With this light philosophy Verena beguiled the transit to the library, into which she introduced her companion with the air of a person familiar with the sanctified spot. This edifice, a diminished copy of the chapel at King's College, at the greater Cambridge, is a rich and impressive institution; and as he stood there, in the bright, heated stillness, which seemed suffused with the odour of old print and old bindings, and looked up into the high, light vaults that hung over quiet book-laden galleries, alcoves and tables, and glazed cases where rarer treasures gleamed more vaguely, over busts of benefactors and portraits of worthies, bowed heads of working students and the gentle creak of passing messengers—as he took possession, in a comprehensive glance, of the wealth and wisdom of the place, he felt more than ever the soreness of an opportunity missed; but he abstained from expressing it (it was too deep for that), and in a moment Verena had introduced him to a young lady, a friend of hers, who, as she explained, was working on the catalogue, and whom she had asked for on entering the library, at a desk where another young lady was occupied. Miss Catching, the first-mentioned young lady, presented herself with promptness, offered Verena a low-toned but appreciative greeting, and, after a little, undertook to explain to Ransom the mysteries of the catalogue, which consisted of a myriad little cards, disposed alphabetically in immense chests of drawers. Ransom was deeply interested, and as, with Verena, he followed Miss Catching about (she was so good as to show them the establishment in all its ramifications), he considered with attention the young lady's fair ringlets and refined, anxious expression, saying to himself that this was in the highest degree a New England type. Verena found an opportunity to mention to him that she was wrapped up in the cause, and there was a moment during which he was afraid that his companion would expose him to her as one of its traducers; but there was that in Miss Catching's manner (and in the influence of the lofty halls) which deprecated loud pleasantry, and seemed to say, moreover, that if she were treated to such a revelation she should not know under what letter to range it.

"Now there is one place where perhaps it would be indelicate to take a Mississippian," Verena said, after this episode. "I mean the great place that towers above the others—that big building with the beautiful pinnacles, which you see from every point." But Basil Ransom had heard of the great Memorial Hall; he knew what memories it enshrined, and the worst that he should have to suffer there; and the ornate, overtopping structure, which was the finest piece of architecture he had ever seen, had moreover solicited his enlarged curiosity for the last half-hour. He thought there was rather too much brick about it, but it was buttressed, cloistered, turreted, dedicated, superscribed, as he had never seen anything; though it didn't look old, it looked significant; it covered a large area, and it sprang majestic into the winter air. It was detached from the rest of the collegiate group, and stood in a grassy triangle of its own. As he approached it with Verena he suddenly stopped, to decline responsibility. "Now mind, if you don't like what's inside, it isn't my fault."

He looked at her an instant, smiling. "Is there anything against Mississippi?"

"Well, no, I don't think she is mentioned. But there is great praise of our young men in the war."

"It says they were brave, I suppose."

"Yes, it says so in Latin."

"Well, so they were—I know something about that," Basil Ransom said. "I must be brave enough to face them—it isn't the first time." And they went up the low steps and passed into the tall doors. The Memorial Hall of Harvard consists of three main divisions: one of them a theatre, for academic ceremonies; another a vast refectory, covered with a timbered roof, hung about with portraits and lighted by stained windows, like the halls of the colleges of Oxford; and the third, the most interesting, a chamber high, dim, and severe, consecrated to the sons of the university who fell in the long Civil War. Ransom and his companion wandered from one part of the building to another, and stayed their steps at several impressive points; but they lingered longest in the presence of the white, ranged tablets, each of which, in its proud, sad clearness, is inscribed with the name of a student-soldier. The effect of the place is singularly noble and solemn, and it is impossible to feel it without a lifting of the heart. It stands there for duty and honour, it speaks of sacrifice and example, seems a kind of temple to youth, manhood, generosity. Most of them were young, all were in their prime, and all of them had fallen; this simple idea hovers before the visitor and makes him read with tenderness each name and place—names often without other history, and forgotten Southern battles. For Ransom these things were not a challenge nor a taunt; they touched him with respect, with the sentiment of beauty. He was capable of being a generous foeman, and he forgot, now, the whole question of sides and parties; the simple emotion of the old fighting-time came back to him, and the monument around him seemed an embodiment of that memory; it arched over friends as well as enemies, the victims of defeat as well as the sons of triumph.

"It is very beautiful—but I think it is very dreadful!" This remark, from Verena, called him back to the present. "It's a real sin to put up such a building, just to glorify a lot of bloodshed. If it wasn't so majestic, I would have it pulled down."

"That is delightful feminine logic!" Ransom answered. "If, when women have the conduct of affairs, they fight as well as they reason, surely for them too we shall have to set up memorials."

The Bostonians (London and New York, 1886).

George Birkbeck Hill

HOW FEW ARE THE SIGNS OF UNIVERSITY LIFE!

(1893)

George Birkbeck Norman Hill (1835–1903), Honorary Fellow of Pembroke College, Oxford, and one of the foremost Johnsonians of his time, visited Cambridge during 1893 and was so taken with Harvard University during his stay that he went home to write a book about the place. Harvard College by an Oxonian *is a rambling, largely factual account of Harvard which both describes the past and contemporary history of the college and summarizes in a pleasant fashion Harvard life of the time. Hill was attracted to Harvard from his first sight of it. In his journal he wrote of the Yard: "There is no quadrangle in Oxford more delightful on a hot summer day. Harvard surely is a College that a man can love."*

OF MY first impressions of the undergraduates, I made the following record in my journal: "They are shorter and slighter than our Oxford men, with much less colour; a year or two older, I think, unless the hot climate makes them look older. I do not see so many gross, stupid faces, but, on the other hand, I have not as yet noticed any of those fresh-coloured, pleasant, inno-cent faces which are so attractive at Oxford." On seeing more of the men, I came to doubt whether in appearance they were older than our undergrad-uates. Near the end of my residence in Cambridge, I thus sum up my obser-vations:

How few are the signs here of university life compared with those seen in Oxford! In Oxford, a real town though it is, and not a suburban village like Cambridge, the presence of the students, nevertheless, is much more conspicuous. No one can walk about its streets and roads without noticing the large number of young men—often moving in a long stream—young men, moreover, who, as their very appearance, their dress, their manner of walking, their features show, are not in business. In the afternoon their suit of flannel makes it clear that they are bent on pleasure, or, at all events, on exercise; in the morning and evening the cap and gown indicate the student. The style, the very make of their clothes, are not those of the young business man. Their easy, confident step distinguishes them from the ordinary youth of a town. The separation of the Colleges distributes this life over the city, so that undergraduates and graduates are constantly passing along the streets from College to College, or from College to the University buildings. The Parks, the upper river, the lower river, and the Cherwell increase this diffusion. It is increased, moreover, by the Englishman's love of walking and riding.

In the American Cambridge there is very little of this open and palpable university life. The College buildings, which are numerous, are mostly in one enclosure, the Yard. Those which are not there—the more modern additions—are separated from them only by a road. The students, therefore, in going to and from lectures, do not cross the town. Outside the Yard I have never seen them moving in a stream, except on the days of some great baseball or football match, and then they have but a few yards to traverse. Beyond the immediate surroundings of the College they are scarcely noticeable. A stranger, whose walks did not lead him past the Yard, might for some time live within a quarter of a mile of the College, without discovering that he was in a University town. Boston attracts the students in large numbers, and to Boston they go, not on foot but on the tram-cars. In their dress, their general appearance, their gait, I discover little of the undergraduate. In England and Germany this clan does not hide itself. An Oxford man lets the world know that he is an Oxford man. His self-satisfaction gives an assurance, sometimes even a kind of swagger, to his whole behaviour. He walks along the High Street as if it belonged, not to the Corporation, but to himself. His apparel too oft proclaims the *man*. There is nothing of this here. The Harvard undergraduate talks of himself and his comrades as boys. He has not learnt to swagger. Probably it takes many years at a great English public school to acquire the true manner. Like the art of beating the French at Waterloo, it is best learnt on the Playing Fields of Eton. His dress, too, is much less costly and showy; for the most part it is of a dark cloth. I notice none of those waistcoats with which an Oxford man dazzles the poorer scholars of his college and startles his friends at home. The ordinary Harvard man might have stepped out of a city office or a Normal School for Teachers. He belongs to a poorer class. Clothing, moreover, is so expensive that many have to be content with one suit a year. An undergraduate who had visited Europe in the previous Long Vacation, told me that the clothes he was wearing, for which he had paid three pounds in England, in Cambridge would have cost him six. Every afternoon there are no doubt men to be seen in the dress of young athletes; but though there is the greatest possible interest taken in the yearly boat-race with Yale, and in the baseball and football matches, nevertheless, those who share in these sports are far fewer than we should find in an English university. It is, I am sure, a picked few rather than the mass of men who play. Nowhere is there such a sight as is to be seen any afternoon at Oxford on the river and in the Parks on the days when there is no great race or match. The build of the men proves, moreover, that they have not gone through that long course of rough games which has formed the active and powerful frames of the young English undergraduates. I am told, however, that during the winter half of the year, North Avenue is a training-ground for runners, who in the afternoon and evening sweep along the "sidewalks," as if the smooth pavement had been laid down for them, and not for quiet, decent Christians. A noble gymnasium, moreover, has been lately built, which is much frequented. "The fever of renown," gained not by the brain, but by the body, is spreading rapidly through the veins of young America. By its "strong contagion" Harvard has been badly caught. One of my friends, whose three sons have recently graduated, lamented to me the excessive interest they all took in the contests of athletes. How different it was when he was young! In those happy days his brother, when home from College, used to talk of books. His sons' talk was of running and jumping, of rowing, baseball, and football. The change is great, indeed, since the time when Dr. Wendell Holmes lamented the general indifference of the youth of New England to bodily exercise . . .

Harvard has not been quite free from a certain kind of affectation which is only too common in the English Universities, but which is known in America as "Harvard indifference." It was not from their forefathers that the New Englanders got this poor quality. It was never carried across the sea in the ships of the early settlers. It is the very opposite of that stubborn strength of character, and of that burning zeal which sent them to the wilderness, and their descendants, "the embattled farmers," to Concord, Lexington, and Bunker Hill. It is the contempt for all that eagerness of heart and thought and life which inspires "the young enthusiast" when first "he quits his ease for fame." "I do not love a man," said Goldsmith, "who is zealous for nothing." These lovers of indifference he would have shunned. Long indulged, it becomes ingrained in the character. It is a great maker of bad citizens. In a young man it almost always begins with affectation, and happily often dies an early death. It is killed by his nobler qualities, or by some strong influence from without.

More than sixty years ago Channing rebuked it. When the Revolution of 1830 broke out in France, he was

> astonished that the freemen of America, especially the young, should be so moderate in their expressions of joy. He went back in memory to his boyish days, when the Cambridge collegians had processions, speeches, and bonfires. Now all was still. One evening a graduate called upon him. "Well, Mr. ———," said he, "are you too so old and so wise, like the young men at Harvard, as to have no foolish enthusiasm to throw away upon the heroes of the Polytechnic School?" "Sir," answered ———, "you seem to me to be the only young man I know." "Always young for liberty, I trust," replied Dr. Channing with a bright smile and a ringing tone, as he pressed him warmly by the hand.

Thirty years had to pass, and then this Harvard indifference was swept away by the Southern revolt. In the presence of that dreadful strife, indifference would no longer have been ridiculous, it would have become hateful.

Professor Goodwin thinks that it was by "the equable pressure" of a revised system of instruction and examination that "the older enthusiasm" of the place was mainly repressed, and this indifference was encouraged. Free play was no longer given to the student's mind. He was forced to attain to mediocrity in many subjects, and was not encouraged, and was scarcely allowed to secure excellence in one or two. There had been students who had refused to cramp themselves in the narrowness of the prescribed course. Lowell read widely, and was rusticated in consequence. Motley escaped this disgrace, but not the reproach of his tutor, who one day "remonstrated with him upon the heaps of novels upon his table. 'Yes,' said Motley, 'I am reading historically, and have come to the novels of the nineteenth century. Taken in the lump, they are very hard reading.'" At the present day the author of *The Biglow Papers* and the historian of the Dutch Republic could have indulged their tastes to the full. This "Harvard indifference" cannot surely long survive the great reforms in education which have already done so much to transform the University from a mere place of teaching to a place of learning.

There is another fault for which Harvard men are reproached by their rivals and enemies. They are distinguished, it is said, by a certain priggishness, a certain consciousness too openly shown that they are not only the salt, but the superfine salt, of the earth—a priggishness and a self-consciousness which, it is said, sometimes cling to them throughout life. What Boston is to Massachusetts, what Massachusetts is to New England, what New England is to the United States, what the United States are to the Universe, that Harvard is to Boston. Among "the five points of Massachusetts decency" laid down by Wendell Phillips, to be a graduate of Harvard College holds the second place. The "old Harvard spirit" on which they prided themselves, was thought by some to be the spirit of a gentleman carried to preciseness. They are fond of telling a story of a man who had twin sons, one of whom he sent to Harvard, and the other to Yale. Before they entered College, no one, not even their father, could tell them apart; but after graduation the difference was plain. One was a Harvard gentleman, the other a Yale *tough*. Wealth and family are said to count for much at Harvard. The New Englander is as proud of his pedigree, and often with as much reason, as any English nobleman or squire. A Bachelor of Arts of Yale, who recently spent two years at Harvard, the first as a graduate-student, and the second as an instructor,—evidently a fair-minded man,—writes:

> I have lived long enough at Yale to know that Yale students are not commonly ruffians; and I have seen enough of Harvard to know that Harvard students are not as a class snobs. Yet there is a slight element of truth

even in these gross caricatures; it is the difference between "Fair" Harvard and "Dear Old" Yale. The Harvard atmosphere occasionally produces "an affectioned ass," and the Yale spirit sometimes turns out an insolent rowdy.

I have been told by one familiar with the Continental Universities that, measured by their standard, the Harvard students are deficient in those graces which were so dear to Lord Chesterfield's heart. In formal politeness, in the lesser morals, the students in their behaviour towards a Professor fall short of the standard which is observed in Germany and France in their behaviour towards each other. Nevertheless, beneath this somewhat unpolished outside much real kindness lies hidden. A young Professor, who had but recently joined the University, told me that in the midst of the work of his first term he had been struck down by diphtheria. His pupils not only every day sent flowers and fruit, but begged that one of them in turns should always sleep in his house as long as the illness lasted, so that in case of sudden need there might be a swift messenger close at hand to summon the doctor. He had won their hearts, as I learnt from another source, by his courage and his devotion to his work. As soon as he knew the nature of his illness, he had sent them word that he was attacked by a dangerous malady, which would very likely carry him off; but that he hoped that they would go on with the experiments on which he had left them engaged. To such students as these might be applied Goldsmith's saying about Johnson: "He has nothing of the bear about him but the skin."

Whatever pride of wealth and birth may exist in Harvard or in Yale, no student in either of these great Universities need hang his head for honest poverty. Many of them gain their own living more or less, and gain it by bodily labour.

Harvard College by an Oxonian (London and New York, 1894).

Rupert Brooke

BOSTON AND HARVARD

(1913)

Rupert Brooke, "young, happy, radiant, extraordinarily endowed and irresistibly attaching" as Henry James called him, wrote this commentary about the Harvard of Commencement Week for the Westminster Gazette *during a tour of the United States, Canada, and the South Seas in 1913. It was published posthumously as one of fifteen sketches called* Letters from America, *edited by Brooke's friend, Edward Marsh, with a note on Brooke by James who first met "the charmed commentator" just before the latter won a Fellowship from King's College in 1909. Brooke died of blood poisoning on a French hospital ship to which he had been transferred while on his way with his contingent to the Dardanelles campaign.*

IT IS RIGHT to leave Boston late in a summer afternoon, and by sea. Naval departure is always the better. A train snatches you, hot, dusty, and smoky, with an irritated hurry out of the back parts of a town. The last glimpse of a place you may have grown to like or love is, ignobly, interminable rows of the bedroom-windows in mean streets, a few hovels, some cinder-heaps, and a factory chimney. As like as not, you are reft from a last wave to the city's unresponsive and dingy back by the roar and suffocation of a tunnel. By sea one takes a gracefuller, more satisfactory farewell.

Boston put on her best appearance to watch our boat go out for New York. The harbour was bright with sunlight and blue water and little white sails and there wasn't more than the faintest smell of tea. The city sat primly on her little hills, decorous, civilised, European-looking. It is homely after New York. The Boston crowd is curiously English. They have nice eighteenth-century houses there, and ivy grows on the buildings. And they are hospitable. All Americans are hospitable; but they haven't *quite* time in New York to practise the art so perfectly as the Bostonians. It is a lovely art ... But Boston also makes you feel at home without meaning to. A delicious ancient Toryism is to be found here. "What is wrong with America," a middle-aged lady told me, "is this *Democracy.* They ought to take the votes away from these people, who don't know how to use them, and give them only to *us,* the Educated." My heart leapt the Atlantic, and was in a Cathedral or University town of South England.

Yet Boston is alive. It sits, in comfortable middle-age, on the ruins of its glory. But it is not buried beneath them. It used to lead America in Literature, Thought, Art, everything. The years have passed. It is remarkable how nearly now Boston is to New York what Munich is to Berlin. Boston and Munich were the leaders forty years ago. They can't quite make out that they aren't now. It is too incredible that Art should leave her goose-feather bed and run away to the raggle-taggle businessmen. And certainly, if Berlin and New York are more "live," Boston and Munich are more themselves, less feverishly imitations of Paris. But the undisputed palm is there no more; and its absence is felt.

But I had little time to taste Boston itself. I was lured across the river to a place called Cambridge, where is the University of Harvard. Harvard is the Oxford and Cambridge of America, they claim. She has moulded the nation's leaders and uttered its ideals. Harvard, Boston, New England, it is impossible to say how much they are interwoven, and how they have influenced America. I saw Harvard in "Commencement," which is Eights

Week and May Week, the festive winding-up of the year, a time of parties and of valedictions. One of the great events of Commencement, and of the year, is the Harvard-Yale baseball match. To this I went, excited at the prospect of my first sight of a "ball game," and my mind vaguely reminiscent of the indolent, decorous, upper-class crowd, the sunlit spaces, the dignified ritual, and white-flanneled grace of Lord's at the 'Varsity cricket match. The crowd was gay, and not very large. We sat in wooden stands, which were placed in the shape of a large V. As all the hitting which counts in baseball takes place well in front of the wicket, so to speak, the spectators have the game right under their noses; the striker stands in the angle of the V and plays outwards. The field was a vast place, partly stubbly grass, partly worn and patchy, like a parade-ground. Beyond it lay the river; beyond that the town of Cambridge and the University buildings. Around me were undergraduates, with their mothers and sisters. "Cambridge!" . . . but there entered to us, across the field, a troop of several hundred men, all dressed in striped shirts of the same hue and pattern, and headed by a vast banner which informed the world that they were the graduates of 1910, celebrating their triennial. In military fashion they moved across the plain towards us, led by a band, ceaselessly vociferating, and raising their straw hats in unison to mark the time. There followed the class of 1907, attired as sailors; 1903, the decennial class, with some samples of their male children marching with them, and a banner inscribed "515 Others. No Race Suicide"; 1898, carefully arranged in an H-shaped formation, dancing along to their music with a slow polka-step, each with his hands on the shoulders of the man in front, and at the head of all their leader, dancing backwards in perfect time, marshalling them; 1888, middle-aged men, again with some children, and a Highland regiment playing the bagpipes.

When these had passed to the seats allotted for them, I had time to observe the players, who were practising about the ground, and I was shocked. They wear dust-coloured shirts and dingy knickerbockers, fastened under the knee, and heavy boots. They strike the English eye as being attired for football, or a gladiatorial combat, rather than a summer game. The very close-fitting caps, with large peaks, give them picturesquely the appearance of hooligans. Baseball is a good game to watch, and in outline easy to understand, as it is merely glorified rounders. A cricketer is fascinated by their rapidity and skill in catching and throwing. There is excitement in the game, but little beauty except in the long-limbed "pitcher," whose duty it is to hurl the ball rather further than the length of the cricket-pitch, as bewilderingly as possible. In his efforts to combine speed, mystery, and curve, he gets into attitudes of a very novel and fantastic, but quite obvious, beauty. M. Nijinsky would find them repay study.

One queer feature of this sport is that unoccupied members of the batting side, fielders, and even spectators, are accustomed to join in vocally.

You have the spectacle of the representatives of the universities endeavoring to frustrate or unnerve their opponents, at moments of excitement, by cries of derision and mockery, or heartening their own supporters and performers with exclamations of "Now, Joe!" or "He's got them!" or "He's the boy!" At the crises in the fortunes of the game, the spectators take a collective and important part. The Athletic Committee appoints a "cheer-leader" for the occasion. Every five or ten minutes this gentleman, a big, fine figure in white, springs out from his seat at the foot of the stands, addresses the multitude through a megaphone with a "One! Two! Three!" hurls it aside, and, with a wild flinging and swinging of his body and arms, conducts ten thousand voices in the Harvard yell. That over, the game proceeds, and the cheer-leader sits quietly waiting for the next moment of peril or triumph. I shall not easily forget that figure, bright in the sunshine, conducting with his whole body, passionate, possessed by a demon, bounding in the frenzy of his inspiration from side to side, contorted, rhythmic, ecstatic. It seemed so wonderfully American, in its combination of entire wildness and entire regulation, with the whole just a trifle fantastic. Completely friendly and befriended as I was, I couldn't help feeling at those moments very alien and very, very old—even more so than after the protracted game had ended in a victory for Harvard, when the dusty plain was filled with groups and lines of men dancing in solemn harmony, and a shouting crowd, broken by occasional individuals who could find some little eminence to lead a Harvard yell from, and who conducted the bystanders, and then vanished, and the crowd swirled on again.

Different enough was the scene the next day, when all Harvard men who were up for Commencement assembled and, arranged by years, marched round the yard. Class by class they paraded, beginning with veterans of the 'fifties, down to the class of 1912. I wonder if English nerves could stand it. It seems to bring the passage of time so very presently and vividly to the mind. To see, with such emphatic regularity, one's coevals changing in figure, and diminishing in number, summer after summer! . . . Perhaps it is nobler, this deliberate viewing of oneself as part of the stream. To the spectator, certainly, the flow and transiency become apparent and poignant. In five minutes fifty years of America, of so much of America, go past one. The shape of the bodies, apart from the effects of age, the lines of the faces, the ways of wearing hair and beard and moustaches, all these change a little, decade by decade, before your eyes. And through the whole appearance runs some continuity, which is Harvard.

The orderly progression of the years was unbroken, except at one point. There was one gap, large and arresting. Though all years were represented, there seemed to be nobody in the procession between fifty and sixty. I asked a Harvard friend the reason. "The War," he said. He told me there had always been that gap. Those who were old enough to be conscious of the war had lost a big piece of their lives. With their successors a new America began. I don't know how true it is. Certainly, the dates worked out right. And I met an American on a boat who had been a child in one of the neutral States. He used to watch the regiments forming in the main street of his town, marching out, some north and some south. He said it felt as though pieces of his body were being torn in different directions. And he was only nine.

The procession filed in to an open court, to hear the speeches of the recipients of honorary degrees, and the President's annual statement. There was still, in every sense, a solemn atmosphere. The President's speech floated out into the great open space; fragments of it were blown to one's ears concerning deaths, and the spirit of the place, and a detailed account of the money given during the year. Eleven hundred thousand dollars in all—a record, or nearly a record. We roared applause. The American universities appear still to dream of the things of this world. They keep putting up the most wonderful and expensive buildings. But they do not pay their teachers well.

Yet Harvard is a spirit, a way of looking at things, austerely refined, gently moral, kindly. The perception of it grows on the foreigner. Its charm is so deliciously old in this land, so deliciously young compared with the lovely frowst of Oxford and Cambridge. You see it in temperament, the charm of simplicity and good-heartedness and culture; in the Harvard undergraduate, who is a boy, while his English contemporary is either a young man or a schoolboy, less pleasant stages; and in the old Bostonian who heard, and still hears, the lectures of Dickens and Thackeray. Class Day brings so many of that older generation together. They reveal what Harvard, what Boston, was. There is something terrifying in the completeness of their lives and their civilisation. They are like a company of dons whose studies are of a remote and finished world. But the subject of their scholarship is the Victorian age, and especially Victorian England. Hence their liveliness and certainty, greater than men can reach who are concerned with the dubieties and changes of incomplete things. Hence the wit, the stock of excellent stories, the wrinkled wisdom and mirth of the type. They are the flower of a civilisation, its ripest critics and final judges. Carlyle and Emerson are their greatest living heroes. One of them bent the kindliness and alert interest of his eighty years upon me. "So you come from Rugby," he said. "Tell me, do you know that curious creature, Matthew Arnold?" I couldn't bring myself to tell him that, even in Rugby, we had forgiven that brilliant youth his iconoclastic tendencies some time since, and that, as a matter of fact, he had died when I was eight months old.

Letters from America (New York, 1916).

Norman Mailer

MR. MAUGHAM'S PARTY

(1942)

Once upon a time, long before he wrote The Naked and the Dead, *and before a professional career as novelist, critic, and reporter brought him both fame and notoriety, Norman Kingsley Mailer was a member of the Harvard* Advocate. *That was in the period just before the temporary collapse of the magazine in the war years, a heyday of now distinguished names that made the late thirties and early forties a notable period in the* Advocate's *fortunes—James Laughlin, Gerard Piel, Julian Bach, Arthur Schlesinger, Jr., Wayne Andrews, Harry Brown, Seymour Lawrence, Howard Nemerov—and of course Mailer. Mailer's recollection of the reception the* Advocate *was persuaded to extend to the visiting British literary personality W. Somerset Maugham is one of the most delicious tales in Harvard literature.*

LET ME tell you about the Somerset Maugham party that we gave at the *Advocate* in the Spring of 1942. The magazine was housed then in a dark gray flat-roofed three-story building across the street from the stern of the *Lampoon* (and indeed we were much aware of being in their wake—*Lampoon* editors usually went to *Time*; ours to oblivion). In those days the *Advocate* building was as ugly from the exterior as it is now. A few small and dingy stores occupied the ground floor, some mysterious never-seen tenants were on the second, and the *Advocate* offices took up the third. They were beautiful to me. One climbed a dull carpeted staircase as dusty as a back road in Guerrero, used one's *Advocate* key to go through the door at the top, and the suite opened, an entire floor-through of five rooms, five mystical chambers full of broken-down furniture, and the incomparable odor that rises from old beer stains in the carpet, and syrup-crusted empty Coke bottles in the corners. It is a better odor than you would think, sweet and alcoholic and faintly debauched—it spoke of little magazines and future lands of literature, and the offices were almost always empty in late afternoon when the sunlight turned the dust into a cosmos of angels dancing on a pin. Magicians would have felt a rush of aphrodisia amid all this pendant funk and mote. Maybe I loved the *Advocate* offices more than anyone who was taken in my competition—I spent the spring of sophomore year at Harvard drinking Cokes by a table at the window that faced on the *Lampoon*, and I read old issues of the magazine. Once I was an authority on the early published work in the *Advocate* of T. S. Eliot, Edwin Arlington Robinson, Van Wyck Brooks, John Reed, Conrad Aiken, E. E. Cummings, and Malcolm

Cowley—it must have been the nearest I ever came to extracting genealogical marrow from old print. Occasionally Marvin Barrett, the President, or Bowden Broadwater, Pegasus, would come through the office, give a start at seeing me at the same chair and table where they had glimpsed me on the last visit, and go off to do their work.

The following academic year, '41–42, Bruce Barton, Jr., was elected President and John Crockett became Pegasus. We had troubles instantly. Barton, called Pete, was the son of Bruce Barton, Sr., an advertising magnate as well known in his period as Nicholas Murray Butler, and for that matter one could find similarities. (Barton must have been the last of the advertising tycoons who believed passionately in a strenuous Jesus with muscles.)

His son, in compensation, was a gentleman. Pete Barton was the nicest guy a lot of us met at Harvard, and with his blond hair, good if somewhat pinched features, and fundamental decency, he could have passed for Billy Budd if he had not (1) gone to Deerfield, which left him a little more patrician than yeoman in manner, and (2) if he had had more beef. But he was gentle, he was quietly literary, and his father had millions. Since the *Advocate* was in its usual cauldron of debt, no other man would have been so appropriate to serve as President. Barton might even have had a benign, well-financed, and agreeable administration if not for the new Pegasus, John Crockett, a man as talented as Claggart, and equally riven in his soul by detestation of our Billy Budd.

Being innocent of Crockett's propensities for literary evil, we were a happy group coming into office. The magazine would be ours. We would print what we wished. Our first issue, therefore, consisted of each of us putting in his own story. Crockett then took our pearls to a printer in Vermont. This was, I think, in November. By February we still did not have a magazine. Crockett kept assuring us the printer would soon deliver. None of us ever called him. Crockett had assured us that the inexpensive rate he had managed to extract from the linotype mills of the Vermont woods would be ruined forever if we broke any of our voices on the printer's ear. Therefore, we waited. Nervously, impatiently, suspiciously, we waited for the issue with our stories.

Instead Crockett came back with the (75th) anniversary edition of the *Advocate*, a little work of love Crockett had gotten together by himself over the last year, in truth, a prodigious push of Pegasusmanship collecting poems, pieces, and comment from the fine ranks of Wallace Stevens, Horace Gregory, Djuna Barnes, Marianne Moore, Robert Hillyer, Frederic Prokosch, Mark Schorer, John Malcolm Brinnin, Richard Eberhart, Bowden Broadwater, and William Carlos Williams, plus a poem by John Crockett, "The Sulky Races at Cherry Park." It was a mammoth virtuoso critico-literary crypto-CIA affair back in March '42, and none of us on the *Advo-*

cate had had the first clue to what Crockett was cooking. As for our issue with the stories—Crockett promised to get to that next. The expression on his young but sour face told us what he thought of our stories. Crockett, incidentally, while not as well-featured as John Dean, had a great resemblance to him—I remember his tortoise-shell glasses, high forehead, and thin pale hair.

Pete Barton had been agitated for weeks at the long wait of our first issue. Painfully aware of his father's weight in the world, he was invariably over-scrupulous never to push his own. He had suspended himself into a state of forebearance worthy of a Zen warrior, considering the immense agitation the late appearance of the magazine had caused. When the anniversary issue appeared (to rich critical reception in the Boston papers, worse luck!), Barton finally demonstrated his father's blood. He called an emergency meeting where he calumniated himself for his derelictions of attention, took the full blame for the financial disaster of the issue (it had cost something like three times as much as more modest issues; our debt on the consequence had doubled overnight) and—Billy Budd to the last—absent even to intimations of a further notion to evil, stated that he would not ask for Crockett's resignation if he could expect his cooperation on future projects.

Crockett replied with a nod of his head and a profound turning of our collective head. Having heard, he said, that Somerset Maugham would be in the Boston area during April, he had sent an invitation to Maugham to come to a party that the *Advocate* would be happy to throw in his honor. Maugham had accepted. Maugham had accepted.

That piece of news ran around the ring of Cambridge like a particle in a cyclotron. Nothing in four years at Harvard, not Dunkirk, Pearl Harbor, or the blitz, not even beating Yale and Princeton in the same season for the first time in ten years could have lit Harvard up more. Not to be invited to that party was equal to signifying that one had mismanaged one's life.

The literary grandees of the faculty sent their early acceptance, F. O. Matthiessen, Theodore Spencer, and Robert Hillyer in the van; the officers of the *Lampoon* sucked around; House Masters' wives asked how things were *going* at the *Advocate*. On the night of the party, four hundred souls in four hundred bodies as large as Patrick Moynihan's and as delicate as Joan Didion's came to the small rooms on the third floor and packed themselves in so completely that you ended by bringing your drink to your lips around the wrist of the forearm in front of your face. The noise of cocktail gabble anticipated the oncoming shapings of time—one would not hear the sound again until the first jet planes fired up their engines at an airport. Drinks were passed overhead. If you did not reach at the right time, another hand plucked the drink. It did not matter. More was on its way. Glasses bounced like corks over white choppy Harvard hands. From time to time, word would pass like wind through grass that Maugham had just entered the building, Maugham was having trouble getting up the stairs, Maugham was through the door, Maugham was in the other room. We formed phalanxes to move into the other room; we did not budge. A phalanx cannot budge a volume that is impacted. The lovely smile of resignation was on the lips of faculty wives: it is the establishment smile which says, "Life is like that—the nearest pleasures are not to be tasted." After a half hour of such smiling into the face of a stranger as one brought one's arm around her neck to get at one's drink, the wind came through the grass again. Maugham, we heard, was at the door. Maugham was slowly going down the stair, Somerset Maugham was gone.

Hands passed drinks above the impacted mass. Eyes flashed in that hard gem-like smile of pride retained when opportunity is lost. In another half-hour, there was a lessening of pressure on one's chest, and bodies began to separate. After awhile, one could walk from room to room. What was the point? Maugham was gone.

It was only on the next day, after the claims of liars had been checked against the quiet evidence of reliable witnesses who had found themselves analogously empretzeled in every room and on the stairs, that the news came back. By every sound measure of verification, Somerset Maugham had never been in the *Advocate* building that night. Crockett, now confronted, confessed. Out of his unflappable funds of phlegm, he allowed that he had known for weeks Somerset Maugham was not coming—the great author had been kind enough to send a telegram in answer to the invitation. "Certainly not" the telegram said.

It was too late to ask Crockett to resign. Due to the war and an accelerated graduation, our term as *Advocate* officers was up; the new President and Pegasus were in. Because of the party, we left with a debt that had just doubled again. The *Advocate* has never been solvent since.

A postscript: Pete Barton became a navy officer and commanded a ship, came home, worked as quietly for *Time* as if he had been a *Lampoon* man, and died before he was forty. The only time I saw John Crockett again was about ten years ago in New York on a reunion at the Harvard Club. He was now in the State Department and had been stationed for years in Yugoslavia. He told delicious stories about idiotic conversations with Madame Tito at banquets in Zagreb. He looked to be as wicked as ever. Our cause was being well served in Yugoslavia. It occurs to me that the mag across the street never knew what a talent it missed when the *Advocate* got Crockett. Rest in peace, Pete Barton.

First Flowering: The Best of the Harvard Advocate (Reading, Massachusetts, 1977).

Robert Ellis Smith

HOW THE MARSHALL PLAN
WAS BORN

(1947)

*One of the cherished peculiarities of Harvard ceremonial is an alumni group
called the Committee on the Happy Observance of Commencement. They
charge themselves with responsibility for the afternoon events of Commencement Day—the smooth operation of the alumni procession, the good
order of the Chief Marshal's spread, and the review of the classes in front of
Widener. Above all, they and the officers of the associated alumni wage a
ceaseless campaign to insure that—through the efforts of the Governing
Boards and the Faculty committee on honorary degrees—the list of hon-
orands include a man or woman capable of attracting and holding the attention of a large audience on a usually hot June day. The favorite example
of such a candidate is the late Secretary of State, George Catlett Marshall,
whose appearance at Harvard on Commencement Day, June 5, 1947, became a historic moment in American history. Indeed, General Marshall's address on that occasion led naturally and helpfully to the popular Harvard
argument that there is no better place for a political leader to announce an
important direction in national policy than the Harvard Commencement
platform. Robert Ellis Smith, A.B. 1962, was only six years old at the time of
General Marshall's speech, but his reconstruction of the events of that day
reads as if he had been present with the advantage of all the background. A
journalist by profession, Smith has been successively reporter for the Detroit*
Free Press *and the* Trenton Times, *editor of the* Southern Courier, *press
liaison officer in the Office of Civil Rights, a member of the District of Columbia bar, and editor and publisher of* Privacy Journal.

IT WAS Harvard's first fully normal Commencement since the start of World
War II. As the long line of degree candidates and dignitaries formed in the
Old Yard, George C. Marshall chatted with Edmund M. Morgan, then
Royall Professor of Law. Mr. Morgan, who was to escort the Secretary of
State in the procession to the steps of Memorial Church, expressed surprise
at Marshall's apparent anxiety about his coming performance.

"He assured me that he was expected to say something of importance,"
Mr. Morgan recalled later. "Who expected it? He did not say."

Even President James B. Conant, who had entertained the 67-year-old
general at his house the evening before, was not led to expect a major address from Secretary Marshall. But word of Harvard's honorary degree to
the Secretary had leaked to the press 24 hours earlier. The New York *Times*
said on the morning of June 4, 1947, "He is expected to deliver a speech

which perhaps will include an important pronouncement on foreign affairs."

In Cambridge, however, a capacity crowd of 15,000 had showed up not in expectation of seeing history made, but to see the usual parade of prominent persons and to see friends or relatives receive degrees.

Morgan escorted the Secretary of State ahead of a group of eleven other distinguished honorary-degree recipients. Among them were T. S. Eliot, James Wadsworth, I. A. Richards, J. Robert Oppenheimer, George Henry Chase, formerly dean of Harvard, W. Hodding Carter, Jr., the editor of the *Delta Democrat-Times* in Mississippi, Frank L. Boyden, the headmaster of Deerfield Academy, and General Omar N. Bradley, the other afternoon speaker.

In the parade of caps and gowns, Secretary Marshall was dressed in a business suit and carried his hat in his hand. He walked slowly to the platform and acknowledged the appreciative applause along the way. A loud ovation greeted him and the other dignitaries as they reached the stage.

After awarding the first eleven honoraries in the traditional morning ceremonies, President Conant came to Secretary Marshall, "an American to whom freedom owes an enduring debt of gratitude, a soldier and statesman whose ability and character brook only one comparison in the history of this nation."

When the assemblage of dignitaries adjourned to the Twenty-Fifth Reunion Class Marshal's luncheon, the crowd thought it had seen most of the show. But Secretary Marshall's speech at the afternoon Alumni Association meeting was still to come.

What later became known as the Marshall Plan had been conceived in a place closer to the Kremlin than the Harvard Yard. Shortly after accepting President Truman's call to return from China (where he had been ambassador) and to become Secretary of State, Marshall led the American delegation to the Moscow Foreign Ministers Conference in April 1947. After a fruitless private meeting with Russian Premier Joseph Stalin and Foreign Minister V. M. Molotov, Secretary Marshall became convinced that the Soviet Union was not prepared to participate in a European recovery program, that Europe needed help fast, and that only the West could and would provide that help. Piecemeal aid to Greece and Turkey—the "Truman Doctrine" of 1946–47—had not only failed to help Europe as a whole, but also failed to "scare" Russia.

On the return plane trip from Moscow to Washington, Secretary Marshall conveyed his thoughts to other members of the U.S. delegation: John Foster Dulles, Benjamin V. Cohen, Walter Bedell Smith, James Burns. Out of the failure of the Moscow Conference came an offensive strategy for the United States.

In late April and early May, Secretary Marshall combined his own ideas with recommendations from the State Department staff and the White House. As the proposal for American aid to a unified Europe developed, it was generally referred to as "the Marshall plan" in meetings. President Truman encouraged the use of this term, as he recalled in his memoirs, "because I wanted General Marshall to get full credit for his brilliant contribution to the measure which he helped formulate." This may be why Mr. Truman chose not to make a speech similar to Secretary Marshall's when an appropriate occasion arose—two weeks after Harvard's Commencement, when Mr. Truman was the main speaker at Princeton's graduation.

The Administration launched a trial balloon for its European recovery program on May 8, 1947. Mr. Truman's mother was sick in Kansas City at the time, and he authorized Dean Acheson, then Undersecretary of State, to replace him at a meeting of plantation owners in Cleveland, Mississippi. Mr. Acheson omitted the particulars, but his general message was clear: The United States ought to be conscious of Europe's postwar plight and ought to be offering substantial aid.

Meanwhile, Harvard was looking for speakers at its Alumni Association meeting on Commencement Day. The man responsible for inviting speakers was Laird Bell '04, LL.D. '55, then President of the Association and a prominent Chicago attorney. Bell later recalled that the public reaction to the Acheson speech had been satisfactory, and "the Secretary of State [had] determined to go all out for what has become known as the Marshall Plan, and a speech was prepared accordingly. The question was then the rostrum from which it should be delivered. Two or three suggestions were made, and then the Secretary remembered that he had been invited to receive a Harvard degree and that seemed a highly suitable occasion. He therefore indicated that he would like to accept, and of course was welcome."

In accepting, Secretary Marshall was reversing himself. He had not been available in earlier years, when a number of leading generals and admirals of World War II were nominated for honors; degrees are awarded only when the candidate is present in person (General Douglas MacArthur never did pick his up). Some time before the Commencement of 1947, Mr. Bell had renewed an invitation to Secretary Marshall to attend Harvard's ceremonies and to speak in the afternoon. The Secretary had declined. Mr. Bell, as president of the Alumni Association, was authorized to select speakers from the Corporation's confidential list of honorary-degree candidates. Mr. Bell had told President Conant that he was not about to name any high military brass to speak. But, according to Mr. Bell, President Conant argued in favor of a military man. So Mr. Bell selected General Omar N. Bradley, at that time Administrator of Veterans' Affairs.

Two days before Commencement, the State Department called Mr. Bell to say that the Secretary of State would be glad to speak at Harvard after all, although he did not want to make the major speech of the day. "Thus, I wound up with two generals, instead of none," recalled Mr. Bell. "I did not realize how historic the occasion would be."

There is no evidence that anyone in the audience at the afternoon Alumni Association meeting realized, either. First came the National Anthem; then a talk by Mr. Bell; an address by the Governor of Massachusetts Robert F. Bradford '23, LL.B. '26; the two scheduled addresses, and a reading of the 78th Psalm. Then Governor Bradford rose and announced, "Ladies and gentlemen—the Secretary of State." There was appreciative applause as Secretary Marshall stepped to the rostrum.

"President Dr. Conant, members of the Board of Overseers, ladies and gentlemen," Secretary Marshall began. "I am grateful—touched by the honor accorded me by the authorities of Harvard—overwhelmed, as a matter of fact. These historic and lovely surroundings, this perfect day . . . this wonderful assembly, a tremendously impressive thing for a person in my place."

From there, the Secretary of State began his prepared text: "I need not tell you, gentlemen, that the world situation is very serious." Fidgeting with his glasses, rarely looking up from his notes, speaking undramatically and sometimes inaudibly, George Marshall went into a somber description of Europe's losses—"the visible destruction of cities . . . factories, mines, railroads . . . long-standing commercial ties, private institutions, banks, insurance companies, and shipping companies"—in short, the "dislocation of the entire fabric of European economy."

It was a simple, twenty-minute speech without oratorical flourish or wasted words; it revolved around one unmistakable point: "It is logical that the United States should do whatever it is able to do to assist in the return of normal economic health in the world, without which there can be no political stability and no assured peace."

This undoubtedly was not the first time, in public or in private, that this thought had been expressed, but from that point historians would date America's foreign aid to Europe and America's policies in the Cold War. It was to be regarded as a landmark in American foreign policy. And from that point, Harvard University would come to expect—or at least hope for—a major policy pronouncement from its Commencement speakers. Upon invitation, many would be reminded of Marshall's history-making address, and many would allude to it in their own speeches.

Secretary Marshall then began to lead into the main point of the speech, saying: "The remedy lies in breaking the vicious circle and restoring the confidence of European people in the economic future of their own countries and of Europe as a whole."

The audience and the press considered this the keynote of Secretary

Marshall's talk. (MARSHALL PLEADS FOR EUROPEAN UNITY, said the *New York Times* the next day.) The General continued:

> Our policy is directed not against any country or doctrine but against hunger, poverty, desperation, and chaos. Its purpose should be the revival of a working economy in the world, so as to permit the emergence of political and social conditions in which free institutions can exist. Such assistance, I am convinced, must not be on a piecemeal basis as various crises develop. Any assistance that this government may render in the future should provide a cure rather than a mere palliative.
>
> Any government that is willing to assist in the task of recovery will find full cooperation, I am sure, on the part of the United States government. Any government which maneuvers to block the recovery of other countries cannot expect help from us. Furthermore, governments, political parties, or groups which seek to perpetuate human misery in order to profit therefrom politically or otherwise will encounter the opposition of the United States.

Here, and at the end of his talk, Secretary Marshall cut off the applause and lessened the impact by moving on to his next point. As the audience rose to applaud at the end of the speech, the Secretary took off his glasses, leaned forward on the lectern, and reached into his pocket for some scribbled remarks. He reiterated his earlier point, "the vast importance that our people reach some general understanding of what the complications really are, rather than react from a passion or prejudice or an emotion of the moment." It was this gesture that led some members of the audience to believe—to this day—that "the Marshall Plan" was an impromptu stroke of genius that the Secretary happened to toss out at the end of his prepared address.

"After the speech, the applause was tremendous, and the distinguished guests crowded around the Secretary," recalled Mr. Bell. The audience surely grasped Marshall's plea for European unity, but few could have been fully aware of the significance of his plans for the role of the United States in European recovery.

"I was much impressed . . . as were many of the others I talked to," President Conant said later. "However, I am frank to say I had no suspicion that the speech would turn out to be so epoch-making. That it was a major speech there could be no doubt, but since none of us knew that it would be immediately picked up by high-ranking officials of foreign countries, we could not anticipate the subsequent developments."

The immediate favorable response by foreign officials was not accidental. "Unbeknownst to Marshall, Undersecretary Acheson had called in key English correspondents, briefed them on the upcoming proposal, and urged them to dispatch the full text of Marshall's remarks in their papers," according to one of that year's degree candidates, Douglass Cater, Jr., '46, later a White House assistant to President Johnson.

"I am told that the British Embassy in Washington, for economy reasons, failed to cable the text. Thus it was that when Foreign Minister Ernest Bevin and others sought to find out more about what Marshall said, they had to turn to the press," Cater said. The speech evoked great enthusiasm from Bevin, and it was he who later organized Europe's unified positive response.

At the time Secretary Marshall spoke, the United States had already given $11 billion in postwar aid. In the summer of 1947, England and France invited the European nations to a conference to plan cooperative efforts. Russia declined the invitation. The Commission of European Economic Cooperation then set its specific needs in September, as President Truman investigated the capacity of the U.S. economy to help.

In November, Mr. Truman was apparently satisfied that the United States could give considerable help without seriously disrupting the domestic economy. He called a special session of Congress to appropriate half a billion dollars for interim aid to Europe. On December 19, immediately after the failure of the Big Four Conference in London, Mr. Truman submitted the first official version of the Marshall Plan to Congress. On April 3, 1948, one year after the Moscow conference, President Truman signed the Foreign Assistance Act, appropriating $17 billion for grants and loans over a four-year period, to be administered through the Economic Cooperation Administration and other agencies.

At the midpoint ceremony of the Marshall Plan in 1950, General Marshall said, "Looking again at the conditions prevalent in the spring of 1947, and again considering the situation at this moment, I can only feel that one near miracle has been accomplished. We must work for, and expect, another miracle."

President Conant, in a letter to Marshall a year later, wrote, "Your speech at the Harvard Commencement of 1947 will always remain an honored memory at Harvard." So it does, but perhaps its most enduring memorial is the European economic miracle of the fifties—the "other miracle" that George Catlett Marshall would live to see completed before his death in 1959.

Harvard Alumni Bulletin, June 17, 1967.

Michael Steinberg

SANDERS—I LOVE IT!

(1974)

For fifteen years Michael Steinberg was intimately involved in the musical
life of Greater Boston and beyond. A native of Breslau who found his way to
the United States at the age of fifteen during World War II, Steinberg gra-
duated from Princeton and had made a name for himself as a critic (for the
Saturday Review *and other publications) and teacher (at the Manhattan*
School of Music) when he accepted in 1964 an invitation to become music
critic of the Boston Globe. *For the next dozen years he was a household word*
in local musical circles, known for his sharp opinions well based in musical
knowledge, and strongly held positions often caustically stated. Erich
Leinsdorf's regime at Symphony Hall was a steady target, but in 1976
Steinberg joined Seiji Ozawa and his orchestra as Director of Publications
and three years later moved to San Francisco, where Ozawa was also music
director, to become artistic adviser and publications director of the San Fran-
cisco Symphony Orchestra. Here is his tribute to a favorite auditorium, that
glorious sound box Sanders Theater.

JANOS STARKER, the eminent cellist, was playing Dvorak's Concerto with the
Harvard-Radcliffe Orchestra in Sanders Theater, when suddenly, at a quiet
place in the slow movement, there was a racket as though a snare-drummer
had gone beserk . . . The real noise at the concert turned out to come from a
popped radiator valve, and it was loud and persistent so that the performance drifted quickly to a halt. Having sneaked in ticketless at intermission, a
displaced person from another and awful concert nearby, I was standing at
the back of the balcony and couldn't see in detail what was happening, only
some general rushing about of purposeful-looking young men. In the interval, James Yannatos, the conductor, said something I didn't catch, but
which made the people around him laugh. Then Starker, as coolly imper-
turbable now as he had been while unreeling his sinuously elegant, fabu-
lously controlled playing, said, "It looks as though Harvard needs a new
concert hall," a remark greeted with a spatter of applause.

As a mid-Westerner (from Budapest), Mr. Starker doesn't understand
about Harvard and Sanders Theater. Sanders is not a concert hall, though it
is where most big concerts at Harvard are given, and of course many others
in Cambridge independent of Harvard: it is a monument and part of a way
of life, and the day it comes down or is otherwise replaced by "a new concert hall" will be a day of mourning.

I love it. Considered as a concert hall, it is both wonderful and impossible. It is impossible, or at least maddening, because of the absence of tem-

perature control (I hope that's what it is, not sadism or playfulness) and because of noise. The inside of the hall is subtropical, summer and winter, though winter adds piercing, icy drafts. The lobby in winter is Arctic. The passage from Memorial Hall, which serves as greenroom and which is larger than many a concert hall, across the lobby into Sanders is hell for musicians and instruments. Once, John Harbison, whose musicianship combines practical with spiritual, intellectual, and artistic values, canceled the intermission of a Cantata Singers concert, substituting a stretch-break, so as to spare his singers and players that trip. Sanders also welcomes street noise. The fire-house at the corner of Broadway and Quincy turns every concert into an adventure: will they, won't they, and if so, when? Then it comes, almost surely in the slow movement or during something very quiet—earlier in that Dvorak performance we lost the lovely horn solo in the first movement—first the warning bell, in itself quiet, but presaging the whoo-a whoo-a whoo-a of the sirens and the roar of motors. And you get trucks and buses, Hondas, people just living their Cambridge lives, and sometimes WHRB, whose studio is in the basement.

Two summers ago, the Harvard Summer School concerts were moved into Burden Hall, a new air-conditioned auditorium at the Business School. It was cool, quiet and acoustically satisfactory. It has comfortable chairs very different from the penitential pews in Sanders. It was awful—a green, faceless, plastic place. Everyone was glad when this past summer they moved the series back into the heat, discomfort, and noise of Sanders. Sometimes that heat and discomfort oddly add to the pleasure of the concert. People stuck here for the summer are music-starved and resentful of their friends who have gone somewhere cool, and then, on a July evening, when the temperature is still close to 90 (and something more than that inside Sanders) to be offered the gift of Mozart's G-minor Quintet and the great Schubert C-major Cello Quintet is to know that it is better to be here than among the clams and mosquitos. I remember just such an evening: a group led by Alexander Schneider was playing, and how they managed it all I don't know, but I have never seen an audience—and the house was packed (and the warmer for it)—more moved by music and more grateful for it.

Partly I love Sanders for associations, including ones I have only at second-hand: Copland gave his "Music and Imagination" lectures there, and Schoenberg conducted the Boston Symphony. The first music I ever heard in Sanders was Schubert four-hand-music—the A-flat Variations and the F-minor Fantasy—played by Luise Vosgerchian and Leon Kirchner, enough to invest any hall with an aureole forever. And Ernst Haefliger's Schubert-Schumann recital with Paul Ulanowsky, Peter Serkin playing the Goldberg Variations, Jan Curtis singing Mahler's "Kindertotenlieder" with Kirchner conducting, F. John Adams conducting the St. Matthew Passion, some of Harbison's Cantata Singers concerts; the Juilliard Quartet playing the new

Carter No. 3, are among the experiences whose memory I shall never cease to treasure.

But all that aside, Sanders is so good. The sound is rich, resonant, vivid. The semicircular shape has an indrawing quality that always makes you feel close to the music (the sense of contact, I know from my two scary times of standing on that stage, works beautifully in the opposite direction, too). And if the concert should disappoint, why, Sanders is the most boredom-proof hall in the world. Of its kookily noble kind, it is a masterpiece of architecture and decoration, and to the hungry eye it offers a prodigal, incredible play of planes and surfaces, to say nothing of more superficial diversions like the mirrors over the stage which turn every fiddler left-handed, the grey guardian statues on either side, the lights and windows, the long Latin inscription to figure out on the wall straight ahead. No—long live Sanders (though I don't undertake to stop complaining about the climate and the noise—and perhaps, if not a new concert hall, Harvard needs some new radiators . . .)!

Harvard Today, Winter, 1974, reprinted from the *Boston Globe Sunday Magazine*.

CREDITS AND ACKNOWLEDGMENTS

INDEX

CREDITS AND ACKNOWLEDGMENTS

Roger Angell for permission to use "Harvard Wins, 29–29," printed originally in *Harvard Football News*, November 18, 1978 (pp. 9–11).

Barnes & Noble Books, Totowa, New Jersey, for excerpts from the *Journal of Jasper Danckaerts, 1679–1680*, edited by Bartlett Burleigh James and J. Franklin Jameson. Copyright 1913, 1941, Barnes & Noble, Inc., reprinted 1952.

Sallie Bingham, her agents, Literistic, Ltd., and her publisher, Houghton Mifflin Company, for "Winter Term," originally published in the Harvard *Advocate* (April, 1957), revised and republished in *Mademoiselle* (July, 1958), and included in her short story collection *The Touching Hand*, Boston, 1967. Copyright © 1967 by Sallie Bingham. Reprinted by permission of Houghton Mifflin Company.

The Boston Herald American and the Hearst Corporation for Walter Prichard Eaton's "Here's to the Harvard Accent" and Lucius Beebe's "Notes on a Dry Generation," two articles printed in the Harvard Tercentenary supplement of the *Boston Herald*, September 13, 1936 (pp. 22 and 23).

Carey J. Chamberlin, Secretary of the Harvard College Class of 1913, for the quotation from the biographical sketch of Richard C. Evarts, published in the 25th Anniversary Report of the Class.

Colonial Society of Massachusetts for various quotations from the publications of the Society, in particular from Volume XIV (p. 193), for the text of Thomas Shepard's letter to his son, and from Volume XXXI (pp. 327 *et seq.*), for selections from "College Laws and Customs" and from the official printing of "The Laws of Harvard College."

Grace Richards Conant and Harper & Row, Publishers, Inc., for permission to use "I Hadn't the Stomach to Apologize," from James B. Conant, *My Several Lives*, New York, 1970 (pp. 168–171). Copyright © 1970 by James B. Conant.

Constable and Company for the brief quotation from *Unforgotten Years* by Logan Pearsall Smith, London, 1938 (p. 115).

Laurence Curtis, Secretary of the Harvard College Class of 1916, for the quotation from the biographical sketch of Robert Nathan appearing in the 25th Anniversary Report of the Class.

Lee A. Daniels for permission to use "I'm a Harvard Man Now," a portion of a work in progress.

Elizabeth H. Dos Passos for the brief quotation from John Dos Passos, *Nineteen Nineteen* in his trilogy *U.S.A.*, published by Harcourt, Brace and Company, New York, 1933 ("Harvard stood for the broad *a* . . .") and for the first chapter of his novel *Streets of Night*, George H. Doran Co., New York, 1923 (pp. 9–30).

David Graham Du Bois, heir of Shirley Graham Du Bois, for permission to use "That Outer Whiter World of Harvard" from W. E. Burghardt Du Bois, *Dusk of Dawn: An Essay Toward an Autobiography of a Race Concept*, Harcourt, Brace and Company, New York, 1940 (pp. 34–40).

Elsevier-Dutton Publishing Company for permission to use "Dr. Parkman Takes a Walk," from *The Proper Bostonians*, by Cleveland Amory (Chapter 10, pp. 207–227). Copyright 1947, © 1975 by Cleveland Amory. Reprinted by permission of the publisher, E. P. Dutton.

Anne Fadiman and Harvard Magazine, Inc., for "Where Is the Grace of Yesteryear?" originally titled "A la recherche de Harvard perdu," first printed in the *Harvard Bulletin*, December, 1972 (pp. 18–19).

John H. Finley, Jr., and the Saturday Club for "A Cambridge Horatian," from Edward W. Forbes and John H. Finley, Jr., eds., *The Saturday Club: A Century Completed, 1920–1956*, Houghton Mifflin Company, Boston, 1958. Copyright © 1958 The Saturday Club.

The Reverend Peter J. Gomes and the President and Fellows of Harvard College for permission to use "Our Secular Sacrament," first printed in the *Harvard University Gazette*, June 7, 1979 (p. 14).

David Halberstam for "The Greatest House Crew Ever," originally printed in *Harvard Today*, May, 1958 (pp. 18–21). Copyright © 1958 the President and Fellows of Harvard College.

Harper and Row for the quotation beginning "All my memories of the four years were happy ones . . ." from Thomas William Lamont's *My Boyhood in a Parsonage; Some Brief Sketches of American Life Towards the Close of the Last Century*, New York, 1946 (pp. 187–188), and for the quotation beginning "Students at Harvard . . ." taken from the *Journals of Francis Parkman*, edited by Mason Wade, Harper and Brothers, New York, 1947 (I, 256).

The Harvard Lampoon for numerous references and quotations and especially the excerpts from *Rollo's Journey to Cambridge*, originally published in 1880, and for the selection from R. C. Evarts, *Alice's Adventures in Cambridge*, illustrations by E. L. Barron, copyright 1913 by the Harvard Lampoon (pp. 7–15).

Harvard Magazine, Inc., proprietors of the copyright of the *Harvard Graduates' Magazine*, for numerous quotations from comments and reviews, but particularly for William James, "The True Harvard," a paper delivered at the Harvard Commencement Dinner, June 24, 1903, first printed in the issue of September, 1903 (pp. 6–8); "Harvard on the Eve of the Revolution," selections from the diary of Samuel Chandler by Sarah E. Mulliken, March and June, 1902; and the passages from Grace Hollingsworth Tucker, "The Gods Serve Hebe," June, 1933 (pp. 207–214); and for "Reunions Improve with Age," by Edward Weeks, a portion of "The Graduate's Window" in the issue of September, 1933 (pp. 47–50).

Harvard Magazine, Inc., for many and various excerpts from the *Harvard Alumni Bulletin*, particularly John T. Bethell, "Listening to Music with Woody," September 15, 1969 (p. 56); extracts from the undergraduate diary of James Woodbury Boyden, September 24, 1949 (pp. 6 and 30); the brief quotation from Karl M. Elish, May 6, 1961 (p. 604); Alan Gregg's "Forty Years After," originally published anonymously in the issue of April 7, 1951 (pp. 546–548); Barklie Henry, "Ladies in the Yard: An Alumni Report," February 2, 1954 (pp. 391–392); Frederick West Holland's undergraduate diary for the years 1827 and 1828, first published in the September 29, October 6, and October 13 issues in 1927; Howard Mumford Jones's remark about a Harvard man, printed in the October 28, 1961, issue (p. 130); Victor O. Jones, "When Riots Were Riots," reprinted with Mr. Jones's permission from the Boston *Globe* in the March 29, 1954, issue; Bishop Lawrence's account of Phi Beta Kappa Day in 1871 from the issue of December 14, 1940 (pp. 343–345); "Emerson Hall Revisited," by Jacob Loewenberg, January 29, 1949 (pp. 348–351); "The Lights Come On," an unsigned editorial by David McCord, and various quotations from the Charles Garden sequence of David McCord, as well as the excerpt "Enter a Former Naval Person," taken from the news columns of the issue of September 18, 1943 (pp. 11–15); "Harvard's Past," by Samuel Eliot Morison, November 22, 1935 (pp. 265–274); "The Shining Moments," John Lord O'Brian's remarks to the Associated Harvard Clubs, meeting in Washington, printed in the May 25, 1957, issue (p. 640); "Senior in the Long Procession," Henry Richards's letter to his classmate printed in "The College Pump," April 23, 1955 (p. 540); "The Alumnus," by Willard L. Sperry, April 26, 1947 (pp. 587–590); and the letter to her family written by Barbara Ward (Lady Jackson of Lodsworth) and published with her permission in the December 14, 1957, issue (pp. 257–259).

Harvard Yearbook Publications, for the brief quotation from Kerry Gruson's "To Faye Before Retiring," in *333: The Yearbook of Harvard and Radcliffe*, Cambridge, 1969 (p. 132).

Hawthorn Properties (Elsevier-Dutton Co., Inc.) for permission to reprint the excerpt from Lee Simonson's autobiography, *Part of a Lifetime: Drawings and Designs, 1919–1940*, Duell, Sloan and Pearce, New York, 1943 (pp. 6–9), Copyright 1943, © 1975 by Lee Simonson.

Houghton Mifflin Company for permission to use "What a Day for Our Race!" from *Charles W. Eliot*, by Henry James, Boston and New York, 1930 (pp. 80–84), copyright 1930 by Henry James, and to quote the letter describing President Walker's inauguration from *The Letters of Horace Howard Furness*, edited by H. H. F. J., Boston and New York, 1922 (pp. 16–19), copyright 1922 by H. H. F. Jayne; and for selections from *The Heart of Emerson's Journals*, edited by Bliss Perry, Boston, 1926 (pp. 10 and 103); for quotations from Bliss Perry's autobiography *And Gladly Teach*, Boston, 1935 (pp. 232–233 and 253–254); and for the quotation from *Bret Harte, Argonaut and Exile*, by George R. Stewart, Jr., Boston and New York, 1931 (p. 201), included in Bishop Lawrence's account. Copyright 1935, © 1959 by George R. Stewart, Jr.

E. J. Kahn, Jr., and the Harvard Magazine, Inc., for "The Harvardization of E. J. Kahn," printed in the *Harvard Bulletin*, December 8, 1969 (pp. 23–26).

Steven Kelman and Houghton Mifflin Company for "Meeting Mr. McNamara," from *Push Comes to Shove*, Boston, 1970 (pp. 54–61). Copyright © 1970 by Steven Kelman. Reprinted by permission of Houghton Mifflin Company.

Janet King and the Radcliffe Quarterly for permission to reprint "A Letter to My Freshman Daughter at Radcliffe," from the *Radcliffe Quarterly*, December, 1976 (pp. 2–4). Copyright © 1976 Radcliffe College.

Faye Levine and Harvard Yearbook Publications for permission to use "The Girls Who Go to Harvard," from *329: The Yearbook of Harvard and Radcliffe*, Cambridge, 1965 (pp. 108–114).

Little, Brown and Company and the Atlantic Monthly Press for the use of "Jane Toppan's Case," taken from pp. 79–85 of *The Happy Profession* by Ellery Sedgwick, Boston, 1946; Little, Brown and Company for "Mr. Hilliard Tells All" (Chapter II, pp. 15–28) in *H. M. Pulham, Esquire* by John Phillips Marquand, Boston, 1941, copyright 1940, 1941 by John P. Marquand and Adelaide H. Marquand.

Malcolm J. Logan, Secretary of the Harvard College Class of 1915, for the quotation from the biographical sketch of John P. Marquand, which appeared in the 25th Anniversary Report of the Class.

Archibald MacLeish for "When We Think Now of the Greatness of the University," remarks at the memorial service for his colleague, Kenneth B. Murdock, printed in *Harvard Magazine*, February, 1976 (p. 16C).

The Macmillan Publishing Company, Inc., for permission to use a portion of *Philosophy 4* by Owen Wister (pp. 45–95), New York, 1903. Copyright 1901, 1903, 1931, The Macmillan Company. Reissued 1937.

Norman Mailer and the Harvard Advocate for permission to use "Mr. Maugham's Party," his preface to *First Flowering: The Best of the Harvard Advocate*, edited by Richard M. Smoley and published by Addison-Wesley Publishing Company, Reading, Massachusetts, copyright © 1977 by the Harvard Advocate (pp. xii–xiii). The article was also published in *Esquire*, April, 1977.

The Manchester Guardian and Alistair Cooke for Mr. Cooke's account of the Harvard-Yale cricket match, which was published in the May 21, 1951 issue of the *Guardian* (p. 5).

The Massachusetts Historical Society for permission to make use of the typescript entitled "Extracts from the diaries of John Quincy Adams, 1787, and his son, Charles Francis Adams, 1825, relating to Harvard College from 1786 to 1880," selected and transcribed by Henry Adams and William G. Roelker (entry for Thursday 16th July [1857], pp. 45–48); selections from *The Education of Henry Adams*, Houghton Mifflin Company, Boston and New York, 1918 (the first part of Chapter 4, pp. 54–55); for David Sewall's account of his journey to Portsmouth, New Hampshire, and return, with Tutor Henry Flynt in the year 1754, which was edited by Charles Deane and printed in the Proceedings of the Society,

First Series (Volume XVI, 1878–1879, pp. 5–11); and for the biography of Joseph Mayhew from *Sibley's Harvard Graduates: Biographical Sketches of Those Who Attended Harvard College* (Volume VIII, 1726–1730, pp. 730–734), compiled by Clifford K. Shipton.

Robert Nathan for permission to use portions of the second chapter of *Peter Kindred*, Duffield & Co., New York, 1919 (pp. 21–28).

The New Republic for permission to reprint John Reed's "Almost Thirty" from the issue of April 29, 1936 (pp. 332–333). Copyright 1936 by The New Republic, Inc.

Séan O'Faoláin for portions of the Harvard chapter excerpted from *Vive Moi* (New York: Charles Scribner's Sons; London: Rupert Hart-Davis, Ltd.). Copyright © 1964 by Séan O'Faoláin. Reprinted by permission of Curtis Brown, Ltd., and A. P. Watt Ltd. All rights reserved.

President and Fellows of Harvard College for extracts from the addresses and annual reports of Presidents Eliot, Conant, Pusey, and Bok.

President and Fellows of Harvard College for the use of manuscript materials in the Harvard University Archives—Thomas Hill's letters to his family and the typescript of an address about Louis Agassiz, included among the Hill papers; Oliver Wendell Holmes's letters from 1828 to 1830, now in the Houghton Library; Eliphalet Pearson's "Journal of Disorders," 1788; Richard Waldron's "Admittatur"; and selections from the official letter books of Presidents Quincy, Sparks, Felton, and Hill.

President and Fellows of Harvard College and the Harvard University Press for the selection from *On Writing the Biography of a Modest Man*, by Rollo Walter Brown, Cambridge, 1935 (later published as one of the sketches in Mr. Brown's *Harvard Yard in the Golden Age*, A. A. Wyn, New York, 1948); John F. Kennedy, "Sower of the Seed," and Nathan M. Pusey, "Island of Light," from *College in a Yard*, edited by Brooks Atkinson, Cambridge, 1957 (pp. 125–127 and 9–15); for quotations from William G. Land's *Thomas Hill*, Cambridge, 1933; for quotations from the addresses of A. Lawrence Lowell, printed in President Lowell's *At War with Academic Traditions in America*, Cambridge, 1934; for excerpts from Donald Moffat's introduction to *Fair Harvard*, photographs by Samuel Chamberlain, Cambridge, 1948 (pp. 5–10); for numerous quotations from Samuel Eliot Morison's *Three Centuries of Harvard*, Cambridge, 1936, *The Founding of Harvard College*, Cambridge, 1935, and *Harvard College in the Seventeenth Century*, Cambridge, 1936; for the selections from Jacob Rhett Motte's diary, *Charleston Goes to Harvard, the Diary of a Harvard Student of 1831*, edited by Arthur H. Cole, Cambridge, 1940 (pp. 87–93); for the description of President Lowell by Theodore Pearson, published in Henry Aaron Yeomans's biography, *Abbott Lawrence Lowell, 1856–1943*, Cambridge, 1948 (pp. 369–370); for the selections from *The Age of the Scholar* by Nathan M. Pusey, Cambridge, 1963; for the excerpt from the diary of Maria Sophia Quincy included in *The Articulate Sisters*, edited by M. A. DeWolfe Howe, Cambridge, 1946 (pp. 176–189); and for quotations from the undergraduate letters of Edwin Arlington Robinson to Harry de Forest Smith, 1890–1905, published in *Untriangulated Stars*, edited by Denham Sutcliffe, Cambridge, 1947 (pp. 18 and 38–48).

Radcliffe College for paragraphs from the *Radcliffe Guide 1980–81*, and for permission to reprint "A Letter to My Dear Girls," published in Lucy Allen Paton's *Elizabeth Cary Agassiz: A Biography*, Houghton Mifflin Company, Boston and New York, Copyright 1919 Radcliffe College (pp. 245–248).

Radcliffe Quarterly for permission to use Le Baron Russell Briggs's remarks at the laying of the cornerstone of Briggs Hall, first printed in the January, 1925 issue; and Ada Louise Comstock's address to the alumnae, June, 1943, printed in the August, 1943 issue (pp. 15–18).

Charles Scribner's Sons for permission to reprint chapter 4, "Boston and Harvard," from Rupert Brooke, *Letters from America*, with a preface by Henry James, copyright 1916 by Charles Scribner's Sons, copyright 1944 by Edward Marsh; part of the chapter entitled "The Harvard Yard" from George Santayana, *Persons and Places, the Background of My Life*, New York, 1944 (pp. 186–202); and Chapter 7 (pp. 89–93) from Thomas Wolfe, *Of Time and the River*, copyright 1935 by Charles Scribner's Sons.

Erich Segal and Harper & Row, Publishers, Inc., for permission to use "Love on the Ice," from *Love Story*, New York, 1970 (pp. 7–12). Copyright © 1970 by Erich Segal.

Robert Ellis Smith and Harvard Magazine, Inc., for permission to use "How the Marshall Plan Was Born," *Harvard Alumni Bulletin*, June 17, 1967 (pp. 18–21).

Kevin Starr and Harvard Magazine, Inc., for permission to reprint "Memories and Reflections on the Occasion of Reading *Samuel Johnson* by My Former Neighbor, Mr. Walter Jackson Bate," *Harvard Magazine*, March–April, 1978 (pp. 28–32, 54–58).

Michael Steinberg and the President and Fellows of Harvard College for "Sanders—I Love It," originally printed in the *Boston Globe Sunday Magazine*, reprinted in *Harvard Today*, Winter, 1974.

Barbara Tuchman and Radcliffe Quarterly for the transcript of her extemporaneous remarks on receiving the Radcliffe Alumnae Annual Recognition Award, *Radcliffe Quarterly*, September, 1975 (p. 1).

John Updike for "The Folly on Bow Street," taken from his foreword to *The Harvard Lampoon Centennial Celebration, 1876–1973*, edited by Martin Kaplan. Copyright © 1973 by Harvard Lampoon, Inc. Reprinted by permission of Little, Brown and Company in association with the Atlantic Monthly Press. The essay was included in Updike's *Picked-Up Pieces*, published by Alfred A. Knopf, Inc., New York, 1975.

George Weller and Harold Ober Associates, Inc., for permission to use the quotation beginning "Generalizing about Harvard . . ." on p. 109, and for the chapter "Eleven O'clock in November" taken from his novel *Not to Eat, Not for Love*, Harrison Smith and Robert Haas, New York, 1933 (pp. 47–52).

INDEX OF NAMES

The index includes authors of selections as well as persons mentioned in the text; page references to their contributions are followed by an asterisk. For reasons of space, individuals are not identified except by birth and death dates, Harvard College class, or Harvard degrees.